Microsoft Certified Professional

Windows® NT™ Server 4.0 Enterprise Exam Guide

Microsoft Certified Professional

Windows® NT™ Server 4.0 Enterprise Exam Guide

Written by Steve Kaczmarek

Windows NT Server 4.0 Enterprise Exam Guide

Copyright© 1998 by Que® Corporation.

Library of Congress Catalog No.: 97-67038

ISBN: 0-7897-1191-5

99 98   6 5 4 3 2

Interpretation of the printing code: the rightmost double-digit number is the year of the book's printing; the rightmost single-digit number, the number of the book's printing. For example, a printing code of 98-2 shows that the second printing of the book occurred in 1998.

Screen reproductions in this book were created using Collage Plus from Inner Media, Inc., Hollis, NH.

Credits

President
Roland Elgey

Senior Vice President/Publishing
Don Fowley

Publisher
Joseph B. Wikert

Publishing Director
Brad R. Koch

General Manager
Joe Muldoon

Editorial Services Director
Carla Hall

Managing Editor
Thomas F. Hayes

Acquisitions Director
Cheryl D. Willoughby

Acquisitions Editors
Don Essig, Nancy Maragioglio

Senior Product Director
Lisa D. Wagner

Product Directors
Dana Coe, Kevin Kloss, Jeff Sparks

Production Editor
Brian Sweany

Editors
*Lisa Gebken, Kate Givens,
Rebecca Mounts, Sarah Rudy*

Web Master
Thomas H. Bennett

Product Marketing Manager
Kristine R. Ankney

Assistant Product Marketing Manager/Design
Christy M. Miller

Assistant Product Marketing Manager/Sales
Karen Hagen

Technical Editors
*Robert Bogue, Nadeem Muhammed,
Stan Spink*

Media Development Specialist
David Garratt

Technical Support Specialist
Nadeem Muhammed

Acquisitions Coordinator
Tracy M. Williams

Software Relations Coordinator
Susan D. Gallagher

Book Designer
Ruth Harvey

Cover Designer
Ruth Harvey

Production Team
*Jennifer Earhart, Trey Frank,
Tim Neville, Paul Wilson*

Indexer
Tim Wright

Composed in **Bembo** and **Avenir** by Que Corporation.

To my partner, Bill Glewicz, who has supported and encouraged me throughout this and many other efforts; to my Cairn terrier, Scruffy, who contentedly warmed my feet while I typed away at my computer; and to my parents, Donald and Pearl Kaczmarek, who fostered in me the pursuit of knowledge and a determination to succeed.

Acknowledgments

The author would like to thank the following for their support during this project:

Don Essig, Nancy Maragioglio, Lisa Wagner, Dana Coe, and Sarah Rudy at Que Corporation, who made this book possible.

Pam Bernard, Pam Riter, and Elaine Avros at Productivity Point International for their support and assistance, especially when balancing training and writing schedules.

My fellow authors for agreeing to undertake this project with me and for sharing their expertise and their time to make it a reality.

My fellow partners and trainers at Productivity Point International for their assistance and expertise when my mental active RAM failed to work properly.

Productivity Point International, a truly world–class training organization, for its ongoing investment and conviction in me and for offering me such an exciting career opportunity.

About the Authors

Steven D. Kaczmarek, MCSE, MCT, has been associated with Productivity Point as a training consultant since October of 1991. During that time he has focused on providing operating system, network management, and personal computer support training to its clients. Since January of 1996, he has also provided independent consulting services. He holds training and professional certifications (MCT and MCP) from Microsoft Corporation for Windows 3.1, Windows for Workgroups 3.11, Windows 95, Windows NT 3.51 and Windows NT 4.0, Microsoft Systems Management Server 1.2 and TCP/IP, as well as the Microsoft Certified Systems Engineer (MCSE) certification for both Windows NT 3.51 and Windows NT 4.0. Later this summer he plans to begin work on another book tentatively titled *Understanding and Implementing Microsoft Systems Management Server*.

Prior to joining Productivity Point, Steve provided a variety of client personal computer support services through the IS departments of

Heller International, McDonald's Corporation, and Continental Bank, which included purchasing and installation of personal computer hardware and software, network management, maintenance and help desk support, and customized training. He jokes that he started working with personal computers when they were in their "terrible twos" and has survived them into their "teen years."

Steve has a Master of Science degree from Loyola University with a specialization in computational mathematics.

Steve can be reached through e-mail at **sdkacz@aol.com** (America Online) or **105000,1756@compuserve.com** (CompuServe).

James P. O'Connor, MCT, is a Corporate Technical Trainer for Productivity Point International and is based out of Hinsdale, Illinois. Since working for PPI, Jim has conducted Microsoft certified courses on Windows NT 3.1 through Windows NT 4.0, Windows 95, Windows 3.1/3.11, plus numerous PPI Windows NT and Windows 95 courses.

Prior to PPI, Jim was employed by Burroughs/Unisys Corporation for 28 years. The first 13 years were spent as a field engineer supporting numerous mainframe and peripheral equipment throughout the state of Wisconsin and within the Minneapolis district. The last 15 years of Jim's career with Burroughs/Unisys were spent in the training department in California and Illinois where he taught classes and developed courses on Burroughs/Unisys proprietary mainframe and peripheral equipment. Jim has also taught classes in England and Australia. The last two years with Unisys were spent conducting Microsoft NT, Windows 3.1, Windows for Workgroups 3.11, and DOS classes.

Jim resides in Bolingbrook, Illinois, a Chicago suburb, with his wife, Donna, and two daughters, Nicole and Michelle. His Internet address is **joconnor@ppiptc.com**.

Teri Guendling launched her career over 20 years ago and has successfully managed a career of technical training, corporate consulting, and authoring. Taking advantage of a solid educational foundation, she has been able to play a leading role in corporate projects, including systems analysis and design, expert systems development, and enterprise level networking systems.

Teri holds an undergraduate degree in Computer Science and a Master of Science degree in Management Information Systems. Studying as a doctoral candidate, she was able to develop graduate-level courses in the design and implementation of corporate expert systems. Teri was a tenured instructor of Computer Science and taught undergraduate as well as graduate-level courses. She is a Microsoft Certified Systems Engineer (MCSE) and a Microsoft Certified Trainer (MCT).

Teri began her career working on large-scale mainframe systems. Her career progression has paralleled technological advances, positioning her for enterprise networking consulting, authoring, and technical training. Her special areas of interest are Microsoft Windows 95, Microsoft Windows NT, Systems Management Server (SMS), and SQL Server.

Teri is a published author, having co-authored *SMS 1.2 Administrators Guide* (SAMS Publishing) and *Microsoft Windows NT Exam Guide* (Que). Additionally, she has edited several books on these topics and has developed, authored, and taught courses for Productivity Point International.

Teri resides in the Chicago area with Bill, her husband of over 30 years. As founder and owner of TMG & Associates, she has developed a widespread reputation within the computer industry and is recognized as an industry expert. She can be reached at **102415.3262@COMPUSERVE.COM**.

Michael LaBarbera, MCPS, MCT, has successfully combined over 14 years of experience and knowledge with hardware and software ranging from high end main frames to low end controlling logic circuits. He configures, installs, upgrades, and supports networks, hardware, and primarily Microsoft operating systems. With over seven years experience in the technical education environment, Michael has worked closely with design and technical engineers in order to develop, maintain, and train proprietary courseware. He has developed numerous impromptu seminars and workshops for his clients.

Michael began his career with computers and software from his fascination with electricity and a hobby analog computer. Michael graduated with honors from DeVry Institute of Technology in Digital Electronics. Michael has several years experience as a Microsoft Certified Trainer and Product Specialist.

Productivity Point International (PPI) provides integrated computer software training and support services to the corporate market. PPI's more than 110 state-of-the-art training centers throughout North America serve the needs of both computer users and information technology professionals in subjects such as end-user applications, local area networks, application development, system migrations and client/server computing. PPI offers results-oriented training in more than 1,000 professional instructors.

Since launching its computer training network in 1990, PPI has trained more than four million students from thousands of companies. PPI specializes in designing and delivering customized solutions that fullfill its clients' specific computer training needs. Its roster of blue-chip clients includes leaders in manufacturing, financial and other information-intensive industries, as well as government institutions.

PPI offers a unique, proprietary methodology—*ProductivityPlan*—which integrates the sofware training process, products and services under an umbrella of strategic planning. This consultative methodology delivers a customized productivity solution for people who use software as an integral part of their jobs. *ProductivityPlan* consists of three components: DISCOVERY (needs analysis and skills assessment), DESIGN (training plans, products and support services) and DELIVERY (implementation and evaluation).

PPI has developed proprietary, objective evaluation and measurement techniquies that qualify the results of *ProductivityPlan* and the return on investment. PPI's evaluation system also provides a formal method of channeling feedback into the ongoing Discovery process, delivering a "closed loop" process that lets the client company refine its software productivity solution through time. These results yield a number of important benefits:

- More cost-effective use of training dollars.
- Improved skill retention and transfer to the job.
- Better employee time-utilization.
- Increased on-the-job productivity.

We'd Like to Hear from You!

Que Corporation has a long-standing reputation for high-quality books and products. To ensure your continued satisfaction, we also understand the importance of customer service and support.

Tech Support

If you need assistance with the information in this book or with a CD/disc accompanying the book, please access Macmillan Computer Publishing's online Knowledge Base at:

http://www.superlibrary.com/general/support

Our most Frequently Asked Questions are answered there. If you do not find the answer to your questions on our Web site, you may contact Macmillan Technical Support by phone at **317/581-3833** or via e-mail at **support@mcp.com**.

Also be sure to visit Que's Desktop Applications and Operating Systems team Web resource center for all the latest information, enhancements, errata, downloads, and more:

http://www.quecorp.com/desktop_os/

Orders, Catalogs, and Customer Service

To order other Que or Macmillan Computer Publishing books, catalogs, or products, please contact our Customer Service Department:

Phone: 800/428-5331

Fax: 800/835-3202

International Fax: 317/228-4400

Or visit our online bookstore:

http://www.mcp.com/

Comments and Suggestions

We want you to let us know what you like or dislike most about this book or other Que products. Your comments will help us to continue publishing the best books available on computer topics in today's market.

Dana Coe
Product Director
Que Corporation
201 West 103rd Street, 4B
Indianapolis, Indiana 46290 USA
Fax: 317/581-4663
E-mail: **dcoe@que.mcp.com**

Please be sure to include the book's title and author as well as your name and phone or fax number.

We will carefully review your comments and share them with the author. Please note that due to the high volume of mail we receive, we may not be able to reply to every message.

Thank you for choosing Que!

Contents at a Glance

Table of Contents

IV • Managing Domain Resources   317

12 Domain Users and Groups   319

Introduction

This book was written by Microsoft Certified Professionals, for Microsoft Certified Professionals and MCP candidates. It is designed, in combination with your real-world experience, to prepare you to pass the Implementing and Supporting Windows NT Server 4.0 in the Enterprise Exam (70-68), as well as give you a background in performance monitoring, optimizing, enterprise management, and troubleshooting in a Windows NT Server environment.

The reader should already have a strong working knowledge of the following subjects before beginning a study of this product:

- ◆ *Windows 95.* It is strongly suggested that you be well acquainted with the look and feel of Windows 95 as this is also the interface used by Windows NT 4.0.

- ◆ *Windows NT Server 4.0.* It is not the intention of this book to teach you Windows NT Server 4.0. Rather, it is designed to build on your existing knowledge of the product. Wherever it is appropriate, however, functions and procedures will be reviewed.

◆ *Basic networking concepts.* Again, it is not the intention of this book to teach you how to network, or what networking is all about. Rather, it is designed to explain how Windows NT Server 4.0 can be used to create and manage a network environment.

As of this writing, the exams cost $100 each. Each exam consists of 50 to 100 questions and is timed from one to two hours each. Depending on the certification level, you may have to take as many as six exams, covering Microsoft operating systems, application programs, networking, and software development. Each test involves preparation, study, and for some of us, heavy doses of test anxiety. Is certification worth the trouble?

Microsoft has cosponsored research that provides some answers.

Benefits for Your Organization

At companies participating in a 1994 Dataquest survey, a majority of corporate managers stated that certification is an *important factor* to the overall success of their companies because:

◆ *Certification increases customer satisfaction.* Customers look for indications that their suppliers understand the industry and have the ability to respond to their technical problems. Having Microsoft Certified Professionals on staff reassures customers; it tells them that your employees have used and mastered Microsoft products.

◆ *Certification maximizes training investment.* The certification process specifically identifies skills that an employee is lacking or areas where additional training is needed. By so doing, it validates training and eliminates the costs and loss of productivity associated with unnecessary training. In addition, certification records enable a company to verify an employee's technical knowledge and track retention of skills over time.

Benefits Up Close and Personal

Microsoft also cites a number of benefits for the certified individual:

- Industry recognition of expertise, enhanced by Microsoft's promotion of the Certified Professional community to the industry and potential clients.
- Access to technical information directly from Microsoft.
- Dedicated CompuServe and The Microsoft Network forums that enable Microsoft Certified Professionals to communicate directly with Microsoft and with one another.
- A complimentary one-year subscription to *Microsoft Certified Professional Magazine.*
- Microsoft Certified Professional logos and other materials to publicize MCP status to colleagues and clients.
- An MCP newsletter to provide regular information on changes and advances in the program and exams.
- Invitations to Microsoft conferences and technical training sessions, plus a special events program newsletter from the MCP program.

Additional benefits, depending upon the certification, include:

- Microsoft TechNet or Microsoft Developer Network membership or discounts.
- Free product support incidents with the Microsoft Support Network seven days a week, 24 hours a day.
- A one-year subscription to the Microsoft Beta Evaluation program, providing up to 12 monthly CD-ROMs containing beta software for upcoming Microsoft software products.
- Eligibility to join the Network Professional Association, a worldwide independent association of computer professionals.

Some intangible benefits of certification are:

- Enhanced marketability with current or potential employers and customers, along with an increase in earnings potential.

◆ Methodology for objectively assessing current skills, individual strengths, and specific areas where training is required.

How Does This Book Fit In?

One of the challenges that has always faced the would-be Microsoft Certified Professional is to decide how to best prepare for an examination. In doing so, there are always conflicting goals, such as how to prepare for the exam as quickly as possible, and yet still learn how to do the work that passing the exam qualifies you to do.

Our goal for this book is to make your studying job easier by filtering through the reams of Windows NT 4.0 technical material. Through the chapters and lab exercises, this book presents only the information that you actually need to *know* to pass the Windows NT 4.0 Certification Exam (plus a little bit extra). Other information that we think is important for you to have available while you're working has been relegated to the appendixes, sidebars, and notes.

How to Study with This Book

This book is designed to be used in a variety of ways. Rather than lock you into one particular method of studying, force you to read through sections you're already intimately familiar with, or tie you to your computer, we've made it possible for you to read the chapters at one time, and do the labs at another. We've also made it easy for you to decide whether you need to read a chapter by giving you a list of the topics and skills covered at the beginning of each chapter, and describing how the chapter relates to previous material.

Labs are arranged topically, so that you can use them to explore the areas and concepts of Windows NT 4.0 that are new to you, or that you need reinforcement in. We've also decided not to intermix them with the text of the chapter, because nothing is more frustrating than not being able to continue reading a chapter because your child is doing his homework on the computer, and you can't use it until the weekend.

The chapters are written in a modular fashion, so that you don't necessarily have to read all the chapters preceding a certain chapter to be able to follow a particular chapter's discussion. The prerequisites for each chapter specify what knowledge you need to have to successfully comprehend the current chapter's contents. Frequently, subsequent chapters build on material presented in previous chapters. For example, Chapter 2, "Windows NT 4.0 Directory Services Overview," explains Microsoft's concept of Directory Services. Without a thorough understanding of the implications of this concept, the rest of the material presented in the book will be less than satisfying.

Don't skip the lab exercises, either. You certainly can practice what you read on your PC while you are reading. Some of the knowledge and skills you need to pass the Windows NT 4.0 MCP exam can only be acquired by working with Windows NT 4.0. Lots of practice and the lab exercises help you acquire these skills.

How This Book Is Organized

The book is broken up into 22 chapters in 5 sections. Each section contains chapters relating to a common subject or theme. Each chapter focuses on a particular topic that is an important piece of the overall picture.

◆ Section I, "Certification Overview," consists of Chapter 1, "Microsoft Certified Professional Program," which gives you an overview of the Microsoft Certified Professional program, what certifications are available to you, and where Windows NT 4.0 and this book fit in.

◆ Section II, "Planning for Windows NT 4.0 Server in the Enterprise," consists of four chapters that explore the subject of Windows NT domains, trusts, models, and planning issues.

◆ Chapter 2, "Windows NT 4.0 Directory Services Overview," provides an overview of Microsoft's concept of Directory Services, discussing single point of logon, centralized account administration, and resource management across Windows NT domains.

◆ Chapter 3, "Trust Relationships," explores how Windows NT domains are linked together to create enterprise computing units.

◆ Chapter 4, "Domain Models," reviews the four Windows NT domain models and the trusts implemented to create and manage them.

◆ Chapter 5, "Capacity Planning and Performance," discusses various planning issues to consider when implementing your Windows NT domain model including number and placement of domain controllers, the size of the account database, and replication of the account database.

◆ Section III, "Installation and Configuration," consists of six chapters that explore various network-related configuration considerations such as the Computer Browser service, network printing, client configuration, and the Windows NT Registry.

◆ Chapter 6, "Domain Installation Considerations," discusses server roles and their requirements.

◆ Chapter 7, "The Role of the Registry," presents a detailed discussion of the Windows NT Registry and its components, and explores how it can be used to troubleshoot problems.

◆ Chapter 8, "Configuring Domain Network Core Services," covers the various protocol choices you have with Windows NT 4.0 and explores certain particular services such as Computer Browser and Directory Replication.

◆ Chapter 9, "Disk Management and Fault Tolerance," discusses the options for implementing fault tolerance available through the Disk Administrator utility on Windows NT Server 4.0.

◆ Chapter 10, "Managing Printers in the Domain," provides an overview of the Windows NT 4.0 printing process, and specifically explores printing considerations in the enterprise.

◆ Chapter 11, "Network Client Configuration and Support," discusses the Windows NT Network Client Administrator utility used to configure Windows NT client connectivity, and discusses Macintosh clients as well.

◆ Section IV, "Managing Domain Resources," consists of four chapters that deal with the subject of users, groups, security, resource access, and server management within and across domains.

◆ Chapter 12, "Domain Users and Groups," reviews the process for creating user and group accounts, and specifically discusses global groups, account policies, and user rights in the domain.

◆ Chapter 13, "Security and Permissions," discusses how to make resources available across the network and how to secure and audit access to them.

◆ Chapter 14, "Policies and Profiles," explores how user profiles and system policies can be used to standardize computer configurations and user environments.

◆ Chapter 15, "Remote Server Management," covers the remote management tools available in Windows NT 4.0 that enable an administrator to manage the network from a central location.

◆ Section V, "Connectivity," consists of four chapters, each of which deals with a different aspect of network connectivity with Windows NT 4.0.

◆ Chapter 16, "Novell NetWare Connectivity Tools," explores the Windows NT 4.0 Server-based services that provide connectivity to Novell NetWare networks, such as Gateway Services for NetWare, File and Print Services for NetWare, Directory Service Manager for NetWare, and the NetWare Migration utility.

◆ Chapter 17, "Multiprotocol Routing," discusses implementation of routing between protocols within a Windows NT network.

◆ Chapter 18, "Internet Information Server," introduces Windows NT Server 4.0's Internet Information Server which provides intranet and Internet Web services on your Windows NT 4.0 Server.

◆ Chapter 19, "Remote Access Server," examines Windows NT's Remote Access Service including configuration, gateway services, and security.

◆ Section VI, "Monitoring and Optimization," consists of three chapters chock full of information relating to performance measuring, optimization, and troubleshooting techniques and tools.

◆ Chapter 20, "Performance Monitor," explores the Performance Monitor tool and how it can be used to create and log performance baselines on a Windows NT system, and use that information to identify, predict, and resolve performance issues.

◆ Chapter 21, "Network Monitor," explores the Network Monitor utility now included with Windows NT Server 4.0, which provides a frame analyzing tool to help identify, predict, and resolve network traffic generated and received by a Windows NT server.

◆ Chapter 22, "Advanced Troubleshooting," presents some additional useful tools to help problem solve your Windows NT server, including interpreting blue screens, using kernel debugger, and generating memory dumps.

Lab Exercises can be found in Appendix K. As mentioned earlier, you can do these exercises at your own pace, when you want to—you're not tied down to the computer for every chapter. However, any dependencies among the labs will be noted at the beginning of each lab. Also, most of the labs will assume that the very first lab has been completed, which configures the computers initially.

All of the Windows NT Server 4.0 Enterprise exam objectives are covered in the material contained in the text of the chapters and the lab exercises. Information contained in sidebars is provided to give history, extend the topic, expound on a related procedure, or provide other details. It is useful information, but not primary exam material.

Finally, the many appendixes in this book provide you with additional advice, resources, and information that can be helpful to you as you prepare and take the Implementing and Supporting NT Server 4.0 in the Enterprise Certified Professional exam, and later as you work as a Windows NT 4.0 Certified Professional:

◆ Appendix A, "Glossary," provides you with definitions of terms that you need to be familiar with as a Windows NT 4.0 MCP.

◆ Appendix B, "Certification Checklist," provides an overview of the certification process in the form of a to-do list, with milestones you can check off on your way to certification.

◆ Appendix C, "How Do I Get There from Here?" provides step-by-step guidelines for successfully navigating from initial interest to final certification.

◆ Appendix D, "Testing Tips," gives you tips and pointers for maximizing your performance when you take the certification exam.

◆ Appendix E, "Contacting Microsoft," lists contact information for certification exam resources at Microsoft and at Sylvan Prometric testing centers.

◆ Appendix F, "Suggested Reading," presents a list of reading resources that can help you prepare for the certification exam.

◆ Appendix G, "Windows NT 4.0 Overview," provides a brief look at the features and functionality offered by Windows NT 4.0.

◆ Appendix H, "Internet Resources for Windows NT," is a list of places to visit on the Internet related to Windows NT.

◆ Appendix I, "Using the CD-ROM," gives you the basics of how to install and use the CD-ROM included with this book. This appendix also includes skill self-assessment tests and simulated versions of the Microsoft exam, as well as the Microsoft TechNet sampler, with over 400M of Microsoft technical information, including the Microsoft Knowledge Base.

◆ Appendix J, "Sample Tests," provides performance-based questions designed to test your problem-solving capabilities.

Special Features of this Book

There are many features in this book to make it easier to read and make the information more accessible. Those features are described in the following sections.

Chapter Overview

Each chapter begins with an overview of the material covered in that chapter. The chapter topics are described in the context of material already covered, and material coming up. Also, any prerequisite information needed to fully appreciate the contents of a chapter is presented.

Notes

Notes present interesting or useful information that isn't necessarily essential to the discussion, but will enhance your understanding of Windows NT Server 4.0 in the Enterprise. Notes look like this:

 Note   Microsoft posts beta exam notices on the Internet (**http://www.microsoft.com**), and mails notices to certification development volunteers, past certification candidates, and product beta participants. ▪

Tips

Tips present short advice on quick or often overlooked procedures. These include shortcuts that save you time. A tip looks like this:

 Tip
Use the Windows NT taskbar to quickly switch between open programs and windows.

Key Concepts

Key Concepts present particularly significant information about a Windows NT function or concept. Count on this material being on the test. Here's an example of a key concept:

Key Concept
When you share a resource in Windows NT, the default is to provide everyone with complete access to the resource. If you want additional security, you must add it yourself by restricting access with permissions.

Sidebar

Sidebars are used to provide additional information and enhance the discussion at hand. If a particular topic has a different twist in Windows NT server, it will be discussed in a sidebar. A sidebar looks like this (but longer):

Network Monitor on Windows NT Server

Another useful performance tracking tool is packaged with Windows NT Server 4.0. It is called the Network Monitor and provides network packet analysis to the administrator.

Caution

A Caution is meant to draw your attention to a particularly tricky twist in a concept, or to point out potential pitfalls. Cautions look like this:

Caution

If you do not keep your Emergency Repair Disk up-to-date, and you use it to restore Registry information, you can wipe out your existing account database by overwriting it with the old information.

In addition to these special features, there are several conventions used in this book to make it easier to read and understand. These conventions are described in the following sections.

Underlined Hotkeys or Mnemonics

Hotkeys in this book appear underlined, as they appear on-screen. In Windows, many menus, commands, buttons, and other options have these hotkeys. To use a hotkey shortcut, press Alt and the key for the underlined character. For example, to choose the Properties button, press Alt and then R. You should not study for the MCP exam by using the hotkeys, however. Windows is a mouse-centric environment, and you will be expected to know how to navigate it using the mouse—clicking, right-clicking, and using drag and drop.

Shortcut Key Combinations

In this book, shortcut key combinations are joined with plus signs (+). For example, Ctrl+V means hold down the Ctrl key, while you press the V key.

Menu Commands

Instructions for choosing menu commands have this form:

Choose File, New.

This example means open the File menu and select New, which in this case opens a new file.

This book also has the following typeface enhancements to indicate special text, as indicated in the following table.

Typeface	Description
Italic	Italics are used to indicate new terms and variables in commands or addresses.
Boldface	Bold is used to indicate text you type, as well as Internet addresses and other locators in the online world.
Computer type	This typeface is used for on-screen messages and commands (such as DOS copy or UNIX commands).
My Filename.doc	File names and folders are set in a mixture of upper- and lowercase characters, just as they appear in Windows NT 4.0.

Part I.

Certification Overview

1 Microsoft Certified Professional Program

Chapter Prerequisite

This chapter has no prerequisites, only a desire to become
a Microsoft Certified
Professional.

1

Microsoft Certified Professional Program

As Microsoft products take an increasing share of the marketplace, the demand for trained personnel grows, and the number of certifications follows suit. As of April of 1996, the team of Microsoft Certified Professionals increased in number to more than 40,000 product specialists, more than 8,000 engineers, and more than 1,600 solution developers. There were also more than 4,900 certified trainers of Microsoft products.

There is every indication that these numbers will continue to grow, given Microsoft's commitment to its products and to the certification program, as well as the continued market interest in these products and in those certified to administer them. The best place to look for changes would be Microsoft's Web site at **www.microsoft.com**.

This chapter covers the Microsoft Certified Professional Program and describes each certification in more detail. Microsoft certifications include:

- ◆ Microsoft Certified Professional (MCP)
- ◆ Microsoft Certified Systems Engineer (MCSE)
- ◆ Microsoft Certified Product Specialist (MCPS)
- ◆ Microsoft Certified Solutions Developer (MCSD)
- ◆ Microsoft Certified Trainer (MCT)

Exploring Available Certifications

When Microsoft started certifying people to install and support their products, there was only one certification available, the Microsoft Certified Professional (MCP). As time went on, employers and prospective customers of consulting firms demanded more specialized certifications. There are now four certifications available in the MCP program, as described in the following sections.

Microsoft Certified Systems Engineers (MCSE)

Microsoft Certified Systems Engineers are qualified to plan, implement, maintain, and support information systems based on Microsoft Windows NT and the BackOffice family of client-server software. The MCSE is a widely respected certification because it does not focus on a just one aspect of computing, such as networking. Instead, the MCSE has demonstrated skills and abilities on the full range of software, from client operating systems to server operating systems to client-server applications.

Microsoft Certified Solution Developers (MCSD)

Microsoft Certified Solution Developers are qualified to design and develop custom business solutions with Microsoft development tools, platforms, and technologies such as Microsoft BackOffice and Microsoft Office. MCSD candidates are required to demonstrate a full understanding of 32-bit architecture, OLE, WOSA, and other related topics.

Microsoft Certified Product Specialists (MCPS)

Microsoft Certified Product Specialists have demonstrated in-depth knowledge of at least one Microsoft operating system. Candidates may pass additional Microsoft certification exams to further qualify their skills with Microsoft BackOffice products, development tools, or desktop applications.

The Microsoft Certified Product Specialist Areas of Specialization (AOS) that lead to the MCSE certification include:

- *Networking.* This AOS requires the candidate to pass the Implementing MS Windows NT Server exam (version 3.51 or 4.0); one desktop operating system exam, such as the Implementing MS Windows NT Workstation 4.0 exam; and one networking exam, such as the Networking Essentials for BackOffice exam.

- *TCP/IP.* This AOS requires the candidate to pass the Implementing MS Windows NT Server exam (3.51 or 4.0) and the Internetworking TCP/IP on Windows NT exam.

- *Mail.* This AOS requires the candidate to pass the Implementing MS Windows NT Server exam (3.51 or 4.0) and the Microsoft Mail (Enterprise) exam.

- *SQL Server.* This AOS requires the candidate to pass the Implementing MS Windows NT Server exam (3.51 or 4.0) and both SQL Server exams.

- *Systems Management Server.* This AOS requires the candidate to pass the Implementing MS Windows NT Server exam (3.51 or 4.0) and the SMS exam.

- *SNA Server.* This AOS requires the candidate to pass the Implementing MS Windows NT Server exam (3.51 or 4.0) and the SNA Server exam.

◆ *Internet Systems.* This newly introduced AOS requires the candidate to pass the Implementing MS Windows NT Server 4.0 exam, as well as two new exams—Internetworking TCP/IP on MS Windows NT 4.0 and Implementing and Supporting MS Internet Information Server.

The Microsoft Certified Product Specialist product-specific exams are your first steps into the world of Microsoft certification. After establishing a specialty, you can work toward additional certification goals at the MCSE or MCSD level.

Microsoft Certified Trainers (MCT)

Microsoft Certified Trainers are instructionally and technically qualified to deliver Microsoft Official Curriculum through Microsoft authorized education sites. These sites are comprised of Authorized Technical Education Centers (ATECs), including companies such as Productivity Point International, which specialize in offering technical and application training to corporate clients; and Authorized Academic Training Partners (AATPs), which represent educational institutions that offer certified classes for continuing education. In order for a trainer to be certified by Microsoft as a MCT, that trainer must also have attended and completed, or in some cases studied, each certified class that he or she expects to teach.

Understanding the Exam Requirements

The exams are computer-administered tests that measure your ability to implement and administer Microsoft products or systems; troubleshoot problems with installation, operation, or customization; and provide technical support to users. The exams do more than test your ability to define terminology and/or recite facts. Product *knowledge* is an important foundation for superior job performance, but definitions and feature lists are just the beginning. In the real world, you need hands-on skills and the ability to apply your knowledge—to understand confusing situations, solve thorny problems, optimize solutions to minimize downtime, and maximize current and future productivity.

To develop exams that test for the right competence factors, Microsoft follows an eight-phase exam development process:

◆ In the first phase, experts analyze the tasks that make up the job being tested. This job analysis phase identifies the knowledge, skills, and abilities relating specifically to the performance area to be certified.

◆ The next phase develops objectives by building on the framework provided by the job analysis. This means translating the job function tasks into specific and measurable units of knowledge, skills, and abilities. The resulting list of objectives (the *objective domain*) is the basis for developing certification exams and training materials.

◆ Selected contributors rate the objectives developed in the previous phase. The reviewers are technology professionals who are currently performing the applicable job function. After the objectives are prioritized and weighted based on the contributors' input, they become the blueprint for the exam items.

◆ During the fourth phase, exam items are reviewed and revised to ensure that they are technically accurate, clear, unambiguous, plausible, free of cultural bias, and not misleading or tricky. Items are also evaluated to confirm that they test for high-level, useful knowledge, rather than obscure or trivial facts.

◆ During alpha review, technical and job function experts review each item for technical accuracy, reach consensus on all technical issues, and edit the reviewed items for clarity of expression.

◆ The next step is the beta exam. Beta exam participants take the test to gauge its effectiveness. Microsoft performs a statistical analysis based on the responses of the beta participants, including information about difficulty and relevance, to verify the validity of the exam items and to determine which items are used in the final certification exam.

◆ When the statistical analysis is complete, the items are distributed into multiple parallel forms, or versions, of the final certification exam, usually within six to eight weeks of the beta exam.

 Note Microsoft posts beta exam notices on the Internet (**http://www.microsoft.com**), and mails notices to certification development volunteers, past certification candidates, and product beta participants. ▪

Tip

If you participate in a beta exam, you may take it at a cost that is lower than the cost of the final certification exam, but it should not be taken lightly. Beta exams actually contain the entire pool of possible questions, about 30 percent of which are dropped after the beta. The remaining questions are divided into the different forms of the final exam. If you decide to take a beta exam, you should review and study as seriously as you would for a final certification exam. Passing a beta exam counts as passing the final exam—you receive full credit for passing a beta exam.

Also, because you will be taking *all* of the questions that will be used for the exam, expect a beta to take significantly longer than the final exam. For example, the beta tests for Windows NT 4.0 have so far had a time limit of four hours each, and more than three times as many questions as the final versions of the exams!

Also during this phase, a group of job function experts determine the cut, or minimum passing score, for the exam. (The cut score differs from exam to exam because it is based on an item-by-item determination of the percentage of candidates who answered the item correctly.)

◆ The final phase—Exam Live!—is administered by Sylvan Prometric, an independent testing company. The exams are always available at Sylvan Prometric testing centers worldwide. Exams can be scheduled by calling 1–800–755–exam.

Note If you're interested in participating in any of the exam development phases (including the beta exam), contact the Microsoft Certification Development Team by sending a fax to (206) 936-1311.

Include the following information about yourself: name, complete address, company, job title, phone number, fax number, e-mail or Internet address, and product areas of interest or expertise. ■

Microsoft Certified Systems Engineer Core Exams

To achieve the Microsoft Certified Systems Engineer certification, a candidate must pass four required "core" exams, plus two elective exams. There are two possible paths, or tracks, that lead to an MCSE certification: the Windows NT 4.0 track, and the Windows NT 3.51 track.

Microsoft Windows NT 4.0 Track to an MCSE

The Microsoft Windows NT 4.0 track to an MCSE is significantly different from the earlier Windows NT 3.51 track, although there are still four core exams. These first two exams are required:

◆ Implementing and Supporting Microsoft Windows NT 4.0 Server (70-67). This exam covers installing and supporting Windows NT 4.0 in a single-domain environment. This exam also qualifies a candidate as an MCPS.

◆ Implementing and Supporting Microsoft Windows NT 4.0 Server in the Enterprise (70-68). This exam covers installing and supporting Windows NT 4.0 in an enterprise computing environment with mission critical applications and tasks. This exam does *not* qualify a candidate as an MCPS.

The third required core exam can be fulfilled by one of four different exams:

◆ Microsoft Windows 3.1 (70-30). Legacy support.

◆ Microsoft Windows for Workgroups 3.11 (70-48). Legacy support.

◆ Implementing and Supporting Microsoft Windows 95 (70-63). Tests a candidate's ability to implement and support Microsoft Windows NT 4.0 in a variety of environments, including as a network client on Novell NetWare. This exam qualifies a candidate as an MCPS.

◆ Implementing and Supporting Microsoft Windows NT Workstation 4.0 (70-73). Tests a candidate's ability to implement and support Microsoft Windows NT Workstation 4.0. This exam qualifies a candidate as an MCPS.

The fourth core exam can be fulfilled by one of the following:

Note This exam is waived for those candidates who are also Novell Certified NetWare Engineers (CNE) or Banyan Certified Banyan Engineers (CBE). ■

◆ Networking with Windows for Workgroups 3.11 (70-46). Legacy support.

◆ Networking with Windows 3.1 (70-47). Legacy support.

◆ Networking Essentials (70-58). Tests the candidate's networking skills required for implementing, administrating, and troubleshooting systems that incorporate Windows NT 4.0 and BackOffice.

Windows NT 3.51 Track to the MCSE Certification

Most current Microsoft Certified Systems Engineers followed, or are following, this track, which will continue to be a valid track.

There are four core exams. The first two, the Windows NT 3.51 exams are required:

◆ Implementing and Supporting Microsoft Windows NT Server 3.51 (70-43). This exam covers installing and supporting Windows NT Server 3.51 in a variety of environments. This exam also qualifies a candidate as an MCPS.

◆ Implementing and Supporting Microsoft Windows NT Workstation 3.51 (70-42). This exam covers installing and supporting Windows NT Workstation 3.51. This exam qualifies a candidate as an MCPS.

The third required core exam can be fulfilled by one of three different exams:

◆ Microsoft Windows 3.1 (70-30). Legacy support.

◆ Microsoft Windows for Workgroups 3.11 (70-48). Legacy support.

◆ Implementing and Supporting Microsoft Windows 95 (70-63). Tests a candidate's ability to implement and support Microsoft Windows 95 in a variety of environments, including as a network client on Novell NetWare. This exam qualifies a candidate as an MCPS.

The fourth core exam can be fulfilled by one of the following:

Note This exam is waived for those candidates who are also Novell Certified NetWare Engineers (CNE) or Banyan Certified Banyan Engineers (CBE). ■

◆ Networking with Windows for Workgroups 3.11 (70-46). Legacy support.

◆ Networking with Windows 3.1 (70-47). Legacy support.

◆ Networking Essentials (70-58). Tests the candidate's networking skills required for implementing, administrating, and troubleshooting systems that incorporate Windows NT 4.0 and BackOffice.

Electives for the Microsoft Certified Systems Engineers

Besides the core exam requirements, you must pass two Elective exams to complete a Microsoft Certified Systems Engineer certification. The list of electives in Table 1.1 was current as of January 1997.

Table 1.1 Microsoft Certified Systems Engineer Electives	
Exam	Number
Microsoft SNA Server	70-12
Implementing and Supporting Microsoft Systems Management Server 1.0	70-14
System Administration of Microsoft SQL Server 6.0	70-26

continues

Table 1.1 Continued	
Exam	**Number**
Implementing a Database Design on Microsoft SQL Server 6.0	70-27
Microsoft Mail for PC Networks—Enterprise	70-37
Internetworking Microsoft TCP/IP on Microsoft Windows NT 3.5	70-53
Internetworking Microsoft TCP/IP on Microsoft Windows NT 4.0	70-59
Implementing and Supporting Microsoft Exchange	70-75
Implementing and Supporting Microsoft Internet Information Server	70-77
Implementing and Supporting Microsoft Proxy Server	70-78

Continuing Certification Requirements

After you gain an MCP certification, such as the Microsoft Certified Systems Engineer certification, your work isn't over. Microsoft requires you to maintain your certification by updating your exam credits as new products are released, and old ones are withdrawn.

A Microsoft Certified Trainer is required to pass the exam for a new product within three months of the exam's release. For example, the Windows NT Server 4.0 exam (70-67) and Enterprise Exam (70-68) were released in December of 1996. All MCTs, including the authors of this book, were required to pass these exams by March 31, 1997, or lose certification to teach the Windows NT 4.0 Core Technologies course.

Holders of the other MCP certifications (MCPS, MCSD, MCSE) are required to replace an exam that gives them qualifying credit within six months of the withdrawal of that exam. For example, the Windows for

Workgroups 3.10 exam was one of the original electives for the MCSE certification. When it was withdrawn, MCSEs had six months to replace it with another elective exam, such as the TCP/IP exam.

Once you become a certified trainer, you begin receiving monthly up-dates regarding the tests and courses that have become obsolete, as well as the introduction of new courses and tests and certification require-ments via Microsoft's Education Forum newsletter. Updates can also be found by browsing Microsoft's Web site at **www.microsoft.com**.

Part II.

Planning for Windows NT 4.0 Server in the Enterprise

Chapter Prerequisite

There is no prerequisite for this chapter other than a desire to learn how to extend your knowledge of Windows NT 4.0 into an enterprise computing environment. You should already be familiar with Windows NT 4.0 features, as well as basic networking. Appendix G, "Windows NT 4.0 Overview," can help to familiarize you with some of these topics.

Windows NT 4.0 Directory Services Overview

This chapter is designed to introduce you to Windows NT 4.0's fundamental concept of directory services, or what Microsoft calls the "enterprise challenge." In this chapter, we will cover the following topics:

◆ Workgroup versus domain network models

◆ Windows NT 4.0 Directory Services concept

◆ Centralized account administration

◆ Centralized resource management and universal resource access

◆ Account synchronization

◆ Domain structure and trust overview

Distinguishing a Workgroup from a Domain

There are two distinct types of networking supported by Windows NT: *workgroup computing* and the *domain model*. As you plan your network, you need to distinguish between these two and decide which model best meets your networking needs. Let's compare the two models.

Workgroup Model

The workgroup model of networking is more commonly referred to as the *peer-to-peer model*. In this model, all computers participate in a networking group. They can all make resources available to members of the workgroup and access each other's resources as well. In other words, each computer acts as both a workstation and a server.

Computers using Windows NT, Windows 95, and Windows for Workgroups have the ability to participate in a workgroup network model as shown in Figure 2.1. In fact, both Windows NT Workstations and Windows NT Servers can be members of a workgroup. However, only Windows NT offers the added capability to provide security for network resources.

FIG. 2.1 ⇒

Here is an example of the workgroup network model.

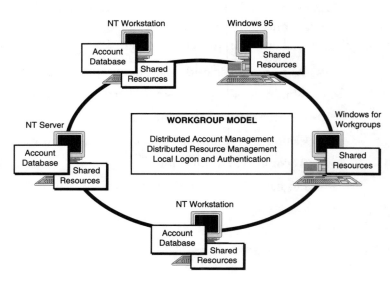

On computers using Windows NT, access to resources is provided by authenticating the inbound user at the resource computer. Each Windows NT computer participating in a workgroup must maintain a list of users who will be accessing the resources on that computer.

Potentially, this means that each computer will have at least as many user accounts as there are participating members in the workgroup. Account administration in a workgroup is thus considered to be distributed, as is resource administration. In other words, the responsibility for maintaining the integrity of user account and resource access generally falls to the owner of the computer. A workgroup model, then, might be construed to have limited security potential.

The workgroup model works quite well within smaller networks where the number of users requiring access to workgroup resources is small and easily managed. This number has been suggested to be between 10 and 20 computers/users. As mentioned before, a Windows NT Server can participate in a workgroup. If a larger number of computers or users is required within a workgroup model, the more heavily used resources might be located in a Windows NT Server participating in the workgroup. This could help to simplify the management of large groups of users accessing resources. Nevertheless, the main characteristics of this network model are distributed account management, distributed resource management, and limited security.

Domain Model

The domain model of networking, also known as the *enterprise model*, was introduced by Microsoft as a response to the management challenges presented by the growing workgroup model.

Unlike the workgroup model, the domain model (see Figure 2.2) maintains a centralized database of user and group account information. Resource access is provided by permitting access to users and groups that are members of the domain, and thus appear in the domain's account database. Recall that in the workgroup model, each computer maintains its own account database which is used for managing resource access at that computer. In the domain model, by virtue of their participation in the domain, the resources utilize the same central account database for managing user access. Resource managers also enjoy a higher level of security for their resources.

FIG. 2.2 ⇒

Here is an example of the domain network model. The domain model answers what Microsoft refers to as the "enterprise challenge."

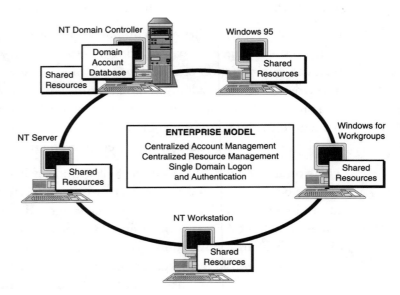

Taking the Enterprise Challenge

When planning a large wide area network for an organization—hereafter referred to as the enterprise—Microsoft advocates implementing a structure that answers the following challenges:

◆ A single network logon account for the user regardless of the user's location or domain affiliation

◆ Centralized account administration

◆ Easy user access to network resources regardless of the location of the user or the resource in the enterprise

◆ Focusing network resource administration in the hands of the resource owner or administrator

◆ Synchronization of account and security information across the enterprise

The structure should be able to support enterprise networks of varying size, with servers, computers, and users in a variety of geographic locations. It should also support, and in some cases use, a variety of network architectures, protocols, and platforms to provide a completely flexible and open architecture.

Microsoft responds to this challenge with its Directory Services solution. Windows NT's Directory Services provides a domain model of enterprise computing that centralizes account information and management into a single domain account database, while focusing network resource management with the owner/administrator of the resource.

A *domain* can be thought of as a logical grouping of computers in a Microsoft network. A *domain controller* (discussed in more detail in Chapter 5, "Capacity Planning and Performance," and Chapter 6, "Domain Installation Considerations") establishes the domain's identity and is used to maintain the database of user, group, and computer accounts for that domain. Besides the domain controller, a Windows NT domain can include member servers and workstation computers. A member server might be a Windows NT 4.0 Server configured as an application server, a database server, a RAS server, a print server, or a file server. Workstation computers might be running Windows NT Workstation 4.0, Windows 95, Windows for Workgroups 3.11, MS-DOS, Apple Macintosh System 7, or LanMan 2.2c for DOS or OS/2.

All of the computers that identify themselves as belonging to a particular domain are part of the same logical grouping. As such, they have access to the account database on the domain's domain controller for authenticating users as they log on, and for creating access control lists (ACLs) for securing network resources stored on those computers. An enterprise may consist of one domain, or several domains following one of the domain models suggested by Microsoft. See Chapter 4, "Domain Models," for more information.

For example, a domain might be centered around the organizational hierarchy and reflect its departmental structure. Perhaps the MIS department has assumed all responsibility for maintaining user and group accounts, while placing resource management within each department.

Possibly, the enterprise is organized according to regional areas such as the West, Midwest, and East domains. The domain structure might even be global in nature reflecting the enterprise's international presence. Windows NT's Directory Services provides a fit for each of these structures because Windows NT domains are logical groupings of computers; therefore, they are extremely flexible. While the physical layout of your network may affect the type of domain model that you choose to establish, domains simply don't care what the network topology looks like.

Single Network Logon

The concept of a single network logon is really quite simple: Provide the user with a single logon account that can be used to access the network from anywhere within the enterprise. An account executive based in Chicago should be able to fly to her company's office in London, use her same account to log on to the network at any computer in the London office, and access the same resources she has access to in Chicago.

Windows NT 4.0's Directory Services is designed to provide just that capability by combining the domain model of networking with a security relationship called a *trust*. Trusts are discussed in greater detail in Chapter 3, "Trust Relationships." Briefly, however, a trust relationship allows users from one Windows NT domain to be allowed access permissions to the network resources in a second Windows NT domain.

Let's assume that a trust exists between the London and Chicago domains. If the account executive's account is maintained in the Chicago domain, she can still log on to the company network at any computer in the London domain. Directory Services allows the account executive's request to log on to be passed through the trust, back to the Chicago domain for authentication (see Figure 2.3). This process of passing the logon request back through the trust to the account domain is called *pass-through authentication*. Once her account has been validated, she can access any resource in the enterprise to which she has been given permission. Note that she needs only one logon account and password to access the network and its resources. Her physical location is not important, nor is the location of the resources.

FIG. 2.3 ⇒
UserX's logon information is passed through the trust relationship to be authenticated in the appropriate domain, as depicted here.

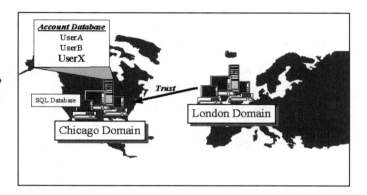

Centralized Account Administration

Recall that in a workgroup model, account administration tends to be decentralized to the desktop of each member of the workgroup. Each user might maintain his or her own workstation's account database, making it difficult to establish or maintain consistency or security.

By contrast, in a domain model, accounts are centralized on a specific domain server called the domain controller. The domain controller for the domain establishes the domain's identity in the enterprise. In fact, a domain is established by the installation of a *primary domain controller* (PDC). The PDC maintains the master account database for the domain. The PDC can also authenticate users on the network (or log users on), but its primary function is to maintain the domain's account database.

While a domain can consist of only the primary domain controller for managing accounts and authenticating users, very often the domain will also include one or more *backup domain controllers*, or BDC. The BDC receives a *copy* of the master account database maintained on the PDC. Its primary function is to authenticate users who are trying to log on to the network.

Windows NT 4.0 includes two utilities that can be used to manage user, group, and Windows NT computer accounts: User Manager for Domains and Server Manager. Both of these will be discussed in greater detail in Chapters 12, "Domain Users and Groups," and Chapter 15, "Remote Server Management."

Briefly, User Manager for Domains allows an administrator to manage the account database from any computer in the enterprise that supports the utility. That would of course include any Windows NT workstation or server, but could also be a Windows 95 or Windows for Workgroups 3.11 computer using add-on server management tools that are available. Remote server management tools are discussed in Chapter 15.

Similarly, Server Manager lets the administrator use directory services to remotely view and administer domains, workgroups, and computers. For example, the administrator could use Server Manager on her Windows NT 4.0 Workstation desktop to start and stop services on a Windows NT 4.0 Server, or to synchronize account databases among domain controllers in a domain.

Network Resource Access

Through a combination of single logon accounts, centralized administration, and trust relationships, a user can easily access any resource that he has been given permission to use from anywhere in the enterprise. Let's return to our account executive in Chicago.

She has an account in the Chicago domain that she uses to log on to the company's network. She regularly accesses a SQL database of client information that is located on a member server in the Chicago domain and to which she has been given access permission. She frequently visits the company's London office which has its own domain and its own SQL database. There is also a trust relationship between the Chicago and London domains.

As we have seen so far, when she sits down at a computer in the London domain, she can still log on to the network using her same logon account and password, just as if she was sitting at her computer in

Chicago. Also, because of the trust relationship and pass-through authentication, she can still access the SQL database on the member server in the Chicago domain (see Figure 2.4). The entire access process is transparent to her—as it should be for every user in the enterprise.

FIG. 2.4 ⇒
When UserX logs on, whether in Chicago or in London, he has access to any resources to which his account has been given permission, such as the SQL database.

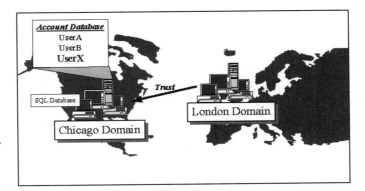

We can take this concept a step further by giving resources their own domain. This means that in most organizations, each department, unit, project team, and so on, usually has its own set of resources that they want to manage. Human Resources manages the company's Employee Handbook in Lotus Notes and maintains a SQL database of employee performance reviews, résumés, and other confidential information. Finance manages the company's budget spreadsheets, including the investment options for the retirement fund.

Each department wants to securely manage its own resources, ensuring that only authorized persons have access and that the level of access is controlled. But, they do not want to deal with day-to-day account management, such as forgotten passwords, locked out accounts, new users, users changing group memberships, and so on. In a large organization, the number of resources and resource managers may make a single large domain impractical.

In this particular scenario, each department could be given its own domain for the purpose of managing its own resources as shown in Figure 2.5. Account management would still be maintained in the account domain. By establishing trust relationships between each resource domain and the account domain, the resource managers can use the account domain's account database to create access control lists for each of their resources. Users can still log on to the network with the same single logon account and password, and access any resource to which they are given access permission. Everyone uses the same account database, yet account and resource management is centralized where it should be—with the appropriate account and resource managers.

FIG. 2.5 ⇒

The trust relationship between each resource domain and the account domain allows resource managers to use one central account database to secure access to their resources.

TRUST RELATIONSHIPS

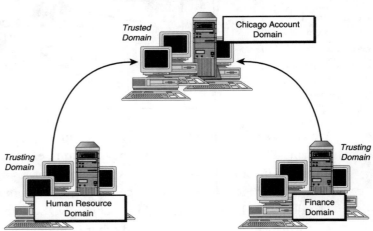

Once again, Windows NT's Directory Services provides a flexible set of options for resource management that can fit the needs of most enterprise models.

Synchronization of Account and Security Information

As we pointed out, a domain is established by the installation of a primary domain controller (PDC). As with all security objects in Windows NT, such as user and group accounts, trust relationships, and computer accounts, the creation of a PDC establishes a security identifier (SID) for the domain that is used for any security-related function, such as establishing trust relationships, implementing backup domain controllers, and effecting account synchronization.

Creating a domain controller is an implementation of Windows NT Server 4.0. Besides establishing the existence of the domain, the primary role of the PDC is to maintain the account database for the domain, hereafter called the *master* account database. If the PDC is the only domain controller created for the domain, it will also serve as the validation server and authenticate users' requests to log on to the network.

In most networks, however, in addition to the PDC, one or more backup domain controllers (BDCs) will be created for the domain. The primary role of the BDC is to authenticate users' logon requests. To do so, it must receive a copy of the master account database from the PDC for that domain. In fact, when the BDC is created, you must tell it to join a specific domain as a backup domain controller. A security relationship is established between the PDC and the BDC, and they share the same account database. The relationship between these domain controllers is so integral that any local group created on the PDC is considered local to *all* the domain controllers for the domain.

Key Concept

Any change that is made to the account database for the domain affects only the master copy maintained by the PDC. Changes are never directly registered on a BDC. BDCs only receive copies of the changes made to the master account database according to a regular schedule.

If you are using User Manager for Domains on your Windows NT 4.0 Workstation on your desk in London, and the PDC for the domain you are administering is located in Chicago (accessible through a fibe-optic connection), your change requests will be sent through the fiber-optic connection to the PDC in Chicago, even though you may have one or more BDCs located locally in London. This is easy to test. Shut down your PDC temporarily. Then try to use User Manager for Domains to add a new user account. User Manager for Domains will display a blank screen. It could not open the master account database because the PDC was not currently active. However, as long as there is a BDC available on the network, the users will continue to be able to log on successfully and access any resource they have permissions to access, provided the resource is not on the PDC that is down.

> **Caution**
> If you try the User Manager for Domains test, be sure you restart your PDC!

As stated earlier, the BDC receives a copy of the master account database and any changes made to it according to a regular schedule. On a regular interval, by default every five minutes, the PDC checks the master account database for changes. When it detects a change, it sends a notification to the BDCs in the domain. This notification interval is called a *pulse* and can be modified in the PDC's Registry. More about setting this and other Registry values related to synchronization can be found in Chapter 5, "Capacity Planning and Performance."

When the BDC receives a pulse from the PDC, it then copies the changes from the PDC. In networking terms this is called a *pull* operation because the BDC copies the changes rather than the PDC sending them. Until the BDC receives the changes, however, its copy of the master account database will still contain "old" information.

Let's consider the following scenario. Our administrator in London has added three new user accounts for three new employees that have joined the London office. He uses User Manager for Domains to add the accounts, and we know that the changes are registered in the master account database on the PDC in Chicago. We also know that, by default, it will take up to five minutes for the PDC to note the change and "pulse" the BDCs, including the BDC in London. Let's add the additional time it will take for the BDC to copy the changes across the fiber-optic connection. Depending on the amount of other network traffic, the BDC may not get the changes immediately. In fact, if the new users are particularly motivated to get on to the network to start working, and they try to log on before the changes reach the BDC in London, they won't be able to because the BDC will still have the old information that does not include the new users.

The Server Manager utility includes two functions related to the synchronization process. Again, these will be discussed in more detail in Chapter 5. Briefly, however, the administrator can force a synchronization to take place at any given point in time between the PDC and any specific BDC, or between the PDC and all the BDCs. If the PDC is down, access to the master account database is unavailable and synchronization cannot take place. So, our administrator in London could use Server Manager to have the London BDC synchronize with the Chicago PDC as soon as he creates the new user accounts. Then, the new employees could log on as soon as they wanted.

A domain may have none or several BDCs. The number and location of these BDCs will likely be determined by the number and location of the users in the enterprise, as well as by network performance and traffic concerns. For example, if the domain consists of 1,000 users all located in the same building with little or no routing taking place, then the domain might consist of the PDC and perhaps 1 or 2 BDCs. On the other hand, if your network consists of the same 1,000 users dispersed in 10 regional offices connected by various WAN connections (RAS, T1, 56K, and so on), your domain might then consist of the PDC and one BDC located at each regional office. Number and placement of BDCs will more likely be driven by issues of performance than by the number of users. Chapter 5 discusses this topic in more detail.

However you plan for your BDCs, the synchronization process will ensure that the master account database maintained on the PDC is kept up-to-date on each of the BDCs, allowing your users to log on to the network from wherever they are located in the enterprise.

Integrating Directory Services with Microsoft BackOffice

Microsoft designed its BackOffice product suite to take advantage of the Directory Services environment offered by Windows NT. The Microsoft BackOffice suite is engineered to use the master account database to identify users and groups that have access to its product functions and information, such as mail folders, databases, and management functions. As a result, the user can use the same logon account to log on to the network, access her home directory, print to a print server's print devices, send and receive mail through Exchange, query a SQL database, and remotely control another computer through System Management Server (SMS).

Security, or permissions, as with all Windows NT network resources, are granted at the resource level. Thus, permissions to access the SQL database, the Exchange mail folder, or to use remote control in SMS are granted at the BackOffice application level. The manager of the SQL database in Human Resources can have the account administrator create a domain group called HRSQL, and place certain Human Resource users in that group. The SQL database manager then grants that HRSQL group appropriate permissions to the database through the SQL Security Manager. Thereafter, if the group membership changes, the change only needs to take place in the master account database. Nothing else needs to happen at the SQL database level. As far as the user is concerned, access is transparent. The user merely needs to log on to the network to gain access to any and all network resources to which the user was given permission.

Taking the Disc Test

 If you have read and understood the material in the chapter, you are ready to test your knowledge. Insert the CD-ROM that comes with this book and run the self-test software as described in Appendix I, "Using the CD-ROM."

From Here...

We have introduced the concept of Directory Services for Windows NT 4.0 and have described how it meets the enterprise challenge envisioned by Microsoft. The next three chapters in this section of the book—Chapter 3, "Trust Relationships," Chapter 4, "Domain Models," and Chapter 5, "Capacity Planning and Performance"—will take this concept to a more detailed level examining the impact and effect it can have in establishing your enterprise network.

Trust Relationships

One of the security relationships that allows Directory Services to accomplish its objectives as stated in Chapter 2, "Windows NT 4.0 Directory Services Overview," is the trust relationship. This chapter will focus on the following topics relating to trusts:

◆ The nature of trust relationships

◆ How and when to implement trusts

◆ Managing accounts across trusts

◆ Managing resources across trusts

◆ Authenticating user requests for logging on in the domain and across the trust

Understanding the Nature of a Trust Relationship

As you read in the last chapter ("Windows NT 4.0 Directory Services Overview"), the primary objectives of the enterprise challenge are to provide network users a single logon account, easy access to resources regardless of the location of the user or the resource in the enterprise, and centralized administration of accounts and resources.

For example, let's hypothesize that in my enterprise, I have two domains. Domain A has network resources that the users of Domain B would like, or need, to access. Recall that each domain is established by the creation of its primary domain controller (PDC). Each domain is therefore considered completely separate from any other. The users from Domain B could not access the resources on Domain A unless they had access to a valid user account in Domain A which was included in the Access Control Lists (ACLs) for the resources on Domain B (see Figure 3.1). Even then, the user would effectively have to log on again to Domain A to access the resource, and this would violate one of the goals of Directory Services.

FIG. 3.1 ⇒
UserB logging on to a computer in Domain B cannot access a resource in Domain A without a valid user account in Domain A. The two domains, as is, are completely separate security objects in the enterprise.

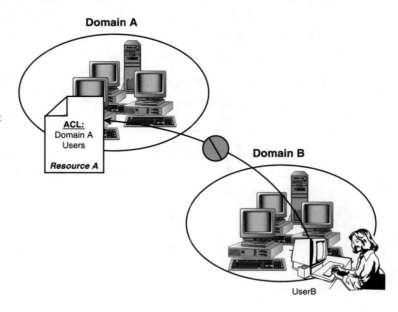

Domain A

ACL:
Domain A
Users

Resource A

Domain B

UserB

A *trust relationship* establishes a security relationship, or secure connection, between the two domains. It allows secure user authentication and resource access to occur between the two domains. Once the trust has been established, users from one domain can access resources in another domain to which they have been given access. Thus, the user need only log in once, and can have easy access to resources elsewhere in the enterprise—two of our Directory Services goals. Also, account management can be centralized in one of the domains in the trust, thus satisfying yet another Directory Service goal: centralized account management.

Trusts can only be established between two Windows NT Server domains. In fact, trusts are created between the PDC servers for each domain. The domain which has the resources that are needed by the users in another domain is referred to as the *trusting domain* because it trusts the users to use the resources responsibly. The domain which contains the users that need access to the resources in the trusting domain is referred to as the *trusted domain* because the users are trusted to use the resources responsibly. The trusting domain has the resources; the trusted domain has the accounts.

Once the trust has been established, resource managers in the trusting domain can create ACLs for their resources by adding accounts from their own domain, as well as from the account database on the trusted domain. So, if UserB from Domain B needs access to a resource in Domain A, the resource manager for the resource in Domain A can add UserB to the ACL for the Domain A resource by virtue of the trust. When UserB logs on in Domain B, UserB has access to all her usual resources in Domain B and any resource she is given permission to use in Domain A, again by virtue of the trust. In addition, the trust gives UserB the ability to log on to a computer that is a member of Domain A and still access the same set of network resources (see Figure 3.2).

FIG. 3.2 ⇒

When the trust is established be-tween Domain B and Domain A, UserB can access any resource in Domain A or Domain B to which she has been given access from any computer in Domain A or Domain B.

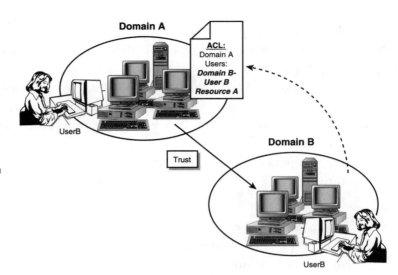

The type of trust relationship just described is known as a *one-way trust*. In fact, trust relationships are by nature unidirectional. They are always directed from the domain that contains the resources toward the do-main that contains the users and groups that require access. The rela-tionships are generally represented by Microsoft as an arrow drawn from the resource (trusting) domain to the account (trusted) domain. This book follows that convention as well.

In Chapter 2, "Windows NT 4.0 Directory Services Overview," we discussed a scenario in which an organization decided to centralize management of accounts in the MIS department, while allowing all departments the ability to manage their own resources. To further ex-pand this scenario, let's give each department—Human Resources, Fi-nance, Accounting, and so on—its own resource domain. MIS is given the master account domain for the organization—read: enterprise (see Figure 3.3).

One-way trusts from the resource domains to the master account do-main allow the resource managers for each resource domain to create and manage ACLs for their resources is by selecting users and groups from the master account domain through the trust. They also allow a user to log on at a computer belonging to any of the domains in the enterprise and still have access to the same set of network resources.

FIG. 3.3 ⇒
Here, MIS is established as the account domain as all users and groups are managed by this department. Finance, Accounting, and Human Resources each manage their own resources, and so are given their own resource domains.

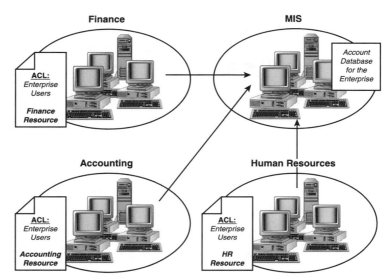

As we have seen, a one-way trust allows users from the trusted domain to access resources in the trusting domain by logging into a computer belonging to either domain. However, users in the trusting domain do not have the ability to access resources in the trusted domain, nor to log on and authenticate through computers belonging to the trusted domain.

Key Concept

A one-way trust is directed from the resource domain to the account domain (trusting to trusted). This allows users from the account domain to access resources in the resource domain and even to log on and authenticate at computers belonging to the resource domain. Users in the resource domain can only access their domain's resources and log on and authenticate only on computers belonging to their domain.

If both domains have users and resources, and users from both need to access resources in the other, then a trust can be established each way between the two domains. These two one-way trusts establish a *two-way trust* between the two domains. This effectively allows users from both domains to access any resources in either domain to which they have been given access, as well as the ability to log on and authenticate at computers belonging to either domain.

Key Concept

Trust relationships are not transitive. A trust is established between two domains. If Domain A trusts Domain B, and Domain B trusts Domain C, it does not automatically follow that Domain A trusts Domain C. For Domain A to also trust Domain C, a separate trust relationship must be established between Domain A and Domain C.

Like domains, trusts are logical communication channels. The physical location of the domains is not important. Neither, as we have seen, is the physical location (where they log on) of the users important. What is important for you as an administrator is to make the administration of your network as streamlined as possible. This means identifying:

◆ The location of resources and accounts—for example, resource domains and account domains

◆ Which domains require trusts

◆ Whether the trust needs to be one-way or two-way

◆ What is the minimum number of trusts to establish in order to satisfy the Directory Services goals of your enterprise

Setting Up a Trust Relationship

Let's begin this discussion by reviewing the elements necessary to successfully set up a trust between two domains:

◆ A trust is established between two domains. A *domain* is identified by its PDC and retains its own *SID (Security IDentifier)*. Therefore, the PDCs for both domains must be up and accessible.

◆ Be sure to disconnect any currently established sessions between the PDCs of the two domains involved in the trust.

◆ Once the trust is established, users authenticating through the trust will authenticate on either the PDC or the backup domain controllers (BDCs) for their domain. Therefore, the BDCs for the trusted domains must be set up properly and regularly synchronized with the PDC.

◆ Administrators can establish the trust relationship. Be sure that you have access to an administrator account in both domains.

◆ User Manager for Domains is the tool used to set up trust relationships. You must have access to a computer in both domains on which the server tools have been installed. This would probably be a Windows NT 4.0 Workstation or Server computer, but could also be a Windows 95 or Windows for Workgroups client on which remote server tools have been installed. Remote server tools are discussed in Chapter 15, "Remote Server Management."

Once you have determined that these prerequisites have been met, you can begin to set up the trust.

As you recall, the domain which has the users and groups that desire access to another domain's resources is referred to as the trusted, or account, domain. The domain that has the network resources to which users from another domain desire access is referred to as the trusting, or resource, domain. The terms *trusted*, *trusting*, *account*, and *resource* will be used throughout this discussion to help familiarize you with the terminology and the concept.

Establishing a trust relationship is a two-step process. The trusted domain must identify which domain will do the trusting (has the resources that the trusted users want to use). The trusting domain must identify which domain is to be trusted (has the accounts that want to use the resources). While it doesn't greatly matter which domain goes first, it is generally recommended that the trusted domain first permit the trusting domain to trust it. Then the trusting domain can complete the relationship.

Part

II

Ch

3

> **Caution**
>
> When the trusted domain goes first, the trust is generally established immediately after the trusting domain completes the trust. However, if the trusting domain goes first (before the trusted domain permits it to trust), the trust can take up to 15 minutes to complete.

Follow these steps to permit a trusting domain to trust you:

1. At a computer on which the server tools have been installed, log on as an administrator to the domain which will be the trusting domain.

2. Start User Manager for Domains.

3. Choose Policies, Trust Relationships. The Trust Relationships dialog box will appear (see Figure 3.4).

4. Choose the Add button alongside the Trusting Domains list box.

5. Enter the name of the trusting domain in the Trusting Domain text box.

6. Optionally, enter a password in the Initial Password text box and confirm it in the Confirm Password text box. This password must be provided by the trusting domain when it completes the trust. It is used only once—at the time the trust is established—and is designed as an optional level of security because only an administrator who knows the password can complete the trust from the trusting domain.

7. Choose OK. The trusting domain name will appear in the Trusting Domains list box.

8. Complete steps 4–7 for any additional trusting domains.

9. Choose Close.

FIG. 3.4 ⇒

In this example, the domain DOMAINB has the resources our domain users want to access and is therefore added as the trusting domain.

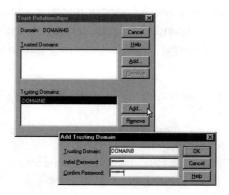

Follow these steps to identify which domains will be trusted to use your resources:

1. At a computer on which the server tools have been installed, log on as an administrator to the domain which will be the trusting domain.

2. Start User Manager for Domains.

3. Choose Policies, Trust Relationships. The Trust Relationships dialog box will appear (see Figure 3.5).

4. Choose the Add button alongside the Trusted Domains list box.

5. Enter the name of the trusted domain in the Domain text box.

6. If a password is required to complete the trust, enter the password in the Password text box.

7. Choose OK. If the trusted domain has permitted your domain to trust it, and the passwords match, then a message will appear within a few moments indicating that the trust has been successfully established. If the trusted domain has not yet permitted your domain to trust it, a message to that effect will be displayed.

8. Repeat steps 4–7 for any additional trusted domains.

9. Choose Close.

Part

II

Ch

3

FIG. 3.5 ⇒

In this example, DOMAINA has the accounts that desire access to our resources. Therefore, it is added as our trusted domain.

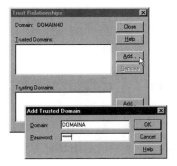

The Trust Relationships dialog box can be confusing. An easy way to remember which list box is which is to ask yourself the following questions:

◆ *I have network resources; who do I trust?* Fill in the Trusted Domains list box.

◆ *I have users that want to access network resources; who trusts me?* Fill in the Trusting Domains list box.

If a two-way trust is necessary—that is, if the users from both domains want to access the resources from each other's domain—you must create two one-way trusts. Simply perform the process twice, reversing the roles of the domains for each time through the steps. The Trust Relationships dialog box will look similar to that in Figure 3.6.

FIG. 3.6 ⇒
Here both Domain A and Domain B have resources that each other's accounts want to access. Each domain indicates the other as both the domain they trust and the domain which trusts them.

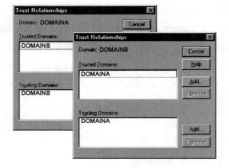

Managing Users and Groups Across Trusts

Now that the trust relationship has been established, communication can take place between the two domains. Users from the trusted domain have the ability to log on at a computer belonging to either their own domain or the trusting domain. The ACLs for the resources

in the trusting domain can now include accounts from the trusted domain. The next section discusses account management and authentication across trust relationships.

The Net Logon Service and Pass-Through Authentication

The *Net Logon service* is a Windows NT Server service that is started by
default every time you boot your computer. Within a domain, it is responsible for locating a domain controller for the domain and validating
a user when the user logs on. It also keeps the domain account database
synchronized between the PDC and its BDCs. Chapter 5, "Capacity
Planning and Performance," discusses the synchronization process in
more detail.

More pertinent to our discussion, however, is *pass-through authentication*.
This Net Logon function is what allows a user from a trusted domain
to log on and validate at a computer belonging to the trusting domain.
When the user logs on at a computer belonging to the trusting domain,
the Erom box on the NT Welcome screen displays not only the trusting
domain as a valid domain option, but also any trusted domains that have
been set up.

Let's say that Domain A trusts Domain B. Domain A is therefore the
trusting domain and Domain B is the trusted domain. UserB is a member of Domain B. When UserB tries to log on to an NT computer that
belongs to Domain A, when he selects the Erom box on the NT Welcome screen, he will see a choice for both Domain A *and* Domain B.
By selecting Domain B, the Net Logon service determines that this
account cannot be validated by a domain controller for Domain A.
Therefore, the request is *passed through* the trust to Domain B where it
can be validated by a domain controller for that domain. Once UserB
is validated, the user's access token information is returned to the computer at which he is logging on.

Part
II

Ch
3

Local versus Global Accounts

When a user or group account is created on a Windows NT Workstation or member server, that account is considered to be *local* in that it can only be used to access resources on that computer. A user or group account created on a Windows NT PDC is by default a *global* account. This means that it can be used to access resources anywhere it has been used within a domain—for example, in the ACL of any resource on any member computer in the domain. It also can be used across trusts to access resources in other domains. By virtue of the trust relationship, the ACLs for resources in the trusting domains can include global accounts from the trusted domain. Whenever and wherever a user with a global account logs on, that user can access any resource to which that global account has been given permission.

A local account can also be created for the domain, but it does not share the same benefits for the global account. A local account in a domain has two very specific purposes:

◆ It allows a user in an untrusted domain to access a resource in another domain. This could be thought of as peer-to-peer networking between domains because a user must have a valid account in the other domain in order to access a resource there.

◆ It allows a user in a network that does not support trust relationships, such as Microsoft LAN Manager, to access a resource in a Windows NT domain.

Group Management in the Domain

Similar in concept to a local user account, global groups provide a means of managing users within a domain environment as well as across trusts. Local groups reside on the computer at which they are created and are used to more effectively manage user access to resources on that computer. Local groups can include local users from the local account database as well as global users and global groups from the domain account database. With the trust in place, a local group on a computer in the trusting domain can additionally include global users and groups from the trusted domain.

Key Concept

Microsoft's recommended strategy for managing resources effectively is to create local groups to manage the local resource, and populate it with global groups from its own domain and from the trusted domain. More simply stated, create user accounts and make them members of global groups. Then add the global groups to local groups for more effective resource management.

Table 3.1 describes the local groups that are created by default when installing Windows NT Server 4.0 as a domain controller.

Table 3.1   Built-in Domain Local Groups

Group	Default Members	Description
Administrators	Administrator; Domain Admins global group	Members of this group can fully administer the computer, or the domain. Only administrators can modify this group.
Users	Domain Users global group	Members of this group have the necessary level of access to operate the computer for daily tasks such as word processing, database access, and so on. Only administrators and Account Operators can modify this group.
Guests	Domain Guests global group	Members of this group have the least level of access to resources. Only administrators and Account Operators can modify this group.

continues

Table 3.1 Continued		
Group	Default Members	Description
Backup Operators	None	Members of this group have only enough access to files and folders as is needed to back them up or restore them on this server. Only administrators can modify this group.
Replicator	None	When Directory Replication is configured, this group is used to identify the specific user account, often called a service account that Windows NT uses to perform the replication function. Only administrators can modify this group.
Server Operator	None	Members of this group can log on at the server, manage shared resources on the server, lock or override the lock of a server, format server hard disks, back up and restore the server, and shut down the server. Only administrators can modify this group.
Account Operator	None	Members of this group can log on at the server, create and manage accounts (except those groups as identified in this table), and shut down the server. Only administrators can modify this group.

Group	Default Members	Description
Print Operators	None	Members of this group can log on at the server, create and manage printers, and shut down the server. Only administrators can modify this group.

Key Concept

A group that is local to the PDC is also local to all the BDCs for that domain because they share the same database.

This means that if a user is made a member of the Backup Operators group on the PDC, that user will not only be able to back up and restore files on the PDC, but also all the BDCs because all the domain controllers for a domain share the same account database (see Chapter 5, "Capacity Planning and Performance").

Three global groups are created by default as well. These are described in Table 3.2. A *global group account*, like a global user account, can be used anywhere within the domain, or through a trust, to facilitate the management of user access to network resources. In other words, you don't have to create individual local groups of domain users on individual computers. You can use the same global groups of domain users that are available to all resource managers in the network. Global groups can only be created and maintained on domain controllers and can only contain global users from their domain as members.

Table 3.2 Domain Global and Local Groups		
Group	Default Members	Description
Domain Admins	Administrator	Members of this group enjoy all the benefits of the local Administrators group. This group is also used to assign its members administrative privileges on local computers by making it a member of that local Administrators group. It automatically becomes a member of the Administrators local group on the domain controller. Only administrators can modify this group.
Domain Users	Administrator	This group contains all domain user accounts that are created and is itself a member of the Users local group on the domain controller. If made a member of a workstation's local Users group, its members will assume the user privileges that the local Users group has been given on that workstation. Only administrators and Account Operators can modify this group.
Domain Guests	Guest	This group contains the domain Guest account which is disabled by default. Its members enjoy only the level

Group	Default Members	Description
		of access that has been assigned to it. If made a member of a workstation's local Guests group, the domain guest account will also have guest access to the workstation resources. Only administrators and Account Operators can modify this group.

Local groups can have as its members any local users as well as global users and groups from the domain that computer participates in. It can also contain global users and groups from trusted domains. However, it cannot have another local group as a member.

Key Concept

Global groups can only have users from their own domain as a valid member.

As stated earlier in this section, Microsoft's group strategy for domains recommends that domain users be grouped into as many global groups as is appropriate. Local resource managers should then create local groups for maintaining access to the resources. The members of the local groups then become the global groups of domain users. While this may at first seem to be a bit of over-management, in large networks with hundreds or thousands of users, this strategy makes much sense and can actually facilitate user management and resource access.

This strategy is actually implemented by default through Directory Services. When a new user account is created on the PDC, it is made a member of the Domain Users group, which is itself a member of the Users (local) group for the domain. When a Windows NT Workstation or Server computer joins a domain, the Domain Users and Domain

Part

II

Ch

3

Admins groups automatically become members of the computer's local Users and Administrators groups, again to facilitate administration and management of all the Windows NT-based computers in the domain and to preserve the goals of Directory Services—for example, a single logon account to provide the same level of access throughout the domain.

Extending this concept to the trust relationship follows naturally. Because the trust gives a resource administrator access to the account database of a trusted domain, the resource administrator can use the global groups created in the trusted domain as members of the local groups she creates to manage access to her resources. For example, if you wanted the administrators of the trusted domain to also be able to administer your trusting domain's domain controllers, you would make the Domain Admins group from the trusted domain a member of the Administrator's local group for the trusting domain. Or, if you had a database that certain users from the trusted domain need to access, you could have an Administrator or Account Operator for the trusted domain create a global group for those users. You would then make that global group a member of your local group that manages access to the database.

Resource Management Across Trusts

You should already be familiar with Windows NT's share level, file level, and folder level permission structure and how to assign permissions, because that is a prerequisite for this chapter and for this book. This section briefly covers the steps involved in sharing a folder and demonstrates how the trust expands your ability to manage resource access.

You have already seen that when the trust relationship is established, the user from the trusted domain can log on either from a computer that participates in the trusted domain or the trusting domain. The trusted domain becomes a valid domain logon option for computers that are members of the trusting domain. Trusted domains appear in the From box on the Windows NT logon screens for Windows NT-based computers.

Similarly, the permissions dialog boxes for shares, files, folders, printers, and any other network resources—as well as local group management through User Manager and User Manager for Domains—are also modified to display a choice of domain account databases from which to select users and groups.

For our example, let's say that Domain A trusts Domain B once again. This makes Domain A the trusting domain and Domain B the trusted domain. We have a folder called Data on a Windows NT-based server in Domain A that we want to share to the Global Finance group in Domain B with Read permission. How do we do that? You would proceed just as you always would when sharing the folder:

1. Select the folder that you want to share (through Windows Explorer or My Computer, as an example).

2. Right-click the folder and choose S_haring.

3. On the Sharing tab of the Data Properties dialog box, choose S_hared As.

4. Leave the default share name (the same as the folder name) or change it in the S_hare Name text box.

5. Modify the User Limit if appropriate.

6. Select P_ermissions.

7. Use the A_dd and R_emove buttons to make changes to the existing permission list—the ACL for this resource. The A_dd button displays the Add Users and Groups dialog box. The R_emove button merely removes the selected account from the list.

8. In the Add Users and Groups dialog box, use the L_ist Names From drop-down list and scroll up and down to see the list of valid domains, including the trusted domains, from which you can select accounts (see Figure 3.7).

9. Choose Domain B from the list. Available global groups from Domain B will be displayed in the N_ames list box (and users if you select Show U_sers).

10. Choose the Global Finance group from the list, select A_dd, modify the T_ype of Access if necessary (Read is the default), and then select OK.

Part

II

Ch

3

FIG. 3.7 ⇒
Once the trust has
been established,
accounts can be
added from both
the trusting and
trusted domains.
Notice how both
domains are listed
in the List Names
From box.

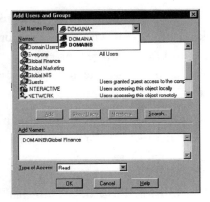

Wherever you have a choice to select users or groups, the trusting and trusted domains will appear as valid domain selections.

Troubleshooting Trust Relationships

There are generally two main categories into which trust-related problems might fall: either the trust isn't working, or access does not take place as expected.

Failure to Establish a Trust

Recall that in order for a trust relationship to be successfully established, the following conditions must be met:

◆ Because a trust is established between two domains, and a domain is identified by its PDC, the PDCs for both domains must be up and accessible or else the trust will fail to be established.

◆ Be sure to disconnect any currently established sessions between the PDCs of the two domains involved in the trust. If a session does exist, the trust will fail to be established.

◆ Once the trust is established, users authenticating through the trust will authenticate on either the PDC or the BDCs for their domain. Therefore, the BDCs for the trusted domains must be set up properly and regularly synchronized with the PDC. If the BDCs are not regularly or properly synchronized, a user from a trusted domain may not be able to log on successfully from a computer participating in the trusting domain.

◆ Administrators can establish the trust relationship. Be sure that you have access to an administrator account in both domains, or you will not be able to set up the trust.

◆ User Manager for Domains is the tool used to set up trust relationships. You must have access to a computer in both domains on which the server tools have been installed. This would probably be a Windows NT 4.0 Workstation or Server computer, but could also be a Windows 95 or Windows for Workgroups client.

◆ Establishing the trust is a two-step process: The account domain must permit the resource domain to trust it, and the resource domain must complete the trust. If either the account or resource domain fails to do its part, the trust will not be established.

◆ If a password is used to permit the resource domain to complete the trust, be sure that you know what it is, keeping in mind that it is case-sensitive. If the passwords do not match, the trust cannot be completed.

◆ The resource domain is considered to be the trusting domain, and the account domain is considered to be the trusted. If you are unable to add users from a domain to the ACLs for resources in your domain, check the direction of the trust. Be sure that your domain is actually trusting the other domain.

Broken Trusts

No, this has nothing to do with soap opera plot lines. What we are referring to here is what happens when one side of the trust fails for some reason. A trust can be broken when one of the domains in the trust is renamed, the Net Logon service stops, or an administrator purposely removes the trust. Once the trust has been broken, it must be re-established following the steps outlined in the section "Establishing a Trust."

Part
II

Ch
3

→ also, the trust is merely controlled by passwords that the PDCs periodically change!

A trust relationship has a SID associated with it, just like user and group accounts do when they are created. As such, when an administrator chooses to break the trust, it must be broken on both sides and then re-established to create a new SID. A trust can be broken by following these steps:

At the trusted domain:

1. At a computer on which the server tools have been installed, log on as an administrator to the trusted domain.
2. Start User Manager for Domains.
3. Choose Policies, Trust Relationships. The Trust Relationship dialog box will appear.
4. In the Trusting Domains list box, highlight the trusting domain whose trust you want to break and choose the Remove button alongside the list box.
5. Choose OK and confirm that you want to break the trust.
6. Choose Close.

At the trusting domain:

1. At a computer on which the server tools have been installed, log on as an administrator to the trusting domain.
2. Start User Manager for Domains.
3. Choose Policies, Trust Relationships. The Trust Relationship dialog box will appear.
4. In the Trusted Domains list box, highlight the trusted domain whose trust you want to break and choose the Remove button alongside the list box.
5. Choose OK and confirm that you want to break the trust.
6. Choose Close.

Resource Access Anomalies

Anomalies refers to two specific situations that might occur:

- ◆ Access to a resource fails or is denied when logged on as a trusted account.

- ◆ A user *can* access a resource in a remote domain that he should not be able to access.

Of course, the first thing to check when a user cannot access a resource, whether you are using a trusted account or not, is if that account actually has been given appropriate levels of access. Recall that a user's effective permissions are determined by adding up all the access the user has either explicitly or through group membership at the file/folder level and at the share level. When both share level and file or folder level security are in use, the effective access is whichever of the two (share or file/folder) is more restrictive. So, of course, check the user's permissions and effective access.

However, if the same account exists in both the trusting and the trusted domains, the user could be denied access as well because the account SIDs will not match.

> **Caution**
> When a trust relationship exists, the user account should only exist in one domain—not both.

Conversely, it could happen that a user who is logged in to one domain might find that she has access to a resource in another domain that she should not have. This can also occur when an account exists in both domains. See Figure 3.8. Domain A is trusted by both Domain B and Domain C. UserB has an account in both Domain A and Domain B. Through the trust, a resource in Domain C gives access to the UserB account from Domain A. Suppose UserB logs on to Domain B using Domain B's account rather than the UserB account available from the trusted domain Domain A. It is possible that UserB can access the resource on Domain C, even though he is not logged in as that account.

FIG. 3.8 ⇒
Domains B and C both trust Domain A. However, a duplicate user account exists in both Domain A and Domain B, thus making it possible for a user logging in as one account to gain resource access meant for the other account.

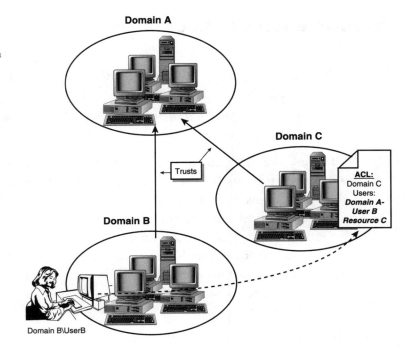

Here's how: When UserB attempts to access the resource in Domain C, the request is passed to Domain C which cannot validate it. As a result, the request is passed through the trust (pass-through authentication) to Domain A to be validated. Pass-through authentication just passes the user name and password to the validating domain—not the SID. Consequently, Domain A successfully validates the account, and gives UserB access to the resource.

Caution
When a trust relationship exists, the user account should only exist in one domain—not both.

Taking the Disc Test

 If you have read and understood the material in the chapter, you are ready to test your knowledge. Insert the CD-ROM that comes with this book and run the self-test software as described in Appendix I, "Using the CD-ROM."

From Here...

Now that you have learned the concept of trust relationships and the implications of account and resource management, you can apply them to our enterprise. Chapter 4, "Domain Models," explores the four basic domain models, how trusts are used to implement each model, and how to determine which model is appropriate for the enterprise.

Part

II

Ch

3

4

Domain Models

This chapt er explores the significance of the domain for Microsoft's Directory Services and discusses four domain models that can be used as the basis for implementing Directory Services within a networked organization. Specific topics include:

- Domains and Directory Services
- Single Domain Model
- Master Domain Model
- Multiple Master Domain Model
- Complete Trust Domain Model
- Group management considerations

Understanding the Role of the Domain for Directory Services

As we have discussed in the last two chapters, a Windows NT 4.0 domain is characterized by a centralized database of user and group account information. When users log on to the domain, their user account is passed on to an available authenticating server in the enterprise called a *domain controller*. Because each user's account is centralized at the domain level rather than the local level, the user can log on to the domain from any workstation participating in the domain.

Likewise, resource access is provided by adding users from the domain database to resource *Access Control Lists (ACLs)*. Thus, only one account database is necessary to manage any resource available within the domain. Recall that in the workgroup model, each computer maintains its own account database which is used for managing resource access at that computer. Resources may actually reside on various server and workstation computers within the domain. By virtue of their participation in the domain, the resources use the same central account database for managing user access. These are, of course, two of the primary goals of Directory Services and why the domain plays a significant role in implementing Directory Services.

A *domain* is best thought of as a logical grouping of computers for the purpose of authenticating users and sharing resources.

Key Concept

While the physical layout of the network may affect the type of domain model you choose to implement—as well as the number and location of domain controllers and servers—nevertheless, the domain does not depend on the physical layout of the network, nor does it depend on the physical location of the computers or the users.

This is not meant to imply that you can just throw together a domain without some thought and planning. Quite the contrary, it is important that you carefully consider what the domain structure should look like and how it will best meet the needs of your enterprise. Perhaps one large domain will more than adequately serve the networking needs of your organization. Often, there may be multiple enterprise models or domains within an organization, each with its own resources and in some cases with its own account database, as well as joined by trust relationships.

There are four domain models that Microsoft affirms as the foundations for any network enterprise. They are:

◆ Single Domain Model

◆ Master Domain Model

◆ Multiple Master Domain Model

◆ Complete Trust Model

These domain models will be discussed in more detail in the upcoming sections of this chapter.

The following considerations may ultimately affect which type of model or models will best meet the networking needs of your enterprise.

User and Group Accounts

The number of users and groups that will participate in the network will drive your decisions somewhat. Chapter 5, "Capacity Planning and Performance," addresses this issue in some detail. In brief, there is an outside limit to the number of accounts a domain can support, and that number is 40,000 or a 40M account database consisting of user, group, and computer accounts. Once you reach the database limit, you must create another account domain for additional accounts.

When you think about it, however, you will probably have already decided to split your account database into two or more domains just for ease of administration. If you are the administrator for a network resource and are creating an ACL for that resource, do you really want to scroll through 40,000 user and group accounts to find the ones you want? Would you want to go through 10,000? It is not enough to think

Recommend by Microsoft not a physical limitation?

about how many accounts you have to manage. You must also consider how, where, and by whom those accounts will be used.

Another consideration here might be the location of the users and groups. If the company is located in one campus location, it may be easily managed by one centralized account domain. However, if the users are localized by region (such as West, Midwest, and East), they might more effectively be managed by account domains located in those regions.

However your decision is impacted by the number or location of users, keep in mind that the goal of Directory Services is to keep account management centralized. Database size, domain controller placement, and other optimization issues are discussed in Chapter 5, "Capacity Planning and Performance."

Resource Management

Your choice of domain model is dependent on the management of network resources. You must know where the network resources are and who will manage them. This affects not only the kind of model you choose, but also as we saw in Chapter 3, "Trust Relationships," the number of trust relationships that need to be established. For example, an organization that is relatively localized and whose resources are in the same general location may be best served by a single domain model. All resource servers participate in the same domain. Perhaps the same persons who administer the users also administer the resources. No trust relationships are necessary in this scenario.

But what if the company is multinational, and resources are regionally or departmentally located? Perhaps each region wants or needs to administer its own resources. Indeed, perhaps each region needs to administer its own accounts. A single domain model will not suffice in this scenario. This environment may be best suited for a Master or Multiple Master Domain Model.

Organizational Culture

This leads directly to another important consideration called the *cultural factor*. The makeup of the organization will necessarily drive decisions related to the domain structure and implementation. Is your organization built around departments, regions, or hierarchies? Is the management philosophy territorial or team-oriented? Are there politics that must be employed when establishing the enterprise? Remember that domains are logical groupings of computers. As such, they can span locations such as cities, regions, or countries.

For example, perhaps the Finance department for Global Enterprises has offices in six major cities around the world. It also has several SQL databases on which it maintains the company's financial history, and it must administer these databases internally.

In one scenario, each office maintains its own databases for that location. You might then give each office its own domain for managing its database resources. In another scenario, all the offices use the same databases. You might then create one Finance domain that all the offices participate in.

The domain doesn't care that the offices are in different physical locations. A domain is identified, remember, by its *primary domain controller (PDC)* and has its own *SID (Security ID)*. The workstations and servers need only identify that they are members of the domain. Windows NT-based computers do this by creating a computer account for themselves in the domain's account database. Other Windows NT network clients do this by identifying in their network properties which domain they belong to.

Part
II

Ch
4

Understanding the Single Domain Model

In the *Single Domain Model*, shown in Figure 4.1, all accounts and all resources are contained within one enterprise-wide domain. Thus, trust relationships are not necessary. Account management is centralized to the PDC, and resources are maintained on resource servers that are members of the domain.

FIG. 4.1⇒

In the Single Domain Model, all accounts and resources are maintained in the same domain structure, so trust relationships are unnecessary.

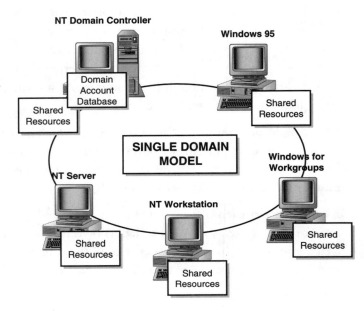

This model scales well for small businesses, or where the computers do not participate in a larger WAN environment. A single domain model can accommodate up to 40,000 accounts. However, if the domain controller hardware is unable to handle the number of accounts, it will certainly experience performance problems. Also, as the number of resource servers increases in this model, the browsing of shared resources becomes slower. (See Chapter 5, "Capacity Planning and Performance," for a discussion of the hardware issues that are related to the account database.)

limit recommended by Microsoft, not a physical limitation

Understanding the Master Domain Model

In the *Master Domain Model*, demonstrated in Figure 4.2, there is one domain that maintains the account database, and one or more domains that administer resources. The resource domains trust the account domain. This was the type of domain model referred to when trust relationships were first introduced in Chapter 3. This is also the type of model that you create when you complete the one-way trust in the Trust Relationship Lab for Chapter 2. The resource domains are the trusting domains, and the account domain is the trusted domain.

FIG. 4.2⇒
Here is an example of a Master Domain Model with two resource domains trusting one account domain. Accounts are still centrally administered in the account domain. Resources are now grouped logically and administered where they need to be.

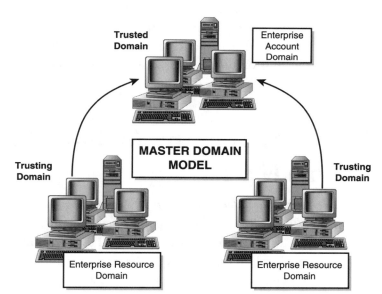

Part II Ch 4

This model is common in organizations where resources belong to various departments, and those departments want or need to maintain authority over access to their resource, because it allows resources to be grouped according to the needs, or culture, of the organization. Recall from Chapter 2 that Microsoft's recommended group strategy is to create global groups for managing domain users, and local groups for managing local resources, then populate the local groups with the global groups.

The resource domains therefore need not maintain user accounts. In fact, resource managers need only create local groups on the resource servers to manage access to their resources. Because a trust relationship exists with the account domain in this model, the resource managers would simply add the appropriate global groups—and in some cases, global users—to their local groups. Any changes to group membership take place on the PDC. The resource manager need only be concerned with the ACL permissions granted to the local groups.

The model is transparent to the users. Because the trust relationship exists, users can log on any computer that is a member of any of the domains and still access any network resource that the user has been given permission to use. Thus, our Directory Services goals are once again preserved.

Understanding the Multiple Master Domain Model

The *Multiple Master Domain Model* is similar to the Master Domain Model in that the accounts are managed centrally, the resources are grouped logically and managed where they need to be managed, and trust relationships exist between the resource and account domains. The main difference in this model is that the account database may be distributed between two or more account domains. This may be a result of the way users are distributed through a WAN, their physical location, the size of the account database(s), the hardware of the domain controller, or the organizational culture or structure.

This model scales well for large organizations with users located in several different areas, but who still want to centralize account management within a particular administrative group, such as MIS. The biggest disadvantage is that there are more trust relationships to create and manage.

In this model, each resource domain trusts each account domain. In other words, each resource domain will have one trust relationship for every account domain, and each account domain will trust the other. As shown in Figure 4.3, if there are two account domains, each resource domain will have two trust relationships—one for each account domain. The formula for calculating the number of trusts in the master domain model is $M*(M-1)+(R*M)$ where M represents the number of master account domains and R represents the number of resource domains. Thus, if your master domain model has two account domains and three resource domains, you will need $2*(2-1)+(3*2)$ or eight trusts total.

FIG. 4.3⇒

In this example of a Multiple Master Domain Model, there are two account domains that are trusted by each resource domain. Each account domain also trusts the other to facilitate account management.

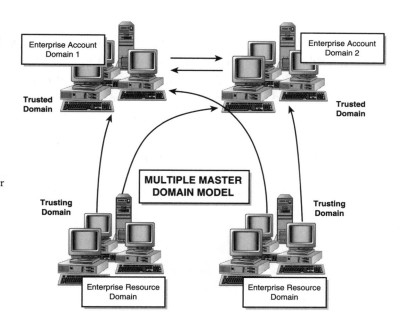

Part

II

Ch

4

Account and resource management takes place just as in the Master Domain Model. Domain users are created once in the appropriate account domain, and then grouped into global groups in their respective domains. Resource managers manage access to their resources by assigning permissions to local groups, and making global groups—and in some cases, global users—members of the local groups.

The account domains also trust each other—that is to say there are two one-way trusts established between the account domains. This facilitates the administration of accounts from either account domain. It also ensures that a user can log on any computer that is a member of any of the domains and still access any network resource that the user has been given permission to use. Thus, our Directory Services goals are once again preserved.

Understanding the Complete Trust Domain Model

The *Complete Trust Model* shown in Figure 4.4 is perhaps the simplest to describe, though perhaps it also provides the least amount of integrity. In this model, every domain trusts every other domain. Account administration as well as resource management are distributed throughout the enterprise. Every domain maintains a copy of its own account database. Resource administrators can provide resource access to users from any other domain. The number of trust relationships required for the Complete Trust Model can be obtained by using the following formula supplied by Microsoft: $n \star (n-1)$, where n represents the number of domains to be included in the model.

> **Caution**
> Resource access and security in this model are only as secure as the *worst* administrator in the enterprise.

Because there is no one person or group overseeing the administration of user accounts and resource access, duplicate users can be created, and inappropriate access can be granted to secure network resources. It is difficult to ensure the overall integrity of your network. Because of this, I sometimes call this model the *chaos model*. This is not to say that this model has not been successfully implemented in several large organizations, especially those that do not have a central or corporate MIS group. It does, however, require a greater degree of control to remain secure.

FIG. 4.4⇒

In this example of a Complete Trust Model, all four domains contain both accounts and resources. All domains trust each other in this model. Note that there are 4★(4–1) or 12 trusts in all to create and manage.

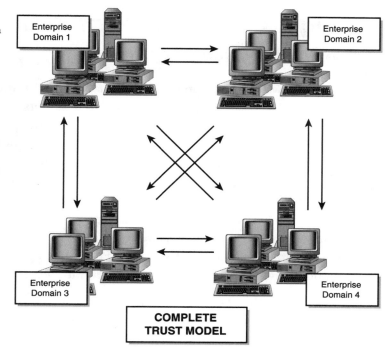

Enterprise Domain 1

Enterprise Domain 2

Enterprise Domain 3

Enterprise Domain 4

COMPLETE TRUST MODEL

This model also happens to be more common than you might expect. In companies for which there is no high-level strategy for implementing a Domain Model, departmental or regional Windows NT networks are introduced independently. Over time, they find the need to communicate with each other and share resources. To accommodate that need, trust relationships are established among the domains and—voilá!—you have a Complete Trust Model.

> **Note** The domain models presented here represent the purest form of the model. For example, the ideal Multiple Master Model would have each resource domain trust every account domain. However, given your organization's structure, culture, and networking needs, not every resource domain may need to trust every account domain, and every user may not need to be able to log on anywhere in the enterprise. Microsoft recommends creating all the trusts for the chosen model to preserve the Directory Services goals of one logon account, centralized administration, and universal resource access. ∎

Managing Global Groups in the Domain Models

Let's review Microsoft's strategy for managing users through group accounts. Recall that Microsoft recommends that users be managed at the PDC by being grouped into one or more global groups. Global groups are global to the domain and as such can be used by any computer that is a member of the domain to manage local resources on that computer. Microsoft recommends that local resources be managed by creating local groups and assigning permissions to these local groups. Local group membership then should consist of global groups from the domain (and when appropriate, global users from the domain). This provides a rather flexible and easy method of managing local resources without having to deal with the user accounts directly.

As you saw when you read about trusts in Chapter 3, "Trust Relationships," the establishment of a trust relationship between the resource (trusting) domain and the account (trusted) domain makes it possible for resources to be grouped into their own domains (by department, region, or function, for example) without sacrificing the Directory Services' goal of centralized account management. Local resource managers in each resource domain still manage their resources by creating local groups, assigning them access to their resources, and then making global groups (and users) members of the local groups. However, the global groups now can come from the trusted domain by virtue of the trust relationship.

Three of the domain models discussed in this chapter rely on trusts for their foundation: Master Domain, Multiple Master, and Complete Trust models.

Master Domain Model

The Master Domain Model is precisely what is just described in the second paragraph of the last section. The user and group accounts are centralized into one master account domain, perhaps managed by an

MIS group. Resources are localized in the hands of those users, departments, regions, and so on that want or need to manage them. The local resource managers create ACLs for their resources which consist of local groups. Those local groups' members consist of global groups (and users) from the trusted domain.

This is easy enough to comprehend. However, the next question to consider from a planning point of view is, how many global groups need to be created? If the same logical grouping of users in a global group can be used in all resource domains, then the one global group is sufficient. If each resource domain requires a variation of the users in a global group, then ideally a separate global group should be created in the trusted domain for each resource domain.

Here's an example. Let's say that the Finance department has three database files that contain the company's financial records. These database files are distributed across three regional resource domains—West, East, and Midwest. There are nine managers in the Finance department, each region having three managers. All company users and groups are managed by MIS in the CORP account domain, and each resource domain trusts the CORP domain.

In the first scenario, all the managers need access to the database files in all regions. Access to the file in each region has been given to a local group called FINMGR on the resource server in each resource domain. The Finance managers have been grouped into a logical global group in the CORP domain called FINMANAGERS. To give all the Finance managers access to each database file in each region, the resource manager in each region adds the FINMANAGER global group to the local FINMGR group. Now all nine managers have access to all the database files.

In another scenario, suppose that only the three managers for each region should be able to access the database file in their respective regions. The global group FINMANAGER will not suffice here because it contains *all* the managers.

In this scenario, you need to create three global groups in the CORP domain. Let's call them FINMGR-EAST, FINMGR-WEST, and

FINMGR-MID. Each of these would contain the three managers for their respective regions. The FINMGR-EAST global group would then be added to the FINMGR local group in the EAST resource domain; the FINMGR-WEST global group would then be added to the FINMGR local group in the WEST domain; the FINMGR-MID global group would be added to the FINMGR local group in the MID-WEST domain. Now only the appropriate managers will have access to the database file in each region.

Multiple Master Domain Model

The Multiple Master Domain Model is much the same as the Master Model, except that the user and group accounts have themselves been grouped into two or more account domains, again perhaps by region or country, for example. Resources are still localized in the hands of those users, departments, regions, and so on, that want or need to manage them. Trust relationships exist from each resource (trusting) domain to *each* account (trusted) domain. The local resource managers create ACLs for their resources which consist of local groups. Those local groups' members consist of global groups (and users) from one or more of the trusted domains.

Let's return to the Finance department example introduced in the last section. The Finance department has three database files that contain the company's financial records. These database files are distributed across three regional resource domains—West, East, and Midwest. There are nine managers in the Finance department, each region having three managers. All company users and groups are managed by MIS in three account domains: CORPEAST, CORPWEST, and CORPMID, and each resource domain trusts each account domain. The Finance managers for each region have accounts in the appropriate account domain for their region.

In the first scenario, all the managers need access to the database files in all regions. Access to the file in each region has been given to a local group called FINMGR on the resource server in each resource domain. The Finance managers have been grouped into logical global groups in each account domain called FINMANAGERS, such as CORPEAST\ FINMANAGERS, CORPWEST\FINMANAGERS, and CORPMID\FINMANAGERS. To give all the Finance managers access to each database file in each region, the resource manager in each region adds the FINMANAGER global group *from each* account domain to their local FINMGR group. Now all nine managers have access to all the database files.

In another scenario, suppose that only the three managers for each region should be able to access the database file in their respective regions. Because the managers for each domain are already grouped into a global FINMANAGERS group in their region's account domain, the resource manager for each domain should add the FINMANAGERS global group from their respective account domains to their local FINMGR local group.

However, this solution does not offer the greatest flexibility. Suppose that management changes and that one of the new managers for the EAST region has her account in the CORPWEST domain, and a manager for the MIDWEST region has an account in the CORPEAST domain. Clearly, the global groups that have been created will not provide the level of access that we require.

Microsoft suggests that when creating global groups in a Multiple Master Domain Model, you can achieve the greatest flexibility by creating the same set of global groups *in each account domain* and then adding the global group from each domain to the local group in the resource domain. Let me show you what I mean.

In this scenario, we need to create three global groups in each account domain—FINMGR-EAST, FINMGR-WEST, and FINMGR-MID. This means we have created nine global groups in total. Each of these would contain the three managers for their respective regions. The FINMGR-EAST global groups from CORPEAST, CORPWEST, and CORPMID would then be added to the FINMGR local group in the EAST resource domain; the FINMGR-WEST global groups from CORPEAST, CORPWEST, and CORPMID would then be added to the FINMGR local group in the WEST domain; the FINMGR-MID global groups from CORPEAST, CORPWEST, and CORPMID would be added to the FINMGR local group in the MIDWEST domain. Now it does not matter where the manager's account resides. As long as the account is a member of the appropriate global group in that account domain, the appropriate managers will have access to the database file in each region.

Note At this point, it is worth reiterating that global groups can only have user accounts *from their own domain* as valid group members. ▪

Complete Trust Model

In the Complete Trust Model, all domains manage resources and all domains manage users and groups. Every domain trusts every other domain. The local resource managers in each domain create ACLs for their resources which consist of local groups. Those local groups' members consist of global groups (and users) from their own domain, and one or more of the trusted domains.

Returning one more time to the Finance department example, the Finance department still has three database files that contain the company's financial records. These database files are distributed across three regional domains—WEST, EAST, and MIDWEST. There are nine managers in the Finance department, each region having three managers. All company users and groups are managed in each regional domain as well, and each domain trusts the other for a total of $3\star(3-1)$ or six trust relationships. The Finance managers for each region have accounts in their respective regional domain.

In the first scenario, all the managers need access to the database files in all regions. Access to the file in each region has been given to a local group called FINMGR on the resource server in each regional domain. The Finance managers have been grouped into a logical global groups in each regional domain called FINMANAGERS, such as EAST\FINMANAGERS, WEST\FINMANAGERS, and MIDWEST\FINMANAGERS. To give all the Finance managers access to each database file in each region, the resource manager in each region adds the FINMANAGER global group from its own, as well as from each regional domain to their local FINMGR group. Now all nine managers have access to all the database files.

In another scenario, suppose that only the three managers for each region should be able to access the database file in their respective regions. This is easy. Because the managers for each domain are already grouped into a global FINMANAGERS group in his or her region's domain, the resource manager for each domain should add the FINMANAGERS global group from his/her respective domains to their FINMGR local group.

You know what's coming next. This solution does not offer the greatest flexibility. Suppose that management changes and that one of the new managers for the EAST region has her account in the WEST domain, and a manager for the MIDWEST region has an account in the EAST domain. Clearly, the global groups that have been created will not provide the level of access that we require.

Once again, Microsoft suggests that you can achieve the greatest flexibility by creating the same set of global groups in each regional domain and then adding the global group from each domain to the local group in the resource domain. Let me show you what this means for the Complete Trust Model.

In this scenario, we need to create three global groups in each regional domain—FINMGR-EAST, FINMGR-WEST, and FINMGR-MID. This means we have created nine global groups in total. Each of these would contain the three managers for their respective regions. The FINMGR-EAST global groups from EAST, WEST, and MIDWEST would then be added to the FINMGR local group in the EAST resource domain; the FINMGR-WEST global groups from EAST, WEST, and MIDWEST would then be added to the FINMGR local group in the WEST domain; and the FINMGR-MID global groups from EAST, WEST, and MIDWEST would be added to the FINMGR local group in the MIDWEST domain. Now it does not matter where the manager's account resides. As long as the account is a member of the appropriate global group in that account domain, the appropriate managers will have access to the database file in each region.

You can see that as the number of domains in a Complete Trust Model increases, the number of global groups that must be created and maintained increases exponentially. You can also see that the security of resource access relies heavily on the integrity of the resource managers in each domain. This model can require a great deal of monitoring and planning.

Taking the Disc Test

 If you have read and understood the material in the chapter, you are ready to test your knowledge. Insert the CD-ROM that comes with this book and run the self-test software as described in Appendix I, "Using the CD-ROM."

From Here...

Chapter 5, "Capacity Planning and Performance," will take the concepts of Directory Services, trust relationships, and domain models, and apply them when planning your enterprise. You will learn how to determine the appropriate number and placement of domain controllers, various considerations for the account database, and the synchronization process that takes place among the domain controllers.

Chapter Prerequisite

Before reading this chapter, you should have a basic understanding of LAN and WAN concepts, Directory Services, domain models, and trust relationships (see Chapter 2, "Windows NT 4.0 Directory Services Overview," Chapter 3, "Trust Relationships," and Chapter 4, "Domain Names").

5

Capacity Planning and Performance

This chapter contains important information about the planning and implementation of a Windows NT enterprise environment. Planning is one of the most important steps in designing a network. Proper planning can ease the enterprise implementation and administration, and save a substantial amount of time and money. The plan has to provide for both your present and future requirements. It should provide for easy administration of revisions and updates as your environment changes, and it should include cost-effective decisions.

Topics for this chapter include:

◆ Establishing a baseline performance database

◆ Planning for effective WAN performance

◆ Choosing the proper protocol for various situations

◆ Establishing the size of the account database

◆ Determining the type and number of domain controllers

◆ Account database replication considerations

Planning a Baseline of Performance Database Procedure

One of the steps in planning an enterprise is to establish a procedure to evaluate the baseline performance of your equipment, applications, and network soon after installation. Then, set up another plan to monitor the above at regular intervals and compare the results to the initial baseline database. From these results, a determination can be made if your equipment, network, and software performance are above, at, or below your baseline standard. If performance is above or at expectations, no modifications have to be made. However, if performance is below expectations, there are a number of changes that can be considered.

If users are complaining that access to resources, both applications and data, is slow, consider moving resources to where the users are located or relocating users to where the resources are located. Consider analyzing server load and balancing applications and data across multiple servers by adding more servers or adding more resources (memory and disk) to your servers. If the network is the problem, consider revamping it; for example, replace currently installed network cards with faster hardware. Also, consider using fast LAN links such as bridges and routers rather than slow WAN links such as 56K lines or modems.

Your plan for creating a performance baseline database must also include the method of data collection and the procedure for viewing and analyzing the data after collection.

Initially, manual data collection is probably the way to go because a determination of the required performance monitor objects pertaining to your enterprise must be made. Also, a determination has to be made as to whether each and every system must be monitored, or whether all monitoring can be done from a centralized location. If monitoring is done on each machine, processor, memory, and disk object performances are affected; however, if it is done from a centralized location, network traffic is affected. Another consideration is the size of the baseline database. This database can become very large very fast. Whether collection is done on each machine or from a central system, adequate resources, memory, and disk space must be available. You should collect data for at least one week to get accurate and reliable baseline data. Plan to collect data only at peak use periods to conserve resources.

Once a determination of performance monitor objects is made, plan to automate the collection process on remote systems by using the Windows NT AT scheduler service and monitor.exe (resource kit utility) to monitor remote systems on the network. This service is used to monitor computers without a user being logged on to the network. To automate the process, a performance monitor workspace file (.pmw) must be used to specify what performance monitor objects and interval times are going to be used. Examples to start and stop the monitor service are:

- at \\<*computer name*> 14:00 /date:M,W,F "monitor start"
- at \\<*computer name*> 15:30 /date:M,W,F "monitor stop"

Part
II

Ch
5

The most important system resources to monitor on all Windows NT systems, whether they are file, print, application servers, or domain controllers, are:

- Memory
- Processor
- Physical Disk
- Network

Planning decisions on other required objects to monitor depend on specific server usage such as a SQL Server, a RAS server, an SNA server, or an Exchange server. A few of the more useful counters are listed here. A more complete discussion of these objects and their counters is presented in Chapter 20, "Performance Monitor."

Memory Monitoring Considerations

Performance monitor objects used to establish memory performance are *cache, memory, paging file, physical disk, process, redirector,* and *server.* The amount of caching and paging done on a system will greatly affect system performance.

Processor Monitoring Considerations

Processor, server work queues, system, and *thread* are performance monitor objects used to check processor performance.

Physical Disk Monitoring Considerations

Objects used to monitor physical disk in performance monitor are *cache, logical disk, memory, paging file, physical disk, process, redirector,* and *server.*

Note Before any disk monitoring can be accomplished, the disk performance counters must be activated. At the Windows NT command prompt, type **diskperf -y**.

To turn the disk performance counters off, type **diskperf -n**. ■

Note If RAID disks are being monitored, the following syntax is required to turn on the counters:

diskperf -ye

The disk counters are turned off by typing **diskperf -ne**. ■

Network Monitoring Considerations

Performance monitor objects used to establish a network baseline are browser, client service for NetWare, Gateway Service for NetWare, FTP server, ICMP, IP, NBT connection, NetBEUI, NetBEUI resource, network interface, network monitor statistics, network segment, NWLink IPX, NWLink NetBIOS, RAS port, RAS total, redirector, server, TCP, UDP, and WINS Server.

Another plan that must be formulated is how the collected data is to be stored and viewed. Many applications other than performance monitor can be used to accomplish this and include:

- ◆ Microsoft Excel
- ◆ Microsoft SQL Server
- ◆ Microsoft Access
- ◆ Microsoft FoxPro

Simply collect performance data with Performance Monitor and select the Export <View> choice on the File drop-down menu to export the chart or alert, log, or report as a .tsv or .csv file to be opened by an application such as Microsoft Excel.

Network monitor is another tool used to gather enterprise performance statistics. Depending on your network characteristics and installed components and services, plan to monitor and establish a baseline for any of the following:

- ◆ Browser announcements, elections, and backup browser updates
- ◆ Logon validation and pass-through authentication
- ◆ DHCP address leasing and renewal
- ◆ WINS database building and updating
- ◆ Directory services database replication
- ◆ Client/server application, file, and data transfers
- ◆ Directory and file replication

Part
II

Ch
5

Both performance monitor and network monitor provide tools to collect and store or archive data to institute and maintain a performance baseline.

The actual mechanics of using performance and network monitoring tools are covered in Chapter 20, "Performance Monitor" and Chapter 21, "Network Monitor."

Planning Effective WAN Performance

Planning for effective WAN performance includes three issues:

- ◆ Logon validation
- ◆ Pass-through authentication
- ◆ Directory services database synchronization

Depending on the enterprise layout, establishing ideal performance regarding these three issues can be a chore.

A WAN consists of a number of network segments all connected to form a network enterprise. WAN segments could conceivably be connected using slow 56K links, 256K links, T1 links, fast T3 links, or any combination of these. WAN links, although not recommended, could also be connected by RAS connections.

The physical location of domain controllers, users, and resources all interact to result in WAN enterprise performance. Careful planning will provide the best performance possible.

Logon Validation

Both types of domain controllers, the PDC and all BDCs, in a domain and/or trusted domain provide logon validation for users in the enterprise. The location of the PDC and BDCs combined with the location of users is the key to WAN performance.

The following is an example of a Windows NT domain consisting of two offices separated by a WAN link.

Office A in the domain contains the PDC and three BDCs to provide logon validation for 6,000 users and backup for the PDC. One thousand management personnel are located in office A and 5,000 workers are located in office B. Office A is connected to office B over a 56K link.

In Figure 5.1, all 6,000 users must be validated from the domain controllers physically located in office A; 5,000 of which have to be validated over a 56K WAN link. Logon validation performance, in this case, would be slow and would probably not be acceptable.

FIG. 5.1 ⇒ 5.2

This Windows NT domain suffers from slow and inefficient logon validation performance.

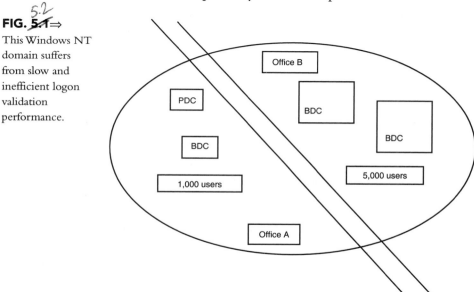

Figure 5.2 shows that two BDCs were physically located in office B. Logon validation for the 5,000 users is now local to that office and not over the 56K link. This provides much faster and efficient logon validation performance.

In addition, the third BDC could be placed in office B for even faster logon validation; however, a BDC should be located in office A for backup to the PDC.

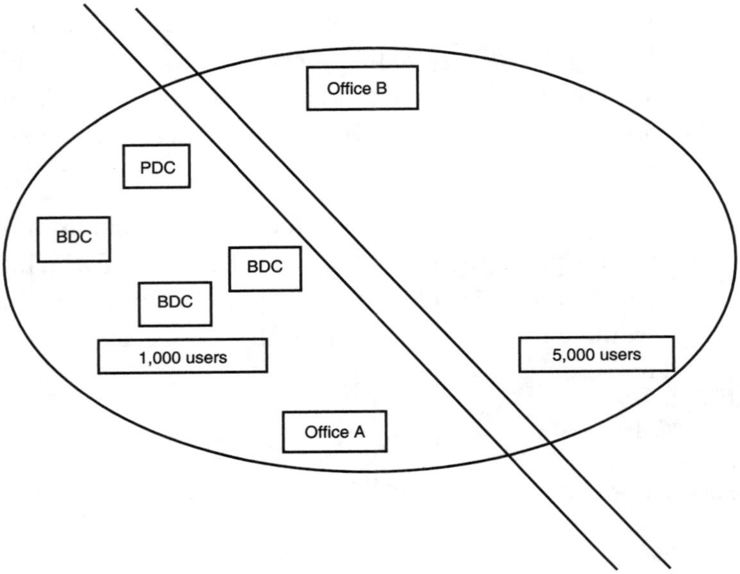

5.1

FIG. 5.2 ⇒
This Windows NT
domain provides
fast and efficient
logon validation
performance.

Also, notice the size of the BDCs in Figure 5.2. Because more users
are located in office B, the BDCs are actually more powerful than the
PDC or BDC in office A. This will also contribute to better logon
performance.

The above examples illustrate that if slow logon is the problem in the
enterprise, the solution is to place BDCs at locations where most of the
users are logging on. This alleviates the possibility of numerous logon
validations being performed over a slow WAN link.

Pass-Through Authentication

In addition to logon validation, pass-through authentication performance must also be planned for. Pass-through authentication will occur
at three different times during Windows NT operation: two times during logon validation and once during resource access.

If a user logs on to a local domain (the local domain name is specified
in the Logon Information dialog box) from a Windows NT Workstation or a Windows NT Member Server, the Net Logon service in the

workstation or server will pass the user name and password through to the Net Logon service on a domain controller. If the user name and password are valid, the domain controller will authenticate the logon.

If a user logs on to the trusted domain (the trusted domain name is specified in the Logon Information dialog box) from a workstation or member server in a trusting domain, the Net Logon service in the workstation or server will pass the user name and password through to the Net Logon service on the local domain controller. The local domain controller will check to see if the domain name is a trusted domain, and if it is, will pass the user name and password through to a trusted domain controller to authenticate the logon. If the domain name is not that of a trusted domain, the logon will fail.

Pass-through authentication also occurs in the same way it does for logon validations when a user tries to connect to a resource in a trusting domain.

Figure 5.3 shows an example of resource access pass-through authentication. There is a trust relationship between domain A and domain B. Domain A is the trusted domain and domain B is the trusting domain. User Jim sitting at a workstation in domain A tries to access a resource on a server in domain B.

FIG. 5.3⇒

This is an example of pass-through authentication.

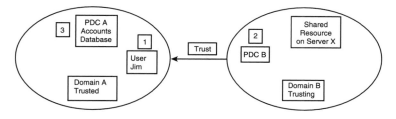

1. User Jim, located at a workstation computer in domain A, tries to access a resource in domain B.

2. PDC B requests authentication from PDC A accounts database.

3. PDC A authenticates the request and Jim gets access to the shared resource.

The properties of pass–through authentication for logon validation in the first scenario, such as speed and efficiency, are simply based on the speed of the local network and the efficiency of the domain controller doing the validation.

In the second scenario, logon validation is being provided by a trusted domain. The trusted domain and the trusting domain could be connected by a WAN. As illustrated in Figure 5.1 and 5.2, it is a good idea to place domain controllers where the majority of users are located.

The third scenario, illustrated in Figure 5.3, could be a similar situation where the users are accessing resources not only through a trust relationship but also across a WAN. In this case, it is a good idea to place resources where the users that use them are located, if possible.

Database Synchronization

The third performance issue in an enterprise is directory services database synchronization, which is the process of replicating the accounts and policies database from the PDC to all BDCs in the domain or network.

If the domain or enterprise problem is slow or incomplete synchronization, and not slow logon validation over a WAN, the solution would be to locate the BDCs on the same side of the WAN as the PDC as illustrated in Figure 5.4.

Note It is important to note the number of users located in each office of the following figure. This figure differs from Figure 5.1 in this regard.

A variation to this example would be to locate one BDC in office B for user validation in that office. Only one BDC in this case would require synchronization over the WAN.

The second issue that requires an enormous amount of planning is a combination of user logon validation and directory services database synchronization.

FIG. 5.4⇒

BDCs can be located on the same side of the WAN as the PDC to fix synchronization problems.

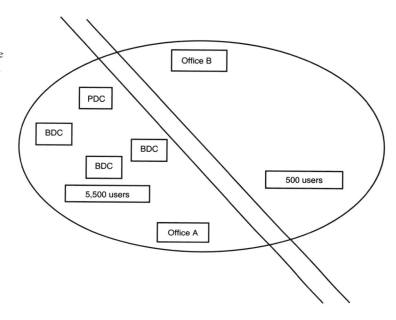

Previously, the problem of slow logon validation was corrected by placing BDCs on the side of a WAN where the majority of the users were located. Next, the problem of slow synchronization was fixed by placing the BDCs in the same location as the PDC.

Because of the BDC placement, one problem is fixed; however, another situation becomes apparent. The challenge is now to arrive at an acceptable performance level on both logon validation and database synchronization with the infamous slow WAN link in the middle.

In Figure 5.5, office A and office B have an equal amount of users. It has been determined that the PDC and one BDC will be physically located in office A and that two BDCs will be physically located in office B. This configuration provides excellent logon validation performance.

Part

II

Ch

5

FIG. 5.5⇒

This configuration allows for acceptable logon validation and database synchronization performance.

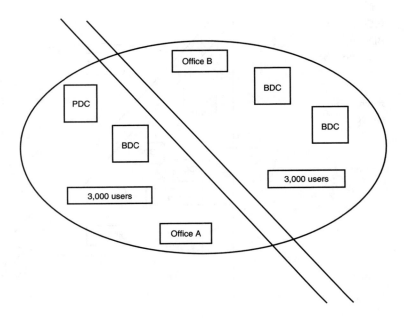

The plan now calls for a way to configure the network for acceptable synchronization performance. This can be accomplished by configuring the following replication parameters in the Registry.

The following parameters are a function of the Net Logon service in Windows NT, and are found at this Registry location:

```
HKEY_LOCAL_MACHINE\System\CurrentControl\Set\Services\
Netlogon\Parameters
```

◆ *Pulse*

◆ *PulseConcurrency*

◆ *ReplicationGovernor*

Pulse

The `pulse` parameter defines the pulse frequency in seconds. All changes made to the SAM/LSA during this time are collected. When this parameter expires, the PDC will signal or pulse all the BDCs that require updating. BDCs that do not require updating will not receive a pulse.

The default value for this parameter is 300 seconds (five minutes), with a range of 60 seconds to 3,600 seconds (one minute to one hour).

Increasing this value will result in less frequent notifications of database changes to the BDCs.

PulseConcurrency

This NETLOGON parameter defines the maximum number of BDCs that the PDC will send pulses to at one time. Once a BDC gets a pulse, it will acknowledge the pulse by asking for the database changes.

The default value for this parameter is 20, with a range of 1 to 500. Increasing this value will result in more load or stress on the PDC, so make sure that the PDC is powerful enough to handle this number of calls. Decreasing this parameter will increase the time it takes for a PDC to replicate the database changes to all of the BDCs.

ReplicationGovernor

This parameter must be set at each BDC to be involved with the synchronization process in the domain.

The `ReplicationGovernor` NETLOGON parameter is set to a value of 100 percent by default and has a range of 0 to 100 percent. This value controls two different functions of the Net Logon service. It defines how much data is transferred to the BDC on each call to the PDC, and it also defines how often the Net Logon service on the BDC will make a replication call to the PDC. The default value of 100 will cause 128K of data to be replicated on each call, and will allow the Net Logon service to make calls 100 percent of the time.

If, for example, this value is set to 50, 64K of data will be transferred on each call and the Net Logon service will only make calls 50 percent of the time. With synchronization calls being made only 50 percent of the time, the network is open to be used by other applications or services.

If this number is too low, replication will not complete because all of the data will not be replicated in the time frame allotted. If this value is set to 0, the Net Logon service will never replicate the database which would result in a completely out-of-sync database on the BDCs involved.

Part
II
Ch
5

Depending on the layout of the domain, some BDCs may be physically located on the same LAN as the PDC, and others may be located on different speed WAN segments. BDCs of different speed WAN segments can be adjusted individually for different rates of synchronization.

It should also be noted that the Windows NT AT scheduler service can be used in conjunction with regini.exe and a script file to automatically change this value at different times of the day as required. An example batch file that will change the *ReplicationGovernor* value to 50 is:

```
net stop NETLOGON
regini \registry\machine\system\currentcontrolset\services\
NETLOGON\parameters
ReplicationGovernor = REG_DWORD 50
net start NETLOGON
```

If many database changes take place often, the *ChangeLogSize* parameter in the Registry may also have to be adjusted. The *change log* is used to control whether a full or partial synchronization will take place between the BDCs and the PDC. Changes made to the directory services database normally place an entry in the change log that takes 32 bytes of data. By default, the size of the change log is 64K that will allow for around 2,000 changes. The maximum size of the log can be set to 4M that would allow for approximately 125,000 changes.

If the change log becomes full, older entries at the beginning of the log will start to become overwritten. When this happens, the BDC will implement a full synchronization process (the entire database), rather than a partial synchronization operation (only database changes). The *ChangeLogSize* parameter is located in the same Registry location as the *ReplicationGovernor* parameter previously mentioned.

Planning Protocol Selection of a Network Enterprise

Planning a network enterprise includes the selection and configuration of the required protocol or protocols. Use information presented earlier in this chapter in the section "Planning Effective WAN Performance," regarding WAN topology to assist in determining proper protocol selection. More information on protocols is presented in Chapter 8, "Configuring Domain Network Core Services."

Windows NT Server supports the following transport protocols:

NetBEUI	NetBIOS Extended User Interface
NWLink	NetWare Link
TCP/IP	Transmission Control Protocol/Internet Protocol
DLC	Data Link Control
AppleTalk	

NetBEUI

The Microsoft Windows NT implementation of NetBEUI is the *NBF (NetBIOS Frame)* protocol. NBF is a fast, efficient, and compact protocol designed to be implemented and used in small departmental LANs of anywhere from 2 to 200 workstations.

NBF can be used to connect different LAN segments through bridges, but cannot be used with routers because it is not a routable protocol. NBF is primarily used in a Microsoft client/server local area network and does support existing LAN Manager and IBM LAN Server installations.

Another feature of NBF includes self-tuning capabilities relating to memory and slow LAN links. NBF only uses as much memory as is needed to support current established connections. As for slow LAN links, NBF dynamically adjusts link timer T1 (response timer) on a per link basis, depending on line conditions and characteristics. The T1 timer value determines how long the sending computer waits for a response from the receiving computer. T2 (acknowledge timer) and Ti (inactivity timer) are not adjusted dynamically, but can be adjusted manually in the Registry.

There are virtually no NetBIOS session limits with the present version because it uses a 32-bit handle that contains the session number and the network address of the remote computer to identify a session. The 32-bit handle is used in place of the 8-bit session number used by the previous version that resulted in a per computer session limit of 254.

NBF offers extremely good error protection and, by default, is configured for fast LAN performance and requires very little configuration. Client computers that require remote connections to Windows NT RAS servers can use the NBF protocol to establish these sessions.

The Registry location of available NBF configuration parameters is shown here:

```
HKEY_LOCAL_MACHINE\System\CurrentControlSet\Services\Nbf
```

NWLink

If your enterprise plan includes Novell servers and networking issues, you will require NWLink as one of your chosen protocols. *NWLink* is Microsoft's version of Novell's *IPX/SPX (Internetwork Packet Exchange/Sequence Packet Exchange)* transport protocol. In addition to connecting Microsoft networks or network segments together, it is required to provide communication between Microsoft computers and Novell server and client computers. NWLink is a routable transport protocol.

NWLink by itself will not allow Windows NT computers to access Novell resources such as directories, files, and printers. However, because Windows NT supports both Windows sockets and NetBIOS over NWLink, it will, by itself, allow Windows NT computers to act as an application server to a Novell client in a client/server application environment. The reverse is also true. Windows NT computers can run the client portion of the application with the server portion being run on the Novell server.

If Windows NT computers must access NetWare resources on a Novell server, a NetWare redirector is required. If a Windows NT Workstation platform is used, the redirector required is *CSNW (Client Service for NetWare)*, and if a Windows NT Server platform is used, the required redirector is *GSNW (Gateway Service for NetWare)*. Together, with both the NWLink protocol and the correct NetWare redirector installed on a Windows NT Workstation or Server platform, the Windows NT computer can access Novell server resources.

Novell has also created a 32-bit NetWare redirector that can be installed on a Windows NT system in place of the Microsoft redirectors and used to access resources on a NetWare server.

As mentioned earlier, Gateway Service for NetWare is the NetWare component installed on a Windows NT server platform to access NetWare resources. As its name implies, this redirector supplies a gateway service that allows Microsoft clients that do not have NetWare software installed (NWLink and/or a NetWare redirector) to access Novell server resources. For example, Microsoft clients with just NetBEUI installed can connect to a share point on the Windows NT Server with NetBEUI installed. In addition, through the NWLink and GSNW software on the Windows NT Server, they can connect directly to the Novell resource through the gateway service.

Other software services available for the Windows NT Server platform are *FPNW (File and Print Service for NetWare)* and *DSMN (Directory Service Manager for NetWare)*. FPNW is add-on software that allows NetWare clients to use Windows NT file and print resources. DSMN is add-on software that allows Windows NT administrators to manage NetWare accounts from a Windows NT domain controller.

The Registry locations of available NWLink configuration parameters are:

```
HKEY_LOCAL_MACHINE\System\CurrentControlSet\Services\NlinkIpx
HKEY_LOCAL_MACHINE\System\CurrentControlSet\Services\NlinkNb
HKEY_LOCAL_MACHINE\System\CurrentControlSet\Services\NlinkSpx
```

TCP/IP

TCP/IP is an industry standard suite of protocols that was developed in 1969 by the Department of Defense and designed for use on Wide Area Networks (WANs). It is a routable protocol and provides the capability of connecting a large variety of host systems. It provides for connections to TCP/IP networks using NetBIOS such as UNIX-based systems with NetBT (NetBIOS over TCP/IP).

Part

II

Ch

5

In addition to the features mentioned here, Microsoft TCP/IP offers *Simple Network Management Protocol (SNMP)* support, *Dynamic Host Configuration Protocol (DHCP)* support, *Windows Internet Name Service (WINS)* support, and access to the Internet.

Enterprise plans have to include not only TCP/IP protocol requirements such as IP addresses, subnet mask, and default gateway parameters, but also requirements of all services related to each protocol. Protocol parameters and configuration will be covered in Chapter 8, "Configuring Domain Network Core Services."

SNMP

SNMP is a network management protocol that can be installed as a service in addition to the Microsoft TCP/IP protocol and is used to monitor and manage other host computers and gateways on the network. SNMP will run on any computer running Windows NT that has TCP/IP installed. As a management service running on a Windows NT system, it will request and receive status information from a host or gateway. As an agent service, it will send status information to the administrator running the management service when a serious event happens or when status information is requested. Windows NT Server 4.0 is not itself an SNMP manager. However, there are a variety of SNMP managers available in the network market, and Windows NT's SNMP service is used to communicate information to these managers.

For example, if the SNMP service is installed on a Windows NT 4.0 server or workstation, and the Resource Kit Utility snmputil.exe is run from the command prompt with the following syntax:

```
snmputil get <computername where service is installed> public
system.sysDescr.0
```

the return message would consist of system description information similar to the following:

```
Variable = system.sysDescr.0
Value    = OCTET STRING - Hardware: x86 Family 5 Model 2
Stepping 12 AT/AT COMPATIBLE - Software: Windows NT Version
4.0  (Build Number: 1381 Uniprocessor Free)
```

Note The SNMP service must be installed on a Windows NT system for any of the TCP/IP objects to appear in Performance Monitor. ■

DHCP

DHCP is a service included in Windows NT that provides dynamic IP address assignment to DHCP clients. DHCP clients can include Windows NT, Windows 95, Windows for Workgroup 3.11, and Windows 3.1 and DOS client computers.

Note Windows for Workgroup 3.11, Windows 3.1, and DOS clients must support DHCP. All software to support this requirement is located in the client's folder on the Windows NT Server CD. ■

Planning for this service includes a number of issues. First of all, if DHCP is being used, WINS should also be used so NetBIOS names to IP address for clients are dynamically mapped.

The enterprise topology and number of DHCP clients must also be included in the plan. If DHCP is to be used on one subnet, it is recommended that a DHCP server, along with a backup or standby server, be implemented for every 10,000 clients. If a multiple subnet network is necessary, it is very possible that multiple DHCP servers will be required.

> **Caution**
> If multiple DHCP servers are used on any type of network, either single or multiple subnet, verify that none of the DHCP servers include the same scope of addresses. Duplicate IP addressing can occur if DHCP servers contain duplicate scopes.

It is important to note that the physical placement or location of DHCP servers is not the most important item to consider. DHCP servers are not required to be physically located on each network subnet unless the routers used do not conform to RFC 1542 that supports BOOTP relay agent. The relay agent will pass DHCP packets to other

Part
II

Ch
5

subnets on the network even with broadcast messaging being used. It is recommended, however, that each subnet include a DHCP server for performance and administration reasons.

It is also important to know that the DHCP service does not follow the Windows NT domain structure; therefore, a DHCP server is not necessarily required in each Windows NT domain. Placement depends more on the physical network layout than the domain structure.

DHCP parameters and configuration are covered in Chapter 8.

WINS

WINS provides Windows NT with the capability of dynamically resolving IP address with NetBIOS names. All planning issues mentioned for DHCP servers also pertain to WINS servers, with some additions and considerations. WINS performance will increase approximately 25 percent if the WINS server has two processors, and more if using the NTFS file system.

If using more than one WINS server, another consideration is to designate one of the WINS servers as a central server and designate all other WINS servers as push-and-pull partners to this central server. This will ensure that each WINS server will have a consistent database of all node addresses.

WINS parameters and configuration are covered in Chapter 8.

Internet Access

With TCP/IP, Windows NT computers can connect directly to the Internet, provided that you have acquired a valid Internet IP address. Internet addresses can be obtained through the *Internet Network Information Center (InterNIC)* or from an Internet Service Provider. The InterNIC can be contacted at **http://internic.net** or call 1-800-444-4345.

The Registry location of available TCP/IP configuration parameters is:

```
HKEY_LOCAL_MACHINE\System\CurrentControlSet\Services\TCP/IP
```

DLC

DLC is used in Windows NT for the purpose of communicating with IBM mainframes, primarily through 3270 and 5250 emulation, and printing to HP network printing devices. It is not used in Windows NT for normal computer-to-computer communication because it does not provide for or use the NetBIOS interface layer. It only provides applications direct access to the Data Link Layer. DLC can be used on both an Ethernet or Token-Ring network, and if using Ethernet, it can communicate using the *DIX (Digital Intel Xerox)* frame format.

The DLC protocol only needs to be installed on the Windows NT computer that is performing the mainframe communication or the print server services. For example, the protocol would have to be installed on the Windows NT computer acting as the print server for the HP JetDirect printers and not on all the client computers that are using the printers.

Note   The DLC protocol must be installed on the Windows NT print server before the self-test is performed on the network printing device. Once the protocol is installed, a self-test is manually performed on the printer that will report the NIC address to the protocol. ▪

The Registry location of available DLC configuration parameters is:

```
HKEY_LOCAL_MACHINE\System\CurrentControlSet\Services\DLC
```

AppleTalk

The AppleTalk protocol is used to communicate with Macintosh systems. With Services for Macintosh installed on a Windows NT Server platform, Macintosh Accessible Volumes can be created and shared between the Macintosh users and the Microsoft users on the network. Microsoft users can also use Macintosh AppleTalk PostScript printers, and Macintosh users can use non–PostScript printers controlled by Windows NT print servers.

Part

II

Ch

5

Planning for Windows NT and Macintosh connectivity is dependent on the type of network and the type of hardware presently being used. Services for Macintosh supports LocalTalk, Ethernet, Token Ring, and FDDI topology. If the existing Macintosh computers are presently communicating with their own LocalTalk hardware and software, connectivity can be accomplished by installing a LocalTalk adapter in the Windows NT machine. This is in addition to the Ethernet, Token Ring, or FDDI hardware and attaching it to the existing Macintosh network. This would be the least expensive way because only one hardware adapter is required; however, the speed of a LocalTalk network is only 230K.

Another option would be to install EtherTalk, TokenTalk, or FDDI hardware in the Macintosh machines. This option is the most expensive choice, but the speed of the network would be greater. Ethernet networks operate up to the 10M range; Token Ring up to 16M; FDDI, 100M.

The third option is to involve an Ethernet/LocalTalk router. If Windows NT with Services for Macintosh will be configured as the router, the Windows NT computer must have both a LocalTalk adapter and an Ethernet adapter installed. If a third-party router is installed, the AppleTalk protocol must be installed and bound to the Ethernet adapter.

Windows NT with Services for Macintosh can also function as a seed router or a nonseed router in this environment. A *seed router* is a router that will initialize and broadcast routing information about other physical networks on the enterprise. If it is acting as a seed router, it must be the first server started so it can initialize other routers and computers in the network. If it is functioning as a nonseed router, it must be started after a seed router such as an AppleTalk router or Windows NT seed router is running and has initialized all ports.

Planning the Size of the Directory Services Database

The directory services or *Security Accounts Manager (SAM)* database in a Windows NT domain environment has limits pertaining to its physical size and number of accounts. The recommended physical or maximum size limit of the database is 40M. This limit is based on how long it takes a domain controller to boot. The recommended limit of the number of accounts in the database is 40,000 and includes the following four different types of accounts:

◆ User

◆ Local group

◆ Global group

◆ Computer

The type and size of the domain controllers required to accommodate databases of various sizes is discussed in the next section.

Each type of account created will require a certain amount of space in the database. Determining the number of each type of account required both now and in the future is crucial to setting up a network.

User Accounts

A unique user account is required and must be created for each person who requires access to the network. Planning of user accounts includes naming conventions, password policies, group associations, profile considerations, hour and computer logon restrictions, account information, and RAS dialing permissions. User accounts, by default, do not have any system rights associated with them and obtain system rights by their association with local built-in groups.

Part
II

Ch
5

Local Group Accounts

The first determination dealing with group creation is to decide if all or any of the built-in local groups and their built-in system rights can be used in your enterprise. The built-in local groups included by default with Windows NT Server are:

- ◆ Account Operators
- ◆ Administrators
- ◆ Backup Operators
- ◆ Guests

- ◆ Print Operators
- ◆ Replicator
- ◆ Server Operators
- ◆ Users

Local group planning includes naming conventions, user account membership, and system right associations. By default, local groups are the only account that automatically have system rights associated with them. Local groups and their functions and default system right associations will be covered in Chapter 12, "Domain Users and Groups."

Global Group Accounts

The use of global groups is another determination that has to be made when planning a network layout. If the enterprise contains a number of domains, global groups can ease the administration of user accounts and resource permissions immensely. As with local groups, determine if any of the built-in global groups fit your needs. By default, the included global groups are:

- ◆ Domain Admins
- ◆ Domain Guests
- ◆ Domain Users

Global group planning includes naming conventions, user account and local group membership, and system right associations. Like user accounts, by default, global group accounts do not have any system rights associated with them. Global groups and their functions are covered in Chapter 12.

Computer Accounts

Each Windows NT computer that is a member of a domain will require a computer account which is also an account in the directory services or SAM database. With the computer registered in the domain database, each system can be administered and monitored from a central location, normally from an administrator's computer. Users can be assigned certain computers from which they can log in.

Table 5.1 indicates the disk space required for each type of account within the directory services database.

Table 5.1	Account Disk Space Requirements
Account Type	Required Disk Space
User Account	1.0K
Local Group Account	0.5K+ 36 bytes per user
Global Group Account	0.5K+ 12 bytes per user
Computer Account	0.5K

The following will assist you in determining the total size of the directory services database once you have determined the number of user, local group, global group, and computer accounts required.

Number of
Users _____ x 1.0K = _____

Number of
Computers _____ x 0.5K = _____

Number of
Local Groups _____ x 0.5K + 36 bytes/user = _____

Number of
Global Groups _____ x 0.5K + 12 bytes/user = _____

Total Bytes
Required _____

Part
II

Ch
5

The following worksheet example illustrates a number of database size requirements using a variety of users, local groups, global groups, and computer accounts.

Users	Computers	Local Groups	Global Groups	Total Size
100	100	10	5	158K
1,000	1,000	25	15	1.6M
5,000	5,000	50	20	8.7M
10,000	20,000	100	30	20.6M
25,000	25,000	200	50	38.9M

Planning the Type and Quantity of Enterprise Domain Controllers

A number of issues must be thought out, and calculations must be made when planning for the correct number of domain controllers in a Windows NT enterprise. The following list illustrates the most important concerns:

◆ Size and speed
◆ Number of domains, both master and resource
◆ Location
◆ Number of backup controllers

Size and Speed of Domain Controllers

Size, speed, and amount of resources domain controllers require to perform properly is largely dependent on the physical size of the directory services database. Obviously, the more user, group, and computer accounts in the database, the larger and faster the domain controller must be to provide acceptable operation and performance. Table 5.2 offers recommendations to consider when planning the size, speed, and resource considerations of domain controllers.

Table 5.2	**Domain Controller Properties**		
Database Size	**Accounts**	**Minimum CPU Size**	**Minimum Amount of RAM**
10M	7,500	486DX/66	32M
20M	15,000	Pentium or RISC	64M
30M	20,000–30,000	Pentium or RISC	96M
40M	30,000–40,000	Pentium or RISC	128M

Note Database sizes are approximate. Accounts include user, group, and computer accounts and are approximate. RISC includes MIPS, Alpha AXP, or PowerPC computers. ∎

Another consideration in planning the size of domain controllers is where the administrative unit of the enterprise will be located and where the majority of users and computers are physically located. If the administrative unit or MIS department is located at one location requiring few logon validations, and a large number of users and computers are located at another location requiring a large number of logon validations, the BDC should be a physically larger computer with more resources and speed than the PDC.

Number of Domains, Master Domains, and Resource Domains

The total number of domains required is based on the number of accounts, the location of users and administrative units, and the location and number of resources. Each and every domain will require a PDC.

The number of master domains is almost totally dependent on two issues: the total number of accounts in the domain, and the layout of the organization. As stated previously, the directory services database suggested limit is 40,000 accounts (40M) including user, group, and computer accounts. If more than 40,000 accounts are required, then more than one master domain is needed.

Another example may be that a corporation has only 20,000 accounts; however, the organization has four departments and each department requires total control over its own account's database. One department is located in New York with 8,000 accounts, another in Los Angeles with 5,000 accounts, another in Chicago with 4,000 accounts, and the last in Miami with 3,000 accounts. This situation would require four master domains, one for each administrative department, each with its own PDC. It would be a good idea for each location to have a BDC, also.

The following can be used to calculate the directory services database size and domain controller requirements:

Number of User Accounts × 1K	a)_____K
Number of Computer Accounts × .5K	b)_____K
Number of Local Groups × .5K + 36 bytes/user	c)_____K
Number of Global Groups × .5K + 12 bytes/user	d)_____K
Total SAM Size (Total a + b + c + d)	e)_____K
Convert SAM Size to M (total e × .001024)	f)_____M
Number of Domains (total f ÷ x)	g)_____ (x = the largest SAM database size supported by domain controllers)

Location of Domain Controllers

One of the most common approaches to designing a Windows NT enterprise is to organize users and computers by their location. If a user is physically located in Green Bay, that user will be a member of the Green Bay domain. If a user is physically located in Milwaukee, that user will be a member of the Milwaukee domain. This approach may work for some organizations, but not for others. Access to resources with this approach is an issue. If the resources needed by all users in the

Green Bay domain are located in the Green Bay domain, then the location organization approach can be effective. If engineers in Green Bay require access to resources both in Green Bay and Milwaukee, then it would make more sense to organize domains and users by job function rather than location. This would result in more efficient resource administration.

Proper planning of the location of your domain controllers in your enterprise will result in efficient logon validation, directory services database synchronization, and pass-through authentication.

To establish effective logon validation and pass-through authentication in your enterprise, plan to physically locate master domain BDCs in resource domains where the users actually log on to the network. Using this approach will provide for fast and efficient network validation and authentication within a well-connected LAN rather than across a slow WAN link, but there are trade-offs.

The speed and quality of any installed WAN links in your enterprise directly affect directory services database synchronization. As stated in the preceding paragraph, placing a master domain BDC in a resource domain provides fast and efficient logon validation rather than validating across a slow WAN link. However, if only a few users require validation across a WAN link, it may be more efficient to log on and authenticate across the WAN than to continuously synchronize the directory services database across the link.

As a rule, locate the master domain BDCs where the majority of users are located, but avoid placing a BDC on each side of a WAN link if only a few users are going to be affected.

Backup Domain Controllers

For logon validation purposes, one BDC is suggested for every 2,000 users. There are a number of other issues that must be taken into consideration, and every enterprise will have different requirements. It will be up to the network administrator to plan for the required amount of

Part

II

Ch

5

redundancy in the network. The following are suggestions of BDC requirements:

◆ One master domain, one administrative unit, one physical location of users, and resources with 12,000 user accounts and 12,000 computer accounts. One PDC will be used. What are the BDC requirements?

  The need is for one administrative unit with 24,000 user and computer accounts all located in one physical location; one master domain will satisfy the requirement. The PDC and six BDCs, one for every 2,000 users, will share the logon validation load of the domain. Total suggested number of BDCs is six.

◆ One master domain, one administrative unit, one logical location of user accounts with 12,000 users, four resource domains with 3,000 physical users, and computers in each. Trust relations will be established between the resource domains (trusting) and the master domain (trusted). The PDC in the master domain will contain the directory services database for the entire enterprise. The PDCs in the four resource domains will be used for resource administration. What are the BDC requirements?

  The requirement is one administrative unit; however, the resources and users are located in four different locations with the account administrator at the master domain and the resource administrators located at each of the resource domains. Nine BDCs should be installed in the master domain with one physically located in the master domain and two physically located in each of the resource domains. The one BDC in the master domain is for redundancy in case the PDC goes down; the two BDCs in each of the resource domains will handle the 3,000 logon validation in each resource domain with room for expansion. There should also be a BDC installed in each of the four resource domains for redundancy. Total suggested number of BDCs is 14.

Planning the Effects of Directory Services Database Replication

Recall that the Directory Services database replication service copies the SAM database from the PDC to all BDCs in the domain.

Proper planning for this service is essential for efficient enterprise operation. Consider the following items pertaining to the connection between the PDC and BDCs and the characteristics of the SAM database when planning your network:

- ◆ Type, speed, and reliability
- ◆ Protocol
- ◆ Number and location of users
- ◆ Administrator location

Type, Speed, and Reliability of Network Connections

These items greatly affect Directory Services database replication. The type, speed, and reliability of the line go hand in hand to provide efficient replication.

Line types range from very fast, well-connected LAN connections (directly through cables and hubs or through bridges and routers) to very slow RAS connections through telephone lines like T1, 56K, ISDN, or modem connections.

Protocol Considerations

Protocol selection can also affect database replication. Virtually any protocol (NetBEUI, NWLink, or TCP/IP) can be used if the PDC and BDC systems are communicating through a direct LAN connection. The only considerations are that the same protocol be used at both ends and if NWLink is used, the same frame type must be used. If the LAN connection is through a router, either locally or over a WAN, then

Part

II

Ch

5

only NWLink or TCP/IP can be used because NetBEUI is not a routable protocol.

Number and Location of User Considerations

The size of the SAM database and the speed and reliability of the connection between the PDC and BDCs will determine how long database replication will take. If BDCs remain on, only changes (partial synchronization) are replicated. If BDCs were shut down, a full synchronization must be completed when BDCs are powered on and initialized. Full synchronization increases network traffic.

The location of users, computers, and groups in a network and the user logon and authentication requirements must also be included in the enterprise plan. As discussed earlier, if BDCs are located on slow WAN connections, plan to adjust the `ReplicationGovernor` parameter in the Registry for effective and complete synchronization.

Recall that the `ReplicationGovernor` parameter is located in the Registry at the following location:

```
HKEY_LOCAL_MACHINE\SYSTEM\CURRENTCONTROLSET\SERVICES\
NETLOGON\PARAMETERS
```

The following can be used to calculate replication times depending on the size of the directory services database:

Number of User Accounts	a)_____
Passwords Expire in How Many Days	b)_____
Divide b by 30	c)_____
Password Changes Per Month (a × c)	d)_____
New User Accounts Per Month	e)_____
New Group Accounts Per Month	f)_____
New Computer Accounts Per Month	g)_____
Amount of Data Per Month (d + e + f + g) × 1K	h)_____
Compute WAN Throughput in BPS	i)_____

Compute i ÷ 8 bits/byte   j)_____

Compute j × 60 seconds/minute   k)_____

Compute k × 60 minutes/hour   l)_____

Total Synchronization Time (h ÷ l)   m)_____

For fast and efficient logon validation and pass-through authentication, place the master domain BDCs where the majority of the users and resources are located. At the same time, keep directory services database replication issues in mind to establish an effective balance between the two.

Registry values such as the `ReplicationGovernor` parameter can be changed on-the-fly by running a batch file through the AT scheduler service and using resource kit utilities such as Regini.exe or Regchg.exe. In this way, values can be automatically adjusted at times during the day when it is possible that WAN links are slow but re-adjusted at night when the links have less traffic on them.

Location of the Enterprise Administrator

Locate the PDC where the administrative unit or MIS department is located. If a database change is made at a BDC, the change is physically made in the database located on the PDC, therefore generating additional network traffic.

If a PDC is extremely busy performing logon validation, pass-through authentication, and is also involved in SAM database synchronization, all of its time can be devoted to the synchronization process by pausing the Net Logon services. The PDC will not perform logon validations or pass-through authentication operations but will perform database synchronization with its BDCs.

Part

II

Ch

5

Taking the Disc Test

 If you have read and understood material in the chapter, you are ready to test your knowledge. Insert the CD-ROM that comes with this book and run the self-test software as described in Appendix I, "Using the CD-ROM."

From Here...

Installation and configuration of Microsoft Windows NT is the next section of this manual. Understanding of Windows NT directory services, domain models, trust relationships, and capacity planning and performance will all aid dramatically in the concepts presented in the next chapter.

Part III.

Installation and Configuration

Chapter Prerequisite

You should be familiar with
Windows NT directory ser-
vices, trust relationships, and
domain models. You should
also be familiar with the concepts of capacity planning and
performance. These topics are
covered in Chapters 2–5.

Domain Installation Considerations

This chapter will discuss the different Windows NT 4.0 Server configurations that are available and the considerations that you must make
prior to the actual installation of the Windows NT software. The concepts that you will learn will assist you with maximizing the potential
of your software and hardware performance. You will reduce bottlenecks and keep costs to a minimum.

Topics covered in this chapter include:

- Identifying the three Server types
- Deciding the Server role that is needed for a specific use
- The resources that maximize a particular Server function
- Troubleshoot improperly configured servers

Identifying the Three Server roles

Windows NT 4.0 Server computers configure in one of three different ways:

- ◆ Primary Domain Controller (PDC)
- ◆ Backup Domain Controller (BDC)
- ◆ Stand-alone or member server

Primary Domain Controller

Also known as the PDC, the primary domain controller is the computer that creates the domain. Only one PDC exists per domain. This computer contains the master accounts database for the domain. All Windows NT computers and users that are listed in this encrypted database are members of this server's domain. The PDC also authenticates users and is responsible for synchronizing the database information with the BDCs that belong to its domain. All updates using the administrative utility tool User Manager for Domains will modify the master account database.

Backup Domain Controller

In a Windows NT Domain environment, you may install an unlimited number of BDCs for each domain. You should create a new BDC for every 2000 users in your Domain. Each BDC receives updated account information from the PDC automatically. The BDC only contains a copy of the account information, and no changes may be directly applied to it. BDCs authenticate users and logs them on just as a PDC would.

> **Caution**
> More than 200 BDCs in any one domain will result in an excessive processing burden on the PDC.

When the PDC fails, the authentication and logon processes of the BDC continue unaffected. At any later point, any of the BDCs can be promoted to a PDC. Normally, you promote a BDC as a result of a PDC failure. However, you can also promote the BDC simply to replace the PDC. The result of promoting a BDC when the PDC is online is that all changes will be forcibly synchronized.

Stand-Alone or Member Server

A stand-alone or member server has the same services as the domain controllers. It does not participate in the domains account authentication or logon process. Also, it does not share the domain *security identifier (SID)* and cannot be promoted to a domain controller. This configuration is used to dedicate more CPU time toward services.

What is the difference between a stand-alone server and a member server? Upon installation of a stand-alone server, the server can be a member of either a workgroup or a domain. This is the same for a Windows NT Workstation. If the server belongs to a workgroup, it is known as stand-alone server. When the stand-alone server joins any domain, it is now a member server, and resources can be assigned permissions using the domains' accounts.

Features and services that are available to all servers include:

- ◆ Unlimited inbound connections
- ◆ Remote Access Service (RAS) support for 256 connections
- ◆ Fault-tolerant disk configurations including Redundant Array of Inexpensive Disk (RAID) 1 and 5
- ◆ File and print services for Macintosh
- ◆ Dynamic host configuration protocol (DHCP)
- ◆ Windows Internet Naming Services (WINS)
- ◆ Domain Name Services (DNS)
- ◆ Internet Information Server (IIS)
- ◆ Remote program load (PRL) support for MS-DOS, Windows, and Windows 95 clients

Part
III

Ch
6

Selecting the Appropriate Server Role

When you begin planning your site's configuration, logical and physical locations of the servers must be taken into consideration. Decide what resources there are and where the greatest demand for the resources will be before you install one piece of hardware or software. Careful planning, good server role selections, and network positioning will save you time, money, and energy spent handling complaints. Future additions to the network will be easy.

Primary Domain Controller

The PDC is the first server we will visit. This server may appear to be the ruler of the domain with little to do. The reality is that it has many housekeeping chores. As mentioned earlier in this chapter, it houses the master accounts database now called the *directory services database*. All account, trust, or policy changes are made here. For example, say you have implemented account policies to change user passwords every seven days; the changes are made directly to the PDC. Because changes have been made to the directory services database, these changes must be synchronized to all of this domain's BDCs. The PDC is also the domain master browser for the domain. The Computer Browser service will be discussed in more detail in Chapter 8, "Configuring Domain Network Core Services."

The greater the number of accounts, the more the demand on the PDC. Limit the use of the PDC to these functions to improve performance. It is very easy to add numerous other services to this machine and not realize the processing load that already exists.

Backup Domain Controller

To a few, the BDC server may seem to be an expensive and unnecessary proposition. Remember that it will keep your domain running, such as when the PDC is offline for service or failure so that users may still be authenticated and logged on. This is because the BDC contains a copy of the directory services database from the PDC. Likewise, the trust relationships with other domains continue to function. This server shares the same domain SID as the PDC of the domain it joined. This SID can only be changed by re-installing the BDC software.

As discussed in Chapter 5, "Capacity Planning and Performance," placement of the BDCs in your enterprise environment impacts the time it takes to log on and can minimize the traffic on the WAN. Each LAN should contain at least one BDC. Place the BDCs near the users. Microsoft recommends as a guide one BDC per 2,000 users.

More BDCs than required is not the answer, either. If forecasting or performance monitoring indicates a need for more BDCs, then add them. Sometimes adding more BDCs increases the workload for the PDC with the synchronization and directory replication processes. The use of the BDC should be limited to the same functions as the PDC to improve performance. It is easy to add more services to this machine and not realize the existing processing load that exists. By not using the BDC or some of the BDCs, you make it possible to promote it to a PDC without affecting the end user. If this server has additional duties such as being a print server, the users of that resource will be dropped during the promotion.

Member Server

The member server role is considered the enterprise workhorse. This server does not participate with the domain controllers as far as account synchronization and authentication; therefore, the server does not have the additional overhead of the domain controllers. There is more processing time available. It also does not share the domain SID. Because the domain SID is unique and integrated into the security database on a PDC and BDC, they must be reinstalled to be moved to another domain. Since a stand-alone or member server doesn't have this ID, it can be easily dropped from one domain and added to another domain just as a workstation.

Part

III

Ch

6

There are two main categories for the member server:

◆ File and print server

◆ The application server

Permissions to these resources can be granted to users or groups from the domain this server has been a member of or through a properly installed trust relationship. Many times, servers are used for all three of the mentioned functions. For application servers, optimally it is dedicated for use as a SQL, SNA, and client server application.

 Note Regardless of the server role, place the resources physically near the users of the resource for the best performance. ■

Maximizing the Resources Used by Each Server Role

Each role that a server participates in—whether PDC, BDC, file and print server, or application server—demands that a different set of requirements be considered which will affect the overall performance of that server.

Primary Domain Controller

As discussed in Chapter 5, once you have determined the account database size, ensure this machine has that much memory and the equivalent free space on disk. Ranking the importance of resources needed for the PDC are memory, network subsystem, processor, and disk subsystem. The recommended minimum RAM is 2.5 times the Security Account Manger (SAM) database size.

Memory is of vital importance due to the fact the SAM will be loaded into the RAM. This design speeds up the logon process.

The network subsystem is just as important as the amount of physical RAM. The *Network Interface Card (NIC)* should be a high performance card capable of handling communications with the network with a minimal involvement of the CPU.

If the server is connected to multiple network environments, you should consider multiple NICs to segment the network traffic. The number of protocols installed on the server should be minimal as well, as Windows NT "paths" through the installed protocols to find the one appropriate for its synchronization requests. A BDC is best placed physically near each group of users to reduce overall wide area network (WAN) traffic.

The processor is one of the most important resources for a PDC. When performing analysis on the bottleneck of a PDC, pay particular attention to CPU utilization. Since the PDC manages the entire domain, it uses a processor more than a traditional member server will.

The disk subsystem is last on the list for resources due to the fact the PDC is intended to store the Directory Services database and domain policies only. Because the account data is loaded into the RAM for authentication, the subsystem does not have to be the fastest and most expensive configuration in your domain.

Once the PDC has completed the bootup sequence, very little will be read or written to the disk until changes occur. Compared with the traffic that a file server will get with file requests, or a print server will get with print spooling requests, the PDC's disk requirement seems almost non-existent.

Backup Domain Controller

The BDC resource-wise requires the same considerations as the PDC—memory, network subsystem, processor, and disk subsystem, in that order. The difference is that the system overhead is slightly reduced on a BDC because it is not responsible for contacting the PDC when the directory services database is not up-to-date. The BDC only responds to the PDC for synchronization when called by the PDC.

Many BDCs are multifunctional, and additional resources may be necessary. For example, the BDC may require a faster fault-tolerant disk configuration because it has been set up at a remote location that uses directory replication and is the local file and print server. The addition of the DHCP server and WINS will require additional resources. Many BDCs are configured this way to take advantage of the equipment that has been purchased. After considering baseline performance monitor readings and network monitor readings, you will find that the BDC will have more resources installed on it than the PDC.

When determining your domain controller requirements for your enterprise, consider the following factors:

◆ The number of accounts and simultaneous logons

◆ The closer the PDC or BDC, the quicker the logon

◆ If you have more BDCs, it takes longer to synchronize accounts.

◆ If you have more BDCs, it takes longer to replicate the directory.

Member Server as File and Print Server

Remember that the member server can be used as a file and print server or an application server. First let's look at the member server resource requirements when used for file and print services. In order starting with the most significant impact, they are memory, processor, disk subsystem, and the network subsystem.

Memory is at the top of the list to exploit the caching inherent to the Windows NT Server. The more available physical RAM available, the more Windows NT caches. Any local and network requests for folder and file access will be cached.

Installing a server with a minimal amount of memory will yield a small cache, decreasing the effectiveness of this important performance feature. Disk access will be greater because fewer requests will be handled in memory, and because of a greater dependence on virtual memory.

The processor is almost as important as memory; it is needed to handle all the I/O requests from the NIC and disk subsystem. Installing bus mastering cards, you will reduce the number of processor interrupts, thereby releasing processor cycles for more work. Again, consider adding additional processors for performance. When the server is a print server, the processor will be used extensively for rendering the final spooled data and sending that data to the printing device.

The disk subsystem is next on the list. The subsystem should include multiple fast access disk drives and multiple fast disk controllers. Use RAID 0 (Striping with no parity) disk configuration for resources that do not require fault tolerance. Because this server is supplying shared folders, possibly home folders, and network printers, the disk will be heavily accessed for information and the spooler functions. Recall that striping allows data to be read and written across anywhere from 2 to 32 physical disks concurrently in equal-sized blocks. This configuration can increase disk I/O significantly.

Caution

RAID 0, disk striping, provides no fault tolerance. The greater the number of physical disks involved in a strip set, the greater the chance for data loss in the event that one disk crashes.

Last on the resource list is the network subsystem. That statement should not indicate to you to use the slowest 8-bit NIC. If the data cannot get into or out through the card fast enough, it really will not matter how much memory or processors you have; the server will respond poorly.

Member Server as Application Server

By using the member server as an application server, the resource requirements' priorities shift a little. The order starts with the processor, memory, disk subsystem, and the network subsystem.

Part

III

Ch

6

The processor is the most important component. With a true client/server application installed on the server, the processor is needed to handle all the I/O requests from the NIC and disk subsystem, just as with the file and print server; however, the applications run on the server's processor and not on the client that requested the service. This translates to many additional threads competing for processor time. To improve this situation, consider, as with the PDC, symmetric multiprocessing. Add another processor to handle the additional threads.

Memory places second on the resource list. You may exploit the caching inherent to the Windows NT server. The more physical RAM available, the more it caches. Local and network requests for folder and file access are cached. Memory is critically important because after your application server starts using the pagefile, your performance will drop drastically. You can monitor paging using Performance Monitor.

Do your homework on the applications you intend to install on these servers. Know the resources they require. For example, installing Microsoft SQL Server software automatically tunes the server for its performance, including handling its own memory cache and network buffer caching. By default, SQL leaves very little memory resources for Windows NT or any other application you add to this server. Manually modify the SQL settings for your particular need.

After reviewing the disk subsystem, there usually is a significant amount of data on an application server. Once again, consider the faster disk controllers, faster disk drives, and most likely a RAID 5 (fault-tolerant striping with parity) configuration. Hardware RAID subsystems are also a possibility for increasing performance and reducing the need for additional physical drives. Hardware RAID also reduces system overhead involved in tracking Windows NT's software RAID.

The network subsystem most likely will not have the connection demand that a file and print server does, mainly because most of the client/server requests are of the query type and the data is relatively small.

Key Concept

The common elements with any type of server configuration are to plan out the needs of the servers. Any additional unnecessary services and protocols will impact the server's performance. Wise placement of the servers in the enterprise domain can greatly improve performance, reduce costs, and meet expectations. Specific server performance optimization will be covered in the "Monitoring and Optimization" section, later in this book

Troubleshooting Server Problems

The following sections discuss some common situations that arise when dealing with the various server roles, and potential actions to consider to resolve them.

Slow Logon

If you're finding that it takes too long to log on in the morning, you may need an additional BDC. The current BDCs could be becoming overwhelmed with the number of logon requests that they receive. You could also increase the power of the BDCs. When attempting to improve logon performance make sure that you place BDCs as close to the users logging in as possible.

Post-Installation SQL Performance Problems

If you're dissatisfied with SQL performance after installation, review the memory and paging of the server. Make sure that the server has enough memory to operate. SQL server requires a significant investment in memory to perform well. SQL Server also requires a fast CPU. Pay particular attention to the SQL Cache Hit Ratio, the Paging Activity, and processor activity on the server, as explained in Chapter 20, "Performance Monitor."

Part
III

Ch
6

Slow Access to the Corporate Policy Folder

You might discover that it takes an extended period of time to access the Corporate Policy folder. File servers need memory and a good processor. More memory will provide better throughput because the data requested returns to the client, and it is also cached in memory. Subsequent read requests will be fast. The processor must also be able to keep up with the demand.

Poor Performance after Converting Workstations to Servers

Perhaps you have converted some ~~servers~~ *ws* into ~~workstations~~ *servers*, only to find that your system's performance has seriously declined. Be aware that the stresses placed on a server are much greater than those placed on a workstation. Review each of the resources in the system. Look for the most important resources for each type of server. Generally, these are the resources that need to be upgraded to improve performance.

Taking the Disc Test

If you have read and understood material in the chapter, you are ready to test your knowledge. Insert the CD-ROM that comes with this book and run the self-test software as described in Appendix I, "Using the CD-ROM."

From Here...

Continuing your examination of configuration methods, concerns, and utilities, the next chapter guides you through the Windows NT Registry. Everything that you have learned up to this point—server roles, synchronization values, database size, and so on—are values that are stored in the Registry.

Chapter Prerequisite

The only prerequisite that the reader should have for this chapter is a familiarity with the Control Panel and other utilities that affect entries in the Windows NT Registry.

The Role of the Registry

The Windows NT Registry is the primary configuration database for Windows NT. Any change made through a Control Panel applet, an Administrative Tool group application, Windows NT Setup, or any other Windows NT program is saved in the Registry. This chapter will explore the Windows NT Registry, examine its significance, and discuss some troubleshooting techniques. Topics covered include:

◆ Understanding the Registry structure

◆ Working with the Registry

◆ Troubleshooting techniques

◆ Exploring the Windows NT boot process as it relates to the Registry

◆ Registry-related tools in the Windows NT Resource Kit

Examining the Windows NT 4.0 Registry

The Windows NT 4.0 Registry is perhaps the single most important element of the Windows NT operating system architecture. The Registry is an encrypted database of configuration and environment information relating to the successful booting of Windows NT 4.0. Think of this file as being the DOS AUTOEXEC.BAT and CONFIG.SYS files rolled into one—and then some.

Key Concept

The Registry is central to the operation of Windows NT 4.0. User environment settings are stored here. Driver information, services, hardware profile information, security objects and their permissions, and account information are all stored in the Registry. Microsoft considers the Registry so integral a part of Windows NT that it strongly discourages you from making changes to it.

In fact, the Control Panel, Administrative Tools group, and various properties sheets give you all the utilities you need to modify and customize your installation of Windows NT 4.0 for normal maintenance. All of these utilities modify one or more Registry entries. Therefore, there are only limited and specific reasons for you to make changes to the Registry directly.

Caution

A good rule of thumb for modifying the Registry: If there is a utility that can do the modification, *use the utility!* If you make substantial changes to the Registry that result in problems during boot-up or execution, Microsoft will disallow your support call.

That said, there are specific instances when you have to modify the Registry directly. These usually have to do with the absence of a utility to make a necessary change, or troubleshooting purposes. Some of the more common of these are discussed later in this chapter in the section "Using the Registry to Configure Windows NT 4.0."

Navigating with the Registry Editor

The Registry can be accessed by starting the Registry Editor utility. This utility can be accessed in several ways. Here are two:

◆ Open the Windows Explorer and select the SYSTEM32 folder under the Windows NT system folder (by default called WINNT). Double-click the file REGEDT32.EXE.

◆ Choose Run from the Start menu and type in **REGEDT32.EXE**. Then choose OK.

If you access the Registry often, you can also create a shortcut to REGEDT32.EXE on your desktop. Most Windows NT Registry settings can be viewed through the Windows NT Diagnostics utility located in the Administrative Tools program group. If needed, the Registry Editor can then be accessed through the utility's File, Run menu option.

> **Caution**
>
> If you are a support professional, it may be convenient or advantageous for you to add the Registry Editor icon to your desktop. However, this would probably not be appropriate to add to users' desktops as inappropriate modifications can cause Windows NT to become unstable.

Note Because the installation directory name default for Windows NT 4.0 is WINNT, throughout the remainder of this book, the Windows NT system directory is referred to as *WINNT*. ▪

Note Upon installation, Windows NT Setup includes both the Windows NT Registry Editor (REGEDT32.EXE, stored in the WINNT\SYSTEM32 folder) and the Windows 95 Registry Editor (REGEDIT.EXE, stored in the WINNT folder). The primary difference between the two is that the Windows 95 Registry Editor includes a tool that can search keys as well as values and data strings. The Windows NT Registry Editor can only search keys.

Part
III

Ch
7

continues

continued

The Windows 95 Registry Editor does not allow security changes to the Access Control List (ACL) of the subkey entries and does not provide a read-only mode. Also, the Windows 95 Registry Editor may not allow you to modify all entries in the Windows NT Registry. For example, You can only add values of data type string—binary and DWORD—whereas Windows NT values may require other data types. ■

The Registry Editor displays the five main windows, called *subtrees*, of the Windows NT 4.0 Registry for the local computer as shown in Figure 7.1. They are:

- HKEY_LOCAL_MACHINE
- HKEY_CURRENT_CONFIG
- HKEY_USERS
- HKEY_CURRENT_USERS
- HKEY_CLASSES_ROOT

FIG. 7.1 ⇒

This screen shows the five subtrees of the Windows NT Registry, tiled for better viewing.

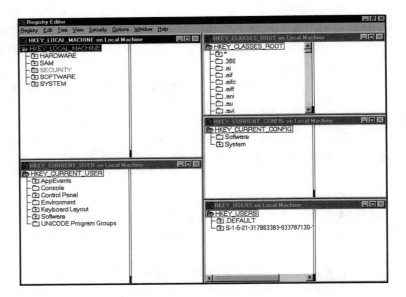

By default, only users with Administrator access can make modifications to the Registry. Other users can only view the information contained there.

Tip

I recommend setting the View option to Read Only, even for administrators. This guards against any accidental modifications that can lead to serious boot and operation problems. Enable it by selecting <u>R</u>ead Only Mode from the <u>O</u>ptions menu in Registry Editor.

From <u>O</u>ptions, choose <u>F</u>ont to change the font style and size to facilitate viewing, and <u>C</u>onfirm on Delete to guard against accidental deletions.

Why Is It Called HKEY?

When an application developer needs to access a resource for some reason, the developer needs to identify it by its unique value called a *handle*. For example, when opening a resource for write access, a write handle is allocated for that resource, and no other process can access that resource until the write process is completed and the write handle is released. The H in HKEY refers to "handle" and indicates to software developers that the subtree is a resource with a unique handle that can be used by a program. Because all applications installed under Windows NT 4.0 need to be able to store its configuration information in the Registry, this provides a way for application developers to modify the Registry.

At first glance, these windows look a lot like File Manager or the Windows Explorer, and in fact, you can navigate them in much the same way. The left pane of each subtree window displays the keys pertinent to that subtree. As each key is selected, the parameters and values assigned to that key are displayed in the right pane. You can think of a key as being a more sophisticated .INI file.

You may recall that an .INI file (see Figure 7.2) consists of section headings, with each section containing one or more parameters unique to that section, and each parameter having an appropriate value or values assigned to it. The values can be text strings, file names, or simple "yes" or "no" or "1" or "0" values.

FIG. 7.2 ⇒

Here is part of a Windows .INI file. Notice the section headings in square brackets. Each section has at least one parameter. The values assigned to each parameter represent what the parameter "expects."

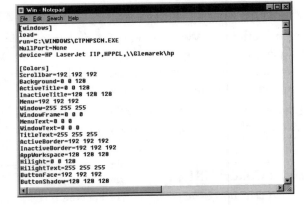

A Registry key is quite similar. Think of it as a "nested" .INI file. A key can consist of parameters with assigned values, or it can consist of one or more subkeys, each with its own parameters as displayed in Figure 7.3.

FIG. 7.3 ⇒

A Windows NT Registry key can go several levels deep before finally displaying parameter values.

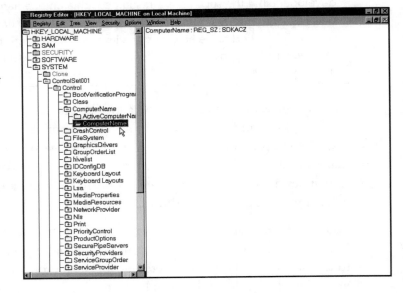

HKEY_LOCAL_MACHINE

HKEY_LOCAL_MACHINE contains all the system configuration data needed to boot and run the operating system successfully. This includes services that need to be run, device drivers, hardware profiles (including what is currently loaded), login parameters, and so on. It is composed of five primary keys called *hives*, which represent a discrete set of keys, subkeys, and parameter values. Each hive can contain subtrees several folders deep (refer to Figure 7.3). The five hives are:

- ◆ Hardware (volatile hive or key)
- ◆ Software
- ◆ System
- ◆ SAM
- ◆ Security

Each of the hives relates to a corresponding Registry file saved in the WINNT\SYSTEM32\CONFIG directory, except for the Hardware hive which is built when the computer is booted. The Hardware hive, more properly referred to as a *volatile* hive or key because it is created during the boot process, can change as hardware changes and is not written to disk.

Hardware

The Hardware hive, or key, contains data related to detected hardware devices installed on your computer. It includes information such as processor type and power, keyboard class, port information, SCSI adapter information, drive data, video, and memory. This information is primarily stored as binary data, and because it is built during startup, is useless to modify. The Windows NT Diagnostics utility is the best tool to use to view this data.

The information for Hardware is viewed through the Registry Editor in four subkeys described in Table 7.1.

Part

III

Ch

7

Table 7.1 HKEY_LOCAL_MACHINE\HARDWARE Subkeys

Subkey Entry	Description
DESCRIPTION	The data displayed here is collected from NTDETECT.COM, NTOSKRNL.EXE, or on non-Intel platforms by the firmware or the manufacturers' Hardware Recognizer. Data includes bus type, adapter type, port information, drive information, keyboard, SCSI adapter information, and mouse.
DEVICEMAP	This subkey contains information relating specific devices to the location in the Registry where driver information for each can be found. This could be an actual port name or the path for a subkey in HKEY_LOCAL_MACHINE\System\ControlSet\Services.
RESOURCEMAP	This subkey contains information used by applications and device drivers for accessing devices and updating information about them in DEVICEMAP.
OWNERMAP	This subkey appears in the Registry when certain device buses such as PCI are installed on the computer and is used to associate drivers with devices of the same type on each bus.

Tip

These values can be viewed more easily, and with considerably more understanding through the Windows NT Diagnostics utility. This utility can be found in the Administrative Tools group.

SAM and Security

The SAM and Security hives contain security-related information. *SAM* stands for *Security Accounts Manager* and, as you may suspect, contains user and group account information as well as workgroup or domain membership information. The Security hive contains *Local Security Account (LSA)* policy information such as specific user rights assigned to user and group accounts.

Neither of these hives or their subtrees are viewable. It is part of Microsoft's security policy to hide this information even from the system administrator. Even if you could look at it, it probably would not make a lot of sense, or give you any insight into violating account information.

Unlike the Hardware key, SAM and Security *are* written to files on the hard disk. Each has a Registry and log file associated with it—SAM and SAM.LOG, and SECURITY and SECURITY.LOG, respectively. You can find them in the WINNT\SYSTEM32\CONFIG subdirectory on the Windows NT system partition.

SOFTWARE

The Software hive consists of computer-specific software installed on your computer, as opposed to user-specific settings. This includes manufacturer and version; installed driver files; descriptive and default information for Windows NT-specific services and functions such as the Browser, NetDDE, and Windows NT version information; and the WINLOGON service. This hive also has two files associated with it that can be found in the WINNT\SYSTEM32\CONFIG subdirectory: SOFTWARE and SOFTWARE.LOG.

SYSTEM

While the Software hive contains more descriptive information regarding the installation of applications, drivers, and so forth, on your computer, the *System* hive provides configuration and parameter settings necessary for Windows NT to boot successfully and correctly maintain your computer's configuration. A quick look at the subtrees below SYSTEM shows at least three *control set* entries, as shown in Figure 7.4.

FIG. 7.4 ⇒

Here is
HKEY_LOCAL_
MACHINE with
the SYSTEM hive
expanded to show
the boot control
sets.

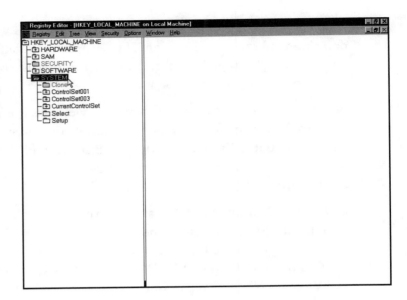

Control sets are used to control the startup process, indicating which services should load, which drivers to load and initialize, and so on. Any changes you make to existing driver settings, or any new drivers you install and configure, are added to a control set in the SYSTEM hive. Its corresponding files in the WINNT\SYSTEM32\CONFIG subdirectory are SYSTEM and SYSTEM.ALT. The System hive will be explored in more detail later in this chapter in the section "Understanding Control Sets and the Last Known Good Option."

HKEY_CURRENT_CONFIG

HKEY_CURRENT_CONFIG is a new subtree added to Windows NT 4.0. It is a subset of HKEY_LOCAL_MACHINE and reflects only the current software and system modifications made during the current session, as well as the current startup settings. This is useful for isolating data specific to a hardware profile from other data stored in the Registry. It also facilitates changes to the current settings that need to be made by the administrator.

HKEY_CLASSES_ROOT

HKEY_CLASSES_ROOT will look familiar to administrators of previous versions of Windows. It represents OLE and file association data specific to file extensions. This is information similar to that which was stored in Windows' REG.DAT file. This subtree is also a subset of HKEY_LOCAL_MACHINE and its values map back to the Classes subkey under the HKEY_LOCAL_MACHINE\SOFTWARE hive.

HKEY_USERS

HKEY_USERS consists of two subkeys relating to user settings. DEFAULT contains system default settings used when the LOGON screen is first displayed. The second entry represents the user who is currently logged on to the system. The long alphanumeric value you see is the user's security identifier, hereafter called the *SID* of the user.

Tip

All the entries you see under the SID subkey represent changes that can be made to the user's environment, primarily through the Control Panel. If the user changes his color scheme, cursor pointers, wallpaper, and so on, the values can be found in his respective keys here. If you need to modify a user's entries, perhaps remotely, you can do so here as well. The values stored here correspond to an actual file like the HKEY_LOCAL_MACHINE hives do. Windows NT creates a subfolder in WINNT\Profiles for each user who logs on and changes his or her profile—for example, change a color scheme or mouse pointer. This subfolder contains two files that correspond to the Registry entries for that user's profile: NTUSER.dat.LOG and NTUSER.DAT.

HKEY_CURRENT_USER

HKEY_CURRENT_USER represents a subset of HKEY_USERS, and points back to the settings of the current user (the SID entry in HKEY_USERS). Like HKEY_CURRENT_CONFIG, HKEY_CURRENT_USER facilitates changes to the current user's settings that need to be made by the administrator.

Using the Registry to Configure Windows NT 4.0

This section is designed with two purposes in mind. The first is to introduce you to the method for looking up keys and making changes to them. The second is to point out some specific modifications that you can *only* accomplish by changing the Registry.

Let's begin by stating the not-so-obvious. As you navigate through the Registry and select various keys, you may or may not see parameter values displayed in the windows. That does not necessarily mean that there are *no values* present. It may simply mean that Windows NT is using the *default* values for that entry.

For example, if you select the HKEY_CURRENT_USER\ CONTROL PANEL\CURSORS subkey, and you have made no changes to your mouse pointers, you will see no entries here. However, it is obvious that you do, in fact, have default mouse pointers displayed on your screen. In this case, Windows NT does use parameter values—the default values.

Tip

Here is the general rule of thumb: If the Registry does not display parameter values when you select a subkey, assume that Windows NT is using the defaults for that subkey, realizing that a default can be to have *no* values loaded at all.

Let's use the example of changing the cursor pointer. A user has selected the peeling banana to replace the hourglass "wait" cursor, and wants to change it to the running horse. Also, this user wants to change the application starting cursor (hourglass with an arrow) to the lumbering dinosaur. You can simply and easily do this through the Mouse applet in the Control Panel, but you feel particularly bold today.

There are basically three pieces of information that you need to know before modifying this particular entry, and in general for changing any Registry entry:

◆ Know which Registry entry you are going to change, what subkey or subkeys are involved (yes, there might be more than 1!), and where they are located.

◆ Know which parameter needs to be added, modified, or deleted to effect your change.

◆ Know what value needs to be assigned to the parameter and its type.

Now, let's look at this step-by-step.

First, to determine what the subkey is, and where it is, is not always easy. If the change you are making modifies the way the system operates (new device driver, changing the video display, adding a new hardware profile), those subkeys are most likely found under HKEY_LOCAL_MACHINE in the SYSTEM hive under one of the control set entries. If the change you are making affects the working environment of a particular user (desktop wallpaper, cursors, colors, window properties), those subkeys are most likely found under HKEY_USERS in the current user's subkey identified by the user's SID, or in HKEY_CURRENT_USER which maps to the same place.

Also, sometimes the subkeys that need to be modified are easy to identify, like "cursors." Sometimes they are not. Who would know that the HKEY_LOCAL_MACHINE\SYSTEM\ CURRENTCONTROLSET\SERVICES\NMCMACE entry refers to the driver settings for the PC Card Ethernet Adapter installed in my laptop? So how do you find out? Sometimes your documentation tells you. Most times, you find them by exploration, trial, and error. But re-member, Microsoft recommends that you *not* affect configuration changes through the Registry directly, especially when there is a utility that can do it for you. In the case of my network adapter, I don't really need to know where its configuration values are stored in the Registry because I can configure it through the Network applet in the Control Panel or through the Properties sheet of the Network Neighborhood.

Part

III

Ch

7

Finding Subkey Names in the Registry

If you are not sure of the subkey name you are looking for, but know what it might be called or a category that it might fall into, you can use the Registry's FIND KEY function to look it up. Follow these steps:

1. Place your cursor at the top (root) of the directory structure in the subtree where you think the key is located.
2. Choose View, Find Key.
3. Type in the key name you are looking for.
4. Choose Match Whole Word Only or Match Case if you are relatively sure of the key entry; otherwise, deselect these options.
5. Choose Find Next.

Find Key places a box around the first subkey entry that matches the text string you entered. You can move the Find window out of the way if it blocks your view. Choose Find Next again until you locate the appropriate subkey.

Find Key only works with key entries. It does not work on parameter value entries. If you need to search parameter values, consider running the Windows 95 Registry Editor (WINNT\REGEDIT.EXE) which provides that function.

Getting back to the mouse pointer example, because this is a user environment change, you can assume you will find the subkey in the HKEY_USERS subtree under the user's SID entry. You can also select the HKEY_CURRENT_USER subtree because it points to the same location in the Registry.

From there, because you are modifying cursors, you want to look for a subkey called Cursors. Because you modify cursors through the Control Panel, it is a pretty safe bet that you will find a Cursors subkey under the Control Panel subkey. You now know the location and the subkey to modify: HKEY_CURRENT_USER\CONTROL PANEL\Cursors.

The second thing you should know is which parameter needs to be added, modified, or deleted to effect your change.

Once again, finding out which parameter value is difficult unless someone gives you the parameter and value to enter. In this example, the parameter corresponding to the working hourglass is called WAIT, and the parameter corresponding to the application start hourglass-with-arrow is called APPSTARTING.

Finally, you need to know what value needs to be assigned to the parameter and its data type.

By now, you get the idea. Again, in this example, the file names that correspond to the various cursors either have a .CUR or .ANI extension. You can find these listed in the WINNT\SYSTEM32 subdirectory. Recall that the WAIT cursor needs to change from the banana (BANANA.ANI) to the running horse (HORSE.ANI), and that the APPSTARTING cursor needs to be the lumbering dinosaur (DINOSAUR.ANI).

There are five data types that can be applied to a parameter value. Again, you usually know which one to use, either because it is obvious or because someone has told you. Table 7.2 lists the value types and a brief description of each.

Table 7.2 Parameter Value Data Types

Data Type	Description
REG_SZ	Expects one text string data value.
REG_DWORD	Expects one hexadecimal string of one to eight digits.
REG_BINARY	Expects one string of hexadecimal digits, each pair of which is considered a byte value.
REG_EXPAND_SZ	Expects one text string value that contains a replaceable parameter such as %USERNAME% or %SYSTEMROOT%.
REG_MULTI_SZ	Expects multiple string values separated by a NULL character.

Part

III

Ch

7

In this example, cursors can only be associated with one file name (a text string). Therefore, your parameter value will have a data type of REG_SZ, and the value will be the file name. Now you can modify the Registry. Just follow these steps:

1. Open the Registry Editor. From Options, deselect Read Only Mode, if it is selected.

2. Maximize the HKEY_CURRENT_USER subtree window to make it easier to work with.

3. Expand the Control Panel key.

4. Highlight the Cursors key. In the right pane, because the WAIT cursor has already been modified once, there is an entry called WAIT, of data type REG_SZ and value BANANA.ANI.

5. Double-click the parameter entry (WAIT) to display the String Editor (see Figure 7.5).

FIG. 7.5 ⇒

The WAIT cursor currently has the value BANANA.ANI. Double-click it to display the String Editor and change the value to HORSE.ANI.

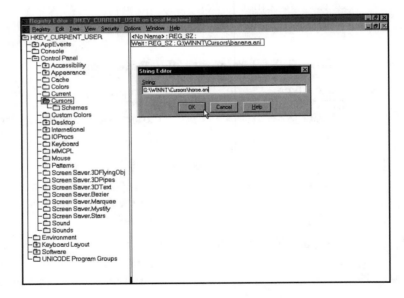

6. Enter the new parameter value (**D:\WINNT\SYSTEM32\HORSE.ANI**).

7. To add a new parameter and value, choose Edit from the Registry Editor menu bar, then Add Value.

8. In the Add Value dialog box, enter in the Value Name (APPSTARTING) and choose the appropriate Data Type (REG_SZ). Then choose OK (see Figure 7.6).

FIG. 7.6 ⇒

Choose Edit, Add Value to add the new cursor parameter APPSTARTING with a data type of REG_SZ, and click OK. In the String Editor, type **DINOSAUR.ANI**.

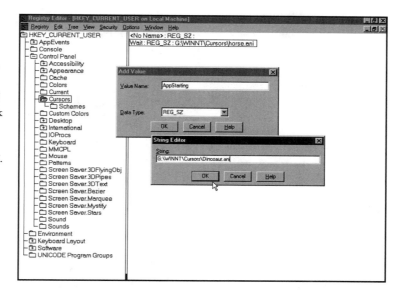

9. In the String Editor dialog box, enter the appropriate parameter value (**G:\WINNT\SYSTEM32\DINOSAUR.ANI**), and click OK.

10. Reselect Read Only Mode from the Options menu, then close the Registry Editor.

The change does not take effect immediately.

Tip

In general, if this is a user environment change, the user has to log off and log back on before the change takes effect. In general, if this is a system change, the computer has to be shut down and restarted before the change takes effect.

> **Caution**
>
> Parameter names are *not* case-sensitive. However, because they can be quite lengthy, Microsoft uses proper case when displaying these values to make them easier to read.
>
> If you misspell a parameter name, the result may simply be that Windows NT ignores it, or it can result in a service stopping altogether. This is also true with parameter values. If in doubt, look it up in the Windows NT Resource Kit, or test it first. Before testing, back up your original Registry or, at the very least, save the original subkey.

Following are some other modifications that you can make to the Registry for which a utility does not exist.

System Policy Editor

Windows NT Server 4.0 includes a configuration management utility called the *System Policy Editor*. This utility is not included with the Workstation version. It is intended for managing server-based workstation and user policies—that is, configuration information that is stored on a login server (domain controller) and downloaded to the user's workstation when the user logs on to the network. Most of the administrative changes you will need to make to the system configuration that are not already handled by an existing utility can be made more safely through the System Policy Editor. Also, the configuration is assured to "follow" the user and, thus, be consistent and standard.

In Figure 7.7, for example, a system policy has been created for user SDKACZ. Note that simply by pointing and clicking through a variety of intuitive screens, the user's access and environment can be fixed. In this example, the user's ability to modify the screen is reduced, a wallpaper has been selected, and the RUN and Settings folders have been removed. This policy affects the user wherever SDKACZ logs on.

Similarly, a system policy can be established by workstation name, thus regulating a user's environment and access by workstation. For example, you could disable the last user name from displaying, or modify the legal notice dialog box again by simply pointing and clicking the appropriate check box. These settings then would affect every user who logged on to this specific workstation.

FIG. 7.7 ⇒

Here is a sample System Policy Editor screen from Windows NT Server 4.0.

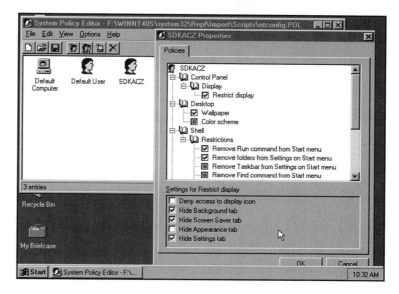

The workstation and user policies are saved in a file called NTCONFIG.POL and stored in the WINNT\SYSTEM32\REPL\ IMPORT\SCRIPTS subdirectory of each domain controller. This directory is also known by the share name NETLOGON.

System Policy Editor will be discussed in more detail in Chapter 14, "Policies and Profiles."

Accessing the Registry Remotely

It can happen that a computer's Registry has been modified either through a utility or directly, and now the computer is not quite functioning as it should. The Registry Editor provides a facility for accessing the computer's Registry remotely. If you have an administrator account on your computer that matches one on the other machine (including

Part

III

Ch

7

password), you can access the other computer's Registry. Just follow these steps:

1. Open your Registry Editor.

2. From the <u>R</u>egistry menu option, choose <u>S</u>elect Computer.

3. In the Select Computer dialog box, enter the name of the computer or select it from the browse list, and then click OK.

    The Registry Editor now displays the HKEY_LOCAL_MACHINE and HKEY_USERS subtrees from that computer. The title bar of each window displays the remote computer's name.

4. When you have finished working with the remote Registry, choose <u>C</u>lose from the <u>R</u>egistry menu option, being sure that the remote Registry window is highlighted.

If you do not close the remote Registry windows, they reappear the next time you start the Registry Editor on your computer.

Managing Remote Access to the Registry

While remote Registry management is allowed to administrators by default, there is an optional security subkey that can be configured called *WINREG*. It is added to the HKEY_LOCAL_MACHINE\ System\CurrentControlSet\Control\SecurePipeServers subkey with the following parameter value: Description, with Data Type REG_SZ and value Registry Server. The ACL for the WINREG subkey restricts access to Administrators with Full Control. Hence, any administrator can remotely access the Registry. By modifying the ACL for WINREG, you can further restrict which users have the ability to access remotely the Registry on a given Windows NT computer. If you make a change to the ACL for WINREG, you will need to shut down and restart the computer for the new ACL to take effect.

> **Caution**
> If the WINREG subkey is not added to the Registry, then all users have the ability to connect remotely to the computer's Registry.

Modify the ACL for WINREG by following these steps:

1. Using the Windows NT Registry Editor, select the HKEY_LOCAL_MACHINE\System\CurrentControlSet\Control\SecurePipeServers\Winreg subkey.

2. Select Security, Permissions.

3. Modify the permissions as you would for a file or folder by adding or removing the appropriate users or groups and assigning Full Control, Read, or Special Access to each.

4. Choose OK.

5. Close the Windows NT Registry Editor, shut down, and restart the system.

There is also an optional subkey that can be added below WINREG called *AllowedPaths*, which specifies Registry entries that can be read by everyone regardless of the ACL for WINREG. AllowedPaths contains a parameter value called `Machine` with a data type of REG_MULTI_SZ and whose value contains multiple strings representing the appropriate Registry paths. This subkey is used to ensure that system functions like print status work regardless of the ACL set on WINREG. Both WINREG and AllowedPaths are created by default on Windows NT Server installations.

> **Caution**
>
> Once again, any changes made to the Registry are done on an at-your-own-risk basis. Microsoft cannot guarantee that any problems that result from a change to the WINREG, AllowedPaths, or any other Registry subkey or value can be corrected.

Remotely Managing Through the Command Line

The Windows NT 4.0 Resource Kit contains two utilities that can facilitate remote management of the Registry through the command line:

◆ WINMSDP.EXE

◆ Remote Command Service—RCMD

WINMSDP.EXE

WINMSDP.EXE is a command-line version of the GUI Windows NT Diagnostics utility. As with the GUI utility, WINMSDP also reads the Registry and provides information regarding configuration and status of the system. However, WINMSDP writes this information to a text file called MSDPRPT.TXT which is stored in the current directory. The text report can then be viewed with a text editor or printed out, and the administrator has the same information that could be obtained through the GUI interface.

Because WINMSDP can be run from a command line, no user interaction is necessarily required. In fact, it can be run from a remote command prompt using Remote Command Service. It can also be included as a batch file with the Windows NT AT command and scheduled to run at certain times to gather Registry information.

The first time that WINMSDP is run, it presents a menu of switches that can be used to determine how much information is gathered. These switches are outlined in Table 7.3.

Table 7.3   WINMSDP Command-Line Switches

Switch	Information Collected
/A	Reports all Registry settings
/D	Reports Drive settings
/E	Reports Environment settings
/I	Reports Interrupt settings
/M	Reports Memory settings
/N	Reports all Network parameter settings
/O	Reports Operating System version
/P	Reports Port resource settings
/R	Reports Driver settings

Switch	Information Collected
/S	Reports Service status
/U	Reports DMA resource settings
/W	Reports Hardware hive settings
/Y	Reports Memory resource status

For example, if you would like to create a report on the memory and service settings for a system, you would initiate the command:

```
WINMSDP /M /S
```

If a previous version of the MSDRPT.TXT file exists, WINMSDP renames it (MSDRPT00.TXT, MSDRPT01.TXT, and so on) before creating the new version.

Remote Command Service

Remote Command Service (RCMD) provides a secure channel between two Windows NT computers that facilitates remote management of a Windows NT computer. It consists of a client component called *RCMD.EXE* that is run from the command line, and a server component called *RCMDSVC.EXE* which is installed and managed like any other Windows NT service. When a client initiates RCMD.EXE, a secure connection is made to the computer running RCMDSVC.EXE. The mechanics of RCMD will be discussed in more detail in Chapter 22, "Advanced Troubleshooting."

Modifying the Registry Through the Command Line

Another useful Resource Kit utility is *REGINI.EXE*. This command-line utility provides a means of modifying the Registry when the Registry Editor is unavailable, such as through a remote connection or when you would like certain Registry changes to be affected at certain time intervals. For example, if you want to change the Replication Governor value before initiating account synchronization between domain controllers on opposite ends of a slow WAN connection. You may want this to happen at 11 p.m. and want to be sure that the Registry on the computers involved is modified before that time, and set back afterwards.

Part
III

Ch
7

continues

continued

The syntax for REGINI is really fairly straightforward:

    REGINI VALUE.TXT

where *VALUE.TXT* is a text file that you create that contains the subtree, hive, subkey, and parameter setting values that you want to have changed.

For example, if you want to change the Replication Governor value to 50 (representing 50 percent bandwidth usage with a transfer of data at every other interval from the PDC), the *VALUE.TXT* file might look like this:

```
\Registry\Machine
    System
        CurrentControlSet
            Services
                NetLogon
                    Parameters
                        ReplicationGovernor = REG_DWORD 50
```

The change can then be effected by entering **REGINI *VALUE.TXT*** from the command prompt, or remotely using the Remote Command Server services.

If you make this command part of a batch file, say REPGOV.BAT, you could use the Windows NT AT command-line scheduler to schedule the change to take place at a particular time. For example, to have the command execute on a remote computer called ServerX at 11 p.m., you would enter the following command at a command prompt:

AT \\ServerX 23:00 /interactive "c:\FOLDER\REPGOV.BAT"

where *C:\FOLDER* represents the location of the REPGOV.BAT file. For more information about REGINI and AT, consult the *Windows NT 4.0 Resource Kit* and the *Windows NT Server 4.0* online books.

Examining the Windows NT Boot Process

The Windows NT 4.0 boot process, while a bit more complicated during the operating system load phase, is still pretty much like booting most any other operating system. There are five basic steps:

1. Power On Self Test (POST). This occurs with every computer when you first power it on. This is the BIOS check of installed hardware, interrupts, I/O, memory, and so on.

2. The Master Boot Record (MBR) is read to determine which operating system (OS) will govern the boot process.

3. The OS system file recorded in the MBR is loaded, and the operating system is initialized, the hardware is initialized, and drivers and configuration files are loaded.

4. The OS kernel is loaded.

5. Environment settings are initialized.

Windows NT 4.0 follows these same basic steps with some variation for steps 3, 4, and 5.

The Windows NT boot process has two primary phases: boot and load.

The *boot phase* consists of the pre-boot sequence during which the operating system is initialized, hardware is detected, and the Executive Services is loaded. When Windows NT is installed, it replaces the MS-DOS entries in the Master Boot Record with its own system file NTLDR. Along with NTLDR, the following boot files are read during the boot phase: BOOT.INI, NTDETECT.COM, NTOSKRNL.EXE, and NTBOOTDD.SYS (all some combination of the hidden, read-only and system file attributes stored in the root directory of the active system partition), NTOSKRNL.EXE and HAL.DLL (stored in the WINNT\System32 subdirectory), and the HKEY_LOCAL_MACHINE\ SYSTEM hive.

The process advances as follows:

1. NTLDR loads a mini-OS and changes memory to a flat, 32-bit model and loads mini-file-system drivers for FAT and NTFS so that the Windows NT System directory can be located and read.

2. NTLDR next reads the BOOT.INI file to display the operating system (OS) menu on the screen called the Boot Loader menu.

3. If the user chooses Windows NT or if Windows NT is the default operating system, NTLDR loads NTDETECT.COM.

NTDETECT.COM determines what hardware is installed in the computer and uses this information to build the HKEY_LOCAL_MACHINE\HARDWARE hive.

If the system boots Windows NT from a SCSI drive whose SCSI adapter BIOS is disabled, NTLDR will load NTBOOTDD.SYS to initialize and access that device.

If the user chooses MS-DOS or Microsoft Windows (for Windows 95), NTLDR loads BOOTSECT.DOS (which recorded the boot sector location of the alternate OS system files during Windows NT's installation) and loads the alternate OS system files. OS initialization then proceeds as normal for that OS.

4. NTLDR next loads NTOSKRNL.EXE which initializes the Executive Services of the operating system. Think of this as Windows NT's COMMAND.COM.

5. NTLDR then loads the HAL.DLL and the SYSTEM hive and any drivers that need to initialize at boot time to continue the building of the Executive Services, then passes control back to NTOSKRNL.EXE.

6. At this point, the screen displays progress dots across the top indicating the loading and initialization of drivers. At this time, the user is also prompted to press the spacebar to invoke the Last Known Good boot configuration. Control is passed to NTOSKRNL.EXE and the load phase begins.

During the *load phase*, the rest of the kernel and user modes of the operating system are set up. The kernel is initialized, control set information is created, Windows NT services are loaded, and the WIN32 subsystem starts. The process continues:

1. The blue screen is displayed indicating the kernel is initializing, drivers are initialized, and the CurrentControlSet is created and copied to the CLONE control set.

2. The Services Load Phase begins with the starting of SMSS.EXE, the session manager. The session manager runs the programs listed in HKEY_LOCAL_MACHINE\SYSTEM\CURRENTCONTROLSET\

CONTROL\ SESSION MANAGER\BootExecute, usually
AUTOCHK.EXE, that performs a CHKDSK of each partition. If
a drive has been flagged to be converted to NTFS, this will also
have been added to BootExecute and conversion takes place at
this time as well. Next, the pagefile is configured as defined in
HKEY_LOCAL_MACHINE\SYSTEM\CURRENTCONTROLSET\
CONTROL\ SESSION MANAGER\MEMORY MANAGE-
MENT parameters.

Finally, the required subsystem defined in HKEY_LOCAL_MACHINE\
SYSTEM\CURRENTCONTROLSET\CONTROL\
SESSION MANAGER\SUBSYSTEMS\Required is loaded.
The only required subsystem at this time is WIN32.

3. With the loading of the WIN32 subsystem, WINLOGON.EXE
   (the service that governs the logon process) is loaded and started.
   WINLOGON in turn starts the Local Security Authority
   (LSASS.EXE) that displays the Ctrl+Alt+Delete screen, and
   the Service Controller (SCREG.EXE) that starts services which
   are configured to start automatically such as Computer Browser,
   Workstation, and Server.

4. The user enters the user name and password and logs on to the
   computer or domain. If the logon is successful, the CLONE
   control set is copied to Last Known Good. If the boot is not
   successful, the user can power off or shut down and choose Last
   Known Good to load the last values that resulted in a successful
   logon.

The Boot Process for RISC-Based Computers

The boot process for RISC-based computers is essentially the same.
During the boot phase, the resident ROM firmware of the system
selects the boot device from a preference table stored in RAM and
controls the selection of the boot partition and the appropriate OS file.
In this case, the firmware finds and loads OSLOADER.EXE which is
Windows NT's operating system file for RISC-based computers.

continues

Part

III

Ch

7

continued

OSLOADER in turn finds and loads NTOSKRNL.EXE, HAL.DLL, *.PAL files (for ALPHA systems) and the System hive, and then the load phase continues as usual.

Note that because the computer's firmware controls the initialization of hardware and the selection of the boot partition, there is no need for the NTLDR, NTDETECT.COM, BOOT.INI, or BOOTSECT.DOS files on a RISC-based computer.

BOOT.INI

The BOOT.INI file is a read-only, system, ASCII text file created by Windows NT during installation. It is stored in the root directory of the primary boot partition of the computer and flagged with the Read Only and System file attributes. It contains the information that Windows NT uses to display the Boot menu when the computer is booted (see step 2 in the previous section for boot phase). It is divided into two sections: Boot Loader and Operating System. The *Boot Loader section* contains the default operating system and timeout values, and the *Operating System section* displays operating system choices and the location of the system files. It can be modified using any ASCII text editor after first turning off the system and read-only attributes.

Note You can locate the BOOT.INI using Windows Explorer, Windows Find, or My Computer. To change its properties, right-click the file and choose Properties. Deselect Read-Only and System. Be sure to reselect these attributes again when you have finished modifying the file. ■

In the following example, you see that the default timeout value is 30 seconds. If the user does not make a selection during that time, the default operating system will be loaded. Notice that the unusual looking path to the WINNT directory matches a line under the Operating Systems section.

```
[Boot Loader]
Timeout=30
Default=multi(0)disk(0)rdisk(0)partition(4)\WINNT
[Operating Systems]
multi(0)disk(0)rdisk(0)partition(4)\WINNT="Windows NT Server
➥Version 4.00"
```

```
multi(0)disk(0)rdisk(0)partition(4)\WINNT="Windows NT Server
➥Version 4.00
  [VGA mode]" /basevideo /sos
C:\="Microsoft Windows"
```

That unusual looking path (`multi(0)disk(0)...`) is called an *ARC path (Advanced RISC Computer)*. The best way to think of an ARC path is as a hardware path. By now, everyone has used a DOS path. It indicates the drive and directory location of a specific file. An ARC path indicates the *physical* disk location of the Windows NT system files—the specific partition on a specific physical disk connected to a specific physical controller.

Referring to the example, the ARC path

```
multi(0)disk(0)rdisk(0)partition(4)\WINNT
```

can be interpreted as follows.

The first value can be either `multi` or `scsi`. This really has no direct relation as to whether the controller is a SCSI controller. Windows NT will choose SCSI if the controller does *not* have its card BIOS-enabled. Otherwise, the choice will be `multi`. The number that appears in parentheses is the ordinal number of the controller.

The next two values are `disk` and `rdisk`. If the first value choice was `scsi`, then the `disk` number will represent the SCSI bus number and will be incremented accordingly (the physical disk attached to the card), and the `rdisk` value will be ignored. If the first value is `multi`, then the `disk` value will be ignored and the `rdisk` value representing the physical disk on the adapter will be incremented accordingly.

Next, the `partition` value indicates on which partition on the disk the directory \WINNT can be found. Recall that this is the Windows NT system directory that you selected during installation.

So, putting it all together for the example, during boot, if the user lets the timeout value expire or specifically selects Windows NT from the menu, Windows NT can find the Windows NT system files (specifically the location of the NTOSKRNL.EXE file) in the WINNT directory on the fourth partition of the first disk attached to the first controller in

Part

III

Ch

7

this computer. If the user selects Microsoft Windows from the menu, then NTLDR will load BOOTSECT.DOS and proceed to boot (in this case) Windows 95.

The Boot Menu

The Operating Systems section values are what build the boot menu that you see during startup. Each ARC path has a text menu selection associated with it that is enclosed in quotes. By default, there are always two entries for Windows NT, and one for the other operating system, usually MS-DOS (`C:\= MS-DOS"`) or Windows 95 (`C:\="Microsoft Windows"`). The first entry represents the default installation of Windows NT and generally loads the current configuration settings. The second entry for Windows NT represents a fall-back entry that loads Windows NT with a generic VGA driver.

If you make changes to the display settings that make it difficult or impossible to read the screen, selecting this choice during startup ignores those settings and loads a generic VGA driver so that you can see the screen and rectify the problem. This is accomplished through the `\Basevideo` switch that you see at the end of that line in the sample BOOT.INI file displayed in the last section.

Tip

Windows NT provides a variety of switches that can be added to these or additional Windows NT boot entries to modify the way Windows NT boots. For example, I might want to create another entry in my Boot Menu that displays all the driver files that are loaded during boot. I could copy the first line in the Operating Systems section to a new line, modify the text to read Windows NT Server 4.0 Driver Load, and add the /SOS switch to the end of the line.

Thus, if I was having trouble booting, or wasn't sure whether a particular driver was being found, I could select this choice and they would be displayed during the Load Phase (step 6 in the section "Examining the Windows NT Boot Process").

Table 7.4 lists the more practical boot switches that can be used in the BOOT.INI file. An exhaustive list can be found in the Windows NT Resource Kit.

Table 7.4	Windows NT Boot Switches for BOOT.INI
Switch	Description
`/Basevideo`	Boots Windows NT with the standard VGA display driver in 640×480 resolution.
`/SOS`	Displays driver file names instead of progress dots during the load phase.
`/Crashdebug`	Used for troubleshooting, enables Automatic Recovery and Restart mode for the Windows NT boot process, and displays a system memory dump during the blue screen portion of the load phase.
`/Maxmem:`*n*	Specifies the maximum amount of RAM in megabytes that Windows NT will recognize and work with. This is helpful when you suspect a bad SIMM or memory chip and you are trying to pinpoint its location.

Understanding Control Sets and the Last Known Good Option

In the HKEY_LOCAL_MACHINE\System hive, there are several control set subkeys. These are used by Windows NT to boot the system, keep track of configuration changes, and provide an audit trail of failed boot attempts. In general, there are four control sets:

◆ Clone

◆ ControlSet001

◆ ControlSet002

◆ CurrentControlSet

Part
III

Ch
7

In addition, there are three other subkeys that contain specific boot startup configuration information:

◆ Select
◆ Disk
◆ Setup

HKEY_LOCAL_MACHINE\SYSTEM\Clone

Clone is used by Windows NT during the boot process (step 7 in the section "Examining the Windows NT Boot Process") as a temporary storage area for the boot configuration. Settings from CurrentControlSet are copied into Clone during the load phase. When a user logon results in a successful boot, the configuration settings in Clone are copied to another control set such as ControlSet002 and are referred to as the *Last Known Good*. If the boot attempt is unsuccessful, these values are copied to a different control set number. Clone is unavailable after the user logs on.

HKEY_LOCAL_MACHINE\SYSTEM\ControlSet001

ControlSet001 is generally the default control set and is created from either the CurrentControlSet or the Last Known Good control set. As such, it also by default contains the Windows NT boot configuration.

HKEY_LOCAL_MACHINE\SYSTEM\ControlSet00x

ControlSet00x represents other control sets. There are generally two control sets that are maintained by the Windows NT operating system. The control set with the highest number increment usually reflects the Last Known Good configuration. Other control sets can be created depending on the frequency of configuration changes or whether there are problems with a configuration set. Those which refer to failed boot configurations can be determined by viewing the HKEY_LOCAL_MACHINE\SYSTEM\Select subkey.

HKEY_LOCAL_MACHINE\SYSTEM\Select

The *Select* subkey displays information about the control sets, such as which one did Windows NT boot from, which one(s) failed, and which one represents the Last Known Good.

This subkey contains four parameter values, as outlined in Table 7.5. Each value has a data type of REG_DWORD (hexadecimal string) that represents a ControlSet number.

Table 7.5   HKEY_LOCAL_MACHINE\SYSTEM\Select Parameter Values

Parameter	Description
Current	Its value identifies which control set was used to create CurrentControlSet. If the value, for example, is 0x1, it means that CurrentControlSet is mapped to ControlSet001, 0x2 means ControlSet002, and so on.
Default	Its value identifies from which control set Windows NT boots by default. If the value is 0x1, it means that Windows NT boots with the values of ControlSet001.
Failed	Its value identifies which control set(s) contained configuration values that resulted in a failed boot attempt. If the value is 0x3, for example, it means that ControlSet003 contains configuration values that resulted in a failed boot attempt. If the value is 0, then no failed boot has been recorded.
LastKnownGood	Its value identifies the control set whose configuration settings are known to result in a successful boot. If ControlSet001 was used to boot Windows NT successfully, and there

continues

Part

III

Ch

7

Table 7.5   Continued

Parameter	Description
	was no failed control set, then LastKnownGood would be written to ControlSet002 and the select value would identify it with the value 0x2. This means that ControlSet002 contains configuration settings from the last successful boot.

Key Concept

Changes made to CurrentControlSet are mapped back and saved in the default control set identified by the Select subkey, generally ControlSet001. During the load phase, the settings in ControlSet001 are copied to Clone and used to determine service order, driver files to load, startup configurations, hardware profiles, and so on. If the boot is successful—a user logs on to Windows NT successfully—Clone is copied to the control set designated as the Last Known Good, say ControlSet002. If changes made by the administrator result in a failed boot attempt, the failed configuration in Clone is copied to ControlSet002, what used to be the Last Known Good control set becomes ControlSet003, and the user has the option of selecting to boot with the Last Known Good control set.

What Is the Last Known Good Control Set?

The *Last Known Good* control set contains the last boot configuration that resulted in a successful logon to the computer. The user is given the option to use Last Known Good when the load phase begins, and the progress dots are displayed on the screen. The user has five seconds within which to press the spacebar to invoke the Last Known Good.

Caution

If the system itself detects a severe or critical device initialization or load error, it will display a message asking the user whether choosing Last Known Good might not be a good option. Users can choose to bypass this message, but do so at their own risk.

Tip

The Last Known Good helps to recover in the event of a failed boot. But remember that a failed boot is one in which a user cannot successfully log on to Windows NT. The user *may be able to* log on successfully and still have a system that fails to run correctly due to a configuration error. The Last Known Good will not be helpful in this situation because it is created as soon as the boot is successful, such as when you log on successfully.

HKEY_LOCAL_MACHINE\SYSTEM\Disk and Setup

The *Disk* subkey entry contains setting information related to disk configurations. This information includes volume sets, drive letters, stripe sets, and fault tolerance settings—such as striping with parity and disk mirroring, and mapped drives. In short, changes made through the Disk Administrator utility are stored in the Disk subkey.

The *Setup* subkey provides configuration settings relating to Windows NT's Setup. For example, this subkey defines the system partition, the location of the Windows NT system files (the boot partition), and the setup type.

HKEY_LOCAL_MACHINE\SYSTEM\ CurrentControlSet

CurrentControlSet is mapped back to the default control set as identified by the Select subkey. This is generally ControlSet001. These settings are copied to Clone during the load phase of the boot process. Whenever an administrator makes a change to the configuration of the computer, such as modifying the virtual memory parameters, adding a new driver, or creating a hardware profile, those changes are saved to CurrentControlSet (and thus to the default control set). CurrentControlSet also identifies which devices and services need to load during the Windows NT boot process, the order in which services need to load, and service and device dependencies.

CurrentControlSet contains four subkeys, which are described in Table 7.6. The Services subkey is described in detail in the next section

Part

III

Ch

7

"Understanding HKEY_LOCAL_MACHINE\SYSTEM\
CurrentControlSet\Services."

Table 7.6 HKEY_LOCAL_MACHINE\SYSTEM\ CurrentControlSet Subkeys	
Subkey	Description
Control	This subkey identifies startup settings for the current session, including the currently logged on user, active computer name, file system support, location of Registry hive files from which users can remotely administer the Registry, configuration settings for the WOW subsystem that supports WIN16 applications, and the maximum Registry size.
Enum	This subkey identifies Plug and Play bus enumerator settings. (Windows NT 4.0 is not truly Plug and Play compatible, but performs some Plug and Play enumeration functions during the hardware detection phase of the boot process.
Hardware Profiles	This subkey contains settings specific to hardware profiles created through the Control Panel.
Services	This subkey contains configuration settings for most devices and services installed on the computer. It links drivers to devices, identifies the order in which devices and services need to load, and which devices and services need to load during the boot process.

Understanding HKEY_LOCAL_MACHINE\ SYSTEM\CurrentControlSet\Services

As you learned in the last section, the Services subkey contains configuration settings for most devices and services installed on the computer. The values for these settings are much more easily viewed using the Windows Diagnostics utility. Changes to these values are most safely effected through the appropriate Control Panel, Setup, or Administrative Tools group utility. While browsing through these values in the Registry Editor, be sure to first enable the Read Only option from the Options menu. Changes made to this subkey in CurrentControlSet will take effect the next time you boot Windows NT.

Because this key displays subkeys for most every device and service installed on the computer, it would be impractical to list all possible subkey entries in this chapter. From an administrative and troubleshooting point of view, you will only need to view or modify a smaller subset of these anyway.

Each service that is installed maintains several similar parameter values which define how that service should be handled by Windows NT— for example, what to do if the service fails, what other services does this one depend on to function properly when is it loaded, and so on. These parameter values are displayed in Figure 7.8 and described in Table 7.7.

Table 7.7   Service Subkey Parameter Values

Parameter	Description
DependOnGroup	Services, like users, can be logically grouped to make the boot process more efficient. Windows NT loads these groups in the order defined in HKEY_LOCAL_MACHINE\ SYSTEM\CurrentControlSet\Control\ ServiceGroupOrder. DependOnGroup defines a

Part

III

Ch

7

continues

Table 7.7 Continued	
Parameter	Description
	group or groups that this service depends on to function properly. At least one service from the group(s) defined must be started in order for this service to successfully load and function. In Figure 7.8, you see that the Net Logon service has no group dependencies.
DependOnService	This parameter value is similar to DependOnGroup in that it defines which services must be loaded and running in order for this service to successfully load and function. In Figure 7.8, you see that the Net Logon service will not load successfully unless the LanmanWorkstation, LanmanServer, and LMHosts services have been loaded first.
DisplayName	This parameter displays the service name that appears to the user in utilities listing services, such as Control Panel, Services. In Figure 7.8, you see that the Net Logon service is represented in service lists as Netlogon.
ErrorControl	This parameter identifies how Windows NT should deal with problems encountered during the load of this service. There are four error control values that can be entered for the service: 0, which means ignore the error and continue booting; 1, report the error and continue booting; 2, the error is severe and reverts to Last Known Good to boot; and 3, the error is critical and reverts to Last Known Good to boot. In Figure 7.8, the

Parameter	Description
	`ErrorControl` value for Netlogon is set to 1. This means that if an error is reported while loading the Net Logon service, the error will be reported to the Event Viewer, and the boot process will continue.
ImagePath	This parameter defines the location of the file associated with this service. In Figure 7.8, you see that the file that is associated with the Net Logon service is lsass.exe and is located in %SystemRoot%\System32 (WINNT\System32).
ObjectName	This parameter specifies an object name for the service to use when interacting with the operating system depending on the Type value entered. For example, if the Type value is for a WIN32 subsystem driver or service, then the object name represents the name of the service account that the service will use when interacting with the operating system. In Figure 7.8, you see that because the Net Logon service is a WIN32 subsystem service (see the Type entry in this table), Net Logon will interact with the operating system using the LocalSystem service account.
Start	This parameter defines when and how the service is loaded when the system is booted. There are five start values. 0 indicates that the service is loaded by NTLDR during boot; 1 indicates that the service is loaded at kernel initialization during boot; 2 indicates that the service is set to automatically start during system startup (blue screen); 3 indicates that

continues

Part

III

Ch

7

Table 7.7 Continued

Parameter	Description
	the service is started on demand by either the user or another process; 4 indicates that the service is disabled and will never be started. Start values for adapters are ignored, and start values for WIN32 services must be either 2, 3, or 4. In Figure 7.8, you see that Netlogon is automatically started during the system startup phase of the boot process.
Type	This parameter indicates what kind of service it is and where it fits in the Windows NT architecture. A Type value of 1 indicates that this is a kernel device driver; 2 indicates that this is a file system driver (also a kernel driver); 4 indicates that these are parameter values for an adapter; 10 indicates that this is a WIN32 subsystem program that can run as its own process; 20 indicates that this is a WIN32 subsystem process that can share a process with other WIN32 services. In Figure 7.8, you see that Netlogon has a Type value of 20. Therefore, it is a WIN32 subsystem process that can share with other WIN32 processes. It also means that Netlogon will use the `ObjectName` value as its service account when it interacts with the Windows NT operating system.

FIG. 7.8 ⟹

Here you can see the parameter entries displayed for the Netlogon service that provides pass-through authentication and database synchronization. These entries are representative of those that appear for other subkey entries under HKEY_LOCAL_ MACHINE\ SYSTEM\ CurrentControl-Set\Services.

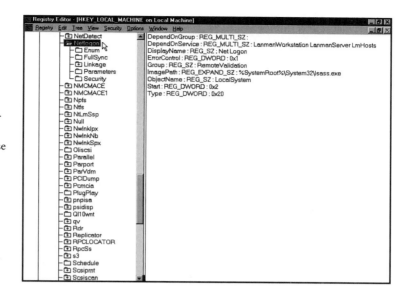

Troubleshooting the Boot Process

The most common errors that you are likely to encounter during the boot process will be due to corrupt or missing boot files. Recall the boot files needed by Windows NT:

NTLDR

BOOT.INI

BOOTSECT.DOS

NTDETECT.COM

NTOSKRNL.EXE

If the NTLDR file is missing or corrupt, the following message will be displayed after the POST:

```
BOOT: Couldn't find NTLDR
Please insert another disk.
```

While there are a variety of reasons for this file to become missing or corrupt, the most common are viruses that attack the MBR, and a user

Part

III

Ch

7

inadvertently reinstalling MS-DOS onto the computer. If the problem involves a virus, use a virus protection program to restore the MBR. If this is unsuccessful, you can use the Emergency Repair Disk to reestablish NTLDR in the MBR. The worst case will be to reinstall Windows NT from scratch—which you should try to avoid.

If the problem involves a user reinstalling MS-DOS, or *sys-ing* the hard drive (restoring the DOS system files to the MBR), again use the Emergency Repair Disk to reestablish the NTLDR. The worst case will be to reinstall Windows NT.

If BOOT.INI is missing or corrupt, Windows NT will look for the default Windows NT system directory name (usually WINNT) on the boot partition. If Windows NT is installed in a directory other than the default name, or if Windows NT cannot otherwise locate it, the following message is displayed after the prompt for Last Known Good:

```
Windows NT could not start because the following file is
➥missing or corrupt:
\winnt root\system32\ntoskrnl.exe
Please reinstall a copy of the above file.
```

If the ARC path to the Windows NT system file directory is incorrect in the BOOT.INI file, NTLDR may display this message:

```
Windows NT could not start because of a computer disk hardware
configuration problem. Could not read from the selected boot
disk. Check boot path and disk hardware. Please check Windows
NT documentation about hardware disk configuration and your
hardware reference manuals for additional information.
```

Incorrect paths are relatively easy to fix. Because BOOT.INI is a text file, turn off its System and Read Only attributes and edit the ARC path using your favorite text editor.

Caution

The ARC path indicated in the Default parameter in the Boot Loader section of the BOOT.INI *must match* an ARC path for a parameter in the Operating Systems section. If it does not, the menu will display a phantom selection option called NT (default), which may result in the same error message discussed for a missing BOOT.INI file.

If BOOTSECT.DOS is missing, NTLDR displays this error message when the user tries to select the other operating system from the Boot menu:

```
I/O Error accessing boot sector file
multi(0)disk(0)rdisk(0)partition(1):\bootsect.dos
```

Because this file is unique to each computer, the best way to recover it would be to restore it from that backup you create regularly (!), or use the Emergency Repair Disk.

If NTDETECT.COM is missing or corrupt, expect the following message after the user selects NT from the Boot Menu, or the menu times out to Windows NT:

```
NTDETECT v1.0 Checking Hardware...
NTDETECT v1.0 Checking Hardware...
```

Again, recover using the Emergency Repair Disk or from a backup.

If NTOSKRNL.EXE is missing or corrupt, NTLDR displays this message after the prompt for Last Known Good:

```
Windows NT could not start because the following file is
➥missing or corrupt:
\winnt root\system32\ntoskrnl.exe
Please reinstall a copy of the above file.
```

As before, this file can be recovered using the Emergency Repair Disk, or from a file backup.

The Emergency Repair Disk

The *Emergency Repair Disk* is usually created during the Windows NT installation process. However, it can be created (and updated) at any time by running the Windows NT Repair Disk utility RDISK.EXE at a Windows NT command prompt.

RDISK.EXE can either update the backup of the Registry files contained in the WINNT\REPAIR folder or create a new Emergency Repair Disk. The Emergency Repair Disk itself is updated by re-creating it. In other words, the old information on the disk is overwritten with the updated information as though a new Emergency Repair Disk was being created.

Part

III

Ch

7

> **Caution**
> RDISK.EXE does not back up the Default, SAM, or Security Registry files by default. The SAM, in particular, because it contains the user and group accounts, can grow to be quite large in size and thus not fit on a disk. If you need to update this information as well—for example, to the WINNT\REPAIR folder—initiate RDISK.EXE with the /S switch.

To use the Emergency Repair Disk, you must first boot the computer using a Windows NT Startup disk.

> **Tip**
> If you do not have an Emergency Repair Disk, but have access to the original installation files, you can create one by typing the command ~~WINNT /OX.~~ *RDISK.EXE* Be sure to have three disks available.

The Setup disk offers a menu of options. From the Startup menu, choose Repair. You'll be prompted to insert the Emergency Repair Disk. The repair process offers four options:

◆ *Inspect Registry Files.*   This option prompts the user for replacement of each Registry file, including System and SAM.

> **Caution**
> The files on the Emergency Repair Disk overwrite the files in the Registry. For this reason, this is *not* the best way to recover damaged security or account information. A backup will be much more useful in maintaining the integrity of existing account entries.

◆ *Inspect Startup Environment.*   This option checks the BOOT.INI file for an entry for Windows NT. If an entry isn't found, one is added for the next boot attempt.

◆ *Verify Windows NT System Files.*   This option verifies whether the Windows NT system files match those of the original installation files. For this option, you will need to have access to the original installation files. This option also looks for and verifies the integrity of the boot files.

Tip

If you updated Windows NT with a service pack, you will need to reinstall the service pack after initiating a repair.

◆ *Inspect Boot Sector.* This option checks the MBR for NTLDR. If it is missing or corrupt, it will restore the boot sector.

If you know specifically which file is missing or corrupt, you can replace the file directly from the source files using the Windows NT EXPAND utility. At a Windows NT prompt, type **EXPAND –R** followed by the compressed file name. If Windows NT is inoperable on your system, use another Windows NT system to expand the file and then copy it to your computer.

Windows NT Boot Disk

Another useful tool to have in your toolkit is a Windows NT boot disk. This is not a disk formatted with NTFS. Rather, it is a disk that has been formatted under Windows NT that has copies of the boot files on it.

When you format a disk under Windows NT, Windows NT creates a boot sector on that disk that references NTLDR. Simply copy the boot files (NTLDR, NTDETECT.COM, BOOT.INI, and NTBOOTDD.SYS if the Windows NT system files are on a disk attached to a SCSI controller with its BIOS disabled) to this disk and— voilà!—you have a Windows NT boot disk. This disk can be used in a variety of Windows NT computers because it is not unique to each installation. The only file you may need to modify for obvious reasons (ARC path differences) is the BOOT.INI file. This makes it much easier to replace missing or corrupt boot files.

Tip

You can format a disk from My Computer. Right-click the A: Drive icon and select Format. Make the appropriate selections and choose OK.

Part

III

Ch

7

Other Troubleshooting Tips

The Hardware and System keys are most useful when it comes to troubleshooting. These have already been described in detail in the preceding sections. The ability to troubleshoot successfully through these keys begins with your ability to understand and interpret entries. A comfort level for doing this comes best through experience.

However, here are some specific tips to help you interpret and use these keys when troubleshooting Windows NT through the Registry.

Network Device Settings

The Services subkey under System contains subkey entries related to network card devices installed in the system. In general, each card has two subkey entries. The first entry contains parameter values relating to the location of the driver, boot settings, and so on. The second entry contains specific parameter entries for the adapter such as interrupt levels, I/O address, transceiver settings, and protocol-specific settings.

For example, Figure 7.9 shows the two subkey entries for the PC Card network adapter in my laptop computer. From its parameter values, you can see that the entry NMCMACE refers to the NMC LiveWire Ethernet PC Card adapter (DisplayName), and that it automatically loads as a kernel device driver during the boot process (Type value 1 and Start value 2). The ImagePath parameter tells us that the driver name and location is WINNT\System32\drivers\nmcmace.sys.

The second entry is NMCMACE1 (see Figure 7.10), where 1 represents the first network adapter card. If I had another, its entry would have the number 2 appended to it, and so on. This entry itself contains additional subkeys that contain card settings. For example, the subkey Linkage tells us which subkey contains the driver file name that initializes this adapter (the Bind parameter). The Parameters subkey shows us the interrupt and I/O address settings. Under Parameters in Figure 7.10, you see there is also a subkey for TCPIP. This displays settings such as the default gateway address, DHCP server address, DHCP lease information, subnet mask, and so on.

FIG. 7.9 ⟹

This example shows the two Service subkeys that refer to the NMC LiveWire Ethernet PC Card adapter.

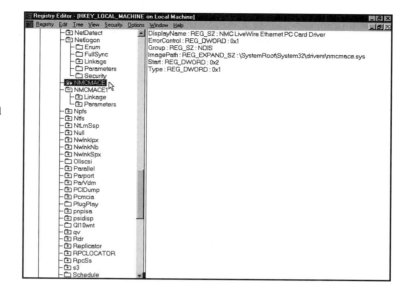

FIG. 7.10 ⟹

Here you see the TCPIP settings for the NMC LiveWire Ethernet PC Card Adapter under the NMCMACE1\ Parameters subkey.

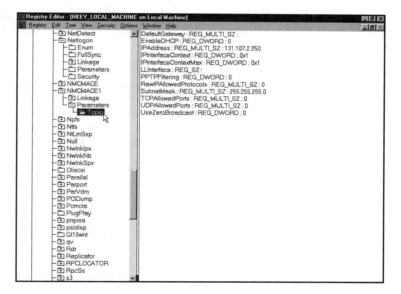

All these settings can be viewed more easily and modified more safely through the Network Properties dialog box. However, if you need to remotely administer a Registry and do not have the GUI interface available, the values can be scanned and, if necessary, modified here.

Part
III

Ch
7

Service Dependencies

As stated previously, services and device drivers often have *dependencies*—that is, they may depend on another service or device driver having been loaded before they can successfully load and function. As a point of troubleshooting, it is helpful to be able to interpret which services depend on other services.

The *Windows NT Diagnostics utility* can be very helpful in identifying dependencies. Both the Services and Devices tabs provide a list of service and group dependencies in the properties of each member of the Services and Devices lists, as shown in Figure 7.11.

FIG. 7.11 ⇒

View the service dependencies for the Computer Browser service through the Windows NT Diagnostics utility.

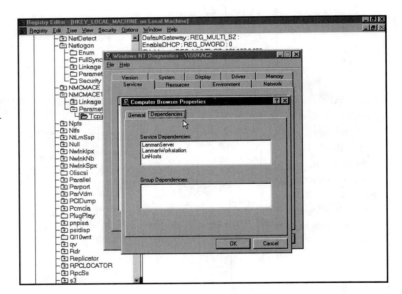

These dependencies can also be determined from the Registry directly by viewing the service parameters (refer to Table 7.7). Let's use Computer Browser as an example (see Figure 7.12).

The DependOnService parameter for the Browser service tells us that Computer Browser (its DisplayName) depends on three other services having already been loaded: Lanman Workstation, LanmanServer, and LMHosts.

FIG. 7.12 ⟹
The same dependency information for Computer Browser is displayed through Windows NT Diagnostics (refer to Figure 7.11) as recorded in the Registry.

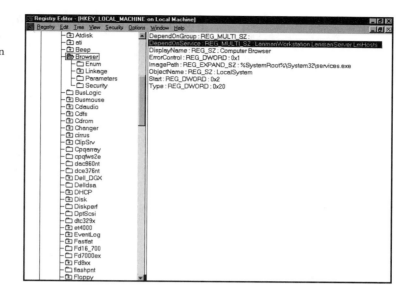

 Note LanmanWorkstation and LanmanServer refer to RDR.SYS and SRV.SYS, respectively, which are Windows NT's workstation and server services. ▇

If any one of these fails to start, the Computer Browser service will also fail to start. Note, however, from the ErrorControl value that if the Computer Browser fails to start, it will not stop the system from booting. It will record the failure in the Event Viewer's System log.

Tip
Failed services can be quickly spotted in the Event Viewer's System log. The source entry for all service-related events is the Service Control Manager. Use the filter in the Event Viewer to just display Service Control Manager events to view the service-related events together.

Now let's take a look at the LanmanServer service and see if it has any dependencies (see Figure 7.13). Note that while it does not itself depend on any specific services, it does have a group dependency: TDI (Transport Device Interface). Windows NT arranges some device drivers and services in groups to facilitate the load process.

Part
III

Ch
7

Groups are loaded in the order specified in another subkey: HKEY_LOCAL_MACHINE\SYSTEM\CurrentControlSet\Control\ ServiceGroupOrder. For example, the entry refers to all the drivers that provide video support. You can see the specific device driver loaded for your monitor by viewing HKEY_LOCAL_MACHINE\ HARDWARE\DeviceMap\Video. In our case, TDI represents the *Transport Device Interface* or binding support between the server service and the network protocols installed on the computer. So, the server service will not load until the TDI support files are loaded and the bindings established.

The Start value for LanmanServer tells you that the server service is loaded automatically during the boot process. If this value had been set to 4, this would tell us that the service failed to start during the boot process and has been disabled. To troubleshoot this, you might start by determining whether its group dependency, the TDI, loaded success-fully.

TDI Trace Utility

The Windows NT Server 4.0 Resource Kit has a variety of tools and utilities—both command line and GUI—to facilitate the management and troubleshooting of Windows NT services and devices. One of these is the TDI Trace utility. This utility can determine whether the TDI loaded successfully, and if not, provide information as to why not. This utility is run from the command line by executing TDISHOW.EXE. After you install this utility from the Resource Kit's CD-ROM, you must install the TDI Trace driver:

1. Open the Network Properties dialog box and select the Protocols tab.

2. Choose Add, and then Have Disk. Enter the path to the location of the TDITRACE.SYS and OEMSETUP.INF files (usually in a directory called NTRESKIT\TDITRACE).

3. Choose OK and then restart the computer.

To run the utility, open a command prompt window, switch to the TDITRACE directory and enter **TDISHOW** at the prompt. A menu of choices will appear. You can now capture and display information relating to TDI.

For more information about running and interpreting the utility and its data, refer to the Resource Kit utilities' online manuals.

You might also check whether the Services.exe file referenced in the `ImagePath` parameter exists or is corrupted. Services.exe is the file that loads WIN32 services.

Tip

The Services applet in the Control Panel allows you to stop, start, and control the startup properties of services. If you try to stop a service that has dependencies associated with it, the applet will display them in a list.

FIG. 7.13 ⇒

This figure displays the LanmanServer parameters showing its dependencies.

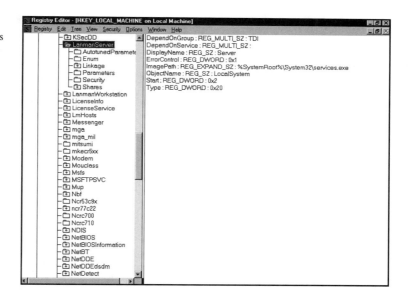

Taking the Disc Test

If you have read and understood the material in the chapter, you are ready to test your knowledge. Insert the CD-ROM that comes with this book and run the self-test software as described in Appendix I, "Using the CD-ROM."

From Here...

In this chapter, we made a rather extensive tour of the Windows NT 4.0 Registry. We especially looked at the System hive, its relation to the boot process, and its usefulness in troubleshooting problems. Chapter 8, "Configuring Domain Network Core Services," discusses some of the network services that Windows NT uses to perform various network tasks. One of these was used as an example in this chapter—Computer Browser.

Chapter Prerequisite

Before reading this chapter, you should have a basic understanding of LAN and WAN concepts, network adapter cards, transport protocols, the Windows NT 4.0 interface, and initial installation concepts. You should also be comfortable with the concepts of directory services, trusts, and domain models as presented in Chapters 2-5.

Configuring Domain Network Core Services

This chapter expands on information relative to protocol choices from Chapter 5, "Capacity Planning and Performance" and then presents installation and protocol configuration options. In addition, this chapter contains important information on the browser service and its configuration options, as well as directory and file replicator setup and configuration.

Topics for this chapter include:

◆ Windows NT protocol choices, installation, and configuration options

◆ The browser service configuration options

◆ Directory replication configuration and implementation

Understanding Windows NT Protocol Choices and Configuration Options

Chapter 5 illustrated the protocols that Windows NT supports with respect to planning your enterprise. Chapter 5 also discussed the different protocols and their attributes such as a protocol being routeable, whether additional services had to be installed to complement the individual characteristics of a protocol, and the Registry locations of protocol keys and values.

As a review, the following is a list of the protocols supported by the Windows NT operating system:

◆ NetBEUI (NetBIOS Extended User Interface)

◆ NWLink (NetWare Link)

◆ TCP/IP (Transmission Control Protocol/Internet Protocol)

◆ DLC (Data Link Control)

◆ AppleTalk

If you need to review protocol characteristics and capabilities, refer back to Chapter 5, "Capacity Planning and Performance."

Most protocols require some configuration to operate properly. Protocol configuration is relatively easy to perform in Windows NT; however, a thorough understanding of all configuration options is essential to proper operation.

NetBEUI

NetBEUI installation, as with any network component installation, begins with accessing the network icon in the Control Panel, or by right-clicking the Network Neighborhood icon on the desktop and selecting Properties followed by selecting the Protocol tab. NetBEUI can also be selected for installation during Windows NT setup.

NetBEUI Installation

The Network dialog box appears with the Identification tab selected by default. Select the Protocols tab to show the installed network protocols and to add required components. Select the Add button to display the Select Network Protocol dialog box required to add protocols. Figure 8.1 shows the Network dialog box and the Select Network Protocol dialog box with NetBEUI Protocol selected. Click OK to add the selected protocol.

FIG. 8.1 ⇒

This is the dialog box used to install the NetBEUI protocol.

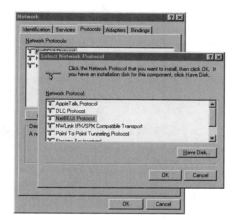

Because NetBEUI is a self-tuning protocol, once installed on a Windows NT platform, there are virtually no mandatory parameters to configure. As with any protocol, options such as disabling, enabling, or changing the binding order are available through the Bindings tab of the Network dialog box. Remote Access Service (RAS) options such as limiting access to a RAS server instead of the entire network are available through the RAS configuration options. Figures 8.2 and 8.3 illustrate screens for both situations.

FIG. 8.2 ⟹
This is the dialog box used to configure the NetBEUI binding order.

FIG. 8.3 ⟹
This is the dialog box used to configure NetBEUI RAS options.

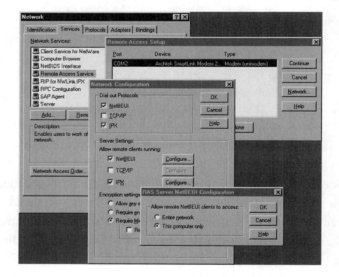

NetBEUI and the Registry

There are, however, various Registry values that can be configured by experienced support personnel that will fine-tune the operation of the NetBEUI protocol. The Registry location of the NBF parameters is:

HKEY_LOCAL_MACHINE\SYSTEM\CurrentControlSet\
Services\Nbf\Parameters

> ### Caution
> Use extreme caution when editing the Registry. Improper use of the Registry Editor can render Windows NT totally inoperable. Microsoft will not support any problems that result from improper Registry configuration using Registry Editor.

The default values configured in the Registry when NetBEUI is initially installed are shown in Figure 8.4.

FIG. 8.4 ⇒
Default NetBEUI
Registry values are
shown here.

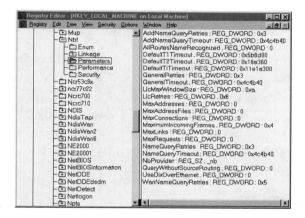

Additional values not shown in the Registry at initial installation time are listed here with default values indicated.

- ◆ InitAddresses   Default 0 (no limit)
- ◆ InitAddressFiles   Default 0 (no limit)
- ◆ InitConnections   Default 1
- ◆ InitLinks   Default 2
- ◆ InitReceiveBuffers   Default 5
- ◆ InitReceivePackets   Default 10
- ◆ InitRequests   Default 5
- ◆ InitSendPackets   Default 30
- ◆ InitUIFrames   Default 5

Note   All the preceding values are REG_DWORD type. ▪

Refer to the Windows NT 4.0 and 3.5/3.51 Resource Kits or consult Microsoft TechNet for full details on NetBEUI Registry values.

NWLink

NWLink is Microsoft's implementation of the Novell IPX/SPX protocol. The installation of NWLink can be selected at installation time, or can be done at any time through the network application in the Control Panel as previously described.

NWLink is required on Windows NT workstation and server platforms that require communication with Novell networks directly. NWLink can also be used for Windows NT to Windows NT communication. NWLink is also a routeable protocol. When NWLink is installed, NWLink NETBIOS is also installed automatically. NWLink NETBIOS requires no configuration; however, fine-tuning can be accomplished by editing the NwlnkNb Registry values, which is discussed later in this chapter.

Frame Types

One of the most important configuration parameters of NWLink is the Frame Type parameter. To communicate using NWLink, the frame type on each end of the connection must be the same. Available frame types for NWLink in Windows NT are:

- 802.2
- 802.3
- Ethernet II
- Ethernet SNAP

When NWLink is installed, frame type detection defaults to auto detect, meaning that when Windows NT boots, it will automatically detect the IPX frame type on the network. If no IPX frames are detected, or if more than one IPX frame type is detected, Windows NT 4.0 will default to frame type 802.2. If only one IPX frame type is detected on the network, Windows NT will default to the detected IPX frame type.

Manual frame type configuration, which can be done during installation as well as anytime after installation, is accomplished through the NWLink IPX/SPX Compatible Transport properties dialog box. The Windows NT Workstation frame type configuration is shown in Figure 8.5. The Windows NT Server frame type configuration is illustrated in Figure 8.6.

FIG. 8.5 ⇒

This is an example of Windows NT Workstation frame type configuration.

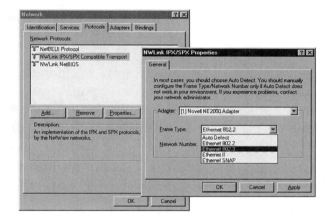

FIG. 8.6 ⇒

This is an example of Windows NT Server frame type configuration.

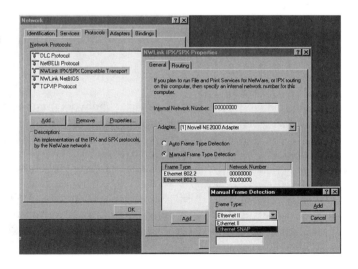

Key Concept

It is important to note that only a single frame type can be configured from the NWLink IPX/SPX Compatible Transport properties dialog box for Windows NT Workstation. Multiple frame types are configured in Windows NT Workstation through manual editing of the Registry.

Multiple frame types can be configured in Windows NT Server through the NWLink IPX/SPX Compatible Transport properties dialog box. Manual editing of the Registry is not required to configure multiple frame types in Windows NT Server.

Also shown in Figure 8.6 on the General tab of the NWLink IPX/SPX Properties sheet is the Internal Network Number window. This number represents a virtual or logical network segment inside the computer and is used to uniquely identify this specific computer in the enterprise. Other than the reasons mentioned on the property sheet, this number may also need to be manually configured with other than a zero value in the following cases:

◆ Multiple frame types are being used on a single network card.

◆ NWLink is bound to multiple network adapter cards in the computer.

◆ The computer is configured to be a SQL or SNA server.

Key Concept

The Internal Network Number, or virtual network number, should not be confused with the External Network Number, or physical network number, which identifies each physical network segment in the enterprise.

To configure multiple frame types in Windows NT Workstation, the Registry location and frame type (packet type) values must be known. The location is HKEY_LOCAL_MACHINE\System\Current-ControlSet\Services\NwlinkIpx \NetConfig\<adapter type>, PktType value. PktType value meanings are as follows:

- ◆ ff   Auto
- ◆ 0   Ethernet_II
- ◆ 1   Ethernet_802.3
- ◆ 2   Ethernet_802.2
- ◆ 3   SNAP
- ◆ 4   ArcNet

Multiple frame type configuration (802.2 and 802.3) through the Registry for Windows NT Workstation is illustrated in Figure 8.7.

FIG. 8.7 ⇒
Configure multiple frame types for Windows NT Workstation using the Registry Editor.

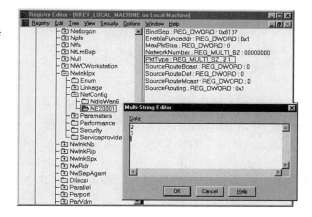

Client Service for NetWare/Gateway Service for NetWare

NWLink by itself, as mentioned in Chapter 5, "Capacity Planning and Performance," cannot access resources on a Novell file server. It can, however, provide access to client/server applications to Novell clients.

Novell resource access is obtained after the installation of a NetWare redirector. For Windows NT Workstation, the built-in redirector is Client Service for NetWare (CSNW) and for Windows NT Server, the built-in redirector is Gateway Service for NetWare (GSNW). Both CSNW/GSNW are installed as a service in Windows NT from the Services tab in the Network dialog box. Novell also makes a 32-bit NetWare redirector for Windows NT, referred to as NetWare Client for Windows NT (NCNT).

In Windows NT Workstation, CSNW is installed from the Services tab of the Network property sheet as shown in Figure 8.8.

FIG. 8.8 ⟹

CSNW installation is initiated from this dialog box.

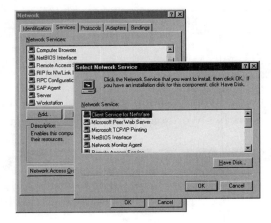

Prior to installing GSNW on Windows NT Server, a group called NTGateway must be configured on the Novell file server from which resources are to be accessed. User accounts that require resource access must be added to the group and permissions must be assigned accordingly. GSNW is then installed on the Windows NT Server. GSNW is installed as shown in Figure 8.9 and configured as shown in Figures 8.10 through 8.12.

FIG. 8.9 ⟹

GSNW installation is done from this dialog box.

After CSNW on Windows NT Workstation or GSNW on Windows NT Server is installed, the appropriate icon (CSNW or GSNW) is displayed in the Control Panel. As illustrated in Figure 8.10, selection of a preferred server, selection of a default tree and context, print options, and logon script options can be configured from either icon properties. Also illustrated in Figure 8.10, the gateway service, (GSNW), is configured from the GSNW icon.

FIG. 8.10 ⟹

Configure the preferred server for GSNW.

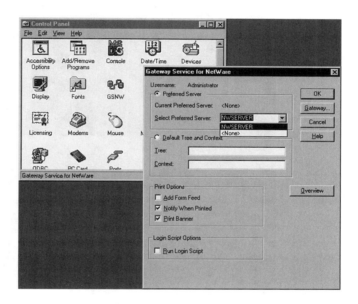

The following steps 1 through 3 show gateway configuration, which is also illustrated in Figure 8.11. Step 4, permission assignment, is shown in Figure 8.12.

1. Enable the gateway.

2. Select a gateway account and password.

3. Configure share points to the gateway.

4. Assign user and group permissions to the share points.

FIG. 8.11 ⟹

Enable the gateway, select a gateway account, and configure a share point from the Configure Gateway dialog box.

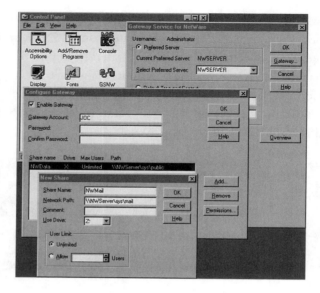

FIG. 8.12 ⟹

These screens show how to assign gateway permissions.

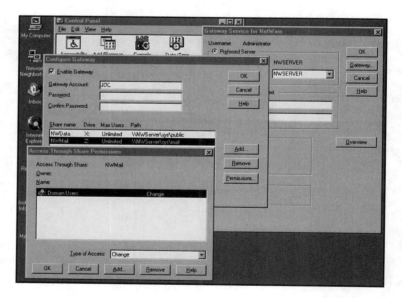

RIP for NWLink IPX/SPX Compatible Transport Service

Another NWLink configuration parameter, one which is new in Windows NT 4.0, is the RIP for NWLink IPX/SPX Compatible Transport service. This service allows a Windows NT Server to function as an IPX router. This service is installed as any other service from the Select Network Services dialog box.

During installation of this service, a determination of whether to use NetBIOS Broadcast Propagation (broadcast type 20 packets) must be made. A dialog box will appear giving you information about why it should be enabled and the consequences of having it enabled.

Key Concept

If any Microsoft clients in your network are using NWLink to connect to this computer, NetBIOS Broadcast Propagation must be enabled. If your Microsoft clients are not using NWLink to connect to this server, disable NetBIOS Broadcast Propagation because it will affect network performance.

Once NetBIOS Broadcast Propagation is enabled, it can be disabled by choosing RIP for NWLink IPX properties as shown in Figure 8.13.

FIG. 8.13 ⟹

Disable NetBIOS Broadcast Propagation.

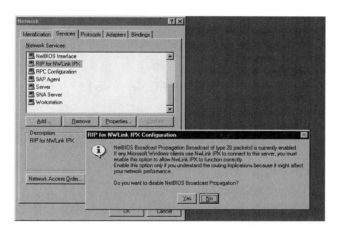

When RIP for NWLink IPX is installed, routing can be enabled or disabled from the Routing tab in the NWLink IPX/SPX Properties dialog box as shown in Figure 8.14.

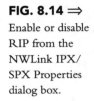

FIG. 8.14 ⟹

Enable or disable RIP from the NWLink IPX/ SPX Properties dialog box.

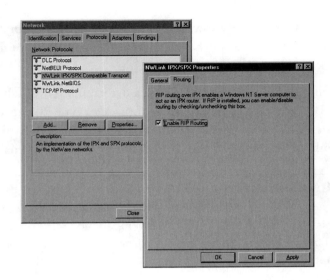

NWLink and the Registry

As with any protocol installed, numerous Registry entries can be made by experienced support professionals to optimize a network. Registry locations pertain to NWLink and NWLink options and are as follows:

HKEY_LOCAL_MACHINE\SYSTEM\CurrentControlSet \Services\NwlinkIpx\Parameters

HKEY_LOCAL_MACHINE\SYSTEM\CurrentControlSet \Services\NwlinkNb\Parameters

HKEY_LOCAL_MACHINE\SYSTEM\CurrentControlSet \Services\NwlinkSpx\Parameters

HKEY_LOCAL_MACHINE\SYSTEM\CurrentControlSet \Services\NwlinkRip\Parameters

HKEY_LOCAL_MACHINE\SYSTEM\CurrentControlSet \Services\NwRdr\Parameters

> **Caution**
>
> Use extreme caution when editing the Registry. Improper use of the Registry Editor can render Windows NT totally inoperable. Microsoft will not support any problems that result from improper Registry configuration using the Windows NT Registry Editor.

Figure 8.15 shows the default Registry values loaded when NWLink is first installed.

FIG. 8.15 ⇒

These are the default NWLinkIPX Registry values.

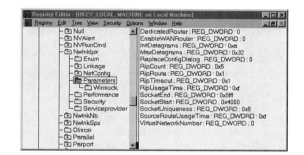

Other Registry value names not shown in Figure 8.15 relating to NWLinkIPX (Global IPX Parameters) and their default values are as follows:

- ◆ ConnectionCount   Default 10
- ◆ ConnectionTimeout   Default 1 (1 second)
- ◆ DisableDialinNetbios   Default 1 (true)
- ◆ DisableDialoutSap   Default 0 (false)
- ◆ EthernetPadToEven   Default 1 (true)
- ◆ KeepAliveCount   Default 8
- ◆ KeepAliveTimeout   Default 12 (6 seconds)
- ◆ RipAgeTime   Default 5 (minutes)
- ◆ RipTableSize   Default 7
- ◆ SingleNetworkActive   Default 0 (false)
- ◆ WindowSize   Default 4

Registry values loaded when NWLink NetBios is first installed are shown in Figure 8.16.

FIG. 8.16 ⇒

These are the default NWLinkNb Registry values.

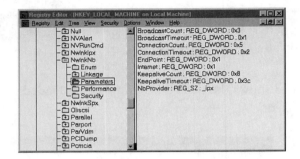

Value names not shown in Figure 8.16 relating to NWLinkNb and their default values include:

- ◆ AckDelayTime   Default 250 (no entry = default)
- ◆ AckWindow   Default 2 (no entry = default)
- ◆ AckWindowThreshold   Default 500
- ◆ EnablePiggyBackAck   Default 1 (true, no entry = default)
- ◆ Extensions   Default 1 (true, no entry = default)
- ◆ InitialRetransmissionTime   Default 500 (no entry = default)
- ◆ RcvWindowMax   Default 4 (no entry = default)
- ◆ RetransmitMax   Default 8 (no entry = default)

Default Registry values pertaining to NWLinkSPX that are loaded when NWLink is first installed are illustrated in Figure 8.17.

FIG. 8.17 ⇒

These are the default NWLinkSPX– Registry values.

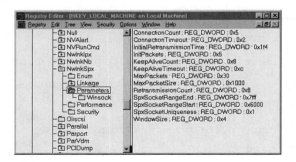

Other important Registry values to consider are the ones that pertain to the specific adapter card installed as illustrated in Figure 8.18. The location of these values is:

HKEY_LOCAL_MACHINE\SYSTEM\CurrentControlSet\
Services\NwlinkIpx\NetConfig\<adapter card name>

FIG. 8.18 ⟹

Here are the
NWLinkIPX
NetConfig
<adapter card
name> values.

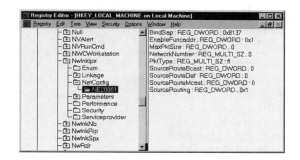

TCP/IP

TCP/IP is the default protocol selected at installation time for Windows NT 4.0, both the workstation and server platforms. At this point in time, TCP/IP is the protocol of choice because of its ability to connect to many types of computing equipment and to the Internet.

Numerous installation options are available pertaining to TCP/IP. This section will address the most common TCP/IP installation issues and options.

TCP/IP Addressing

To install TCP/IP, access the Network property sheet, select the Protocol tab, and click the Add button. During the installation process, an IP address and subnet mask must be configured for at least one network interface card in the machine (a unique IP address is required for every network adapter card using TCP/IP). This IP address and subnet mask can be obtained from a Dynamic Host Configuration Protocol (DHCP) server, or entered manually if no DHCP server exists on the network. Installation of DHCP is covered later in this section.

An IP address consists of 32 bits of address information and is denoted in a dotted decimal notation such as 131.107.2.200. Each node of the address is made up of 8 bits of information with each bit assigned a binary weight. Each byte (8 bits) can contain any value from 0 to 255 as illustrated in Table 8.1.

Table 8.1   Bit Value for an IP Address Node

Most Significant Bit	Least Significant Bit
128	8
64	4
32	2
16	1

An IP address of 131.107.2.200 would have the corresponding bits (bolded) in each node as shown in Table 8.2.

Table 8.2   An Example IP Address

First Node		Second Node		Third Node		Fourth Node	
131		107		2		200	
128	8	128	**8**	128	8	**128**	**8**
64	4	**64**	4	64	4	**64**	4
32	**2**	**32**	2	32	**2**	32	2
16	**1**	16	**1**	16	1	16	1

An IP address consists of two parts, the network address and the workstation address. IP addresses are also divided into classes, class A through class C; each class by default denotes a number of networks and workstations available. The class of an address is resolved by the value in the first node of the address. Table 8.3 illustrates the three classes of addresses and the number of networks and workstations available by default in each class.

Table 8.3 IP Address Class Definitions

Class	Value in First Node	Available Networks	Available Workstations
A	1–126	254	16,777,214
B	128–191	65,534	65,534
C	192–255	16,777,214	254

 Note Address 127 is reserved for loop-back testing. ■

If the address is a class A address, the first node (left-most node) of the address is the network address and nodes 2, 3, and 4 are the workstation address. If the address is a class B address, the first and second nodes are the network address and nodes 3 and 4 are the workstation address. If the address is a class C address, the first, second, and third nodes are the network address and node 4 is the workstation address.

A *subnet mask* is used to divide the address nodes as mentioned in the previous paragraph. If all bits are on (value 255) in the subnet mask for a specific node, the bits are considered *masked out* in that node and the value remains constant. If no bits are on in the subnet mask for a specific node, they are not masked out, and therefore the value can change. For example, a class C address of 192.123.234.xxx will by default have a subnet mask of 255.255.255.0. The values in nodes 1, 2, and 3 (192.123.234), which is the network number, will not change and remain constant; all workstation addresses depicted by node 4 (xxx) will change. All workstations will be on network 192.123.234 and will have a unique value from 1 to 254. In IP addresses, the network number remains constant while the workstation addresses change.

By default, the subnet mask parameter for each class of addresses is listed here:

- Class A   255.0.0.0
- Class B   255.255.0.0
- Class C   255.255.255.0

Note It should be noted that the preceding subnet mask parameter values are default values. It is perfectly legal to have any class of address with any subnet mask, for example, a class B address with any subnet mask (131.107.2.200 and 255.255.255.0). ■

A subnet mask value can be any value from 0 to 255. A subnet mask of 255.255.240.0 would allow 1,048,575 network addresses and 4,096 workstations on each network.

Another parameter that may need to be configured is a default gateway or router parameter if this computer is to communicate with another computer on another TCP/IP network in or outside the enterprise.

Figure 8.19 illustrates the IP address, subnet mask, and default gateway parameters.

FIG. 8.19 ⟹
This is the
Microsoft TCP/IP
Properties dialog
box.

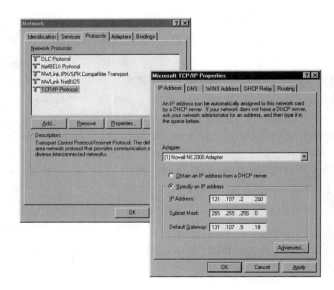

The Advanced button on the Microsoft TCP/IP Properties dialog box presents the opportunity to add up to five additional IP addresses and up to five additional default gateway (router) addresses.

Figure 8.20 shows an additional default gateway address being added to the already configured default gateway address of 131.107.5.18.

FIG. 8.20 ⇒
Here you can add additional default gateway addresses.

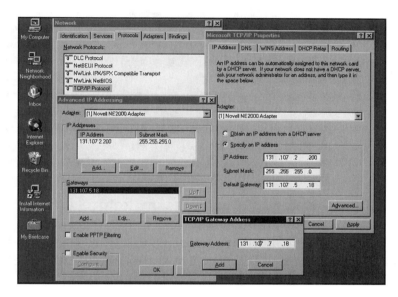

PPTP Filtering and Enable Security Options

In addition to the parameters previously mentioned, Point to Point Tunneling Protocol (PPTP), Filtering and Enable Security for TCP Ports, UDP Ports, and IP Protocols can also be configured from the Advanced button. Figure 8.21 shows PPTP Filtering enabled and shows the TCP/IP Security dialog box with TCP Port 23 (telnet), UDP Port 137 (nbname), and all IP Protocols or ports enabled.

Caution
Enabling PPTP Filtering effectively disables all other protocols from passing through the selected network adapter card. Only PPTP packets are allowed through.

FIG. 8.21 ⇒

Here you can enable PPTP Filtering and TCP/IP security options.

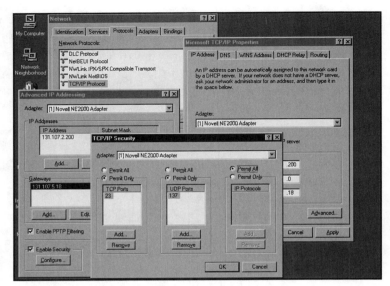

Dynamic Host Configuration Protocol (DHCP)

As mentioned previously, each network card installed in a computer requires an IP address to communicate in a TCP/IP network. Also mentioned was the fact that IP addresses could be configured manually or obtained dynamically from a Dynamic Host Configuration Protocol (DHCP) server. Windows NT 4.0 Server is capable of being configured as a DHCP server and dynamically allocates IP addresses to DHCP-enabled clients in lieu of manual IP address configuration.

To configure a Windows NT 4.0 Server to become a DHCP server, the specific computer must be given a static IP address and subnet mask manually; then the DHCP service can be added. In fact, the following message dialog box is displayed when the DHCP service is loaded:

> If any adapters are using DHCP to obtain an IP address, they are now required to use a static IP address. Press Close on the Network Control Panel and the TCP/IP Property Sheet will be displayed allowing you to enter an address.

Once the service is added, configuration of the DHCP server is performed using the DHCP manager tool in the administrative tools program group. DHCP manager is used to add and remove DHCP servers, create, configure, and manage scopes and reservations, and to configure and manage DHCP options. Figure 8.22 shows the DHCP Manager and the Scope Properties dialog boxes with a scope configured and a range of excluded IP addresses. The figure also shows a default lease duration of three days.

FIG. 8.22 ⇒

Here you can configure a DHCP scope.

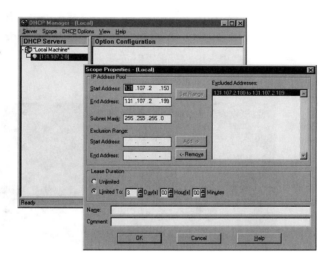

Caution

If more than one DHCP server is configured on a network or an enterprise, it is extremely important to note that each DHCP server must be configured with a unique scope of IP addresses. Failure to comply with this warning will result in duplicate IP addresses on the network.

DHCP options that a DHCP server assigns to clients are configured using the DHCP Options drop-down menu on the DHCP Manager dialog box. Options can be set for a single scope (scope selection) or for all scopes (global selection). If the default choice is selected, default values for the default options can be changed, and default options can be deleted or additional options can be added. Active global options apply unless overridden by scope or client options. Refer to Windows NT 4.0 online help for a description of all default options.

If it is desirable to assign a network card a specific IP address, a reservation can be configured using DHCP Manager. A reservation is made by associating an IP address to a unique 12-digit MAC address of a network card on the network. The 12-digit MAC address is found by activating a command prompt and typing **ipconfig /all**. The resulting display will include a line that indicates the physical address of the network card or cards in the computer. An example of the ipconfig command is shown in Figure 8.23.

FIG. 8.23 ⇒

This is an example of the command prompt IPCONFIG /ALL command.

```
Command Prompt                                                  _ □ ×
C:\>ipconfig /all

Windows NT IP Configuration

        Host Name . . . . . . . . . . : workstation1
        DNS Servers . . . . . . . . . : 131.107.2.200
        Node Type . . . . . . . . . . : Hybrid
        NetBIOS Scope ID. . . . . . . :
        IP Routing Enabled. . . . . . : No
        WINS Proxy Enabled. . . . . . : No
        NetBIOS Resolution Uses DNS : No

Ethernet adapter NE20001:

        Description . . . . . . . . . : Novell 2000 Adapter.
        Physical Address. . . . . . . : 00-80-AD-0E-2E-6F
        DHCP Enabled. . . . . . . . . : Yes
        IP Address. . . . . . . . . . : 0.0.0.0
        Subnet Mask . . . . . . . . . : 0.0.0.0
        Default Gateway . . . . . . . :
        DHCP Server . . . . . . . . . : 131.107.2.200
        Primary WINS Server . . . . . : 131.107.2.200

C:\>
```

Key Concept

The TCP/IP protocol must be running for the ipconfig command to function.

Figure 8.24 displays the Add Reserved Clients dialog box used to specify an IP reservation. A reserved IP address of 131.107.2.180 is being assigned to a client computer named workstation1.

If the routers that connect the IP subnets in an enterprise can function as a DHCP/BOOTP relay agent (specified in RFC 1542), a DHCP server can lease IP addresses to clients in multiple subnets on the network. If the routers are not RFC 1542-compliant, a DHCP server must be configured on each subnet. The DHCP relay option is configured on each client.

FIG. 8.24 ⇒
Here are the
DHCP Manager
and the Add Re-
served Clients
dialog boxes.

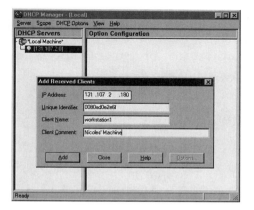

The DHCP Relay tab is found in the TCP/IP Properties sheet and is
shown in Figure 8.25.

FIG. 8.25 ⇒
See how to config-
ure a DHCP relay
agent.

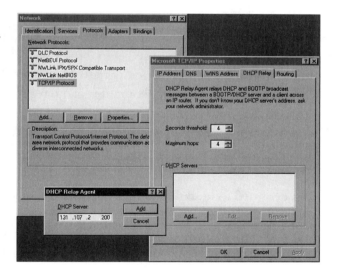

 Note A maximum of 16 hops can be configured in the DHCP Relay
tab of the TCP/IP Properties dialog box. ■

Windows Internet Name Service (WINS)

The TCP/IP protocol communicates with other network devices by
using an IP address. For an application to communicate with another

computer through the NetBIOS session level interface using a computer name, the computer name must be mapped or resolved to an IP address. Methods used to map or resolve NetBIOS computer names to IP addresses are shown in Table 8.4.

Table 8.4   NetBIOS Name to IP Address Resolution Methods

Mapping Method	Configured
IP Broadcasts	NetBIOS Name Queries
Host Files	Manually Configured
LMHOST Files	Manually Configured
DNS Configuration	Manually Configured
WINS Configuration	Dynamically Configured

Windows NT 4.0 Server is capable of being configured as a Windows Internet Name Service (WINS) server and multiple WINS servers can be configured in one network or enterprise. Multiple WINS servers help divide the load of handling computer name registration and queries as well as database backup and redundancy. Unlike DHCP servers, WINS servers can be configured to communicate with each other and replicate their databases with each other to ensure a current database structure.

WINS is designed to lessen the use of IP broadcast messages on the network to establish an IP address of a specific network device. Because WINS maintains a dynamic database of NetBIOS names to IP addresses, the administrative task of maintaining a Host or LMHost file is eliminated.

WINS is installed and configured as a service in the same way as the DHCP service is installed and configured. Figure 8.26 displays the Select Network Service dialog box from where WINS is installed.

Once installed, the WINS is managed from WINS Manager in the administrative tools program group. Figure 8.27 illustrates the WINS Manager dialog box.

FIG. 8.26 ⇒
See how to install
the WINS service.

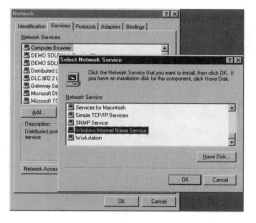

FIG. 8.27 ⇒
Manage the WINS
from the WINS
Manager dialog
box.

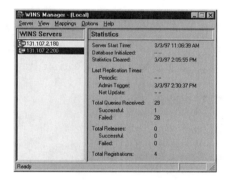

The WINS Manager dialog box displays the configured WINS servers
and a Statistics window. The five drop-down menu choices are Server,
View, Mappings, Options, and Help.

WINS Manager Server Menu

The Server menu provides options to add or delete WINS servers, display detailed information about a WINS server, display a WINS Server
Configuration dialog box, display a replication partner configuration
dialog box, and exit. Figure 8.28 shows the default settings for the
WINS Server Configuration dialog box. In addition, the Advanced button is selected displaying information under the Advanced WINS
Server Configuration section at the bottom of the screen.

FIG. 8.28 ⇒

Here is the WINS Server Configuration dialog box.

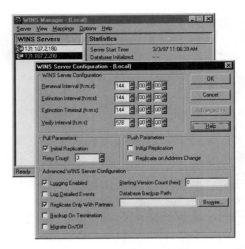

The WINS Server Configuration dialog box is used to configure parameters used to manage the WINS database and replication partner relationships. Figure 8.29 displays the Replication Partners dialog box.

FIG. 8.29 ⇒

Here is the WINS Replication Partners dialog box.

The Replication Partners dialog box is used to add or delete WINS replication partners and to display the status of each WINS server on the network. The display shows if a WINS server is a push partner, a pull partner, or both. The Replication Options area of the dialog box is used to configure the update count for push partners and the time interval for pull partners. If the Configure button is selected adjacent to

Push Partner, an update count parameter for push partners specifies how many changes or additions can be made in the WINS database before a replication is triggered. (The minimum value is 20.) If the Configure button is selected adjacent to Pull Partner, a time interval parameter for pull partners specifies when replication of the WINS database should begin and how often replication should occur.

Another option that can be selected from this dialog box is the Send Replication Trigger Now for both push and pull partners to replicate the WINS database immediately without waiting for the time interval to time out for the pull partners or the update count to be exceeded for the push partners. Also available as a choice is the Replicate Now button to initiate replication in both directions immediately.

WINS Manager View Menu

The WINS Manager View menu is simply used to perform two options: one is to clear the Statistics window on the right pane of the WINS manager dialog box, and the other is to refresh the Statistics window.

WINS Manager Mappings Menu

The WINS Manager Mappings menu is used to display the WINS database, initiate scavenging, add static mappings, and back up and restore the WINS database. Figure 8.30 shows an example of a WINS database.

FIG. 8.30 ⇒

Here is an example of a WINS database.

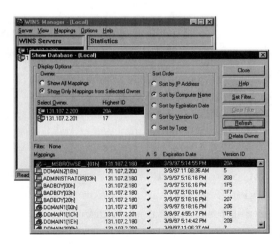

The Show Database dialog box displays the WINS servers and the actual database mappings, either all mappings or individual WINS server mappings.

Scavenging can be initiated from the mappings menu; however, by default, it is performed automatically. Scavenging is the process of cleaning up the database of old released mappings and old mappings from other WINS servers that did not get deleted. Scavenging is automatically done based on the renewal interval time and extinction interval time defined on the WINS Server Configuration dialog box previously shown in Figure 8.28.

Static mapping and importing mapping files like LMHost files can also be accomplished from the <u>M</u>appings drop-down menu. Figure 8.31 is an example of adding a static mapping for a computer named Michelle configured with an IP address of 131.107.2.182.

FIG. 8.31 ⟹

Here is an example of static mapping.

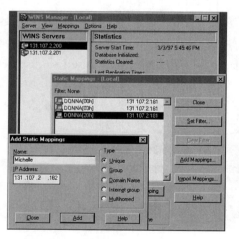

WINS Manager Options Menu

The one option of importance on this drop-down menu is the Preferences option. The Preferences option allows the configuration of a default setting for two parameters discussed earlier. As depicted in Figure 8.32, most options are self-explanatory; however, by selecting the Partners button, two additional parameters become available.

Those parameters are the New Pull Partner Default Configuration and the New Push Partner Default Configuration options. Values entered here will be configured automatically for the pull and push partners if the Set Default Value option is selected in the Pull Partners Properties and the Push Partner Properties dialog boxes. Recall that these two properties sheets are accessed from the Replication Partners dialog box selected from the Server drop-down menu. Figure 8.32 displays the Preferences dialog box with the Partners button selected.

FIG. 8.32 ⟹

Here is the Prefer-
ences dialog box.

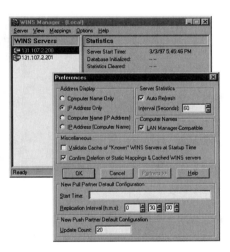

WINS Client Installation and Configuration

When the TCP/IP protocol is installed on a WINS-compliant client such as a Windows NT domain controller or member server, a Windows NT Workstation, or a Windows 95 computer, WINS can be installed and configured. WINS is configured from the WINS Address tab in the TCP/IP Properties sheet (see Figure 8.33). All that has to be configured is the IP address of a primary and/or secondary WINS server. From that point, any time the WINS client is started, it will register its name, IP address, and user with a designated WINS server. WINS client computers should also be shut down properly. By doing so, the clients send a WINS server a name release request and the computer name/IP mapping is released from the WINS database.

Enable DNS for Workstation Resolution can be selected and Enable LMHOST Lookup is selected by default. An LMHOST file can be imported from this screen and a Scope ID can also be configured.

FIG. 8.33 ⟹

This is a WINS client configuration example.

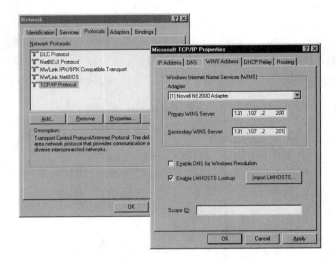

Domain Name System Server

Windows NT 4.0 Server is also capable of being configured as a Domain Name System (DNS) server. DNS is installed from the Select Network Service dialog box by selecting Microsoft DNS Server.

In a DNS or Internet/intranet environment, clients (resolvers) query DNS servers and their databases for computer name resolution. DNS servers map DNS domain names to IP addresses.

DNS Server Configuration

Once the DNS service is installed, open the TCP/IP protocol property sheet from the Network dialog box and select the DNS tab. The first thing that must be defined is a domain name as well as the IP addresses of the DNS servers in the DNS Service Search Order window as illustrated in Figure 8.34.

FIG. 8.34 ⟹

Here is a DNS domain and server configuration example.

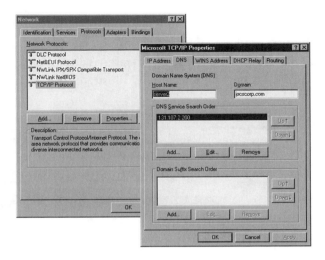

The next step in the process of configuring a DNS server is to start DNS Manager from the Administrative Tools program group and define a new server or group of servers in the Server List that will be managed from this computer's DNS Manager.

The drop-down menu options in DNS Manager include DNS, View, Options, and Help. Except for configuring preferences in the Options menu, all other DNS configuration is performed from the DNS menu. The Preferences selection under the Options menu allows for Auto Refresh Statistics, Show Automatically Created Zones, and Expose TTL (TimeToLive).

Either right-click the Server List icon and choose New Server, or from the DNS drop-down menu, select New Server (see Figure 8.35). The result of entering a server name or IP address and clicking OK is shown in Figure 8.36.

When a DNS server has been successfully created and, if required, forwarder information is defined in the Servers properties sheet, a zone is created by right-clicking the server and selecting a new zone. In the Creating New Zone for Server dialog box, enter the required information by typing the zone name in the Zone Name window, then press the Tab key. A zone file name will automatically appear. Selecting the Next button produces an information screen stating that all the information for the new zone has been entered and to create the new zone, click the Finish button. Figure 8.37 illustrates the creation of a new zone.

FIG. 8.35 ⟹

Here is the Add DNS Server dialog box.

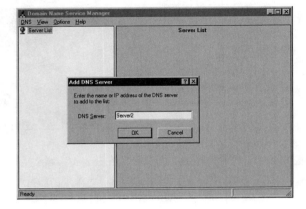

FIG. 8.36 ⟹

Here are the results of adding a DNS server.

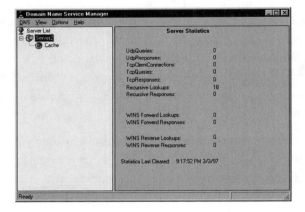

FIG. 8.37 ⟹

This figure shows the creation of a new DNS zone.

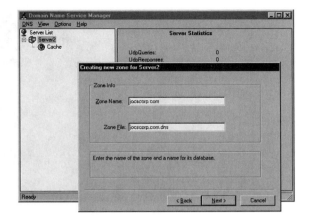

When a new zone is created, the DNS Manager appears as shown in Figure 8.38; however, for illustration purposes, two additional records have been added. The first is the A record (address record) for server2, and the second is the CNAME record (canonical or alias record).

FIG. 8.38 ⟹

Here is an example of the newly cre-ated DNS zone and DNS record associations.

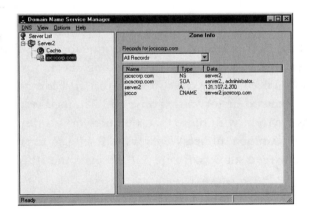

Figure 8.39 illustrates the Ping utility being utilized to both ping server2's address of 131.107.2.200 and also to ping the alias or CNAME of server2. Pinging the alias was successful because of the CNAME record (refer to Figure 8.38). The alias computer name to IP address is resolved by the DNS database.

FIG. 8.39 ⟹

This is an example of pinging an IP address and alias name.

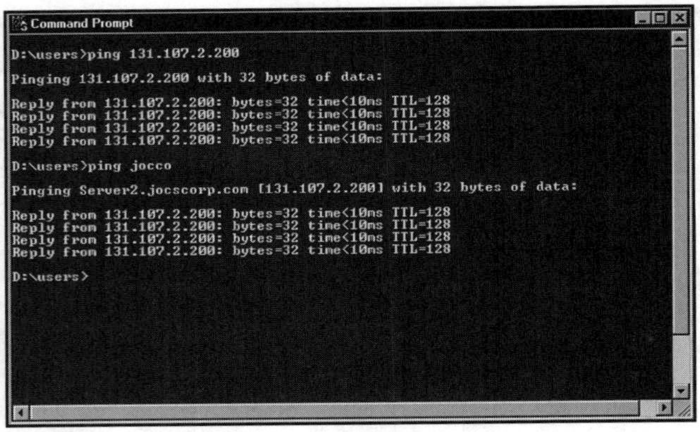

IP Routing

The Routing Information Protocol (RIP) for Internet protocol is another service available in Windows NT 4.0. After it is installed, a Windows NT 4.0 system can act as an IP router in a TCP/IP network. The service is installed in the same fashion as RIP for NWLink mentioned previously (from the Services tab in the network application).

When RIP for IP is installed, the Routing tab in the TCP/IP Properties sheet displays an Enable IP Forwarding check box, which is selected by default. The Routing tab also states that IP Forwarding (IP Routing) allows packets to be forwarded on a multi-homed system. A *multi-homed system* is a system with more than one network card installed, each connected to a unique subnet. Windows NT 4.0 can forward TCP/IP packets between subnets. Figure 8.40 displays the IP Routing tab.

FIG. 8.40 ⇒

The IP Routing tab is displayed here.

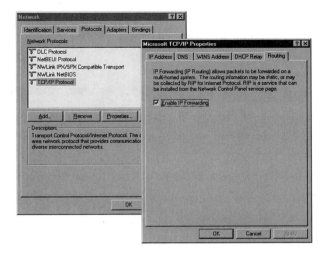

TCP/IP and the Registry

Registry keys and values for the TCP/IP protocol and all its additional services are found in many different locations in the Registry. To display all locations would be virtually impossible as well as impractical; however, a number of default keys and values are shown in the following figures. Figure 8.41 displays the default TCP parameters.

FIG. 8.41 ⇒

These are the default TCP Registry parameter values.

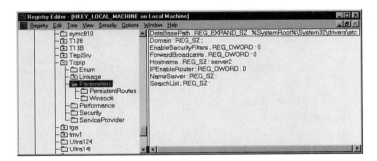

Figure 8.42 shows default NE20001 network adapter card parameters for TCP/IP. Values can change depending on the network adapter card used.

FIG. 8.42 ⇒

This figure shows the default TCP/IP NE20001 compatible network adapter card parameters.

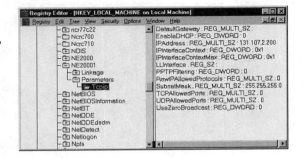

Default NetBIOS over TCP/IP parameters are established in the Registry when TCP/IP is installed. Figure 8.43 displays the NetBT over TCP/IP default Registry values.

FIG. 8.43 ⇒

Here are the default NetBT over TCP/IP Registry parameters.

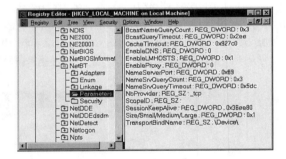

Windows sockets Registry entries by default are shown in Figures 8.44 and 8.45.

FIG. 8.44 ⇒

This figure shows the default Winsock Registry parameters.

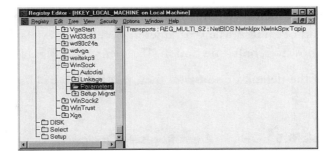

FIG. 8.45 ⇒

Here are the default TCP/IP Winsock Registry parameters.

Default DHCPServer Registry parameters are displayed in Figure 8.46.

FIG. 8.46 ⇒

These are the default DHCP-Server Registry parameters.

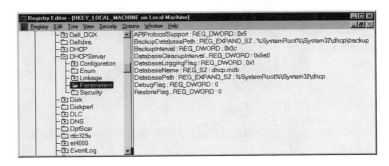

Figure 8.47 shows parameter information relating to the DHCP client portion of DHCP. Many parameters options are available in this location; however, only one option, 15, is shown in Figure 8.47.

All of the default options and their relationship to DHCP are listed in Table 8.5.

Table 8.5	DHCP Client Registry Options
Option	**Relationship**
1	DhcpSubnetMaskOption
15	DhcpDomain (see Figure 8.47)
3	DhcpDefaultGateway
44	DhcpNameServer
46	DhcpNodeType
47	DhcpScopeID
6	DhcpNameServer

FIG. 8.47 ⇒

This figure shows the default DHCP client Registry parameters.

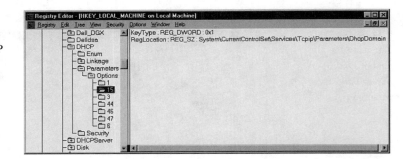

Default Registry parameters for WINS are shown in Figure 8.48. No default parameters are listed in this location; however, in this example, the pull and push partners are shown. Default DNS Registry parameters are shown in Figure 8.49.

FIG. 8.48 ⟹

Here are the default WINS Registry parameters.

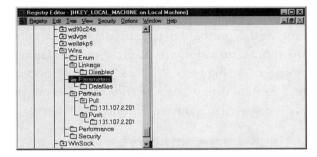

FIG. 8.49 ⟹

This figure shows the default DNS Registry parameters.

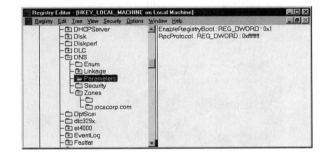

For additional information on the TCP/IP protocol, options, and Registry parameters, refer to the online help files in Windows NT 4.0 and the Windows NT 4.0 Resource Kit.

DLC

Data Link Control (DLC), as stated previously in Chapter 5, "Capacity Planning and Performance," is used by Windows NT to communicate with IBM mainframes and HP JetDirect Printers.

System Network Architecture (SNA), a BackOffice application installed on Windows NT Server, uses 802.2 DLC over token ring, Ethernet, or FDDI as a SNA protocol to communicate directly with either an IBM mainframe or an IBM front-end processor.

DLC is also used with Windows NT to communicate with HP print devices with network adapter cards installed. Configuration of DLC printing is covered in Chapter 10, "Managing Printers in the Domain."

DLC Installation

Installation of this protocol is accomplished the same way as other protocols mentioned previously, from the Protocols tab on the Network property sheet (see Figure 8.50). The Have Disk button on the Select Network Protocol dialog box is used to install other protocols or software that is not available on the Windows NT Server CD-ROM.

FIG. 8.50 ⇒

This is an example of a DLC installation.

DLC and the Registry

DLC does not bind to a MAC driver until a network adapter card open command is issued. When an open command is issued for the first time, the DLC protocol driver writes default values in the Registry specific to the network adapter card. The default DLC Registry values (see Figure 8.51) are specific to the DLC protocol and a NE20001 compatible network card.

FIG. 8.51 ⇒

This is a default DLC Registry values display.

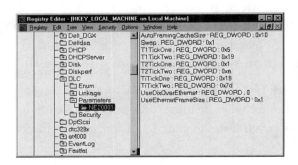

AppleTalk

The AppleTalk protocol in the Windows NT environment is used to communicate with Macintosh systems and AppleTalk Postscript printers. The AppleTalk protocol by itself can be installed on Windows NT 4.0 Workstation to provide print server functions to AppleTalk printers on the network. AppleTalk protocol can also be used for the development of AppleTalk-compliant programs.

On Windows NT 4.0 Server, when Services for Macintosh is installed, two services for Macintosh clients are provided. They are File Server for Macintosh and Print Server for Macintosh. The first service provides Macintosh clients access to files on the Windows NT Server; the second service allows Macintosh clients to print to non-Postscript printers controlled by the Windows NT Server. Services for Macintosh also provides Microsoft clients the same services the other way; they can share files with Macintosh clients and print to AppleTalk Postscript print devices.

AppleTalk Protocol Installation on Windows NT Workstation

The installation of the AppleTalk protocol will be covered here; but the configuration of the AppleTalk printer port will be covered in Chapter 10, "Managing Printers in the Domain."

Installation of the AppleTalk protocol for Windows NT 4.0 Workstation is accomplished from the Network properties sheet. Select the Protocols tab and then click the Add button (see Figure 8.52).

FIG. 8.52 ⇒

This is an example of the AppleTalk protocol installation on Windows NT 4.0 Workstation.

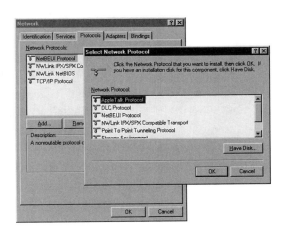

During the binding phase of the installation, a default AppleTalk zone must be configured. Figure 8.53 displays the dialog box used to supply the default zone.

FIG. 8.53 ⟹

This is an example of the AppleTalk default zone name configuration.

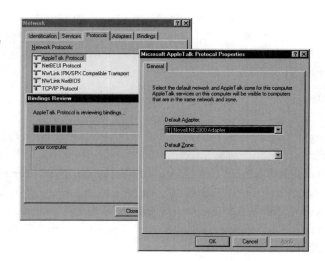

When the AppleTalk protocol is installed on Windows NT Workstation, AppleTalk print devices can be added through the Print Wizard, and the Control Panel devices icon allows starting and stopping of the AppleTalk device. Performance Monitor also has an AppleTalk object choice. Installation of the AppleTalk protocol on Windows NT Workstation does not provide for any routing configuration as it does in Services for Macintosh on Windows NT 4.0 Server.

Services for Macintosh Installation on Windows NT Server

Windows NT 4.0 Server allows for the installation of the Services for Macintosh service, and during the installation of this service the AppleTalk protocol is installed. Installation of Services for Macintosh is accomplished from the Services tab in the network application. Figure 8.54 displays the Services for Macintosh installation screen.

Key Concept

Services for Macintosh requires an NTFS partition to be available when it is installed. A default Mac Volume will be initialized on the NTFS partition when the service is installed.

FIG. 8.54 ⟹

This is an example of the Services for Macintosh installation on Windows NT 4.0 Server.

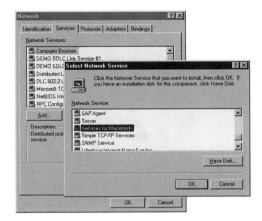

The Microsoft AppleTalk Protocol Property sheet is where both the default AppleTalk zone is configured from the General tab and routing information is configured from the Routing tab.

Figure 8.55 shows the General tab where the default AppleTalk zone must be selected. An AppleTalk zone is a logical collection of computers and/or printers (nodes), similar to a Windows NT Domain or Workgroup.

Routing information is configured on the Routing tab (see Figure 8.56). The Enable Routing check box on the Routing tab is selected if this Windows NT 4.0 Server is to become an AppleTalk router. If multiple network cards are bound to the AppleTalk protocol, and this check box is selected, all Macintosh clients on the bound networks will see this Windows NT Server. If this check box is not selected, only Macintosh clients on the default network will see this Windows NT Server.

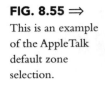

FIG. 8.55 ⇒

This is an example of the AppleTalk default zone selection.

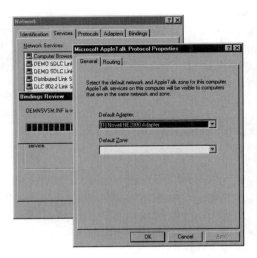

The next section, Adapter, will display all the network cards in the computer that are bound to the AppleTalk protocol. Each will be a separate network.

Once routing is selected, the Use This Router to Seed the Network option becomes available. If this Windows NT 4.0 Server is to provide routing information to other routers on the network, this box should be selected. If selected, the From and To windows become available and will accept a value from 1 to 65,279.

The Get Zones button will display the zone information for the selected network card. To see zone information for another network, select the desired network card in the Adapter window.

When Services for Macintosh is installed and configured, Macintosh clients can use MAC Volumes created on the Windows NT 4.0 Server and can print to printing devices configured on the Windows NT 4.0 Server. Microsoft clients can use resources in the MAC Volumes, provided they are shared, and print to AppleTalk postscript printers.

FIG. 8.56 ⟹

This figure shows how to configure AppleTalk routing.

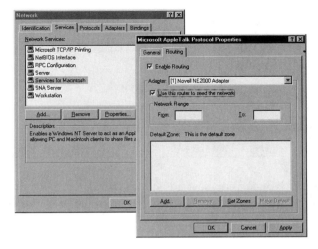

AppleTalk and the Registry

Default Registry locations of AppleTalk protocol and Services for Macintosh parameters are shown in Figures 8.57 (Adapter values), 8.58 (Parameter values), and 8.59 (File Server values).

FIG. 8.57 ⟹

This is an AppleTalk Adapter NE20001 parameters Registry example.

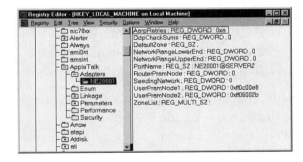

FIG. 8.58 ⟹

This is an AppleTalk parameters Registry example.

FIG. 8.59 ⇒

This is a MacFile parameters Registry example.

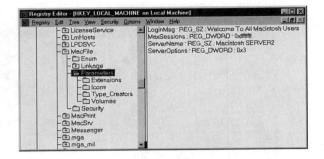

Note Notice in the last figure that there are two other Registry keys associated with Services for Macintosh besides MacFile: MacPrint and MacSrv. ■

Understanding Windows NT Browser Service, Options, and Configuration

The browser service is used in Windows NT 4.0 to provide clients with a list of resources on the network. By default, specific computers on the network take on the task of maintaining a network browse list. These computers work together to provide all other computers, including non-browser computers, with a list of shared network resources.

Resource lists contain the domain name, a computer name of the location of the shared resource, and the name of the shared resource, whether it is physically a folder (directory) or a printer.

Browser Types

Types of browsers within the browser service include the following:

◆ Domain master browser

◆ Master browser

◆ Backup browser

◆ Potential browser

◆ Non-Browser

Domain master browsers and master browsers take on the responsibility of maintaining a master list of computers and resources and, if warranted, will designate backup browsers and send the master list to the designated backup browsers. Backup browsers are designated automatically by the browser service running in a master browser. The PDC in a domain will automatically be the domain master browser and the BDCs will automatically be backup browsers. A BDC can become the domain master browser if the PDC goes offline for some reason.

A general rule is that for every 32 computers in a domain or workgroup, a backup browser is delegated by the master browser.

When a client requires a list of resources located on a specific computer, either a master browser or a backup browser will fulfill the client request.

Key Concept

If the computer name is known, there is a very easy way to obtain a list of shared resources on a specific computer. Simply choose Run from the Start menu and type the computer name preceded by two back-slashes. If any of the computer's resources are shared, they will appear in a window labeled <computer name>. A specific resource can also be accessed from the Run command if its specific share name and computer name are known. If a share called DATA is located on a computer named APPLICATIONS, typing **\\APPLICATIONS\DATA** from the Run command will access that resource.

Browser Announcements

When a computer capable of announcing itself on the network is turned on, it sends a broadcast announcement to the master browser stating that it is available on the network. The following is a list of platforms that announce themselves to master browsers on the network:

◆ Windows NT 4.0 Server and Workstation

◆ Windows NT 3.1/3.51 Server and Workstation

◆ Windows NT 3.1 Server and Workstation

- ◆ Windows 95
- ◆ Windows For Workgroups
- ◆ LAN Manager systems

Non-browsers announce themselves by sending a directed datagram to the master browser every minute. This time is extended up to every 12 minutes. The time increment goes from one minute, then two minutes, then four minutes, then eight minutes, and lastly, every 12 minutes. If a master browser does not hear from a computer for three announcement periods, or 36 minutes, the master browser removes the computer from the browse list.

Potential browsers also announce themselves the same way; however, any potential browser can become a backup browser, or even a master browser. If no master browser is found, these computers send an election announcement.

Backup browsers, in addition to announcing themselves in the same way as non-browsers or potential browsers initially, also contact the master browser every 15 minutes to get an updated list of resources. If no master browser can be found, the backup browser will also initiate an election.

Key Concept

If a client is receiving a resource list from a backup browser, it is possible for a client to see a computer and its resources in a list for up to 51 minutes after a computer is turned off (three announcement periods, 36 minutes, plus 15 minutes). Users should be instructed to do normal shutdown procedures to reduce this time to a maximum of 15 minutes.

Browser Elections

As stated previously, if a master browser cannot be found, the computer trying to notify the master browser will send out an election announcement that includes all of its election criteria. Election criteria include software platform and version, machine size and type, computer name, time online, and other pertinent information. This will force an election of a master browser on the network.

The following list specifies the software platforms that can perform either master browser or backup browser functions if configured to participate in the browser process:

- Windows NT 4.0 Server and Workstation
- Windows NT 3.1/3.51 Server and Workstation
- Windows NT 3.1 Server and Workstation
- Windows 95
- Windows for Workgroups

All computers receive the election announcement. If the computer that sent the announcement has higher criteria than any computer receiving it, that computer will win the election. If a computer receives the announcement and it has higher criteria than the computer that sent the announcement, it will send out its own election announcement. The original computer will lose the election and will then try to find the new master browser.

Key Concept

It is important to realize that there is a master browser elected for each protocol found on the network. For example, in a single workgroup with some computers running NetBEUI, some running NWLink, and others running TCP/IP, there could be three different master browsers.

Browser Monitor

Figure 8.60 displays an example of the Browser Monitor utility located in the Windows NT 4.0 Resource Kit Utilities CD-ROM.

There are four entries for Domain1 under the Transport column. The first entry specifies \Device\Nbf_NE20001, the second \Device\NetBT_NE20001, the third \Device\NwlnkIpx, and the last \Device\NwlnkNb. The following list describes the transport definition of each entry:

- Nbf   NetBEUI Frame
- NetBT   NetBIOS over TCP/IT

◆ NwlnkIpx   NWLink IPX

◆ NwlnkNb   NetBIOS over NWLink IPX

Notice that the NWLink entry that is not using NetBIOS over NWLink has a status of unknown.

FIG. 8.60 ⟹

This is a Browse Monitor display example.

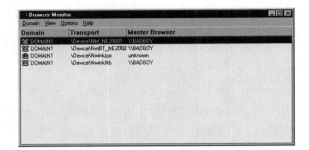

Browser Requests

As stated before, the browser service is used to supply a list of network resources to requesting clients. A resource list request is issued on the network every time a Net Use command is entered at a command prompt or a Map Network Drive is initiated from the desktop. The request is a `NetServerEnum` API call to either a master browser or a backup browser. If it is the first time a client is requesting a resource list, the request is a `GetBackupList` datagram directed to the master browser. The master browser will return a list of available browsers on the network. The client will store up to three browsers from the list and, from that point on, will request a resource list from one of the three browsers.

Browser Shutdowns and Failures

If a non-browser is shut down normally, the master browser removes it from the master list. If it fails, it could remain visible as a resource for up to 51 minutes (3 announcement periods ★ 12 minutes + 15 minutes).

If a backup browser is shut down normally, it will send an announcement to the master browser of this fact and will be removed from the browse list. If a backup browser fails, it could remain in the list for up to

51 minutes. If a client cannot retrieve a resource list from that specific backup browser, it will select another browser from its list of three.

If a master browser is shut down normally, it will send a `ForceElection` datagram so a new master browser can be elected. If the master browser fails, either a backup browser or a client will force an election within 15 minutes.

Browser and the Wide Area Network

Most enterprise designs include more than one network or subnet within a single domain or more than one domain. If this is the case, users will need to acquire a total list of resources from either all subnets within a single domain, or from all domains in the enterprise.

In a single domain, multiple subnet design, each subnet must have its own master browser because each subnet is an independent browsing entity with its own master browser and backup browsers. The PDC in the domain will be the domain master browser, and each master browser in each subnet will send its subnet resource list to the PDC. Subnet master browsers announce themselves to the domain master browser using a `MasterBrowserAnnouncement` directed datagram. This is a different type of announcement than a normal computer uses to announce itself to a master browser. In turn, the PDC will send a total domain resource list to the master browsers in each subnet. The master browsers in each subnet will then ensure that their backup browsers receive their list. This way, any client in any subnet can receive a complete domain resource list.

If a domain master browser should go offline, after a 45-minute time period (three announcement periods multiplied by 15 minutes), clients will only receive a subnet resource list instead of a complete domain resource list. This can be remedied by promoting a BDC to a PDC within the first 45 minutes of a PDC going down.

In a multiple domain enterprise design, each domain master browser (PDC) will send a `DomainAnnouncement` datagram to every other domain's PDC. A `DomainAnnouncement` datagram contains the name of the domain and the name of the domain master browser computer.

Browser and the Registry

Browser parameters in the Registry have to be manually maintained to control the browser service on specific computers. For example, when Windows NT 4.0 Workstation is installed, its `MaintainServerList` parameter, by default, is set to Auto. If it is determined by the browser service on the master or domain master browser that a backup browser is needed on the network, it could be designated as a backup browser. In fact, under certain conditions it could possibly win an election and be a master browser.

If it is determined that a specific workstation computer should not participate in the browser service at any time because of overhead or resource limitations, the `MaintainServerList` parameter in the Registry can be changed from Auto to No. This will prevent a specific computer from being designated to help. By default, workstation and member server computers are set to AUTO, and domain controller computers are set to YES.

Key Concept

It should be noted that even though the specific computer will not ever maintain a server list, it can still function as a non-browser client.

Figure 8.61 shows a display of the Registry location for the browser service.

FIG. 8.61 ⇒

This figure shows Browser parameters in the Registry.

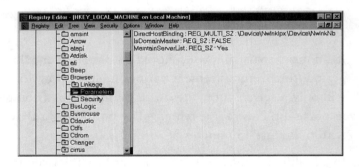

The IsDomainMaster parameter can be set to TRUE or YES to force a specific computer to become a master browser. The default setting for this parameter is FALSE or NO.

To change the time period of how often a client will announce itself to a master browser, a server service Registry parameter can be changed. By default, once up and running a computer will announce itself every 12 minutes. This can be adjusted under the HKEY_LOCAL_ MACHINE\ System\CurrentControlSet\Services\LanmanServer\Parameters by adding the Announce value; type **REG_DWORD**. The default is 720 seconds, or 12 minutes.

Key Concept

If the Announce value is decreased, network traffic will increase. If this value is increased, an improperly shut down computer will appear in a browse list longer.

Browser Optimization

The browser service uses a high percentage of the total network bandwidth to operate when compared to other services. Optimization of the browser service may become an issue in any given network or enterprise.

From a client-to-server perspective, the browser traffic exists on the network (see Table 8.6).

Table 8.6   Browser Service Announcement Traffic from Client to Server

Announcement Type	Announcement Occurrence
Host Announcements	Every 12 minutes
Get Backup List	First browser request
Election	Seldom
Get Browse List	Every browse request
Get Share List	Every browse request

From a server to server perspective, the browser traffic exists on the network (see Table 8.7).

Table 8.7 Browser Service Announcement Traffic from Server to Server

Announcement Type	Announcement Occurrence
Host Announcements	Every 12 minutes
Local Master Announcements	Every 12 minutes
Workgroup Announcements	Every 15 minutes
Elections	Every domain controller restart
Local Domain Updates	Every 15 minutes
Remote Domain Updates	Every 12 minutes
WINS Server Updates	Every 12 minutes

There are a number of ways to optimize the browsing service and these are listed here:

◆ Decrease the number of host announcements. If any computers are not configured to provide resources to other users on the network, disable or stop the server service on those computers. With this service disabled, a computer will not send an announcement to a master browser when it is turned on initially, or every 12 minutes, and the size of the browse list is reduced.

◆ If it is determined that a particular computer or group of computers, such as a number of Windows NT Workstations or Member Servers, are never to participate in the browse service as potential browsers, change the MaintainServerList in the Registry on each computer to NO. This can also be done on Windows 95 computers from the network icon or on Windows for Workgroups computers in the [network] section of system.ini.

◆ Use only the protocols you need. Eliminate the ones you don't need.

◆ Optimize the Registry on client computers by adding the `LanmanServer Announce` parameter: type **REG_DWORD**. The default is 720 seconds. The range is from 300 to 4,294,976 seconds. This can cause client computers to announce themselves less than every 12 minutes.

◆ Optimize the Registry on master browser computers in a domain by adding the `MasterPeriodicity` parameter: type **REG_DWORD** in the HKEY_LOCAL_MACHINE\System\CurrentControlSet \Services\Browser\Parameters location. This controls the time between master browser to domain master browser announcements. The range is from 300 to 4,294,976 seconds.

◆ Optimize the Registry on backup browser computers in a domain or workgroup by adding the `BackupPeriodicity` parameter: type **REG_DWORD** in the HKEY_LOCAL_MACHINE\System\ CurrentControlSet\ Services\Browser\Parameters location. This controls the time between backup browser to master browser announcements. Increasing this time will reduce the frequency of resource list updates between the master browser and backup browsers.

Setting Up and Configuring Folder and File Replication

Once configured, the directory replicator service that is built-in to Windows NT provides for automatic folder and file replication from an export server or computer to an import computer without any manual intervention.

To export folders and files, Windows NT 4.0 Server software must be installed on the system. To be an import computer, either Windows NT 4.0 Server or Workstation software can be installed.

One of the reasons this service is available in Windows NT is to ease domain and workgroup administration. The following list suggests reasons to implement directory replication. The items listed can be maintained in one location and replicated to any number of import computers.

- Logon scripts
- Profiles
- Policies
- Read-only files

If logon scripts are implemented in a domain environment, the logon scripts must be located on the computer that validated the logon. If both the PDC and BDCs are validating logons, the administrator must ensure that the logon scripts are installed on all domain controllers. Directory replication can be implemented in this case and logon scripts have to be maintained in one location only: the \export\scripts folder on the PDC. Directory replication is then configured to export the logon scripts to its own \import\scripts folder and all of the BDC's \import\scripts folders.

Profiles and policies are another reason to implement directory replication. It is much more efficient to have profiles and policies available locally than to implement them over a WAN.

Maintaining read-only files such as company phone directories and employee handbooks in one location is still another reason to implement directory replication.

Directory Replicator Default Folder Structure

On the export side of the service, the default replicator folder is:

\<winnt-root>\System32\Repl\Export

All folders to be replicated must appear in the directory structure after the Export folder. An example of a folder structure is shown in Figure 8.62.

FIG. 8.62 ⟹

Here is an example of a suggested Export folder structure.

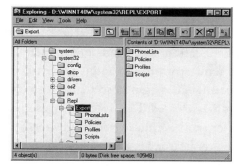

On the import end of the service, the default replicator folder is:

<winnt–root>\System32\Repl\Import

The folder structure that is implemented on the export end will be duplicated on the import end.

Directory Replicator Operation

When the directory replicator is configured and folders and files are set up, the directory replicator service starts the replication process. After the first replication, the export server periodically checks the replicated folders for changes. If changes have occurred, the export server sends a notice to the import domains or computers. It is then up to the import computers to read and copy the changes.

The time period between checking the replicated folders is governed by the interval Registry parameter and will be displayed and discussed later in this chapter.

Directory Replicator Configuration

The process of folder and file replication is started by a series of steps; either the export server or import computer can be configured first. For purposes of illustration, the export server configuration will be discussed first here.

Preparing the Export Server

The first step in configuring the export server is to start the User Manager for Domains application and create a new user. This user account will be used in the replicator process and is normally named Repl or ReplUser. This account is configured so that the password never expires and all logon hours are selected. The account is also made a member of the Backup Operators and Replicator local groups. This user account will be used by the Replicator Service to log on to the computer as a service and have the necessary system rights to replicate folders and files to other computers. Figure 8.63 shows all attributes of the ReplUser account except the logon hours.

FIG. 8.63 ⇒

Here is an example of the Replicator Service user account configuration.

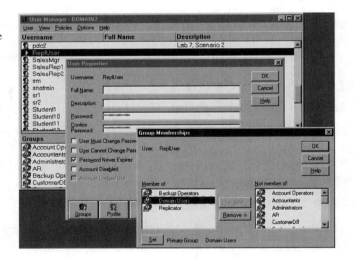

The second step in the process is to configure the Directory Replicator service from the Control Panel Services application. The Directory Replicator service is configured to start automatically and to log on to the network with the previously created user account. Figure 8.64 illustrates the Directory Replicator service configuration process. When OK is selected on the Services dialog box, a Service information dialog box appears indicating that the account configured has been granted the Log On As A Service right.

FIG. 8.64 ⇒

This figure shows configuration of the Directory Replicator Service.

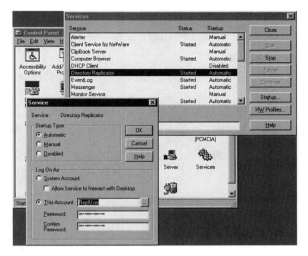

The third step in the process is to manually build the required folder or directory structure. Refer to Figure 8.62 for an example of the folder structure. When the folder structure is built, the desired files must be placed in the proper folders for replication.

The last step in the process is to configure the export server to export the folders constructed in the previous step. This is accomplished by doing the following:

1. Start the Server Manager application from the Administrative Tools menu.

2. From the list of machines shown, select the Windows NT Server that is to be configured as the replication export server.

3. Display the properties for the selected computer.

4. From the Properties for <computer name> dialog box, choose the Replication button (see Figure 8.65).

5. From the export (left) side of the Directory Replication on <computer name> dialog box, select the Export Directories radio button (this enables the directory replicator on this computer).

6. Ensure the From Path is correct.

7. Add the desired import computers and domains by selecting the Add button. In the Select Domain dialog box, enter the proper name in the Domain text box and click OK.

8. Choose the Manage button and configure the folders required to be replicated in the Manage Exported Directories dialog box (see Figure 8.66).

Figures 8.65 and 8.66 illustrate the previous export server configuration steps.

FIG. 8.65 ⟹

Here is the first Export Server configuration example.

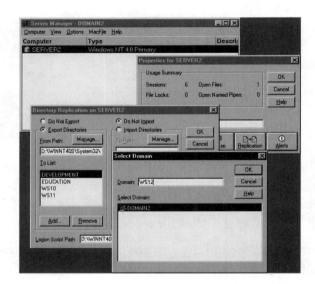

FIG. 8.66 ⟹

Here is the second Export Server configuration example.

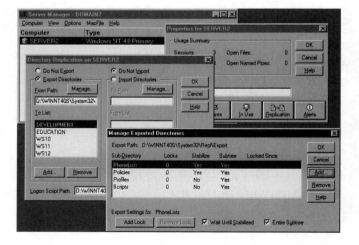

Preparing the Import Computer

The first step in configuring the import computer is to determine if the import computer is a member of the same domain as the export computer. If it is, the user account created for the export server can be used for the import computer. If the import computer is not a member of the export server's domain, a user account will have to be created using the same procedure discussed previously for the export server.

Next, configure the directory replicator service to log on to the network as the identified or created user account, as previously discussed for the export server.

The last step is to configure the import computer to receive the required folders and files from the export server. Figure 8.67 displays the steps required to configure the import computer.

FIG. 8.67 ⇒

Here is an Import Computer configuration example.

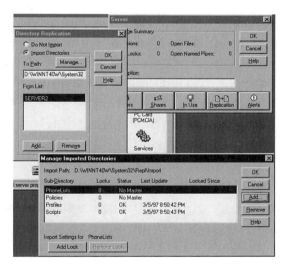

It is important to note that the Manage button on the import computer side of the Directory Replication on <computer name> dialog box is used to troubleshoot the replication process. When the Manage button is selected, the Manage Imported Directories dialog box appears (refer to Figure 8.67). The important item to interrogate is the Status column of each folder.

◆ A status of [blank] indicates replication has never occurred. Configuration on either the export server, the import computer, or both could be the problem.

◆ A status of No Master indicates the replication process is not working and that the export server may be down or the replicator service is not configured correctly.

◆ A status of No Sync indicates that replication has occurred but the data on the import computer is not current with the data on the export server. This could be caused by a communication problem, a permission problem, or an export server malfunction.

◆ A status of OK indicates the replication process is working and that the data on the import computer is current with the data on the export server.

Directory Replicator and the Registry

Registry parameters can also be configured to optimize the directory replicator process. Three important parameters that are manually changed to govern the replicator service are the GuardTime parameter, the Interval parameter, and the Pulse parameter. By default, these parameters are set to 2, 5, and 3, respectively. The replicator service parameter location is HKEY_LOCAL_MACHINE\System\CurrentControlSet\Services\Replicator\Parameters and is illustrated in Figure 8.68.

FIG. 8.68 ⇒

This is an example of Directory Replicator Services Registry parameters.

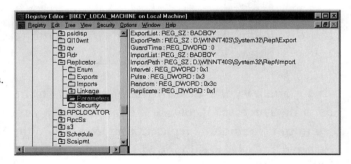

The GuardTime parameter is used by the export server to dictate how many minutes an export folder must be stable (have no changes), before the import computers can copy the files to themselves. The default is 2 minutes with a range of 0 to 1/2 the interval time.

The Interval parameter controls how often an export server will check for updates on the import computers. This parameter default is 5 minutes and the range is from 1 to 60 minutes. This option is ignored on import machines.

The Pulse parameter is a counter to control how often an export server will repeat the last update notice to the import computers. The default is 3 minutes. If an import computer is not pulsed by an export server in "Pulse" times "Interval" time (default 3 * 5 minutes), it will contact the export server for update information.

Note It should be noted that the default values of 2 and 5 for the GaurdTime and Interval parameters in Figure 8.68 have been changed to 0 and 1, respectively. The Pulse parameter has not been changed. ▪

Directory Replicator Optimization

It should be realized that this function will create network traffic. The amount of traffic is, of course, dependent on the number and size of folders and files and the frequency of replication. The number of import computers also helps determine the amount of network traffic generated.

The following is a list of items to consider concerning directory replication and network traffic, because anytime a change to the replication directory structure is at an export server, the following network traffic is generated to every import computer:

◆ Change announcements
◆ Session establishment
◆ Verify directories
◆ Update directories

There are also other ways to optimize the replicator service:

◆ Set up shallow or flat directory structures.

◆ Prevent the service from replicating during extremely busy network times. To stop folders from being replicated, manually add a lock to the folder.

◆ If the Wait Until Stabilized option is selected, the import computer will copy the entire directory structure whenever a file changes in the structure. When this option is not selected, only the changed file is replicated.

◆ Adjust the Registry parameters as required to adjust replication times and traffic.

Taking the Disc Test

 If you have read and understood material in this chapter, you are ready to test your knowledge. Insert the CD-ROM that comes with this book and run the self-test software as described in Appendix I, "Using the CD-ROM."

From Here...

"Disk Management and Fault Tolerance" is the next chapter of this book. Understanding the software fault tolerance options of Windows NT plus the characteristics and uses of volume sets, stripe sets, and stripe sets with parity, along with disk mirroring and duplexing, will greatly enhance your ability to support Windows NT 4.0. Concepts learned in this chapter will aid in understanding performance and troubleshooting options presented in the next chapter.

Chapter Prerequisite

The reader should already be
familiar with the Disk Administrator tool, as this chapter discusses a specific use for the
Disk Administrator.

9

Disk Management and Fault Tolerance

This chapter will discuss the different Windows NT 4.0 Server fault
tolerance disk options available and some decisions you must make
prior to the actual implementation. The concepts that you learn will
help you maintain data integrity and maximize the performance of
your server's disk subsystem.

Topics covered in this chapter include:

- ◆ Windows NT 4.0 Fault tolerance

- ◆ Striping—RAID 0

- ◆ Striping with parity—RAID 5

- ◆ Disk mirroring and disk duplexing—RAID 1

- ◆ Recovering from hard disk failures

- ◆ Performance enhancements

- ◆ Review questions

What Is Fault Tolerance?

Fault tolerance is the capability for your Windows NT server to continue to do its designated tasks, even though the machine has lost one of its disk drives. Another part of fault tolerance is the capability to quickly return to operational status with all the data intact after a power failure. The goal of the enterprise administrator is to have the most "up" time as possible. This translates to no hardware failures and no software restores or rebuilds. The last problem the administrator wants is to have a server disk or any other type hardware failure to cause the server to be "down" for any length of time. The network must be producing 100 percent of the time.

Windows NT provides some inroads to these networking needs. Hardware vendors are also helping to meet these fault tolerance goals with redundant motherboards, power supplies, and other components. Microsoft's new Wolfpack clustering is making even further inroads to the zero-down time objective.

Windows NT uses a fault-tolerant driver FTDISK.SYS and a software-implemented system called Redundant Array of Inexpensive Disk(RAID). Windows NT 4.0 also supports hardware-based RAID subsystems. You should create a RAID subsystem whenever you need to retain data integrity, increase logical disk space, or improve performance. In the event of a drive failure, your RAID subsystem will ensure data integrity and prevent downtime.

Windows NT Controlled Software RAID

Windows NT software fault tolerance supports RAID 1 and 5 only. RAID 1 is called disk mirroring. RAID 5 is called striping with parity. The fault tolerant disk driver is also used for a process know as cluster sparing. Cluster sparing will mark a bad sector, read or regenerate the information from the remaining fault tolerant disk partition(s), and write the data to the new cluster.

Caution

The subsystem solution RAID 0 is known as striping. Striping is *not* fault tolerant.

Hardware-Controlled RAID

Windows NT supports hardware-implemented fault tolerance. Support for most current RAID configurations is widely available through various third-party vendors. Be sure to check the hardware compatibility list (HCL) or the vendor before you purchase the hardware. Hardware RAID solutions use disk array controller cards that handle the processing necessary to protect your data on the drives.

When Windows NT is managing a drive in a fault tolerant manner, it sends separate I/O requests to each drive. It collects all of the data from the drives and assembles it for use. When hardware RAID is involved Windows NT treats the entire array of disks as one large drive and sends a single request to the RAID controller, which in turn sends requests to each of the individual drives.

Tip

You can use both software- and hardware-based RAID systems in the same Windows NT box. However, you should use hardware-based RAID whenever the CPU has the potential of becoming the bottleneck, such as in an application server.

Disk Striping

Disk striping can be implemented either through software or hardware configurations. Once again, disk striping is not part of fault tolerance. The data integrity, or in this case the ability to keep any data, is as good as your last backup. Two reasons to implement striping are: for pure, high-speed transactions both reading and writing; and to address the need for a large logical drive. It is normally configured to be a logical drive larger than the largest physical disk storage devices.

Stripe sets can be created using the Disk Administrator tool. The drives can be composed of the same size segments, but with different types and manufacturers. For example, you can configure a combination of disks including a mix of ESDI, IDE, and SCSI drives and their free space into one logical drive. You can use multiple controllers in your subsystem. You must have a minimum of two physical drives, up to a maximum of 32 drives. Because the drives still function the same whether they are striped or independent, by putting them together as a stripe you have concurrent I/O activity. Data is written and read simultaneously from all drives in this logical unit.

Key Concept

A stripe set isn't the same as a volume set. In a stripe set, Windows NT considers consecutive sectors to occur on each drive in turn. Because Windows NT reads and writes to all drives simultaneously, performance is enhanced. Volume sets, however, don't get written to each disk in turn; instead the information is written to drive one until it fills up, then is written to disk two, then disk three, and so on.

Stripe sets require partitions of the same size and increase performance. Volume sets do not require partitions of the same size and do not enhance performance.

To create a stripe set:

1. Select one area of free space on one of the drives to be used in the stripe set.

2. Select additional areas of free space on all other drives which you want to use for the stripe set. You can only select one area of free space on each drive. Selecting multiple free space areas is accomplished by holding the control key down while clicking the additional free space areas.

3. Choose <u>P</u>artition, Create <u>S</u>tripe Set....

4. Select the size of the stripe set. Windows NT will only allow you to create a stripe set as large as the number of free space segments selected multiplied by the smallest free space area. When the stripe set is created, it will be made of an equally sized partition on each of the drives where free space was selected.

For example, say you have five disk drives; four of them are 1G drives and one drive is a 500M drive. When you combine the free space of all five drives, the smallest is the 500M; therefore Windows NT will allocate 500M on each of the five drives to be considered the maximum stripe size of 2.5G. This is also the case when implementing RAID 5.

 Note   RAID 5 will be discussed in the following section, "Disk Striping with Parity." ■

At this point, you need to select the desired actual logical disk size. You have 2.5G available and you only need 1G; using the spin box, reduce the 2.5G to 1G. The disk administrator will make the adjustments to the drives automatically. You now have occupied 200M of physical space on each drive. Select Partition, then Commit Changes Now.

 Key Concept

Remember that whenever you make changes to the partitions on your system, you must commit changes before formatting the partition.

Now you may format your logical drive as FAT or NTFS. It is ready to use. The remaining free space can be used logical drive, another stripe set, a volume set, or a stripe set with parity.

 Tip

Always format stripe sets, stripe sets with parity, and volume sets with NTFS. The advantages of FAT being able to be read from DOS and Windows 95 are not valid with stripe sets since DOS and Windows 95 don't understand stripe sets and can't use them even if they are formatted FAT.

Windows NT accesses the logical drive using 64K units on each drive. Reading and writing is simultaneous across all physical drives and controllers used in making the stripe set.

Disk Striping with Parity

Disk striping with parity (known as a RAID 5 configuration) is the first fault tolerant disk configuration we will discuss. Windows NT takes care of the configuration process and the control. Microsoft Windows NT 4.0 supports two software RAID configurations: RAID 1 and RAID 5. RAID 1 is disk mirroring, discussed later in the "Disk Mirroring or RAID 1" section of this chapter. Microsoft Windows NT 4.0, 3.5, and 3.51, support one striping with parity configuration—that configuration being RAID 5. Using RAID 5 is the best choice for databases or other crucial data you don't want to lose.

If a drive fails, the server continues to function and no data is lost. The failed drive can be replaced and the striping with parity configuration can be rebuilt. The most common configurations are listed in Table 9.1.

Table 9.1	Raid Configurations
Type	Description
RAID 1	Disk mirroring
RAID 2	Disk striping using Error Correction Code
RAID 3	Disk striping with ECC stored as parity
RAID 4	Disk striping parity is stored on one drive
RAID 5	Disk striping parity is stored on all drives evenly

As previously mentioned, stripe sets can be created using the Disk Administrator tool. The steps are the same; however, now you must have a minimum of three physical drives, up to a maximum of 32 drives.

To create a stripe set with parity:

1. Select one area of free space on one of the drives to be used in the stripe set.

2. Select additional areas of free space on all other drives which you want to use for the stripe set. You can only select one area of free space on each drive. Selecting multiple free space areas is accomplished by holding the control key down while clicking the additional free space areas.

3. Choose Fault Tolerance, Striping with Parity....

4. Select the size of the stripe set. Windows NT will only allow you to create a stripe set as large as the number of free space segments selected minus one multiplied by the smallest free space area. When the stripe set is created it will be made of an equal sized partition on each of the drives where free space was selected. The extra segment is necessary overhead to provide fault tolerance.

Let's use the striping example once more. You have five disk drives; four of them are 1G drives and one drive is a 500M drive. When you combine the free space of all five drives, the smallest is the 500M; therefore, Windows NT will allocate 500M on each of the 5 drives to be considered the maximum physical stripe size of 2.5G.

Because we are creating a fault tolerant disk subsystem, and this is RAID 5, we know there will be space used for the parity block. Every time we write to the disk, there is a parity stripe block for each row. Every new row written by the parity block moves to the next physical disk. Remember, RAID 5 parity moves from drive to drive. It is not random; it moves to the next physical drive. Because we do have a parity block, it also takes up space. Our 2.5G physical space being used yields only 2G. You lose $1/n$ storage space, where n is the number of physical drives.

Disk Mirroring or RAID 1

Mirroring is also a fault-tolerant disk configuration. The Windows NT 4.0 fault tolerance disk driver (FTDISK.SYS) will write the same data to only two physical drives. System and boot partitions are eligible for mirroring as well as data drives. You can mirror FAT or NTFS. In the event of a hardware failure, the data on the mirrored drive survives and is up-to-date.

To create a mirror set:

1. Select a previously formatted partition.
2. Select an area of free space on the other drive which you want to use for the mirror set. Selecting the free space area is accomplished by holding the control key down while clicking the free space area. The free space must be at least as large as the existing partition.
3. Choose Fault Tolerance, Establish Mirror....
4. Select the size of the mirror set.

Key Concept

RAID 5 (Stripe sets with Parity) performs better when the data is mixed with both read and write operations since information is written $1+1/n$ times where n is the number of drives in the stripe set, and the reads can be accomplished by reading all of the drives simultaneously.

RAID 1 (Mirroring) performs better when the data is largely read only because Windows NT can read either drive to get the information. However, writing incurs a slight performance penalty since the information must be written twice.

With mirroring, you're prepared for a drive failure; however, you're still susceptible to a controller failure. Disk duplexing is a level above mirroring in terms of fault tolerance and just requires another disk controller. If you want the added protection of disk duplexing, set up a mirror set with one drive on one controller and the second drive on the second controller.

Recovering from Hard Disk Failure

If there is a failure of a hard drive in either fault-tolerant disk configurations (RAID 1 or RAID 5), the fault tolerant driver directs all I/O requests to the remaining drives in the chosen configuration.

The RAID 5 system will use the remaining drives and continue to implement the parity. Mirroring will continue to read and write to the remaining partition. If the system partition being mirrored experiences the failure, you will need to restart using a Windows NT fault tolerance boot disk.

 Note Information on how to create a fault tolerant boot disk can be found in article Q119467 in the Microsoft knowledgebase. ■

Breaking and Building a Mirror Set

To logically break the mirror set, use the following steps.

1. Using the Disk Administrator, select Mirrored Partition.
2. Select Fault Tolerance from the menu bar.
3. Select Break Mirror.
4. Assign the original drive letter to a good drive.
5. Delete the failed partition.
6. Select this drive and free space to make a new mirror.
7. Exit and restart.

Regenerating a Stripe Set with Parity

To rebuild a failed RAID 5 set, use the following steps.

1. Shut down the Windows NT server.
2. Replace the failed disk drive.
3. Run Disk Administrator.
4. Use the left mouse button and select the failed drive set.

5. Choose fault tolerance, Regenerate.

6. Shutdown and restart the server.

Regeneration occurs at boot up time using the parity.

Performance Enhancement

To enhance the performance of any Windows NT disk subsystem, there are a few basic principles you must consider. They are as follows:

◆ Disk Controllers

◆ Caching

◆ Type and performance of the drive

◆ Type of work

Disk Controllers

Disk Controllers can have a huge impact on server performance as well as disk performance. The cost difference between a good, fast, disk controller, and a poor performing disk controller is relatively minor. It makes sence to put good disk controllers in place. The server will perform faster disk requests and general tasks because the disk controller won't be demanding as much CPU attention.

Multiple disk controllers and busses improve performance even more. The more disk controllers, and busses, the more commands that can be taking place simultaneously.

Tip

Microsoft recommends that you use a Fast SCSI-2 controller as the minimum controller. However, a SCSI-3 Ultra Wide controller connected to a PCI bus would be a good choice as well.

Note the following approximate throughput that can be attained by various controller types.

Controller Type	Throughput
IDE controllers	2.5M/sec depending on Bus
ISA Bus standard SCSI controllers	3M/sec
SCSI-2 controllers	5M/sec
Fast SCSI-2 controllers	10M/sec
PCI Bus controllers with SCSI	nearly 40M/sec

You may have not noticed, but the farther you scan down the list, the faster the cards become. Keep in mind that you need the appropriate drive type to connect with the controller chosen.

Caching

Caching is the process of keeping a copy of some information close at hand. This ensures that it doesn't take quite so long to find important information when you really need it.

> **Note** Caching is easy to understand if you think of the process in terms of an address book. Most of the numbers and addresses we keep in our address books are ones that we could look up in the local phone book. However, it would take longer to search a thick phone book than it would to simply flip through our address book; so in a way, our address books are a kind of cache for telephone numbers. ■

Windows NT will use any available memory for cache when running. There are also disk controllers which have cache built in. When information is needed from the disk the cache is checked first to see if the information is available there.

Whenever possible, memory should be added to Windows NT instead of a cache on a disk controller. When system memory is used as cache by Windows NT it can retrieve the information without even going to the bus. The result is faster operations than even a disk controller cache can provide.

In addition, if Windows NT needs the memory, it can utilize it rather than utilizing virtual memory, which will greatly enhance performance.

Drive Types

As stated before, you must match the drive type to the controller. If you have standard SCSI controllers, you need SCSI drives. Additional considerations for disk subsystems include disk access times. Typically, the lower the disk-access time the faster the transfer rate. Also look for transfer rate numbers that the vendor sometimes supplies.

In addition to disk access time, the speed of the drive—specifically, how fast the media is spinning—can have a significant impact on the sustained throughput. Drives originally spun at 3,600 RPM but speeds as high as 10,000 RPM can be found today. Consider drives that spin at a fast rate for server applications.

Type of Work

Knowing the nature of the data greatly helps your decision-making process. If you know that the data is mission critical and you cannot afford any downtime or loss, consider RAID 5. Remember, you can lose a drive and the data is still intact while the drive continues to function. The read performance is approximately a 20 percent improvement over a single drive. The write performance is marginal at best due to the CPU time needed to generate the parity block. If your data is mixed between reads and writes but not critical, consider striping with *no* parity (RAID 0). RAID 0 provides the fastest read and write operations, but it is not fault tolerant.

Taking the Disc Test

If you have read and understood the material in the chapter, you are ready to test your knowledge. Insert the CD-ROM that comes with this book and run the self-test software as described in Appendix I, "Using the CD-ROM."

From Here...

Now that you know how to protect the information on your servers, you can move on to other interesting topics such as:

◆ Chapter 10, "Managing Printers in the Domain," provides an overview of the Windows NT 4.0 printing process, specifically in the enterprise.

◆ Chapter 13, "Security and Permissions," gives insight into protecting your information from other users.

◆ Chapter 20, "Performance Monitor," takes a look at how to use the Performance Monitor tool to resolve performance issues.

Part
III

Ch
9

Chapter Prerequisite

Readers should understand the
concept of directory services
presented in Chapters 2-5.
Readers should also have a
general concept of Windows
NT share-level security.

10

Managing Printers in the Domain

This chapter will provide a short discussion of the Windows NT 4.0
print process, followed by discussions on adding and configuring network printing devices and working with printer pools and printer priorities. Lastly, discussions on troubleshooting network printing will be
presented. The concepts and procedures discussed in this chapter will
apply to both workstation and server installations.

The following topics will be covered in this chapter:

◆ Examining the Windows NT 4.0 print process

◆ Adding and configuring network printing

◆ Working with printer properties

◆ Exploring DLC, TCP/IP, and Macintosh installation options

◆ Troubleshooting network printing

Examining the Windows NT 4.0 Print Process

In the past, configuring a printer was somewhat of a problem; not only from a local desktop, but also across the network. Microsoft has extended great effort in the Windows NT 4.0 operating system to streamline and simplify management of the printing process, particularly on the network.

Microsoft has been aware of the problems associated with local and network printing and has, throughout its history, successfully enhanced the process. For example, each MS-DOS application generally requires its own print driver to be loaded to successfully print to a given printing device. With Windows, Microsoft introduced a single set of print drivers that can be used with all applications. In other words, Windows required the installation of one printer driver, which all its applications would use, instead of a driver for each application.

Windows NT follows this same concept by using a generic set of drivers along with a specific printer mini driver that is used by all applications running under Windows NT. Windows NT 4.0 also takes this concept a step further by requiring a set of drivers to be installed only on the printer server and not on every installation using the printing device.

Before we begin, terminology used in the Windows NT 4.0 print process must be defined. A *printer* in Windows NT 4.0 is the software interface between the application and the physical printing device, which consists of the print driver and the print queue. The physical hardware that does the printing is referred to as the *print device.* A print request or print job can be sent to either a *local print device* (connected directly to the user's local computer) or a *remote print device* (attached to and managed by another computer or print server on the network). Requests can also be sent to a *network interface print device,* which is controlled and managed by a print server on the network, but is connected directly to the network and not to a print server.

The printer, or software interface, interacts with the print device to ensure the print device receives a print job that has been formatted appropriately for that device. The printer also provides the print management interface from which print jobs can be viewed and manipulated.

After a print device has been made available to users on the network, any valid Microsoft network client (Windows NT, DOS, Windows 95, Windows for Workgroups, Windows 3.1, LAN Manager 2.x, NetWare, or Macintosh) and even OS/2 and UNIX clients are able to direct print jobs to that device.

When a print device is made available on the network as a remote printer, you are not actually sharing the print device itself. The actual printer, or the management interface, is being shared. A given print device might have several printers associated with it, each with a different set of characteristics, priorities, or permissions. This concept will be discussed further in the section "Sharing a Printer" later in this chapter.

Windows NT 4.0 Print Process

The print process starts when an application makes a print request. As mentioned previously, print drivers do not have to be installed on each Windows NT installation. Let's explore this further. One of the innovative accomplishments Microsoft has brought about with the Windows NT 4.0 print process is to automatically download the required print drivers to Windows NT clients (all versions), as well as Windows 95 clients. While these clients do need a print driver to process print requests, these clients *do not require* that a print driver be manually installed locally. When any Windows NT or Windows 95 client connects to a network printer server through the Print Wizard application, the Windows NT print server will automatically download the required print driver to the client.

From that point on, if the client is a Windows NT client, any time the client prints to the network printer, a version check is done to make sure the latest print driver exists on the client. If the latest version does not exist on the client, the print server automatically downloads a copy of the newer print driver to the client computer.

Key Concept

At this point in time, no version checking is done between Windows NT 4.0 print servers and Windows 95 clients. If a new print driver is installed on the Windows NT 4.0 print server, each Windows 95 client will require the newer print driver to be installed manually.

The automatic downloading of print drivers to Windows NT and Windows 95 clients allows network administrators the ability to easily provide a greater number and variety of print devices to their clients. Print drivers do not have to be manually installed on every client computer. Figure 10.1 gives a graphic representation of the print process, including six specific print process steps that are explained after the graphic.

FIG. 10.1 ⇒

This figure shows the Windows NT 4.0 Print Process for Windows NT and Windows 95 Clients.

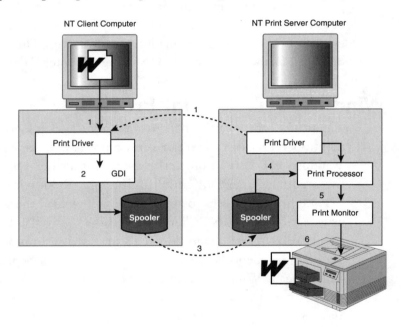

1. When a Windows NT client makes a request for printing on a print device attached to a print server, the client computer checks to see whether it has a local print driver installed. If it does not, or if the local copy is older than the copy on the print server, the print server automatically downloads a copy of the print driver to

the client. (If a Windows 95 client's print driver is older than the print server, the newer print driver must be manually loaded on the Windows 95 client).

2. By default, the Graphics Device Interface (GDI) component of a Windows NT 4.0 client operating system creates a print job in enhanced metafile format. This is sometimes called a journal file, and represents the print job formatted to print on most any print device type such as HPPCL or PostScript. It is then sent to the local spooler.

3. The local *Spooler* service makes a Remote Procedure Call (RPC) connection to the corresponding service on the print server and copies the print job to the print server spooler directory. The bulk of the print process now continues on the print server.

4. The print job is routed to the appropriate *print processor* where the print job is further rendered into a format compatible for the specific print device. This is usually referred to as a RAW file (refer to the section "Print Processor" later in the chapter). If a *separator page* has been requested, then it is attached to the beginning of the print job.

5. The print job is then passed to the appropriate *print monitor* which controls access to print devices, directs jobs to the correct port, and monitors the status of the job.

6. The *print device* receives the print job from the print monitor and generates the final print product.

Printing from other clients is essentially the same, except that the appropriate print driver must be installed on that local client computer. The fully formatted RAW print job file is generated locally and routed to the print server spooler. Because no further rendering is needed, a separator page is added if required and the print monitor sends the print job to the print device.

Windows NT 4.0 supports MS-DOS-based applications and Windows-based applications. In general, these applications will take advantage of the Windows NT print driver and print successfully. Some MS-DOS applications that produce graphic print output, however, will probably require that the print driver native to that application be installed for that application. It is safe to say that if the print output from MS-DOS or Windows-based applications is not correct, you will need to install an application-specific driver.

Print Process Components

There are four basic components of the print process: print driver, print spooler, print processor, and print monitor. Each will be discussed further in the following paragraphs.

Print Driver

As stated earlier, the print driver interacts with the print device to allow applications to generate printed output. It also provides the graphic interface through which the print device and queue can be managed. The print driver consists of three pieces: two DLLs and a characterization data file.

◆ The *printer graphics driver DLL* converts the print job output from an application into a print device-ready format.

◆ The *printer interface driver DLL* provides the interactive management screen through which the print jobs and the print device can be manipulated.

◆ The *characterization data file* provides information concerning device-specific characteristics of the print device such as the amount of memory, internal cartridges, additional form trays, and so on.

An example of the three print driver files for a HP LaserJet 4 printing device are as follows:

◆ Rasdd.dll   printer graphics driver DLL
◆ Rasddui.dll   printer interface driver DLL
◆ Pcl5ems.dll   characterization data file

Print Spooler

The print spooler actually refers to the spooler service running in Windows NT 4.0. The spooler is responsible for making a connection to the spooler on a remote print server. It also tracks print jobs, sends print jobs to the appropriate ports, and assigns jobs an appropriate print priority.

The spooler could be considered the print queue for the Windows NT print process. Because the spooler is a Windows NT service, it can be controlled through the Services applet in the Control Panel. If a print job gets "stuck" or hangs, simply select the spooler service from the list, choose Stop and then choose Start. This will effectively cancel the stuck print job waiting in the spooler. If a print job hangs, or the spooler does not seem to be responding, you can also purge the spooler. If the spooler is purged, all jobs in the spooler will also be purged.

Key Concept

It is always preferable to use the printer interface to try to pause or delete a problem job rather than stopping and starting the spooler service, so as not to lose any other jobs in queue. However, if the spooler is not responding and jobs cannot be deleted, the spooler service must be stopped and then started again.

By default, print job files are spooled to the <winnt root>\ SYSTEM32\SPOOL\PRINTERS directory. Depending on the size of the partition, as well as the number and size of the print jobs spooled, it is possible to run out of disk space.

Tip

The folder compression attribute, available through the properties dialog box for files and folders on an NTFS partition, can be used to compress the spool files and conserve disk space. However, keep in mind that compression does add additional overhead to your system and could, with large print files, result in a performance decrease.

If the spool folder is located on an NTFS partition, the Disk Administrator can be used to extend the partition into a volume set to increase the space available for the spooler folder. Windows NT also provides a Registry entry through which you can modify the location of the spooler folder globally for all printers, as well as for individual printers.

Use the Registry Editor to select the HKEY_LOCAL_MACHINE subtree and expand through to find the following key:

SYSTEM\CurrentControlSet\Control\Print\Printers

Look for a parameter entry called DefaultSpoolDirectory and modify its value to correspond to the new spool location. This change will affect all printers installed on the computer.

On the next level below the Printer key, you will find an entry for each printer you created on the computer. Each of these also has a SpoolDirectory entry that, if modified, will change the spool location just for that printer. Figure 10.2 displays these two Registry locations.

FIG. 10.2 ⇒

Here are two Print Spooler locations in the Registry.

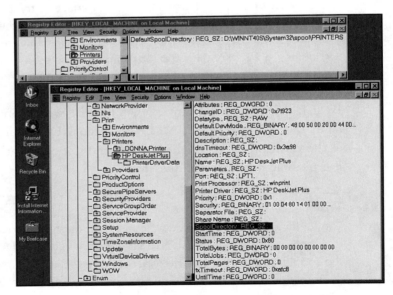

When planning an installation of Windows NT 4.0, especially if the installation will be a print server, allow for enough print spooler disk space.

Print Processor

The print processor is responsible for carrying out any further formatting or rendering of the print job required for the specific printer to understand it. The default print processor for Windows NT 4.0 is WINPRINT.DLL. It recognizes and renders the print job types listed in Table 10.1.

Table 10.1 WINPRINT.DLL Print Job Types

Type	Description
Raw Data	The most common print job type. It represents a print job that has been fully rendered and ready for the specific print device, such as PostScript.
Enhanced Metafile (EMF)	A portable format that can be used with any print device.
Text	Represents a print job rendered with raw, unformatted ASCII text and minimal control codes (linefeeds and carriage returns).
PSCRIPT1	Used on Windows NT servers running Services for Macintosh, it represents Postscript code from a Macintosh client destined for a non-Postscript print device on a Windows NT print server.

Print Monitor

As mentioned previously, the spooler tracks the location of the job and ensures that the print job reaches the appropriate destination. The Windows NT 4.0 print monitor is responsible for tracking the status of the print job. It controls the stream of jobs to the printer ports, sends the job to its destination print device, releases the port when finished, returns print device messages like `out of paper` or `out of toner`, and notifies the spooler when the print device has completed the generation of print output.

Table 10.2 outlines the print monitors supplied by Windows NT 4.0. The print monitor installed will depend on the print driver that you are using, the print device type such as Postscript, HPPCL, or DEC, as well as the network protocol used to direct print traffic.

Table 10.2   Windows NT 4.0 Print Monitors

Print Monitor	Description
LOCALMON.DLL	Monitors print jobs targeted for print devices connected to local ports.
HPMON.DLL	Monitors print jobs targeted for Hewlett-Packard network print devices. The DLC protocol must be installed on the print server, and the printer port identified by supplying the print device's hardware address.
SFMMON.DLL	Monitors Macintosh print jobs routed using AppleTalk protocol to network print devices.
LPRMON.DLL	Monitors print jobs targeted for print devices communicating through the TCP/IP protocol such as UNIX print devices and print spooler services.
DECPSMON.DLL	Monitors print jobs targeted for DEC's Digital PrintServer and other DEC print devices. Either the DECnet protocol or TCP/IP may be used to communicate with these print devices. Obtain the DECnet protocol from DEC (Digital Equipment Corporation).
LEXMON.DLL	Monitors print jobs targeted for Lexmark MarkVision print devices using DLC, TCP/IP, or IPX to communicate.

Print Monitor	Description
PJLMON.DLL	Monitors print jobs targeted for any bi-directional print device that uses the PJL (Printer Job Language) standard such as the HP LaserJet 5Si.

Additional LPD Device Information

The Line Printer Port print monitor (LPRMON.DLL) is loaded when the TCP/IP Printing Support service is installed on the print server. It is designed to facilitate the routing and tracking of print jobs destined for network-ready print devices that communicate using the TCP/IP protocol, or print devices that are connected to certain UNIX-based computers.

Windows NT provides two command-line utilities for directing and monitoring print jobs targeted for UNIX host printers called LPR.EXE and LPQ.EXE. If you are familiar with the UNIX environment you have probably used these commands before.

To direct a print job to a UNIX host print device, open a command prompt window and enter the command:

LPR –S *<IP address of UNIX host>* -P *<printer name>* *<filename>*

where *IP address of UNIX host* is the TCP/IP address of the printer or host computer to which the printer is attached, *printer name* is the shared name of the printer, and *filename* is the name of the print job that you are directing.

To receive queue information on the print server, enter the command:

LPQ –S *<IP address of UNIX host>* -P *<printer name>* –l

Key Concept

Note that the LPR and LPQ command switches (such as -S and -P) are case-sensitive.

Adding and Configuring Network Printing

This section will present how to create and share printers, set their characteristics and properties, assign security, and manage print jobs.

Adding a Printer

Recall the definition of a printer. When we speak of a *printer* in Windows NT 4.0, we are referring to the *print driver* and the interface through which we interact with the print device and from which we can monitor and manipulate print jobs.

The first step in creating a printer is to ensure that the print device is compatible with Windows NT 4.0. This information can be verified from the Hardware Compatibility List (HCL).

Only certain users have the ability to create printers and share them on the network. Administrators, of course, have this ability by default. However, members of the Print Operators and Server Operators groups on domain controllers, and Power Users group members on any other Windows NT Workstation or Server, can also perform this task.

Printers are added and connected to using the Add Printer Wizard, which is accessible through the Printers folder in My Computer or by choosing Start, Settings, Printers. The following paragraphs and figures will step through the process of adding a new printer that is physically connected to a local computer. The local computer (either workstation or server platform) will act as a print server for users on a network (either a workgroup or a domain).

To create a new printer, follow these steps:

1. From the Printers folder in My Computer, start the Add Printer Wizard by double-clicking Add Printer (see Figure 10.3).

2. If the printer is connected directly to this computer, keep the default setting <u>M</u>y Computer. N<u>e</u>twork Printer Server will be used to connect to a remote printer. Choose <u>N</u>ext.

FIG. 10.3 ⇒

This figure shows the Add Printer Wizard dialog box.

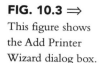
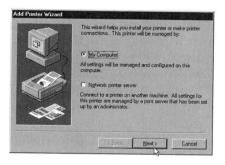

3. Select the port that the printer is physically attached to such as LPT1: or COM1: (see Figure 10.4). Use <u>C</u>onfigure Port to modify transmission retry of an LPT port or baud rate settings of the designated COM port. Choose <u>N</u>ext.

   If the print device is a network printer or is identified through a hardware or IP address, choose Add Por<u>t</u> to provide new port information, or select or add the appropriate print monitor. This information will be covered later in this chapter. You also have the option of enabling a printer pool. Printer pools and their benefits are discussed later in this chapter in the section "Print Pools."

FIG. 10.4 ⇒

In this example, the <u>A</u>vailable Ports window in the Add Printer Wizard dialog box indicates that the print device is physically attached to LPT1.

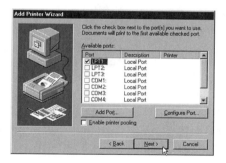

4. The list of supported print driver options has grown tremendously (see Figure 10.5). The driver selection menu has been divided into a <u>M</u>anufacturers list and a <u>P</u>rinters list. If the device you are installing is not represented in the list, and you have an OEM disk with a Windows NT compatible driver on it, choose <u>H</u>ave Disk to install it. Choose <u>N</u>ext.

FIG. 10.5 ⇒

In the Add Printer Wizard Dialog Box, you can see the selection of a print driver for the HP LaserJet 4.

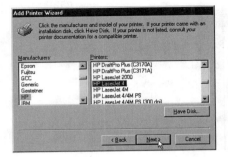

5. Enter a Printer Name that is descriptive of the print device (see Figure 10.6). This is the name that print administrators will use to identify the printer. Also, if the printer is being installed for local use, identify it as the default printer for use by applications if you like. The first installed printer will always be designated as the default. Choose Next.

FIG. 10.6 ⇒

In this example, the Printer Name remains the default name of the print device and will be the default print device for applications run on this computer.

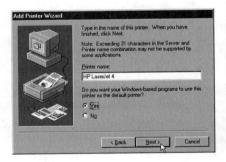

6. If the printer is to be shared, you can do so by selecting the Shared radio button and supplying a share name; otherwise, by default, the Not Shared radio button is selected. The printer can always be shared later. When sharing a printer, enter a Share Name that is descriptive for the users that will connect to this printer (see Figure 10.7). Choose Next.

FIG. 10.7 ⟹

This printer has been shared using the user-friendly name of ACCT-HP4.

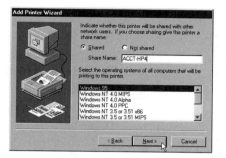

> **Note** Also, in the list box on the lower portion of the Add Printer
> Wizard dialog box, a list of drivers for alternate platforms
> appears allowing all required drivers to be installed. For example, if
> Windows 95 clients will be accessing this printer, and you want to down-
> load the driver to each client rather than installing it separately on every
> Windows 95 client, then select Windows 95 from the list. The Printer
> Wizard will prompt you later for the Windows 95 source files. Any required
> drivers can always be added at a later time.
>
> Note that in this example, the Windows 95 drivers have been selected to
> be installed. ▨

7. The Printer Wizard then asks if you would like to print a test page to the print device. This is usually a good idea, especially if you are identifying a network print device through a hardware or IP address. Choose Finish.

8. As Windows NT installs the print driver, you will note the various driver files, DLLs, monitor files, and so forth being loaded. If asked, supply the path to the location of the Windows NT 4.0 source files.

9. As the installation completes, the Printer Wizard adds an icon to represent the printer in the Printer folder (see Figure 10.8), and asks whether the test page printed successfully. If it did, the installation is complete. If it did not, you have the opportunity to go back and modify your settings. The new printer icon is your access to the print manager for that printer, its jobs, and its print device(s).

FIG. 10.8 ⟹

Notice the new HP LaserJet 4 icon created in the Printers dialog box. By double-clicking the HP LaserJet 4 icon, the print manager window for that printer is displayed.

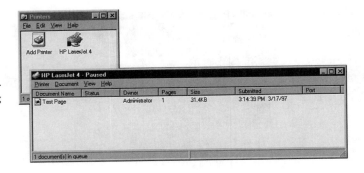

Sharing a Printer

If a printer was not shared during installation, it can be shared at a later time and permissions can also be configured. The default permission for shared printers allows Everyone to print permissions.

To share a printer use these steps:

1. Display the printer's property sheet by secondary-clicking the Printer's icon in the Printers dialog box and choosing Properties. Or, double-click the Printer's icon in the Printers dialog box, choose the Printer drop-down menu, and choose Properties.

2. Select the Sharing tab.

3. Enter a user-friendly share name. This is the name that users will see when they are determining which printer to connect to. Make the share name descriptive and informative.

Note Printer share names, as is true with all share names, must remain within the eight-character range in order for non-Windows NT/Windows 95 clients to be able to see the share name. If the share name is longer than eight characters, MS-DOS and Windows 3.1/3.11 network clients may not be able to connect to the printer. ■

4. Optionally, choose to install an alternate platform printer driver if needed.

5. Choose OK. The printer will now be shared.

Setting Permissions for the Shared Printer

There are no permissions that you can set directly on a printer share. Instead, permissions are set on the printer itself. There are four permissions that can be used to secure a printer in Windows NT 4.0:

◆ *No Access* means just that. Regardless of whatever permission you have been assigned through group membership, if you get No Access explicitly or through a group, you will not be able to access the printer to print *or* view the print jobs.

◆ *Print* permission is the default permission for the Everyone group. It allows users to connect to the printer, send print jobs to the printer, and manage their own print jobs. Users can delete, pause, resume, or restart print jobs owned by the user.

◆ *Manage Documents* allows all the permissions of Print and extends job management to *all* print jobs.

◆ *Full Control*, in addition to the permissions allowed for Manage Documents, lets the user modify printer settings, enable or disable sharing, delete printers, and modify permissions.

Like file and folder permissions, the permission list is actually the Access Control List (ACL) for the printer. By default, Administrators and Power Users are given Full Control on Windows NT Workstations and Member Servers; Administrators, Print Operators, and Server Operators have Full Control on Windows NT domain controllers. On all Windows NT computers, Everyone has Print permission and Creator Owner has Manage Documents permissions. The Creator Owner group is a special internal group that Windows NT uses to identify the owner of a file, folder, or in this case, a print job. By assigning it the Manage Documents permission, you are basically saying that only the owner of any given print job has the ability to pause, resume, delete, resend, or cancel it.

To secure a printer, use these steps:

1. Display the printer's property sheet by secondary-clicking the Printer's icon in the Printers dialog box and choosing Properties.

Or, double-click the Printer's icon in the Printers dialog box, choose the Printer drop-down menu, and choose Properties.

2. Select the Security tab.

3. Choose Permissions to display the Printer Permissions dialog box. The current ACL for the printer is displayed in the Name list box (see Figure 10.9).

FIG. 10.9 ⇒

In the Printer Permissions dialog box for the HP LaserJet 4, the Everyone group has been removed and the Developers group has been added with Print permission.

4. Modify the access of the current ACL entries by selecting the entry and choosing a Type of Access; choose Remove to remove entries from the list (like Everyone, Print); or choose Add to add user and group accounts from the local or domain SAM database.

5. Choose OK to save the permissions.

Auditing the Printer

As with files and folders, access to a printer can be audited, provided auditing has been enabled in User Manager (see Figure 10.10). The audit events are saved as part of the Security log, which can be viewed through the Event Viewer utility after auditing is enabled through User Manager or User Manager for Domains from the Policies drop-down menu. File and Object Access must be selected after auditing is enabled.

Auditing for the printer can be configured by selecting Auditing from the Security tab on the printer's property sheet. Recall that you audit the activities of specific users and groups regarding the printer rather than general access to the printer.

In the Printer Auditing dialog box, select <u>A</u>dd to display the account database. Select the users and groups for whom you want to record printer activity. In the Printer Auditing dialog box, select the activities you want to audit.

FIG. 10.10 ⇒
In this example, users who are members of the Developers and Managers groups that print to this printer will be recorded in the Security log of the Event Viewer.

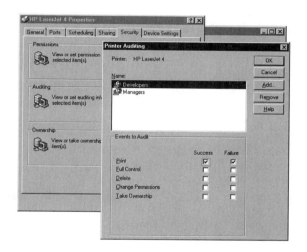

Part

III

Ch

10

> **Caution**
> Auditing causes additional overhead on resources and the processor. It is designed as a troubleshooting technique rather than as a reporting tool.

Taking Ownership of a Printer

The user who creates the printer becomes the owner of the printer (usually an administrator). If for some reason that user is no longer able to manage a printer, another user can be given permission to take ownership of a given printer.

Members of the Administrators, Print Operators, Server Operators, and Power Users groups have the ability to take ownership of a printer. Also, any other user or group that has been given Full Control permission for the printer can take ownership of that printer.

To take ownership of the printer, navigate to the printer's property sheet, select the Security tab, and choose Ownership. Then choose Take Ownership.

Working with Printer Properties

Up to this point, this chapter has reviewed only two tabs of the printer's property sheet: the Sharing tab and the Securities tab. This part of the chapter will explore the remaining printer properties tabs.

General Tab

The General tab gives you the option of entering a descriptive comment about the printer, such as who can use it, what options it provides, and so on (see Figure 10.11). A descriptive location of the printer can also be entered here. This is useful when users are browsing for printers, viewing print manager screens, or receiving device-specific messages.

FIG. 10.11 ⟹

In this printers Properties sheet, a comment and descriptive location have been added. When users view the printers or receive device-specific messages, they will see the location as well.

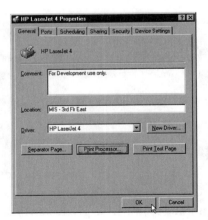

Using the General tab, you can also identify a Separator Page, select an alternate Print Processor, or choose the Print Test Page option.

Separator pages, sometimes called banner pages, identify and separate print output by printing a page before the document that indicates who submitted the document, as well as the date and time it was printed. Separator pages also have the function of switching a printer between modes. Windows NT provides three separator pages located in <winntroot>\SYSTEM32 as shown in Table 10.3. Separator pages can be selected by choosing the Separator Page button.

Table 10.3   Windows NT 4.0 Separator Pages

Separator File	Description
SYSPRINT.SEP	Causes a page to print before each document and is compatible with PostScript print devices.
PCL.SEP	Causes the device to switch to PCL mode for HP devices and prints a page before each document.
PSCRIPT.SEP	Causes the device to switch to PostScript mode for HP devices and does not print a page before each document.

Separator pages are text files and can be created and saved with a .SEP extension in the <winnt root>\SYSTEM32 directory using any text editor. Control characters that you can use to customize a separator page include:

- ◆ \N returns the name of the user who sent the document.
- ◆ \D returns the date the document was printed.
- ◆ \T returns the time the document was printed.
- ◆ \H*nn* sets a printer-specific control sequence based on a specified hexadecimal ASCII code.

Note More information about creating custom separator pages can be found in the online help and in the Books folder on the Windows NT Server CD. Simply choose Find and search for "separator." ■

The Print Processor button lets you specify an alternate print processor for the print device and port, and modify the job types it creates to accommodate your applications. For example, WINPRINT.DLL offers five default print job types including RAW (the default), RAW (FF appended), RAW (FF auto), NT EMF 1.003, and TEXT.

If an application is not adding a form feed to the end of the document when the application sends a print job to a particular printer, the last page may remain stuck in the printer. You might choose RAW (FF appended) to force a form feed on the end of any document sent to the printer, or RAW (FF auto) to let the print processor decide.

Note The Print Test Page button can be used at any time to test a change in printer configuration. ■

Ports Tab

The Ports tab is used for a number of different activities. First, you can use it to view which port the printer and print device are associated with and what kind of print device it is.

From this tab, you could also change the port associated with a given printer. For example, if the LPT1 port has failed and you move the print device to the LPT2 port, you need only change the port designation here rather than create a new printer.

The port associations listed here can also be used to redirect print output from one printer to another. For example, if the printer stalls for some reason—perhaps because of a failed port, broken printer, or problem print job—the output of the printer can be redirected from the current printer to another printer such as a remote printer (see Figure 10.12).

> **Note** It would be good idea to test this type of redirection before implementing it. If the spooling has been done in extended metafile format (EMF), the print job will print correctly. If not, the remote print device needs to be identical to the printer from which you are redirecting. ∎

FIG. 10.12 ⇒
Here the HP LaserJet 4 has been redirected from LPT1 to a remote printer HP on a server named Glemarek.

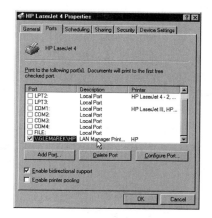

Use the Add Port button to add additional ports such as a network port IP address for an LPD-enabled print device. For example, if you need to redirect print jobs from an existing printer to a network printer, use Add Port to add the remote printer to the list of ports, then select it from the list on the Ports tab. Use the Delete Port button to delete ports that you no longer need. Use the Configure Port button to modify the LPT transmission retry value, COM port settings, and so on.

Bidirectional Support

When the print device associated with the printer you installed supports the sending of setting and status information back to the printer, we say it provides bidirectional support. Any extra information about the print process that you can get will be helpful in troubleshooting. If the print device supports this feature, select Enable Bidirectional Support.

Print Pools

One of the most useful configuration activities you can perform from the Ports tab is the creation of a *printer pool*. A printer pool represents one printer (queue or software interface) associated with two or more print devices. In other words, the same printer driver and management window is used to interact with two or more print devices that are compatible with that printer driver. This type of arrangement is particularly efficient on a network with a high volume of printing. Print jobs sent to the pool will print on the next available print device, thus reducing the time jobs stay in queue. In addition, you only need to manage one printer rather than several.

As shown in Figure 10.13, three print devices are available for use on a print server computer. An HP LaserJet 4 is connected to LPT1, another HP LaserJet 4 is connected to LPT2, and an HP LaserJet III is connected to COM1. Three separate printers (one for each print device) can be created; however, this does not stop users from favoring one printer over another. Users may not choose, for example, the HPIII printer because of its slower performance. Consequently, print jobs may get stacked up on the other two printers.

FIG. 10.13 ⇒

Three printers have been configured as a printer pool in this example.

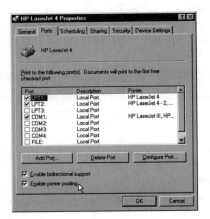

By associating one printer with all three devices, users have only one shared printer choice to make and their print jobs will be serviced by any of the configured print devices. However, the user will not know which printing device the job will be printed to. For this reason, physically position all printing devices in the printer pool in the same location.

To set up a print pool use these steps:

1. Choose Enable Printer Pooling on the Ports tab.

2. Check the ports connected to the print devices you want as part of the pool.

3. Click OK.

> **Caution**
>
> Make sure that the print device you associate with the printer in the printer pool supports that print driver. If it does not, print output may be unintelligible.
>
> For example, while the HP LaserJet 4 printer driver is downward compatible with an HP LaserJet III print device, it definitely will not support an HP LaserJet 5Si. All of the print devices in the print pool must be able to use the same print driver.

Printer pools can be combined with other printers to produce a variety of output control options for the print manager. For example, three shared printers are created: one for Developers, one for Accountants, and one for Managers. Permissions are configured so that members of each group can only print to their specified printer; however, it is imperative that any of the Manager's print jobs get printed as quickly as possible.

The Manager's printer is configured into a print pool by associating it with the other two print devices. Now Developers and Accountants each have one print device that services their print jobs, but all of the Manager's print jobs can be printed on any of three printers.

Scheduling Tab

The Scheduling tab, besides allowing you to define the time when the printer can service jobs, lets you set a priority for the printer and define additional spool settings as shown in Figure 10.14. All three of these option settings will assist a print administrator to further refine how and when print jobs are serviced.

FIG. 10.14 ⟹

This printer will begin sending print jobs to the print device after 10 PM. It will also wait until the entire job has been spooled before it sends it, and will print jobs that have finished spooling ahead of jobs that are still spooling.

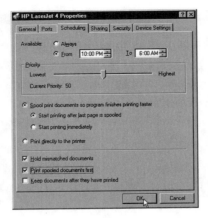

Available Time

Defining the time the printer can service jobs is fairly straightforward. Select the Available: From radio button and select the time range you want. Print jobs sent to this printer will still be spooled, but will not print until the designated time.

For example, suppose that you have a color LaserJet print device to which several different groups of users send print jobs. One group, Graphics, tends to send very large graphic files that cause the other group's print jobs to wait in the spooler. You could create a separate printer for that print device and assign only the Graphics group print access. Then, you could set the printing time to print at off-peak hours. The Graphics group's print jobs will then wait in queue until the print time for their printer is reached.

Priority

When a priority is configured for a printer, the priority is really being set for all print jobs received by that printer. The printer priority can be set from 1 (lowest) to 99 (highest).

Setting a priority on a printer really only makes sense when you want documents sent to the *same* print device to have different priorities to that device. The key to making a priority effective is to associate two or more printers with the *same* print device. This is the exact opposite of creating a printer pool in which only *one* printer is associated with *two or more* print devices.

After you have created and associated a number of printers with one print device, the priority for each printer is configured from the Scheduling tab by using the sliding bar under Priority.

The priority theory can be illustrated as follows. Three groups: Managers, Developers, and Accountants will all be using the same HP LaserJet 5Si network print device. Accountants send large spreadsheets to the printer, while Developers send small to medium source files. Managers, on the other hand, always want their documents to print as soon as possible.

To solve this printing scenario, create three *printers* and associate each with the *same* HP LaserJet 5Si print device. Set permissions so that each group can only print to their respective printer and then set the priority for each printer as follows:

99 (highest) for the printer used by Managers

50 (medium) for the printer used by Accountants

1 (lowest) for the printer used by Developers

Because the Managers' printer has been given the highest priority, their print jobs will print ahead of the Accountants' and Developers' print jobs. Likewise, because the Accountants' printer has been given a medium priority, their print jobs will print ahead of Developers' print jobs. Since the Developers' printer has the lowest priority, their print jobs will always wait until Managers' and Accountants' print jobs finish printing.

Key Concept

Priorities will not affect a job that has begun printing. If a Developers' print job has begun printing, the Managers' print job will wait until it is finished. However, any subsequent Developers' print jobs will wait until Managers' and Accountants' print jobs have completed.

Part

III

Ch

10

Other Spool Options

There are several other options that can be used to determine how jobs are spooled. These options, in combination with print pools and priorities, give the print administrator many choices for affecting how, when, and where print jobs are printed.

The first is Spool Print Documents so Program Finishes Printing Faster. This option is set by default, and simply means that print requests will be spooled in the Printers folder rather than sent directly to the printer, resulting in a faster return to the application for the user.

If you choose Spool Print Documents so Program Finishes Printing Faster, two secondary options are available. Start Printing Immediately—set by default—indicates that the print job will be sent to the print device for printing as soon as enough information has been spooled. Printing, of course, will be faster overall. The other option, Start Printing After Last Page Is Spooled, indicates that the print job will not be sent to the print device for printing until the entire job has been spooled. When used with printers of different priorities, this option can be effectively used to prevent large documents from "hogging" the print device. Smaller documents will be printed first, because they will be spooled first.

The other option is to Print Directly to the Printer. In this case, the print job is not spooled. It decreases printing time because the rendered print job is sent directly to the print device. However, the user will wait until the print job is complete before control is returned to the application.

Did you ever experience the problem of sending a legal size print job to a print device that only had a letter size tray? The print job will hang the print device. The Hold Mismatched Documents option is designed to prevent that from happening by comparing the format of the print job with the configuration of the printer. If they do not match, the print job will be held in queue and not allowed to print while other print jobs in the queue will proceed.

The Print Spooled Documents First option allows print jobs that have completed spooling to print ahead of those that are still spooling, even if their priority is lower. When used with the Start Printing After Last Page Is Spooled option, it virtually assures that smaller print jobs will print ahead of larger print jobs. If no print jobs have finished spooling, larger jobs will print ahead of smaller jobs.

When a print job finishes printing, the spooler deletes the print job from the queue (the printers folder), which deletes it from the printer management window. If you would like to keep the document in queue to see its complete status, to keep open the option of resubmitting the job, or to redirect it to another printer if it prints incorrectly, choose Keep Documents After They Have Printed option. After the print job is completed, it will be held in the spooler rather than be deleted, and its status will be displayed. For example, if you have an end-of-month report that is difficult to reproduce and you would like to resubmit it, use this option to keep the job in the spooler. On the other hand, the jobs do remain in the spooler folder taking up space and it becomes the responsibility of the print administrator to remove these jobs when they are no longer needed.

Device Settings Tab

The Device Settings tab is used to assign forms to paper trays, indicate the amount of memory installed in the print device, specify font cartridges, and configure other device-specific settings such as soft font or halftone settings.

Configuring these options is as easy as selecting the option you want to configure and choosing a setting from the list box displayed in the lower portion of the dialog box. The options that are available, and their settings, will depend on the print device (or the printer) you installed. For example, while an HP LaserJet 4 only has one paper tray, an HP LaserJet 5Si may have several, including an envelope feed. The Device Settings tab will reflect these device features.

Part

III

Ch

10

> **Note**   Some printers offer page protection as a feature, and this option will be displayed on the Device Settings tab. Page protection ensures that the print device prints each page in memory before creating the output page. If you regularly send print jobs whose pages are composed of complex text and graphics, enabling this option will help ensure that the print device prints the page successfully rather than possibly breaking the page up as it prints it. ■

Managing the Printer and Its Documents

Double-clicking a printer icon in the Printers dialog box displays its print management window. There are four menu options to choose from: Printer, Document, View, and Help. View and Help are fairly self-explanatory. Most of your time will be spent using the Printer and Document options.

Printer Drop-Down Menu

From the Printer drop-down menu, you can pause the printer, change the default printer for the computer, manage sharing and permissions, purge all documents from the spooler, and manage printer properties. In addition, you can set document defaults that apply to all print jobs sent to the printer. Among the options that can be set are the paper size, paper tray, number of copies, orientation, and resolution settings.

Document Drop-Down Menu

From the Document drop-down menu, you can pause, resume, restart, and cancel print jobs. Each print job also has individual properties that can be set much like the properties for the printer itself.

Individual print jobs can have their properties set just like printers. However, the most important options, such as scheduling a time and priority for the job, are available (see Figure 10.15). Only users who have Full Control or Manage Documents permissions, or the owner of the document, can modify the print job's properties.

FIG. 10.15 ⇒

The Budget document is scheduled to print between 12 A.M. and 1:30 A.M. with the highest priority.

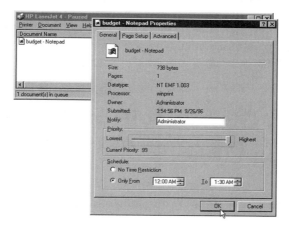

Display a print job's properties by highlighting the document in the printer management window and selecting <u>D</u>ocument, P<u>r</u>operties or by double-clicking the print job.

The General tab displays statistics about the print job such as its size, number of pages, data type, print processor, its owner, and when it was submitted. In addition, you can specify a user account to send a message to when the print job is complete.

You can set an individual priority for the job here like you did for the printer; however, the priority selected here overrides the printer priority. If there is one particular large print job that has been sent to a low priority printer that needs to be printed as soon as possible, you can set its priority higher from this tab. The priority change only affects the specific print job; other jobs will use the priority setting of the printer (print queue).

Finally, time restrictions can be set for the individual print jobs. Using Figure 10.15 as an example, suppose the Budget document is a large job that has been sent to the low priority Developers' printer. Other jobs have undoubtedly been sent to the Managers and Accountants printers that have higher priorities. Budget's individual property settings are being set from this document properties sheet to ensure that it will print with the highest priority between 12 AM and 1:30 AM.

The Page Setup and Advanced tabs let you set additional options for the particular document such as the paper size, paper tray, number of copies, orientation, and resolution settings.

Exploring DLC, TCP/IP, and Macintosh Installation Options

The following paragraphs and figures will illustrate and detail the installation options pertaining to installing and configuring network print devices using the DLC, TCP/IP, and AppleTalk protocols.

DLC Printing

When configuring a print server to communicate with a network interfaced print device using DLC you must first install the DLC protocol on the print server. Installing the DLC protocol is covered in Chapter 8, "Configuring Domain Network Core Services." This must be done in order to select any of the available network interfaced print devices. Once the DLC protocol is installed, the Hewlett-Packard Network Port choice becomes available in the Printer Ports dialog box as shown in Figure 10.16.

When the Hewlett-Packard Network Port is chosen and the New Port button is selected, the Add Hewlett-Packard Network Peripheral Port dialog box appears. In this window where the pointer is shown (refer to Figure 10.16), all available network interfaced print device MAC addresses are displayed. Simply select the desired print device for this port by its MAC address, give the device a name, and choose OK. After a port is created for each available network interface print device, each port can be configured as shared on the print server. Printer pools can also be configured using any number of the DLC ports.

FIG.10.16 ⟹

This figure is an example of adding a Hewlett-Packard Network DLC Printer Port

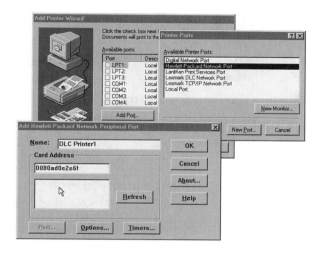

Additional DLC configuration options include selecting the Options and Timers buttons from the Add Hewlett-Packard Network Peripheral Port dialog box. The Advanced Options for All HP Network Ports dialog box is shown in Figure 10.17 and is accessed by selecting the Options button. The HP Network Peripheral Port Timers dialog box is shown in Figure 10.18 and is accessed by selecting the Timers button.

FIG. 10.17 ⟹

This is an example of setting advanced options for All HP Network Ports.

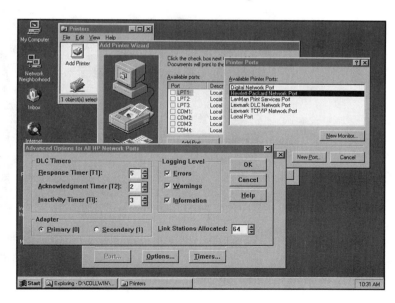

The DLC Timers options control the network timing parameters and include the Response Timer (T1), the Acknowledgment Timer (T2), and the Inactivity Timer (Ti). The only time these parameters should be changed is if timeouts consistently occur on extremely busy networks.

The Logging Level options control how much information is placed in the event log. By default, all errors, warnings, and information events are entered in the event log.

The Adapter Primary (0) or Secondary (1) option allows the HPMON software to use one of two possible adapter cards installed in the computer. The default is shown in Figure 10.17 and is Primary (0).

The Link Stations Allocated option specifies how many network peripherals can be configured on this print server. The default is 64, with a range of 1 to 255. One link station is required for each print device configured.

FIG. 10.18 ⇒

Here is an example of configuring the HP Network Peripheral Port Timers dialog box.

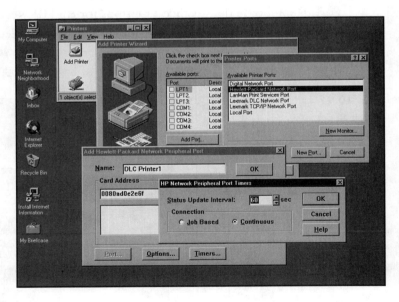

In the HP Network Peripheral Port Timers dialog box, the Status Update Interval is simply the interval in which the status of print devices will be updated. The default is 60 seconds with a range of 1 to 32,767 seconds.

The Connection options control how the print server will communicate with the network interface print device. If Continuous (the default) is selected, the server maintains a connection with the print device until either the server or the peripheral is turned off. This allows a single server to monopolize the network interface print device. If Job Based is selected, the workstation establishes a connection with the print device during each print job. No connection is maintained between jobs. This allows other print servers to use the network interface print device when this specific print server is not using it.

Figure 10.19 displays the Add Printer Wizard dialog box with a DLC Printer1 port configured.

FIG. 10.19 ⇒
Select a DLC configured print device using the Add Printer Wizard dialog box.

TCP/IP Printing

Printing to TCP/IP network interface print devices also requires specific installation configuration. The following paragraphs and figures outline these requirements.

In addition to the TCP/IP protocol, the Microsoft TCP/IP Printing service must also be installed on the print server. Recall that both the TCP/IP protocol and the Microsoft TCP/IP Printing service are installed from the Network icon in the Control Panel. Figure 10.20 covers the Microsoft TCP/IP Printing service installation.

FIG. 10.20 ⇒

This figure shows how to install the Microsoft TCP/IP Printing service.

Once the Microsoft TCP/IP Printing service is installed, the LPR Port option is available for adding and configuring LPR ports in the Printer Ports dialog box as shown in Figure 10.21.

FIG. 10.21 ⇒

This figure shows how to add and configure a LPR Printer Port.

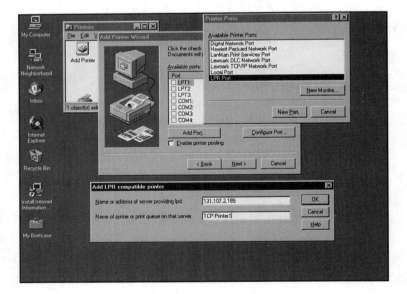

From the Printer Ports dialog box, the New Port button is selected and the Add LPR compatible printer dialog box appears. Two options in this dialog box must be configured: Name or Address of Server

Providing lpd and Name of Printer or Print Queue on That Server. These configuration options can be extremely misleading. The first option, Name or Address of Server Providing lpd, requires the name or address of the MAC installed in the network interface print device, or the address of the MAC installed in a special electronic controller attached to the print device. This could be a UNIX computer that controls a print device, or a Fiery PC controlling a Savin color laser print device.

Key Concept

The address required in the Name or Address of Server Providing lpd text box is *not* the IP address of the print server.

After the port is added, it is accessible in the Available Ports window to be selected and configured with the specific type of print device as shown in Figure 10.22.

FIG. 10.22 ⟹
Select a TCP/IP
configured print
device using the
Add Print Wizard
dialog box.

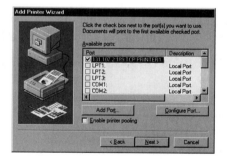

Macintosh Printing

After the AppleTalk protocol is installed on the Windows NT workstation platform or the Services for Macintosh service is installed on a Windows NT Server platform, either platform can function as a print server for AppleTalk print devices. Simply highlight the AppleTalk Printing Devices option in the Printer Ports dialog box and select the Add Port button. The Available Appletalk Printing Devices selection window appears listing the Appletalk print devices available (see Figure 10.23).

FIG. 10.23 ⇒
Select one of the
print devices for
each port and
configure each port
in the print server.

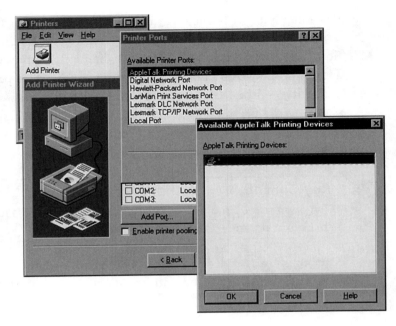

> **Note**   Print devices attached to and configured on the Windows NT
> print server will be available for selection on the Macintosh
> computers in Chooser. ■

Troubleshooting Printing

This troubleshooting discussion contains some extremely basic steps to
follow when the printing process fails. The following bullets outline this
troubleshooting checklist:

◆ Check to see if the print device is turned on and online.

◆ Check to see whether the physical print device connection is
good. Swap out cables, and check the network card and IP address.
Also verify the configured MAC address.

◆ Verify that the printer driver installed is compatible with the print device. Verify that the correct version of print driver is installed (3.1, 3.5/3.51, 4.0, or 95). Also verify that the print driver for the correct platform is installed (I386, Alpha, MIPS, or PowerPC).

◆ Confirm that the printer is available and has been selected. Verify that sharing has been enabled and that the permissions allow printing to take place for the users affected.

◆ Verify that the appropriate print port has been selected and configured by printing a test page.

◆ Monitor network traffic in the case of remote printing to verify that print jobs are being routed correctly and not being dropped.

◆ Check the amount of disk space available for spooling. Recall that the default spool directory is <winnt root>\SYSTEM32\Spool \Printers. The installation partition often only contains the Windows NT files and is kept purposely small. If there is not enough space for the spooled files, printing will fail. Either add more disk space (extend the partition if it is NTFS), or move the spool folder to a disk with adequate space by editing the Registry. Disk compression could also be enabled for the spool directory; however, this could have a negative effect on printing performance for large print jobs. Recall that the Registry location to change the default spool folder is HKEY_LOCAL_MACHINE\System\ CurrentControlSet\Control\Print\Printers.

◆ Determine whether the printing problem is due to a specific application error, or occurs within all applications. Some MS-DOS and Windows 16-bit applications may require their own print drivers installed to successfully print their documents.

◆ Determine whether the printing problem is due to a non-updated print driver installed on a Windows 95 client. Recall that there is not version checking done between a Windows NT print server and a Windows 95 client; the update must be done manually on the Windows 95 client.

Part

III

Ch

10

◆ Resubmit the print job to print to a file and then copy the file to a printer port. If the job prints successfully, the problem may be related to the spooler or transmission process. If not, the problem is probably related to the application or printer driver.

Another source of help for troubleshooting printing problems is the built-in Windows NT Help program. It also provides a set of trouble-shooting steps and tips to help resolve printing-related problems. Access help for printing problems by following these steps:

1. Select Help, Help Topics from the menu of any window opened through My Computer or Network Neighborhood; or select the Start button and choose Help from the Start Menu.

2. Choose the Contents tab in the Help dialog box.

3. Double-click the contents entry titled Troubleshooting.

4. Select the topic If You Have Trouble Printing.

5. Find the problem you are having and click it.

6. Help will guide you through a series of questions and suggestions to help resolve the problem.

7. Exit Help when you are finished by closing the Help window.

Additional Considerations

As noted earlier, most printing problems stem from an improper print driver, inadequate disk space, incorrect port or address settings, or re-strictive permissions. Also, recall that most older MS-DOS based applications, and some Windows-based applications require that their own printer driver be installed. Be sure to consider these possibilities as well when troubleshooting.

Windows-based applications will print just like they did under Windows. Settings saved in WIN.INI or CONFIG.SYS are copied into the Windows NT Registry and will be used for these applications printing under Windows NT. Applications that produce PostScript-specific graphics will probably print incorrectly or not at all. If no default printer has been selected, these applications produce an out-of-memory error message when loading or will not allow selection of fonts.

If print jobs stall in a printer, or no one is able to print to it any longer, the spooler has probably stalled. The spooler can be purged of its documents by starting the Print Manager for that printer, selecting the Print drop-down menu, and choosing Purge Print Documents. The spooler service can also be stopped and restarted through the Services applet in the Control Panel to purge the specific job that is stalled.

If your print server and clients happen to be of different or mixed platforms, and you want the print server to download the appropriate driver to all the Windows NT Workstations, you need to install the appropriate platform drivers on the print server. A given print server may have multiple platform drivers installed for just this purpose.

For example, suppose that your print server is a RISC-based DEC Alpha computer. The Windows NT clients connecting to shared printers on the print server are Intel-based computers. You must install the Windows NT 4.0 Alpha printer driver in order for the print server to interact successfully with the print device. In addition, the Windows NT 4.0 Intel print driver must be installed on the print server for it to automatically download the Intel print driver to Intel clients. When an Intel client accesses the shared printer, the Intel driver will be downloaded to them. The Alpha print server, in turn, will use the Alpha driver to manage the print job on the print device.

Table 10.4 lists the folders in which the drivers will be located for Windows 95 and the different Windows NT versions. The printer driver location starts with <Winnt root>\System32\Spool\Drivers\.

Table 10.4   Windows NT Printer Driver Locations

Location	Description
Win40	Windows 95 Drivers
w32×86\0	Windows NT 3.1 Intel Drivers

continues

Table 10.4 Continued	
Location	Description
w32×86\1	Windows NT 3.5/3.51 Intel Drivers
w32×86\2	Windows NT 4.0 Intel Drivers
Alpha\0	Windows NT 3.1 Alpha Drivers
Alpha\1	Windows NT 3.5/3.51 Alpha Drivers
Alpha\2	Windows NT 4.0 Alpha Drivers
MIPS\0	Windows NT 3.1 MIPS Drivers
MIPS\1	Windows NT 3.1 5/3.51 MIPS Drivers
MIPS\2	Windows NT 4.0 MIPS Drivers
PPC\0	Windows NT 3.1 PPC Drivers
PPC\1	Windows NT 3.5/3.51 PPC Drivers
PPC\2	Windows NT 4.0 PPC Drivers

Taking the Disc Test

 If you have read and understood the material in the chapter, you are ready to test your knowledge. Insert the CD-ROM that comes with this book and run the self-test software as described in Appendix I, "Using the CD-ROM."

From Here...

In the next chapter, "Network Client Configuration and Support," you will look at the network client administrator program and learn how to create an over-the-network installation disk for some clients and make installation disk sets for other clients. You will also become aware of the various types of client software available on the Server CD-ROM. Troubleshooting client connectivity will also be covered along with installing and working with Services for Macintosh.

Network Client Configuration and Support

This chapter discusses the different options for the network administrator to create a network startup installation disk and installation disk sets. You learn about the server tools that are available for administering the Windows NT domain from a Windows NT Workstation or Windows 95 operating system. Also, you learn about the services for Macintosh.

In this chapter, you learn how to:

◆ Use Network client administrator

◆ Use client based server tools

◆ Work with the Macintosh clients

Using Network Client Administrator

Network Client Administrator is a tool provided with the server compact disc to enable the administrator to graphically create an installation startup disk or disk sets. You can make the disks for the following clients:

◆ Microsoft Network Client 3.0 for MS-DOS

◆ LAN Manager 2.2c

◆ Microsoft Windows 95

◆ Network Client Administrator tool

Windows NT software maintains support for the Windows for Workgroups 3.11 client that was available on the Windows NT 3.51 compact disc. It does not ship with Windows NT 4.0. The TCP/IP-32 add-on for Windows for Workgroups does ship with the Windows NT 4.0 CD.

Microsoft Network Client 3.0 for MS-DOS

Microsoft Network Client 3.0 provides MS-DOS computers network connectivity and resource access to Windows NT Servers. Microsoft Network Client for MS-DOS supports NetBEUI, IPX compatible protocol, TCP/IP, and DLC.

In addition, the TCP/IP protocol supports the Dynamic Host Configuration Protocol (DHCP). It does not support Windows Internet Name Service (WINS) or Domain Name System (DNS). Network Client 3.0 for DOS supports Internetwork Packet exchange transport only. It does not support the Sequenced Packet exchange transport.

The client can be installed using either a full redirector or basic redirector. A *full redirector* allows the client to log on to a network domain as a valid user, access services and resources, and run the logon scripts. By default, Microsoft Network Client for MS-DOS supports the full redirector. Basic redirector allows access to a server using a guest account. Of course, the server must have the guest account enabled. The client makes use of this Remote Access Service (RAS) version 1.1, messaging, and Inter Process Communication (IPC) mechanisms such as named pipes, RPC, and Winsock. IPC mechanisms allow programs to communicate with each other, on the same machine or across the network.

LAN Manager 2.2c Clients

Two options exist for LAN Manager clients: LAN Manager 2.2c for MS-DOS and LAN Manager 2.2c for OS/2. *LAN Manager 2.2c for MS-DOS* ships with NetBEUI, Microsoft DLC, and TCP/IP. It supports DHCP, but not DNS or WINS. Also included is a NetWare connectivity disk that allows clients to connect to a NetWare server. LAN Manager 2.2c for MS-DOS supports the Remoteboot service so that MS-DOS or a Windows 95 client may be remotely started. The server in this is used as the replacement for a local active partition.

LAN Manager 2.2c for OS/2 supports OS/2 2.1 and OS/2 2.x. The protocols you can use are NetBEUI and TCP/IP. This version of TCP/IP does not support DHCP or WINS and must have its address manually configured.

Part
III

Ch
11

Microsoft Windows 95

Windows 95 is a full 32-bit operating system with 32-bit networking interface that supports a full redirector using protected mode and/or real mode network drivers. Windows 95 supports NetBEUI, NWLink IPX/SPX, and TCP/IP protocols. TCP/IP supports DHCP, WINS, and DNS.

Network Client Administrator Tool

The Network Client Administrator tool is used to create the aforementioned client disks. It is found within the Administrative Tool's folder. Once you have started the client administrator tool, there are four options to choose from:

◆ Installation startup disk

◆ Make installation disk set

◆ Copy client-based network administration tools

◆ View remoteboot client information

The tool is designed to simplify the process of adding machines to a network, and managing client access to the network. The first two options—Installation Startup Disk and Make Installation Disk Set—create disks that can be used to set up a new computer with connectivity to Windows NT.

The Installation Startup Disk option requires that the server be available to the client when the installation is to occur, and that it have the installation files shared. The client administrator automatically handles this function. The Make Installation Disk Set option can be used when connectivity can't be immediately established with a server.

The Client Administration tool also allows you to prepare the Windows NT Server administration tools to Windows 95 or Windows 3.1. In addition, the Client Administration tool allows you to manage the remote boot settings for clients.

Installation Startup Disk

After you choose the installation startup disk option, you must select the path of the shared client's folder in the Share Network Client Installation Files dialog box from the clients directory on the CD. You can pick from an existing share. Share the client folder directly from the tool itself, or copy the files to a new location and re-share them. Select the client software you desire—for example, Network Client MS-DOS and Windows. Pick the target computer's network adapter card type and to which floppy density this software will be sent (3.5-inch or 5.25-inch).

Now, make the following selections:

1. Enter a unique name for the target computer.

2. Enter a user name that identifies the user to the network and domain.

3. Enter the domain name the target needs to log on to.

4. Choose your Network Protocol.

5. Enable DHCP configuration if you chose TCP/IP and there is a DHCP server.

   If you chose TCP/IP and there is no DHCP server, then enter the IP address, subnet mask, and default gateway.

6. Choose the destination path where files should be sent using the left mouse button to click choice box disk drive A or B.

Installation Disk Set

Installation disk sets are used to manually install software on client computers. Installation disk sets are made for Microsoft Network Client 3.0 for MS-DOS, Microsoft LAN Manager 2.2c for MS-DOS, and Microsoft LAN Manager 2.2c for OS/2. In addition, you can make disk sets for RAS for MS-DOS and TCP/IP 32 for Windows for Workgroups 3.11. Two or more disks are required to create an installation disk set for the clients. To create an installation disk set, use the Network Client Administration Tool then do the following:

1. Select Make Installation Disk Set from the Network Client Administrator dialog.

2. Select the appropriate Network client or Service from the list box.

3. Select the destination drive in the spin box.

4. If necessary, click Format Disks to have the Network Client Administrator format the disks for you.

5. Click the OK button.

Copy Client-Based Network Administration Tools

You use Copy Client-Based Network Administration tools to administer the domain environment from a Windows 95 or Windows NT Workstation. Of course, you must have the appropriate rights to use them. In the following section, you will examine the requirements for Windows 95 and Windows NT Workstation in order to use the tools, and what tools are available for each operating system.

Part
III

Ch
11

The minimum requirements needed to install Windows NT Server tools for Windows 95 are:

◆ CPU must be at least a 486DX/33

◆ 8M of RAM

◆ 3M of free disk space on the system partition because the Srvtools folder is created here

◆ You must be a client for the network you want to administer

The tools available to Windows 95 for managing the Windows NT Servers are:

◆ Event Viewer for the logs

◆ File Security for file and folder permissions

◆ Print Security

◆ Server Manager

◆ User Manager for Domains

◆ User Manager Extensions Services for NetWare, assuming you added on the File and Print Services for NetWare (FPNW) or Domain Services Manager for NetWare (DSMN)

◆ File and Print Services for NetWare (FPNW)

The minimum requirements needed to install Windows NT Server tools for Windows NT Workstation are:

◆ CPU must be at least a 486DX/33

◆ 12M of RAM

◆ 2.5M of free disk space on the system partition

◆ Workstation and Server services must be running. (These services are running by default.)

Located in the Administrative Tools folder, the tools available to manage the Windows NT Servers from a Windows NT Workstation are as follows:

◆ DHCP Manager for the DHCP service running on a server

◆ Remote Access Administer for the RAS on a RAS server

◆ Remoteboot Manager to configure the Remoteboot service

◆ Services for Macintosh to share Server resources with Apple Macintosh computers

◆ Server Manager

◆ System Policy Editor

◆ User Manager for Domains

◆ WINS Manager

Working with the Macintosh Clients

Services for Macintosh enable Microsoft and Apple clients to share files and printer resources with each other. Use the Control Panel and click the Network icon to add the services for Macintosh.

By adding this service, several features are automatically installed and enabled. If you have an NTFS partition, a *Macintosh Accessible Volume (MAV)* is created on the servers for the Mac user. This enables sharing for the Mac, and the Windows NT client will still have share access to the New Technology File System (NTFS) folder following the same Windows NT effective permission rules.

Printer services for Macintosh are also added automatically to allow either Microsoft client to access the Mac's available printer resources. Windows NT operating systems must use a LaserWriter 5.1 or higher level printer driver for the Mac PostScript printer. Printer services for the Mac also allow Macintosh clients to access any printer defined on the Windows NT Server. The postscript is converted to the native language of the printer by the server.

You manage Mac user accounts from the Windows NT Server. AppleTalk routing is supported with zones for establishing an AppleTalk Internetwork. AppleTalk File Protocol is added and supports 2.0 and 2.1 levels. Supported Mac clients must use version 6.07 or later.

Taking the Disc Test

 If you have read and understood the material in the chapter, you are ready to test your knowledge. Insert the CD-ROM that comes with this book and run the self-test software as described in Appendix I, "Using the CD-ROM."

From Here...

Now that you have examined the Windows NT Network Client Administrator utility, Chapters 12 and 13 take you into managing resources in the domain. Specifically, you review account management, especially global group management, security, permissions, and resource access.

Part IV.

Managing Domain Resources

Domain Users and Groups

This chapter will review the creation and management of accounts on Windows NT Server 4.0. This basic administrative function will be addressed primarily from the enterprise perspective, including a discussion of how to administer accounts across a trust relationship and remotely.

Topics covered in this chapter include:

◆ Discussing what user and group accounts are all about

◆ Creating user and group accounts in the domain

◆ Highlighting the uniqueness of account identification

◆ Managing users through global group accounts

◆ Exploring account policies and system rights

◆ Administering accounts through a trust relationship

◆ Troubleshooting account management issues

Understanding User and Group Accounts

The first screen that you see after booting Windows NT and pressing Ctrl+Alt+Delete is the Logon Security dialog box. It is here that you must enter your user name and password in order to gain access to the domain through network authentication—for example, the Net Logon process.

Key Concept

You should consider the user account as the first and foremost security object for access to your local and network resources.

Each user and group account that is created in the domain is unique to that Windows NT domain, and as such has a *unique* security identifier associated with it. This identifier is called the *Security Identifier*, more commonly referred to as the *SID*. All references made by Windows NT to any account, especially those dealing with security access and permissions, are linked to the SID.

If you delete the user account and re-create it *using exactly the same information*, Windows NT will create a new SID for that user, and all security access and permissions will have to be reestablished. The account information is stored in the *Security Accounts Manager (SAM)* database, which you will recall is part of the Windows NT 4.0 Registry—HKEY_LOCAL_MACHINE\SAM.

If the account is a *local account*—in other words, an account that a user uses to log on to a specific workstation at the workstation—the account is included in the SAM database of that workstation's Registry. If the account is a *network account*—meaning an account that is used to log on to the enterprise network from any given workstation—the account is included in the SAM database of the primary domain controller (PDC) for the account domain of the enterprise.

Key Concept

A local account, in general, will only have access to resources on the local workstation. A network account will have access as provided to network resources such as shared printers, files, and folders.

Note Refer to Chapter 2, "Windows NT 4.0 Directory Services Overview," for a review of Windows NT's Directory Services and the significance of the account database. ■

Default User Accounts

When you first install Windows NT Server 4.0, two default accounts are created for you: the Guest and Administrator accounts. Neither of these accounts can be deleted. For this reason, care must be taken to preserve the integrity of these accounts.

The *Guest account* provides the least amount of access for the user and is, in fact, disabled by default on both Windows NT Workstation and Server to prevent inadvertent access to resources. It is strongly recommended that you assign a password to this account (preferably something other than "password") and for additional security, rename the account. This account is automatically made a member of the default domain global group Domain Guests.

The *Administrator account*, as you might expect, provides the greatest amount of access and complete functional rights to the domain. Because this account is created by Windows NT by default, it also is the first account that a user has to log on to the domain controller with. In most organizations, this account is used to perform most every administrative task in the domain. Therefore, it is strongly recommended that this account be password-protected (again, with a unique, though memorable, password) and for additional security, it should also be renamed.

After all, if you were a hacker trying to break in with administrative access, the first account name you would try would probably be **administrator**, and then perhaps **supervisor** or **admin** or **XYZadmin** where *XYZ* is your company name. If this list has exhausted your choices for alternate administrator account names, good! With Internet access especially prevalent, enterprise security has become an extremely significant and sensitive issue.

Another suggestion that Microsoft makes is to create a separate user account for specific functional access. For example, Windows NT provides a default group that is local to the domain controllers called *Account Operators*. Members of this group are given just enough functional access to be able to successfully manage user and group accounts for the domain. The administrator might identify a user or users who have the responsibility of managing accounts, or create a specific user account for that purpose, and add them to the Account Operators group for the domain. The user would then use his or her account or the specific user account to access the domain and manage accounts. This eliminates a potential security "hole"—for example, being logged in as administrator and leaving for lunch without locking the workstation or logging out. This may not be quite so significant when logged on as a local administrator, but becomes far more disconcerting when logged on to a domain as a network administrator.

Default Group Accounts

When you first install Windows NT Server 4.0, eight default local groups are created for you:

- Administrators
- Users
- Guests
- Backup Operators
- Server Operators
- Account Operators
- Print Operators
- Replicator

These groups are considered *local* groups in that they are used to provide a certain level of functional access for that domain. Because the domain controllers share the same account database (see Chapter 2, "Windows NT 4.0 Directory Services Overview" and Chapter 5, "Capacity Planning and Performance"), a local group is considered local when it is created on the PDC to *all* the domain controllers.

Windows NT also creates three global default groups as well:

- ❖ Domain Admins
- ❖ Domain Users
- ❖ Domain Guests

A global group account, like a global user account, can be used anywhere in the domain, or through a trust relationship to a trusting domain, to facilitate the management of user access to network resources. As with local groups, global groups created on a PDC are considered global to all the domain controllers for that domain.

Note   Again, refer to Chapter 3, "Trust Relationships," for a complete treatment of local and global user and group accounts and their impact when managing resources. ▪

There are also four groups created and managed by Windows NT to "place" a user for accessing resources, called *internal* or *system groups*:

- ❖ Everyone
- ❖ Interactive
- ❖ Network
- ❖ Creator Owner

Everyone, of course means just that. Every user that logs on to the workstation or accesses a resource on the workstation or a server locally or remotely becomes a member of the internal group Everyone. It is interesting to note that Windows NT's philosophy for securing resources is *not* to secure them at all. By default, the group Everyone has full access to resources. It is up to the administrator to restrict that access and *add* security.

Everyone, when applied to Directory Services, means everyone within and without the enterprise. A user from one domain could access a resource on another domain if that user has a valid account in the other domain and if no trust relationship exists. This happens through pass-through authentication between the domains. That user then becomes a member of the Everyone group on the other domain.

There is a subtle distinction between the Everyone group and the Domain Users global group. While Everyone always means absolutely everyone who accesses that domain, Domain Users means only those users *from the domain*. Recalling that Windows NT's default permission for network resources is Everyone with Full Control, replacing Everyone with Domain Users now subtly changes the access from absolutely everyone to only users from the domain.

Interactive represents to Windows NT the user who has logged on at the computer itself and accesses resources on that computer. This is also referred to as *logging on locally*.

Network represents to Windows NT any user who has connected to a network resource from another computer remotely.

Creator Owner represents the user who is the owner or has taken ownership of a resource. This group can, for example, be used to assign file access only to the owner of a file. While Everyone may have read access to files in a directory, Creator Owner will have full access; thus, while other users can read a file, only the owner of the file can make changes to it.

The membership of these internal groups is fixed by the Windows NT operating system and cannot be altered. For example, if you create a file, you are the owner of that file, and Windows NT places you in the Creator Owner group for that file.

Group Management in Domains

Microsoft's group strategy for domains recommends that domain users be grouped into as many global groups as is appropriate. Local resource managers should then create local groups for maintaining access to the resources. The global groups are then used as members of the local groups. Whichever domain users are members of the global group will get whatever level of access was given to the local group. While this may at first seem to be a bit of over-management, in large networks with hundreds or thousands of users, this strategy makes much sense and can actually facilitate user management and resource access.

Extending this concept to the trust relationship follows naturally. Because the trust gives a resource administrator access to the account database of a trusted domain, the resource administrators can use the global groups created in the trusted domain as members of the local groups they create to manage access to their resources. For example, if you wanted the administrators of the trusted domain to also administer the domain controllers or resource servers in the trusting domain, you would make the Domain Admins global group from the trusted domain a member of the local Administrators groups of the PDC and resource servers for the trusting domain.

Planning for New User Accounts

Part of setting up new user accounts—or group accounts for that matter, especially on a domain controller—involves some planning. Here are six basic areas to consider before creating new accounts:

- ◆ Account naming conventions
- ◆ How to deal with passwords
- ◆ Group membership
- ◆ Profile information
- ◆ Logon hours (when logon is possible)
- ◆ Which workstations the user can log on from

Naming Conventions

The choice of user name determines how the user will be identified on the network. In all lists of users and groups, the account names will be displayed alphabetically. So the choice of user name can be significant. For example, if your naming convention is FirstnameLastinitial, your user names for the following users would look like this:

User	User Name
Luke Skywalker	LukeS
Han Solo	HanS
Jabba T. Hutt	JabbaTH

Part
IV

Ch

12

Now what if you had several LukeS's or HanS's? In a large corporation, it would not be uncommon to have 20 or 30 persons with the same first name. Looking through a list of users with the same first name and only a couple of letters from the last name to go by could become not only confusing, but irritating as well.

A more effective convention might be LastnameFirstInitial, like so:

User	User Name
Luke Skywalker	SkywalkerL
Han Solo	SoloH
Jabba T. Hutt	HuttJT

Finding the appropriate user in a list will be easier. Many organizations will already have a network ID naming convention in place and it may be perfectly acceptable to follow that.

User names must be unique with Windows NT's Directory Services. Therefore, your naming convention must plan for duplicate names. Han Solo and Hank Solo, for example, would both have the user name SoloH according to the second convention previously suggested. So perhaps the convention could be altered to include middle initials in the event of a tie—such as SoloHA and SoloHB—or include extra letters from the first name until uniqueness is achieved—such as SoloHan and SoloHank. User names are not case-sensitive and can contain up to 20 characters, including spaces, except the following:

" / \ { } : ; | = , + ★ ? < >

You might also consider creating user accounts based on function rather than the user's name. For example, if the role of administrative assistant is assigned from a pool of employees, then it may make more sense to create an account called AdminAsst or FrontDesk. This will ensure that the assistant of the day will have access to everything that person should have access to—as well as minimize your administrative setup for that person.

Considerations Regarding Passwords

Besides the obvious consideration that requiring a password provides the greater level of security, there are some other things to think about. One of these is who controls the password.

When you create a new user account, you have three password-related options to determine:

- ◆ User Must Change Password at Next Logon
- ◆ User Cannot Change Password
- ◆ Password Never Expires

Selecting User Must Change Password at Next Logon allows you to set a blank or *dummy* password for the user. When the user logs on for the first time, Windows NT will require the user to change the password.

Key Concept

It is important to set company policy and educate the users in the importance of protecting the integrity of their accounts by using unique and "unguessable" passwords. Among the most common choices for passwords are children's names, pet's names, favorite sports teams, or team players. Try to avoid the obvious association when choosing a password.

User Cannot Change Password provides the most control to the administrator. This option is particularly useful for temporary employees, or the administrative assistant pool account.

Password Never Expires ensures that the password will not need to be changed, even if the overall password policy requires changes after a set period of time has elapsed. Again, this is useful for the types of accounts just mentioned or for service accounts.

Passwords are case-sensitive and can be up to 14 characters in length. It is generally suggested among network administrators to require a minimum password length of eight characters, using alphanumeric characters and a combination of upper- and lowercase. For example, I might use as my password a combination of my initials and the last four digits of my Social Security number—two things I am not likely to forget, but not obvious to anyone else. Thus, my password might be SDK4532, or it might be sdk4532, SdK4532, 4532sdK, 45sdk32, and—oh well, you get the idea.

Group Membership

The easiest way to manage large numbers of users is to group them logically, functionally, departmentally, and so on. Creating local groups for local resource access control is the most common use for creating groups on the resource computers. As already discussed, local group membership consists primarily of domain global groups, although in specific instances it may include domain global users as well.

Determining User Profile Information

User Profiles on a Windows NT Server usually refers to a file of environment settings that is stored on a specific computer and downloaded to whatever Windows NT-based computer that the user is logging in from. The location of the logon script and personal folder might also be located on a remote computer rather than on the local workstation, which is especially useful if the user moves around a lot (like our pool of administrative assistants).

It is helpful, though not necessary, to determine ahead of time where this information will be kept, and how much will be used. Will you need a user profile stored on a server for every user, or only for administrative assistants? Does everyone need a logon script? Should personal files be stored on the local workstation, or on a central computer? (Again, this setup is useful for users who move around.)

A more thorough discussion of user profile files, login scripts, and another related utility called the System Policy Editor will be undertaken in Chapter 14, "Policies and Profiles."

Home Directory

The *Home Directory* simply represents a place where the user can routinely save data files. This is usually a folder (directory) that has been created on a centrally located server in the domain; though in small workgroups, it may actually be found on the user's local workstation—or not identified at all.

The advantages of placing the home directory on a centrally located server somewhere in the domain is primarily that of security. By using NTFS permissions, the users' folders can be secured quite nicely so that only they (and whomever they determine) can have access to them. In addition, these folders can then be included in regular server data backups, thus ensuring the availability of the files in the event of accidental deletion, corruption, or system crashes.

In the Home Directory section of the User Environment Profile dialog box (accessed by viewing the <u>P</u>roperties of the user account and choosing P<u>r</u>ofile), there are two choices:

- ◆ Local <u>P</u>ath
- ◆ <u>C</u>onnect To

The first represents the drive and path to an existing home directory folder, such as C:\USERS in which the user's own profile folder can be created. The other represents a *UNC (Universal Naming Convention)* path that identifies the name of the server that contains an existing home directory share, and a logical drive letter to assign to it that the user can use for saving files in applications, searching, exploring with the Windows Explorer, and so on.

> **Note** A UNC name is very much like a DOS path in that it represents the path through the network to a network resource. In this case, the network resource is a directory that has been "shared" for the creation of a home directory folder for the user. UNC names take the following form:
>
> \\servername\sharename\path
>
> where *servername* represents the name of the server computer that contains the folder, *sharename* represents the name of the directory that has been made available for use as a resource (shared), and *path* represents an optional path to a subdirectory or specific file. ■

When entering the Home Directory location, you can either specify the name of the folder explicitly, or use an environmental parameter to create and name it for you. For example, by using the variable %USERNAME%, Windows NT will create a directory using the user name value as the directory name. This is particularly useful when using a template for creating large numbers of users. Recall that when you create a new user account by copying an existing account, the User Environment Profile information is also copied. Using %USERNAME% will enable individual user home folders to be created by using each user's user name as the directory name. Table 12.1 displays a list of the environment variables that Windows NT 4.0 can use.

Table 12.1   Additional Environment Variables for Home Directories and Logon Scripts

Variable	Description
%HOMEDIR%	Returns the logical mapping to the shared folder that contains the user's home directory.
%HOMEDRIVE%	Returns the logical drive mapped to the home directory share.
%HOMEPATH%	Returns the path name of the user's home directory folder.
%HOMESHARE%	Returns the share name of the folder which contains the user's home directory folder.
%OS%	Returns the operating system of the user's computer.
%PROCESSOR_ARCHITECTURE%	Returns the processor's base architecture, such as Intel or MIPS, of the user's computer.
%PROCESSOR_LEVEL%	Returns the processor type, such as 486, of the user's computer.

Variable	Description
%USERDOMAIN%	Returns the name of the enterprise account domain in which the user is validating.
%USERNAME%	Returns the user's logon ID (User name).

Logon Scripts

If you have had any dealings with networks before, you have encountered a logon script. *Logon scripts* are simply files that contain a set of network commands which need to be executed in a particular order. Often, as is the case with Novell NetWare, logon scripts have a specific command language and structure that should be used. In the case of Windows NT, they are simply batch files and support all the Windows NT command-line commands, or in some cases, an executable file.

Here is an example of a Windows NT logon script called LOGON.BAT:

```
@echo Welcome to the NT Network!
@echo off
Pause
Net use p:\\server5\database
Net use r:\\server4\budget
Net time \\server1 /set /y
```

The two net use commands map drives to existing network resource shares. The net time command synchronizes the system time on the current computer with the system time of the server specified.

The name of the logon script is arbitrary. Windows NT does provide a place for storing logon scripts. In a domain setting, they are usually placed in the WINNT\SYSTEM32\REPL\IMPORT\SCRIPTS folder on a domain controller. Because the user uses any available domain controller to gain access to the network, it makes sense that the logon scripts be stored on all the domain controllers in the domain.

Part

IV

Ch

12

The advantage of storing the logon scripts on a domain controller is that through Directory Replication, the scripts can be distributed to *all* the domain controllers in the network. Because a user may authenticate at any one of the domain controllers, this provides a convenient way to ensure that the logon scripts are always available. Also, it provides the administrator with one central storage place for the scripts, making maintenance of them easier. Refer to Chapter 8, "Configuring Domain Network Core Services," for a discussion on how to set up and use Directory Replication.

Windows NT assumes that you will be storing the login script file in the WINNT\SYSTEM32\REPL\IMPORT\SCRIPTS folder on the domain controller server. Because of this, it is not necessary to use a UNC name when specifying the location of the login script in the User Properties Environment Profile dialog box. In fact, once you have distributed the login scripts to all the appropriate domain controllers, you need only enter the file name in the Logon Script Name text box. More Windows NT environment variables are shown in Table 12.1.

Understanding User Manager for Domains

Domain user and group accounts are created and managed through an Administrative Tool called *User Manager for Domains*. Account policies are also created and maintained through this utility, as well as the assignment of functional user rights, the enabling of security auditing, and the establishment of trust relationships (as outlined in Chapter 3, "Trust Relationships"). Functional rights define what functions a user can perform at a Windows NT computer. For example, shutting down the computer, changing the system time, formatting the hard disk, and installing device drivers are all functional rights.

User Manager for Domains acts as the database manager for user and group accounts stored in the SAM database, as shown in Figure 12.1. There are five menu options:

- *User.* Creates and modifies user and group accounts; copies, deletes, renames, and changes properties of user accounts; and allows you to change the domain focus for remote management of other domain databases.

- *View.* Allows user account entries to be sorted by Full Name or Username (the default).

- *Policies.* Sets account policies, assigns functional user rights, enables security auditing, and establishes trust relationships.

- *Options.* Enables/disables confirmation and save settings, sets display fonts for User Manager, and allows a low-speed setting when administering a domain database across a slow connection, such as a 56K WAN line.

- *Help.* Displays the Windows NT help files specific to User Manager.

FIG. 12.1⟹
User Manager displays the account database showing all user and group accounts. Here we see the two default users, eight default local groups, and three default global groups that are created during installation.

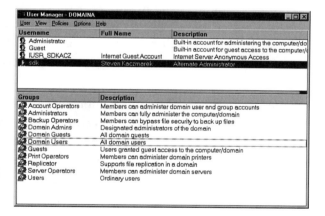

Part IV
Ch 12

Creating a New User

Selecting New User from the User menu displays the New User dialog box shown in Figure 12.2. This is a fairly intuitive screen and is described in Table 12.2.

FIG. 12.2⇒
The New User
dialog box has
options selected,
and has the Group
Memberships
window showing
the default mem-
bership in the
Domain Users
global group.

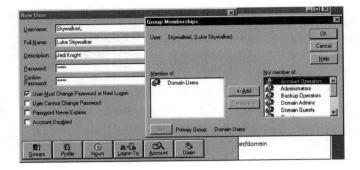

Table 12.2 New User Dialog Box Options

Option	Description
Username	The logon ID that you have chosen for the user. Recall that this name must be unique in the database (or in the enterprise when creating the account on a domain controller) and up to 20 characters including spaces, but excluding " / \ [ ] : ;	= , + ★ ? < >.
Full Name	The user's full name. As with user names, it is recommended that you determine a convention for entering this name (such as "Luke Jedi Skywalker"), because the full name is used by Windows NT as an alternative user account sort order.
Description	A simple description of the account or user, such as `Admin Assistant Account` or `Project Manager`.
Password	The password is case-sensitive and can be up to 14 characters in length. Recall the discussion of password integrity earlier in the section "Considerations Regarding Passwords."

Option	Description
<u>C</u>onfirm Password	You must confirm the password here before Windows NT can create the account.
User <u>M</u>ust Change Password at Next Logon	This password option forces the user to change her password the next time she logs on.
U<u>s</u>er Cannot Change Password	This password option prevents the user from being able to change his password. As mentioned earlier, this setting is useful for accounts for which the password should remain the same, such as temporary employee accounts.
Pass<u>w</u>ord Never Expires	This password option prevents the password from expiring and overrides both the Maximum Password Age option set in the Account Policy as well as the User <u>M</u>ust Change Password at Next Logon option.
Account Disa<u>b</u>led	Prevents the use of the account. This is a useful setting for users who are on vacation, extended leave, or whose accounts should not be available for logging on to the network. It is always more appropriate to disable an account if there is any possibility of the user returning. Remember that deleting a user account also deletes the user's SID, and thus removes all previous network resource access for that user.

continues

Part

IV

Ch

12

Table 12.2 Continued

Option	Description
Account Locked Out	Displays when the Account Lockout account policy is enabled. When a user exceeds the number of allowed incorrect logons, this option is checked by the operating system and can only be deselected by an administrator or account operator.
Groups	Displays the Group Memberships dialog box which displays the user's group membership and from which group membership can be modified.
Profile	Displays the User Environment Profile dialog box from which a server-based profile can be referenced, logon script defined, and home folder (directory) identified.
Hours	Displays the Logon Hours dialog box from which you can determine what times of the day the user can log on to the network. This is useful for shift employees or for backup times.
Logon To	Displays the Logon Workstations dialog box and allows you to identify by computer name the computers at which this account can log on to the network. You can identify up to eight workstations.
Account	Displays the Account Information dialog box in which you can specify an expiration date for the account, and identify whether the account is a global domain account (default) or one for a user from another untrusted domain who needs occasional access to your domain.

Option	Description
Dialin	Displays the Dialin Information dialog box which is used to grant permission to use Dial-Up Networking to the user account and set Call Back options.

As you can see, it is a fairly straightforward process to create user accounts. By double-clicking the account name in the User Manager window, or highlighting the user name and choosing Properties from the User menu, you can view these settings for each user and modify them as is appropriate.

Creating a New Local or Global Group

The process of creating a new local or global group is even more straightforward, as you can see by the Global Group Properties dialog box displayed in Figure 12.3. The options available in the Local Group and Global Group Properties dialog boxes are described in Table 12.3.

FIG. 12.3⟹

The Global Group Properties dialog box shows the new group name and description filled in.

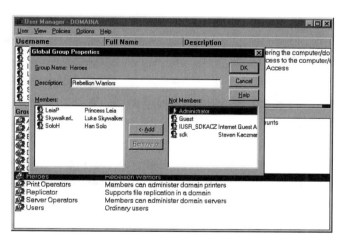

Table 12.3 Global Group Dialog Box Options

Option	Global or Local	Description
Group Name	Both	The name you have chosen for the local group. It can have up to 256 characters except the backslash (\) which, while descriptive, would be somewhat confusing in display lists of groups. Group names, unlike user names, *cannot* be renamed. However, a group name can be copied and its member list preserved for the copied group.
Description	Both	A simple description of the group such as Administrative Assistants or Project Managers.
Show Full Names	Local Only	Displays the full name associated with each user account displayed in the Members list box.
Members	Both	Displays all the current user accounts (or domain user and global group accounts) that are members of this local group.
Not Members	Global Only	Displays the users from the domain who can be added to the group member list.

Option	Global or Local	Description
Add	Local Only	Displays the Add Users and Groups dialog box from which you can select user accounts from your domain's user and global group accounts database on the PDC, or from the accounts database from a trusted domain. Select the trusted domain that has the desired user accounts from the List Names From list box, click the user you want to add to the group in the Names list box, and choose Add, then OK. Use the Search button to look for an account among all possible account databases. If you have selected a global group in the Names list box, use Members to display the members of that global group. You can select multiple accounts at one time by Ctrl+clicking the additional accounts. In the New Global Group dialog box, this button will add whichever users you selected in the Not Members list to the Members list.
Remove	Both	Deletes the account selected in the Members list, thus removing it from group membership.

Part

IV

Ch

12

Note Here's a shortcut to populating a group. Before you create the group, select all the user names you want in the group from the User Manager Username screen by Ctrl+clicking the additional accounts. Then create the group. The <u>M</u>embers list box will display any user account that has been highlighted before the group was created. ■

Key Concept

Remember the primary membership difference between local and global groups. Local groups can contain user accounts from the local account database, global user and global group accounts from the domain database of the domain that the server is a member of, and global user and global group accounts from the domain database of a trusted domain. Global groups can only contain user accounts from their own domain database.

Renaming, Copying, and Deleting Accounts

Recall from the discussion of the default Administrator and Guest accounts that for a higher level of security, you can rename these accounts. Renaming an account does not affect the account's SID in any way. This makes it relatively easy to change a user name without affecting any of that user's access—whether it be changing the Administrator account to enhance its security, or reflecting a name change due to marriage or the Witness Protection Program. Simply highlight the user name in User Manager for Domains, choose <u>R</u>ename from the <u>U</u>ser menu, and type the new user name in the box provided. Group names *cannot* be renamed.

 Key Concept

If you choose to delete an account, remember that the account's SID will also be deleted, and all resource access and user rights will be lost. This means that if you re-create the account even exactly as it was before, the SAM database will generate a new SID for the account, and you will have to reestablish resource access and user rights for that account.

To delete the account, highlight it and press Delete on the keyboard, or choose Ṳser, Ḏelete. Windows NT will warn you that the SID will be lost. Choose OK, and the account will be deleted.

 Note   You cannot delete built-in user or group accounts, global or otherwise. ■

The Ṳser, Ꞔopy menu command is useful for duplicating user account information that is the same for a group of users. Because you cannot rename a group, copying a group to a new name also duplicates its membership list and is the next best thing to renaming. Copying user and group accounts results in new accounts being created. As such, each new account will have its own new SID assigned to it.

When you copy a user account, the following settings are maintained: the Description, the password options that have been checked off, and if Account Disabled has been selected, it will be unchecked for the copy. Also, group membership and profile information is maintained for the copied account, as are Logon Hours, Logon to Workstations, and Account Expiration and Type. This greatly simplifies the task of creating large numbers of similar users.

Creating and Managing Account Policies, System Rights, and Auditing

Account policy information and user rights are considered part of account management and as such are administered through User Manager for Domains. *Account policy* information includes password-specific information such as password, age, minimum length, and account lockout options.

User rights represent the functional rights that a user acquires for a given server when logging in either at the console or remotely. Auditing for file and directory access, print access, and so on, is accomplished by specifying the users or groups whose access you want to audit and is performed at the file, directory, and print level. However, auditing for those security events must first be enabled for user and group accounts; that is performed through User Manager for Domains as well.

Account Policy

Figure 12.4 shows a typical domain account policy. The options presented in this dialog box should be very familiar to network administrators. The policies determined here apply to *all* domain users.

FIG. 12.4⇒

In this example of an account policy, the password must be at least six characters long and expires every 45 days. Also, if the user forgets the password in three consecutive tries, within 30 minutes the account will be locked out until an administrator releases it.

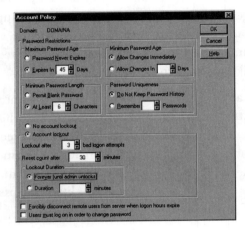

Table 12.4 describes the various entries that can be made for an account policy.

Table 12.4 Account Policy Options	
Option	Description
Maximum Password Age	The password may be set to never expire, or you may select a set number of days after which the user will be prompted to change the password. The default is set to 42 days.

Option	Description
Minimum Password Age	The default here is to allow a user to change the password any time. Many organizations now prefer that passwords cannot be changed whenever the user wants. The user must wait a specified number of days before the password can be changed. This helps to maintain password uniqueness.
Minimum Password Length	The default, oddly enough, is to allow blank passwords. As discussed earlier in the section "Considerations Regarding Passwords," you will probably want to define a minimum length for the password. Most network administrators use eight as the minimum length. The maximum length can be 14.
Password Uniqueness	The default is to not maintain a history of past passwords. This allows a user to reuse passwords when they expire. While being able to reuse a password is convenient for the user, it is not always the most secure way to deal with passwords. Many organizations require passwords to be unique. This is accomplished by specifying the number of passwords to be "remembered" by the system for each user (up to 24), and requiring a maximum password age and a minimum password age. For example, by setting the maximum and minimum password age to 30 days and uniqueness to 24, the user would not be able to reuse the first password for two years. This in effect accomplishes uniqueness simply because the user is not likely to be able to remember that far back.

Part
IV

Ch
12

continues

Table 12.4 Continued

Option	Description
Account Lockout	The default is to not enable account lockout. In the enterprise where security is essential, this option will probably be enabled, and in fact it is recommended.
Lockout After	Specifies the number of bad logon attempts (incorrect passwords) that the system will accept before locking out that account. The default is 5 and can be set from 1 to 999.
Reset Count After	This number represents the number of minutes that the system will wait between bad logon attempts before resetting the bad logon count to 0. For example, if I mistype my password, the bad logon count is set to 1. If the reset count is 15 minutes, and after 15 minutes I do not log on incorrectly again, the bad logon count is set back to 0. If I do log on incorrectly again within 15 minutes, the logon count is set to 2, and so on. The default is 30 minutes, and can be set from 1 to 99,999 minutes (or roughly 70 days, for those of you who couldn't help wondering).
Lockout Duration	You can require an administrator to reset the account after lockout. You could also specify a length of time for the lockout to be in effect before letting the computer hacker try again. The default for this choice is 30 minutes, and can be set from 1 to 99,999 minutes.

Option	Description
Users <u>M</u>ust Log On…	This option will require that the user log on to the system before making password changes. Normally, when a password expires, the user is prompted during logon to change the password. With this option selected, the user will *not* be able to change the expired password, and the administrator will need to reset it. This is useful for short-term employee accounts that expire in a specific amount of time to ensure that the employee cannot change the password on his own.
<u>F</u>orcibly Disconnect…	By default, logon hour settings merely stop a user from logging in during the specified time period. If the user is already logged in, the logon hour settings have no further effect on the user. This option causes the user to be logged off the system when the logon hours have expired.

User Rights

As mentioned previously, user rights are *functional* rights and represent functions or tasks that a user or group can perform locally on a given workstation or server, or while remotely connected to a server. User rights include shutting down the computer, formatting a hard disk, backing up files and directories, and so forth. Contrast this with *permissions* such as read-only, write, and delete which reflect resource access rights.

In the domain, user rights are granted primarily to local groups as they usually represent access at the server console itself. However, user rights can also be granted to global groups, especially when remote access and administration are involved.

For example, the user right Log on Locally defines which users can log on at the server console. Only members of the local Account Operators, Administrators, Backup Operators, Print Operators, and Server Operators are granted this access. Note that, unlike Windows NT Workstation, the group Everyone is not listed on Windows NT Server installations by default.

Let's assume for this discussion that the server in question functions as a print server for a Multiple Master Domain model. I would like Print Operators from all domains to be able to manage this print server; that includes the ability to log on at the print server itself. Following Microsoft's group management strategy, I would create a global group in each trusted domain, perhaps called GlobalPrintOps, and then add it to the local Print Operators group on my print server. Those users have the ability to log on locally at the print server to manage the printers.

However, by virtue of the trust relationship, I could also have added the GlobalPrintOps global group directly to the Log on Locally user right as well to allow them the ability to log on at the print server. As with all security objects, user rights maintain *Access Control Lists (ACLs)*. Groups and users represented by their SIDs are members of the ACL for each user right. Consequently, there is no way to select an account and see what user rights (or file permissions, for that matter) have been assigned to that account because the rights do not "stay" with the account.

Table 12.5 highlights the basic user rights on domain controllers and the default groups assigned to each.

Table 12.5   User Rights on Domain Controllers

User Right	Group(s) Assigned
Access this Computer from the Network	Administrators, Everyone
Add Workstations to Domain	No groups explicitly assigned; a default Administrator function.
Back Up Files and Directories	Administrators, Backup Operators, Server Operators
Change the System Time	Administrators, Server Operators

User Right	Group(s) Assigned
Force Shutdown from a Remote System	Administrators, Server Operators
Load and Unload Device Drivers	Administrators
Log on Locally	
Manage Auditing and Security Log	Administrators
Restore Files and Directories	Administrators, Backup Operators, Server Operators
Shut Down the System	Account Operators, Administrators, Backup Operators, Print Operators, Server Operators
Take Ownership of Files or Objects	Administrators

Accounts assigned to the various user rights can be administered through the User Rights Policy dialog box, displayed by choosing User Rights from the Policy menu (see Figure 12.5). Select the user right from the Right drop-down list. The default groups assigned this user right will be displayed in the Grant To list box. Choose the Add button to display the Add Users and Groups dialog box (described in the section "Creating Groups") and add user and group accounts to the user right's Grant To list. Or choose Remove to delete members from the Grant To list.

Part

IV

Ch

12

FIG. 12.5⇒
The User Rights
Policy dialog box
shows some of the
user rights that can
be selected. Log on
Locally has been
selected, and in the
Grant To box you
can see the groups
assigned this user
right.

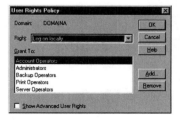

There are advanced rights that can also be displayed by checking the
Show Advanced User Rights option at the bottom of the User Rights
Policy dialog box. These rights are for use primarily by developers.
However, there are two advanced user rights which as an administrator
on a network you may need to modify from time to time:

◆ *Bypass Traverse Checking.* This advanced user right allows the
   specified user or group accounts to change between directories
   and navigate directory trees even if permission has been denied
   to various directories. This might be assigned to power users or
   resource managers.

◆ *Log On as a Service.* This advanced user right is intended for user
   accounts that are used by certain background application tasks or
   Windows NT system functions such as Directory Replication.
   This right allows the service or function to log in as the specified
   account for the express purpose of carrying out that specific task.
   No other user needs to be logged in for the task to be performed.

Audit Policy

Auditing for events relating to file and directory access, print access, and
so on is accomplished by specifying the users or groups whose access
you want to audit. This is performed at the file, directory, and print
level. However, auditing for those security events must first be enabled
for user and group accounts; this is done through User Manager by
selecting Audit from the Policies menu. The Audit Policy box is displayed (see Figure 12.6).

FIG. 12.6⇒

This audit policy
has enabled audit-
ing of failed logon
and logoff attempts,
unsuccessful file
and object access,
and any events
relating to restart,
shutdown, or
system processes
relating to this
domain controller.

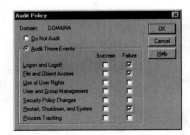

By default, auditing is not enabled because of the additional resources required to monitor the system for related events. There are seven areas for which auditing can be enabled:

- *Logon and Logoff.* Monitors user logon and logoff of the server, the domain, and network connections.

- *File and Object Access.* Monitors user access of files, directories, or printers. This enables the auditing of those objects to take place. The users and groups that are audited are set up at the file, directory, and printer resource level.

- *Use of User Rights.* Monitors when a user right is exercised by a user (such as formatting the hard disk).

- *User and Group Management.* Monitors events relating to user and group management such as the creation of new users, the modification of group membership, or the change of a password.

- *Security Policy Changes.* Monitors changes made to User Rights or Account Policy information.

- *Restart, Shutdown, System.* Monitors events related to these activities.

- *Process Tracking.* Monitors events related to certain process activity such as starting a program, indirect object access, and so on.

Successful and Unsuccessful events can be logged in the Security Log which can be viewed through the *Event Viewer*, another useful Administrative Tools utility. It is generally not at all useful for you to monitor successful and unsuccessful events for all seven options on a server because of the resources involved and the volume of data that would be collected in the Security Log. Auditing, however, can be very helpful in troubleshooting events such as unsuccessful logins or unsuccessful file access.

Part
IV

Ch
12

Troubleshooting Account and Policy Management

If you have been reading carefully, you already have the necessary building blocks for understanding and troubleshooting account management. The best tool for learning is to practice.

Most of the problems that you will encounter regarding user and group accounts will have to do with permissions to use resources rather than with the account setup itself. Nevertheless, here are some things to keep in mind.

User Cannot Be Logged on by System

When a user cannot log on, fortunately the message(s) that Windows NT displays to the screen is self-explanatory. Usually, it involves the user incorrectly typing the user name, or more likely, the password. User names are not case-sensitive, but passwords are. User names and passwords can both have spaces, but that tends to confuse users rather than provide descriptive account names. Be sure to be consistent in your use of user names. Educate your users in the importance of maintaining the integrity of their passwords, and expect a call every now and then from someone who has forgotten a password, or has the Caps Lock on when the password is in lowercase.

If a user forgets a password, the easiest thing for the domain administrator to do is use User Manager for Domains to give the user a new temporary password, and check the User Must Change Password at Next Logon properties option. If an account lockout policy has been established, and the user exceeds the allowed number of incorrect passwords, the Account Locked Out properties option for that user will be checked. Only an Administrator or Account Operator can remove the lock, again through User Manager for Domains.

Unable to Access Domain Controllers or Servers

Another possibility that can slow or inhibit a person's ability to log on successfully is the unavailability of a server. If the user is logging on locally, the user is being validated on the local computer for access to resources on that computer; unless the computer suddenly turns itself off, the user should be able to log on successfully.

When a Windows NT Workstation or Server is made a member of a domain, the From box on the Logon Security screen will display the local computer as well as the domain name. If there are one or more trusts established, the From box will display all available trusted domains. So the first thing to check if a user cannot be authenticated is whether the user chose the correct domain from the list when logging on.

If the user is validating on a network domain controller, the domain controller must be accessible to the user or the user may not be able to log on. For example, if the PDC is down and there is no backup domain controller (BDC) identified to the network, the user will be unable to log on. If the user logged on successfully at the computer in a previous session, a message may display that the domain controller is unavailable and that the user will be logged on with cached information from the Registry. Any changes that may have been made to a profile since the last session will probably not be available.

You troubleshoot this one, of course, by verifying that the domain controller is up, and that the computer in question has a valid connection to the network. If you are using TCP/IP as your protocol, you will want to check that the computer has a valid IP address and subnet mask, and if routing is involved, a valid default router address. If there is a trust relationship involved, verify that the trust is valid and working.

Sometimes the location of the BDC can cause user logon to be slow or to fail due to WAN traffic. Determine whether the location for the BDCs in your domain best meets the needs of your users and the logon traffic they generate. For a more complete discussion of this topic, refer to Chapter 5, "Capacity Planning and Performance." Network traffic and performance can be tracked using the Network Monitor service and utility that comes with Windows NT Server 4.0. This utility will be discussed in some detail in Chapter 21, "Network Monitor."

Sometimes network-based errors cannot be easily tracked down. For example, everything may seem to be functioning okay, but you just can't access the network. Sometimes the network card can get

Part

IV

Ch

12

confused, and the best thing to do is shut down the computer and do a cold boot. A warm boot does not always reset the hardware—in this case, the network card.

Other Logon Problems

Other problems may be related to other settings made through User Manager for Domains. Recall that in this utility the administrator can additionally add logon hour and workstation restrictions for the user, as well as account expiration. Again, the messages that Windows NT displays are pretty obvious in this regard, and will direct you to the appropriate account property to check and modify.

Remote Account Management Tips

Most account management can take place remotely by installing User Manager for Domains on a local Windows NT workstation. Versions also exist for Windows 95 and Windows for Workgroups. Remote server management tools will be discussed in Chapter 15, "Remote Server Management."

There are two options available in User Manager for Domains that can facilitate the remote management of accounts across trust relationships and across slow network connections: Select Domain and Low Speed Connection.

The User menu in User Manager for Domains offers a Select Domain option. Selecting this option displays the Select Domain dialog box. Here you can either choose the domain whose account database you want to administer from the Select Domain list (all trusted domains will be listed), or type it in the Domain text box. User Manager for Domains will display the account database for that domain, provided you have the appropriate level of access. For example, you must be made a member of the trusted domain's Administrators, Server Operators, or Account Operators local groups.

In the Select Domain dialog box, there is a check box option for Low Speed Connection. This is also available from the Options menu. This option is useful for facilitating administration when the network connection is particularly busy, or when administration takes place over a slower connection medium such as a 56K line. Selecting this option will result in the following modification to User Manager for Domains:

◆ The list of user and group accounts will not appear, and the User, Select User menu option is unavailable, though the administrator can administer accounts using the other User menu commands.

◆ The ability to create and manage global group accounts is unavailable, although global group membership can be affected through the group membership of individual user accounts.

◆ The View menu options are unavailable.

Taking the Disc Test

If you have read and understood the material in the chapter, you are ready to test your knowledge. Insert the CD-ROM that comes with this book and run the self-test software as described in Appendix I, "Using the CD-ROM."

From Here...

The next chapter will discuss an issue that is of paramount importance to any type of network—security in the domain. Chapter 14, "Policies and Profiles," continues to expand the discussion of account management by discussing user profiles and the System Policy Editor.

Chapter Prerequisite

The reader should be familiar
with the concepts of Directory
Services, Trust Relationships,
and Domains Models discussed
in Chapters 2, 3, and 4, as well
as the basics of user and group
management discussed in
Chapter 12, "Domain Users and
Groups."

13

Security and Permissions

We have so far encountered two levels of access security: logon and
user rights. Logon security is implemented through the use of user
accounts and passwords. User rights, as you saw in the last chapter, are
functional in nature and define what activities a user can engage in on a
given computer.

In this chapter, we will discuss more thoroughly the Windows NT 4.0
security model. The security model itself applies both to Windows NT
4.0 workstation and server, as does the method of applying permissions
and sharing resources. Specifically, we will cover the following topics:

◆ Examining Windows NT 4.0 security

◆ Exploring the Windows NT logon process for the domain

◆ Examining access tokens and access control lists

◆ Determining access rights to a security object

◆ Determining resource access in the domain

◆ Sharing resources and assigning permissions

◆ Troubleshooting security access

Examining the Windows NT 4.0 Security Model

All security provided by Windows NT 4.0 is handled through a kernel mode executive service known as the *Security Reference Monitor*. When a user logs on, tries to perform a function at the workstation—like formatting a disk—or tries to access a resource, the Security Reference Monitor determines whether and to what extent to allow access to the user. The authentication process provides security through user account location and password protection. User rights are functional in nature and define what actions a user can take at a given workstation, member server, or domain controller, such as shutting down the workstation or formatting a disk. These are discussed in Chapter 12, "Domain Users and Groups."

There are also *permissions*, which define a user's access to network resources. Permissions define what a user can do *to* or *with* a resource, such as delete a print job or modify a file. The terms *rights* and *permissions* are often used interchangeably, and usually refer to resource access. With Windows NT, the term *rights* invariably refers to those functional user rights that you can set through User Manager and User Manager for Domains; the term *permissions* refers to resource access. This is how we use these terms throughout this book.

There are two types of permissions that can be applied in Windows NT:

◆ *Share-level permissions.*   These define how a user can access a resource that has been made available (shared) on the network. This is a resource that resides some place other than the workstation at which the user is sitting and that the user accesses remotely. The owner or administrator of the resource makes it available as a network resource by sharing it. The owner or administrator of the resource also defines a list of users and groups that can access the resource through the share and determines just how much access to give them.

◆ *Resource-level permissions.* These also define a user's access to a resource, but at the resource itself. The owner or administrator of the resource assigns a list of users and groups that can access the resource itself and the level of access to allow. Combined with share-level permissions, the owner and administrator of a resource can provide a high degree of security.

The most common resource-level permissions that you will encounter are those for files and folders. File and folder permissions are only available on NTFS-formatted partitions. If you do not have a partition formatted for NTFS, you will only be able to use the FAT-level properties—read-only, archive, system, and hidden. Under NTFS, you get a more robust set of properties including read, write, delete, execute, and change permissions.

Shared devices, such as printers, also provide a means of assigning permissions to use the device—for example, printing to a print device, managing documents on the print device, and so on.

Key Concept

Any resource for which access can be determined is considered to be a security object. In other network operating systems, such as Novell NetWare, some permissions used to set access to resources are assigned directly to the user or group and stay with the user or group account. This is not true with Windows NT. In all cases, it is important to note that permissions are assigned to and stay with the security object and *not* the user. A user's access to a resource is determined at the time the user tries to access it, *not* when the user logs on.

When a user logs on to Windows NT, whether at the local workstation or through a domain controller, the user is granted an access token. Permissions ascribed to an object (resource) reside in an access control list (ACL) with the object. The Security Reference Monitor compares the user's access token information with that in the ACL and determines what level of access to grant the user. Let's explore these concepts further.

Exploring the Windows NT Logon Process

When a user logs on to Windows NT on a Windows NT-based computer, the user name, password, and point of authentication must be provided. This is part of the WIN32 Winlogon service that monitors the logon process. The Winlogon service passes this information to the Security Subsystem, which in turn passes it to the Security Reference Monitor (see Figure 13.1).

FIG. 13.1 ⟹

This figure shows a diagram of the Windows NT 4.0 local logon process.

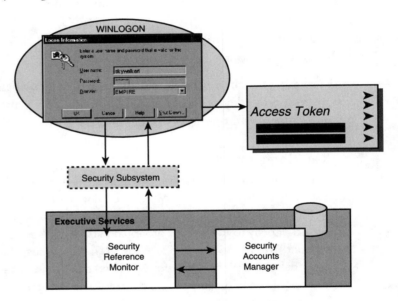

The Security Reference Monitor checks the information entered against the Security Accounts Manager (SAM) and the account database. If the information is accurate, the Security Reference Monitor authenticates the user and returns a valid access token back to the Security subsystem and the Winlogon process. With Directory Services, users are authenticated by a domain controller in the domain for which they are a member. This domain authentication is governed by another process called *Net Logon*. Figure 13.2 demonstrates this process.

FIG. 13.2 ⟹

This example highlights how network authentication takes place in Windows NT 4.0 using Net Logon.

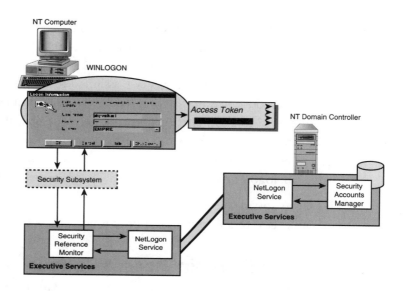

The process is very similar to the local logon process. The difference is that the Security subsystem passes the logon information to the Net Logon process. The Net Logon process on the user's Windows NT computer then establishes a secure network IPC connection with the Net Logon process on an available domain controller (refer to Chapter 5, "Capacity Planning and Performance," for a discussion of the number and placement of domain controllers).

The Net Logon process of the domain controller then passes the logon information to the SAM and database on the domain controller where the user is authenticated. The validation confirmation is sent back through the secure connection to the Security Subsystem on the user's Windows NT computer where the access token is generated.

The Account Access Token

Many companies that have secured areas provide access to those areas through an electronic key card. A magnetic stripe on the back of the card contains the user's information, such as a security ID. The card is read by a card reader at the point of entry. Often, the user may also have to enter a security number or password on a keypad before the door is unlocked.

The *access token* is a lot like a key card. It contains important security information about the user. This information includes, most importantly, the user's SID. Recall from Chapter 12 that the *SID* is the unique security identifier that Windows NT assigned to the user's account when the account was created. All security-related requests made by the user are linked to and matched first and foremost against the user's SID. Other information includes the user name and password, group memberships by name and group SIDs, profile location, home directory information, logon hours, and so on.

The access token is used by Windows NT to determine whether a user can gain access to a resource, and how much access to provide.

Local versus Domain Access Tokens

When a user logs on to a local Windows NT Workstation participating in a workgroup, the user's account resides in the local Windows NT Workstation's Registry (SAM database). Hence, the user's access token is created on that local Windows NT workstation and can only be used to access resources on that workstation.

As you saw in Figure 13.2, when a user logs on to a Windows NT computer that is a member of a domain, the user's account resides in the domain SAM database on the domain controller. Recall that this type of account is called a *domain*, or *global*, account because the user can log on once and access any resource in the network that the account has been given permission to use. Hence, the user's access token is created on the domain controller for that domain and can be used (as it is a global account) to access any resource throughout the enterprise domain that the account has been given permission to use. This is a hallmark of Windows NT's Directory Services.

Because access to remote resources is determined by examining the SIDs for each account in the ACL with the SIDs listed in the user's access token, the point of logon validation affects the user's ability to access a resource.

In a domain, the user and group accounts are global and can be used in the ACL of any resource in the domain. When the user logs on to the domain, the access token contains the user's SID (and group SIDs per group membership) and is global to the network. Both access tokens and ACLs obtain their SIDs from the same SAM database. Thus, the user can access any resource that has given access permission to any SID contained in the user's access token (to the extent that the permission allows).

This is also true where trust relationships exist between domains. As discussed in Chapter 3, "Trust Relationships," the trust relationship allows users to log on and authenticate at a Windows NT computer that participates in either the trusting or trusted domain. Also, the trust relationship allows resource managers to assign access to user and group accounts from any trusted domain as well as their own.

Among domains where no trust relationships exist, a user's access token is only good in the validating domain. The ACLs for network resources in another domain consist of SIDs from that domain's account database. If the user has an account in that other domain, the user's SID in that domain is necessarily different (see Chapter 12, "Domain Users and Groups") from the SID the user gets when he logs in his own domain. When the user tries to access the other domain's resource, the two SIDs (access token and ACL) do not match, and the user cannot access the resource.

Whether a trust exists between two domains or not, Windows NT uses a process called *pass-through authentication* to validate the user on the other domain. When a trust exists, as the user logs on, the Net Logon process determines that the user's account does not reside within the trusting domain and passes it through to the Net Logon service on a domain controller in the trusted domain where it is authenticated (refer to Figure 13.2).

When there is no trust, the user must log in to his domain. Windows NT takes the user name and password from the user's access token on the user's domain rather than the SID, and "passes it through" to the

Net Logon service on a domain controller in the other domain. There, the user is, in effect, logged on to the other domain, and a new access token is created there with the user's account and group SIDs from the other domain's account database. The user can then access resources on that computer to which the ACL grants permission.

This all works great so long as the user name and password match in both domains. The user can use Network Neighborhood or browse lists to point and click and select the resources in the other domain. However, usually the passwords, if not both user name and password, do not match. In this case, the user may still be able to access the resource through pass-through authentication, but generally has to connect to the resource by mapping a drive, entering a valid user name from the other domain in the Connect As box, and supplying a valid password.

Let's look at an example. If DOMAINA has account BrownC with password ABC, and BrownC wants to access a shared printer on Pserver2 in DOMAINB, the first thing the print administrator must do is add BrownC to the ACL for the printer. If DOMAINB trusts DOMAINA, the print administrator need only add the account because it is available through the trust. However, without a trust between the domains, the administrator of DOMAINB can only add members of DOMAINB's account database to the printer's ACL. This means that an account for BrownC must be created in DOMAINB and added to the ACL for the printer.

Let's assume that BrownC's account in DOMAINB also expects password ABC. When BrownC uses the Add Printer Wizard to connect to the printer on Pserver2 in DOMAINB, Windows NT uses pass-through authentication and the Net Logon service to pass BrownC and ABC from BrownC's access token in DOMAINA to the Security Reference Monitor on a domain controller in DOMAINB to be authenticated. A new access token is created for BrownC in DOMAINB. This can be used successfully to access the printer, because now the SID for BrownC in DOMAINB matches the SID for BrownC in the ACL for the printer.

Unlike mapping to shared folders, there is no Connect As text box for shared printers in which the user could supply a valid user name and password for the printer. Thus, if the passwords do not match, BrownC cannot access the printer at all. If this were a folder that BrownC was attempting to access in the same circumstances, he could supply his user name, or a valid user name from DOMAINB in the Connect As text box that appears when mapping a drive through Network Neighborhood or Windows Explorer. He will then be prompted for the appropriate password, and if it is correct, he will gain access to the folder with the appropriate level of permissions.

Examining Access Control Lists

When a key card is read by the card reader, the information on the card is generally checked against a central database to see whether this user has the appropriate level of access to be let in the secured area. The database may indicate that the cardholder has full access and allows the door to open; or the database may indicate that the cardholder has minimum access and only allows a window in the door to open. If the access token is thought of as the key card for access to secured areas, an *access control list (ACL)* can be thought of as the card reader database.

An ACL is just that—a list of users and groups that have some level of access to the resource. It is created at the object (resource or share) level and stays with the security object. It consists of user and group account entries that reference the accounts' SIDs rather than the accounts' names. These entries are called *Access Control Entries*, or *ACEs*. Each entry has a particular level of permission associated with it, such as Read-Only, Full Control, or No Access.

When a user tries to access a resource, the request is passed once again to the Security Reference Monitor. The Security Reference Monitor acts here as the card reader. It checks the SID entries in the access token against the SID entries in the ACL (see Figure 13.3).

FIG. 13.3 ⇒
This figure is a diagram of the security access process.

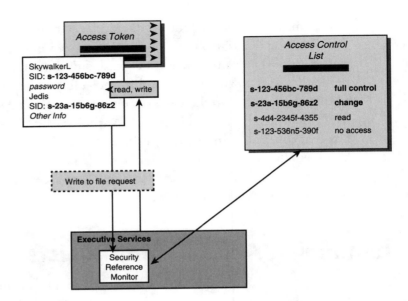

The Security Reference Monitor determines all matches, evaluates the permissions assigned to each matching entry, and calculates an overall permission level for the user which becomes the user's effective access to the resource. It then returns that effective access as a security "handle" to the object—for example, read and write permissions for a file. The security handle becomes part of the access token for as long as the user accesses the object.

Key Concept

As long as the user maintains access to the object, the same security handle is in effect, even if the owner or administrator of the resource changes the user's access. The changed permissions do not take effect for the user until the user releases control of the object and tries to access it again. For example, if BrownC has full access to a file he has opened, and the owner of the file decides to restrict BrownC to Read-Only, BrownC continues to have full control until he closes the file and tries to open it again.

Sharing Resources and Determining Network Access

A resource, such as a folder or printer, is made available as a network resource by sharing the resource. For simplicity, printer sharing is discussed in Chapter 10, "Managing Printers in the Domain."

Only a user who is an Administrator, Server Operator, or Print Operator (or Power User on a member server) has the ability to share a resource on a workstation or server. In addition, the Server service must be running, and the network card operational. If you suspect a problem with the Server service or the network card, a good place to begin troubleshooting is the Event Viewer. Look for any devices or services that failed to start (see Chapter 7, "The Role of the Registry").

Sharing a folder is a relatively simple process. A folder is shared by selecting the file or folder through Windows Explorer or My Computer, right-clicking it, and choosing S̲haring; or through the object's properties sheet. Figure 13.4 shows an example of a folder that has been shared.

FIG. 13.4 ⟹
Rebel Plans has been shared with the name Force. Notice the list of groups and the permissions assigned to each.

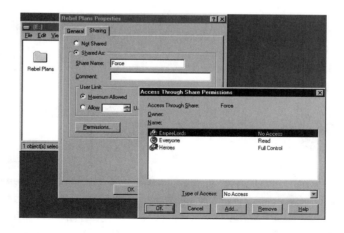

Sharing is enabled by clicking the Shared As option. When you share a folder, the share name defaults to the folder name, but can be changed to be more descriptive for its potential users. You can also indicate the number of users that are allowed to access the share at a time, or accept the default of Maximum Allowed.

 Note Recall that the maximum number of remote connections allowed on a Windows NT workstation is 10. On a server, the number of connections is effectively unlimited, except as defined by the license option chosen. ■

If you go no further, Windows NT shares this resource to any and all users. The default permission for every shared resource is Everyone with Full Control.

Key Concept

Windows NT's philosophy of sharing resources is to make information readily and easily available. Therefore, the default is to give every network user access to the resource. Hence, the default permission is always Everyone with Full Control. With printers, the default for Everyone is Print.

If you want to add a layer of security to the shared folder, you must choose Permissions and Add the appropriate group and user accounts, modifying the permissions as necessary. By doing this, you are creating and modifying the ACL for the folder.

Caution

It is recommended that you either remove the Everyone group and explicitly assign permissions to specific users and groups, or give Everyone the least level of access (Read) to provide a greater level of security. Do not give the Everyone group No Access. Because every network user is automatically a member of Everyone, giving it No Access results in locking every user—even the owner and administrator—out of that shared resource.

There are four share-level permissions that you can assign in your ACL. They are defined in Table 13.1.

Table 13.1 Permissions for Shared Folders

Permission	Effect
Read	Displays the folder and file names; allows files to be opened and programs to be run; allows similar access to subfolders.
Change	In addition to read permissions, allows changes to be made to files and folders, including creating and deleting files and folders.
Full Control	Allows complete access to the folder and its files and subfolders, including the ability to take ownership of files and change permissions of files and folders.
No Access	Denies access to the folder and its contents.

Caution

Share permissions take effect for users accessing the resource remotely over the network. If the user sits down at the computer that has the folder, and no other permissions have been assigned, the user still has complete access to the folder and its files.

Note If two or more users attempt to access the same file at the same time, the first user is able to modify the file, and the rest see the file in a read-only fashion. ▪

Permissions assigned to a folder also apply to all files and folders within the shared folder. For example, if you give the Sales group read permissions for the folder DATA, the members of the Sales group also have read permissions for all files and subfolders within DATA.

Effective Permissions

The Security Reference Monitor checks the user's access token against the entries in the ACL, as you have seen. When it identifies a match or matches, it must then determine the permissions to give the user. The effective share permissions are cumulative. The permissions explicitly assigned to a user, as well as permissions assigned to any groups that the user is a member of, are added together, and the highest level of permission is granted to the user. The only exception to this rule is the No Access permission which will always deny access regardless of any other permissions assigned.

For example, suppose BrownC is a member of Managers and Sales. BrownC has been given Change access, Managers has been given Full Control, and Sales has been given Read access to a shared folder. BrownC's effective permissions are Full Control by virtue of his membership in the Managers group.

The only exception to this rule is No Access. No Access always supersedes any other permission, even Full Control. Using the same example, if BrownC is given No Access explicitly, he is not able to access the shared folder, even though he is a member of the Managers group which has Full Control.

It is important, therefore, that you take sufficient time to plan your shared folders and their permissions. Let's look at the home directory folders as an example. Suppose that users' home directories are created under a share called Users. By default, Users are shared to Everyone with Full Control. This means that all files and folders within Users also give Everyone Full Control. Thus, all network users can see all other users' files in their home directories. This is probably not a good idea.

So how can you fix that? Here is one suggestion: Change the share permissions for Users to remove Everyone and add Administrators with Full Control (or at least Read). Share each home directory to the appropriate user explicitly with Full Control and change the users' properties through User Manager appropriately. Now, while Administrators can access everything for security reasons (and because they like the power), each user can access only his own home directory.

Administrative and Hidden Shares

When Windows NT is installed, it creates several shares, called *administrative shares*, all of which are hidden except for Net Logon. *Hidden shares* are shares that exist, but cannot be seen by any user in lists of available shared resources. They are meant to be used either by the operating system for specific tasks and services, such as IPC$ and REPL$, or by an administrator for security access or troubleshooting, such as the root drive shares.

Table 13.2 summarizes these hidden (and Net Logon) administrative shares.

Table 13.2 Administrative Shares

Share Name	Description
drive$	The root directory of every partition that Windows NT can recognize is assigned an administrative share name consisting of the drive letter followed by $. Administrators, Server Operators, and Backup Operators have the ability to connect to these shares remotely.
Admin$	Used by the operating system during remote administration of the computer, and represents the directory into which the Windows NT system files were installed (such as C:\ WINNT40). Administrators, Server Operators, and Backup Operators have the ability to connect to these shares remotely.
IPC$	Represents the named pipes that are used for communication between programs and systems, and is used by the operating system during remote administration of a computer, and when accessing another computer's shared resources.

continues

Part

IV

Ch

13

Table 13.2 Continued	
Share Name	**Description**
`Netlogon`	Created and used on domain controllers only for authenticating users logging on to the enterprise domain. This share is not hidden.
`Print$`	Similar to `IPC$`, provides remote access support for shared printers.
`REPL$`	Created and used on a Windows NT Server computer when the Directory Replication service is configured and enabled. It identifies the location of the directories and files to be exported.

Hidden shares can be identified by the $ after the share name. As an administrator, you can view all the administrative shares on a computer by starting the Server applet from the Control Panel and viewing Shares (or by starting Server Manager on a Windows NT Server, viewing a computer's properties, and then its Shares).

You can also create hidden shares yourself by adding $ to the end of the share name that you enter. This is a way to keep certain shares more secure. The only users that can connect to them are those who know the share name.

Accessing a Shared Folder

There are several ways that a user can access a shared folder (assuming that the user has been given permission to do so). Shares can be accessed by connecting directly to the resource through Network Neighborhood or the Find command, or by mapping a drive letter to a shared folder through My Computer or Windows Explorer.

All four utilities offer a point-and-click method of accessing the resource, which means that you do not necessarily have to know where the resource is exactly. The Computer Browser service (see Chapter 8, "Configuring Domain Network Core Services") provides you with the lists of domains, computers, and resources that you see. With Network Neighborhood and Find, you do not waste a drive letter on the resource. With My Computer and Windows Explorer, you use a drive letter for every mapping you create—and the alphabet is not an unlimited list.

Network Neighborhood

Perhaps the easiest way to connect to a shared folder is to use Network Neighborhood, especially if you only need occasional or short access to the folder and its contents (see Figure 13.5).

FIG. 13.5 ⇒
Network Neighborhood is used here to display the contents of the Force folder shared on the computer SDKACZ in DOMAINA.

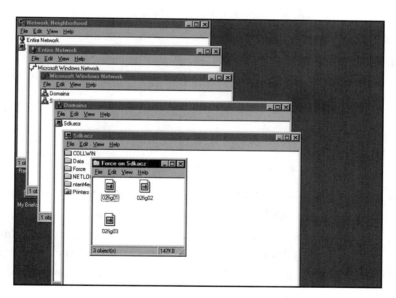

To connect to a shared folder using Network Neighborhood, follow these steps:

1. Double-click Network Neighborhood.

2. All members of your domain are listed under Entire Network. To see members of other domains, double-click Entire Network, then The Microsoft Network, and select the domain from the list.

3. Double-click the computer that has the shared folder to display a list of its shared folders.

4. Double-click the appropriate share name to see the contents of that folder.

Find Command

The Find command on the Start menu can be used effectively to search for computers that do not show up right away in a browse list like Network Neighborhood displays, or for a specific file or folder in a shared folder whose name you cannot recall.

To find a computer, follow these steps:

1. Choose Start, Find and then Computer from the taskbar.

2. In the Computer Name box, enter the name of the computer that has the shared folder.

3. Choose Find Now. Find displays a window showing the computer it finds.

4. Double-click the computer to display its shared folders.

5. Double-click the appropriate share name to display its contents.

To find a file or folder by name:

1. Choose Start, Find and then Files or Folders from the taskbar.

2. In the Look In box, enter the name of the computer that contains the shared folder. Or, you can choose Browse to browse the Network Neighborhood entry to find the computer.

3. In the Named box, enter the name of the file or folder that you are looking for.

4. Choose Find Now. Find displays a window with its search results. Double-click the appropriate file or folder to work with it.

Note   Several Find options are available to help narrow your search, such as Date Modified and Advanced. For example, if you are only looking for a folder contained in some share on a computer, use Advanced to narrow the search only to folders. ▪

My Computer and Windows Explorer

My Computer can be used to map a network drive to a shared folder on a computer. This is similar to the way logical drives are assigned to Novell NetWare resources, for those of you who are familiar with that network operating system (see Figure 13.6).

Using Windows Explorer is probably closest to using File Manager in previous versions of Windows NT or Windows for Workgroups. It displays a Map Network Drive dialog box similar to that used with My Computer, and, in fact, they both operate the same way.

FIG. 13.6 ⇒

Network Neighborhood expands you through The Microsoft Network entry to find the computer SDKACZ in the domain DOMAINA, and display its shares. The drive letter J will be assigned to this resource.

To map to a shared folder using Network Neighborhood, follow these steps:

1. Right-click My Computer and choose Map <u>N</u>etwork Drive. Or, you can start Windows Explorer, choose <u>T</u>ools from the menu, then <u>M</u>ap Network Drive.

2. The next available drive letter is displayed in the <u>D</u>rive box. Select it or make another drive choice.

3. Double-click the appropriate network entry in the <u>S</u>hared Directories list box to display a browse list of Workgroups and Domains.

4. Double-click the Workgroup or Domain that contains the sharing computer to display a list of computers with shared resources.

5. Double-click the appropriate computer to display its list of shared resources.

6. Select the appropriate shared folder from the list.

Or, if you do not see the computer or folder in the browse list but know the name of the computer and share, follow these steps:

1. Right-click My Computer and choose Map Network Drive. Or, you can start Windows Explorer, choose Tools from the menu, then Map Network Drive.

2. The next available drive letter is displayed in the Drive box. Select it or make another choice of letter.

3. In the Path box, enter the UNC name to the shared folder using the convention \\server\share, where server represents the name of the computer that has the shared folder, and share represents the name of the shared folder.

4. Click OK.

Notice in Figure 13.6 that the check box Reconnect at Logon may be selected. This is known as a *persistent connection*. When a user maps a drive through Windows NT Workstation 4.0, this option is selected by default. If you select this box, drive J is reconnected to the share every time the user logs in. If this is a resource that the user accesses frequently, then this is a convenient tool. If not, then you are just taking up extra system resources to locate the shared folder, make the connection, and monitor for access.

Note Mapped drives can be disconnected when no longer needed by right-clicking My Computer and choosing Disconnect Network Drive, or by choosing Disconnect Network Drive from the Windows Explorer's Tools menu. Select the drive from the list that you want to disconnect and choose OK. ▪

Also, it may happen that you need to access a resource on a computer on which you do not have a valid user account. This is particularly possible in workgroup configurations, or in the case of administrative access to various workstations or servers. If you know the name and password of a valid user account on that computer (including Guest), you can enter the UNC name in the Path box, as described in step 3 of the preceding list, and then enter the name of the valid account in the Connect As box. Windows NT asks you for the password, if it is required or different from your own, before connecting you to the resource.

Securing Folders and Files with NTFS Permissions

Up to this point, you have learned how to make resources available to other network users, how to secure those resources that you share on the network, and how you access them. There is another level of security that can be applied to files and folders stored on an NTFS partition. Among the many benefits of formatting a partition as NTFS, Windows NT's own file system, is the ability to assign permissions directly to the file and folder—that is, at the resource level.

Permissions are set for a file or folder by right-clicking the file or folder, displaying its Properties sheet, and selecting the Security tab. Choosing Permissions here displays the file or folders permissions dialog box from which you can make your choices.

Effective File and Folder Permissions

When you assign permissions to a folder or file, you are creating an ACL for that folder or file, much like you did for the share. The Security Reference Monitor checks the user's access token against the entries in the ACL, as you have seen. When it identifies a match or matches, it then must determine the permissions to give the user. The effective file or folder permissions are cumulative. The permissions explicitly assigned to a user, as well as permissions assigned to any groups that the user is a member of, are added together, and the highest level of permission is granted to the user *at the file or folder level*.

For example, suppose BrownC is a member of Managers and Sales. BrownC has been given Change access to a particular file, Managers has been given Full Control, and Sales has been given Read access to the file. BrownC's effective permissions for that file are Full Control by virtue of his membership in the Managers group.

The only exception to this rule is No Access. No Access always supersedes any other permission, even Full Control. Using the same example, if BrownC is given No Access explicitly, he is not able to access the file, even though he is a member of the Managers group which has Full Control.

Unlike share permissions, which are effective for all files and folders within the share, folder and file permissions are effective only for the immediate folder and its contents, or for an individual file if applied to that file. The permissions for files in a folder, or for subfolders, *can* trickle down, but can also be applied individually. If permissions have been applied to an individual file, the file permission *always* supersedes the folder permission.

For example, if BrownC has been given Read permission for the folder DATA, and Change permission to a file budget.doc, BrownC's effective permission for the file budget.doc is Change, even though because of the folder permission he has read to all the other files in DATA.

As you can see, you have a great deal of discretion and control over the application of permissions to folders, subfolders, and files. It is important, therefore, that you take sufficient time to plan your folder and file permissions. Let's take a different look at the home directory folders as an example. Suppose that users' home directories are created under a share called Users. By default, Users are shared to Everyone with Full Control. If the home folders are on an NTFS partition, you can assign each user the NTFS permission Full Control to his own home folder only while assigning the Everyone group List access to the directory. This effectively restricts access to each folder only to the owner of the folder.

Tip

If you create the users' home directories on an NTFS partition using the %USERNAME% variable (see Chapter 12, "Domain Users and Groups"), Windows NT will automatically restrict access to the home directory only to the specific user account.

Assigning File and Folder Permissions

There are six individual permissions that can be applied to files and folders. Table 13.3 describes these permissions.

Table 13.3   NTFS File and Folder Permissions

Permission	Folder Level	File Level
Read (R)	Can display folders, attributes, owner, and permissions.	Can display files and file data, attributes, owner, and permissions.
Write (W)	Can add files and create subfolders, change folder attributes, and display folder owner and permissions.	Can change file contents and attributes, and display file owner and permissions.
Execute (E)	Can make changes to subfolders, and display folder owner, attributes, and permissions.	Can run executable files, and display file owner, attributes, and permissions.
Delete (D)	Can delete a folder.	Can delete a file.
Change Permission (P)	Can change folder permissions.	Can change file permissions.
Take Ownership (O)	Can take ownership of a folder.	Can take ownership of a file.

Part

IV

Ch

13

Files and folders can be assigned these permissions individually or more often by using standard groupings provided by Windows NT security. There are nine standard folder permissions, which include two choices for setting your own custom choice of folder permissions and file permissions to apply to all files in a folder. There are five standard file permissions, which includes an option for setting your own custom choice of file permissions per individual file. Tables 13.4 and 13.5 outline these permissions and what they allow the user to do.

Note that when viewing and setting permissions, Windows NT always displays the individual permissions in parentheses alongside the standard permission. For folder permissions, the first set of parentheses represents the permissions on the folder, and the second set represents the permissions that apply to files globally, including any new file created in the folder.

Table 13.4 Standard Permissions for Folders

Permission	Access
No Access (None)(None)	Supersedes all other file permissions and prevents access to the file.
List (RX)(Not Specified)	Allows user to view folders and subfolders, and file names within folders and subfolders. List is not available as a valid permission option for files.
Read (RX)(RX)	In addition to List access, user can display file contents and subfolders, and run executable files.
Add (WX)(Not Specified)	User can add files to the folder, but not list its contents. Add is not available as a valid permission option for files.

Permission	Access
Add and Read (RWX)(RX)	In addition to Add, user can display the contents of files and subfolders, and run executable files.
Change (RWXD)(RWXD)	Allows user the ability to display and add files and folders, modify the contents of files and folders, and run executable files.
Full Control (All)(All)	In addition to Change, allows the user the ability to modify folder and file permissions and take ownership of folders and files.
Special Directory Access	Allows the selection of any combination of individual permissions (R, W, E, D, P, O) for folder access.
Special File Access	Allows the selection of any combination of individual permissions (R, W, E, D, P, O) for file access.

Table 13.5 Standard Permissions for Files

Permission	Access
No Access (None)	No access is allowed to the file.
Read (RX)	Allows user to display file data and run executable files.
Change (RWXD)	In addition to Read, the user can modify the file contents and delete the file.
Full Control (All)	In addition to Change, the user can modify the file's permissions and take ownership of the file.
Special Access	Allows the selection of any combination of individual permissions (R, W, E, D, P, O) for a file.

Part
IV

Ch

13

> **Caution**
>
> The folder permission Full Control provides the user an inherent ability to delete files in a folder through the command prompt even if the user is given No Access permission to a specific file. This is done to preserve Posix application support on UNIX systems, for which Write permission on a folder allows the user to delete files in the folder. This can be superseded by choosing the Special Directory Access standard permission and checking all the individual permissions.

Permissions are set for a file or folder by right–clicking the file or folder, displaying its Properties sheet, and selecting the Security tab. Choosing Permissions here displays the file or folder permissions dialog box as shown in Figure 13.7 from which you can make your choices.

FIG. 13.7 ⇒

The Force folder's permission list (ACL) shows that Administrators have Full Control access, Everyone has Read access, and Heroes has Change access.

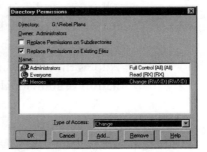

Notice in the Directory Permissions dialog box shown in Figure 13.7 that there are two Replace choices: Replace Permissions on Subdirectories and Replace Permissions on Existing Files (which is selected by default).

> **Caution**
>
> The effect of Replace Permissions on Existing Files is to change any and all permissions that you set on individual files with the permissions that you set at the folder level. Because this option is selected by default, it is easy to forget when setting permissions at the folder level, and you can accidentally change permissions on files that you do not want to change. Bottom line: Read all screens carefully.

Choosing Replace Permissions on Subdirectories causes Windows NT to apply the permissions set at this folder level to all subfolders. Any new files added to the folder will assume the folder's permissions. If Replace Permissions on Existing Files is also left selected, the permissions are applied not only to the subfolders, but to their contents as well.

The Type of Access list box shows all the standard permissions that are available at the folder level, including the two special options, Special Directory Access and Special File Access, from which you can customize your choice of permissions.

As with share permissions, users and groups can be added or removed from the ACL using the Add and Remove buttons.

Determining Access When Using Share and NTFS Permissions

A folder (and its contents) is made accessible across the network by sharing it. As discussed, an ACL can be created for the share. This defines which users and group accounts can access the share, and the level of access allowed. You know that the effective permissions are cumulative at the share level.

When NTFS permissions are assigned to individual folders and files, the level of access can be further refined by creating an ACL at the file and folder level. You know that the effective permissions at the file and folder level are also cumulative.

When a user accesses a file or folder protected by NTFS permissions across the network through a share, the Security Reference Monitor determines the cumulative permissions at the share and the cumulative permissions at the file or folder. Whichever permission is *most restrictive* becomes the effective permission for the user.

Part

IV

Ch

13

For example, if BrownC, a member of the Managers group, has been given Read access individually and Change access through the Managers group to a share called Public, then BrownC's effective permission for Public is Change. If BrownC has been given Read access to a file budget.doc (contained in the folder that has been shared as Public) and Full Control through the Managers group, BrownC's effective permission at the file level is Full Control. However, BrownC's net effective permission to budget.doc, when accessing it through the network share, is Change, which is the more restrictive of the two permissions.

	Public Share Level	**Budget.doc File Level**	**Budget.doc accessed through the Public share**
BrownC Managers	Read + Change	Read + Full Control	
Effective Permissions	Change	Full Control	Change (more restrictive than Full Control)

Through a shrewd use of share and file\folder level permissions, you can create a very effective security structure for resources stored on your Windows NT workstations and servers.

Understanding the Concept of Ownership

The user who creates a file or folder is noted by Windows NT to be the owner of that file or folder, and is placed in the Creator Owner internal group for that file or folder. A user cannot give someone else ownership of her files or folders. However, a user can give someone the *permission* to take ownership of her files and folders.

The Take Ownership permission is implied through Full Control, but can also be assigned to a user or group through the Special Access permission options. A user that has this permission can take ownership of the file or folder. After ownership has been taken, the new owner can modify the file or folder's permissions, delete the file, and so on. Administrators always have the ability to take ownership of a file or folder.

A user who has the Take Ownership permission can take ownership of a folder or file by following these steps:

1. Right-click the folder or file and select P<u>r</u>operties.
2. In the Properties sheet, select the Security tab.
3. On the Security tab, choose <u>O</u>wnership. The current owner is displayed.
4. Choose <u>T</u>ake Ownership, and then choose OK.

> **Note** If any *member* of the Administrators group takes ownership of a file or folder, or creates a file or folder, the owner becomes the Administrators *group*. ▪

Taking ownership of files and folders can be useful, especially when users move around from department to department or position to position, or leave the organization. It provides a way to assign files and folders that are no longer being used by a user to an appropriate replacement.

Copying and Moving Files...and Permissions

When you copy a file from one folder to another, the file assumes the permissions of the target folder. When you move a file from one folder to another, the file maintains its current permissions. This sounds simple enough, except that a move isn't always a move. When you move a file from a folder in one partition to a folder in another partition, you are actually copying the file to the target folder, and then deleting the original file. A move is only a move, where permissions are involved, when you move a file from a folder in one partition to another folder in the *same* partition.

Managing Shares and Permissions Remotely

As an administrator, it is possible to create and manage shares and set permissions for folders and files remotely. If you are working on a Windows NT-based computer, simply map a drive to the hidden drive share—for example, D$—and then proceed as described in the previous section "Assigning File and Folder Permissions."

If you have installed the server tools on your computer (see Chapter 15, "Remote Server Management"), you can also use Server Manager to manage shares. Server Manager displays a list of the Windows NT-based domain controllers, member servers, and workstations in your domain. Manage shares by following these steps:

1. Select the computer on which you want to manage the share from the computer list.

2. Choose Computer, Shared Directories to display the Shared Directories dialog box (see Figure 13.8).

3. Choose New Share and enter a Share Name, folder Path (there is no browse feature here), and set Permissions in the New Share dialog box.

   Select an existing share from the Shared Directories list and choose Properties to modify its current properties, such as permissions.

   Select an existing share from the Shared Directories list and choose Stop Sharing to remove the share.

4. Choose Close to save your changes.

FIG. 13.8 ⟹

Server Manager allows an administrator to remotely create and manage shares on Windows NT computers in the domain.

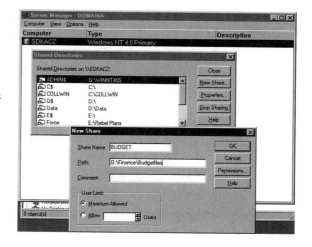

If you have administrative access to other domains either through a valid administrator's account or through a trust relationship, you can remotely administer shares on Windows NT computers in that domain as well. Follow these steps to switch to that domain:

1. Choose Computer, Select Domain to display the Select Domain dialog box.

2. Either select the appropriate domain from the Select Domain list, or enter the domain name in the Domain text box.

3. Choose OK. The Server Manager screen will refresh and list computers in the selected domain.

4. Manage shares as outlined in the steps at the beginning of this section.

Part
IV

Ch
13

Troubleshooting Security

The most likely problem that you will have with security will be when a user is unable to access a resource. There is not much additional advice that can be given besides what has been said. In other words, you must go back and check the share permissions and file and folder permissions. Remember that at the share level and at the file and folder level, permissions are cumulative. However, when comparing share permissions to file and folder permissions, Windows NT assigns the most restrictive permission to the user.

When changing permissions on a share, file, or folder, the user will not notice the effect of the change until the next time the resource is accessed. This is because of the way Windows NT assigns the permission to the user. Recall that when the user's access token is compared to the ACL, and the effective permission established, the user's access token receives a permission handle to the resource. This handle remains in effect until the user releases the resource.

For example, BrownC has effective permission Change to budget.doc. The owner of budget.doc decides to restrict BrownC to Read. While BrownC has budget.doc open and in use, his effective permission remains Change. When he closes budget.doc and opens it later, his effective permission changes to Read.

Suppose BrownC has established a logical drive mapping to the Data share and has effective permission Change to the share. The owner of the share changes BrownC's permission to Read. BrownC continues to maintain Change permission to the share until he disconnects from it and reconnects, or until he logs off and logs back on.

In another case, suppose BrownC is currently a member of the Managers group. BrownC has Read permission to the Data folder but Full Control effective permission through his membership in the Managers group. You take BrownC out of the Managers group to ensure that he only has Read access to the folder. When BrownC accesses the folder, he still has Full Control access to the folder. This is because his access token still maintains that he has membership in the Managers group. Remember that the access token is created during *logon*. Thus, the group change is not effective until BrownC logs off and logs back on.

Taking the Disc Test

If you have read and understood the material in the chapter, you are ready to test your knowledge. Insert the CD-ROM that comes with this book and run the self-test software as described in Appendix I, "Using the CD-ROM."

From Here...

In this chapter, you learned about security and the management of network resources. Chapter 14, "Policies and Profiles," will focus on a different aspect of computer and user management—setting environment and Registry variables. User profiles and system policies and their effects within the domain will be discussed at length.

Part
IV

Ch
13

Chapter Prerequisite

It is important that the reader be comfortable with the concepts of user and group management covered in Chapter 12, "Domain Users and Groups," as well as the Directory Services concepts presented in Chapters 2-5.

Policies and Profiles

In this chapter we will discuss how to manage the user's and computer's environments through the use of user and computer profiles. In particular we will cover these topics:

◆ Understanding user and computer profiles

◆ Creating and managing server-based profiles

◆ Exploring the System Policy Editor

◆ Troubleshooting profiles

Understanding User and Computer Profiles

As discussed in Chapter 12, "Domain Users and Groups," when we speak of the User Profile in Windows NT 4.0, we are really talking about managing the user's working environment. In contrast, when we speak of the Computer Profile, we are talking about managing the computer's environment and configuration settings. Both types of profiles involve modifications that are made to the Windows NT Registry.

Through the User Environment Profile dialog box in User Manager for Domains, various elements of the user's environment can be defined. These include:

◆ *The User Profile Path.* Identifies the location of the Registry files and profile folders for the user.

◆ *The Logon Script Name.* Identifies the name and optional path of a set of commands that are executed when the user logs on.

◆ *The Home Folder.* Identifies the location of the user's personal data folder.

Each of these elements is discussed at length in Chapter 12.

Through the System Policy Editor, Registry settings for both the user's environment and the computer's configuration can be modified. These might include restricting the use of the File, Run command for the user, or configuring a legal notice to display on a Windows NT workstation when a user attempts to log on.

In both cases, the user's computing environment is configured automatically, and according to predetermined settings, when the computer boots and the user logs on.

User Profiles

The User Profile itself represents the user's environment settings such as screen colors, wallpaper, persistent network and printer connections, mouse settings and cursors, shortcuts, personal groups, and Startup programs. These settings are normally saved as part of the Windows NT Registry on the user's computer and loaded when the user logs on to the system.

In Windows NT 3.51 and earlier versions, these settings were kept in the WINNT\SYSTEM32\CONFIG subdirectory with the other Registry files on the local computer, workstation, or server that the user logged on to. The next time that the user logged on, the profile settings were made available and merged into the Registry for that session. If the user moved to another computer, whether the user logged on locally or to the network, a new profile would be created on that computer and saved locally. The settings saved on that computer would in turn be merged into the local Windows NT Registry on that computer.

Under Windows NT 4.0, profiles are still saved on the local computer at which the user logs on. However, all information relating to the user's profile is now saved in a subdirectory structure created in the WINNT\ PROFILES folder which contains the Registry data file as well as directory links to desktop items. An example of this structure is displayed in Figure 14.1.

FIG. 14.1⇒
In this view of Windows Explorer, the WINNT\ PROFILES folder with the profile subdirectory structure for SOLOH is expanded. Notice the Registry files NTUSER.DAT and NTUSER. DAT.LOG.

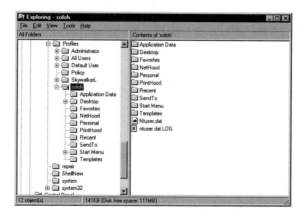

There are three default profile structures created during installation:

- One for the Administrator's account because it is a default account.
- *Default User.* New user accounts can derive their initial environment settings from here.
- *All Users.* Used with the user's profile settings to assign settings that should be common to all users such as startup items and common groups.

The directory structure of the user's profile directory is outlined in Table 14.1.

When the user first logs on, the settings contained in Default User are used to create that user's own profile folders. In addition, the Registry data file, called NTUSER.DAT, is created and stored in the root of the user's profile folder (refer to Figure 14.1). Windows NT also creates and maintains a corresponding transaction log file called NTUSER.DAT.LOG. Changes to the profile are actually recorded in the log file and applied to the NTUSER.DAT file when the user logs off. In the event of a problem, the changes are kept in the log file and can be applied the next time the user logs on. So, as the user modifies the environment by changing settings, creating shortcuts, installing applications, and adding programs to the Start menu, Windows NT adds and modifies entries in the appropriate profile folder and updates the Registry log file.

For example, if SoloH (profile folders shown in Figure 14.1) added a shortcut to his desktop for Word 97, Windows NT would add an entry representing the shortcut to Word 97 in the Desktop folder under WINNT\PROFILES\SOLOH. If SoloH modified his desktop wallpaper, the change would be recorded in his NTUSER.DAT.LOG file and applied to his NTUSER.DAT file when he logged off.

The Registry subtree HKEY_CURRENT_USER is actually a cached copy of the Registry data file NTUSER.DAT, and as discussed in Chapter 7, "The Role of the Registry," it contains information relating to the user's environment settings such as color schemes, cursors, wallpaper, and so on.

Table 14.1   Overview of the Profile Folder Directory Structure

Profile Folder	Description
Application	Contains references to application-specific data and is usually modified by the application during installation or when a user modifies a setting for the application.
Desktop	Contains references to shortcuts created on the desktop and the Briefcase.
Favorites	Contains references to shortcuts made to favorite programs and locations.
NetHood	Contains references to shortcuts made to Network Neighborhood items, such as shared folders.
Personal	Contains references to shortcuts made to personal group programs.
PrintHood	Contains references to shortcuts made to print folder items.
Recent	Contains references to items on the computer most recently accessed by the user.
SendTo	Contains references to the last items that documents were "sent to" or copied such as the A: drive or My Briefcase.
Start Menu	Contains references to program items contained on the Start menu, including the Startup group.
Templates	Contains references to shortcuts made to template items.

Note By default the NetHood, PrintHood, Recent, and Templates folders are hidden from display in Windows Explorer. They can be viewed by choosing View, Options, selecting the View tab, and choosing Show All Files. ■

Server-Based User Profiles

As we have seen, user profile information is stored on the computer(s) that the user logs in on. If a user routinely logs on to several computers, it might be inconvenient for the user to create or modify preferred settings on each computer before beginning to work on that computer. It would be far more efficient if the user's work environment settings followed the user to whatever computer the user logs in to. This type of user is known as the *roaming user,* and their profiles are known as server-based, or *roaming* profiles. This type of profile is used more often in organizations to provide a level of consistency among their users' desktops rather than to accommodate roaming users.

Windows NT 4.0 Workstation and Server computers support two types of server-based profiles: Roaming User Profiles and Mandatory User Profiles. They are both user profile settings that have been copied to a centrally located server for access by the user when logging on. The location and name of the profile is identified in the user's User Environment Profile information through User Manager for Domains.

When the user logs on to a computer, either a mandatory or roaming profile is copied to that local computer to provide the best performance (local as opposed to over-the-network access). Changes made to the roaming profile are updated both on the local computer and the server. The next time that the user logs on, the server copy is compared to the local copy. If the server copy is more recent, then it is copied to the local computer. If the local copy has the same time and date stamp as the server copy, the local copy is used again to facilitate the logon process. If the local copy is more recent, as might happen if the user uses a laptop that is not frequently connected to the network, then the user is notified and asked which copy to use.

The primary difference between mandatory and roaming profiles is that the mandatory profile is created by an administrator for the user and *cannot* be modified by the user. The roaming profile can be, and is meant to be, modified by the user and follows the user as a convenience.

Key Concept

The user may change environment settings while in a particular session, but those settings are *not* saved back to the mandatory profile. Also, a mandatory profile can be configured so that if the profile is unavailable when the user attempts to log on, the user will be prevented from logging on.

Server Profiles over Slow WAN Links

Logging in over a slower WAN connection such as a dial-up line or a 56K link can result in slowed response time for the logon process. This can be particularly painful for the user when a server-based profile must be copied across the slow link. If you have told Windows NT to monitor for slow WAN connections (User Manager for Domains), when Windows NT detects a slow link (more than two minutes to respond for a request for the profile), it displays a dialog box that asks the user to select either a locally cached profile, or the server-based profile. If the user selects the local profile, all changes are saved to the local version.

The user can also make the choice to switch to the local profile during his session. Through the User Profiles tab in the System applet in the Control Panel, the user can choose to change his profile from roaming to local, or from local to roaming. Again, if the user selects local, all changes are saved to the local profile until the user switches back to the server profile.

If the user requires a mandatory profile, the user will not be able to log on unless he or she opts to install the user-based profile over the slow connection.

Creating the Server-Based Profile

Windows NT 4.0 Server no longer provides the User Profile utility that some of you may have been familiar with from Windows NT

Server 3.51. Windows NT Server 4.0 has, however, implemented support for server-based profiles in a couple of interesting ways.

A server-based profile is always identified to the user's account by the account administrator by providing the UNC path and file name of the profile file in the user account's User Environment Profile dialog box as shown in Figure 14.2. This path identifies the server on which the profile will be maintained as well as the shared folder in which it will be kept. If the file specified does not exist, Windows NT will create an empty profile for the user. When the user first logs on and modifies the settings, the server-based profile is updated.

FIG. 14.2⇒

The server-based profile file for user SoloH is stored in the Heroes subfolder in the Profiles shared folder on the server SDKACZ. The .MAN extension on the profile file indicates that this is a mandatory profile.

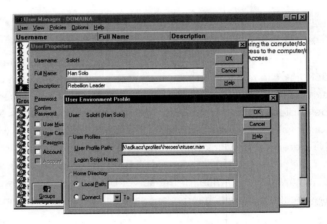

In some cases, the administrator may want or need to predetermine the users' profiles. Windows NT has provided management for this type of user profile through the User Profiles tab of the System applet in the Control Panel.

The User Profiles tab of the System Properties dialog box displays the profiles that have been created and stored on that computer. Remember that a profile is created each time a user logs on. If you plan on deleting a user, you should delete the user's profile first through this tab. If you delete the user first, you will see an entry `Account Deleted` as shown in Figure 14.3. This is not really such a big deal if only one or two accounts are involved; if the account is deleted anyway, it is a pretty safe bet that you can delete its profile information. With large numbers of users, deleting the appropriate profiles can be confusing after the fact. Recall that all settings relating to a user account are linked to the user's SID. Deleting the account deletes the SID and renders all previous settings obsolete, including profile information.

FIG. 14.3⇒

Here we see that there are four user profiles contained on this computer. One of them is for an account that has since been deleted. It should be removed to clean up the Profiles directory on the hard disk.

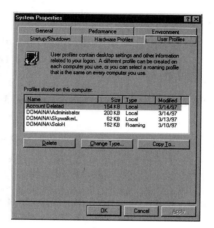

The first step in creating a roaming or mandatory profile is to identify the users or groups that require this type of profile. The Registry file name NTUSER.DAT cannot be changed, and it is this file that will determine whether the profile is mandatory or not. Next, identify the central computer on which you plan to store the users' profiles. This should be a computer that is readily accessible by the users on that network or subnet, particularly if the profiles are mandatory. The directory should then be shared on the network. Within this directory, optionally create subdirectories for the different users or groups that will use various profiles you create.

> **Caution**
>
> If you permit several users or a group of users to use the same roaming profile, remember that profile *can be modified* by the user. It is possible that multiple users may make multiple changes to the profile. Mandatory profiles are better used for groups of users. Individual roaming users should each have their own roaming, changeable profile.

Roaming and mandatory profiles are then configured in the following manner:

1. Identify a server and shared folder location on which you will save the profile.

2. Identify or create a user account, and make the appropriate changes to that account's environment settings.

3. Select that account's profile through the User Profiles tab in the System applet in the Control Panel and choose Copy To.

4. In the Copy Profile To box enter the UNC name to the share and directory that will contain the profiles, or choose Browse to look for the location.

5. Select Change, and from the Choose User dialog box that is displayed, select the user by choosing Show Users, or groups that you are permitting to use this profile.

6. Choose OK to save the profile and exit the System applet.

Next, you must identify the profile file to the user or users in question through the User Manager utility.

1. Open User Manager for Domains.

2. From the User Properties of the user in question, choose Profile to display the User Environment Profile dialog box.

3. In the User Profile Path text box, enter the UNC path to the profile file. For example, if the profile NTUSER.DAT is located in the BROWNC directory in the share PROFILES on the server KITESERVER, you would enter **\\KITESERVER\PROFILES\BROWNC\NTUSER.DAT**.

4. Choose OK and exit User Manager for Domains.

5. Test the profile by logging on as that user.

Mandatory Profiles

As stated earlier, a mandatory profile is one that does not accept user changes. It always provides the same settings for every user who has been identified as using that profile. For this reason, it is the best choice when maintaining the same configuration settings for large groups of users, or for users who should not be allowed to make configuration changes.

The steps for creating a mandatory profile are the same as those for a roaming profile. If you require the profile to become mandatory, you must use Windows Explorer to select the NTUSER.DAT file and change the extension to NTUSER.MAN. This effectively makes the profile mandatory, and any changes that users may make to their desktops will not be saved back to the profile.

Key Concept

Furthermore, if the administrator specifies this file by name in the user's User Environment Profile settings dialog box, the user will be prevented from logging on if the profile is for any reason unavailable.

If the administrator does not specify the file by name, the user will still be able to log on with default user settings.

Default User Profiles

It is possible for an administrator to create a default profile that all users can receive when they first log in. For example, perhaps all users should have the same screen colors, or the company logo as their desktop wallpaper. Again, this profile is created as a regular roaming profile. However, this profile must be copied to the NETLOGON share (WINNT\ SYSTEM32\REPL\IMPORT\SCRIPTS) for every domain controller in the user's account domain. The user accounts must also be configured as outlined earlier to use a personal profile.

When the user logs on, Windows NT checks the user account's specified profile path for the existence of a profile file. If none exist, and there are none stored locally on the computer from which the user is logging in, Windows NT checks the NETLOGON share for a folder named Default User and loads the profile stored there. When the user logs off, these settings, and any changes the user made, are saved to the user's own profile folder.

> **Caution**
> When copying a profile to a server, you must use the Server applet in the Control Panel. Using Windows Explorer will not make the necessary modifications to the Windows NT Registry to record the location of the profile. Only the Server applet makes the appropriate Registry changes. Profile entries are found in the following Registry subkey: HKEY_LOCAL_MACHINE\Software\Microsoft\Windows NT\CurrentVersion\ProfileList.

Supporting Windows 95 Profiles

Windows 95 administrators can also create and maintain profiles for Windows 95 users. Both Windows 95 and Windows NT 4.0 profiles operate similarly, although Windows 95 profiles are created differently and have some functional differences. Windows 95, for example, does not support the concept of common groups or a centrally stored default profile. For that matter, Windows 95 profiles can only be copied from the user's home folder as opposed to a specific profile path. In addition, the Registry files created by Windows 95 to support profiles are different from Windows NT 4.0—USER.DAT, USER.DA0, and USER.MAN as opposed to NTUSER.DAT, NTUSER.DAT.LOG, and NTUSER.MAN.

Nevertheless, Windows 95 users can obtain their profiles when logging in as a member of a Windows NT domain by creating their profiles as usual through Windows 95, storing them in the users' home folders, and referencing the home folders' locations in each user account's User Environment Profile dialog box in Windows NT.

Managing Profiles with the System Policy Editor

The System Policy Editor can alternatively, and perhaps more effectively, be used to control user profile settings. It is only available on Windows NT 4.0 servers. Through the System Policy Editor, you can modify the default settings for all users, or copy the settings and modify them by individual user or groups. The policy file is then saved as NTCONFIG.POL in the WINNT\SYSTEM32\REPL\IMPORT\ SCRIPTS subdirectory on all validating domain controllers. This concept will seem quite familiar to Windows 95 administrators as it is similar to the system policy file that can be created for Windows 95 clients (CONFIG.POL). However, Windows 95 system policies are not compatible with Windows NT 4.0 system policies due, in part, to differences in their registries.

System Policy Editor allows the administrator to affect both computer configurations and settings, such as those saved in the HKEY_LOCAL_MACHINE subtree of the Registry, as well as user environment settings such as those saved in the HKEY_USERS subtree. Settings can affect all computers and users as default or general settings, or they can be created to affect only specific computers or users.

For example, through the System Policy Editor, you can restrict user activity in the Display applet in the Control Panel; specify desktop settings such as wallpaper and color schemes; customize desktop folders; create custom folders and Start menu options; restrict use of Run, Find, and Shutdown; and disable editing of the Registry. Combined with computer system policies applied to the computer at which a user logs on, the administrator can get a finer level of granularity over controlling the user's work environment.

Working with the System Policy Editor

There are two types of policy modes that are provided by the System Policy Editor—Registry mode and Policy mode. The Registry mode allows an administrator to administer local or remote registries without using the Registry Editor. The System Policy Editor provides a point-and-click method of effecting Registry changes, thus the administrator has a safe and relatively intuitive utility for modifying a local or remote Registry. Additionally, changes made through the Registry mode of the System Policy Editor take effect immediately in contrast to those made through the Registry Editor.

Initiate Registry mode by selecting File, Open Registry from the menu. The Local Computer icon displays options that can effect changes to the HKEY_LOCAL_MACHINE subtree of the local Registry. The Local User icon displays options that can effect changes to the HKEY_Users subtree. Access the Registry on a remote Windows NT computer by selecting File, Connect from the System Policy Editor menu and entering the name of the Windows NT computer you want to affect.

 Note You must have administrator privileges on the Windows NT computer whose Registry you want to manage. ∎

The Policy mode provides an administrator with a method of implementing configuration changes for all users or computers, or for selected users and computers. This is done by creating a single policy file that contains references to various computers or users, each with a distinct set of configuration requirements. The policy file can then be saved on a specified server, accessed during user logon and downloaded to the logon workstation.

Initiate Policy mode by selecting File, New Policy from the main menu to create a new policy file; or select File, Open Policy to modify an existing policy file. The Default Computer icon will display options that will affect all computers connecting to the domain, and the Default User icon will display options that will similarly affect all users logging on to the domain. Specific users and computers can also be added to the policy file, each with its own set of configuration options selected.

In both modes, when the user logs on, the settings contained in the system policy are merged with the current Registry settings to provide a specific environment for the computer and the user. The options displayed for both modes are the same, so we will not break them out by mode as we continue our discussion.

Policy Templates
The policy options that are displayed when modifying computer or user settings in either mode are determined by a set of template files

provided by Widows NT 4.0. These templates provide options for the most common configuration settings that administrators modify. The templates are text files with a specific structure, and as such can be modified or customized for specific usage by the administrator.

Two policies are loaded by default when System Policy Editor is started. COMMON.ADM offers options that are common to both Windows NT 4.0 and Windows 95 such as Network, Desktop, Control Panel, System, Shell, and System settings. These options primarily effect changes to HKEY_Users in the Windows NT 4.0 and Windows 95 Registries. WINNT.ADM offers Windows NT 4.0 specific options such as Windows NT Network, Windows NT Printers, Windows NT User Profiles, Windows NT System, Windows NT Remote Access, and Windows NT Shell. These options primarily effect changes to HKEY_LOCAL_MACHINE in the Windows NT Registry.

A third policy is also available called WINDOWS.ADM, which offers options that are specific to Windows 95 computers such as Windows 95 Control Panel, Windows 95 System, Windows 95 Shell, and Windows 95 Network.

Through a combination of these templates, system policies can be created to govern the working environments of all your Windows NT 4.0 and Windows 95 clients from the same policy file.

Setting System Policy Options

When the administrator modifies a system policy by selecting the computer or user icons, a list of option categories is displayed in a manner similar to the Windows Explorer folder screen. The administrator drills down through each option category and makes a selection by checking off the option desired. In many cases, as an option is checked, the bottom half of the screen displays additional settings that can be made, or text that can be entered as demonstrated in Figure 14.4.

Part
IV

Ch
14

FIG. 14.4⇒

The Desktop category for the Default User is selected. With the selection of Color Scheme, the administrator can choose from a list of available color schemes in the Scheme Name list box.

There are three selection possibilities for each policy option.

◆ Checking an option indicates that the option should be merged with the current Registry and override any existing settings.

◆ Clearing a check box indicates that the option should be merged with the Registry if there is no current Registry setting for that option. If there is a current setting, then the policy setting is ignored.

◆ Leaving the check box grey, the default, means that the policy setting is not modified at all.

In fact, only options that are checked or cleared are actually saved to the policy file so as to keep the file to a manageable size when downloading it across network connections.

Default and Specific User and Computer Settings

Changes made to policy settings under Default User or Default Computer are applied to all computers and users affected by this policy file.

When a user logs on, the policy file is checked first for the default settings that should be applied to all computers and users, then the Registry is modified accordingly.

However, policy options can also be set for individual computers and users within a domain. For example, suppose that computer WOOKI5 needs to have a specific network setting configured when a given user logs on. A policy setting can be configured specifically for WOOKI5. When a user logs on at WOOKI5, the policy file is checked for any specific options set for that computer, and then for default settings. It finds WOOKI5 and implements those settings in addition to, or overriding, the default settings. Similarly, specific settings can be provided for individual user accounts. When the user logs on, any specific settings meant for that particular user are implemented in addition to, or overriding, the default settings.

In addition, policy settings can be implemented by group membership. Options for specific groups can be set, along with a group priority, to determine which settings take precedence when a user belongs to several groups for which policies have been set. If a user has a specific policy, however, any group policy that might otherwise have been set for the user will be ignored. The specific order for implementing system policy settings is outlined in Figure 14.5.

Follow these steps to create a specific policy for an individual user.

1. Start System Policy Editor.
2. Choose Edit, Add User.
3. Enter the user name of the user you are adding, or select the Browse button to display the domain database.
4. Double-click the new user's icon in the System Profile Editor dialog box and make your choices as desired.

Follow these steps to create a specific policy for an individual computer.

1. Start System Policy Editor.
2. Choose Edit, Add Computer.

3. Enter the name of the computer you are adding, or select the Browse button to display the list of computers in the Network Neighborhood.

4. Double-click the new computer's icon in the System Profile Editor dialog box and make your choices as desired.

FIG. 14.5⟹
Here is a flow chart for applying system policy settings.

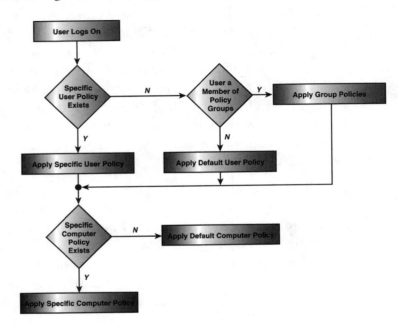

Follow these steps to create a specific policy for an individual group.

1. Start System Policy Editor.

2. Choose Edit, Add Group.

3. Enter the name of the group you are adding, or select the Browse button to display the domain database.

4. Double-click the new group's icon in the System Profile Editor dialog box and make your choices as desired.

When two or more groups are added to the policy file, you can specify the priority order in which group policy settings are applied to users by following these steps.

1. Highlight a group in the System Policy Editor dialog box.

2. Choose Options, Group Priority.

3. Select a group from the Group Order list and choose Move Up or Move Down as appropriate to create the desired priority order for your groups.

Windows NT 4.0 makes use of a predefined policy file name to automatically implement system policies across the domain. The file is called NTCONFIG.POL and must be saved in the NETLOGON share (WINNT\SYSTEM32\REPL\IMPORT\SCRIPTS). When the user logs on, Windows NT automatically looks for the existence of this file in the NETLOGON share on all domain controllers for the domain. If it exists, it is checked for default and specific policy settings (refer to Figure 14.5).

Key Concept

If you are using NTCONFIG.POL to automatically implement system policies, be sure to place a copy of the file on every domain controller in the domain. Recall that when a user logs on to the domain, the Net Logon service locates an available domain controller to authenticate the user. If the user authenticates on a domain controller that does not have the NTCONFIG.POL file on it, then the policy settings will not be implemented. You can use Directory Replication to distribute the NTCONFIG.POL file to all the domain controllers (see Chapter 8, "Configuring Domain Network Core Services").

However, the administrator can choose to create individual policy files for specific users, groups, or computers and save them in an accessible shared directory on a server. These can have any file name, but they must have the extension .POL. Also, these policy files must be specified by a UNC path in the user account's Profile settings dialog box.

> **Caution**
> Windows NT applies system profiles that it finds on the domain from which the user logs in. In a trusted domain environment, this can be confusing as computers may belong to a different domain than that from which the user is logging in. A default computer policy for a computer in a trusting domain that is maintained in an NTCONFIG.POL file in the trusting domain, for example, would not be implemented when a user from the trusted domain logs on at that computer. Windows NT would be looking for the NTCONFIG.POL file on the trusted domain and implementing whatever policy settings it found there.

Taking the Disc Test

 If you have read and understood the material in the chapter, you are ready to test your knowledge. Insert the CD-ROM that comes with this book and run the self-test software as described in Appendix I, "Using the CD-ROM."

From Here...

This chapter dealt with utilities, concepts, and techniques for managing resources in the enterprise. Chapter 15, "Remote Server Management," rounds out the discussion of resource management covered in this section of the book by exploring remote server management tools.

15

Remote Server Management

The first subject presented in this chapter will be the purpose of server tools in the Windows NT environment. Then the chapter explains the server tools available for a number of Windows NT 4.0 clients and what tools are available for each client.

This chapter will also give installation procedures of server tools for all clients including Windows NT 4.0 Workstation and Windows 95. Installation procedures will also be provided for older clients such as Windows for Workgroups 3.11 and Windows 3.1.

Topics in this chapter include:

◆ Server tools introduction

◆ Server tools system requirements

◆ Server tools for Windows NT 4.0 Workstation

◆ Installation of Windows NT 4.0 Workstation server tools

◆ Server tools for Windows 95

◆ Installation of Windows 95 Workstation server tools

◆ Server tools for Windows for Workgroups 3.11/Windows 3.1

◆ Installation of Windows for Workgroups 3.11/Windows 3.1 server tools

The Purpose of Server Tools

Administrators use server tools to administer domain controllers from remote locations. It is quite possible for a domain to be spread out among a number of buildings, towns, cities, or even countries. User and group account changes and additions, password changes, and other administrative duties are all included in the domain administrative functions.

From previous chapters you may recall that to make any change in a directory services database in a domain, an administrator must be located at a domain controller. Even if the administrator is sitting at a Backup Domain Controller (BDC), the change is physically made in the database on the Primary Domain Controller (PDC). It is possible that all locations of the domain do not have a domain controller present. Depending on the location of PDCs and BDCs, it is almost impossible for an administrator to always be at a domain location where a domain controller is located, or to always be in one place and make all database changes from one location.

With server tools, an administrator can be physically located at any client computer and perform a number of domain administrative duties. Server tools also eliminate the need for a domain controller at each and every remote domain location, thereby lowering the overall cost of required software in the domain.

The reason server tools were made available for a number of Microsoft clients is to alleviate the problem of the administrator always having to be located at a domain controller in order to administer a domain.

System Requirements

As with any software or utilities, server tools do require system resources to be installed and function correctly. The following paragraphs summarize the system requirements for the various client platforms.

Required Resources for Windows NT 4.0 Workstation

The following resources are required to install server tools on a Windows NT 4.0 Workstation:

- Microsoft Windows NT 4.0 Workstation software installed
- 486DX/33 or higher CPU
- 12M of memory
- 2.5M of free hard disk space
- Workstation and Server services installed

Required Resources for Windows 95

The following resources are required to install server tools on a Windows 95 computer:

- Microsoft Windows 95 installed
- 486/33 or higher CPU
- 8M of memory
- 3M of free hard disk space
- Client for Microsoft Networks installed

Required Resources for Windows 3.1 or Windows for Workgroups 3.11

The following resources are required to install server tools on Windows 3.1 or Windows for Workgroups 3.11:

- Microsoft Windows 3.1 or Windows for Workgroups 3.11 installed. Both must be running in 386 enhanced mode and have paging (virtual memory, either a permanent or temporary swap file) enabled.
- 8M of memory
- 5M of free hard disk space
- The Microsoft redirector installed

In addition to the above requirements, the FILES statement in config.sys must be set to at least 50.

Windows NT 4.0 Workstation Server Tools

The following 32-bit server tools are available for Windows NT 4.0 Workstation:

- User Manager for Domains
- Server Manager
- System Policy Editor
- Remote Access Administrator
- Services for Macintosh
- DHCP Manager
- WINS Manager
- Remoteboot Manager

Once these tools are installed on a Windows NT 4.0 Workstation, they function exactly the same as they do on a Windows NT 4.0 Server installation.

Tip

Server tools installed on a Windows NT 3.5/3.51 Workstation are the same with the exception of System Policy Editor. User Profile Editor is installed instead.

Installation of Workstation Server Tools

Installation of server tools on a Windows NT 4.0 Workstation is relatively easy and can be accomplished in a number of ways. All the required files for any platform for Windows NT 4.0 Workstation are located on the Windows NT 4.0 Server CD-ROM in the CLIENTS\SRVTOOLS\WINNT folder.

Installation from the CD-ROM

Installation can be accomplished simply by accessing the Windows NT 4.0 Server CD-ROM and running the Setup.bat file in the CLIENTS\ SRVTOOLS\WINNT folder. The Setup.bat file determines the architecture of the client computer and copies all the server tools files and supporting files to the <winntroot>\System32 folder. It will *not* make an Administrative Tools Program Group on the workstation platform. If a specific program group is desired, it must be created manually.

Figure 15.1 displays the autorun screen of the CD-ROM and the CLIENTS\SRVTOOLS\WINNT folder with Setup.bat highlighted. Notice also that server tools files for all Windows NT 4.0 Workstation platforms are available.

FIG. 15.1 ⇒

This figure shows the Windows NT 4.0 Server tools installation file locations.

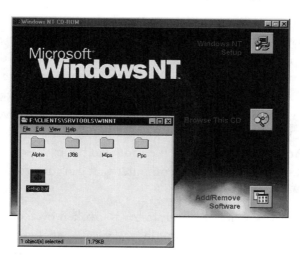

Figure 15.2 illustrates what events take place when the Setup.bat file is executed. Notice that it does display the .exe files that could be manually included in a program group. It does not, however, display the support files loaded with the executables.

FIG. 15.2 ⇒

Here are the Windows NT 4.0 Workstation Server tools files.

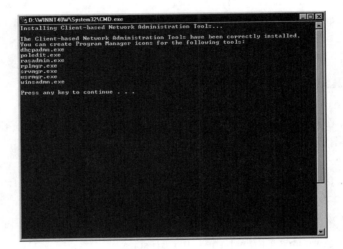

Creating a Server Tools Share Using Network Client Administrator

The Network Client Administrator application, found on Windows NT 4.0 Server, is a tool used to perform four functions. One of these functions is related to Windows NT 4.0 server tools. The Copy Client-based Network Administration Tools option simply copies the CLIENT\ SRVTOOLS folder to a specified location on a network and creates a share for that location. The default location is <diskdrive>\CLIENTS\ SRVTOOLS and the default share name of the srvtools folder is SetupAdm. From this share, the tools can be installed on any Windows NT 4.0 client workstation computer that can map to or access the share.

The Network Client Administrator is invoked by accessing the administrative tools program group on a server and clicking the Network Client Administrator selection. Once started, the Network Client Administrator dialog box appears displaying the four options available. By selecting the third option, Copy Client-based Network Administration Tools, and clicking Continue, the Share Client-based Administration Tools dialog box appears (see Figure 15.3). Enter the path where the server tools files are located, such as a CD-ROM location (<CD-ROM drive>\CLIENTS) or a network location (\\<computername>\ <sharename>\clients). Select the Copy Files to a New Directory, and then Share option. After you click OK, the files will be copied to the specified location.

FIG. 15.3 ⟹

This figure shows the Network Client Administrator and Share Client-based Administration Tools dialog boxes.

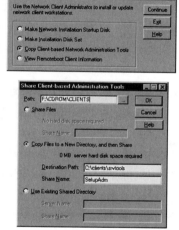

Upon completion of the file copy, a Network Client Administrator information box appears stating how many directories and files were copied; click OK to continue. Next, the srvtools folder is shared and another Network Client Administrator information box appears stating the network administration tools are now available in a shared directory; click OK to continue.

Installing the Server Tools from a Network Share

When a network share is created with the Network Client Administration application, simply map a client computer to that share. For example, secondary-click My Computer or Network Neighborhood, select Map <u>N</u>etwork Drive, and either type the path or select the path from the shared directories window (<computername>\SetupAdm).

From the mapped drive either in Explorer or My Computer, select the WINNT folder and execute the Setup.bat file. Refer to Figure 15.2 for an illustration of the events that take place.

Windows 95 Server Tools

The following 32-bit server tools are available for Windows 95:

- ◆ User Manager for Domains
- ◆ Server Manager
- ◆ Event Viewer
- ◆ User Manager Extensions for Services for NetWare
- ◆ File and Print Services for NetWare (FPNW)

Key Concept

User Manager Extensions for Services for NetWare will only be installed if FPNW or DSNW is installed.

File and Print Services for NetWare will only be installed if FPNW is installed.

In addition, a File Security tab and a Print Security tab will be available to establish file, folder, and print permissions.

When these tools are installed on a Windows 95 computer, they function exactly the same as they do on a Windows NT 4.0 server installation.

Installation of Windows 95 Server Tools

Installing the Windows NT server tools on a Windows 95 platform requires a few more steps than the Windows NT Workstation version. First of all, the source files must be made available; either the Windows NT 4.0 Server CD-ROM or a network share can be used.

Next, on the Windows 95 computer, access the Control Panel and select the Add/Remove Programs icon. When the Add/Remove Programs Properties dialog box appears, select the Windows Setup tab and click the Have Disk button. When the Install from Disk dialog box appears, supply the path to the source files such as <computername>\ SetupAdm\Win95 if the files are on the network, or <CdromDrive Letter>\Clients\Srvtools\Win95 if the Windows NT 4.0 Server CD-ROM is being used. Click OK. Figure 15.4 illustrates these steps.

FIG. 15.4 ⇒

This figure illustrates a Windows 95 Server tools installation procedure, Part 1.

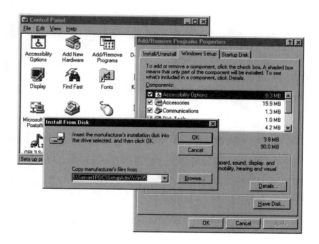

Then, a Have Disk dialog box appears asking you to select the check box next to the Windows NT Server Tools item in the Components window if you want to install the server tools (see Figure 15.5).

FIG. 15.5 ⇒

The Have Disk dialog box is part of the Windows 95 Server tools installation procedure illustration, Part 2.

When the check box is selected, click the Install button and the Windows NT 4.0 Server tools will be installed. After the tools are installed, a new selection will appear in the Start, Programs group as shown in Figure 15.6.

FIG. 15.6 ⟹

This figure shows how to select the Windows NT Server tools.

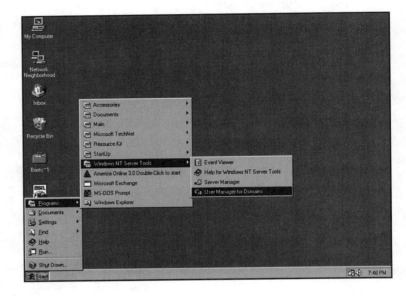

Figure 15.7 displays the Add/Remove Programs Properties dialog box with the Windows Setup tab selected after the server tools are installed. Note the added selection in the components window as shown.

FIG. 15.7 ⟹

The Windows Setup tab is selected in the Add/Remove Programs Properties dialog box.

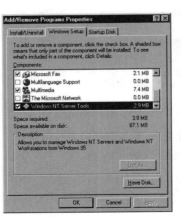

Windows 3.1 and Windows for Workgroups 3.11 Server Tools

The following 16-bit server tools are available for Windows 3.1 and Windows for Workgroups 3.11 installations:

◆ User Manager for Domains

◆ Server Manager

◆ Event Viewer

◆ Print Manager for Windows NT Server

◆ File Manager Security menu

Installation of Windows 3.1 and Windows for Workgroups 3.11 Server Tools

To install Windows NT Server tools on a Windows 3.1 or Windows for Workgroups 3.11 platform, the source files must be made available as mentioned previously in the section "Installation of Windows 95 Server Tools." The server tools for these two platforms can be found on the Windows NT 3.5/3.51 Server CD-ROM in the Clients\Srvtools directory. The Srvtools directory on this CD-ROM has two sub-directories under it; one is the Windows directory, the other is the Winnt directory. The Setup.exe program in the Windows directory is used for the Windows or Windows for Workgroups server tools installation. Once setup is run, the server tools are available in the Windows NT Server Tools program group.

When setup.exe is run, a Windows NT Server Tools Setup screen appears with a Welcome dialog box which gives you the choices to Continue, Exit, or get Help. It also informs you that both the Microsoft Win32s and RPC components and the Windows NT Server tools will be installed. Selecting Continue displays an Installation Options dialog box where you make the decision to either do a Custom Install or Install All Files. The default installation path of C:\SRVTOOLS can also be changed from this window. Choosing Continue proceeds with the server tool installation process.

The next window that appears is the Time Zone Setup window. Select the correct time zone and choose Continue.

The Microsoft Win32s Setup Target Directory is the next window that appears. This window informs you where various components will be installed. Choose Continue.

From this point, the files are copied and when the copy is completed, a Windows NT Server Tools Setup information dialog box appears informing you that some system changes will take effect when the system reboots. Choosing OK will display the final dialog box informing you the installation was successful and that you should reboot your system. Choose Continue to reboot.

Key Concept

Two files of importance are located in the <default>\SRVTOOLS directory: new-conf.sys and new-vars.bat. The statements in these two files must be added to the existing config.sys and autoexec.bat files, respectively, and the system rebooted.

New-conf.sys includes FILES=50

New-vars.bat includes PATH=<default>\SRVTOOLS and SET TZ=UTC+0DST

Without these changes, File Manager will not contain a Security drop-down menu.

Taking the Disc Test

If you have read and understood the material in the chapter, you are ready to test your knowledge. Insert the CD-ROM that comes with this book and run the self-test software as described in Appendix I, "Using the CD-ROM."

From Here...

The next chapter, "Novell NetWare Connectivity Tools," introduces the concept of internetwork connectivity. The next chapters will introduce and discuss Windows NT 4.0 and its interoperability with Novell, multiprotocol routing, the Internet Information Server, and the Remote Access Service. Topics of discussion include Client Services for NetWare (CSNW), Gateway Services for NetWare (GSNW), File and Print Services for NetWare (FPNW), Directory Services Manager for NetWare, the NetWare Migration application, Internet and intranet browsing, and remote access setup and configuration.

Part V.

Connectivity

Chapter Prerequisite

Before reading this chapter, you should be familiar with fundamental protocols and networking concepts. For Windows NT protocol information, see Chapter 8, "Configuring Domain Network Core Services." In addition, refer to Chapters 11-15 for important networking considerations.

16

Novell NetWare Connectivity Tools

Corporations and businesses today are faced with the challenge of a complex computing environment. Most of the issues associated with the management of this environment are related to the integration of components within that architecture. In recognition of that, Windows NT has intensified its efforts for connectivity tools. The efforts have included the development of NWLink, File and Print Services for NetWare (FPNW), Directory Service Manager for NetWare (DSMN), Gateway Services for NetWare (GSNW), Client Services for NetWare (CSNW), and the Migration Tool for NetWare.

In this chapter you will learn about:

◆ The Windows NT connectivity tools for NetWare
◆ File and Print Sharing for NetWare (FPNW)

- Directory Service Manager for NetWare (DSMN)
- Gateway Services for NetWare (GSNW)
- Migration Tool for NetWare

NWLink IPX/SPX Compatible Transport

One of the key components for integrating NetWare is the NWLink protocol. This protocol is an IPX/SPX compatible protocol and is also compatible with SPX II. IPX/SPX stands for Internetwork Packet Exchange/Sequenced Packet Exchange and is the group of transport protocols used in the Novell NetWare environment. Because NWLink is a Microsoft product, NWLink follows the Network Driver Interface Specification (NDIS) and is fully compliant with NDIS.

NWLink provides support for both Windows Sockets APIs, Remote Procedure Calls (RPCs), Novell NetBIOS, and the NWLink NetBIOS. NWLink ships with both Windows NT Server and Windows NT Workstation.

APIs—A Brief Overview

Application programming interfaces (APIs) are a set of program segments used to perform common operating system functions. These functions can be as simple as supplying the look and feel of the Windows interface and as complicated as providing an interprocess communication (IPC) method such as Windows Sockets. The availability of all of the API's is one of the reasons Windows has become so popular. It has allowed the used of standard methods to access system resources and services. Additionally, the availability of the pre-written program segments has reduced the amount of time necessary to develop Windows applications.

NWLink is the transport protocol necessary to implement any of the integration tools and can be loaded with any other transport protocol that might be needed. The protocol is added as other protocols are, from the Network icon in the Control Panel or from the Properties selection from the Network Neighborhood context menu. The access screen is shown in Figure 16.1

FIG. 16.1

From the Select Network Protocol dialog box, high–light the desired protocol and click OK.

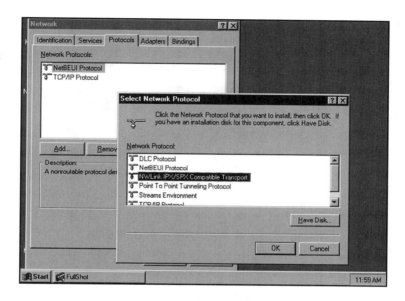

Part
V

Ch
16

The configuration parameters for NWLink are straightforward. Some of these parameters can be provided by the NetWare LAN administrator. NetWare routers use the NetWare Internal Network Number to determine if the packet belongs on that LAN or the network. Additional information regarding these parameters can be found in the Novell manuals. If NWLink does not detect that number, it will default to zeros.

Another configuration parameter relates to selecting Ethernet frame types (see Figure 16.2). On the General tab of the NWLink IPX/SPX Properties dialog box, you are offered two choices: Auto Frame Type Detection and Manual Frame Type Detection. The first option is to set the frame type for the Ethernet card to Auto Frame Type Detection. When automatic detection is selected, Windows NT will go through the list of frame types, as they are listed in the Frame Type selection box, and test each until Windows NT gets a response. When using A<u>u</u>to Frame Type Detection, Windows NT will select the default protocol if there is no response.

FIG. 16.2

The frame type for the Ethernet card can be selected automatically on the NWLink IPX/ SPX Properties screen.

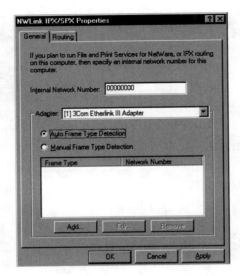

The other possibility is to set the frame type manually using the <u>M</u>anual Frame Type Detection option (see Figure 16.2). If you choose this option, the Manual Frame Detection dialog box opens. Select a frame type from the <u>F</u>rame Type drop-down list and click <u>A</u>dd.

 Note Usually a NetWare 2.x or 3.x server uses 802.3, whereas a NetWare 4.x server will typically use 802.2 frame type. ■

 Tip

When using NWLink, a fast way to determine the frame type is to use the IPXROUTE CONFIG command. The results of this command include the frame type.

When using token ring, the configuration parameters concern the Token-Ring Source Routing Table, which is kept on each computer in a token-ring environment. The Source Routing Table is used in determining the route the packet will take. If there is a packet that is received without a corresponding Mac address in the source routing table, there is a slight problem. When this happens, the packet is passed on as a single route broadcast. The IPXROUTE is useful in this situation also because it will indicate if a single route broadcast packet is being sent.

FIG. 16.3
Manually select a frame type by choosing the Manual Frame Type Detection option and searching the Frame Type drop-down list.

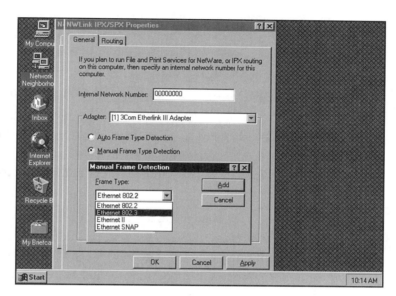

File and Print Services for NetWare

File and Print Services for NetWare (FPNW) is an emulator that presents itself to NetWare clients in the same manner as a NetWare 3.x server, *not* a NetWare 4.x server. It is written to run on all Windows NT platforms, MIPS, Intel, Alpha, and PowerPC machines. It is actually a service that runs on the Windows NT Server. Included in the FPNW package are the Administration Tools and the FPNW product. Generally, the complete package is installed on the Primary Domain Controller and the Administrative Tools are installed on each Backup Domain Controller. When FPNW is running, the Windows NT Server can be a server for any NetWare client—without modifying the client workstation. The file and print services are supported by using either Netx (the NetWare shell) or VLM (the DOS requester).

FPNW is added as other Windows NT services are added, from the Network properties Protocol tab. Because FPNW is an add-on, the Have Disk option is used to install the service.

The installation process requests a Windows NT directory, which is actually going to become the SYS Volume. Microsoft recommends that the directory named to be the SYS Volume be on an NTFS partition. This would allow the maximum amount of security and could duplicate the security found on the NetWare volume. After the installation process, the directory structure has the required NetWare directories MAIL, LOGIN, PUBLIC, and SYSTEM. FPNW provides NetWare-compatible commands in the PUBLIC directory such as SLIST, USERLIST, MAP, CAPTURE, and so on.

Also requested is a server name, which is the Windows NT computer account that the NetWare clients are using to access the SYS Volume. Windows NT uses a default of the server's computer name followed by FPNW.

The installation process creates a Supervisor account, which is added to the Administrators group. A system restart is done at this point and the process is continued when adding new users. The new users are added from the FPNW icon in the Control Panel. When accessing the New User dialog box from User Manager for Domains, notice the additional selection at the bottom. This is a check box to Maintain NetWare Compatible Logon. Checking this box enables the user logon for FPNW.

Directory Service Manager for NetWare

Directory Service Manager for NetWare (DSMN) is like FPNW, it has to be purchased separately. Understanding the advantages of DSMN requires an understanding of working in an environment that has multiple NetWare 3.x file servers. In the NetWare environment, if a user needs access to files on various servers, then that user needs to be defined in the appropriate servers accounts database (bindery). For example, if a user needs access to three NetWare 3.x servers, an account has to be created on each server for that user. While at first glance this may not seem to be a problem, it is. The requirement for multiple definitions of users has been an extra administrative task with associated problems such as password synchronization and directory mappings.

DSMN is a time-saver because it brings the administrative tasks into one location, the Windows NT Server. A user would only have to be created in one location, the Windows NT Server. DSMN updates the NetWare 3.x servers. DSMN is installed on the Primary Domain Controller, and the account information is replicated in the ordinary manner. Essentially, DSMN does not require any changes on the clients workstation. What happens is that core files are replaced in the SYS:PUBLIC directory.

DSMN needs to have Gateway Service for NetWare (GSNW) installed. GSNW is covered in the "Gateway Services for NetWare" section later in this chapter. DSMN is installed as other services, from the Network icon.

> **Caution**
> If FPNW is installed before DSMN, the users defined for FPNW will not be automatically synchronized to the NetWare server.

Gateway Services for NetWare

Gateway Services for NetWare (GSNW) is included with Windows NT. There are a number of ways to understand GSNW. From the bit/byte perspective, GSNW converts the Server Message Block (SMB) packet to Novell's NetWare Core Protocol (NCP). From the user perspective, it allows Microsoft clients to access NetWare resources through the gateway running on the Windows NT Server.

The Microsoft clients do not have to have NetWare client software or Microsoft's Client Service for NetWare (CSNW) on their workstations.

The Windows NT Server shares the NetWare resources and presents these resources to the Microsoft clients for use. The clients attach to the Windows NT Server share, which is actually a NetWare resource. GSNW works for NetWare 3.x and for NetWare 4.x servers which are using bindery emulation mode.

From the NetWare view, there is one attachment to the NetWare server and access rights are assigned to that account. The Windows NT Server can allow multiple attachments to the share, and as a consequence there can actually be many people using the NetWare resource. This could be slow because of speed considerations for the translation between SMB and NCP. Also, because access rights are assigned to that account, all users from the Windows NT side that are accessing the resource have the same rights.

One of the ideal uses for GSNW is to allow access to NetWare print queues. To accomplish this, the Windows NT Server machine needs to add a *logical* printer and direct it to a NetWare print queue (printing device from Windows NT's perspective). After this, the driver is added from the Windows NT installation disk and the printer will appear in the printer folder as if it were a local printer. The Windows NT administrator needs only to share the printer and it will be available for all to use. GSNW allows the creation of a gateway for resources on the NetWare Directory Service (NDS) tree in addition to the resources available on any NetWare server with bindery security.

The installation process for GSNW follows the same process as installing other services. However, there are a few pre-installation tasks.

- ◆ From the NetWare server, create a group called NTGATEWAY. From this group, assign the access rights to the resource.
- ◆ From the NetWare server, create a user and put the user into the group NTGATEWAY.
- ◆ Logon as a member of the Administrators group.

The Network icon is clicked to access the network configuration options. This can also be accessed by secondarily clicking the Network Neighborhood icon and selecting Properties from the Context menu.

After the configuration screen is displayed, select the Services tab. Highlight the Service and Click Add to install the Gateway (and Client) Services for NetWare, as shown in Figure 16.4.

Part
V
Ch
16

FIG. 16.4
The Gateway (and Client) Services for NetWare are installed from the Select Network Service screen.

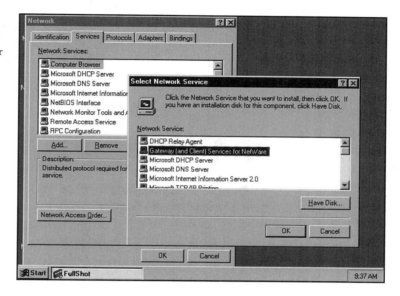

> **Note** If NWLink has not been installed previously, it will be installed automatically when this service is selected. ■

After the selection of the service, the Gateway Service for NetWare dialog box is displayed, as shown in Figure 16.5.

FIG. 16.5
The Gateway Service for NetWare dialog box allows for the entry of configuration information.

In the Preferred Server box, enter the name of the NetWare server to which the Windows NT Server is attaching. If the NetWare server is using NDS, then enter the name of the tree where the resource is located in the Tree box. The Context refers to the position of the object in the tree. The Print Options are for the passing on of further print instructions. The Login Script Options are to control whether the login script should be executed at login time.

Selecting the Gateway button shown in Figure 16.5 displays the Configure Gateway screen as shown in Figure 16.6.

FIG. 16.6

The Configure Gateway screen allows for the input of configuration information.

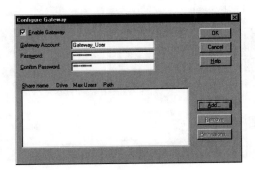

Enter the gateway user name in the Gateway Account text box; here it is Gateway_User. Note that any name can be used, but it is wise to use names that remind the administrator of the original intentions in creating the account. The NetWare configuration, therefore, should have a group named NTGATEWAY, with a user in it named Gateway_User. Remember, of course, that the group and user were created in the pre-installation steps.

Use the Add button to add new shares that are going to be accessed. This is shown in Figure 16.7.

Enter the name of the share in the Share Name text box. The share name should be named as any other Windows NT share is named. The share name appears in the browse list. In the Network Path text box, enter the volume that is being shared, this would be the NetWare volume and path name. In the Use Drive text box, enter the drive letter to be used to establish the gateway share. The User Limit area is used to control the number of users accessing the share.

FIG. 16.7

The New Share screen allows the entry of specific information related to new shares.

After the share is configured as indicated in Figure 16.7, the screen returns to Figure 16.6 with the share information entered. From this screen, the permissions can be set. As with other Windows NT shares, the default is Full Control for the group Everyone. The trustee rights that are set in NetWare override the Windows NT share-level permissions.

After the gateway configurations are made and permissions set, the process is finished. The GSNW icon appears in the Control Panel for future use as shown in Figure 16.8.

FIG. 16.8

Here the GSNW icon can be found in the second row of the Control Panel dialog box.

Client Services for NetWare

The Client Services for NetWare (CSNW) are packaged with Windows NT. This software is also a service, however it runs on the client Windows NT Workstation. The purpose of this service is to allow the users to access NetWare resources. CSNW support NetWare 2.x, 3.x, and 4.x running in bindery emulation mode or NDS.

CSNW is installed on Windows NT Workstation the same way that a service is installed on Windows NT Server. Refer to Figure 16.5 for the screen that shows the needed configuration information of the service. It is significant to note that when the Client Services for NetWare are installed, they are installed on the Windows NT Workstation machine. When that occurs, the Control Panel of the Windows NT Workstation machine has a CSNW icon which brings up a screen similar to the screen on Figure 16.3. The Windows NT Workstation screen is titled Client Services for NetWare and asks for the same information. Of course, the CSNW screen does not have a button for Gateway configuration, which would only apply to Gateway Services.

Migration Tool for NetWare

Windows NT ships with Migration Tool for NetWare. The purpose of this tool is to seamlessly move the users from NetWare to Windows NT. It works in conjunction with FPNW for the migration of the logon scripts; if FPNW is not running, the logon scripts won't be migrated. Essentially, the Migration Tool reads the NetWare bindery and creates the users and groups on the Windows NT Server. File and directory permissions can also be migrated if the receiving Windows NT volume is NTFS.

The Migration Tool has the added capability of migrating more than one NetWare server to the Windows NT primary domain controller (or BDC). The receiving Windows NT Server must have NWLink and GSNW already installed before using this utility. Working with this utility requires both Supervisor (for NetWare) and Administrator (for Windows NT) rights.

The Migration Tool for NetWare dialog box enables you to specify servers for migration (see Figure 16.9). When you select the Add button, another screen is displayed to indicate the selection for the target and destination server. Clicking the ellipses (...) button allows the administrator to select the server from a screen similar to Network Neighborhood, as shown in Figure 16.10.

FIG. 16.9

This is the first Migration Tool screen. This screen keeps the list of the involved servers and allows the setting of user and file options, as well as the actual migration options.

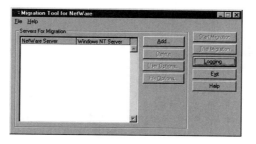

FIG. 16.10

The Select Windows NT Server screen is helpful for the selection of the Windows NT Server participating in the migration.

The Users option box shown in the Migration Tool for NetWare dialog box (refer again to Figure 16.9) allows control over the user accounts and groups. The default of this transfer is that all of the users and groups get migrated to the Windows NT domain, unless there is a name conflict. If the administrator chooses, the administrator can create a mapping file that would have a listing for each user and specific information for their accounts.

Novell NetWare uses an encryption scheme for password storage, hence the passwords from a NetWare server cannot be migrated. In order to assign some type of password, an administrator could use a mapping file to include the password information. If the administrator chooses to use a mapping file, the password information could also be included with the group and user options. Possible options for password information could include assigning all accounts a null password, setting the new password to the users name, indicating a single password for all migrated accounts, and also specifying that the password must be changed at next logon.

The File Options button gives the administrator greater control over the transfer of folders and files. The preferred option is to have these migrated to an NTFS partition so the effective rights are retained.

The most helpful option is to run a trial migration. When the trial migration is run, it creates various log files. These log files are listed in Table 16.1.

Table 16.1   Trial Migration Log Files

Log File Name	Content
Logfile.log	User and group information
Error.log	Failures and error messages
Summary.log	Summary of trial migration, names of server, users, groups, and files

The Migration Tool for NetWare screen also has a convenient feature that allows the administrator the option of saving the configuration. All of the configuration information entered for Users and Files can be saved by selecting File, Save Configuration as shown in Figure 16.11.

FIG. 16.11

The Migration Tool for NetWare screen offers four options under the File command.

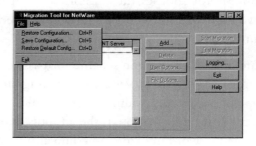

Taking the Disc Test

 If you have read and understood the material in the chapter, you are ready to test your knowledge. Insert the CD-ROM that comes with this book and run the self-test software as described in Appendix I, "Using the CD-ROM."

From Here...

In this chapter, you reviewed material on migrating NetWare users to Windows NT. In Chapter 17, "Multiprotocol Routing," you'll learn about multiprotocol routing, and how to attach Windows NT networks to other networks in the organization. Chapter 18, "Internet Information Server," then introduces you to one of the features of Windows NT that makes it so useful—IIS.

Part
V

Ch

16

Chapter Prerequisite

Readers should have a concept of LAN/WAN topology with regard to the purpose of routers and different subnets or networks. They should also be familiar with protocol characteristics for TCP/IP and NWLink and the DHCP service as discussed in Chapter 8, "Configuring Domain Network Core Services."

Multiprotocol Routing

This chapter adds to the discussion of multiprotocol routing that was presented in Chapter 8, "Configuring Domain Network Core Services." The information presented in that chapter dealt with the installation of the multiprotocol routing services for both TCP/IP and NWLink. Discussions in this chapter include the purpose of the Windows NT 4.0 addition of multiprotocol routing and how multiprotocol routing integrates with Dynamic Host Configuration Protocol (DHCP).

Topics in this chapter include:

◆ Networks, network segments, and the purpose of routers

◆ Windows NT 4.0 and multiprotocol routing

◆ RIP for Internet protocol routing

◆ DHCP relay

◆ RIP for NWLink IPX/SPX-compatible transport routing

◆ AppleTalk routing

Networks, Network Segments, and the Purpose of Routers

Referring back to Chapter 8, "Configuring Domain Network Core Services," recall that NWLink and TCP/IP are considered routable protocols, whereas NetBEUI is considered a non-routable protocol. This means that if a number of computers are configured to communicate with each other using NetBEUI, they have to all be on the same network or physical piece of wire. They cannot be on different network segments connected physically by routing devices. Protocols such as NWLink and TCP/IP, on the other hand, are routable protocols that can communicate with computers on different physical networks through routers.

Routers are devices that pass information from one network segment to another. Routers work up to the Network layer of the Open Systems Interconnection (OSI) model and forward information based on both a network and a device address. Routing devices maintain a table of both network addresses and device addresses to which they are connected. When they receive a packet of information, they can analyze the packet header and determine to which network or device they should route or forward the packet of information. Routers can also determine the best path to route information from one computer to another, thereby optimizing network performance.

Routers pass information packets from one network segment to another without regard to media type. For example, routers can pass information packets between an Ethernet network segment and a token-ring network segment, or between an X.25 network segment and an ARCnet network segment.

Routers are, however, protocol dependent, meaning that they must understand the protocol inclusive of the OSI network layer. The same protocol must be used on each side of the router.

Routing Information Protocol (RIP) routers, in addition to forwarding information packets from one network segment to another, also dynamically exchange routing tables by broadcasting their route information with other routers on the network. This type of communication ensures that all routers on the network contain synchronized routing information.

Windows NT 4.0 and Multiprotocol Routing

After multiprotocol routing is installed and enabled on Windows NT 4.0, the computer will be able to function as a router and forward information packets from one network segment to another, provided more than one network card is installed and configured. Either Internet Protocol (IP) routing or Internetwork Packet Exchange (IPX) routing, or both, can be enabled, provided the required protocol is installed.

A Windows NT 4.0 server can also function as a DHCP Relay Agent by installing the DHCP Relay Agent service, which allows DHCP messages to be relayed across routers in an IP network.

TCP/IP Routing

Windows NT 4.0 provides for both Static and Routing Information Protocol (RIP) IP routing. Fixed or manually maintained routing tables are used in Static routing, whereas routing tables are maintained dynamically when using RIP.

Static IP Routing

To enable Static Routing, simply install TCP/IP, and from the TCP/IP property sheet, choose the Routing tab. Select the Enable IP Forwarding check box.

After Static Routing is enabled, the Route utility is used to maintain a static routing table. Simply start a command prompt and type **route** to display all the Route utility options. Figure 17.1 displays the route options.

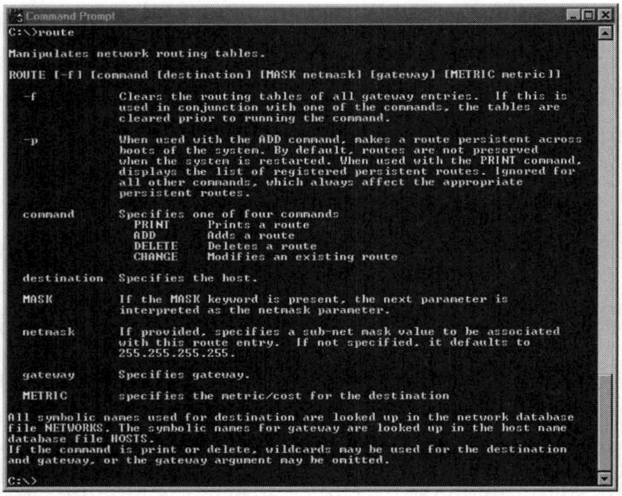

```
C:\>route

Manipulates network routing tables.

ROUTE [-f] [command [destination] [MASK netmask] [gateway] [METRIC metric]]

  -f           Clears the routing tables of all gateway entries.  If this is
               used in conjunction with one of the commands, the tables are
               cleared prior to running the command.

  -p           When used with the ADD command, makes a route persistent across
               boots of the system. By default, routes are not preserved
               when the system is restarted. When used with the PRINT command,
               displays the list of registered persistent routes. Ignored for
               all other commands, which always affect the appropriate
               persistent routes.

  command      Specifies one of four commands
                 PRINT     Prints a route
                 ADD       Adds a route
                 DELETE    Deletes a route
                 CHANGE    Modifies an existing route

  destination  Specifies the host.

  MASK         If the MASK keyword is present, the next parameter is
               interpreted as the netmask parameter.

  netmask      If provided, specifies a sub-net mask value to be associated
               with this route entry.  If not specified, it defaults to
               255.255.255.255.

  gateway      Specifies gateway.

  METRIC       specifies the metric/cost for the destination

All symbolic names used for destination are looked up in the network database
file NETWORKS. The symbolic names for gateway are looked up in the host name
database file HOSTS.
If the command is print or delete, wildcards may be used for the destination
and gateway, or the gateway argument may be omitted.

C:\>
```

FIG. 17.1 ⇒ This figure shows the Route utility syntax and options list.

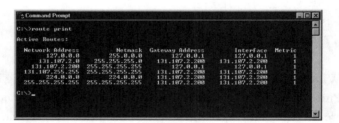

Figure 17.2 displays a route print command. The route print command displays the static route table on the specific computer. This was done on a computer configured with only one network adapter card, a static IP address of 131.107.2.200, and no default gateway assigned.

```
C:\>route print

Active Routes:

  Network Address          Netmask  Gateway Address        Interface  Metric
        127.0.0.0        255.0.0.0        127.0.0.1        127.0.0.1       1
      131.107.2.0    255.255.255.0    131.107.2.200    131.107.2.200       1
    131.107.2.200  255.255.255.255        127.0.0.1        127.0.0.1       1
  131.107.255.255  255.255.255.255    131.107.2.200    131.107.2.200       1
        224.0.0.0        224.0.0.0    131.107.2.200    131.107.2.200       1
  255.255.255.255  255.255.255.255    131.107.2.200    131.107.2.200       1

C:\>_
```

FIG. 17.2 ⇒ Here are the results of the Route utility, Print command.

To add an entry or route to the static route table, the Route Add command is used. The route add syntax and its results are shown in Figure 17.3. The addition establishes a route from computer 131.107.2.200 to a gateway subnet of 131.107.3.0 using a subnet mask of 255.255.255.0 that is configured on computer 131.107.2.180. The Metric value in this case indicates that subnet 131.107.3.0 is one hop or router away from computer 131.107.2.200.

Key Concept

Keep in mind that if a route is added to forward information to another computer or router, the route back to the first computer must also be added to the second computer to establish a path back to the first computer.

FIG. 17.3 ⟹

These are the results of adding a route to the static route table.

The Route utility can also use entries in the Networks file for the purpose of converting destination names to addresses. Figure 17.4 displays an example of the default Networks file.

FIG. 17.4 ⟹

This is a default Networks file example.

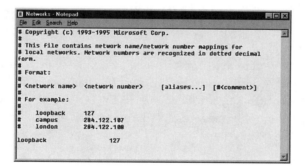

RIP for Internet Protocol Routing

Windows NT 4.0 Server supports RIP for Internet Protocol (IP). RIP for IP will dynamically maintain IP routing tables; therefore, static IP routing tables do not have to be manually maintained.

Tip

The version of RIP for Internet Protocol presently used in Windows NT 4.0 Server at this time does not support RIP over switch or dial-up WANs.

After it is installed, RIP for IP service is configured to start automatically when the computer is started. It also requires that TCP, IP, and UDP be previously installed. TCP provides connection-oriented packet delivery, IP provides address and routing functions, and UDP provides for connectionless-oriented packet delivery.

As mentioned before, routing can take place between two or more network adapter cards installed in a computer. With RIP for IP installed, a Windows NT 4.0 server can forward information from one IP network segment to another IP network segment. That is the purpose of RIP for IP; however, what if RIP is installed on a computer with only one network adapter card installed? If this is the case, the specific Windows NT 4.0 server will be placed in Silent Mode, meaning that the computer will update its own router table from RIP broadcast from other routers on the network, but because it is connected to only one network segment, it does not broadcast its route.

Caution

If, at a later date, one or more network adapter cards are installed, the Registry entry for `SilentRip` must be changed from 1 to 0. The `SilentRip` Registry location is HKEY_LOCAL_MACHINE\System\ CurrentControlSet\Services\IpRip\Parameters. Its value type is REG_DWORD.

DHCP Relay

The DHCP Relay service is used to route DHCP messages from one IP network segment to another. For example, an enterprise has two network segments, segment 1 and segment 2, connected by a router, but has only one DHCP server on network segment 1. If the router is not capable of forwarding DHCP and BOOTP broadcast messages between the DHCP server on segment 1 and a DHCP client on segment 2, a DHCP server would have to be configured on each network segment. However, if the DHCP Relay service is installed on a server computer on segment 2, it will forward DHCP requests through the router to the DHCP server on network segment 1. The DHCP Relay service can be configured to route information up to 16 hops away.

RIP for NWLink IPX Routing

RIP for NWLink IPX, when enabled and configured correctly, allows a Windows NT 4.0 system to function as an IPX router to forward information from one IPX network segment to another. RIP for NWLink IPX, once installed, must be enabled manually, unlike RIP for IP which is enabled automatically when installed. Recall from Chapter 8, "Configuring Domain Network Core Services," that RIP for NWLink IPX is enabled or disabled from the Routing tab on the NWLink IPX/SPX Properties sheet. For the IPX router service to work properly, NetBIOS Broadcast Propagation (type 20 broadcast packets) must be enabled, which allows the computer to use NetBIOS over IPX for browsing and name resolution. If NetBIOS Broadcast Propagation is disabled, client computers will only be able to communicate with systems on the local IPX subnet.

Note RIP for NWLink IPX can only propagate up to eight hops, unlike RIP for IP and DHCP Relay, which can propagate up to 16 hops. ■

When RIP for NWLink IPX is installed, the Service Advertising Protocol (SAP), is automatically installed also. Pertaining to the Windows NT environment, SAP is a service that broadcasts shared files, directories, and printers, first by the domain or workgroup name, then by the server name. In the IPX protocol and routing environment, SAP is used by servers to advertise their services and addresses on a network, and then clients use SAP to determine what network resources are available.

RIP for NWLink IPX also contains a utility to display information and statistics about the IPX route tables. The utility is called IPXRoute. Figures 17.5 and 17.6 display the IPXRoute options.

FIG. 17.5 ⇒

This figure shows the IPXRoute and the IPX routing syntax and options list.

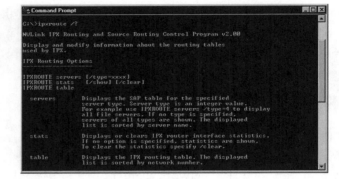

FIG. 17.6 ⇒

Here is the IPXRoute source routing syntax and options list.

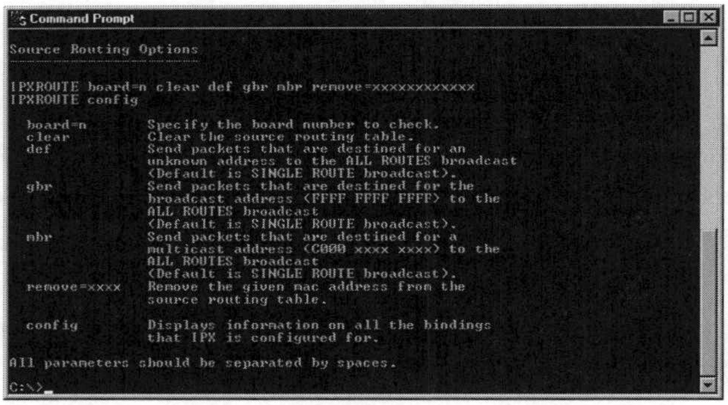

Figure 17.7 displays the results of the IPXRoute servers, IPXRoute stats, and IPXRoute table commands. The type 1600 computers are Windows NT 4.0 installations—one is a Windows NT 4.0 Workstation installation, the other is a Windows NT 4.0 Server installation. The type 4 computer is a Novell 3.12 file server.

FIG. 17.7 ⟹

This figure shows examples of three IPXRoute commands.

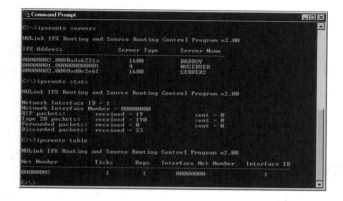

AppleTalk Routing

Windows NT 4.0 Server, with Services for Macintosh (SFM) installed, can function also as an AppleTalk router. After AppleTalk routing is enabled, the Windows NT 4.0 Server can be seen by all Macintosh clients on all bound networks.

Windows NT 4.0 can function as a seed router or as a nonseed router in a Macintosh environment. Seed routers initialize and send routing information to other routers in the enterprise. Each physical network must have at least one seed router configured, and that system must be started first to pass routing information to other routers.

An AppleTalk routing table contains network numbers and ranges, zone names and lists, and the default zone on the network. Each network number must be unique as it identifies a specific AppleTalk network. Network numbers can range from 1 to 65,279.

Key Concept

LocalTalk networks can only have a single network number; however, EtherTalk, TokenTalk, and FDDI networks can support network ranges.

Taking the Disc Test

 If you have read and understood the material in the chapter, you are ready to test your knowledge. Insert the CD-ROM that comes with this book and run the self-test software as described in Appendix I, "Using the CD-ROM."

From Here...

The next chapter, "Internet Information Server," introduces and discusses Windows NT 4.0 and its interoperability with Novell. Topics of discussion include Client Services for NetWare (CSNW), Gateway Services for NetWare (GSNW), File and Print Services for NetWare (FPNW), Director Services Manager for NetWare, and the NetWare Migration application.

Chapter Prerequisite

The reader should be familiar
with the concept of Directory
Services as discussed in Chapter 2, "Windows NT 4.0 Directory Services Overview." It
would also be helpful to be
familiar with basic Internet
concepts and TCP/IP.

18

Internet Information Server

This chapter discusses how the Windows NT computers can provide and gain
access to resources via the Internet or the internal private intranet. The tools to
provide access to resources are the Internet Information Server (IIS) from the
Server NT and the Peer Web Server (PWS) from the Windows NT workstation. To gain access to these resource providers, you will use the Internet Explorer tool.

In this chapter, you learn how to:

◆ Define the Network topics

◆ Configure Windows NT server for Internet and intranet access

◆ Secure Internet and intranet sites

◆ Domain name services and IIS

Overview of Network Topics

Before you build your server for internetworking, you must look to the type of network you are working with. There are two distinct internetworking considerations. They are the Internet and an intranet. Both communication configurations use TCP/IP.

The Internet is outside of your office and part of the global network of computers that communicate using common languages and protocols. The main services on the Internet are the World Wide Web (WWW), e-mail (SMTP/POP), and File Transfer Protocol (FTP). It provides users with a graphical interface that allows them to find pages of information on other computers on the Internet. These Web pages are linked together to comprise a web of information with one source of information pointing to another, which leads to another, and so on. Links can be on both text, which is generally highlighted by a different color, or on pictures where there is no visual indication that the picture is a link.

An intranet is an internal network that uses the same technology and services as the Internet. An intranet is used as a company-wide internal (or private) network using WWW and the Hypertext Transfer Protocol (HTTP) servers to improve the company's internal communications, information publishing, and application development. If you need to access a resource located on your company network, you use the same Web browser with which you access the Internet.

Internet Information Server (IIS), Peer Web Servers (PWS), and Internet Explorer support interoperability with the Internet and intranets. Before you start building your site, it is important to know the difference between them.

The corporate-level intranet and the global Internet can be supported by the same physical network system. However, the security implications must be considered when you combine the two together. Separate the internal information from the external Internet. Corporate information distributed on the intranet, such as internal memos, should remain there. You do not want to distribute corporate research and development projects to the Internet competition.

Internet Information Server (IIS) and Peer Web Services (PWS) provide
Windows NT computers with the capability to publish resources and
services on the Internet and intranet. Both the Internet Information
Server (IIS) and Peer Web Services use HTTP, File Transfer Protocol
(FTP), and the Gopher service for publishing services on the Internet
or an intranet. HTTP is used to create and navigate World Wide Web
(W W W) hypertext documents and applications. HTTP allows you to
click graphics to connect to a resource. FTP is used to transfer files between two computers on any TCP/IP network that supports an FTP
server, as Windows NT does. The Gopher service is used to create links
or pointers to other sites or services. IIS and PWS support the Internet
Server Application Programming Interface (ISAPI). ISAPI is used as a
client/server Internet programming interface. IIS supports large-scale
networking and is installed only on Windows NT Server or Domain
Controllers. PWS supports small-scale networking and is installed only
on Windows NT Workstation.

One tool that can be used to view the information published by IIS
and PWS is Microsoft's Internet Explorer. Of course, Microsoft's
Internet Explorer isn't the only Web browser on the market. Netscape
also produces a Web browser product—Navigator—that runs not only
on Microsoft platforms as does Internet Explorer, but also on UNIX
and other platforms.

Web browsers use Uniform Resource Locators (URL) to locate information on the Internet. The URL is broken down as follows:

Example	Usage
http://	The protocol to be used, HTTP for Web, FTP for File Transfer protocol, Gopher for Gopher services, and Mailto for e-mail.
www.quecorp.com/	The name or IP address of the host to be reached.
kb/	The directory the information exists in.
default.asp	The name of the file to retreive.

Only the host portion of the address is required. Both Microsoft's Internet Explorer and Netscape's Navigator assume http:// for the protocol if it is not included, and Web servers will send a default page if one is not specified.

Configuring Windows NT Server for Internet and Intranet Access

By now you have determined what type of server fulfills your requirements, IIS or PWS server. You also know whether your plans call for the Internet, intranet, or both. Let's look at the requirements for installation of both the IIS and the PWS servers, and discuss the configuration process.

Installing the IIS Server

You need a computer running Windows NT Server 4.0 with TCP/IP and a large amount of disk space for the size of information you expect, and do not expect for your server. Use New Technology File System (NTFS) to secure all the drives and possibly auditing. Auditing will allow you to record access to the pages and can be viewed with the Event Viewer in the Administrative Tools selection under Programs. You should configure the Windows NT Server to operate on the Internet before installing IIS for the Internet. This may reduce some of your troubleshooting time. Configure the Windows NT server default security settings to prevent other Internet users from tampering with the computer.

Before installing IIS, disable any previous versions of FTP, Gopher, or other Web services that may on the Windows NT Server. FTP will be present if you have done an upgrade from Windows NT 3.51. You can install Internet Information Server during or before your installation of Windows NT Server. Figure 18.1 shows the Microsoft Internet Information Server 2.0 Setup dialog box.

FIG. 18.1

The Microsoft
Internet Informa-
tion Server 2.0
Setup screen
begins your
installation of IIS.

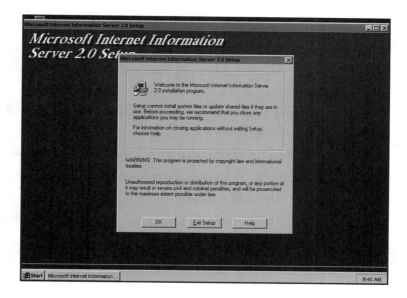

To install Internet Information Server during Windows NT Server
Setup, follow these steps:

1. When prompted, make sure the Install Microsoft Internet Information Server check box is selected and click the Next button.

2. The Internet Information Server Setup program begins.

3. Follow the instructions on the screen.

To install Internet Information Server after installing Windows NT
Server, follow these steps:

Tip

If you want to install Internet Information Server after installing Windows
NT Server, you must be logged on as an administrator.

1. Insert the Windows NT Server compact disc into the CD-ROM
   drive.

2. Double-click the Install Internet Information Server icon on the
   Windows NT Server desktop.

3. Follow the instructions on the screen.

Part

V

Ch

18

You can also install Internet Information Server by using the Windows NT Control Panel:

1. Insert the Windows NT Server compact disc into the CD-ROM drive.
2. On the Windows NT taskbar, click Start, point to Settings, and then click Control Panel.
3. In the Control Panel, double-click the Network icon.
4. On the Network property sheet, click the Services tab.
5. Click the Add button.
6. From the Network Services list, select Microsoft Internet Information Server, and then click OK.
7. In the Installed From box, type the drive letter of your compact disc and click OK.

Installing the PWS Server

To install the PWS Server, you need a computer running Windows NT Workstation 4.0 with TCP/IP (and enough disk space for your expected data). Use NTFS to secure all the drives with permissions and for use with auditing.

Before installing PWS, disable any previous versions of FTP, Gopher, or other Web services that may exist on the Windows NT Workstation. You can install Peer Web Server while installing Windows NT Workstation 4.0 or later.

To install Peer Web Server during Windows NT Workstation Setup, follow these steps:

1. When prompted, make sure the Install Microsoft Peer Web Server check box is selected and click the Next button.
2. The Peer Web Server Setup program begins.
3. Follow the instructions on the screen.

To install Peer Web Server after installing Windows NT Workstation, follow these steps:

Tip

If you want to install Peer Web Server after installing Windows NT Workstation, you must be logged on as an administrator.

1. Insert the Windows NT Workstation compact disc into the CD-ROM drive.

2. Double-click the Install Peer Web Server icon on the Windows NT Server desktop.

3. Follow the instructions on the screen.

You can also install Peer Web Server by using the Windows NT Control Panel.

1. Insert the Windows NT Server compact disc into the CD-ROM drive.

2. On the Windows NT taskbar, click Start, point to Settings, and then click Control Panel.

3. In the Control Panel, double-click the Network icon.

4. On the Network property sheet, click the Services tab.

5. Click the Add button.

6. From the Network Services list, select Microsoft Peer Web Server, and then click OK.

7. In the Installed From box, type the letter of the drive where your compact disc is located, and click OK.

Configuring IIS and PWS Using Microsoft Internet Service Manager (ISM)

Microsoft Internet Service Manager (ISM) is used by both IIS and PWS for configuration and performance changes and is found in the Microsoft Internet Server Tools (common) folder for IIS and the Microsoft Peer Web Services Tools (common) folder for PWS. Using this tool enables you as the administrator to monitor and change Internet services on remote machines. You can connect to and view server properties, as well as start, stop, and pause services. You can also select and adjust services. The Microsoft Internet Service Manager opening screen gives the status of your Internet services (see Figure 18.2).

FIG.18.2

This Microsoft Internet Server Manager screen is showing that the WWW, Gopher, and FTP services are all running.

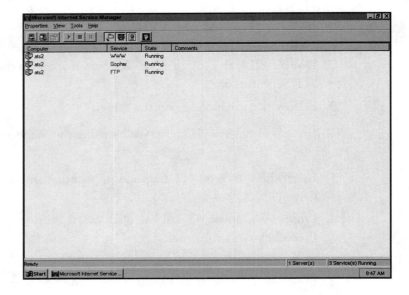

Selecting the Computer property sheet will display the following:

◆ User connections and logon requirements

◆ The Home folder for each service

◆ Server activity

◆ Secured access via IP address for selected service

Clicking any of the individual services listed enables you to modify the settings for that service. For example, click the WWW service and you may change the first page (main page) people see at your site. Click the Gopher service and it helps you to establish links to other information pages. The File Transfer Protocol (FTP) service configuration is set up only through the Internet Service Manager. You may also select from the Directories tab, with UNIX as the Directory Listing Style, for the UNIX-type format. This will allow a UNIX-style presentation of the information. Of course, this must be on an NTFS partition.

Securing Internet and Intranet Sites

As an Administrator, you must protect the integrity of your data. You can specify permissions to this data using specific users and groups. The Internet Guest account is automatically created at setup time for you and is the default account. The Internet Guest account name is ISUR_*computername*. You have the ability to allow Anonymous Access to your pages with the Internet Guest Account. This account is added to the guest group in the directory services database. If remote access is available to only the Internet Guest account, remote users do not need to provide a user name and password, and have only the permissions assigned to the Internet Guest account.

You may select to require a user name and password. There are two ways to do this. One is the basic authentication, meaning that a Windows NT user name and password are not encrypted when they are sent over the wire. The other option is the Microsoft Challenge/Response password authentication, which should be used instead of basic authentication for tougher, better security. Make the passwords difficult and use more than three characters for your password. It is recommended that you use the User Manager for Domains tool. With this tool, you should set the account policies to include a large minimum password length, frequent changes, and a password history to keep users from changing back to their old passwords too soon. Do not make too many users in the administrator group members either. If you make too many users the administrator, then all of those group members have the ability to change the information at any time.

Domain Name Services and IIS

How is the selected resource or site from the Internet or intranet converted to an actual IP address that the machines and software will use to communicate? Part of the answer is Domain Name System (DNS). What the Domain Name System server does is maintain a manually input database of organization names, compound names, and IP addresses. This database may be distributed among multiple servers.

When queried for a particular name it replies with the IP address to the requesting party. The requesting party is referred to as the resolver (client). Located under the administrative tools group, DNS can be used by administrators to manage domain and computer names and addresses.

The database is a tree structure similar to your disk folder layout with subfolders. This structure is called the *domain name space*. Each node in the tree structure is called a domain and may also contain subdomains. The DNS starting domain (referred to as the *root*) is at the top of the tree and is represented by a period. Following the root is the organizational name—for example, ats.com—with the next node or subdomain being computers.ats.com. The extension (.com) is indicative of a commercial organization just as (.gov) is for a government organization. A more complete list of top-level organization names is included in the Windows NT Resource Kit.

DNS servers perform what is called *name resolution*. By querying the known DNS servers, the final address is resolved and is returned to the resolver.

The process starts with the resolver requesting an organization name from the known DNS server. This server is called the *local name server*. If the name requested with the query is not known then the local name server, on behalf of the resolver, queries the other known domain name servers. If that server doesn't know the answer, then that server queries further down the line of DNS servers. When the DNS server with the requested information is found, that server returns the address to the server before it and that server returns the information to the one before it, and eventually the address is sent to the resolver.

The DNS Server Manager, located in the Administrative Tools group on the Windows NT Server, is used to configure DNS objects. Each object has a defined set of attributes. Use this tool to create, change, and delete objects and attributes.

The Resource Record (RR) is the main object in DNS because it contains the actual information elements. The RR contains information properties including information on the owner that applies to this DNS domain record. The Time to Live property identifies how long resource record data will be valid. This property is commonly adjusted for performance. The DNS Domain object is a node in the DNS tree. It contains all of the resource records for this domain or this organization.

DNS Zone will normally contain several records. It may contain information for one or more domains and/or subdomains. An example of a subdomain could be the "Impala" portion of the location **Impala.Chevy.com**. Zone records map domain names to IP address statically unless specified to use a WINS sever for address resolution. If this is the case, there is very little manual intervention for IP address changes of a server because the WINS changes are dynamic. Be sure to enter the IP address for the WINS Server dialog box under the Microsoft TCP/IP Protocol tab.

DNS server allows you to manage one or more zones. They are searched by physical order in the Server List. The Server List may be considered the root of the tool when the manager is first open. All DNS servers in your network may be added here for management purposes. Like the setup of a DHCP server on a Windows NT server, you must manually configure this server's IP address.

Part
V

Ch
18

Taking the Disc Test

 If you have read and understood the material in the chapter, you are ready to test your knowledge. Insert the CD-ROM that comes with this book and run the self-test software as described in Appendix I, "Using the CD-ROM."

From Here...

The next chapter, "Remote Access Server," discusses Windows NT's Remote Access Service (RAS). RAS provides dial-up access to the Windows NT domain and can be used to access your Internet Information Server as was discussed in this chapter.

Chapter Prerequisite

Before reading this chapter, you should be familiar with network protocols, especially the Windows NT 4.0 protocols covered in Chapter 8, "Configuring Domain Network Core Services."

19

Remote Access Server

The Remote Access Service (RAS) is one of the most powerful features of Microsoft Windows NT 4.0 Server. In this day of the "virtual office," corporations are increasingly employing people who work from locations other than the office. One of the most significant features of RAS is that the caller can access corporate resources on the company's networks. Additionally, Microsoft has designed this service to work with any of the common-line protocols and any of the common transport protocols, and has optimized the code with advanced compression techniques to facilitate the interprocess communications necessary for the typical client–server applications.

This chapter covers the Remote Access Server Service and includes the following concepts and topics:

◆ An overview of Remote Service

◆ An example of the installation process for Remote Access Service, including a discussion of the choices that need to be made during the installation process

◆ The administration of the Remote Access Service

◆ Dial Up Networking (DUN), the client component of RAS

An Overview of Remote Access Server

The Remote Access Server Service (RAS) has been a component of Microsoft operating systems for a long time. Windows for Workgroups 3.11 used RAS version 1.1a. Earlier versions of Microsoft Windows NT Server also used RAS. As one would expect, it has been greatly improved over the years. Features of RAS include:

◆ Support for Point-to-Point Protocol (PPP), Serial Line Interface Protocol (SLIP), and the Microsoft RAS Protocol

◆ Support for Point-to-Point Tunneling Protocol(PPTP)

◆ Support for various physical connections including phone lines using modems, X.25, Integrated Services Digital Network (ISDN), null modem cables, and multilink protocol connections

◆ Support for an array of clients, MS-DOS, Windows, Windows 95, Windows For Workgroups, Windows NT, and LAN Manager RAS

Each of these features is significant to the overall operations of RAS and should be understood. Before continuing, it will be helpful to take a closer look at each of these characteristics.

Understanding PPP, SLIP, and the Microsoft RAS Protocol

The Point-to-Point Protocol was first defined by the Internet Engineering Task Force (IETF). It is a protocol that encapsulates the piece of information (packet) as it goes on the line. The encapsulation process causes the addition of bits to the packet for addressing, error-checking, and authentication. The addressing facilitates communications between computer to computer, computer to router, or router to router. The error-checking is handled using a checksum, which is a method of looking at the bits in the packet to determine if they all made it over the line. The authentication methods include Password Authentication Protocol (PAP), Challenge Handshake Authentication Protocol (CHAP), and Shiva Password Authentication Protocol (SPAP). These protocols are called the PPP Control Protocols. PPP is newer and is generally recommended over SLIP.

The Serial Line Interface Protocol is simpler and older than PPP. SLIP does not provide any error-checking or authentication. This protocol is also defined by the IETF and was originally developed for use in the UNIX environment. One limitation with this protocol is that Windows NT Server can be used as a SLIP client but not a SLIP server.

The Microsoft RAS Protocol is used for the older versions of RAS. These older versions are Windows NT 3.51 and Windows for Workgroups. This protocol requires the use of NetBEUI and uses NetBIOS. When the communication is made, the RAS server acts as a gateway for any other protocols that might be running on the corporate network such as IPX or TCP/IP.

Understanding PPTP

At first glance, you might think that this is just a misspelling of PPP. PPTP is Point-to-Point Tunneling Protocol. This is a new protocol for Windows NT Server and is particularly timely due to the fact that it takes advantage of the Internet's popularity: This protocol allows access into the corporate networks through the Internet.

The Internet connection can be either through an Internet provider or directly to the Internet. When either of these connections are made, the PPTP provides tunneling for the connection. The tunneling encapsulates the IP, IPX, or NetBEUI PPP packets for transmission over a TCP/IP network.

Part
V

Ch
19

In other words, PPTP actually allows an Internet connection, and through that call, access to the corporate network. There are many advantages to this, especially the reduction in phone bills. This could also be especially advantageous if the company has already established Internet connections for all of their employees; therefore there is minimal setup. When PPTP is used, it is called a Virtual Private Network (VPN).

PPTP provides a sophisticated level of transport protocol support and is capable of handling TCP/IP, IPX/SPX, or NetBEUI. PPTP uses data encapsulation with encryption and authentication.

Encapsulation, Encryption, and Authentication

Although the following terms are usually covered in preparation for the Networking Essentials Exam Guide, it is helpful to briefly review their definitions for this section of the Windows NT Server 4.0 Enterprise Exam Guide:

Data Encapsulation. A method of inserting one protocol's packet into another protocol's packet.

Encryption. A method of changing data so that it is not readable for any unauthorized purpose. Typically, an algorithm is used to make the data unreadable. After the data is encrypted, it must be decrypted to be read.

Authentication. A method of validation of source, and accuracy.

Defining the Connections

There are various methods of network communication, some more common than others. The most common method is connecting through phone lines using modems. These phone lines are sometimes called Plain Old Telephone Service (POTS) or Public Switched Telephone Network (PSTN). Microsoft Windows NT supports over 200 modems.

Tip

It is strongly recommended that you choose a modem from the Hardware Compatibility List (HCL).

To assist with modem connections, Windows NT uses a device.log file which is intended to be used for tracking of modem problems. This capability is turned on by making a Registry setting change. To use this log file follow these steps:

1. From the Start Menu, select Run, then start the Registry Editor by entering Regedt32.

2. From the HKEY_LOCAL_MACHINE subkey, access this key:

   \SYSTEM\CurrentControlSet\Services\RasMan\Parameters

3. Change the Logging parameter to 1 so that the completed change looks like this:

   Logging:REG_DWORD:0x1

As with other Registry changes, it is necessary to restart the machine to have the change take effect.

If you are taking advantage of the full capabilities of Windows NT Server and are using multiple connections, then it is necessary to purchase special equipment to allow the 256 connections that Windows NT Server is capable of. This equipment is called a multiport I/O board. They allow the addition of the 256 ports that RAS is capable of handling. As with any equipment, make sure that it is listed on the HCL. Typically, the modem standards that are most often used are V.32*bis* which operates at 14.4Kbps and V.34*bis* which runs at 28.8Kbps. It is significant to note that RAS compression can be twice as efficient as the compression algorithms used by the V.42*bis*. A decrease in transmission speed may be experienced if both modem compression and RAS compression are enabled.

Tip

In an ideal network, it is a good rule to use the same modem model at both ends of the communications. While this is not a requirement (and perhaps, considering the exponential growth of Internet users, extremely difficult), it is a good idea.

X.25 has been around for awhile. It is a protocol that has been defined to control the connection between computers and a *packet-switched network*. A packet-switched network is a communications network that sends the data to the destination in packets, a defined groups of bits. A message may consist of many packets, each having a header. A header is a group of bits that contains the address of the destination. When a communication link is established in the X.25 scheme, the connection is called a *virtual circuit* because the connection is not a dedicated connection. Generally, X.25 connections experience performance problems, however the primary advantage of this type of connection is that it is a well established technology and is very common. X.25 uses a Packet Assembler Disassembler (PAD). As the name suggests, the PAD puts the packets together and disassembles them as the communications are going on.

ISDN is a technology with a lot of promise. The idea of ISDN is integrated communications, meaning a connection that can handle data, voice, and video. The signals that are carried on ISDN are digital as opposed to the standard analog signal that is carried on a standard phone line. The primary advantage of ISDN is speed. It is considered the communication choice of the future. ISDN connections also require special equipment and special arrangements through the phone carrier. The equipment needed is called an ISDN card. The type of card used is determined by the details of the connection. ISDN offers a Basic Rate Interface (BRI) and a Primary Rate Interface (PRI).

Null modem cables can be used between two machines for a RAS connection. The null modem cable is connected at the serial port of the machines. A nine or 25-pin cable is used with special pin definitions for each.

Multilink capabilities are possible with Windows NT 4.0. This is a new feature that allows the combining of dial-up lines so that they act as a single channel. The purpose of multilinking is to increase the bandwidth. When it is being used, both client and server must have the capability turned on. A multilink channel can contain both digital and analog signals. This protocol is defined by the Internet Engineering Task Force (IETF) in the Request For Comment (RFC) 1717.

 Note Any clients that connect to the RAS server must also have support for the PPP Multilink standard as described in RFC 1717. ▨

User Security Options

One of the important implementation options is how to handle security. The most basic form of dial in security is the user name and password. Windows NT augments this with support for Call back security.

Call back security is used to further verify the caller by their location, or at least log their location. There are three options for call back security defined by Windows NT.

- ◆ No call back security
- ◆ Call back to a administrator defined number
- ◆ Call back to a user assigned number

The highest security is to utilize an administrator-defined number. This insures that the user calling in will always be where the administrator expects them to be.

Unfortunately, this doesn't always work. For instance, what about sales people who travel from remote office to office? You can't establish a single call back number for them since they move around.

In that case, you still might be able to use call back security. In this case, however, the client, your salesman, must provide the number where they are located.

At this point you're not really adding security to the system, but you are building an audit trail. If you do detect a break in, you'll have the information needed to locate the culprit.

However, there are cases where even call back security with the user setting the call back number won't work. Going back to the salesmen again, if they travel and are in hotels, you won't be able to use call back security at all, since call back security requires that the RAS server be able to directly dial the call back number. Most hotels don't have automated attendants which can allow a RAS server to call back.

Key Concept

Use call back security set to an administrator assigned number wherever possible. This increases security. Use call back security set to a user assigned number when the user moves around. This increases audibility.

Most installations of RAS server do not use any kind of call back security; however, it should certainly be considered for companies with security concerns.

Who Can Be a RAS Server and RAS Client?

RAS communications capabilities are a Microsoft technology; therefore, RAS is not limited to Windows NT Server. MS–DOS 5.0, Windows for Workgroups, OS/2 1.31, Windows 3.1, and Windows 95 can participate in RAS communications. The difference with RAS versions is related to the RAS features. The enhancements made to RAS include support for the newer, faster modems, newer line protocols, flow control, and number of connections supported.

RAS Installation

RAS is a service and is installed as other services are. RAS can be installed during the installation of Windows NT Server, or it can be installed at a later time. The following list of steps is the installation procedure.

Tip

Before the RAS service is installed, you must have the appropriate network protocols installed. It is recommended that the appropriate hardware is installed.

1. The RAS installation is started from the Network icon in the Control Panel after logging on as administrator.

    It is also accessible from the Network icon on the desktop. Secondary click (in other words, right-mouse click) and select Properties from the Context menu. Figure 19.1 shows the Network dialog box that appears.

FIG. 19.1 ⟹

The Services tab is selected, listing the <u>N</u>etwork Services that are already installed.

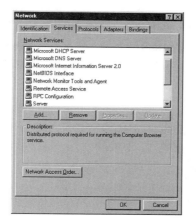

2. After selecting the Services tab, click the <u>A</u>dd button. Windows NT shows a selection of the services that are available (see Figure 19.2). Highlight and select the Remote Access Service.

FIG. 19.2 ⟹

The Select Network Service dialog box lists the services that are available for installation.

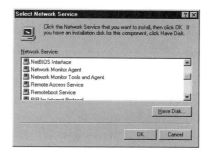

Part

V

Ch

19

The installation process accesses the setup files to start the installation. The typical location of these files is on the Windows NT CD in the \i386 directory. A status screen appears indicating the progress of the file access.

3. Next, you must add the RAS devices. The administrator has a choice of either using the already listed RAS-capable devices or installing other devices.

   The Add RAS Device dialog box lists the RAS Capable Devices (see Figure 19.3). The install buttons—Install Modem and Install X25 Pad—start the Installation Wizards if other devices need to be installed.

> **Note**   A PAD is a Packet Assembler Disassembler and is used in conjunction with X.25 public switched networks. The sending PAD accepts and buffers characters from the source machine. The sending PAD then assembles the characters into X.25 packets and transmits the packets. The receiving PAD disassembles the packet and passes the characters to the destination machine. ■

FIG. 19.3 ⇒
The Add RAS Device screen allows the installation of RAS devices during the installation of the RAS service.

4. The next screen is the Remote Access Setup dialog box, shown in Figure 19.4. This screen contains the list of RAS devices and servers as the entry point for the specific configuration screen associated with each device. From this screen you can Add a new device, Remove an existing device, and Configure either a new or existing device.

In this example, you configure the modem ports by selecting the particular modem device and then clicking the Configure button.

FIG. 19.4 ⇒

The modem to be configured should be selected from the Remote Access Setup screen.

5. When you click the Configure button in the Remote Access Setup dialog box, the Configure Port Usage screen is displayed (see Figure 19.5). Select the Dial Out Only option if the computer is going to be set up as a client. This prevents anyone from calling into the machine. Choose the Receive Calls Only option if the machine is being set up as the RAS server. The last option, Dial Out and Receive Calls, allows the most flexibility. In this case, the machine can be either a RAS client or a RAS server.

FIG. 19.5 ⇒

The Dial Out and Receive Calls port usage option is very flexible, allowing your machine to be either a RAS client or server.

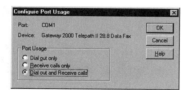

Part
V

Ch
19

6. After selecting your port usage option and clicking OK, the Network Configuration screen appears (see Figure 19.6). Table 19.1 lists the protocol and setting options from which you must choose.

FIG. 19.6 ⇒
The Network
Configuration
screen is used for
both RAS client
and servers.

Table 19.1 Network Configuration Options

Option	Description
Dial Out Protocols	Protocols used by the machine when the machine is calling out as a client.
Server Settings	Protocols used when the machine is acting as the RAS server.
Encryption Settings	Allow Any Authentication Including Clear Text indicates that the authentication method is selected by the client; useful when there are different kinds of clients calling in; the least secure of the RASconnections.
	Require Encrypted Authentication permits any kind of connection with the exception of PAP. (See the following sidebar for details on PAP, MS-CHAP, and other specific protocols).
	Require Microsoft Encrypted Authentication permits authentication using the MS-CHAP method only; a very secure protocol. Require Data Encryption causes all data to be encrypted during the data transfer phase and allows a high level of security by disallowing clear text authentication.

Option	Description
Enable Multilink	Selected if the administrator is combining communication links in order to increase bandwidth.

More About Protocols—PAP, CHAP, and SPAP

Within the three categories of encryption settings listed in the preceding table, there are specific protocols you might encounter. One of the more popular (and least secure) connections is Password Authentication Protocol (PAP). This method does not support encryption of the data needed for authentication.

Microsoft's encryption settings, however, revolve around a more secure protocol—Microsoft Challenge Handshake Authentication Protocol (CHAP). MS-CHAP uses a one-way hash function combined with a checksum procedure.

There are other encrypted authentication protocols, one of which is Shiva Password Authentication Protocol (SPAP). This is a proprietary methodology that was developed by SHIVA. Using SPAP provides compatibility for SHIVA clients.

The most interesting part of setting up RAS is in the configuration of the network settings (refer to Figure 19.6). For NetBEUI configuration, select the NetBEUI check box under Server Settings, then click the Configure button. The RAS Server NetBEUI Configuration appears as shown in Figure 19.7.

Part
V

Ch
19

FIG. 19.7 ⇒

If you want to allow remote NetBEUI clients full access to the network, choose the Entire Net–work option.

In Figure 19.7, the determination is made to use the RAS server as a NetBIOS gateway. This gateway gives NetBEUI clients the opportunity to use the corporate resources on the network. If the network is using another protocol, such as TCP/IP or IPX, the RAS server translates the packets to permit communications. One disadvantage is that if an application needs or requires the participating client to have TCP/IP or IPX on the client workstation, then the application won't run.

The next possible configuration selection is TCP/IP (refer again to Figure 19.6). After choosing the TCP/IP check box and clicking the Configure button, the RAS Server TCP/IP Configuration dialog box appears as shown in Figure 19.8.

FIG. 19.8 ⇒

It makes sense that TCP/IP configuration is more complicated than NetBEUI configuration because of the abundance of configuration parameters in the TCP/IP scheme.

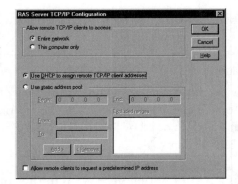

At the top of the TCP/IP configuration screen, the administrator indicates whether or not the caller can access the rest of the network or the RAS server only. This is a straightforward decision and is determined by the company's security policies.

The Use DHCP to Assign Remote TCP/IP Client Addresses option is for those computing environments that have Dynamic Host Configuration Protocol (DHCP) servers. These are the servers that have a service running on them that allows the automatic allocation of the IP addresses.

> **Note** For more information on Dynamic Host Configuration Protocol and other various Windows NT 4.0 protocol choices, refer to Chapter 8, "Configuring Domain Network Core Services." ■

The Use Static Address Pool option is for computing environments that use other methods of IP address assignment. This section permits the designation of the addresses that are set aside for the RAS clients. To enter the static address pool, enter the numbers into the Begin and End boxes. Also permitted in this section is the designation of addresses that need to be excluded. In the From and To boxes you enter the address or range of address that are to be excluded. Therefore, if it is necessary to exclude an address(s), type the address(s) in the From and To box and then choose the Add button, which will add it to the Excluded Ranges box.

In the last area of the TCP/IP configuration screen you can select the Allow Remote Clients to Request a Predetermined IP Address option. The administrator should be sure that the number that the client uses is a unique IP address.

To configure the third and final server setting, select the IPX check box under Server Settings and click the Configure button (refer again to Figure 19.6). The RAS Server IPX Configuration screen appears (see Figure 19.9).

Part

V

Ch

19

FIG. 19.9 ⟹

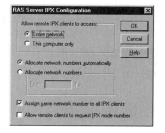

As with the other configuration screens, the top of the RAS Server IPX Configuration screen denotes network permissions for its clients, followed by options specific to the IPX protocol.

After deciding again to allow IPX clients access to either the Entire Network or This Computer Only, the next configuration item enables you to specify how to allocate the network numbers.

Selecting Allocate Network Numbers Automatically causes the RAS server to use the Router Information Protocol (RIP) to assign a number to the client.

The next selection, Allocate Network Numbers, is used when the administrator needs more direct control for the assignment of the numbers. It may be necessary for security or tracking purposes that the administrator knows which numbers are being used for RAS clients, and this is a convenient way to do it. The administrator needs to enter the first number of the group of available numbers. The first number is entered into the From box.

The Assign Same Network Number to All IPX Clients option is used in the case where the administrator wants the clients to be seen as being on the same IPX network. This can be used whether the assignment of the numbers is automatic or manual.

The Allow Remote Clients to Request IPX Node Number allows the client to select its own number. This probably is not a good idea because of security issues and the possibility of a hacker impersonating another client.

The completion of the configuration brings the installation process to an end. There is a final Setup Message screen as shown in Figure 19.10.

FIG. 19.10 ⇒

This screen indicates a successful installation.

The service has been successfully installed and the machine needs to be rebooted. Because RAS is a service, the administration of RAS is the same as with other services. Verify that in fact the service is running and start the administration of the service.

RAS Administration

The administration of RAS starts by finding the RAS Administration Manager on the menu. From the Start menu, choose Programs, Administrative Tools (Common), Remote Access Admin (see Figure 19.11).

FIG. 19.11 ⟹
The Remote Access Admin selection is available after installation.

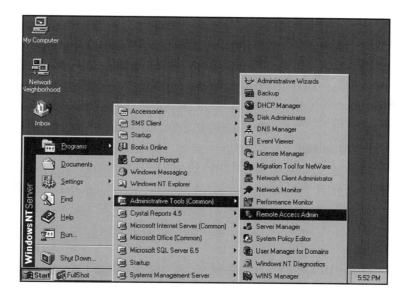

The administrative functions include selections for control of the service, for example starting, stopping, and pausing. Other selections include verification of port status and, of course, the settings for the users that are going to be calling in. The first administration screen that is shown is Figure 19.12.

The first administration screen lists the RAS server that is being administered; in this case, the server is named Instructor and has one port that is available for RAS. If there is another RAS server it would be listed here. It is also possible to access another domain.

Double-clicking the INSTRUCTOR server name displays the Communication Ports screen (see Figure 19.13). This screen shows information related to each port.

Part
V

Ch
19

FIG. 19.12 ⇒

The Remote Access Admin in CLASSROOM screen shows the INSTRUCTOR machine running properly.

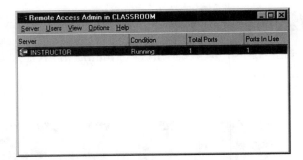

FIG. 19.13 ⇒

Specific information on the staus of a port can be gathered from the Communication Ports screen.

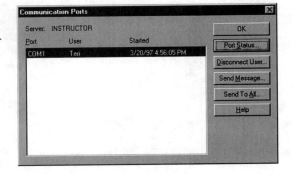

For specific configuration information about each port, select the Port Status button. The Port Status dialog box is displayed (see Figure 19.14).

The Users menu selection from the Remote Access Admin screen (refer to Figure 19.12) is of particular interest because that gives access to the screen that allows the setting of permissions for users. You set permissions in the Remote Access Permissions dialog box shown in Figure 19.15. This screen is accessed from the Remote Access Admin screen by selecting Users, Permissions.

FIG. 19.14 ⇒
The Port Status screen gives information related to the connection from the selected port.

FIG. 19.15 ⇒
Remote Access Permissions can be set for each user.

Figure 19.16, the Remote Access Users screen, shows the activity of the users that are connected to the machine at that point in time. This is available from the Remote Access Admin screen (refer to Figure 19.12) from the Users menu selection and the selection of Active Users. If it becomes necessary to disconnect a user or send a message to a user, this is the screen that is used.

Part
V
Ch
19

FIG. 19.16 ⇒
Remote Access Users can be controlled from this screen.

The Remote Access Administration tool controls the configuration of the RAS server after the installation process is complete. It offers comprehensive status information and tracking of connections.

The Dial-Up Networking Component of RAS

The Remote Access Administration is the first administrative task after the installation is complete. Another part of the equation is from the client's side—the Dial-Up Networking (DUN) setup. DUN allows the connection to the RAS server and essentially converts the communication port to a network card. When the client dials in, the caller needs to be defined on the server, just as they would for any network access.

The DUN selection is available from the Start menu on Windows 95, Windows NT Workstation, and other Windows NT Server machines. It is located under the Accessories selection as shown in Figure 19.17. The DUN Wizard walks the client through the installation of the client component, DUN.

FIG. 19.17 ⇒

The Dial Up Networking component is available from the Accessories selection.

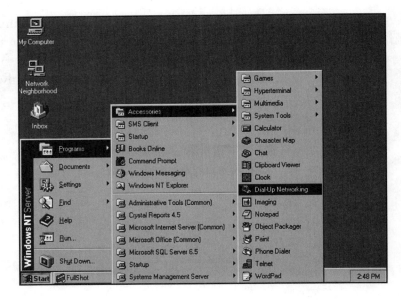

Automatic Logon from DUN

One of the major points of interest for the DUN client installation is the automatic logon feature. This is a feature that will remember the location of a file that has previously been accessed from a DUN connection. In other words, Windows NT RAS automatically connects to the remote Windows NT RAS Server.

When the remote file is accessed, Windows NT will automatically start the dialing procedure to get the file. This is assuming that all connecting authentication information is correct. Additionally, from the DUN Phonebook Entry dialog box, the Authenticate Using Current User Name and Password check box has been checked.

This capability is in effect if the DUN client and the RAS server are both using NT 3.5x or NT 4.0 and if the Remote Access Autodial Manager service is running. This is accessed and controlled from the Services dialog box (see Figure 19.18). The Services icon is accessible from the Control Panel.

> **Note** Windows 95 works in a similar manner from the Window 95 Dial Up Networking component. When a user accesses a resource that requires a connection, Windows 95 automatically activates Dial Up Networking.

FIG. 19.18 ⇒

The Remote Access Autodial Manager is another

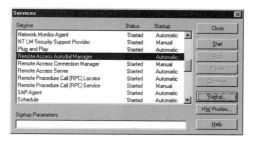

Using a RAS Server as a Router

A RAS server can act as both an IPX router and a TCP/IP router. First, the server involved needs to be configured with the protocol of interest. Additionally, it should be noted that the routing that is performed is a static routing, not dynamic routing. This means that the routing tables are not automatically updated. Also, the routing is only for the networks that are connected to the RAS server. Some third-party software is involved, and the software most often used is written by SHIVA.

The IPX routing allows the passing of IPX messages from the RAS client to the IPX host. Similarly, the IP routing allows the passing of the TCP/IP messages to the associated hosts.

It is because of this routing capability that a RAS server can be used to provide routing between a network and the Internet over a dedicated PPP account from an Internet Access Provider.

Troubleshooting RAS

RAS is a mature, well-behaved, complex Microsoft Windows NT service. Occasionally, there might be a need to do some troubleshooting. The following information contains some insights about where to look for help in the troubleshooting process.

DUN Monitor from the Client's Perspective

One of the first troubleshooting techniques for RAS is checking the status of the remote machine. This can easily be done on the Windows NT client's machine by looking at the System Tray. The System Tray is the part of the taskbar that is located in the lower-right hand corner. Programs and services frequently use this area to convey status information. As shown in Figure 19.19, holding the mouse pointer over the status icon tells what the icon is for.

By double-clicking the status icon for DUN, the DUN monitor is displayed, as shown in Figure 19.20.

FIG. 19.19 ⇒
The System Tray holds the status icon for the Dial Up Networking Monitor.

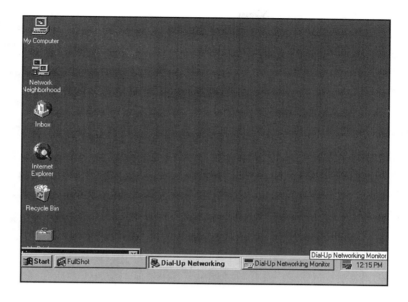

FIG. 19.20 ⇒
Dial Up Networking Monitor Status information is given from the Status Tab.

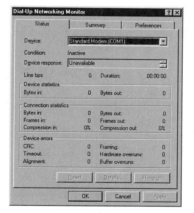

There are three tabs on the DUN Monitor: Status, Summary, and Preferences. The Dial Up Networking Monitor should be the first line of investigation for troubleshooting. The Status tab gives device information including device statistics, connection statistics, and device errors.

The Summary tab gives information about multilink connections. This is the screen to check for information about remote networks and devices that are being used.

FIG. 19.21 ⟹
The Summary tab gives information on remote networks and devices.

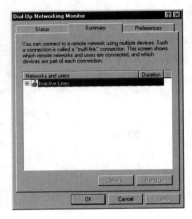

The Preferences tab is the location for controlling associated sounds, the listing of DUN in the task list, and the display of status lights (see Figure 19.22).

FIG. 19.22 ⟹
The Preferences tab is for customizing features to personal preference.

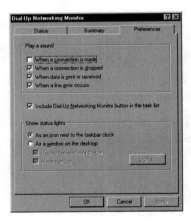

Hardware Considerations for Troubleshooting RAS

There are a number of hardware considerations for this troubleshooting process. First, the state of the communication device (modem, PAD, or ISDN card) should be considered. Consult the manual for the detailed instructions to verify operations. As noted earlier, it is an excellent idea to make sure that the device is on the Windows NT HCL.

Phone line quality could be another issue. This can be easily checked by using a phone and listening to the line quality. If static and clicking noises are heard, then this could be the source of the problem. Line quality problems will typically cut out the connection, generally line quality problems do not prevent the connection from being made.

Software Considerations for Troubleshooting RAS

Verifying that the RAS service is operational is the most obvious software consideration. This should be checked from the Services icon in the Control Panel. All considerations that are true for other Windows NT services are also true for the RAS service. Occasionally, it is necessary to stop a service and then restart it. In even worse cases, it is sometimes necessary to uninstall a service and reinstall it.

Another area of problems might be related to security issues. If a user is being denied access, then it would be helpful to check the user rights and perhaps any trust relationships that might come into play. This would come under the area of typical network administration tasks. Also, consider looking at the Remote Access Administration program and checking User Permissions again. The administrator should check the Event Viewer because RAS generates audit trails of remote connections.

Part
V

Ch
19

Also to be considered are protocol issues. RAS enables NetBEUI, TCP/IP, and IPX on the RAS server by default so there might need to be an adjustment there. Binding order might be significant also; for example, if the protocol being used was NetBEUI and the user was communicating with an application that needed Windows Sockets, then TCP/IP needs to be brought into the picture. Examine the applications that are being used to determine dependencies between the method of interprocess communication and the transport protocol.

One of the most helpful tools that Windows NT provides for troubleshooting is the Event Viewer. This will log all system activities including success and failures for operations of services. The Event Viewer can also audit other RAS activities by turning on the auditing feature. This is controlled by the following key:

> HKEY_LOCAL_MACHINE\SYSTEM\CurrentControlSet\
> Services\RemoteAccess\Parameters

The data field for that key needs to be set to 1 for the enhanced auditing. Extra information will include regular connections, disconnects, timed out authentication, and line error problems.

Taking the Disc Test

 If you have read and understood the material in the chapter, you are ready to test your knowledge. Insert the CD-ROM that comes with this book and run the self-test software as described in Appendix I, "Using the CD-ROM."

From Here...

Now that you've completed learning about the connectivity objectives of the enterprise exam, it's time to move on to a new topic. Chapter 20 starts Section VI by talking about Performance Monitor. All of Section VI is targeted at teaching the skills related to Monitoring and Optimization.

Part VI.

Monitoring and Optimization

Performance Monitor

This chapter explores Windows NT 4.0's Performance Monitor utility. This
utility provides an administrator the ability to chart a Windows NT-based
computer's performance in a given situation. Specific topics that will be discussed include:

◆ Exploring the benefits of Performance Monitor

◆ Creating a baseline of performance

◆ Examining specific objects and counters

Monitoring System Performance with Performance Monitor

Windows NT Server 4.0 contains a performance-tracking tool called Performance Monitor, which collects data about system resources and presents them in a graphical chart-based format. It can be used to:

◆ Create a baseline of normal system performance

◆ Monitor use of system resources for given periods of time

◆ Identify periods of abnormal system activity

◆ Predict system resource usage given specific parameters

◆ Justify upgrades to hardware and resources

The Performance Monitor treats system resources as *objects* with characteristics, or *counters* that can be tracked (see Figure 20.1). Multiple occurrences of an object and counter, or variations on them, are called *instances*. For example, the processor is an object that can be monitored. It has counters that can be charted such as the total percent of processor usage, the percent of the processor used by the kernel mode, and so on. Recall that Windows NT Server 4.0-based computers can support up to 32 processors. If there are multiple processors on a given system, each is considered an instance. You can then track each processor's total percent of usage, total percent of kernel mode usage, and so on for each instance of the processor.

Most counter instances include a *Total* selection, which provides activity generated by all the instances. For example, each of four processors installed in a computer has a `Processor>%Processor Time` instance. You can monitor data for each processor. However, if you want a total value for processor usage by all four processors, you can select the `Total` instance.

With Performance Monitor, you can also create and view log files, view summary statistics, and create system alerts based on monitored values. Performance Monitor is used primarily for two purposes: creating baselines of performance, and monitoring aberrations from the baseline—in other words, troubleshooting.

FIG. 20.1⇒

The Add to Chart dialog box displays some of the objects and instances that can be tracked through the Performance Monitor.

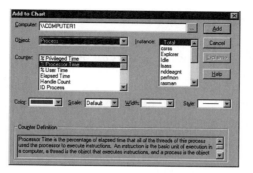

Key Concept

It does you no good as an analyst to turn on Performance Monitor to monitor system activity once a problem has been detected if you have no "normal" baseline of activity against which to measure the problem.

There are 11 core objects that can always be selected in Performance Monitor. These are described in Table 20.1. However, there are numerous other objects that also appear as services and devices are installed. Each object has numerous counters, also available by default. Every additional protocol, service, driver, and in some cases application, you install on your Windows NT Workstation or Server will likely add additional objects and counters to the list. The number of instances varies greatly with each object.

Note In this chapter, Performance Monitor counters will be referred to using the following notation: *Objectname>countername* where *objectname* represents the object to select, and *countername* the corresponding counter for that object. ■

There are three types of counters which are described in the following list.

◆ *Instantaneous*. Display the most recent values for a counter. For example, the `Processor>%Processor Time` counter shows the current total usage of the processor on a system.

◆ *Averaging*. Measure a counter's value over a period of time and show the averaged value of the last two measurements.

◆ *Difference.* Sometimes included with other applications that are installed on your system. Difference counters subtract a measurement from the previous measurement and display the difference if the value is positive. Otherwise, a zero is displayed.

Tip

The Add to Chart dialog box contains an Explain button. This button expands the dialog box to display a full explanation of the counter and the resource that it monitors (refer to Figure 20.1). This is very useful, especially for those counters that you might use infrequently.

Table 20.1   Core Objects in Performance Monitor

Object	Description
Cache	Monitors the most recently accessed data stored in RAM.
Logical Disk	Monitors disk activity by logical partitions and drives.
Memory	Monitors RAM activity.
Objects	Monitors software objects.
Paging File	Monitors page file activity.
Physical Disk	Monitors disk activity for each physical disk installed in the system.
Process	Monitors activity of programs that are currently running on the system.
Processor	Monitors activity of the CPU or CPUs installed on the system.
Redirector	Monitors the activity of network requests generated by this system.
System	Monitors the activity of network requests that this system responds to.
Thread	Monitors activity of process threads.

Of the objects listed in Table 20.1, there are five specific objects that are of particular concern when troubleshooting your system, and we will concentrate on them in this chapter: processor, memory, disk, process, and network.

This is not to say other objects aren't important to monitor. These are simply the objects most often looked at first to determine aberrations from the baseline and bottlenecks in the system. After all, if the system is running with poor performance, it is likely slowing due to poor performance at the processor (too many I/O requests for its power), in memory (not enough RAM to handle all address requests), on disk (not enough disk space or excessive paging), or with the process itself (an application that overuses resources).

Configuring Performance Monitor

Performance Monitor can be found with the other Administrative Tools. There are four types of views that you can configure with Performance Monitor: Chart, Report, Log, and Alert.

Creating a Performance Monitor Chart

The most frequently used view is the Chart view, which plots a real-time graph of the system activity being generated by the objects and counters selected (see Figure 20.2). Here are the basic steps to follow when configuring a Performance Monitor chart:

1. From the taskbar, select Start, Programs, Administrative Tools, Performance Monitor.
2. Choose Edit, Add to Chart to display the Add to Chart dialog box.
3. In the Computer text box, type or browse for the computer you want to monitor.

Part
VI

Ch
20

FIG. 20.2⇒
Here is a sample chart created in Performance Monitor. This chart tracks `Processor>%Processor Time` for the total system, as well as for three individual processes.

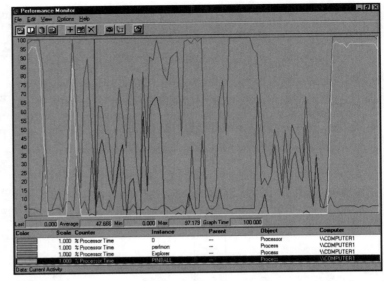

Tip
If you have a valid administrator's account or participate in a domain in which you are a domain administrator, you can monitor other Windows NT computers remotely by selecting them from the browse list. While Performance Monitor is designed to use minimal system resources, nevertheless, depending on what resources you are charting on a system, you can skew performance results somewhat because Performance Monitor itself will be using resources. In such situations, Microsoft recommends monitoring resources on those systems remotely.

4. Select the Object that you want to monitor.

5. As you select an object, the Counter list will display counters associated with the chosen object that you can chart. Select the counter that you want to track. Select multiple counters by clicking the first counter, then holding down the Ctrl button while clicking the others.

6. If you are unsure about what a counter measures, select Explain to display descriptive text about the counter.

7. If appropriate, choose an Instance for each object counter. Again, select multiple instances for each counter by selecting the first and then Ctrl+ clicking the rest.

8. Modify the legend characteristics as you desire (Color, Scale, Width, and Line Style).

9. Choose Add to add the counter(s) to the chart window.

10. Repeat steps 3-9 for any additional objects you want to monitor.

11. Choose Done when you are finished.

Tip

Performance Monitor, by default, displays a line chart that charts activity for every second in time. These defaults can be modified by selecting Options, Chart to display the Chart Options dialog box.

Most of the options in the Chart Options dialog box are self-explanatory. However, note the Update Time section. The Periodic Interval is set to 1 second, the default. If you want to capture information in smaller or larger time intervals, modify the value accordingly. The value you enter will affect the Graph Time value on the Statistics bar at the bottom of the graph itself. At a setting of 1 second, it will take 100 seconds to complete one chart pass in the window. A setting of 2 seconds will take 200 seconds to make a complete pass. A setting of .6 second will take 60 seconds, or 1 minute, to complete a pass, and so on.

Tip

To save chart settings for future use such as creating a chart to compare against baseline activity, choose File, Save Chart Settings. The chart settings can then be loaded later to monitor system activity as designed.

Part

VI

Ch

20

Creating a Performance Monitor Log

As mentioned, charting values really is ineffective unless you have some baseline values against which you can compare activity. Log files are designed to collect this kind of information for viewing later. Object and counter values can be collected and saved in a log file, as well as values from multiple computers (see Figure 20.3).

FIG. 20.3⇒

This example shows the log file as it is recording data for specific objects.

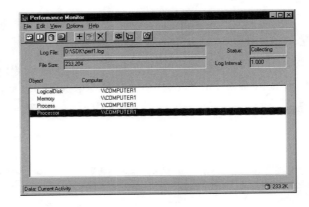

While the log file is collecting data, you cannot view its contents. If you want to monitor what kinds of data the log view is recording, you must start another copy of Performance Monitor and configure the Options, Data From option so that it will view chart data from the running log.

To create a log file, use these steps:

1. Start Performance Monitor.

2. Choose View, Log to display the log window.

3. Choose Edit, Add to Log. Select all the objects whose data you want to capture and choose Add. This will cause the log to record activity for every counter associated with each object. Choose Done when you are finished.

4. Choose Options, Log.

5. Enter a name for the log file and a directory to save it in, and set the Periodic Update interval if you desire.

6. Choose Start Log to begin recording system activity.

7. Monitor the file size counter (shown in bytes) until the file grows as large as you like, or simply use your watch to collect data over a specific period of time.

8. When you have collected the desired amount of data, choose Options, Log, Stop Log.

9. Choose Options, Log, Save to save the log file.

To view the contents of a log file use these steps:

1. Start Performance Monitor.

2. Choose View, Chart to display the chart window.

3. Choose Options, Data From to display the Data From dialog box.

4. Choose Log File and enter the path and file name of the log file, or browse for it. Choose OK.

5. Choose Edit, Add to Chart. The only objects listed will be those you captured in the log file. Select the object and each appropriate counter for which you want to view chart values. Choose Add to add them to the chart. A static chart view will be created.

6. Adjust the time view of the chart by choosing Edit, Time Window and make your adjustment.

Note There is no facility in Performance Monitor to print out charts. However, you can press Print Screen to copy a chart window to the Clipboard, then paste it into a word processing document and print it that way. You can also export the data to an Excel spreadsheet and use its utilities to create graphs and analyze the data. ▪

You can make the log file even more useful by placing bookmarks at various points while you are recording data to the log. For example, perhaps you are performing a series of benchmark tests for which you are creating a log file.

Tip

Before each benchmark test, choose Options, Bookmark. Enter a bookmark name and choose Add. Later, when you are viewing the log, you can more accurately perceive the effects of each benchmark test by the bookmarks placed in the log.

Part
VI

Ch
20

Creating a Performance Monitor Report

The Report view allows you to see a summary window of the object and counter values recorded in a given log file, or collected dynamically for specified values from a current chart (see Figure 20.4). Each object and its counters and instances are summarized in this view.

FIG. 20.4⇒

This sample report is based on and summarizes the same values charted in Figure 20.2.

To create a report, use these steps:

1. Choose View, Report from the menu.
2. Choose Edit, Add to Report. The Add to Report dialog box displays, which is similar to the Add to Chart dialog box.
3. Add the desired objects, counters, and instances as you did when creating a chart. This is described earlier in the section "Creating a Performance Monitor Chart."

Creating a Performance Monitor Alert

The Alert view allows the administrator to monitor a system, and record and receive alerts when a specified threshold is reached for given counters and instances. Alert settings are configured through the Add to Alert dialog box (see Figure 20.5). This allows an administrator to continue to work, perhaps remotely, until notified of an alert.

FIG. 20.5⇒

An alert is generated when the `Processor>%Processor Time` counter exceeds 80 percent for a period of 5 seconds.

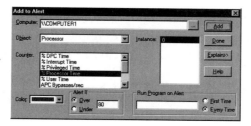

Many counters can be measured concurrently in Alert view, and up to 1,000 alerts can be recorded before the oldest are overwritten with new information. As with charts, logs, and reports, alerts can be saved for future reference. For example, you might use alerts as documentation of increases in resource usage when specific applications are run, or when services are started. The saved files can then be used for troubleshooting or as growth prediction tools.

To create an alert, use these steps:

1. Choose View, Alert.

2. Choose Edit, Add to Alert to display the Add to Alert dialog box (surprisingly similar to the Add to Chart and Add to Report dialog boxes).

3. Add the desired objects, counters, and instances as you did when creating a chart. This is described earlier in the section "Creating a Performance Monitor Chart."

4. Enter an alert threshold appropriate to the counter selected in the Alert If area. For example, select Over and 80 for the `Processor>% Processor Time` counter if you want to generate an alert when the counter exceeds 80 percent over a default period of time. (The default is 5 seconds.)

5. Optionally, enter the name of a program or command prompt command to execute when the threshold is reached in the Run Program on Alert text box. The program or command can be

Part

VI

Ch

20

configured to execute the first time the alert is generated, or every time the alert is generated. For example, you might enter the command: **NET SEND COMPUTER1 Processor Limit Exceeded** to send a system message to COMPUTER1, where the administrator is currently working, to notify her of the alert.

Considering Specific Objects to Monitor

There are five useful objects to monitor, especially when creating a baseline of "normal" system activity. They are: processor, process, disk, memory, and network. The following sections outline specific counters that can be useful to monitor for each object.

Monitoring the Processor

The `Processor` object monitors processor usage by the system. There are four counters that you may want to chart.

`Processor>%Processor Time` (refer to Figure 20.2) tracks the total processor usage and gives a picture of just how busy the processor is. This counter, in and of itself, is not enough to tell you what is driving the processor to a particular level of usage, but it does help to indicate whether the problem or bottleneck is related in any way to the processor.

`Processor>%User Time` and `Processor>%Privileged Time` define processor usage by displaying what percentage of the total processor usage pertains to the user mode (application) or the kernel mode (executive services) components of the Windows NT 4.0 operating system activities. Again, these do not indicate what specific activities are driving the percentages. Microsoft recommends that these three counters (`%Processor Time`, `%User Time`, and `%Privileged Time`) should, in general, remain below 75–80 percent, depending on computer use. For example, you would expect these values to be lower on a desktop computer, but consistently higher on a server running a client/server or system management application—for example, Microsoft Systems Management Server.

`Processor>Interrupts/Sec` tracks the number of device interrupt requests made from hardware devices, such as network cards or disk controllers, which are serviced by the processor. The number of requests considered optimum will vary from processor to processor. For example, you would expect a Pentium-based processor to handle perhaps three times as many requests as a 486 processor. In general, the higher the number (greater than 1,000 suggested for 486), the more likely the problem is related to the hardware rather than the processor.

If this is true, one might next monitor queue lengths for the suspected hardware devices such as the disk controller or network card. Optimally, there should only be one request waiting in queue for each device. Queue lengths greater than two indicate which device is the likely culprit causing the bottleneck and may need to be replaced or upgraded.

> **Caution**
>
> Processor object counters, as with all object counters, should never be monitored alone. As pointed out previously, the mere indication of activity beyond the norm does not in itself point to the processor as the focus of the problem. Use these and the other object counters recommended to draw attention to a problem. Then add additional object counters to help pinpoint and troubleshoot the problem.

There are two additional counters other than `Processor` object counters that can be used to identify the processor as a potential bottleneck. The first is the `System>Processor Queue Length`. This counter tracks the number of requests currently waiting for processing. At least one process thread must also be monitored for any data to be collected for this counter. Microsoft suggests that the queue length value should not be greater than two. Even if it is greater than two, it may not necessarily mean that the processor is the bottleneck. A particular application or process may be generating excessive requests. Your next step is to monitor `%Processor` usage for individual suspected processes to obtain further results.

Part
VI

Ch
20

The other counter is the Server Work Queues>Queue Length counter. Similar to the System>Processor Queue Length counter, this one indicates the number of requests for network resources currently in queue. Again, this value should not exceed two on average.

Monitoring Processes

For every service that is loaded and application that is run, a process is created by Windows NT—a process that can be monitored by Performance Monitor. Each process is considered an instance in this case, and each Process object instance has several counters that can be charted.

Notice that %Processor Time can be tracked for each process instance (see Figure 20.6). This is how you can determine which specific process is driving the processor to higher-than-normal usage.

FIG. 20.6⇒

The Performance Monitor (indicated as Perfmon in the legend and the white chart line in the graph) is driving the total percent of processor usage. You can also see from the thick dark line (ntvdm in the legend) when the screen capture program took the snapshot of this chart and contributed to an overall increase in processor usage.

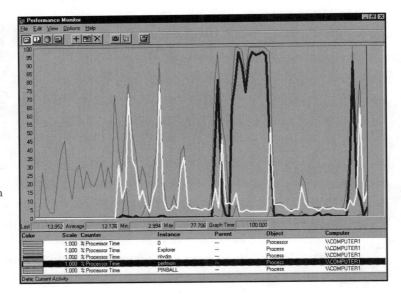

Another useful process counter is `Process>Working Set`. This counter actually tracks the amount of RAM required by the process and can be used to help determine when additional RAM is necessary. For example, if paging appears to be excessive, you might monitor the working sets of the processes suspected of causing the increased paging. The `Memory>Pages/Sec` example in the next section, "Monitoring Memory," gives a complete scenario for combining counters to determine a need for additional RAM.

Monitoring Memory

Perhaps the most common problem encountered on heavily used computers is inadequate RAM for the processes to perform at their optimum rates. There are several `Memory` object counters that can be of particular service to you. Some of these are displayed in Figure 20.7.

FIG. 20.7⇒
In this chart, the `Memory>Pages/Sec` counter (thick dark line) is somewhat high, with the `Memory> Committed Bytes` counter (highlighted in white) at about 22M larger than available RAM (16M on this computer). This indicates that the computer may need to add more RAM to improve performance and reduce paging.

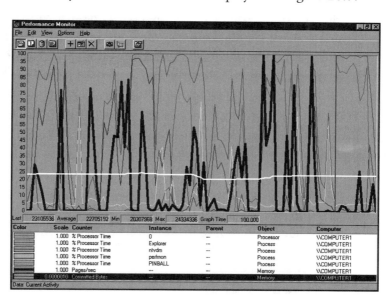

`Memory>Committed Bytes` indicates the amount of virtual memory that is currently stored in either physical RAM or the pagefile. If this value is consistently larger than the total installed RAM on the computer, you may need to install additional RAM to accommodate the system's memory requirements and reduce paging.

`Memory>Commit Limit` indicates the number of bytes that can be written (committed) to the pagefile without extending or growing it. As this number falls, the pagefile is more likely to grow. Whenever the page file needs to expand or grow, it must allocate additional disk storage space. Any time additional disk I/O is generated, your system will experience a performance hit. Use this counter to help you determine whether you need to "right-size" your pagefile.

For example, if you are running several large applications simultaneously, which is quite probable on a Windows NT server, it is likely that the initial size of your pagefile may be inadequate. If, as you load and run each application, the `Memory>Commit Limit` quickly drops and the pagefile expands, you can assume that the initial size is inadequate. Determine what the "expanded" size of the pagefile is. You could use Windows Explorer to see what size the pagefile is. Then modify the pagefile size so that the initial size matches the expanded size. This way you are *starting* with a "right-sized" pagefile and can eliminate the disk I/O involved with growing the pagefile.

> **Note**   While you can use Windows Explorer to monitor the size of the pagefile, the size shown for the pagefile stored on an NTFS volume will probably be inaccurate. This is because in NTFS, file size is not updated while the file is open. It is only updated when it is closed. Of course, the pagefile is always opened to its initial size when Windows NT boots.
>
> There is a way around this phenomenon. Try to delete the pagefile through Windows Explorer. You will get a message that the file is in use by another process (of course, Windows NT). Now refresh Windows Explorer, or type **DIR** at a command prompt, to display the correct pagefile size. ■

Memory>Pages/Sec (refer to Figure 20.7) indicates the number of pages requested by an application or other process that were not in RAM and had to be read from disk, or had to be written to disk to make room available in RAM for another process. In itself, this value should remain rather low—between 0 and 20 pages per second is suggested by Microsoft.

Multiply this counter's average value by that of the Logical Disk object's Avg. Disk sec/Transfer counter. This counter indicates the average number of seconds for each disk I/O. The resulting value shows the percent of disk I/O used by paging. Microsoft suggests that if this value consistently exceeds 10 percent, then paging is excessive and you probably need more RAM. The actual threshold is based on the function of the particular computer. You might expect more paging to occur on an SQL server than on a desktop, for example. When combined with the Process>Working Set counter described in the section "Monitoring Processes," you can determine approximately how much additional RAM you may need to install in the computer.

Consider that you have determined that paging is excessive by multiplying the Memory object's Pages/Sec counter by the Logical Disk>Avg. Disk sec/Transfer counter and got a value of 20 percent. You presume that you need additional RAM. But how much?

You have also been tracking Processor>%Processor Time for the processor as a whole, and for several suspect processes. You note three that really push the processor.

For each process, also monitor that process' Process>Working Set counter. Recall that this is the amount of RAM required by the process. Make note of the amount of RAM used by each process. Now, terminate one of the processes. Check the percent of disk I/O used by paging. Has it dropped below the acceptable threshold (10 percent as recommended by Microsoft)? If so, then the amount of RAM required by that application is the minimum amount of additional RAM to add to your computer. If not, terminate another application and check the results again. Keep doing this until the pagefile I/O drops to an acceptable level, and add the working set values for the terminated processes. The total represents the minimum amount of RAM to add to your computer. Administrators often round this value up to the nearest multiple of four.

Monitoring Disk Activity

There are actually two objects related to disk activity: *physical disk* and *logical disk*. The PhysicalDisk object counters (see Figure 20.8) track activity related to the disk drive as a whole, and can be used to determine whether one disk drive is being used more than another for load-balancing purposes. For example, if the activity of a disk is particularly high due to operating system requests and pagefile I/O, then you might want to move the pagefile to a disk that is being underused, especially if the disk controller can write to each disk concurrently. The number of instances will be the number of physical drives installed on the computer.

FIG. 20.8⇒

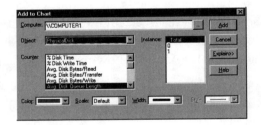

Some of the counters available for tracking activity on the Physical Disk. Note that there is an instance for each of two disk drives, as well as a Total option, which measures both drives together.

The LogicalDisk object counters track activity related to specific partitions on each disk and can be used to locate the source of activity on the disk—for example, on what partition the pagefile is located. The number of instances will be the number of partitions created by drive letter.

Both objects have pretty much the same group of counters for tracking activity. Five counters in particular can be useful and are listed here:

- `Avg. Disk sec/Transfer`. You saw this counter when reviewing `Memory` object counters in the "Monitoring Memory" section of this chapter. It shows the average amount of time for disk I/O to complete and can be used with the `Memory` object's `Pages/sec` counter to determine whether paging is excessive.

- `Current Disk Queue Length`. This counter represents the number of requests for disk I/O waiting to be serviced. This number should generally be less than two. Consistently high numbers indicate that the disk is being overused, or should be upgraded to a faster access disk.

- `Disk Bytes/sec`. This counter indicates the rate at which data is transferred during disk I/O. The higher the value, the more efficient the performance.

- `Avg. Disk Bytes/Transfer`. This counter is the average number of bytes of data that are transferred during disk I/O. As with `Disk Bytes/sec`, the larger the value, the more efficient the disk transfer.

- `%Disk Time`. This counter represents the amount of time spent servicing disk I/O requests. A consistently high number indicates that the disk is being heavily used. You may choose to determine which processes are driving this usage and partition or move the applications to a less heavily used disk to load-balance disk activity.

These counter values, used with the others previously discussed, can help you determine bottlenecks and possible courses of action to alleviate disk-related problems (see Figure 20.9).

Key Concept

Disk object counters, while they are visible in the Add to Chart dialog box, are not enabled by default. This is because the resource required to monitor disk activity is, itself, rather demanding. Disk object monitoring must be enabled before any charting can take place; otherwise, your chart will always display a flat-line graph.

continues

continued

Enable disk monitoring by typing the following command at a DOS command prompt:

DISKPERF -Y *computername* where *****computername* optionally references a remote computer whose disk activity you want to monitor.

When you are finished capturing your data, type **DISKPERF -N ***computername* to disable disk monitoring.

FIG. 20.9⇒

In this sample chart, the %Disk Time, Avg. Disk sec/Transfer, and Current Disk Queue Length values are consistently high, indicating that the disk is being heavily used. Additional analysis can determine what is being accessed (files, applications, and so on) and whether anything can be done to improve disk performance.

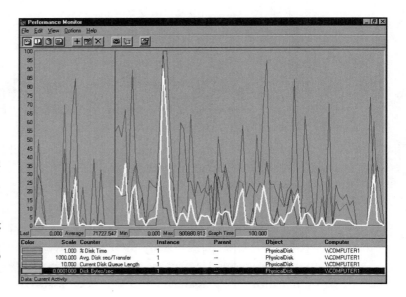

Disk bottlenecks are generally resolved by upgrading the disk or its controller, increasing the amount of controller caching that can take place if that is possible, implementing striping on a server and load-balancing applications across physical disks, or even moving heavily used applications to their own servers.

Monitoring Network-Related Objects

Perhaps one of the more difficult components of system activity to monitor and analyze is the network activity. Windows NT Server 4.0 provides a rather thorough network analysis tool called Network Monitor. This is a frame analysis tool that helps isolate and identify network traffic related to different types of network activity generated between two or more computers. This tool is explored in detail in the next chapter, "Network Monitor."

However, there are also some network-related objects and counters that can be used to determine the performance of network-related processes on the computer itself. These include Server, Redirector, and entries for the protocols installed on the computer such as TCP/IP, NWLINK, and NetBEUI. As additional network services are installed—RAS, DHCP, WINS—objects and counters relating to those services are added to Performance Monitor. If you have multiple network adapter cards installed on your computer, each of them will be considered an instance, and network objects and counters can be charted for each network adapter as well.

Protocol counters include `Bytes Total/sec`, `Datagrams/sec`, and `Frames/ sec`. A high value, in general, is desired because this indicates a high rate of throughput for network activity. However, high values could also indicate excessive generation of traffic, such as excessive frames due to browser broadcasts.

> **Note** TCP/IP counters are enabled only if the SNMP (Simple Network Management Protocol) service agent is installed on the computer. When the SNMP service is installed, it also adds some TCP/IP-related counters to the Performance Monitor. For example, `SNMP>TCP Segments/sec` indicates the number of TCP/IP specific frames that are being generated or received by the computer. `SNMP>UDP Datagrams/sec` identifies the number of broadcast, or UDP (User Datagram Protocol), frames that are generated. ▪

Part
VI

Ch
20

The workstation service on a computer can be monitored by charting `Redirector` object counters. One counter of interest is `Redirector>Network Errors/sec`. This counter indicates the number of errors detected by the workstation service as it attempted to direct frames onto the network. The higher this number goes, the more serious the problem may be. Use Network Monitor to observe and detect network traffic as a whole, especially to and from this computer.

Two more Redirector counters are `Redirector>Reads Denied/sec` and `Redirector>Writes Denied/sec`. If this number rises significantly, it may indicate that the server with which this computer is communicating may be having difficulty handling the number of network requests for resources it is receiving. You want to monitor activity on that server to pinpoint the problem and posit a solution, perhaps using one or more of the following `Server` object counters:

◆ `Server>Bytes Total/sec`. Indicates the number of bytes sent and received by the computer responding to network resource requests. This gives an idea of how busy the server service on the computer is.

◆ `Server>Logon/sec`. Indicates how many logon attempts took place during the last second on the computer either locally, over the network, or by a service account.

◆ `Server>Logon Total`. Indicates the total number of logon attempts that took place during the current computer session. This counter, together with `Server>Logon/sec` and the protocol counters, is particularly beneficial when used with Network Monitor to achieve a complete view of network activity relating to a domain controller.

◆ `Server>Pool Nonpaged Failures`. Indicates how frequently the server tried to allocate memory for server-based request handling and was unable due to a lack of physical RAM. Similarly, `Server>Pool Paged Failures` indicates how frequently the server tried to allocate paged memory and was unable to because either physical RAM was inadequate or the paging file was full. In either case, it may be appropriate to reconfigure memory usage by the server. This can be done by accessing the server service properties through the Network Properties dialog box. There are four memory options that can be selected:

- Minimize Memory Used allocates the smallest amount of memory to handle server-based requests for network resources. This value is adequate for workgroups where the number of users accessing the server is small—no more than 10—or where the server functions primarily as a workstation.

- Balanced allocates enough memory to handle up to 64 network connections to the server. This might be a member server in a moderately used network environment.

- Maximize Throughput for File Sharing is an optimal choice for file and print servers as it allocates enough memory for heavier user access.

- Maximize Throughput for Network Applications allocates the greatest amount of memory for network connections to the server while minimizing the memory cache. This setting is most appropriate for servers running client/server applications as it also takes into account that the applications will need to perform some functions in RAM on that computer. It is also recommended for domain controllers with large numbers of users configured in a master or multiple master domain model.

Summarizing Performance Monitoring and Optimization

Here are some suggestions for collecting meaningful performance data, analyzing it, and using it effectively for problem solving and planning.

First, establish a performance baseline for the computer. If you do not understand what normal performance is like, you will not be able to accurately identify, resolve, or predict abnormal performance. For example, Microsoft recommends that processor usage should not consistently exceed 80 percent. However, some BackOffice applications normally exceed 80 percent processor utilization or more when performing their regular functions and service cycles. Your baseline should include counters from each of the objects discussed in this chapter.

Tip

You will notice that as you select an object, one counter will already be highlighted by default. This is the counter that is considered by Microsoft to be most commonly included in a measurement baseline.

Next, analyze performance for specific functions and during specific periods. For example, if this is a file and print server, you might monitor the `Server>Pool Nonpaged Failures` and `Pool Paged Failures` to determine if the server memory is configured appropriately. You might also want to keep track of the number of users connected to the server concurrently as well as the number of files open by monitoring `Server>Server Sessions` and `Server>Files Open`, respectively. Because you would expect a high level of disk activity on a file and print server (for example, file reads and writes, and print spooling), it would be beneficial to track `Physical Disk>Avg. Disk Bytes/Transfer`, `%Disk Time`, `%Disk Read Time`, and `%Disk Write Time`. These can help you to determine, among other things, whether one disk is enough, whether additional disks should be added and the files load-balanced, or even whether disk striping might be considered as a viable optimizing solution.

On a domain controller, you might monitor the number of simultaneous logons the server is receiving and can handle at peak logon periods throughout the day using `Server>Logon/sec` and `Server>Logon Total`. Other useful counters include `Memory>Available` bytes and `Committed` bytes to identify how RAM and the pagefile are being used.

On servers functioning as WINS, DHCP, and DNS servers, it would be advantageous to monitor the object counters associated with those services as they affect performance on a given computer, in conjunction with the Network Monitor utility as it tracks network traffic associated with that service. For example, WINS servers perform NetBIOS name registration and resolution. The WINS `Server>Total Number of Registrations/sec` and `Queries/sec` counters can provide data relating to those functions as they take place on this computer and affect resources. Network Monitor can identify how many frames are generated for each function, how large they are, how long it took to send them, and where the requests for registration and name resolution originated.

Remember that you can monitor performance on computers remotely. This is suggested particularly so as not to skew data collected with the activities of Performance Monitor itself. Remotely monitoring a computer can be especially useful when trying to pinpoint network bottlenecks. For example, if you suspect that a particular server may be the source of a network bottleneck, you might consider remotely monitoring the `Server` object counters described in the section "Monitoring Network-Related Objects." A consistently high `Server>Pool Paged Failures` counter indicates that the server is trying to allocate paged memory and cannot perhaps because it doesn't have enough RAM, or the page file is full or inadequately sized. This would cause server performance to denigrate, resulting in a potential bottleneck of network requests.

Document your performance measurements and convey the information appropriately. If the system configured as it is—hardware purchased, software installed, network traffic generated—can perform only at a particular level, document that fact. If a higher level of performance is required, use your data to justify upgrading in hardware, load-balancing heavily used applications by purchasing additional servers and moving applications to them, upgrading WAN links, and so on.

Part

VI

Ch

20

Predict performance changes due to growth by using data collected for the current system and usage patterns, and extrapolating that information proportionately to the amount of growth expected. This is more commonly referred to as *trend analysis*. Performance Monitor can help facilitate the identification of potential resource requirements, hardware and software upgrades, and potential budget needs.

Taking the Disc Test

 If you have read and understood the material in the chapter, you are ready to test your knowledge. Insert the CD-ROM that comes with this book and run the self-test software as described in Appendix I, "Using the CD-ROM."

From Here...

This chapter concentrated on performance testing that takes place on the computer itself, such as disk I/O performance, processor usage, memory requirements, and network activity. The next chapter, "Network Monitor," explores a companion utility called the Network Monitor that can facilitate the analysis of network traffic generated and received by your computer.

Chapter Prerequisite

The reader should have a firm
understanding of basic networking terminology and concepts before studying this
chapter. Additionally, the
reader should understand
DHCP, WINS, and the Com-
puter Browser service. These
are covered in Chapter 8,
"Configuring Domain Network
Core Services."

21

Network Monitor

This chapter concentrates on one particular monitoring and troubleshooting tool provided in Windows NT Server 4.0 called the Network
Monitor. Those of you who have used or observed network monitoring
tools such as hardware-based sniffer products will understand the concept and practical use of Windows NT's Network Monitor utility
immediately.

This chapter discusses the following topics:

◆ Review the concept and use of the Network Monitor

◆ Analyze specific types of network traffic including the domain
logon process, connecting to resources, and obtaining IP addresses

◆ Discuss techniques for identifying and planning for network traffic
problems and usage

Understanding Network Monitor

The Network Monitor utility is a Windows NT Server 4.0 tool that provides a mechanism for monitoring and analyzing network traffic between clients and servers in your Windows NT domain. It can be used to identify heavily used subnets, routers, and WAN connections; help spot and troubleshoot network bottlenecks; optimize network traffic patterns and plan for future growth in network traffic, bandwidth needs, transmission speed, and so on.

The Network Monitor utility was actually first introduced as part of Microsoft's BackOffice server management application System Management Server (SMS). This full-featured software implementation of a network monitoring program provides a relatively low-cost alternative to the more expensive (and expansive) hardware-based network sniffer products available on the market today—roughly $900 compared to $10,000 or more.

Windows NT Server 4.0's version of Network Monitor has most of the functionality of the SMS product. The SMS version of Network Monitor allows you to monitor network activity directly for a specific computer or remotely for all devices on the subnet such as determining which protocol consumed the most bandwidth, which devices are routers, and the editing and re-transmitting of network packets. By contrast, Windows NT Server 4.0's version provides local capturing only, to and from the computer running the utility.

Key Concept

Because Network Monitor is used primarily to analyze network traffic with an eye toward identifying and troubleshooting potential problems, this entire chapter can be considered a performance troubleshooting chapter for the network, much as Chapter 20, "Performance Monitor," could be considered a performance troubleshooting chapter for the computer.

However, as we also saw with Performance Monitor, network troubleshooting is always facilitated when you can identify how far off the normal activity your network performance seems to be. Thus, it is important to understand what normal network activity is like on your subnets and across your domains. Only then can you accurately posit how well or how badly your network is performing at a given point in time and predict how it may perform under a given set of conditions.

Exploring Network Frames

Network Monitor is a packet, or frame-analyzer, tool. It provides the ability to not only capture network traffic, but also to filter what is captured and displayed. The full version of Network Monitor, which is part of SMS, also allows for the editing and re-transmission of network frames, as well as the capture of frames from a remote network device.

The frames that are captured represent segments of network traffic related to a particular type of network communication. A frame could be related to a request from a computer for an IP address from a DHCP server, or a user's request to log on and validate at a domain controller. It could represent part of the transfer of data from a client/server application server. In all cases, the frames themselves consist of various parts that will be described shortly.

There are three general categories of frames: broadcast, directed, and multicast. *Broadcast* frames are sent to all hosts on the network and use the unique destination address FFFFFFFF. All computers on the network accept the broadcast frame and pass it through their protocol stack to determine whether it is destined for that computer. If it is, it is processed appropriately. If it is not, it is discarded. The NWLink protocol bases much of its traffic on broadcasts, and TCP/IP uses broadcasts for some of its network communications.

A request for an IP address from a DHCP server is an example of a TCP/IP broadcast frame. The request for the IP address is sent to all computers in the network. The first DHCP server that receives the request responds to it with a directed frame.

A *directed* frame, as the name implies, is directed or sent to a specific computer on the network. All other computers discard it because it is not destined for those computers. TCP/IP relies primarily on directed frames to communicate between computers. This helps to minimize both the number of broadcasts that must take place as well as the amount of bandwidth used by TCP/IP.

Finally, a *multicast* frame is sent to a subset of the computers on the network depending on how that computer has registered itself on the network as opposed to its MAC (media access control) address. The NetBEUI protocol uses multicast frames to communicate on the network.

As mentioned earlier, a frame is itself composed of different pieces that identify what it is, where it came from, where it is going, and what it is carrying. It's kind of like public transportation, but usually more reliable. The components of a frame vary according to the frame type, but generally they consist of the same pieces.

An Ethernet 802.3 frame consists of the following components:

◆ Preamble

This portion of the frame signals the receiving transceiver that the frame has arrived. It is 8 bytes, and is not captured by Network Monitor.

◆ Destination Address

This portion identifies the MAC address of the target computer. If this address is FFFFFFFF, then all computers must accept the frame and determine whether it is meant for them or not. Its length is 6 bytes.

◆ Source Address

This portion identifies the MAC address of the computer at which the frame originated and is 6 bytes in length.

◆ Type or Length

This portion specifies the protocol that originated the frame, or the amount of data that it contains. Its length is 2 bytes.

◆ Data

This portion may be up to 1,500 bytes in length and may contain the actual data, or more specific information about the protocol such as headers and descriptions.

◆ CRC

This 4-byte portion contains a checksum value that is used to determine whether the data arrived intact. CRC stands for Cyclic Redundancy Check.

As you can see in Figure 21.1, the data portion of the frame may not necessarily contain only data. Often, especially when the TCP/IP protocol is used as the network protocol of choice, the data portion of the frame contains additional protocol-specific data. With TCP/IP, for example, the data component consists of an IP datagram that contains IP header and data information such as the IP source address and destination address. The IP data component itself contains TCP header and data information such as the source and destination port for NetBIOS or Windows Sockets.

FIG. 21.1 ⇒

Here are the components of a typical frame along with the size of each. You can also see an example of a captured frame showing each component and its value. Notice that the Ethernet Data portion of the frame in this example consists of an IP piece and a TCP piece.

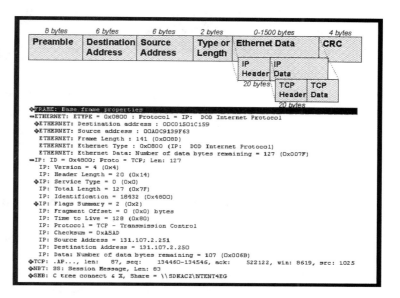

Implementing Network Monitor

The version of Network Monitor that comes with Windows NT Server 4.0 is a subset of the full product that is part of Microsoft SMS. It is meant to be installed on a Windows NT Server 4.0 computer and monitors network traffic sent and received by that computer.

The full product version can be installed on any Windows NT Workstation or Server-based computer, as well as computers running Windows for Workgroups and Windows 95.

The Network Monitor utility consists of two parts: the application itself, and the Network Monitor agent. The agent allows a computer to capture network traffic and report it to the Network Monitor application. When using the full version of the product (SMS), installing the agent on a Windows NT or Windows 95-based computer allows remote monitoring of those computers. Remote monitoring is not a feature of the Windows NT Server 4.0 version. Therefore, it is not necessary to install the Network Monitor agent on your Windows NT or Windows 95-based computers. However, if you would like to use Performance Monitor's Network Segment object to track network performance on a given Windows NT computer, then you must install Network Monitor to activate the Network Segment object.

Tip

The more services that you install on a Windows NT computer, the more overhead that computer will require to manage those services. In general, it is recommended that you only load those services that are necessary to facilitate optimal system performance.

For example, you may load the Network Monitor agent on a Windows NT Workstation to activate the Network Segment object for the purposes of establishing a Performance Monitor baseline for normal system performance on that computer. After you have done that, stop or remove the agent to release the resources needed to manage it. Turn it back on when you need to troubleshoot suspected network-related problems.

When you install the Windows NT Server 4.0 version of Network Monitor, both the application and the agent are installed on the server computer. Network traffic to and from the server will be monitored and recorded.

The full version of Network Monitor requires a compatible network card that can run in promiscuous mode. (It's not what you think.) Promiscuous mode indicates that the adapter is capable of accepting all frames on the network regardless of their true destination. While this does allow for remote monitoring of network traffic, it also places a greater processing load on that computer.

By contrast, Windows NT Server 4.0's version of Network Monitor, while requiring a supported network adapter card, does not require that the card run in promiscuous mode. This is an enhancement that is part of NDIS 4.0 which allows a local capture mode for Network Monitor. As always, check the Windows NT 4.0 compatibility list for those network cards that are supported by Network Monitor.

Because this book deals with Windows NT Server 4.0, we will concentrate on its version of Network Monitor in this chapter. It is installed like any other service through the Network Properties of the Windows NT Server 4.0 computer. To install Network Monitor, follow these steps:

1. Open the Network Properties dialog box and select the Services tab.

2. Choose the Add button and select Network Monitor Tools and Agent from the Network Service list. Choose OK.

3. When prompted for the location of the Windows NT Server 4.0 source files, enter the appropriate path.

4. After the service has been installed, choose Close to save your configuration and update the bindings. You will need to restart the computer when you are finished.

Once Network Monitor has been installed on a Windows NT server, a new program icon will be added to the Administrative Tools group on that computer. Choose the Network Monitor icon to start the utility. Figure 21.2 shows an example of a Network Monitor screen.

Part

VI

Ch

21

FIG. 21.2 ⇒
Going counter-
clockwise from
the upper-left
window, the
default windows
are the Graph
pane, Session
Statistics pane,
Station Statistics
pane (bottom
window), and the
Total statistics
pane. Network
Monitor is run-
ning on
SDKACZ.

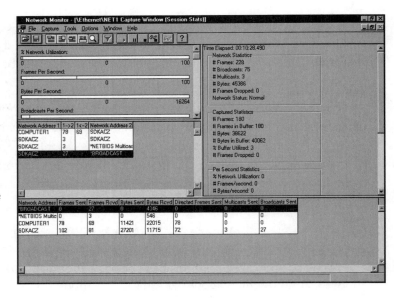

The interface itself is fairly intuitive to use, especially if you are familiar
with other network–sniffer products. As shown in Figure 21.2, there are
five menu choices: File, Capture, Tools, Options, Window, and Help.

- ◆ File   Allows you to open an existing file of captured
         frames for viewing, or to save the existing
         captured data as a file.

- ◆ Capture Allows you to start, stop, view, and otherwise
         manage the capture session. You can identify
         what and how much information is collected,
         set filters, and trigger events based on captured
         information.

- ◆ Tools   Provides the most functionality when the full
         version of the product is used (SMS). In the
         Windows NT Server 4.0 version, you can
         identify Network Monitor users and start the
         local version of Performance Monitor.

- ◆ Options Allows you to decide how to configure your
         viewing screen, for example, how much

information is displayed. By default, all options are selected.

◆ <u>W</u>indow   Presents options for the usual window management functions such as tile and cascade. Also allows you to decide which statistics window to display on-screen.

◆ <u>H</u>elp   Provides online help for Network Monitor.

To start capturing data with Network Monitor, simply choose <u>C</u>apture, <u>S</u>tart. You could also click the Start Capture button (it looks like the forward button on a VCR), or press the F10 key.

The capture window begins to record and visually display statistical information regarding the network traffic sent and received by the computer. The capture window features four default panes (refer to Figure 21.2).

◆ Graph   This pane displays current network traffic as a set of five bar charts—% Network Utilization, Frames Per Second, Bytes Per Second, Broadcasts Per Second, and Multicasts Per Second.

◆ Session Statistics   This pane displays a summary of the frames that were communicated between this computer and other computers. Notice in Figure 21.2 that there were 78 frames sent from Computer1 to SDKACZ, and 69 sent from SDKACZ to Computer1.

◆ Station Statistics   This pane provides specific frame data on a computer-by-computer basis such as the number of frames sent and received, total bytes sent and received, directed frames sent, multicasts sent, and broadcasts sent. Note that computer SDKACZ, which is running Network Monitor, originated 102 frames and received 81, 78 of which came from Computer1.

Part
VI

Ch

21

◆ Total Statistics   This pane displays statistics for network traffic detected as a whole, as well as for frames that were captured, per second statistics, and Network Card statistics.

When you are finished capturing data, select Capture, Stop, click the Stop Capture button on the toolbar, or press F11 on the keyboard. Captured data can be viewed immediately by choosing Capture, Stop and View, or saved to a file with a .CAP extension and viewed later by choosing File, Open.

Note   In this version of Network Monitor, you can set a limited capture filter that identifies what type of frames you want to collect. Network Monitor provides no remote monitoring, so you will only capture frames relating to the computer running the utility. However, you can specify the capturing of frames from specific other computers, or identify and capture frames containing a specific pattern of hexadecimal or ASCII data. ▨

To set a capture filter:

1. Select Capture, Filter from the menu.
2. Modify the existing address from the default setting Any to a specific computer by selecting an entry under Address Pairs and clicking the Address button. Enter the appropriate information in the Address Pairs dialog box.
3. Create or modify a pattern to match by selecting Pattern Matches (or an entry below it) and clicking the Pattern button. Enter the appropriate data in the Pattern Match dialog box.

Viewing Captured Data

Data that has been captured can be viewed immediately by selecting Capture, Stop and View. Data that has been captured and saved can be displayed by selecting File, Open from the menu and choosing the appropriate capture file. The capture file displayed in Figure 21.3 was created by having a Windows NT Workstation 4.0 computer (Computer1) log in to a Windows NT Server 4.0 computer (SDKACZ) acting as a primary domain controller and DHCP server. Computer1 requests and obtains its IP address from SDKACZ, logs a user on to the domain from Computer1, connects a network drive to a share on SDKACZ, and downloads a file. The capture file represents all the frames relating to this network activity that were recorded by the Network Monitor running on SDKACZ.

FIG. 21.3 ⇒

This is an example of the capture file data displayed in a default, three-pane format: Summary (top), Detail (middle), and Hex (bottom).

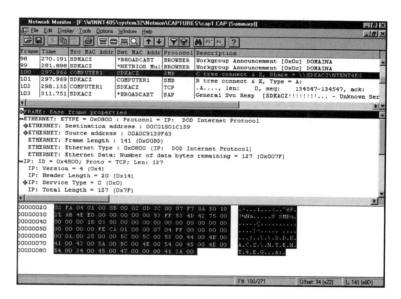

By default, the capture file is displayed in a three-pane window format. The top pane is called the Summary pane and displays all the frames that were captured along with summary details about each frame. The middle frame is called the Detail pane and displays data specific to each frame selected in the Summary pane. In Figure 21.3, frame 100 has been selected in the Summary pane, and its detail is displayed in the Detail pane. The bottom pane is called the Hex pane and displays the content of the frame selected in the Summary pane in hexadecimal format. It also provides an ASCII view column that is used to see data more easily.

Part
VI

Ch
21

Tip

Each pane can be viewed alone by choosing Window and then selecting or deselecting Summary, Detail, and Hex as desired, or by highlighting a pane and clicking the Zoom button (magnifying glass) on the toolbar, or by pressing F4. This is most useful for viewing the Summary or Details pane. As the Hex pane displays the hexadecimal version of the contents of a frame, it is best viewed in the default window by selecting a frame from the Summary pane. Nevertheless, you have the option to configure your display to best meet your needs.

Summary Pane

As stated earlier, the Summary pane lists all the frames that were captured and summary information about each. There are actually nine columns of information that are displayed for each frame. These are described in Table 21.1. Each column can be resized, moved by dragging and dropping it, or resorted by double-clicking the column header.

Table 21.1 Summary Pane Columns

Column Heading	Description
Frame	Displays the frames by number in the order in which they were captured.
Time	Displays the time relative to the beginning of the capture in seconds. This value can be displayed alternately as the time of day, or the number of seconds from that last frame.
Src MAC Addr	Displays the media access control (MAC) address of the computer that sent the frame.
Dst MAC Addr	Displays the media access control (MAC) address of the computer receiving the frame.
Protocol	Identifies the protocol used to transmit the frame.

Column Heading	Description
Description	Summarizes the frame's contents.
Src Other Addr	Displays an address other than the MAC address for the source computer such as an IP address.
Dst Other Addr	Displays an address other than the MAC address for the computer receiving the frame such as an IP address.
Type Other Addr	Identifies the type of "other" address such as an IP or IPX address.

In Figure 21.3, frame 100 occurred 297.966 seconds into the capture period. Because the next frame occurred at 297.969, we know that frame 100 took .003 seconds to complete. It was sent by Computer1 to SDKACZ using SMB and was a request to connect to a share called NTENT4EG on SDKACZ. Though you cannot see it in the figure, the Src Other and Dst Other Addresses were the computers' NetBIOS names as resolved by IP—Computer1 and SDKACZ, respectively.

Tip

The frames displayed in the Summary pane can be configured to show only those frames relating to a particular protocol, address, function, or property. This can be accomplished by selecting Display, Filter from the menu to open the Display Filter dialog box (see Figure 21.4).

The Display Filter dialog box functions as a filter script writer. You will notice buttons to add, modify, and delete expressions, and create logical filtering using AND, OR, and NOT. This can be used effectively to reduce a long capture file down to those frames that are of interest to you. For example, if you only want to see those frames dealing with the request for and assignment of an IP address from a DHCP server, you would edit the Protocol == Any line to read Protocol == DHCP.

Part

VI

Ch

21

FIG. 21.4 ⇒

Here an expression for the property DHCP Request Exists is being added to the filter for this capture file.

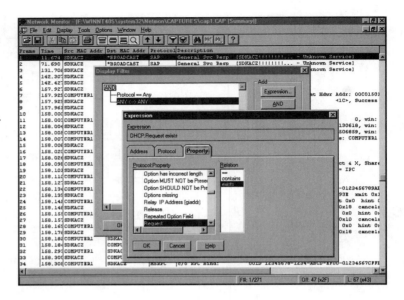

Detail Pane

The Detail pane displays frame-specific data for the frame selected in the Summary pane. This pane can be displayed in full screen by highlighting the pane and clicking the Zoom button on the toolbar. The details for frame 100 are shown in Figure 21.5.

As you can see, there is a detail entry that corresponds to each component of the frame (refer to Figure 21.1). If a particular entry has sub-entries or more data, a plus sign displays before the entry. Double-clicking the entry will expand it to show its additional information.

In Figure 21.5, we can see the source and destination MAC addresses (00C01501C159 for Computer1 and 00A0C9139F63 for SDKACZ). We see that the length of the frame is 141 bytes and that the data length is 127 bytes. The IP section displays Time to Live (TTL) data, Protocol type (TCP), and the IP addresses of the source and destination computers (131.107.2.251 and 131.107.2.250, respectively). Among the TCP data not shown in the figure is that the frame is using the NetBIOS service to make its request. The SMP entry shows us that the request is to connect to a share called NTENT4EG on SDKACZ.

FIG. 21.5 ⇒

In this example, we are looking at the detail data for frame 100 as selected in the Summary pane of Figure 21.3.

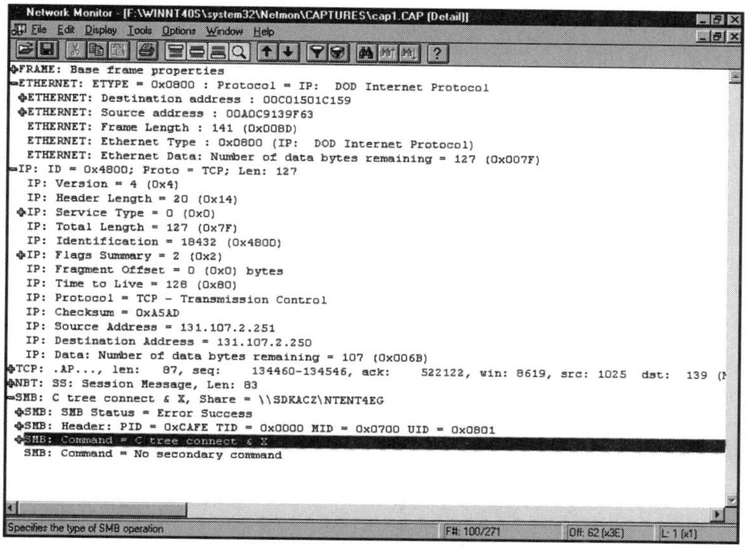

Hex Pane

As you can see back in Figure 21.3, the Hex pane is relatively useless unless you can read hexadecimal notation. However, notice that in the third column of data, you can see the UNC request for the NTENT4EG share on SDKACZ (\\SDKACZ\NTENT4EG). This column can be helpful in identifying more specific information about the frame. For example, if the frame was a request for creating new users on the PDC, you would see the new user information listed in this column.

Interpreting Frames in a Capture File

In this section we will begin to dissect the frames we have captured. We will identify which frames are part of various processes and services, and how they impact the network performance as a whole. This discussion is by no means exhaustive and may prove tedious in its examination of minutiae. Nevertheless, it will provide you with the basic understanding needed to successfully interpret frames captured within your own network.

Let's begin this discussion with a look at the communication that takes place between a client computer and a server. The following functions represent those most frequently associated with network traffic generated between a client and a server.

◆ IP address requests from DHCP server

◆ NetBIOS name registration with a WINS server

◆ Logon validation of a user at a domain controller

◆ Network browsing for resources

◆ Establishing file sessions

DHCP Frames

DHCP, as you learned in Chapter 8, "Configuring Domain Network Core Services," provides a service whereby IP address information is maintained on a DHCP server. When a client boots up, it obtains its IP address information from the DHCP server. This reduces the amount of IP administration that needs to take place at each client computer.

The DHCP process involves four frames (see Figure 21.6). The *DHCP Discover* frame is the client's broadcast attempt to find an available DHCP server on its subnet. The DHCP server that receives the DHCP Discover frame responds with an IP address that the client can lease contained in a *DHCP Offer* frame. The client responds back that it accepts the IP address with the *DHCP Request* frame, which the DHCP acknowledges with the *DHCP ACK* frame. This last frame also contains any additional IP address information needed by the client such as the lease duration, router address, and WINS address.

Each frame, as we can see from Figure 21.6, is 342 bytes long and together take about 1/4 of a second to complete. Figure 21.6 does not show a DHCP Discover frame. The two computers used to generate this capture file are the only two on the subnet, thus this frame is not generated. However, you can see the other frame types clearly. Frame 529 represents a DHCP Request frame generated by a release renewal request by the client (IPCONFIG /renew). Frame 531, 536, and 537 represent frames generated first by a lease release by the client (IPCONFIG /release), followed by a release renewal.

FIG. 21.6 ⇒

In this filtered capture display, we see only the frames relating to the DHCP protocol. You can see three of the four types of DHCP frames.

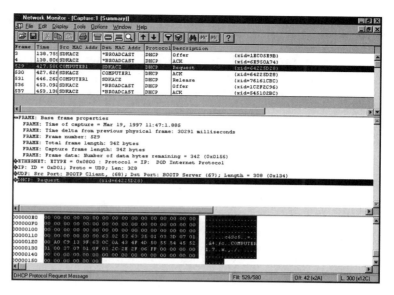

The DHCP process usually takes place once a day, when the computer boots up. After that, additional DHCP traffic is generated by the lease renewal process. When a DHCP server assigns an IP address to the client, it does so in a lease arrangement. The default lease is three days. At the half-way point of the lease, the client automatically requests a lease renewal (DHCP Request) for an additional three days, or whatever the lease period happens to be, to which the DHCP server responds with an acknowledgment (DHCP ACK). The lease renewal process only requires two, 342-byte frames, and takes about half as long as the original DHCP process.

Key Concept

As you can see from the size and frequency of these frames, DHCP-related traffic is relatively minor and generally takes up less than 1 percent of the total bandwidth. While the number of DHCP-related frames on a given subnet will certainly be influenced by the number of clients requesting IP addresses, as well as by the length of the lease period established, because the size and duration of the frames is so small, it should still not significantly affect the overall network traffic.

Part

VI

Ch

21

For example, a lease duration of one day will generate lease renewal requests every half-day (half of the lease period), whereas a lease duration of the default three days will generate lease renewal requests every day and a half. But the total length and duration of the two renewal frames is 684 bytes and less than 200 milliseconds.

If a network contains routers that can support BOOTP-relay agents and RFC 1542, those routers have the ability to forward DHCP Discover frames to other subnets with DHCP servers. These are usually employed via a time out parameter to resolve IP address requests when a local DHCP server is busy or otherwise unavailable.

> **Caution**
>
> It is possible that a particular subnet can receive an unusually high number of DHCP-related frames in this configuration. If this occurs, it can begin to affect network traffic on that subnet. The full version of Network Monitor can help to identify those routers and monitor remote DHCP traffic as well as the local traffic.

WINS Frames

WINS (Windows Internet Name Service) provides a means of resolving IP addresses to NetBIOS names. Most network resources are accessed by name rather than by address. For example, when you connect to a shared folder on a remote server, you generally map a drive to that resource by using its UNC (universal naming convention) name. The Public shared folder on the server ABCCorp would be addressed as \\ABCCorp\Public. When using IP addresses, this name must map back, or be resolved, to an IP address. There are a variety of ways in which name resolution can be effected, and at least as many books that explain the process. Briefly, here is how a NetBIOS name is resolved to an IP address.

1. As you make connections to network resources and resolve NetBIOS names to IP addresses, the names are stored in a local NetBIOS name cache. This cache is checked first. If the name can be resolved, it is. Resolved names stay in the cache for 10 minutes by default.

2. If the NetBIOS name cache does not contain the name, and a NetBIOS Name Server (in this case a WINS server) has been implemented, the name is sent to the WINS server to be resolved.

3. If, after three attempts the WINS server cannot resolve the address, a b-node broadcast is generated on the local subnet. A b-node broadcast is essentially a name request that is sent to every computer on the subnet. The computer whose name matches responds using ARP (address resolution protocol) and the source computer's hardware address.

4. If after three b-node broadcasts the name is still not resolved, the local LMHOSTS or HOST file is checked. Think of these files as IP address books, sort of like your company directory.

5. Finally, if there is still no resolution, the name request may be sent to a DNS (domain name server). If the name still cannot be resolved, an error message is returned to the originating computer.

We are concerned with the WINS portion of this process for this discussion as Microsoft recommends using WINS for name resolution in an IP network.

Note   This section is not intended as a primer for WINS, but rather as a guide to monitoring WINS traffic on the network using Network Monitor. ▪

There are six frames associated with WINS traffic: Name Registration, Name Response, Query Request, Query Response, Release Request, and Release Response. These frames can be filtered by viewing NBT protocol frames.

Part

VI

Ch

21

Key Concept

Think of WINS as being a dynamic host file. When a computer boots up and receives its IP address from a DHCP server, it then broadcasts its name and IP address to the subnet. When a WINS server is implemented and identified to the client computer (either manually or through DHCP), the name and IP address are registered on the WINS server. Registration involves not only the NetBIOS name of the computer, however. NetBIOS names must also be registered for every server or application that supports the NetBIOS API (Application Programming Interface).

Network Monitor supports NetBIOS, and as such the NetBIOS name of the computer acting as the Network Monitor "server" needs to be registered. PDCs and BDCs need to be registered for logon validation and database synchronization. It is not unusual for a client computer to register two or more names.

A NetBIOS Name Registration frame is sent to the WINS server for each name that needs to be registered. As you can see in Figure 21.7, in which frame 7 is highlighted, each name registration frame is 110 bytes long and contains the computer name of the client and its IP address. Frame 8 (see Figure 21.8) shows the WINS server's name response.

Notice that the name response frame is 104 bytes in size and note in the NBT: Flags Summary line that the registration was a success. As with DHCP leases, the registration is good for a specific period of time—six days, by default. This is indicated in the NBT: Time to Live line as 518,400 seconds. And as with DHCP leases, the client will automatically renew the registration at the half-way point with another name registration request.

Note in the Summary pane for every registration request the hex code in brackets: <00>. This code represents the type of name registration that is being requested. In this case, the <00> refers to the computer name registered by the workstation service of the client computer. Table 21.2 outlines the more common registration codes used.

FIG. 21.7 ⇒

This example shows the name registration requests for COMPUTER1 to the WINS server SDKACZ.

FIG. 21.8 ⇒

This example shows the WINS server's response to the first name registration request for COMPUTER1.

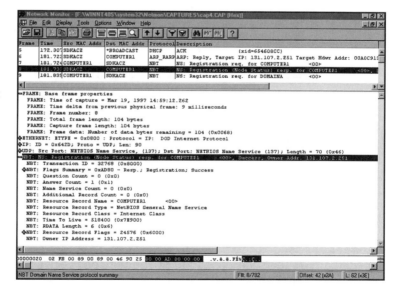

Table 21.2   WINS Registration Codes

Code	Description
Computername <00>	NetBIOS name registered by the client's workstation service.
Computername <03>	NetBIOS name registered by the client's messenger service to receive network messages.
Username <03>	User's logon name registered by the client's messenger service to receive network messages.
Computername <20>	NetBIOS name registered by the client's server service.
Workgroup or Domainname <00>	Identifies the user as a member of the workgroup or domain.
Workgroup or theDomainname <1E>	Identifies the user as a member of workgroup or domain for browser elections.
Workgroup or Domainname <1D>	Identifies the computer as being the subnet Master Browser for that domain.
Domainname <1B>	Identifies the computer as being the Domain Master Browser for that domain.
Domainname <1C>	Identifies the computer as a domain controller for that domain.

Every name resolution request also generates WINS frames. For example, when the user logs on, a request is made to find a domain controller to do the authentication and resolve the domain controller name to an IP address. In Figure 21.9, frame 11 shows the 92 byte request for name resolution for DOMAINA to handle the logon request generated in frame 13. Frame 12 shows the WINS server's 104 byte response.

Note the IP address of the domain controller contained on the last line of the Detail pane.

FIG. 21.9 ⇒

This example shows the two frames involved in resolving a name request for a domain controller.

Finally, when the computer stops a service or shuts down, it generates a 110 byte release request frame notifying the WINS server that the name is no longer needed, and could be used to register another computer. The WINS server responds, as with registration, with a 104 byte release response with a Time To Live value of 0. Frames 780 and 781 in Figure 21.10 show the two release frames with the Time To Live value of 0.

As with DHCP frames, WINS frames generate less than 1 percent of total network traffic on average. The size is never larger than 204 bytes, and the frames generally complete in less than 100 milliseconds. As a rule of thumb, recall that:

◆ Each name registration takes two frames (214 bytes) when the client boots, and every service, NetBIOS application, and so on must be registered.

◆ The client renews its name registration at the half-way point of the Time To Live value, or by default, every three days. Two frames (214 bytes) are generated.

Part
VI

Ch
21

◆ Every attempt to access a computer through the network, such as
with a net use command, generates two frames (196 bytes).

◆ When the client stops a service or shuts down, a registered name is
released generating two frames (214 bytes).

FIG. 21.10 ⇒

This example
shows the two
release frames
generated when
COMPUTER1
shuts down.

Considerations for Optimizing WINS Traffic

If you do need to reduce WINS traffic on the network, recall the order
in which name resolution takes place. The first place that the client
checks is the NetBIOS name cache on the local computer. By default,
resolved names stay in the cache for 10 minutes. This default can be
increased by modifying the following Registry entry:

HKEY_LOCAL_MACHINE\System\CurrentControlSet\
Services\NetBT\Parameters\CacheTimeout

As the resolved name entries will stay in the cache longer, presumably
fewer WINS frames will be generated attempting to resolve names. You
could also create an LMHOSTS file that contains the addresses most
frequently accessed and place it on each computer. These addresses can
be configured to be pre-loaded into the NetBIOS cache, thus reducing
WINS name resolution traffic.

Another consideration would be the disabling of unnecessary services on the computer. Recall that every service, application, and so on that supports or uses NetBIOS must register itself. Each name registration will generate two additional frames. If you disable unnecessary services, you will generate fewer registration frames. For example, if the computer doesn't use NetDDE, disable the service. Or, if the computer is not sharing any network resources to the network, disable its server service.

Tip

Disabling unnecessary services also has the added benefit of releasing unused resources on the computer, resulting in an overall performance gain.

File Session Frames

Before you can access a network resource, the client and server computers must establish a session between them. This generates on average 11 frames and totals a little more than 1K. After a session is established to a resource server, the only additional frames that are generated will be for every additional resource connection that is made during that session. These connection frames tend to average 360 bytes.

If users establish multiple sessions in a day by connecting and disconnecting drives, connecting to multiple servers, and so on, and depending on how many users are on the network, this can have an impact on your overall network traffic. Unfortunately, there is usually little you can do to avoid this type of traffic as it is primarily user-generated. Keeping resource servers close to the users who need access, especially on the same subnet, certainly facilitates overall network traffic within the enterprise. Also, connection requests are sent over all protocols that are installed on the client or server simultaneously. Removing protocols that are not needed will reduce the number of session frames that are generated.

There are, in general, six steps that establish a file session.

1. As we saw with WINS, the NetBIOS name must be resolved to an IP address, and there are two frames generated for this step.

2. Next, the IP address must be resolved to the hardware, or MAC address of the computer. ARP (address resolution protocol), part of the IP protocol stack, is used to accomplish this step. Two frames are generated for this step: *ARP Request* and *ARP Reply*, both 60 bytes in length. As this address resolution is also cached for 10 minutes (like the NetBIOS name cache), these frames will be regenerated every time the two computers need to communicate outside 10 minutes.

3. Now a TCP session must be established to allow two-way communications to take place between the client and the server computers. This is commonly known as the three-way TCP handshake, and, as you might have guessed, generates three frames:

   - *TCP S* from the client to the server requesting a NetBIOS session.

   - *TCP A S* from the server to the client acknowledging the request.

   - *TCP A* from the client to the server establishing the session.

   Figure 21.11 shows the three TCP frames (a total of 180 bytes) generated. Once this TCP session is established, the user can make any number of file connections to the same server.

4. A NetBIOS session is then established generating two frames of 126 bytes and 58 bytes each, respectively: *NBT Session Request* and *NBT Positive Session Response*. Like the TCP frames, these only need to be generated once per session between the client and server.

FIG. 21.11 ⇒
This example shows the three TCP handshake frames (113, 114, 115) with the final frame detailed, as well as the two NetBIOS session frames (116, 117).

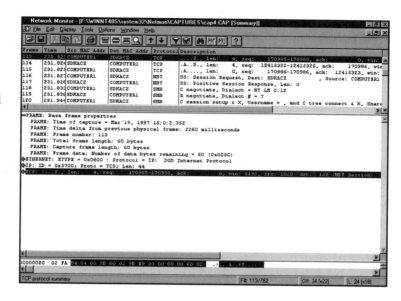

5. The two computers next negotiate their server message block protocols (SMB). The client sends a list of the protocols it understands (called dialects) through an *SMB C negotiate* frame (see Figure 21.12). The server finds the highest common SMB protocol understood by both the client and the server and notifies the client through an *SMB R negotiate* frame. The two frames average 360 bytes total. As with TCP and NetBIOS session frames, these need only be generated once per session.

6. At last the connection to the resource can be made. This involves three more SMB frames. The *SMB C session setup* frame sent by the client indicates the name of the share, and the user name and password of the user requesting access (pass-through authentication). The server validates the user and establishes the connection responding with an *SMB R session setup* frame. The total size of these frames depends largely on the type of command issued and can be anywhere from 360 bytes to more than 500 bytes on average.

Part
VI

Ch
21

In Figure 21.13, you can see all the SMB frames involved in establishing a connection from COMPUTER1 to the NTENT4EG share on server SDKACZ. Beginning with frames 120 and 121, the session is established. Two additional sets of background connections are made for remote API support (frames 130 and 131) before the connection to the share is finally established.

FIG. 21.12 ⇒

This example shows the two SMB negotiation frames (118 and 119) with the dialect list sent from the client in the Detail pane.

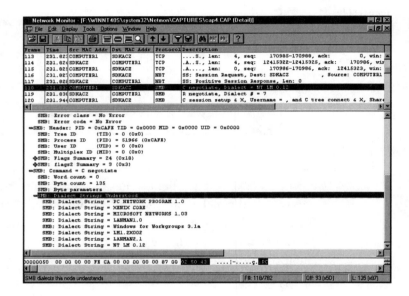

The number of frames that may be generated by the transfer of a file from the shared folder to the client disk varies greatly as it is generated by the size of the file, the frequency with which the file is accessed (saving changes, for example), the overall traffic burden already on the network, and so on. Figure 21.14 shows the frames generated by an application remotely accessing a file on a server. The file is 08FIG46.PCX (frame 424). From start to finish, about 50 frames were generated totaling nearly 40K.

FIG. 21.13 ⟹

This example shows the frames generated between COMPUTER1 and SDKACZ that establish a connection to the NTENT4EG share of SDKACZ.

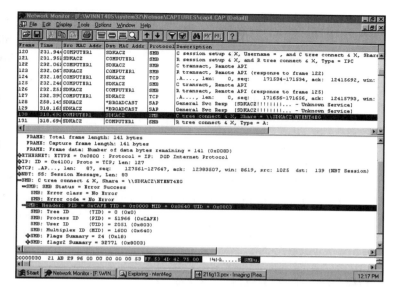

FIG. 21.14 ⟹

This example shows some of the frames generated when a file is accessed on a remote server from the client.

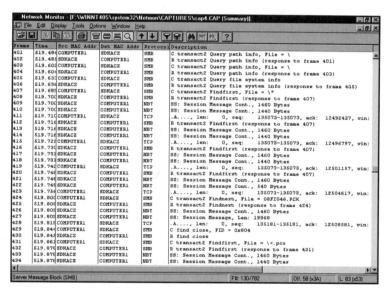

When a connection is disconnected, the client initiates the request with an *SMB C tree disconnect* request frame that identifies which connection is to be terminated, to which the server responds with an *SMB R tree disconnect* request frame. The two frames total about 186 bytes, and two additional frames would be generated for every connection that is disconnected.

Finally, when the last file connection between the client and the server is disconnected, the TCP session is closed. As when we established the TCP session, three frames are generated for a total of 180 bytes: *TCP A F* from the client requesting termination of the session, *TCP A F* from the server acknowledging the request, and *TCP A* from the client terminating the session.

Logon Validation Frames

The logon process is one of the first network functions generated by a user. A user logs on by supplying the user name, password, and the authenticating domain. The Net Logon service then looks for an available domain controller for the requested domain and passes the logon information to it for validation where the authentication process completes. This, of course, generates some network traffic. The amount varies from network to network and depends on whether logon scripts need to be executed, profiles loaded, or any other network task run. The ultimate impact that logon traffic has on the network as a whole also depends on when and how frequently users log on. This is determined easily enough using Network Monitor to establish baselines for your network. However, being user-based, it is also difficult to control.

The first step in the process as stated above is finding an appropriate and available domain controller. This could take the form of a broadcast request to the Net Logon mailslot (UDP Port 138), or by sending a query request to a WINS server for a registered domain controller.

Broadcasting for the Domain Controller

The broadcast request generates a *NETLOGON Logon Request* frame that contains the NetBIOS name of the authenticating domain. This can be anywhere from 260 bytes for Windows 95 to 300 bytes for Windows NT. Each logon server responds with a *NETLOGON Response to Logon Request* frame which is directed back to the originating computer. Again, this frame can be anywhere from 230 bytes for Windows 95 to 270 bytes for Windows NT.

Using WINS to Find the Domain Controller

If the client is configured to use WINS for name resolution, an *NBT NS: Query request* frame (92 bytes) for the authenticating domain is generated and sent to the WINS server.

The WINS server responds with an NBT NS: Query response frame that contains a list of the first 25 domain controllers in the WINS database for that domain. The size will vary according to the number of domain controllers in the list. For example, two domain controllers generates a 116–byte frame.

The client sends a *NETLOGON SAM LOGON Request* frame directed to each domain controller in the list, ignoring any responses until it has completed sending the requests. Each frame is 328 bytes in length.

Each domain controller responds in kind with a *NETLOGON SAM Response* frame similar to that generated for Net Logon broadcast.

Validating the Logon Request

The client establishes a session with the first domain controller that responds to its NETLOGON SAM LOGON Request in a manner similar to that outlined in the "File Session Frames" section earlier in this chapter:

- ◆ The NetBIOS name of the domain controller is resolved.
- ◆ The IP address is resolved to the MAC address of the domain controller.
- ◆ A TCP session is established between the client and the domain controller.
- ◆ A NetBIOS session is also established.

◆ SMB protocol negotiation takes place and a dialect is identified.

◆ An SMB connection to the IPC$ administrative share on the domain controller is established.

This takes about 11 frames for a total of about 1.4K, depending on whether the client is Windows 95 or Windows NT. Figure 21.15 clearly shows the frames discussed from frame 11, the query request for the list of domain controllers from the WINS server (SDKACZ), to the IPC connection established in frame 25.

FIG. 21.15 ⇒

This example shows all the frames involved in connecting to a domain controller for user validation.

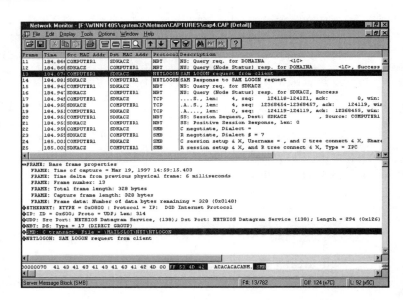

On Windows NT–based computers, the validation process consists of three steps.

1. Through a series of 12 frames and about 2,000 bytes of traffic, a list of trusted domains is returned if any exist.

2. Next, a secure channel is established between the client and the domain controller generating another eight frames and about 1,400 bytes of traffic.

3. Finally, an *RPC client call* frame is generated which contains the user name, password, and domain and is sent to the domain controller. The server responds with a successful *RPC Server response* frame. Any additional named pipes that are necessary to the Net Logon share (for logon scripts, system policies, and so on) are also established.

The IPC$ connection is closed and the NetBIOS and TCP sessions are terminated as discussed in the section "File Session Frames."

Optimizing Logon Validation

The amount of traffic generated by logon validation depends on several factors. To minimize validation traffic and optimize the authentication process for the user, you need to have enough domain controllers to service those needs.

Tip

Microsoft recommends one domain controller for every 2,000 users.

However, the number and placement of domain controllers will itself depend largely on the type of domain model you have chosen, the location of users and the resources they need to access, the type of WAN connections you have in place, and so on.

In general, you will want to place a domain controller near the users who need to log on. For example, in a worldwide organization with users located in Chicago, London, and Tokyo, you would want at least one domain controller in each of those locations so that users are validating locally rather than across WAN connections. The kind of hardware that you are using for the domain controller may itself determine how large an account database it can support and how long validation requests may take to process. All of these concepts have been ably explored in Chapter 5, "Capacity Planning and Performance."

Another possibility for increasing throughput on a domain controller would be to increase the number of simultaneous logons that it can process. By default, domain controllers have their Server service memory management buffer configured as Maximize Throughput for File Sharing. This allows for about six or seven simultaneous logons per second. By changing this setting to Maximize Throughput for Network Applications, this number can increase to about 20. Modify this setting as follows:

1. Open the Network Properties dialog box and select the Services tab.

2. In the Network Services list box, select Server, then choose Properties.

3. In the Server dialog box, choose Maximize Throughput for Network Applications, then choose OK.

4. Choose OK to update the Registry and bindings. Shut down and restart the computer as directed.

Exploring Browser Traffic

The most common, and perhaps the easiest, way for users to access resources is to browse for them. When users open Network Neighborhood, for example, a list of computers and their resources in their workgroup or domain is presented, as well as a list of other domains, and their computers and resources. Users browse through the lists of domains and computers using a point-and-click method to find and connect to resources. The Windows NT service that furnishes this list is the Computer Browser. This service is discussed in some detail in Chapter 8, "Configuring Domain Network Core Services." The Computer Browser service is responsible for creating, maintaining, and distributing lists of computers and their resources. We will briefly review the basic concepts of browsing here.

A domain master browser is selected for a domain, and master browsers for subnets within a domain by means of a predefined election process. Master browsers select one or more backup browsers for their subnets depending on the number of computers in the workgroup or domain on that subnet. When a computer boots up, it announces itself to the master browser once every minute for the first five minutes, and then every 12 minutes thereafter.

The master browsers create a list of the computers and their shared resources from their subnets and announce it to the domain master browser. The domain master browser creates and maintains a master list of all its own domain resources. It also receives lists of resources from other domain master browsers. It then distributes this list back to the master browsers. The master browsers in turn distribute the list to their backup browsers. Eventually, all the browsers in the domain maintain a copy of the same list of domains, workgroups, computers, and their shared resources.

Key Concept

A PDC will always become a domain master browser. BDCs will become master browsers, if on their own subnet, as well as backup browsers. Master browsers announce themselves to the domain master browser every 15 minutes, and update their browse list from the domain master browser every 12 minutes. The domain master browser contacts the WINS server for a list of all domains every 12 minutes. Every backup browser contacts its master browser every 12 minutes to update its browse list.

When a user requests a list of resources, for example, by opening Network Neighborhood, the Computer Browser service contacts the master browser and obtains from it a list of backup browsers. The client computer then contacts a backup browser from the list to obtain a list of computers. When a computer is selected from the list, it responds with a list of its shared resources.

Not surprisingly, this entire process generates some network traffic. Given average usage, Microsoft estimates that 30 percent or more of total network traffic can consist of browser-related traffic.

Browser Elections and Announcements

Let's begin with the election process. There must always be a master browser to maintain the browse list for the subnet or domain. If it is determined that a master browser is needed, for example, a client is looking for a list of backup browsers to contact and cannot find a master browser to provide that list, then an election for a new master browser is initiated. Chapter 8, "Configuring Domain Network Core Services," discusses the election process. Here we will look at the frames generated.

It all begins with a host announcement. All computers that have the ability to share resources are de facto servers and can be included in browse lists. This includes Windows NT-based computers, of course, as well as Windows 95 and Windows for Workgroups-based computers. These computers announce themselves to the master browser every 12 minutes with a *Browser Host Announcement* frame. This is a broadcast frame sent out to all computers in the subnet rather than a directed frame, and is about 250 bytes in length. It contains a list of its browser criteria.

If the computer making this announcement has the potential to become a master browser, it must first determine whether it should be or not. This means finding out who the master browser is, and checking that computer's qualifications against its own. The computer generates a 220-byte *Browser Announcement Request* frame to find the master browser. The master browser responds with a 220-byte *Browser Local Master Announcement* frame which includes its qualifications (see Figure 21.16).

If there is no master browser, or if the originating computer thinks its qualifications are better than the master browser, it generates a *Browser Election [Force]* frame of about 225 bytes that is again broadcast to all other host computers. A host with higher browser criteria will respond with a *Browser Election* response frame of about the same size. These frames continue to be generated until the host with the highest criteria wins the election and generates a Browser Local Master Announcement frame to celebrate the victory and let all the other computers know.

FIG. 21.16 ⇒
Frame 101 represents a Local Master Announcement from the master browser. Note the criteria listed in the Detail pane that make this a master browser.

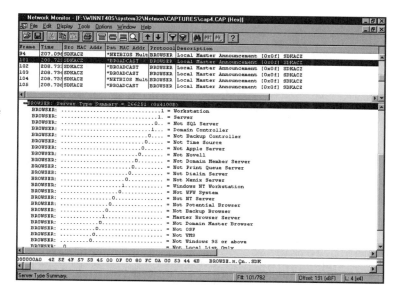

Finally, the master browser will determine if any of the potential browsers need to become backup browsers for the subnet. It will do so by generating a *Browser Become Backup Browser* frame (again, about 220 bytes) naming that computer as the backup browser (see Figure 21.17).

FIG. 21.17 ⇒
Frame 108 announces that Computer1 will become the backup browser for the subnet.

Part

VI

Ch

21

Every 15 minutes every master browser announces itself to other master browsers and the domain master browser with a 250-byte Browser Workgroup Announcement frame. You can see two of these in the Summary pane of Figure 21.17.

Every 12 minutes, the domain master browser contacts the WINS server for a list of registered domains with an *RPC Client call winsif:R_WinsGetBrowserNames* frame to which the WINS server responds with an *RPC Server response winsif:R_WinsGetBrowserNames* frame. As a benchmark, for a list of four domains, the entire process generates 22 frames and about 2.1K of traffic. This includes establishing the session with the WINS server, resolving names, and so on, as we discussed earlier.

Master browsers, in turn, contact the domain master browser to retrieve the master browse list in a similar fashion every 12 minutes. Backup browsers, in their turn, retrieve an updated browse list from the master browser every 12 minutes. Frames are generated to establish the session, resolve the computer name and address, request the list, and retrieve it. Using four domains with four servers for a benchmark, the process of updating the backup browser list could generate up to 15 frames and 2,000+ bytes of traffic on average, every 12 minutes.

What happens, then, when a user innocently requests a browse list by browsing through Network Neighborhood? The client computer begins by broadcasting a *Browser Get Backup List Request* frame to the master browser. The master browser responds with a *Browser Get Backup List Response* frame, which contains a list of browser computers for the client to choose from. Frame 289 in Figure 21.18 shows the response to a client's request. The Detail pane shows that the response frame was 233 bytes in length, it took about 8 milliseconds to complete, and returned two browser computer names.

Next, the client computer connects to one of the backup browsers in the list and retrieves the browse list. This process can generate up to 19 frames and 2,150 bytes. Finally, the user selects a server from the browse list and obtains its list of available resources. The number and size of the frames generated depends on the number of shared resources on the server, its location, which domain is being browsed, and whether there is a trust.

FIG. 21.18 ⇒

This figure shows the request and response for a backup browser list.

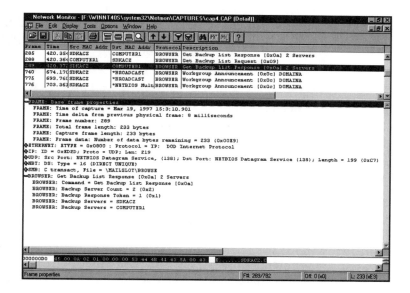

Suggestions for Optimizing Browse Traffic

Needless to say, browsing, while providing an easy and intuitive way for users to locate and connect to shared network resources, also generates a fair amount of network traffic. Unfortunately, you can do little to optimize this type of traffic.

One way to reduce browser host server announcements would be to disable the Server service on any computers that will not share resources. This eliminates the host announcements that these computers will make. They will also never become members of a browse list. You can also affect the number of browsers by modifying the Registry entries for potential browsers and preferred master browsers as described in Chapter 8, "Configuring Domain Network Core Services."

In addition to those Registry entries, here are two more that can be added to HKEY_LOCAL_MACHINE\System\CurrentControlSet\ Services\Browser\Parameters: `MasterPeriodicity` and `BackupPeriodicity`. Like many Registry parameters, these will not show up in the list of parameters when you look at this subkey. You will need to add them to the subkey parameters with a data type of REG_DWORD.

As you recall, the master browser contacts the domain master browser every 12 minutes to update its browse list. This is its `MasterPeriodicity`, and the default value is 720 seconds, or 12 minutes. You can modify this value to be anywhere from 300 seconds (five minutes) to 0x418937 (4,294,967 seconds, or about 50 days). The computer will not need to be restarted after making this change.

Each backup browser also contacts its master browser every 12 minutes to update its browse list. This is its `BackupPeriodicity`, and the default is also 720 seconds, or five minutes. It can be configured like the `MasterPeriodicity`; however, modifying this value will require restarting the computer. Increasing the value for either of these parameters reduces the frequency of browse list updates and the associated network traffic.

Note If you don't want a Windows NT-based computer to become a browser, set the HKEY_LOCAL_MACHINE\System\ CurrentControlSet\Services\Browser\Parameters\MaintainServerList value to No. For Windows 95 computers, disable the File and Printer Sharing Properties Browse Master parameter in the Network Properties dialog box. For Windows for Workgroups computers, set the `MaintainServerList` parameter in the Network section of the System.ini file to No. ▪

Tip
Browsing is protocol-dependent. Browser announcements and elections are generated for every protocol that is installed on a computer. For a server with all three protocols installed (TCP/IP, NWLink, and NetBEUI), this means that browser traffics are, effectively, tripled. If you can disable or remove unused protocols, this can help to reduce browser-related traffic.

Analyzing Traffic Between Domain Controllers

In the previous section we dealt primarily with the traffic that is generated between the client computer and a server. In this section, we want to discuss some common traffic generated between servers. In particular, we will discuss traffic associated with account database synchronization, trust relationships, and directory replication.

Account Database Synchronization

You will recall from Chapter 5, "Capacity Planning and Performance," that when a user logs on to the domain, a domain controller performs the authentication process. We discussed the network traffic that the logon process generates earlier in this chapter in the section titled "Logon Validation Frames." While either a PDC or a BDC may authenticate a user, it is usually the BDC that performs this service. However, any changes made to the account database are always made on the PDC. The BDCs obtain copies of the master account database from the PDC during a process called account synchronization. Because BDCs are primarily responsible for validating user requests for logon, it is of critical importance that their copies of the account database remain consistent with the master copy maintained on the PDC.

There are actually three databases that maintain the accounts and are involved in the synchronization process.

- ◆ The SAM Accounts database (0) contains user and group accounts, built-in global groups, and computer accounts. SAM stands for Security Accounts Manager.
- ◆ The SAM Built-in database (1) contains built-in local groups and their members.
- ◆ The LSA database (2) contains the Local Security Account Secrets used for trust relationships, account policy settings, and domain controller computer account passwords.

Account synchronization takes place automatically according to default parameters that can be modified in the Registry as outlined in Chapter 5, "Capacity Planning and Performance."

Key Concept

Account synchronization also occurs when the BDC is first installed, whenever the BDC is restarted, and when it is forced to take place by the administrator using either the Server Manager utility or a net accounts /sync command issued from the BDC.

Every five minutes by default, the PDC checks its master account database to see if any changes have been made. This is called its pulse interval. If the PDC finds that the master account database has been modified, it notifies the backup domain controllers that need the changes that they need to retrieve the changes. The PDC knows which BDCs need the changes by maintaining a record of the version ID that each BDC has. If the version ID is current, that BDC does not receive the notification.

For example, if there are five BDCs, and the administrator has already forced synchronization to take place with one of the BDCs, that one has a more current version ID than the others. At the next pulse interval, the other four BDCs will be notified of the changes.

The PDC generates a *NETLOGON Announce Change to UAS or SAM* frame that is sent to each BDC (see Figure 21.19, frame 363 and 365). This frame contains an encrypted date and time, the version IDs or serial numbers of the three databases, the domain's name and SID, the PDC name, and the `Pulse` and `Random` parameter values stored in the Registry.

The BDC checks the version IDs in the Announce Change frame. If they are more current than the BDC's version, the BDC connects to the IPC$ administrative share of the PDC and establishes a secure channel to the PDC if none already exists. It will also establish a TCP session if any previous TCP session connections have timed out. The frames that are generated are similar to those already discussed earlier in the sections "File Session Frames" and "Validating the Logon Request," and may take up to 15 frames.

FIG. 21.19

This figure shows some of the network traffic generated when the account database is synchronized between the PDC and the BDC.

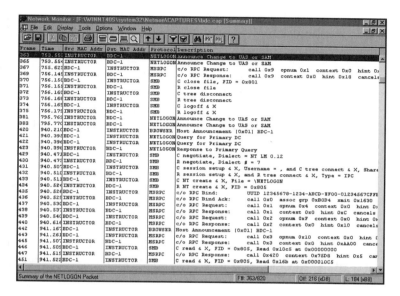

Next, the BDC verifies the account database by making a named pipe request for the Net Logon service on the PDC through a series of four frames sent to the PDC generating a total of 719 bytes: *SMB C NT Create, SMB R NT Create, MSRPC c/o RPC Bind*, and *MSRPC c/o RPC Bind Ack*. The BDC then retrieves the data using either SMB or RPC calls and the NetrDatabaseDeltas API (that only a developer can appreciate): *R_LOGON RPC Client call logon:NetrDatabaseDeltas* and *R_LOGON RPC Server response logon:NetrDatabaseDeltas*, or *SMB C read & X* and *SMB R Read & X*. A set of these two frames is generated for each database with changes. The number of response frames will depend on how much data needs to be transferred. Adding two new users generally averages 12 frames, about 3,300 bytes, and completes in about one second.

Part

VI

Ch

21

When the BDC is first installed, or when an account synchronization is forced, a full transfer of the database takes place. The process begins as always with the discovery of the PDC. The BDC uses a standard name query of the type we discussed in the section "WINS Frames" to the WINS server for the registered name of the domain. Because this name is only registered by the PDC, the WINS server responds with the PDC name and address.

The BDC then generates a 270 byte *NETLOGON Query for Primary DC* frame sent to the PDC. (Refer to Figure 21.19 beginning with frame 422.) The PDC responds with a *NETLOGON Response to Primary Query* frame of about the same size. A session is established between the BDC and the PDC as described in the section "File Session Frames."

Next, a secure channel is created between the PDC and the BDC. First an *SMB C NT Create & X* frame and an *SMB R NT Create & X* frame are generated to establish a named pipe to the Net Logon service on the PDC. Then an RPC connection is made between the BDC and the PDC through a *MSRPC c/0 RPC Bind* and *MSRPC c/o RPC Bind Ack* frame.

The secure channel is then established. The BDC verifies that its account name exists at the PDC by generating two NetrServerReqChallenge frames: R_LOGON RPC Client call logon:NetrServerReqChallenge and R_LOGON RPC Server Response logon:NetrServerReqChallenge. The BDC generates two similar frames (NetrServerAuthenticate2) to verify its account password.

Altogether, eight frames are generated to establish the secure channel for a total of about 1,550 bytes. After the secure channel is in place, the BDC can verify the accounts databases. An RPC Client Call and Response is generated for each account database. The frames that are generated are the same as those described previously when we discussed the automatic update of database changes. The number and size of the frames that are generated in response to these calls depend on the size of the databases.

Optimizing Account Synchronization Traffic

Truly, the only way to optimize synchronization traffic is to modify the Registry defaults that govern the synchronization process. These are discussed in detail in Chapter 5, "Capacity Planning and Performance," and can all be found in the HKEY_LOCAL_MACHINE\System\ CurrentControlSet\Services\NetLogon\Parameters Registry subkey. However, some of them are briefly discussed here.

The `ReplicationGovernor` parameter can be modified on the BDC, and provides a way to control how much bandwidth is consumed by the Net Logon service for synchronizing the databases. The default is, of course, 100 percent. This means that Net Logon will use 100 percent of the available bandwidth while the PDC buffers 128K of synchronization data. Across slow WAN links, or on networks where traffic is already peaking, this can be a concern. Modifying the value to, say, 50 percent would result in a 50 percent use of bandwidth, while the PDC buffers only half as much data, or 64K. Also, synchronization frames will be generated and sent with half the frequency.

> **Caution**
> Setting this value too low may result in the databases never fully synchronizing. Microsoft recommends testing synchronization after changing the value to ensure that the account databases do, in fact, become synchronized within an acceptable time period.

On the PDC, the `Pulse` value can be modified so that the PDC checks its master accounts database less frequently. Recall that the default is five minutes. It can be set from one minute to 48 hours.

> **Caution**
> Similar to the `ReplicationGovernor` caution, setting this value too high could result in the BDC not being updated in a timely fashion, and possibly forcing a full synchronization (and therefore generating much more network traffic) to occur.

Part
VI

Ch
21

The `PulseConcurrency` governs the number of BDCs that the PDC contacts when it has changes. The default value is 10. This means that in a network with 15 BDCs, 10 will be contacted when the PDC has changes. When one of those completes its update, the 11th BDC will be contacted; when another BDC completes, the 12th will be contacted, and so on. If you need to be sure that all domain controllers are updated within a shorter period of time, consider increasing this value. In our example, increasing the value to 15 results in all the BDCs being contacted when the PDC has changes. On the other hand, more synchronization traffic is also generated concurrently, and this effect will need to be evaluated against the benefit of having all BDCs updated at the same time.

Another PDC parameter that can be modified is the `ChangeLogSize` parameter. By default, the PDC maintains a 64K change log of database modifications, about 2,000 changes of an average 32 bytes each. If the change log fills up before synchronization takes place—many users with a large number of changes, setting the `Pulse` value to high—older entries in the log may be overwritten and a full synchronization may occur to ensure that the BDCs have the most current information. Increase this value to increase the size of the change log and reduce the possibility of forcing a full synchronization.

Analyzing Trust Traffic

Another process that generates a certain amount of network traffic is the trust relationship. Chapter 3, "Trust Relationships," provides a thorough discussion of trusts and how they are created and used. Here we look at the traffic they generate.

Trust relationships allow accounts to be maintained in a centralized domain and resources to be focused in the domains where they need to be managed. They allow user accounts from the trusted domain to be granted access to resources located in the trusting domain, usually through global and local group management. There are three basic events related to trust relationships that generate network traffic:

◆ Establishing the trust

◆ Using accounts across the trust

◆ Pass-through authentication

Traffic Generated when Establishing a Trust

A trust is established between two primary domain controllers (PDCs). The PDC that has the accounts to be used across the trust is called the *trusted domain* and must permit the resource domain to trust it. The domain that has the resources that the user accounts want to access is called the *trusting domain* and must complete the trust relationship. The traffic associated with these two steps occurs only once, when the trust is established and generates about 110 frames for a total of about 16K. (see Figure 21.20)

FIG. 21.20 ⇒

This example displays the network traffic generated during the establishment of a trust relationship.

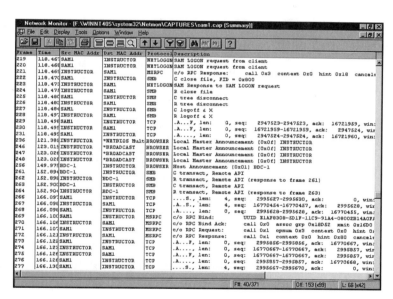

When a PDC permits a resource domain to trust it, there is actually no trust traffic generated as such. The process of permitting the resource domain is just a change to the SAM database on the PDC. So, the network traffic that is generated would be the normal traffic that occurs when the PDC announces a change to the accounts database, and the BDCs update their copies. This traffic is already described in the section titled "Analyzing Traffic Between Domain Controllers."

Part
VI

Ch
21

The PDC of the resource domain completes the trust by adding the account domain as a trusted domain. The first traffic that is generated when the domain is added relates to the name and address resolution that needs to take place, the establishment of TCP and NetBIOS sessions with the PDC of the trusted domain, and the negotiation of SMB protocols. These frames are discussed earlier in sections titled "WINS Frames" and "File Session Frames."

The PDC of the trusting domain attempts to connect to the IPC$ administrative share on the trusted domain's PDC as a regular user from the trusting domain with an *SMB C Session setup & X, Username =* frame. This attempt will fail because this account cannot make normal file session connections, and it generates an *SMB R Session setup & X - NT error* frame. The point of this process is to verify that the account used to create the trust was created in the trusted domain.

The session is then terminated generating three frames totaling about 180 bytes. The PDC of the trusting domain then retrieves a list of the BDCs in the trusted domain generating about 15 frames (2,400 bytes) as described in the section titled "Logon Validation Frames." It then connects to one of the domain controllers in the trusted domain and retrieves the domain name of the trusted domain, which it will use for allowing logon validation and pass-through authentication through the trust. The trusting domain's PDC also will initiate the synchronization process with its own BDCs.

Lastly, the PDC of the trusting domain attempts to log on to a domain controller in the trusted domain using the special Interdomain Trust User Account. Three frames are generated:

- ◆ *NETLOGON SAM LOGON Request from Client* broadcast to the trusted domain controllers (see Figure 21.20, Frame 219)
- ◆ *NETLOGON SAM LOGON Request from Client* to a specific trusted domain controller or the trusted PDC (see Figure 21.20, Frame 220)
- ◆ *NETLOGON SAM Response to SAM LOGON Request* from the trusted domain controller to the trusting PDC (see Figure 21.20, Frame 223)

If the logon attempt is successful, the trust has been successfully established. Along with these frames include, of course, the appropriate traffic associated with establishing and ending the session—altogether about 17 frames totaling 2,300 bytes. Whenever the PDC is restarted, it must verify the trust again by logging on using the Interdomain Trust User Account and regenerating these last 17 or so frames.

Traffic Generated when Using Trusted Accounts

More trust traffic centers around the use of trusted accounts. Traffic is generated whenever a trusted account is added to a local group in the trusting domain or to an access control list (ACL) directly. Also, displaying the list of trusted accounts on a computer in the trusting domain generates network traffic. This traffic involves frames that we have already seen. For example, a connection needs to be made to the IPC$ administrative share on a trusted domain controller. This involves, as we have seen numerous times in this chapter, resolving names and addresses, establishing TCP and NetBIOS sessions if necessary, and disconnecting the sessions when you are finished.

Tip

As a benchmark, Microsoft notes that retrieving a list of 12 trusted accounts generated a total of about 53 frames and 9.5K. One frame contained the list of global groups in the trusted domain, and another frame contained the list of users. These frames are generated for every list request made by a server in the trusting domain.

Traffic is also generated when viewing the membership of local groups in the trusting domain that have trusted domain members. This should make sense, because lists of users are actually enumerated by their SIDs. The SIDs for trusted users are kept in the trusted domain, so traffic will necessarily be generated by the trusting domain which has to look up the SIDs for the trusted users in the trusted domain. Again, only two frames are needed to actually look up the SID and return the account name, but up to 43 frames will be needed to—you guessed it—resolve names and addresses, establish sessions, and so on.

Traffic Generated when Using Pass-Through Authentication

When a user from a trusted domain accesses a resource in the trusting domain, its account information must be verified, or validated. Because the account does not exist in the trusting domain, pass-through authentication is used to validate the user account in the trusted domain. Pass-through authentication is also used to validate a user when the user tries to log on to or access a resource in a domain other than the domain the user's computer is a member of. This is kind of like peer-to-peer networking among domains. Again, please refer to Chapter 3, "Trust Relationships," for a more complete discussion. In any event, pass-through authentication is probably among the more common types of user and trust processes to generate network traffic.

The process begins with the user's request to see a browse list of resources available among the trusting domain's servers. Frames are generated as described in the section titled "Exploring Browser Traffic" earlier in this chapter. Of course, names and addresses may need to be resolved and sessions established.

The user selects a resource from the list and attempts to connect to it. The user may also have simply entered in the UNC path to the resource in the Path box of a connect dialog, or at the command prompt using a NET USE statement. However the user connects, it is at this point that pass-through authentication occurs. The domain controller in the trusting domain contacts a domain controller in the trusted domain establishing TCP and NetBIOS sessions, negotiating SMB protocols, and connecting to IPC$.

A named pipe connection is created between the domain controllers to implement a secure channel between them—a process similar to that which takes place when the user logs on. Two frames generate and complete the validation request, which is really a logon request, sort of like an "attach" command in Novell's NetWare. The frames are: *R_LOGON RPC Client call logon:NetrLogonSamLogon* and *R_LOGON RPC Server Response logon:NetrLogonSamLogon.* Altogether, including all the ancillary frames needed to resolve names and addresses and establish sessions, a pass-through authentication request across a trust generates about 20 frames totaling anywhere from 3,200 to 4,200 bytes.

Optimizing Trust Traffic

There are really two considerations to keep in mind when trying to optimize trust traffic. The first is quite obvious, though not always practical or even possible within some organizations: Minimize the number of trusts you must maintain. In other words, only create the trusts you need to have. Chapter 4, "Domain Models," outlines how trusts are used to build various models of enterprise computing. These represent the basic building blocks of domain models. However, all the trusts described may not be necessary. Eliminate those you don't really need. If you have to re-establish a trust between two domains, remember that the amount of traffic that will be generated to establish the trust is relatively small (110 frames and about 16K) and takes place once.

The other consideration involves Microsoft's recommended strategy for dealing with user accounts across trusts. This strategy was thoroughly outlined in both Chapter 3, "Trust Relationships," and Chapter 12, "Domain Users and Groups." In brief, Microsoft recommends that trusted users be maintained in global groups, and that the global groups be used as members of local groups on resource servers in the trusting domain. This will reduce the traffic generated when displaying local group membership lists and adding accounts to local groups across the trust because only the SIDs of global groups will need to be validated as opposed to the SIDs of each individual user.

Key Concept

If you compare the amount of data transferred from a global group lookup as opposed to that generated with one or two users, the difference is only a few bytes. However, when large numbers of users are involved, the difference can quickly add up to a significant reduction in network traffic.

Traffic Generated Through Directory Replication

The Directory Replication service, described in Chapter 8, "Configuring Domain Network Core Services," provides an automatic means of duplicating a directory tree among multiple computers. The administrator identifies a Windows NT Server to act as an export server, identifies other Windows NT Servers, Windows NT Workstations or LanMan servers to be the import computers, and creates the directory tree structure including any files and subfolders that need to be replicated from the export to the import computers.

This service is most often used to copy logon scripts and system policy files to all the domain controllers in the domain, thus ensuring that no matter which domain controller validates the user, the appropriate logon script and policy file are implemented. Because these types of files generally do not change frequently, Directory Replication should not generate an inordinate amount of traffic. However, if Directory Replication is used to send other files as well, or if the files tend to be large or change frequently, then a great deal more traffic may be generated by this service.

Every five minutes, by default, the export server generates a notification to all the import servers that are export servers and either have or don't have changes to their export directory trees. If there are no changes, that is the extent of the process. If there are changes, then the Directory Replication process kicks in.

The export server notifies the import servers in its list that it has changes in its directory tree through an *SMB C Transact, File=\Mailslot\Net\Repl_cli* broadcast frame sent to the NetBIOS UDP Port 138. The size of this frame will vary with the size of the export directory tree. From this point on, the import computers generate most of the traffic.

In response, the import computers make an SMB connection to the REPL$ administrative share on the export server. Again, they are resolving names and addresses and establishing a session as we have seen many times throughout this chapter. About nine frames are generated, totaling about 1,300 bytes.

Next, the import computer needs to check its system time against that of the export server. If the two times are not within 10 minutes of each other, Directory Replication will fail to complete. The import computer generates an *R_SRVSVC RPC Client call srvsvc:NetrRemoteTOD* frame directed to the export server which responds back with an *R_SRVSVC RPC Server response srvsvc:NetrRemoteTOD* frame.

The import computer checks the export server's replication parameters to determine what it needs to replicate (for example, all files, changed files), if it has to wait for a specific time, whether any directories are locked, and so on. To do so, it must establish a named pipe session and a file open to \Winreg on the export server. Altogether, 18 frames are generated totaling about 3,500 bytes of data. The four frames specific to making the named pipe connection and checking the Registry are: *SMB C NT create & X, File=\Winreg, SMB R NT create & X, FID=0x809, MSRPC c/o RPC Bind*, and *MSRPC c/o RPC Bind Ack*.

Through another 30 frames and 5,000 bytes the import computer verifies the parameters and the export directory tree. If all the files need to be copied, the import computer queries the export server to find all the files in the directory tree. If an update of a file or files is necessary, the updated file or files are copied from the export server to the import computer.

Tip

As a benchmark, Microsoft tells us that replicating 16 files totaling about 426K of data can generate 1,425 frames and take about 42 seconds to replicate.

Optimizing Directory Replication Traffic

When the Directory Replicator detects that a file in its top level directory has changed, it will copy the entire directory during the replication process. Consequently, large, deep directory structures can generate a lot of replication traffic because among large numbers of files it is more likely that at least one file will change.

Key Concept

Microsoft recommends that you keep the export directory tree flat and very shallow. Fewer files in a directory reduces the possibility that any one file may have a change; and if a file does change, a smaller directory is replicated, generating less network traffic overall.

Directory Replication parameters are configured through each computer's properties as accessed through Server Manager. There are two options that are frequently overlooked which can help to control what is replicated and how much. One is the Add Lock option. The administrator can choose to lock one or more directories. This effectively removes it from consideration for being replicated. This can be an effective way to keep large directories from replicating during busy times of the day, for example.

Also, each directory has a Wait Until Stabilized Option which is enabled by default. With this option enabled, the import computer will wait for activity in the directory to cease for a period of two minutes (default) or more before replicating all the files in the directory. Disabling this option will cause the import computer to check the time, date, attributes, name, and size of each file individually and just copy the changed files.

Implement these two options through these steps:

1. Start Server Manager.
2. Open the computer properties of the export server.
3. Click the Replication button, then choose the Manage button under Export Directories.
4. Select the appropriate directory.
5. Choose Add Lock to keep the directory from being replicated. Deselect Wait Until Stabilized to disable the option.
6. Choose OK.

Another obvious change involves the Registry. Recall that by default the export server checks its directory structure and announces itself every five minutes. This is known as the *interval* value and can be set from one minute to 60 minutes or more on the export server. The import computer maintains a *pulse* value of 2 minutes (default)—not to be confused with the pulse value that can be modified on a PDC for account database synchronization. This pulse value controls how often the import computer contacts the export server directly according to the formula *pulse* ⋆ *interval*. This means that, by default, if the import computer does not hear from the export server after 10 minutes (pulse 2 ⋆ interval 5), it will initiate a connection with the export server to see if it needs to copy anything. By increasing the pulse value, you increase the period of time within which the export server can contact the import computer to notify it of a change.

Summarizing and Planning Network Traffic

Throughout this chapter, we have looked at various common events, processes, and services that generate network traffic. We have analyzed their effect on the network, and offered suggestions for their optimization. As you can probably guess, predicting network traffic is hardly an exact science. However, by now you have a better idea of what kinds of traffic to expect and what to look for. The following is a check list of things to look for when trying to analyze or project traffic patterns, bottlenecks, and growth.

◆ Begin by determining the traffic generated by the event or service when it is started; focus on the computers involved, the frequency of the frames generated, and the average size of the frames.

◆ Identify any variables relating to the event or service. For example, the number of BDCs in the domain will effect how much synchronization traffic is generated.

Part
VI

Ch
21

◆ Identify how many client and server computers will participate in the traffic generated. Determine the amount of traffic generated between one set of computers, determine the frequency of the traffic generated, then extrapolate that number to the total number of computers involved.

◆ Determine whether the service or event can be optimized.

◆ Weigh the benefits provided by the service or event against the traffic that is generated.

Table 21.3 summarizes the services discussed in this chapter by the traffic each generates and its frequency. The values stated are approximate and will vary depending on your network implementation.

Table 21.3   Traffic Summary by Service

Service	Traffic Generated	Frequency of Frames Generated
DHCP Service	Obtain IP Address 4 frames, 1368 bytes	Once when client boots
	Renew IP address lease 2 frames, 684 bytes	At startup and at 1/2 lease interval
WINS Service	Registration 2 frames, 214 bytes	Once for every computer, service, and application
	Renewal 2 frames, 214 bytes	At 1/2 the TTL value
	Name resolution 2 frames, 196 bytes	Whenever a connection needs to be established and the resolved name is not in cache

Service	Traffic Generated	Frequency of Frames Generated
Establishing File Sessions	Address resolution 2 frames, 120 bytes	When connecting to another TCP/IP host and address is not in ARP cache
	TCP session 3 frames, 180 bytes	Once per TCP host connection
	NetBIOS session 2 frames, 186 bytes	Once per NetBIOS host connection
	SMB protocol negotiation 2 frames, 350 bytes	Once per SMB connection to target host
	Connection sequence 2 frames, 350 bytes	Once per resource access
	Session disconnect 5 frames, 360 bytes	Once at final disconnection from TCP host
User Logon	Session Establishment 15 frames, 2,000 bytes	Whenever a user logs on
	NT-based validation 20 frames, 3,700 bytes	Whenever a user logs on
	Session breakdown 5 frames, 360 bytes	Whenever a user logs on

Part

VI

Ch

21

continues

Table 21.3   Continued

Service	Traffic Generated	Frequency of Frames Generated
	Implementing logon scripts, profiles, and policies	Whenever a user logs on; when they exist, traffic varies
Computer Browser Service	Host announcement 1 frame, 243 bytes	From every computer with resources, once every announcement period (12 minutes by default)
	Master browser announcement 1 frame, 250 bytes	Whenever requested by a computer or backup browser, and after every election
	Workgroup announcement 1 frame, 250 bytes	From each master browser once every announcement period (15 minutes by default)
	Master Browser Election frames dependent on the number of computers taking part in the election; each frame 225 bytes	Whenever a computer or backup browser determines that the master browser is unavailable, or when a computer that can become a master browser starts up

Service	Traffic Generated	Frequency of Frames Generated
	Requesting a backup browser 2 frames, 450 bytes	When browsing is first initiated at a computer.
	Retrieving a browse list 20 frames, 2150 bytes	Whenever the client browses for resources or whenever the backup browser updates its list from the master browser (every 12 minutes by default)
	Retrieving a list of shared resources from Windows NT servers 19 frames, 3,300 bytes	Whenever the client selects a server in the browser list
Account Database Synchronization	Request for PDC 4 frames, 745 bytes	Whenever the BDC starts up
	Establish a session between PDC and BDC 11 frames, 1,280 bytes	Every time synchronization tales place
	Establish a secure channel between PDC and BDC	Whenever the BDC starts up

continues

Part

VI

Ch

21

Table 21.3 Continued

Service	Traffic Generated	Frequency of Frames Generated
	Verify the databases 6 frames, 1,350 bytes	Whenever the BDC starts up
	Update the PDC 1 frame, 400 bytes	Every time synchronization takes place
	Synchronize the databases 2 frames, 1,400 bytes	Every time synchronization takes place; value based per user change
Establishing a Trust Relationship	110 frames, 16,000 bytes	When the trust relationship is first created
Using accounts across a trust	12 frames, 1,550 bytes per trusted account	Every time an account is selected at a computer in a trusting domain
Verifying trusted accounts	45 frames, 7,000 bytes	Every time you view an ACL or local group membership that contains a trusted account; value based per trusted account

Service	Traffic Generated	Frequency of Frames Generated
Pass–Through Authentication	20 frames, 3,700 bytes	Whenever user logs on to a domain across the trust, or accesses a resource on a computer in the trusting domain
Directory Replication	Export server announcement 1 frame, 340 bytes	Whenever the directory tree is updated on a given interval (5 minutes by default)
	Establish session from import to export computer 9 frames, 1,300 bytes	Whenever the import computer needs to copy an updated directory tree from the export server
	Verify the directory 30 frames, 5,100 bytes	Whenever the import computer needs to copy an updated directory tree from the export server
	Update the import computer directory tree traffic depends on amount of data to be updated	Whenever the import computer needs to copy an updated directory tree from the export server

Taking the Disc Test

 If you have read and understood the material in the chapter, you are ready to test your knowledge. Insert the CD-ROM that comes with this book and run the self-test software as described in Appendix I, "Using the CD-ROM."

From Here...

In this chapter, we took a rather detailed look at some common network traffic generated between Windows NT computers. We saw how the Network Monitor utility can help to identify traffic patterns, and provide some insight into how the network is being utilized. This utility, together with Performance Monitor, are the two best tools in Windows NT 4.0 to analyze and troubleshoot network systems. The final chapter coming up, "Advanced Troubleshooting," rounds out this section's discussion of monitoring and optimization techniques. It will discuss such topics as how to interpret the dreaded blue screen and how to use the kernel debugger tool.

Chapter Prerequisite

The reader should have a good knowledge of PC hardware, Windows NT installation and configuration, Windows NT architecture, and the boot process. Information presented in Chapters 6, 7, 8, and 15 will also be helpful in understanding the troubleshooting concepts and procedures presented in this chapter.

Advanced Troubleshooting

This chapter introduces the reader to Kernel Stop Errors, also referred to as blue screen errors or trap errors, and describes and identifies the data areas of a stop error that are pertinent to finding the cause of the problem. The precise time that a stop error occurs is also relevant to isolating the cause of the malfunction such as during installation, after installation, or during the Windows NT initialization or boot process, and is discussed in this chapter. Software problems that cause stop errors are also discussed in this chapter.

Another topic of interest discussed in this chapter is crash dumps. You will learn how to configure the Windows NT Recovery options and how to configure the required memory resources. Tools to check, analyze, and copy a crash dump such as dumpchk, dumpexam, and dumpflop are also presented.

Next, the Kernel debugger programs and options are discussed along with how to configure Windows NT systems to do live debugging procedures, both at local sites and from remote sites. Discussions include setting up and connecting the host and target computers, locating the kernel debugger programs, and locating, expanding, and using the symbols files.

The last topic of discussion in this chapter is Event Viewer. The three types of event logs, event details, log settings, and other pertinent event viewer information is presented.

Topics in this chapter include:

◆ Windows NT kernel messages

◆ Stop errors

◆ Crash dumps

◆ Kernel debugger

◆ Remote troubleshooting

◆ Event Viewer

Windows NT Kernel Messages

There are three types of Windows NT kernel messages; they are hardware-malfunction messages, status messages, and stop messages. Stop messages, also referred to as blue screens or traps, will be discussed in detail in this chapter.

Hardware Malfunction Messages

Hardware-malfunction messages are caused by a hardware condition that is detected by the processor. The Windows NT Executive will display a message such as `Hardware malfunction, call your hardware vender for support`, the actual message being dependent on the manufacturer. Other information is also displayed indicating the nature of the problem such as a memory parity error, a bus-data error, or a specific adapter error (with slot number), again dependent on the type of error and the manufacturer of the hardware.

Status Messages

Status messages, in most cases, are not as critical. This type of message is displayed when the Windows NT Executive detects a condition within a process or application where the action required is simply clicking OK to terminate the process or application. Messages indicating the action are displayed in a window or dialog box on the screen.

There are three types of status messages: system-information, warning, and application-termination messages. System-information messages could include indications of an invalid current directory, a suspended thread, or a working set range error. Warning messages indicate information such as buffer overflow, a busy device, or an out-of-paper message. Application-termination messages range from access denied, to a corrupt disk, to a data error. Missing system files and out of virtual memory messages are other examples.

Stop (Blue Screen/Trap) Messages

Stop messages, on the other hand, are probably the most severe. They always require the computer to be restarted because the Windows NT Executive cannot recover from the error. Also provided is a mechanism for dumping memory information into a memory dump file if configured prior to the error.

Stop errors can happen virtually at any time: during and after installation, during and after initialization (booting), or from a specific software condition.

Stop Messages During Installation

Stop errors that occur during installation are usually a result of incompatible hardware. Refer to the latest version of an HCL to determine if all hardware on the computer is listed. The latest HCL can be found by doing a search on HCL from Microsoft Corporation's home Web page, **www.microsoft.com**.

Tip
If specific hardware is not on the HCL, contact the manufacturer for information on new hardware or updated BIOS and firmware revisions.

Another approach to determining the specific piece of hardware causing the problem is to configure the system to minimize requirements and try the installation again.

Stop Messages After Installation

It is very apparent that various hardware problems can happen after Windows NT is installed and operational. Also, any drivers such as device drivers or file system drivers can cause the Windows NT Executive to generate a stop error. Problems of this nature can be fixed by replacing hardware or reinstalling Windows NT components.

Tip

In some cases, Microsoft NT Service Packs can solve various types of stop error problems. Service packs can be obtained by accessing Microsoft Corporation's home Web page at **www.microsoft.com**.

Stop Messages only During Windows NT Executive Initialization

A small group of stop errors can only happen during Phase 4 of the boot process, part of which is when the Windows NT Executive initializes. There are two parts to the initialization of the Windows NT Executive, phase 0 and phase 1. During phase 0, interrupts are disabled and only a few Executive components are initialized. One of the components initialized during phase 0 is the Hardware Abstraction Layer (HAL). During phase 1, the Executive is fully operational and the Windows NT subcomponents are initialized.

Key Concept

If a phase 0 initialization stop message is experienced, run all the hardware diagnostic routines to try to solve the problem. If no hardware errors are found, reinstall Windows NT 4.0 and reinitialize to see if the problem persists.

If a phase 1 initialization stop message is obtained, reinstall Windows NT and reinitialize the system.

Tables 22.1 and 22.2 display the Windows NT Executive Phase 0 and Phase 1 Initialization stop messages, respectively.

Table 22.1   Windows NT Executive Phase 0 Initialization Stop Error Messages

Error Code	Error Code Meaning
0x0031	PHASE0_INITIALIZATION_FAILED
0x005C	HAL_INITIALIZATION_FAILED
0x005D	HEAP_INITIALIZATION_FAILED
0x005E	OBJECT_INITIALIZATION_FAILED
0x005F	SECURITY_INITIALIZATION_FAILED
0x0060	PROCESS_INITIALIZATION_FAILED

Table 22.2   Windows NT Executive Phase 1 Initialization Stop Error Messages

Error Code	Error Code Meaning
0x0032	PHASE1_INITIALIZATION_FAILED
0x0061	HAL1_INITIALIZATION_FAILED
0x0062	OBJECT1_INITIALIZATION_FAILED
0x0063	SECURITY1_INITIALIZATION_FAILED
0x0064	SYMBOLIC_INITIALIZATION_FAILED
0x0065	MEMORY1_INITIALIZATION_FAILED
0x0066	CACHE_INITIALIZATION_FAILED
0x0067	CONFIG_INITIALIZATION_FAILED
0x0068	FILE_INITIALIZATION_FAILED
0x0069	IO1_INITIALIZATION_FAILED
0x006A	LPC_INITIALIZATION_FAILED

continues

Table 22.2 Continued

Error Code	Error Code Meaning
0x006B	PROCESS1_INITIALIZATION_FAILED
0x006C	REFMON_INITIALIZATION_FAILED
0x006D	SESSION1_INITIALIZATION_FAILED
0x006E	SESSION2_INITIALIZATION_FAILED
0x006F	SESSION3_INITIALIZATION_FAILED
0x0070	SESSION4_INITIALIZATION_FAILED
0x0071	SESSION5_INITIALIZATION_FAILED

Stop Messages Caused by Software Problems

Software conditions detected by the processor in a system can also produce stop error messages. This event is also called a Software Trap and is caused by the processor executing an instruction in a process or application when it encounters an error such as a divide by zero or a memory segment not present. All 12 software traps produce the same stop error message format as follows:

★★★ STOP: 0X0000007F (0x0000000n, 0x00000000, 0x00000000, 0x00000000) UNEXPECTED_KERNEL_MODE_TRAP

In the first parameter 0x0000000n, n indicates which of the 12 stop messages has been encountered. These are displayed in Table 22.3.

Table 22.3 Windows NT Executive Software Trap Stop Error Messages

Parameter	Stop Message Meaning
0x00000000	An attempt to divide by zero.
0x00000001	A system–debugger call.
0x00000003	A debugger breakpoint.
0x00000004	An arithmetic operation overflow.

Parameter	Stop Message Meaning
0x00000005	An array index that exceeds the array bounds.
0x00000006	Invalid operands in an instruction or an attempt to execute a protected–mode instruction while running in real mode.
0x00000007	A hardware coprocessor instruction, with no coprocessor present.
0x00000008	An error while processing an error (also known as a double fault).
0x0000000A	A corrupted Task State Segment.
0x0000000B	An access to a memory segment that was not present.
0x0000000C	An access to memory beyond the limits of a stack.
0x0000000D	An exception not covered by some other exception; a protection fault that pertains to access violations for applications.

Normal User Stop Messages Procedures

Normal users cannot be expected to diagnose the causes of stop errors. When stop errors occur, these users should be instructed to record the first few lines of the message and then restart the system. If the stop error happens again, a Last Known Good configuration can be invoked; however, the system administrator should ensure that the Recovery option is properly configured in the system to obtain memory dump information. The dumps can then be analyzed to determine the cause of the error message.

General Stop Message Troubleshooting Procedures

Microsoft recommends that the following procedure be followed when stop errors are encountered:

1. Gather information about the problem.
2. Determine whether the problem is a known issue.

3. Determine whether the problem is caused by hardware.

4. Troubleshoot well-known stop codes.

5. Determine whether the problem is caused by non–HCL hardware.

6. Contact Microsoft Service Advantage.

Step 1: Gather Information About the Problem

Record, at a minimum, the following information when experiencing stop errors:

◆ The top four lines of a stop error includes the stop error codes, and other pertinent information. An example of the information to be recorded is shown as follows:

STOP:
0X0000000A(0x0000000B,0x00000002,0x00000000,0xFE34C882)
IRQL_NOT_LESS_OR_EQUAL
ADDRESS 0xFE34C882 has base at 0xFE000000:
NTOSKRNL.EXE

◆ All hardware information including system statistics such as BIOS, CMOS settings, controllers/adapters installed and their BIOS version.

◆ The platform and version of Windows NT installed including any service packs, hotfixes, or third-party drivers such as a Novell redirector.

◆ How often and when the stop error is occurring (whether it is random or when a specific operation is performed such as a certain application or process).

Step 2: Determine Whether the Problem Is a Known Issue

The next step is to see if someone has been there before. Try and determine if this error has been a common occurrence and if there is an already established workaround or hotfix.

Search Microsoft's Knowledge Base (from Microsoft's home Web page and choose support, then technical support) by searching for the word stop, followed by the stop error code, followed by the program module name. An example is as follows:

> STOP 0x0000000A NTOSKRNL.EXE

If no results are received, search for just the word stop and try to locate any general stop error troubleshooting methods.

Step 3: Determine Whether the Problem Is Caused by Hardware

Stop errors are caused by hardware errors and outdated BIOS even if the hardware is on the HCL. Hardware configurations may also cause stop errors. The following examples indicate various situations:

- ◆ A system was working properly; however, when a specific operation is performed such as booting the system, formatting a disk, or performing a backup operation, stop errors occur. Check the specific hardware involved for that operation. A software problem usually occurs only when a certain set of conditions is present. Try to isolate exactly what conditions are present when the failure happens.

- ◆ A system was working fine until a new piece of hardware was installed, then stop errors started occurring. Check the HCL for the new piece of hardware. Check for IRQs, IO addresses, and Direct Memory Access (DMA) conflicts. Check BIOS versions, driver versions, and configuration settings.

Step 4: Troubleshoot Well-Known Stop Codes

Some common stop errors are listed here for your information. Most of the illustrated stop error descriptions indicate the specific reason or cause of the problem.

- ◆ STOP 0x0000000A IRQL_NOT_LESS_OR_EQUAL
- ◆ STOP 0x00000019 BAD_POOL_HEADER
- ◆ STOP 0x0000001E KMODE_EXCEPTION_NOT_HANDLED
- ◆ STOP 0x00000024 NTFS_FILE_SYSTEM

- STOP 0x0000002E DATA_BUS_ERROR
- STOP 0x0000003E
  MULTIPROCESSOR_CONFIGURATION_NOT_SUPPORTED
- stop 0x00000051 REGISTRY_ERROR
- STOP 0x00000058 FTDISK_INTERNAL_ERROR
- STOP 0x00000077 KERNEL_STACK_OVERFLOW
- STOP 0x00000079 MISMATCHED_HAL
- STOP 0x0000007A KERNEL_DATA_INPAGE_ERROR
- STOP 0x0000007B INACCESSIBLE_BOOT_DEVICE
- STOP 0x0000007F USEXPECTED_KERNEL_MODE_TRAP
- STOP 0x00000080 NMI_HARDWARE_FAILURE
- STOP 0x0000008B MBR_CHECKSUM_MISMATCH
- STOP 0x00000218
  STATUS_CANNOT_LOAD_REGISTRY_FILE
- STOP 0x0000021A
  STATUS_SYSTEM_PROCESS_TERMINATED
- STOP 0x00000221
  STATUS_IMAGE_CHECKSUM_MISMATCH

Step 5: Determine Whether the Problem Is Caused by Non-HCL Hardware

Microsoft, as a rule, does not totally support stop errors from hardware such as motherboards, disk drive controllers, network or video adapter cards, or multimedia devices that are not on the HCL. Because hardware that is not on the HCL has not been tested with Windows NT 4.0, diagnostic information is not available.

The first thing to do is to contact the manufacturer of the device for any information regarding Windows NT 4.0, such as device drivers.

Two articles in the Microsoft Knowledge Base on the Internet provide information concerning Microsoft's policy for supporting hardware that is not on the HCL. The two articles are Q142865 and Q143244.

The first article, Q142865 Microsoft PSS Support Policy on Hardware Not on Windows NT HCL, discusses details on troubleshooting problems with non-HCL hardware.

The second article, Q143244 How to Check if Unsupported Hardware Allows Windows NT Install, provides troubleshooting tips on hardware that will allow Windows NT 4.0 to be installed.

Step 6: Contact Microsoft Service Advantage

If a solution to the stop error has not been found by performing the previous steps 1 through 5, Microsoft Service Advantage should be contacted for support. The Microsoft Service Advantage home page on the Internet can be found at **http://www.microsoft.com/servad/**.

Stop Error Screen Layout and Section Meanings

Probably one of the most intimidating errors that Windows NT can produce is a stop error. The entire screen turns blue and a mass of numbers and letters appear, which usually causes panic and disillusion to the user. Enterprise administrators and support personnel, on the other hand, accept a stop error as a challenge and proceed to interpret the information presented to locate the cause of the error.

The first objective in diagnosing stop errors is to define the areas or sections of a stop error screen. Use Figure 22.1 and the following paragraphs to locate and define the five distinct sections:

- Debug port status indicators
- BugCheck information
- Driver information
- Kernel build number and stack dump
- Debug port information

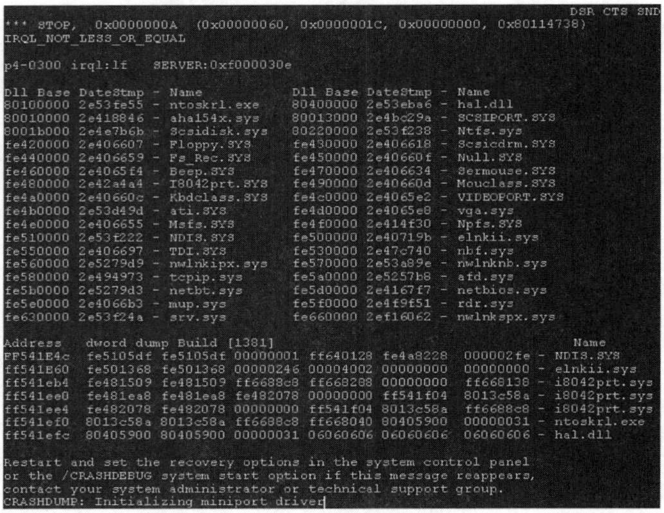

FIG. 22.1 ⇒

Here is an illustration of a Windows NT 4.0 Stop Error Screen (Blue Screen).

Debug Port Status Indicators

If a modem or null modem cable is connected to the computer and the Kernel Debugger program is running, indicators will appear in the upper-right corner of the stop screen on the top line. These indicators will show the serial communication port status of the communication between a host and target computer. The following is a list of the various port status indicators that can appear in this section:

- ◆ MDM   Debugger is using modem controls
- ◆ CD   Carrier Detected
- ◆ RI   Ring Indicator
- ◆ DSR   Data Set Ready
- ◆ CTS   Clear To Send
- ◆ SND   Byte of information being sent
- ◆ RCV   Byte of information being received
- ◆ FRM   Framing error
- ◆ OVL   Overflow
- ◆ PRT   Parity error

BugCheck Information

The next four lines (beginning with the line that starts with ★★★ STOP) contain the error code (or BugCheck code) and other pertinent error code information. This information is critical to finding the cause of the error, and, as mentioned previously in the section "General STOP Error Troubleshooting Procedures," should be recorded. In the example shown in Figure 22.1, the first line is as follows:

> ★★★ STOP: 0x0000000A (0x0000006c, 0x0000001c, 0x00000000, 0x80114738) IRQL_NOT_LESS_OR_EQUAL

◆ The 0x0000000A indicates the stop error.

◆ The parameter 0x0000006c identifies the address that was not referenced correctly.

◆ The parameter 0x0000001c identifies the Interrupt Request Level (IRQL) that was required to access memory.

◆ The parameter 0x00000000 indicates a Read operation was in progress. (A value of 1 would indicate a Write operation.)

◆ The parameter 0x80114738 indicates the instruction address that tried to access memory referenced in the first parameter.

Driver Information

The next section begins with the line Dll Base and continues for a number of lines, depending on the error. The example in Figure 22.1 displays an area of 17 lines and lists 34 drivers. Three columns of information are displayed on the left half of the screen, and three more columns are displayed on the right half of the screen. The first column in each half displays the base address of the driver in memory with the second column displaying the time stamp information. The third column in each half will display the names of all drivers loaded in the system at the time of the error.

Kernel Build Number and Stack Dump

Section 4 contains the version and build level of the Windows NT 4.0 Kernel, Ntoskrnl.exe. Any service pack or third-party driver information is *not* displayed in this section. This section can be extremely useful because it may indicate, depending on the stop error, the driver that failed and caused the stop error.

Debug Port Information

Additional COM port information such as what port and the speed of the port, if Kernel Debugger is running, is displayed here. Other data in this area will confirm if a memory dump has been created or give instructions on how to further troubleshoot the problem.

Crash Dumps (Memory Dumps)

Once the stop error is analyzed, and the solution to the error cannot be determined, it is necessary to obtain more data and information about the problem. One of the ways to retrieve more information concerning a particular stop error is to have the computer dump the entire contents of memory at the time of the error. From this point, either an administrator or a support team can analyze the memory dump to determine the solution for the error.

The first step in initiating a memory dump if a stop error is encountered is to ensure the Recovery option is configured correctly. This option can be configured to invoke a number of different procedures; however, it should be configured to take memory dumps if the error persists.

The Recovery option is configured from the System Properties sheet, on the Startup/Shutdown tab. The Recovery configuration options are shown in Figure 22.2.

The following is a list of the options available in the Setup/Shutdown tab of the System Properties dialog box.

◆ Write an Event to the System Log

If selected, an event will be written to the system log when a stop error occurs.

FIG. 22.2 ⇒

This figure shows the Windows NT 4.0 Recovery option configuration location.

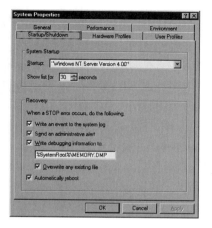

◆ Send an Administrative Alert

If this option is selected, and alerts have been configured in Server Manager or from the Server icon in the Control Panel, an administrative alert is sent to a designated computer on the network if a stop error occurs.

◆ Write Debugging Information To:

This option, when selected, enables the entire contents of system memory to be written to a file specified in the space provided. This file will be written to %SystemRoot%\MEMORY.DMP by default. A DUMPEXAM utility can then be used to analyze the memory dump to isolate the cause of the error.

In addition to this option being selected, four other requirements must be met to provide for a memory dump and are listed here.

- A pagefile must exist on the same partition where Windows NT 4.0 has been installed (the boot partition).

- The pagefile must be at least 1M larger that the physical size of RAM in the system.

- The boot partition must have at least as much free space as the size of the pagefile.

- Automatically Reboot should be selected.

> **Caution**
> The first three requirements listed in the preceding text *must* be met to obtain a memory dump of the system. The memory dump process will put the entire contents of RAM memory in the pagefile on the boot partition. Prior to the reboot process, the pagefile information will be written to the specified .DMP file.

◆ <u>O</u>verwrite any Existing File

If this option is selected and a MEMORY.DMP file exists in the %SystemRoot% folder, it will be overwritten.

◆ Automatically <u>R</u>eboot

This option is selected to invoke a reboot operation following a stop error. If the memory dump option has also been selected, that operation will take place prior to the reboot.

Crash Dump Analysis Utilities

The Windows NT 4.0 Server and Workstation CD-ROMs include three utilities that can be used to analyze the results of a memory dump. A copy of each of these utilities is located in a platform-specific folder (Alpha, I386, Mips, and PPC) under the Support\Debug folder. These utilities are:

◆ Dumpchk.exe

◆ Dumpexam.exe

◆ Dumpflop.exe

Dumpchk.exe

This utility is used to verify the validity of a memory dump and to assure it can be read by a debugger application. It verifies all the virtual and physical memory addresses and displays basic information about the memory dump. It will also display any errors found in the memory dump. The command-line syntax is shown in Figure 22.3.

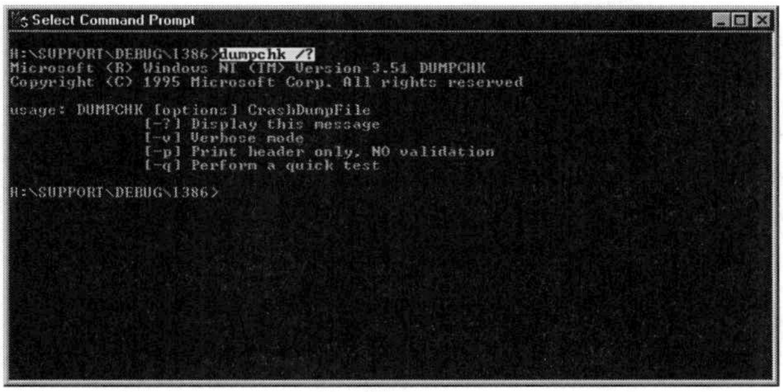

FIG. 22.3 ⇒
This is an example of the Dumpchk.exe utility command-line syntax.

Resultant information from this utility can be used to determine what stop error occurred and what version of Windows NT was being used when the error occurred. An example of dumpchk results using the –v and –q options is shown here.

D:\>dumpchk –v –q memory.dmp

Filename . . . . . . .memory.dmp
Signature. . . . . . .PAGE
ValidDump. . . . . . .DUMP
MajorVersion . . . . .free system
MinorVersion 1381
DirectoryTableBase . .0x00030000
PfnDataBase. 0x81fcf000
PsLoadedModuleList . .0x8014dd90
PsActiveProcessHead. .0x8014dc88
MachineImageType . . .I386
NumberProcessors . . .1
BugCheckCode 0x0000000a
BugCheckParameter1 . .0xfed7a026
BugCheckParameter2 . .0x00000002
BugCheckParameter3 . .0x00000000
BugCheckParameter4 . .0xfed7a026

ExceptionCode. 0x80000003
ExceptionFlags 0x00000001
ExceptionAddress . . .0x8013f46c

```
NumberOfRuns . . . . .0x3
NumberOfPages. . . . .0x1f9d
Run #1
 BasePage . . . . . .0x1
 PageCount. . . . . .0x9e
Run #2
 BasePage . . . . . .0x100
 PageCount. . . . . .0xeff
Run #3
 BasePage . . . . . .0x1000
 PageCount. . . . . .0x1000


★★★★★★★★★★★★★★★
★★★★★★★★★★★★★★★ . . ->Validating the integrity of the PsLoa
★★★★★★★★★★★★★★★
validating ntoskrnl.exe 0x80100000 0x000d4cc0
validating hal.dll 0x80010000 0x0000c920
validating atapi.sys 0x80001000 0x00006000
validating SCSIPORT.SYS 0x80007000 0x00007e80
validating Disk.sys 0x801d5000 0x00003a60
validating CLASS2.SYS 0x801d9000 0x000032e0
validating Ftdisk.sys 0x801dd000 0x00007b60
validating Ntfs.sys 0x801e5000 0x00058000
validating Floppy.SYS 0xfc6f8000 0x00005000
validating Null.SYS 0xfc9c9000 0x00001000
validating KSecDD.SYS 0xfc874000 0x00003000
validating Beep.SYS 0xfc9ca000 0x00001000
validating i8042prt.sys 0xfc738000 0x00007000
validating mouclass.sys 0xfc87c000 0x00003000
validating kbdclass.sys 0xfc884000 0x00003000
validatingVIDEOPRT.SYS 0xfc750000 0x00006000
validating cirrus.SYS 0xfc420000 0x0000c000
validating Msfs.SYS 0xfc780000 0x00006000
validating Npfs.SYS 0xfc430000 0x0000a000
validating NDIS.SYS 0xff09c000 0x0001f000
```

```
validating win32k.sys 0xa0000000 0x00133000
validating cirrus.dll 0xfc580000 0x0000d000
validating Fastfat.SYS 0xfef29000 0x00023000
validating TDI.SYS 0xff084000 0x00003000
validating sfmatalk.sys 0xfeee2000 0x0001f000
validating nbf.sys 0xfeec9000 0x00019000
validating tcpip.sys 0xfeea6000 0x00023000
validating netbt.sys 0xfee89000 0x0001d000
validating amdpcn.sys 0xfc770000 0x00008000
validating afd.sys 0xfc640000 0x00010000
validating netbios.sys 0xfc7b0000 0x00008000
validating Parport.SYS 0xfef54000 0x00003000
validating Parallel.SYS 0xfef4c000 0x00004000
validating ParVdm.SYS 0xfc924000 0x00002000
validating Serial.SYS 0xfc410000 0x0000b000
validating srv.sys 0xfee28000 0x00039000
validating rdr.sys 0xfede9000 0x0003f000
validating mup.sys 0xfedb0000 0x00011000
validating sfmsrv.sys 0xfed67000 0x00021000

★★★★★★★★★★★★★★
★★★★★★★★★★★★★★--> Performing a quick check (^C to end)
★★★★★★★★★★★★★★
★★★★★★★★★★★★★★
★★★★★★★★★★★★★★-->Validating all physical addresses
★★★★★★★★★★★★★★
★★★★★★★★★★★★★★
★★★★★★★★★★★★★★-->Validating all virtual addresses
★★★★★★★★★★★★★★
★★★★★★★★★★★★★★
★★★★★★★★★★★★★★-->This dump file is good!
★★★★★★★★★★★★★★
```

This utility should be run before a memory dump is analyzed and sent to Microsoft Support.

Dumpexam.exe

The Dumpexam utility is used to analyze a memory dump, extract specific information from the memory dump file, and create a text file containing specific memory dump information. This text file is considerably smaller than the raw memory dump file, Memory.dmp (recall that a raw memory dump file can be at least the size of physical memory). The default file that Dumpexam creates will be named Memory.txt and located in the %SystemRoot% folder. Memory.txt can, in some cases, provide a solution to the problem.

Two other files besides Dumpexam.exe are required to analyze a memory dump. One of the files is Imagehlp.dll; the other file is dependent on the platform being used, Kdextx86.dll, Kdextalp.dll, Kdextmip.dll, or Kdextppc.dll for x86, Alpha, MIPX, or PowerPC computers respectively. All files can be found on a Windows NT 4.0 Server or Workstation CD-ROM in the Support\Debug\<platform> folder.

The command-line syntax is shown in Figure 22.4.

FIG. 22.4 ⇒

This is an example of the Dumpexam.exe utility command-line syntax.

Examples and Explanations of Command-line Syntax for the Dumpexam Utility

Dumpexam

Will examine a memory dump file named Memory.dmp located in the %System% folder and use the platform-specific Symbols files located on the CD-ROM.

*Dumpexam -y d:\sp1\symbols;f:\support\debug\i386 -f
d:\memdump\m1dump.txt d:\memdump\memory.dmp*

Will examine a memory dump file named Memory.dmp located in the d:\memdump folder and use the symbols files located in the d:\sp1\symbols folder first, then use the symbols files located in f:\support\debug\i386 folder. It will place an output file named m1dump.txt in the d:\memdump folder.

> **Note** Symbols files are used in the order they are listed in the command-line syntax; therefore, the most recently installed service pack or hot fix symbols files must be listed in the order in which Windows NT was updated. ■

A partial example of Memory.txt is shown as follows. The intent here is to display the various areas of the Memory.txt file, not to show an error indication.

```
********************************************************************
** Windows NT Crash Dump Analysis
********************************************************************

Filename . . . . . . . .memory.dmp
Signature. . . . . . . .PAGE
ValidDump. . . . . . .DUMP
MajorVersion . . . . .free system
MinorVersion . . . . .1381
DirectoryTableBase . .0x00030000
PfnDataBase. . . . . .0x81fcf000
PsLoadedModuleList . .0x8014dd90
PsActiveProcessHead. .0x8014dc88
MachineImageType . . .I386
NumberProcessors . . .1
BugCheckCode . . . . .0x0000000a
BugCheckParameter1 . .0xfed7a026
BugCheckParameter2 . .0x00000002
BugCheckParameter3 . .0x00000000
BugCheckParameter4 . .0xfed7a026
ExceptionCode. . . . .0x80000003
ExceptionFlags . . . .0x00000001
ExceptionAddress . . .0x8013f46c
```

```
********************************************************************
** Symbol File Load Log
********************************************************************

********************************************************************
** !drivers
********************************************************************

Loaded System Driver Summary

Base Code Size Data Size Driver Name Creation Time

********************************************************************
** !locks -p -v -d
********************************************************************

**** Dump Resource Performance Data ****

0012fec8: No resource performance data available

********************************************************************
** !memusage
********************************************************************

********************************************************************
** !vm
********************************************************************
*** Virtual Memory Usage ***
  Physical Memory: 0 ( 0 Kb)

************ NO PAGING FILE *********************

  Available Pages: 0 ( 0 Kb)
  Modified Pages: -2146140568 (5372320 Kb)
  ********** High Number Of Modified Pages ********
  ********** High Number Of Modified No Write Pages ********
  Modified No Write Pages: -18306857 (-73227428 Kb)

Running out of physical memory
  NonPagedPool Usage: -515849464 (-2063397856 Kb)
  ********** Excessive NonPaged Pool Usage *****
  PagedPool Usage: 0 ( 0 Kb)
```

Shared Commit: -59289440 (-237157760 Kb)
Shared Process: 0 (0 Kb)
PagedPool Commit: 0 (0 Kb)
Driver Commit: 0 (0 Kb)
Committed pages: 0 (0 Kb)
Commit limit: 0 (0 Kb)

```
********** Number of committed pages is near limit ********

************************************************************
** !errlog
************************************************************

************************************************************
** !irpzone full
************************************************************

************************************************************
** !process 0 0
************************************************************

**** NT ACTIVE PROCESS DUMP ****
************************************************************
** !process 0 7
************************************************************

**** NT ACTIVE PROCESS DUMP ****
************************************************************
** !process
************************************************************

************************************************************
** !thread
************************************************************

************************************************************
** Register Dump For Processor #0
************************************************************
eax=00143ce0 ebx=77f02a81 ecx=00000000 edx=00140000
esi=0012ff04 edi=00000665
```

```
eip=732deba0 esp=77f13f17 ebp=0526e190 iopl=0 nv up di pl nz na
pe nc
cs=0000   ss=0000   ds=77f028fa   es=12ff00   fs=0000
gs=0000      efl=732d0000
cr0=0012fed4 cr2=00000000 cr3=0012ff28 dr0=77f3be08 dr1=ffffffff
dr2=0012ff38
dr3=05262c22 dr6=00143ce0 dr7=00000001 cr4=77f3ae5c
gdtr=00000000 gdtl=0014 idtr=0012ff10 idtl=0014 tr=ff34 ldtr=0012
```

```
*******************************************************************
** Stack Trace
*******************************************************************
ChildEBP RetAddr Args to Child
ffffffffc 00000000 00000000 00000000 00000000
0x00143ce0+0x12d0e4

 FFFFFFB0: 00 00 add byte ptr [eax],al
 FFFFFFB2: 00 00 add byte ptr [eax],al
 FFFFFFB4: 00 00 add byte ptr [eax],al
 FFFFFFB6: 00 00 add byte ptr [eax],al
 FFFFFFB8: 00 00 add byte ptr [eax],al
 FFFFFFBA: 00 00 add byte ptr [eax],al
 FFFFFFBC: 00 00 add byte ptr [eax],al
 FFFFFFBE: 00 00 add byte ptr [eax],al
 FFFFFFC0: 00 00 add byte ptr [eax],al
 FFFFFFC2: 00 00 add byte ptr [eax],al
 FFFFFFC4: 00 00 add byte ptr [eax],al
 FFFFFFC6: 00 00 add byte ptr [eax],al
 FFFFFFC8: 00 00 add byte ptr [eax],al
 FFFFFFCA: 00 00 add byte ptr [eax],al
 FFFFFFCC: 00 00 add byte ptr [eax],al
 FFFFFFCE: 00 00 add byte ptr [eax],al
 FFFFFFD0: 00 00 add byte ptr [eax],al
 FFFFFFD2: 00 00 add byte ptr [eax],al
 FFFFFFD4: 00 00 add byte ptr [eax],al
 FFFFFFD6: 00 00 add byte ptr [eax],al
```

```
FFFFFFD8: 00 00 add byte ptr [eax],al
FFFFFFDA: 00 00 add byte ptr [eax],al
FFFFFFDC: 00 00 add byte ptr [eax],al
FFFFFFDE: 00 00 add byte ptr [eax],al
FFFFFFE0: 00 00 add byte ptr [eax],al
FFFFFFE2: 00 00 add byte ptr [eax],al
FFFFFFE4: 00 00 add byte ptr [eax],al
FFFFFFE6: 00 00 add byte ptr [eax],al
FFFFFFE8: 00 00 add byte ptr [eax],al
FFFFFFEA: 00 00 add byte ptr [eax],al
FFFFFFEC: 00 00 add byte ptr [eax],al
FFFFFFEE: 00 00 add byte ptr [eax],al
FFFFFFF0: 00 00 add byte ptr [eax],al
FFFFFFF2: 00 00 add byte ptr [eax],al
FFFFFFF4: 00 00 add byte ptr [eax],al
FFFFFFF6: 00 00 add byte ptr [eax],al
FFFFFFF8: 00 00 add byte ptr [eax],al
FFFFFFFA: 00 00 add byte ptr [eax],al
FFFFFFFC: 00 00 add byte ptr [eax],al
FFFFFFFE: 00 00 add byte ptr [eax],al
--->00000000: 00 00 add byte ptr [eax],al
00000002: 00 00 add byte ptr [eax],al
00000004: 00 00 add byte ptr [eax],al
00000006: 00 00 add byte ptr [eax],al
00000008: 00 00 add byte ptr [eax],al
0000000A: 00 00 add byte ptr [eax],al
0000000C: 00 00 add byte ptr [eax],al
0000000E: 00 00 add byte ptr [eax],al
00000010: 00 00 add byte ptr [eax],al
00000012: 00 00 add byte ptr [eax],al
00000014: 00 00 add byte ptr [eax],al
00000016: 00 00 add byte ptr [eax],al
00000018: 00 00 add byte ptr [eax],al
0000001A: 00 00 add byte ptr [eax],al
0000001C: 00 00 add byte ptr [eax],al
```

```
0000001E: 00 00 add byte ptr [eax],al
 00000020:  00  00  add  byte  ptr  [eax],al
00000022: 00 00 add byte ptr [eax],al
00000024: 00 00 add byte ptr [eax],al
00000026: 00 00 add byte ptr [eax],al
00000028: 00 00 add byte ptr [eax],al
0000002A: 00 00 add byte ptr [eax],al
0000002C: 00 00 add byte ptr [eax],al
0000002E: 00 00 add byte ptr [eax],al
00000030: 00 00 add byte ptr [eax],al
00000032: 00 00 add byte ptr [eax],al
00000034: 00 00 add byte ptr [eax],al
00000036: 00 00 add byte ptr [eax],al
00000038: 00 00 add byte ptr [eax],al
0000003A: 00 00 add byte ptr [eax],al
0000003C: 00 00 add byte ptr [eax],al
0000003E: 00 00 add byte ptr [eax],al
00000040: 00 00 add byte ptr [eax],al
00000042: 00 00 add byte ptr [eax],al
00000044: 00 00 add byte ptr [eax],al
00000046: 00 00 add byte ptr [eax],al
00000048: 00 00 add byte ptr [eax],al
0000004A: 00 00 add byte ptr [eax],al
0000004C: 00 00 add byte ptr [eax],al
0000004E: 00 00 add byte ptr [eax],al
```

Dumpflop.exe

The Dumpflop utility is used to copy a dump file in pieces to floppy disks to send to support personnel to analyze. This method is probably the least efficient way to send information; however, it may be the only way at a particular time because of other problems.

Compression is used when copying information to the floppies. A 16M memory dump will fit on five or six floppy disks. The command-line syntax is shown in Figure 22.5.

FIG. 22.5 ⇒
This is an example of the Dumpflop.exe utility command-line syntax.

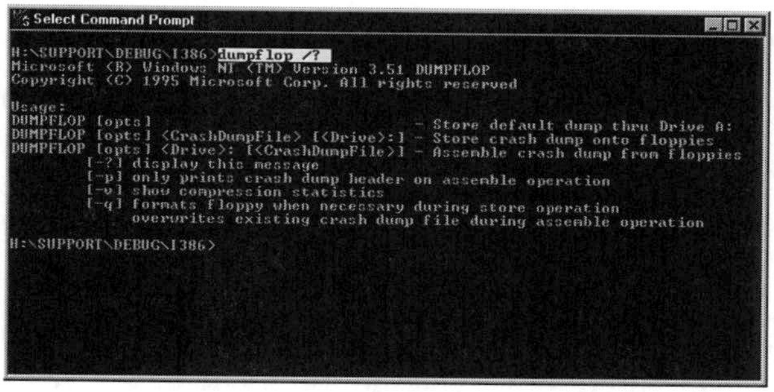

```
H:\SUPPORT\DEBUG\I386>dumpflop /?
Microsoft (R) Windows NT (TM) Version 3.51 DUMPFLOP
Copyright (C) 1995 Microsoft Corp. All rights reserved

Usage:
DUMPFLOP [opts]                                  - Store default dump thru Drive A:
DUMPFLOP [opts] <CrashDumpFile> [<Drive>:]       - Store crash dump onto floppies
DUMPFLOP [opts] <Drive>: [<CrashDumpFile>]       - Assemble crash dump from floppies
        [-?] display this message
        [-p] only prints crash dump header on assemble operation
        [-v] show compression statistics
        [-q] formats floppy when necessary during store operation
             overwrites existing crash dump file during assemble operation

H:\SUPPORT\DEBUG\I386>
```

Kernel Debugger Sessions

If a system is continually crashing during the boot process, the Kernel Debugger option to find the cause of the crash is to configure a Kernel Debugger session. However, before you dive into the process of configuring and using the Windows NT 4.0 Kernel Debugger programs, you must understand debugging terminology.

Host Computer

A host computer is one that is used to troubleshoot a failing computer (target computer). The host computer is the system that runs the debugger programs and has access to the Symbols files. It is physically attached to the target computer by a null modem cable or a modem connection. It must also be running at least the same version of Windows NT software as the target computer.

Target Computer

A target computer is the system on which stop errors are occurring. It is the system that is connected to the host computer by a null modem cable or a modem connection and configured to send information to the host computer to be analyzed. It is the system that needs to be debugged.

Symbols Files and Trees

When source code for executable programs, drivers, dynamic-link libraries, and various other files is compiled for Windows NT, the resultant object code is in two forms or versions: a debug or checked version, and a non-debug or free version. All files that Windows NT normally uses are a much smaller version of the object code, the non-debug version. However, each and every non-debug file has a corresponding debug version used for troubleshooting. The debug versions of the files are referred to as Symbols files; they contain debug codes and are only used as reference codes to debug a broken system.

Symbols files are located on the CD-ROM for both Windows NT Server and Workstation in the Support\Debug\<platform>\Symbols folder. Also note that Symbols files exist for both service packs and hot fixes, and must be obtained to troubleshoot stop errors if Windows NT updates are installed.

The Symbols folder for each platform contains a number of subfolders that contain the actual compressed Symbols (.db_) files. There is a subfolder for each type of Symbols file such as .exe or .dll. These files must be decompressed before using. Decompressing Symbols files is accomplished by running a program called Expndsym.cmd located in the Support\Debug folder on the Windows NT 4.0 Server and Workstation CD-ROMs.

Figure 22.6 presents the directory structure of a Windows NT 4.0 Server CD-ROM with the Support\Debug\I386\Symbols\Exe folder displayed.

Kernel Debugger Programs and Files

There are a number of executable files needed to perform Kernel Debugging. These programs are executed on a host computer and used to debug the kernel on a target computer. The programs listed in Table 22.4 are found on the Windows NT Server or Workstation CD-ROM in the Support\Debug\<platform> folder (<platform> = Alpha, I386, Mips, or Ppc).

FIG. 22.6 ⇒

Here is an example
of the Symbols files
and the Symbols
tree structure.

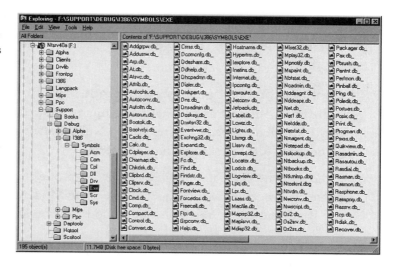

Table 22.4   Kernel Debugger Programs

Program/File	Usage
Alphakd.exe	Kernel Debugger for Alpha computers
I386kd.exe	Kernel Debugger for Intel computers
Mipskd.exe	Kernel Debugger for MIPS computers
Ppckd.exe	Kernel Debugger for PowerPC computers

Configuring Kernel Debugger Session

To configure a Kernel Debugger session, a minimum of two computers
must be used: a host computer and the target computer. The two computers must be connected together, either locally with a null modem
cable, or remotely with a modem connection. The host computer must
be running the same platform and version of Windows NT software as
the target computer. Use the following steps to enable Kernel Debugging:

1. Connect the host computer and the target computer together.

2. Configure the host computer.

3. Configure the target computer.

4. Start the Kernel Debugger on the host computer.

5. Reboot the target computer.

Connect the Host and Target Computers

If the host computer and the target computer are in close proximity, they can be connected together with a Null Modem cable attached to an unused COM port in each computer.

If the computers are in remote locations from one another, they can be connected together using modems. Select the Modem icon in the Control Panel and ensure the following options are configured:

Auto Answer	On
Hardware Compression	Disabled
Error Detection	Disabled
Flow Control	Disabled

The default baud rate for Intel computers is 9,600 baud, for RISC computers it is 19,200 baud.

Configure the Host Computer

The host computer, during the debugger process, requires access to the Symbols files. Copying these files to the host computer is accomplished using the Expndsym.cmd program found on the Windows NT 4.0 Server and Workstation CD-ROMs in the Support\Debug folder. An example of the required syntax for Expndsym.cmd is:

expndsym <Windows NT CDROM drive> <destination path>

expndsym f: c:\debug   will copy and expand the Symbols files from a CD-ROM drive f: to the c:\debug\symbols folder.

The next step in the Kernel Debugger process is to either set up a batch file or run the required commands from the command prompt to start the platform-specific Kernel Debugger program. An example batch file is illustrated later in the section "Start the Kernel Debugger."

The following list describes Kernel Debugger startup options:

- **-b** Causes the debugger to stop execution on the target com puter as soon as possible by causing a debug breakpoint (INT 3).

- **-c** Causes the debugger to request a resync on connect.

- **-m** Causes the debugger to monitor modem control lines.

- **-n** Causes symbols to be loaded immediately rather than in a deferred mode.

- **-v** Verbose mode, displays more information.

- **-x** Causes the debugger to break in when an exception first occurs, rather than letting the application or module that caused the exception deal with it.

 Note The most common used startup options are the -m and -v options. ▦

Configure the Target Computer

If the target computer is an Intel system, the debugger process is started simply by configuring the boot.ini file to include one of the following options at the end of the specific boot.ini selection used to start the system.

/debug	Causes the Kernel Debugger to be loaded during the boot process and is kept in memory. Because the Kernel Debugger stays in memory, the system can be accessed remotely and debugged.
/debugport	Specifies the serial port to be used by the Kernel Debugger. Default is com2 for Intel computers and com1 for RISC computers.
/crashdebug	Causes the kernel debugger to be loaded during boot but swapped out to the pagefile after the boot process. Remote access and debugging cannot be done in this mode.
/baudrate	Sets the speed that the Kernel Debugger will use in bits per second. Default is 9,600 for Intel computers and 19,200 for RISC computers.

Note If the /baudrate option is used, the /debug option is assumed and does not have to be entered. ■

If the target computer is a RISC system, one line in the startup file has to be edited; however, that file is accessed differently on an Alpha system than on a MIPS or PowerPC system.

On an Alpha or PowerPC system, access the Boot Selections menu by selecting the Supplementary choice from the System Boot menu, then select the Setup the System choice from the Supplementary menu.

On a MIPS system, select the Run Setup choice to access the Setup menu, then select Manage Startup to display a boot options menu.

Start the Kernel Debugger

The Kernel Debugger program can be started from the command line or from a preconfigured batch file. Shown in the following figure is an example batch file that will configure the COM port, path to the Symbols files, open a debug.log file, start a remote session, and execute the I386 debugger program with the v (verbose) and m (modem monitoring) options using the Remote utility, which also starts a session named "debug." The results of the batch file are shown in Figure 22.7.

FIG. 22.7 ⇒

This is an example of how to start a Kernel Debugger session.

```
i386kd - [Remote /C WORKSTATION1 debug]
C:\debug>kd
C:\debug>REM local debug batch file named kd.bat
C:\debug>set _NT_DEBUG_PORT=com2
C:\debug>set _NT_DEBUG_BAUD_RATE=19200
C:\debug>set _NT_SYMBOL_PATH=c:\debug\symbols
C:\debug>set _NT_LOG_FILE_OPEN=c:\debug\debug.log
C:\debug>REMOTE /S "i386kd -M -v" debug
***********************************************
**********    REMOTE    ***********
**********    SERVER    ***********
***********************************************
To Connect: Remote /C WORKSTATION1 debug

Microsoft(R) Windows NT Kernel Debugger
Version 4.00
Copyright (C) Microsoft Corp. 1981-1996

Symbol search path is: c:\debug\symbols
KD: waiting to reconnect...
```

Once the Kernel Debugger program is running, commands can be entered to view various types of information or get a list of options.

Before any of the following commands can be entered at the host computer, the Ctrl + C key sequence must be entered (see Table 22.5).

Table 22.5   Kernel Debugger Commands Entered at the Host Computer

Command	Action
!reload	Reloads the Symbol files.
!kb	Displays a stack trace from the last frame dumped by !trap (see below).
!errlog	If not empty, will display information about the component or process that caused the STOP error.
!process	Lists information about the process running on the active processor.
!thread	Lists currently running threads.
!kv	Verbose stack trace used to find the trap frame.
!trap <trap frame address>	Dumps the computer state when the trap frame occurred.
!process 0 0	Lists all processes and their headers.
!drivers	Lists the drivers currently loaded.
!vm	Lists the system's virtual memory usage.
.reboot	Restarts the target computer.
g	Releases the target computer.

If the Kernel Debugger is started using the Remote utility as in the following example, other computers on the network can connect to the session "debug" and view the debugger information. The Remote utility can be found on the Windows NT 4.0 Resource Kit utility CD-ROM. Example syntax for the Remote utility is shown in Figure 22.8.

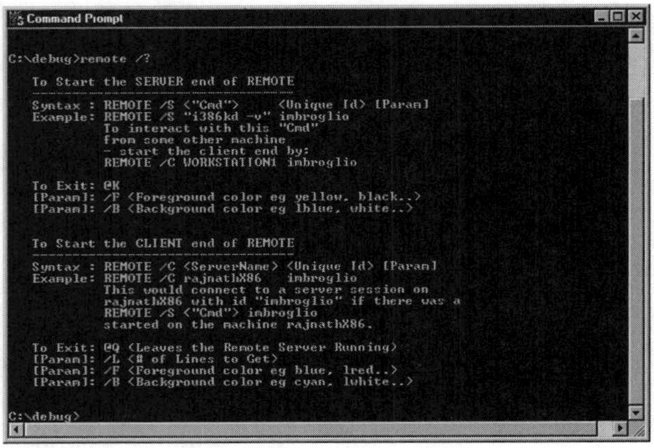

FIG. 22.8 ⇒

This figure shows examples of the Remote utility command-line syntax.

Reboot the Target Computer

To start recording the boot information on the host computer, simply reboot the target computer. As various drivers and dynamic link libraries load, they are displayed on the host computer. When the target computer halts with a stop error, the exact point of failure can be determined.

The following are the results of a Kernel Debugger session retrieved during the boot process of a Windows NT 4.0 Workstation, Build Level 1381 with Service Pack 2 installed without a failure.

KD: waiting to reconnect

Kernel Version 1381 UP Free
Kernel base = 0x80100000 PsLoadedModuleList = 0x8014dd90
KD ModLoad: 80100000 801d4cc0 ntoskrnl.exe
KD ModLoad: 80010000 8001c920 hal.dll
KD ModLoad: 80001000 80007000 atapi.sys
KD ModLoad: 80007000 8000ee80 SCSIPORT.SYS
KD ModLoad: 801d5000 801d8a60 Disk.sys
KD ModLoad: 801d9000 801dc2e0 CLASS2.SYS
KD ModLoad: 80086000 800872e0 Diskperf.sys
KD ModLoad: 801dd000 801ff000 Fastfat.sys
KD ModLoad: 77f60000 77fbc000 ntdll.dll
KD ModLoad: f96e0000 f96e48e0 Floppy.SYS

```
KD ModLoad: f9900000 f9901fa0 Sfloppy.SYS
KD ModLoad: f985c000 f985e500 Scsiscan.SYS
KD ModLoad: f96f0000 f96f5560 Cdrom.SYS
KD ModLoad: f9906000 f9907c40 Changer.SYS
KD ModLoad: f9708000 f970d0a0 Cdaudio.SYS
KD ModLoad: f990a000 f990b820 Fs_Rec.SYS
KD ModLoad: f99c9000 f99c99e0 Null.SYS
KD ModLoad: f9864000 f9866380 KSecDD.SYS
KD ModLoad: f99ca000 f99caea0 Beep.SYS
KD ModLoad: f9400000 f940ae40 sndblst.SYS
KD ModLoad: f9870000 f9873720 sermouse.sys
KD ModLoad: f9730000 f9736120 i8042prt.sys
KD ModLoad: f987c000 f987e340 mouclass.sys
KD ModLoad: f9884000 f9886340 kbdclass.sys
KD ModLoad: f9748000 f974d3e0 VIDEOPRT.SYS
KD ModLoad: f988c000 f988f840 vga.sys
KD ModLoad: f9760000 f97670e0 tgiul40.sys
KD ModLoad: f9894000 f9897840 vga.sys
KD ModLoad: f9778000 f977d680 Msfs.SYS
KD ModLoad: f9410000 f9419360 Npfs.SYS
KD ModLoad: fec44000 fec62fc0 NDIS.SYS
KD ModLoad: f989c000 f989e020 ndistapi.sys
KD ModLoad: febe9000 fec435c0 Ntfs.SYS
KD ModLoad: a0000000 a0132580 win32k.sys
KD ModLoad: febab000 febc00c0 vga.dll
KD ModLoad: f97d8000 f97dde00 tgiul40.dll
KD ModLoad: f98c8000 f98ca1a0 framebuf.dll
KD ModLoad: febab000 febc00c0 vga.dll
KD ModLoad: f97e8000 f97ede00 tgiul40.dll
KD ModLoad: f9620000 f962eec0 Cdfs.SYS
KD ModLoad: f998c000 f998dea0 rasacd.sys
KD ModLoad: feab5000 feab74e0 TDI.SYS
KD ModLoad: fea52000 fea70820 sfmatalk.sys
KD ModLoad: fea39000 fea51560 nbf.sys
KD ModLoad: fea27000 fea38560 nwlnkipx.sys
```

KD ModLoad: fea16000 fea261a0 nwlnknb.sys
KD ModLoad: fe9f5000 fea15820 tcpip.sys
KD ModLoad: fe9d9000 fe9f4040 netbt.sys
KD ModLoad: f9430000 f94397e0 asyncmac.sys
KD ModLoad: febe1000 febe4f40 ne2000.sys
KD ModLoad: f9440000 f944de00 ndiswan.sys
KD ModLoad: f9450000 f945f6c0 afd.sys
KD ModLoad: f9710000 f97170c0 netbios.sys
KD ModLoad: fea7d000 fea7f640 Parport.SYS
KD ModLoad: fea75000 fea78900 Parallel.SYS
KD ModLoad: f99a8000 f99a9780 ParVdm.SYS
KD ModLoad: f98e0000 f98e25a0 Scsiprnt.SYS
KD ModLoad: f94a0000 f94aaf20 Serial.SYS
KD ModLoad: f9780000 f9785ee0 nwlnkrip.sys
KD ModLoad: fe922000 fe960d60 rdr.sys
KD ModLoad: fe835000 fe8595c0 nwrdr.sys
KD ModLoad: fe7fc000 fe834ba0 srv.sys
KD ModLoad: f9550000 f955e3c0 nwlnkspx.sys
KD ModLoad: fe7eb000 fe7fb700 mup.sys
LDR: Automatic DLL Relocation in Explorer.exe
LDR: Dll SHLWAPI.dll base bfe50000 relocated due to collision with
Dynamically Allocated Memory
KD ModLoad: fe621000 fe632be0 RASDD.DLL

 Note Explorer.exe started after the logon process and RASDD.DLL was loaded when a word processor was started in the host computer. ■

Remote Troubleshooting

As mentioned previously, the host computer and the target computer can be near each other and connected together using a Null Modem cable; however, if the systems are apart from each other, modems can be used. This type of troubleshooting scenario implies that someone from a support team is available to diagnose the error. If this is not the case, a remote session can be established with technical support such as Microsoft Technical Support team through RAS.

The procedure is very similar to the one covered previously with some additions. RAS must either be configured on the host computer or some other system on the network that can access the host server; and another computer is required at some remote technical support area. Here are the steps required to access a Kernel Debugger session from a remote location:

1. The target computer is connected to a host computer. The host computer is either a RAS server or can access a RAS server.

2. The host computer is configured as previously mentioned in the section "Configure the Host Computer."

3. The target computer is configured as previously mentioned in the section "Configure the Target Computer."

4. The Kernel Debugger program is started on the host computer with the Remote utility as previously mentioned in the section "Start the Kernel Debugger." The example given was REMOTE /s "i386kd -m -v" debug.

5. From the Remote computer, establish a RAS session with the RAS server (the host computer if it is a RAS server, or a RAS server that has access to the host computer).

6. From the Remote computer, establish a connection with the Kernel Debugger session from the Remote computer using the Remote utility. An example would be:

   REMOTE /c <host computer name> debug

7. The target computer is then rebooted as previously mentioned in the section "Reboot the Target Computer."

8. The Kernel Debugger session can now be monitored and controlled by the technical support person at the remote computer.

Events and Event Log Viewer

An *event* is defined as a significant incident in the system, the security of the system, or in an application that requires someone to be notified.

Some events, such as a disk drive becoming full, are considered critical events and cause a message to be presented on the screen immediately to alert the user of the problem. Other events that do not need immediate attention are recorded in one of three types of event logs and can be viewed by the Event viewer.

Event viewer is a diagnostic tool within Windows NT 4.0 that can be extremely useful in troubleshooting various types of problems encountered with the system, with security, or with applications. Events of each type can also be viewed from other computers on the network.

Event logging is a service in Windows NT 4.0 and is, by default, started each time Windows NT is booted. As stated previously, events are logged in three categories: system, security, and application.

◆ System   The system log contains entries logged by system components or services such as a network adapter card or the browser service.

◆ Security   The security log contains entries caused by activities such as someone accessing a resource or logging on to the system. By default, security log auditing is disabled. Auditing must be enabled from User Manager for Domains before a security log will be produced. How to enable auditing and what events are available for security log auditing will be covered later in this chapter.

◆ Application   An application log contains entries logged from various applications being run in the system. Dr. Watson and Autochk events can be found in this log.

Key Concept

The system and application logs can be viewed by everyone including normal users; however, security logs can only be viewed by administrators. If a normal user tries to access the security log, an `Access is Denied` message is displayed.

Event Log Options

Event viewer is started from the Start, Programs, Administrative Tools program group. Once started, by selecting the <u>L</u>og drop-down menu, either the S<u>y</u>stem, the Se<u>c</u>urity, or the <u>A</u>pplications log can be selected. Figure 22.9 displays the <u>L</u>og drop-down menu.

FIG. 22.9 ⇒

This figure shows the Event Viewer, <u>L</u>og drop-down menu.

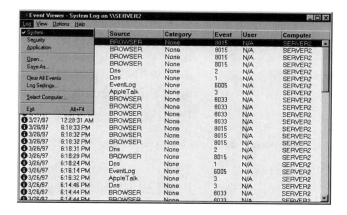

Other options available from the <u>L</u>og drop-down menu are as follows:

- ◆ <u>O</u>pen   Allows you to open and view any .evt file that was previously saved.

- ◆ Sa<u>v</u>e As   Allows you to save a log file.

- ◆ C<u>l</u>ear All Events   Allows you to clear an event log. Before the log is cleared, a message is displayed asking you if you want to save the log.

◆ Log Settings

Allows you to change the default log settings. Settings can be adjusted for each log independently and include size and wrapping settings. Default maximum log size is 512K with a range of 64K to 4,194,240K in 64K increments. Wrapping settings include Overwrite Events as Needed, Overwrite Events Older Than <days> Days, or Do Not Overwrite Events (Clear Manually). The default setting is to overwrite events older than seven days.

◆ Select Computer

Allows you to select any Windows NT computer on the network. LAN Manager 2.x servers can also be selected to view system and security logs only. When Select Computer is chosen, a Select Computer dialog box appears. If the computer selected is available over a slow WAN link, select Low Speed Connection on the dialog box.

◆ Exit

Exit Event Viewer.

The View drop-down menu has the following options:

◆ All Events

This is the default setting; Event viewer will list all events in the selected log.

◆ Filter Events

From this option, you can specify time ranges of when events should be displayed. You can also select event types to be displayed, and from what source, category, user, computer, or by event ID.

◆ Newest First

This is the default setting. As events occur, they are put on top of the list and displayed that way.

◆ Oldest First

Can be selected to list the oldest events first.

◆ Find

Events can be searched for by type, or by source, category, ID, computer, user, or description.

◆ <u>D</u>etail   Displays more information about the selected
                 event. The Event Detail dialog box can also be
                 accessed by double-clicking any event in the
                 Event Viewer display box.

◆ Refresh   Causes the Event Viewer display box to be
                 refreshed.

The <u>O</u>ptions drop-down menu allows for selecting low speed connections, save settings on exit (set by default), or a different font for the
Event viewer display. Select Low Speed Connection if you are analyzing
event logs from other computers over a slow WAN connection. The
only other drop-down menu is <u>H</u>elp.

Event Log Headings

Once an Event Log is displayed using Event viewer, various headings
appear across the top of the display. Their meanings are displayed in
Figure 22.10 and described in the following list.

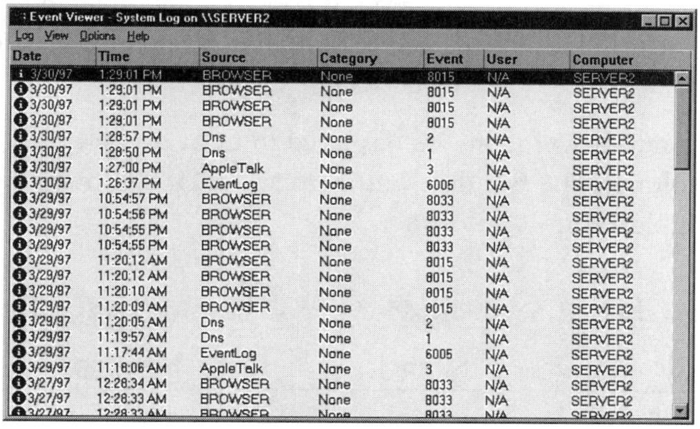

FIG. 22.10 ⇒

Here is a display of
the Event Log
screen headings.

◆ Date   Date the event occurred.

◆ Time   Time the event occurred.

◆ Source   Software that logged the event. This could be an
             application, a network adapter driver, a service, and
             so on.

◆ Category   This heading has meaning mostly in the security log but also is used in the application log. It is how the event source has classified the event. In the security log, whatever classification of event was configured in User Manager for Domains will appear in this column. For example, if the logon/logoff service logged the event, logon/logoff will appear in this column.

◆ Event   The Event column identifies an event type or ID. This relates back to source code and can be used by support personnel to cross-check events with the source code.

◆ User   The user logged on to the system or the client name if the event was caused by the server service when a client was accessing this computer.

◆ Computer   The name of the computer where the event occurred. This value is usually the local computer; however, if you are looking at an event log from another computer on the network, that computer name will be displayed.

A number of icons are displayed in front of the events under the Event column. The five different icons and their meanings are described in Table 22.6.

Table 22.6   Event Icons and Their Meanings

Icon	Symbol	Meaning
Error	Stop Sign	Serious Problem. If services did not load because of network adapter card settings, the services will be displayed with this type of error.

Icon	Symbol	Meaning
Warning	Exclamation Point	Not as serious as Error events; however, could cause more serious problems at a later time such as disk space getting low on a particular disk drive.
Information	Blue Circle	Usually describes successful operations such as browser, DNS, and AppleTalk events. They are for information only.
Success Audit	Paddle Lock	A security event that was successful such as a successful logon.
Failed Audit	Key	A security event that was not successful such as an unsuccessful logon attempt.

Event Details

Select an event in the Event Viewer display screen and press Enter, or double-click the selected event, or select the View drop-down menu and choose the Details selection. In any case, an Event Detail screen is displayed. This screen, in addition to the information already displayed on the Event Viewer display, will show a description window with additional information about the selected event. This information varies depending on the selected event; for example, a master browser was successfully elected, a duplicate IP address was detected on the network, an unsuccessful logon attempt was made in the security log, or a printer became available to the AppleTalk network in the application log.

The Data window at the bottom of the Event Detail screen can contain optional data in the form of either bytes or words. It is additional data created by the event source and is displayed in hexadecimal format. The meaning of this data can be interpreted by support personnel familiar with the source application. Not all events display information in this area. On the very bottom of the Event Detail screen are the Close, Previous, Next, and Help buttons. An example of the Event Detail screen is shown in Figure 22.11.

FIG. 22.11 ⟹

This is an example of an Event Detail dialog box for an event log.

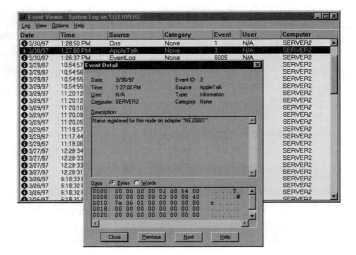

Troubleshooting Problems Using Event Viewer

To mention or display each and every possible event would be impossible; however, some general guidelines can be mentioned for using Event Viewer to troubleshoot system, security, and application problems.

◆ Monitor the system event log regularly on file and print servers to look for low disk space warning errors and bad sector retry warnings.

◆ Monitor the application event log if an application is crashing and you need to try to find out why by searching for any events concerning that application.

◆ Monitor the security event log for any of the security event choices selected in User Manager or User Manager for Domains, by choosing Policies, Audit selection.

♦ When analyzing events, always look for events that happened in a specific time frame. Start viewing detailed information of these events from the newest to the oldest. This will give you a complete picture of a failure. For example, the browser did not start because the workstation or server service did not start because the network adapter card settings were detected wrong. In this case, the browser was not the problem; the network adapter card setting configuration was the problem.

♦ Through Registry editing, you can halt the computer if the security log is full. First of all, either the default Overwrite Events Older Than x Days setting or the Do Not Overwrite Events (Clear Log Manually) must be selected from the Log drop-down menu, Settings option. Next, in the HKEY_LOCAL_MACHINE\System\CurrentControlSet\Control\Lsa key, add the CrashOnAuditFail value, type **REG_WORD**, to set it to 1. If the system halts, it has to be restarted by an administrator, the auditing security events must be turned off, and the security log cleared.

♦ An event log can be saved three different ways, in an Event Log File (.EVT), a regular Text file (.TXT), or in a Comma Delimited Text (.TXT) file. If a log is saved in Event Log File format, the log can be viewed later by Event Viewer. If it is saved in a regular Text file, it can be incorporated into a word processor application; and if saved in a Comma Delimited Text file, it can be incorporated into a spreadsheet or database application. All hexadecimal data is lost if saved in any of the three types of text format.

Taking the Disc Test

 If you have read and understood the material in the chapter, you are ready to test your knowledge. Insert the CD-ROM that comes with this book and run the self-test software as described in Appendix I, "Using the CD-ROM."

From Here...

This is the final chapter in the book. Following this chapter are a number of appendixes including the Glossary, "Windows NT 4.0 Overview," "Certification Checklist," "Testing Tips," "Contacting Microsoft," "Suggested Reading," "Networking Basics," "Internet Resources for Windows NT," "Using the CD-ROM," and "Sample Tests."

Good luck on your test!

Part VII.

Appendixes

Glossary

A

access-control entry (ACE) An entry in an access-control list that defines a set of permissions for a group or user.

access-control list (ACL) A list containing access-control entries. An ACL determines the permissions associated with an object, which can be anything in a Win32 environment.

access time The last time a file was run (if the file is executable). Otherwise, it is the last time the file was read or written to.

ACE See *access-control entry*.

ACK Short for acknowledgment. A control character sent to the other computer in a conversation. Usually used to indicate that transmitted information has been received correctly, when using a communications protocol such as Xmodem.

ACL   See *access-control list*.

active window   The window the user is currently working with. Windows identifies the active window by highlighting its title bar and border.

Advanced Program-to-Program Communications (APPC) A method of interprogram communication, usually used by applications intended for use with IBM SNA-based networks.

Advanced Research Project Agency (ARPA)   The agency responsible for the formation of the forerunner of the Internet. See *Defense Advanced Research Projects Agency*.

agent   Software that runs on a client computer for use by administrative software running on a server. Agents are typically used to support administrative actions, such as detecting system information or running services.

Alerter Service   A Windows NT Executive service that notifies selected users or computers of system-generated administrative alerts.

American National Standards Institute (ANSI)   A standards-making organization based in the U. S.

American Standard Code for Information Interchange (ASCII)   A scheme that assigns letters, punctuation marks, and so on, to specific numeric values. The standardization of ASCII enabled computers and computer programs to exchange data.

ANSI   See *American National Standards Institute*.

ANSI character set   An 8-bit character set used by Microsoft Windows that enables you to represent up to 256 characters (0-255) using your keyboard. The ASCII character set is a subset of the ANSI set. See *American National Standards Institute*.

API   See *application programming interface*.

APPC   See *Advanced Program-to-Program Communications*.

application   A computer program that is designed to do some specific type of work. An application is different from a utility, which performs some type of maintenance (such as formatting a disk).

application programming interface (API)   An API is a list of supported functions. Windows NT 4.0 supports the MS-DOS API, Windows API, and Win32 API. If a function is a member of the API, it is said to be a supported, or documented function. Functions that make up Windows, but are not part of the API, are referred to as *undocumented* functions. An API can also be a low-level software routine that programmers can use to send requests to the operating system.

ARPA   See *Advanced Research Project Agency*.

ASCII   See *American Standard Code for Information Interchange*.

ASCII character set   A 7-bit character set widely used to represent letters and symbols found on a standard U.S. keyboard. The ASCII character set is identical to the first 128 characters in the ANSI character set.

association   The process of assigning a file name extension to a particular application. When an extension has been associated with an application, Windows NT 4.0 will start the application when you choose to open the file from the Windows Explorer. Associations are critical to the concept of document-centric computing.

attributes   A characteristic of a file that indicates whether it is hidden, system, read-only, archive, or compressed.

Audio Video Interleaved (AVI)   The format of the full-motion video files used by Windows NT 4.0.

Audit Policy   A definition of the type of security-related events that will be recorded by the Event Viewer.

authentication   The validation of a user's access to a computer or domain by either the local computer (local validation) or a backup domain controller for the domain that the user is accessing.

Autoexec.bat   A file in the root directory of the boot disk that contains a list of MS-DOS commands that are automatically executed when the system is started. Autoexec.bat can be created by either the user or the operating system. Windows NT 4.0 Setup examines the Autoexec.bat file looking for configuration information such as user environment variables.

auxiliary audio device   Audio devices whose output is mixed with the *Musical Instrument Digital Interface* (MIDI) and waveform output devices in a multimedia computer. An example of an auxiliary audio device is the compact disc audio output from a CD-ROM drive.

AVI   See *Audio Video Interleaved*.

B

background window   Any window created by a thread other than the thread running in the foreground.

Backup Domain Controller (BDC)   The Windows NT controller server which performs the validation of user logon requests. The Backup Domain Controller obtains a copy of the master account database for the domain from the Primary Domain Controller.

Basic Input/Output System (BIOS)   The bootstrap code of a PC. The low-level routines that support the transfer of information between the various parts of a computer system, such as memory, disks, and the monitor. Usually built into the machine's read-only memory (ROM). The BIOS can have a significant effect on the performance of the computer system.

batch program   A file that contains one or more commands that are executed when you type the file name at the command prompt. Batch programs have the .BAT extension.

BID   See *board interface drivers*.

binding   The process that links a protocol driver with a network adapter driver.

BIOS   See *Basic Input/Output System.*

BIOS enumerator   In a Plug and Play system, the BIOS enumerator is responsible for identifying all of the hardware devices on the computer's motherboard.

bit   Short for binary digit, the smallest unit of data a computer can store. Bits are expressed as 1 or 0.

bitmap   Originally, an array of bits, but now expanded to include arrays of bytes or even 32-bit quantities that specify the dot pattern and colors that describe an image on the screen or printed paper.

BMP   The extension used for Windows bitmap files.

Boot Loader   This defines the location of the Windows NT boot and system files.

Boot Partition   The partition that contains the Windows NT system files.

Bootstrap Protocol (BOOTP)   This is an internetworking protocol that is used to configure TCP/IP networks across routers.

branch   A segment of the directory tree, representing a directory and any subdirectories it contains.

browse   To look through a list on a computer system. Lists include directories, files, domains, or computers.

buffer   A temporary holding place reserved in memory, where data is held while in transit to or from a storage device or another location in memory.

buffering   The process of using buffers, particularly to or from I/O devices such as disk drives and serial ports.

bus enumerator   A driver, responsible for building the hardware tree on a Plug and Play system.

byte   8 binary digits (bits) combined to represent a single character or value.

C

Card Services A protected-mode *VxD*, linked with the *PCMCIA* bus drivers. Card Services passes event notifications from socket services to the PCMCIA bus driver, provides information from the computer's cards to the PCMCIA bus driver, and sets up the configuration for cards in the adapter sockets.

cascading menu A menu that is a submenu of a menu item. Also known as a hierarchical menu. The menus accessed via the Windows NT 4.0 Start button are cascading menus.

CCITT See *International Telephone and Telegraph Consultative Committee*.

CD See *compact disc*.

CD-DA See *Compact Disc-Digital Audio*.

CD-ROM See *Compact Disc Read-Only Memory*.

CD-ROM/XA See *Compact Disc Read-Only Memory Extended Architecture*.

CD-XA See *Compact Disc-Extended Architecture*.

CDFS See *compact disc file system*.

central processing unit (CPU) The computational and control unit of a computer; the device that interprets and executes instructions. The CPU, or microprocessor in the case of a microcomputer, has the ability to fetch, decode, and execute instructions as well as transfer information to and from other resources over the computer's main data-transfer path, the bus. The CPU is the chip that functions as the "brain" of a computer.

character A letter, number, punctuation mark, or a control code. Usually expressed in either the ANSI or ASCII character set.

character mode A mode of displaying information on the screen, where all information is displayed using text characters (as opposed to graphical symbols). MS-DOS applications run in character mode.

check box   In the Windows NT 4.0 interface, a square box that has two or three states, and is used by the user to select an option from a set of options. A standard check box is a toggle, with two states: checked and unchecked. A three-state check box has an additional state: disabled (grayed).

class   For OLE, a data structure and the functions that manipulate that data structure. An object is a member of a class. For hardware, a grouping of devices and buses for the purpose of installing and managing devices and device drivers, and allocating the resources used by them. The Windows NT 4.0 hardware tree is organized by device class.

clear-to-send   A signal sent from one computer to the other in a communications conversation to indicate readiness to accept data.

client   A computer that accesses shared network resources provided by another computer, called a server. See also *server*.

code names   A name assigned to conceal the identity or existence of something or someone. The code name for Microsoft Windows NT 4.0 was "SUR," which sometimes appears as an identifier in several places in the released product, including hardware setup files. The next major release of Windows NT is code named "Cairo."

codec   **Co**mpression/**dec**ompression technology for digital video and stereo audio.

Command.com   The command processor for MS-DOS. Windows NT 4.0 loads its version of Command.com (compatible with MS-DOS version 5.0) to process commands typed in MS-DOS mode, or in an MS-DOS prompt.

communications protocol   The rules that govern a conversation between two computers that are communicating via an asynchronous connection. The use of a communications protocol ensures error-free delivery of the data being communicated.

communications resource   A device that provides a bidirectional, asynchronous data stream. Examples include serial and parallel ports, and modems. Applications access the resource through a service provider.

Compact Disc–Digital Audio (CD–DA)   An optical data-storage format that provides for the storage of up to 73 minutes of high-quality digital-audio data on a compact disc. Also known as Red Book audio or music CD.

Compact Disc–Extended Architecture (CD–XA)   See *Compact Disc-Read-Only Memory Extended Architecture (CD-ROM/XA).*

compact disc file system (CDFS)   Controls access to the contents of CD-ROM drivers.

Compact Disc–Read-Only Memory (CD-ROM)   A form of storage characterized by high capacity (roughly 600 megabytes) and the use of laser optics rather than magnetic means for reading data.

Compact Disc–Read-Only Memory Extended Architecture (CD-ROM/XA)   An extended CD-ROM format developed by Philips, Sony, and Microsoft. CD-ROM/XA format is consistent with the ISO 9660 (High Sierra) standard, with further specification of ADPCM (adaptive differential pulse code modulation) audio, images, and interleaved data.

Computer Browser Service   This Executive Service identifies those Windows NT clients which have resources available for use within a workgroup or domain.

computer name   A unique name that identifies a particular computer on the network. Microsoft networking uses NetBIOS names, which can have up to 15 characters, and cannot contain spaces.

Config.sys   An ASCII text file that contains configuration commands. Used by MS-DOS, OS/2, and Windows NT 4.0 to load real-mode device drivers.

Configuration Manager   One of three central components of a Plug and Play system (one for each of the three phases of configuration management). The configuration managers drive the process of locating devices, setting up the hardware tree, and allocating resources.

context menu   The menu that appears at the location of a sub-menu that is displayed when you right-click. It is called the context menu because the contents of the menu depend on the context it is invoked in.

Control Panel   The primary Windows NT 4.0 configuration tool. Each option that you can change is represented by an icon in the Control Panel window.

Controller   See *Domain Controller.*

conventional memory   The first 640K of memory in your computer, used to run real-mode MS-DOS applications.

cooperative multitasking   A form of multitasking in which threads cooperate with each other by voluntarily giving up control of the processor. Contrast with *preemptive multitasking.*

CPU   See *central processing unit.*

crash   A serious failure of the software being used.

CTS   See *clear-to-send.*

cursor   A bitmap whose location on the screen is controlled by a pointing device, such as a mouse, pen, or trackball. See also *bitmap.*

D

DARPA   See *Defense Advanced Research Projects Agency.*

data frame   The structured packets into which data is placed by the Data Link layer.

datagram   A packet of information and delivery data that is routed on a network.

default   An operation or value that the system assumes, unless the user makes an explicit choice.

Defense Advanced Research Projects Agency (DARPA)   An agency of the U.S. Department of Defense that sponsored the development of the protocols that became the TCP/IP suite. DARPA was previously known as ARPA, the *Advanced Research Project Agency*, when ARPANET was built.

desktop   The background of your screen, on which windows, icons, and dialog boxes appear.

destination directory   The directory to which you intend to copy or move one or more files.

device   A generic term for a computer component, such as a printer, serial port, or disk drive. A device frequently requires its own controlling software (called a *device driver*).

device contention   The method that Windows NT 4.0 uses to allocate access to peripheral devices when multiple applications are attempting to use them.

device driver   A piece of software that translates requests from one form into another. Most commonly, drivers are used to provide a device-independent way to access hardware.

device ID   A unique ASCII string created by enumerators to identify a hardware device and used to cross-reference data about the device stored in the Registry.

device node   One of the data structures that make up the hardware tree, a device node is built by the Configuration Manager into memory at system startup. Device nodes contain information about a given device, such as the resources it is using.

DHCP   See *Dynamic Host Configuration Protocol.*

dialog box   The type of window that is displayed by Windows NT 4.0 when user input is needed. Usually contains one or more buttons, edit controls, radio buttons, and drop-down lists.

dial-up networking   Formerly known as **remote access service (RAS)**, it provides remote access to networks. Dial-up networking allows a remote user to access his or her network. Once connected, it is as if the remote computer is logically on the network—the user can do anything that he or she could do when physically connected to the network.

DIP switch   Short for Dual In-line Package Switch. Used to configure hardware options, especially on adapter cards.

Direct Memory Access (DMA)   A technique used by hardware adapters to store and retrieve information from the computer's RAM memory without involving the computer's CPU.

directory   Part of a structure for organizing your files on a disk. A directory can contain files and other directories (called subdirectories).

Directory Replication Service   This service provides a means of copying a directory and file structure from a source Windows NT server to a target Windows NT server or workstation.

disk caching   A method to improve performance of the file system. A section of memory is used as a temporary holding place for frequently accessed file data. Windows NT 4.0 dynamically allocates its disk cache.

disk operating system (DOS)   See *MS-DOS*.

DLL   See *dynamic-link library*.

DMA   See *Direct Memory Access*.

DMA channel   A channel for DMA transfers, those that occur between a device and memory directly, without involving the CPU.

DNS   See *Domain Name Service*.

DNS name servers   The servers that hold the DNS name database, and supply the IP address that matches a DNS name in response to a request from a DNS client. See also *Domain Name Service*.

dock   To insert a portable computer into a base unit. Cold docking means the computer must begin from a power-off state and restart before docking. Hot docking means the computer can be docked while running at full power.

docking station   The base computer unit into which a user can insert a portable computer to expand it to a desktop equivalent. Docking stations usually include drives, expansion slots, AC power, network and SCSI connections, and communication ports.

domain   For DNS, a group of workstations and servers that share a single group name. For Microsoft networking, a collection of computers that share a security context and account database stored on a Windows NT Server domain controller. Each domain has a unique name. See also *Domain Name Service*.

Domain Controller   The Windows NT Server computer that authenticates domain logons and maintains a copy of the security database for the domain.

Domain Name Service (DNS)   A static, hierarchical name service for TCP/IP hosts. Do not confuse DNS domains with Windows NT domains.

DOS   See *Microsoft Disk Operating System*.

DOS Protected Mode Interface (DPMI)   A technique used to allow MS-DOS-based applications to access extended memory.

dpi   Short for dots per inch, a measurement of the resolution of a monitor or printer.

DPMI   See *DOS Protected Mode Interface*.

drag and drop   Selectively moving or copying one or more objects between dialog boxes, using a mouse or other pointing device.

DRAM   See *Dynamic Random-Access Memory*.

Dynamic Data Exchange (DDE)   A form of interprocess communication (IPC) implemented in the Microsoft Windows family of operating systems. DDE uses shared memory to exchange data. Most DDE functions have been superseded by OLE.

Dynamic Host Configuration Protocol (DHCP)   A protocol for automatic TCP/IP configuration that provides static and dynamic address allocation and management.

dynamic-link library (DLL)   File functions that are compiled, linked, and saved separately from the processes that use them. Functions in DLLs can be used by more than one running process. The operating system maps the DLLs into the process's address space when the process is starting up or while it is running. Dynamic-link libraries are stored in files with the .DLL extension.

dynamic random-access memory (DRAM)   A computer's main memory.

E

Eform   See *electronic mail form.*

EISA   See *Extended Industry Standard Architecture.*

electronic mail (e-mail)   A message sent across a network between two or more store-and-forward messaging systems.

electronic mail form (Eform)   A programmed form used to send e-mail in an electronic mail system.

electronic messaging system (EMS)   A system that allows users or applications to correspond using a store-and-forward system.

e-mail   See *electronic mail.*

EMM   See *Expanded Memory Manager.*

EMS   See *Expanded Memory Specification* and *Electronic Messaging System.*

encapsulated PostScript (EPS)   A file format used to represent graphics written in the PostScript page description language.

enumerator   A Plug and Play device driver that detects devices below its own device node, creates unique device IDs, and reports to Configuration Manager during startup.

environment variable   A symbolic variable that represents some element of the operating system, such as a path, a file name, or other literal data. Typically used by batch files, environment variables are created with the SET command.

EPROM   See *Erasable Programmable Read-Only Memory.*

EPS   See *encapsulated PostScript.*

EPS file   A file containing code written in the encapsulated PostScript printer programming language. Often used to represent graphics for use by desktop publishing applications.

Erasable Programmable Read-Only Memory (EPROM)
A computer chip containing non-volatile memory. It can be erased (for reprogramming) by exposure to ultraviolet light.

event   An action or occurrence to which an application might respond, such as mouse clicks, key presses, mouse movements, or a system event. System events are any significant occurrence that may require user notification, or some other action by an application.

expanded memory   Memory that complies with the Lotus-Intel-Microsoft Expanded Memory specification. Used by MS-DOS-based spreadsheet applications.

Expanded Memory Manager (EMM)   The device driver that controls access to expanded memory.

Expanded Memory Specification (EMS)   The specification that controls and defines Expanded Memory. Also known as the Lotus-Intel-Microsoft (LIM) specification, after the three major companies that designed it.

Extended Industry Standard Architecture (EISA)   An enhancement to the bus architecture used on the IBM PC/AT, which allows the use of 32-bit devices in the same type of expansion slot used by an ISA adapter card. EISA slots and adapters were formerly common in server computers, but have been mostly replaced with PCI slots.

extended memory   Memory that occupies physical addresses above the 1 megabyte mark.

Extended Memory Manager (XMM)   The MS-DOS device driver that provides access to XMS memory.

Extended Memory Specification (XMS)   The specification for the application program interfaces that allow an application to access and use extended memory.

F

family name   The name of a given font family. Windows employs five family names—*Decorative, Modern, Roman, Script,* and *Swiss.* A sixth family name, *Dontcare,* specifies the default font. See also *font family.*

FAT   See *file allocation table.*

FAT file system   A file system based on a file allocation table. Windows NT 4.0 uses a 32-bit implementation called VFAT. See also *file allocation table* and *virtual file allocation table.*

FIFO   See *First In, First Out.*

file   A collection of information stored on a disk, and accessible using a name.

file allocation table (FAT)   A table or list maintained by some operating systems to keep track of the status of various segments of disk space used for file storage. See also *virtual file allocation table.*

file attribute   A characteristic of a file that indicates whether the file is read-only, hidden, system, archived, a directory, or normal.

file sharing   The ability of a network computer to share files or directories on its local disks with remote computers.

file system   In an operating system, the overall structure in which files are named, stored, and organized.

file time   A 64-bit value representing the number of 100-nanosecond intervals that have elapsed since January 1, 1601.

file transfer program (FTP)   A utility defined by the TCP/IP protocol suite that is used to transfer files between dissimilar systems.

file transfer protocol (FTP)   The standard method of transferring files using TCP/IP. FTP allows you to transfer files between dissimilar computers, with preservation of binary data, and optional translation of text file formats.

First In, First Out (FIFO)   Used to describe a buffer, where data is retrieved from the buffer in the same order it went in.

floppy disk   A disk that can be inserted in and removed from a disk drive.

focus   The area of a dialog box which receives input. The focus is indicated by highlighted text or a button enclosed in dotted lines.

folder   In Windows Explorer, an object that can contain other objects (a container object). Examples include disk folders, the fonts folder, and the printers folder.

font   A collection of characters, each of which has a similar appearance. For example, the Arial font characters are all sans serif characters.

font family   A group of fonts that have similar characteristics.

font mapper   The routine within Windows that maps an application's request for a font with particular characteristics to the available font that best matches those characteristics.

frame   See *data frame*.

free space   Unused space on a hard disk.

friendly name   A human-readable name used to give an alternative to the often cryptic computer, port, and share names. For example, "Digital 1152 Printer In The Hall" as opposed to "HALLPRT."

FTP   See *file transfer program* and *file transfer protocol*.

G

gateway   A computer connected to multiple networks, and capable of moving data between networks using different transport protocols.

GDI   See *graphics device interface*.

graphical user interface (GUI)   A computer system design in which the user interacts with the system using graphical symbols, tools, and events, rather than text-based displays and commands, such as the normal Windows NT 4.0 user interface.

graphics device interface (GDI)   The subsystem that implements graphic drawing functions.

GUI   See *graphical user interface.*

H

handle   An interface (usually a small black square) added to an object to enable the user to move, size, reshape, or otherwise modify the object.

hardware branch   The hardware archive root key in the Registry, which is a superset of the memory-resident hardware tree. The name of this key is HKEY_LOCAL_MACHINE\HARDWARE.

hardware tree   A record in RAM of the current system configuration, based on the configuration information for all devices in the hardware branch of the Registry. The Hardware tree is created each time the computer is started or whenever a dynamic change occurs to the system configuration.

high memory area (HMA)   A 64K memory block located just above the 1M address in a Virtual DOS Machine (VDM). Originally made possible by a side effect of the 80286 processor design, the memory is usable when the A20 address line is turned on.

High-Performance File System (HPFS)   File System primarily used with OS/2 operating system version 1.2 or later. It supports long file names but does not provide security. Windows NT 4.0 does not support HPFS.

hive   A discrete body of Registry information, usually stored in a single disk file.

HKEY_CLASSES_ROOT   The Registry tree that contains data relating to OLE. This key is a symbolic link to a subkey of HKEY_LOCAL_MACHINE\SOFTWARE.

HKEY_CURRENT_USER   The Registry tree that contains the currently logged in user's preferences, including desktop settings, application settings, and network connections. This key maps to a subkey of HKEY_USERS.

HKEY_LOCAL_MACHINE   The Registry tree that contains configuration settings that apply to the hardware and software on the computer.

HKEY_USERS   The Registry tree that contains the preferences for every user that ever logged on to this computer.

HMA   See *high memory area.*

home directory   A directory that is accessible to a particular user and contains that user's files and programs on a network server.

host   Any device that is attached to the internetwork and uses TCP/IP.

host ID   The portion of the IP address that identifies a computer within a particular network ID.

host name   The name of an Internet host. It may or may not be the same as the computer name. In order for a client to access resources by host name, it must appear in the client's HOSTS file, or be resolvable by a DNS server.

host table   The HOSTS and LMHOSTS files, which contain mappings of known IP addresses mapped to host names.

HOSTS file   A local text file in the same format as the 4.3 Berkeley Software Distribution (BSD) UNIX /etc/hosts file. This file maps host names to IP addresses. In Windows NT 4.0, this file is stored in the \WINNT directory.

hotkey   Letters or combinations of keystrokes used in place of mouse clicks as shortcuts to application functions.

HPFS   See *High-Performance File System.*

I-J

ICMP   See *Internet control message protocol.*

icon   A small bitmap (usually 16×16 pixels or 32×32 pixels) that is associated with an application, file type, or a concept.

IEEE   See *Institute of Electrical and Electronic Engineers.*

IETF   See *Internet Engineering Task Force.*

IFS   See *installable file system.*

IHV   See *independent hardware vendor.*

I/O address   One of the critical resources used in configuring devices. I/O addresses are used to communicate with devices. Also known as *port.*

I/O bus   The electrical connection between the CPU and the I/O devices. There are several types of I/O buses: *ISA, EISA, SCSI, VL,* and *PCI.*

I/O device   Any device in or attached to a computer that is designed to receive information from, or provide information to the computer. For example, a printer is an output-only device, while a mouse is an input-only device. Other devices, such as modems, are both input and output devices, transferring data in both directions. Windows NT 4.0 must have a device driver installed in order to be able to use an I/O device.

independent hardware vendor (IHV)   A manufacturer of computer hardware. Usually used to describe the makers of add-on devices, rather than makers of computer systems.

Industry Standard Architecture (ISA)   A computer system that is built on the Industry Standard Architecture is one that adheres to the same design rules and constraints that the IBM PC/AT adhered to.

INF file   A file, usually provided by the manufacturer of a device, that provides the information that Windows NT 4.0 Setup needs in order to set up a device. INF files usually include a list of valid logical configurations for the device, the names of driver files associated with the device, and other information.

INI files   Initialization files used by Windows-based applications to store configuration information. Windows NT 4.0 incorporates .INI files into its Registry when upgrading from a previous version of Windows.

installable file system (IFS)   A file system that can be installed into the operating system as needed, rather than just at startup time. Windows NT 4.0 can support multiple installable file systems at one time, including the *FAT file system* and *NTFS*, network redirectors, and the *CD-ROM file system (CDFS)*.

instance   A particular occurrence of an *object*, such as a window, module, named pipe, or DDE session. Each instance has a unique *handle* that distinguishes it from other instances of the same type.

Institute of Electrical and Electronic Engineers (IEEE)   An organization that issues standards for electrical and electronic devices.

Integrated Services Digital Network (ISDN)   A digital communications method that permits connections of up to 128Kbps. ISDN requires a special adapter for your computer. An ISDN connection is available in most areas of the United States for a reasonable cost.

internal command   Commands that are built into the command.com file.

International Organization for Standardization (ISO)   The organization that produces many of the world's standards. Open Systems Interconnect (OSI) is only one of many areas standardized by the ISO.

International Telephone and Telegraph Consultative Committee (CCITT)   International organization that creates and publishes telecommunications standards, including X.400. The initials CCITT actually stand for the real name of the organization, which is Comité Consultatif International Téléphonique et Télégraphique in French.

Internet   The worldwide interconnected wide-area network, based on the TCP/IP protocol suite.

App
A

Internet control message protocol (ICMP)   A required protocol in the TCP/IP protocol suite. It allows two nodes on an IP network to share IP status and error information. ICMP is used by the ping utility.

Internet Engineering Task Force (IETF)   A consortium that introduces procedures for new technology on the Internet. IETF specifications are released in documents called Requests for Comments (RFCs).

Internet group names   A name known by a DNS server that includes a list of the specific addresses of systems that have registered the name.

Internet protocol (IP)   The Network layer protocol of TCP/IP, responsible for addressing and sending TCP packets over the network.

interprocess communications (IPC)   A set of mechanisms used by applications to communicate and share data.

interrupt   An event that disrupts normal processing by the CPU, and results in the transfer of control to an interrupt handler. Both hardware devices and software can issue interrupts—software executes an INT instruction, while hardware devices signal the CPU by using one of the *interrupt request lines (IRQ)* to the processor.

interrupt request level (IRQL)   Interrupts are ranked by priority. Interrupts that have a priority lower than the processor's interrupt request level setting can be masked (ignored).

interrupt request lines (IRQ)   Hardware lines on the CPU that devices use to send signals to cause an interrupt. Normally, only one device is attached to any particular IRQ line.

IP   See *Internet protocol*.

IP address   Used to identify a node on a network and to specify routing information on an internetwork. Each node on the internetwork must be assigned a unique IP address, which is made up of the network ID, plus a unique host ID assigned by the network administrator. The subnet mask is used to separate an IP address into the host ID and network ID. In Windows NT 4.0, you can either assign an IP address manually or automatically by using DHCP.

IP router   A system connected to multiple physical TCP/IP networks that can route or deliver IP packets between the networks. See also *gateway*.

IPC   See *interprocess communications*.

IPX/SPX   Internetworking Packet eXchange/Sequenced Packet eXchange. Transport protocols used in Novell NetWare networks. Windows NT 4.0 includes the Microsoft IPX/SPX-compatible transport protocol (NWLINK).

IRQ   See *interrupt request lines*.

IRQL   See *interrupt request level*.

ISA   See *Industry Standard Architecture*.

ISDN   See *Integrated Services Digital Network*.

ISO Development Environment (ISODE)   A research tool developed to study the upper layer of OSI. Academic and some commercial ISO products are based on this framework.

ISO   See *International Organization for Standardization*.

ISODE   See *ISO Development Environment*.

K

K   Standard abbreviation for kilobyte; equals 1,024 bytes.

Kbps   Kilobits per second

kernel   The Windows NT 4.0 core component responsible for implementing the basic operating system functions of Windows NT 4.0 including virtual memory management, thread scheduling, and file I/O services.

L

LAN   See *local area network*.

legacy   Hardware and device cards that don't conform to the Plug and Play standard.

link   A connection at the *LLC* layer that is uniquely defined by the adapter's address and the destination service access point (DSAP). Also, a connection between two objects, or a reference to an object that is linked to another.

list box   In a dialog box, a box that lists available choices. For example, a list of all files in a directory. If all the choices do not fit in the list box, there is a scroll bar.

LLC   See *logical link control*.

LMHOSTS file   A local text file that maps IP addresses to the computer names of Windows networking computers. In Windows NT 4.0, LMHOSTS is stored in the WINNT directory. (LMHOSTS stands for LAN Manager Hosts.)

local area network (LAN)   A computer network confined to a single building or campus.

local printer   A printer that is directly connected to one of the ports on your computer, as opposed to a network printer.

localization   The process of adapting software for different countries, languages, or cultures.

logical drive   A division of an extended partition on a hard disk, accessed using a drive letter.

logical link control (LLC)   One of the two sublayers of the Data Link layer of the OSI reference model, as defined by the IEEE 802 standards. See "Logical Link Control (LLC) Sublayer" in Chapter 15 for more information.

login   The process by which a user is identified to the computer in a Novell NetWare network.

logon   The process by which a user is identified to the computer in a Microsoft network.

logon script   In Microsoft networking, a batch file that runs automatically when a user logs on to a Windows NT Server. Novell networking also uses logon scripts, but they are not batch files.

M

M   Standard abbreviation for megabyte, or 1,024 kilobytes.

MAC   See *media access control*.

MAC address   The address for a device as it is identified at the media access control layer in the network architecture. MAC addresses are usually stored in ROM on the network adapter card, and are unique.

mailslot   A form of interprocess communications used to carry messages from an application on one network node to another. Mailslots are one-way.

mailslot client   A process that writes a message to a mailslot.

mailslot server   A process that creates and owns a mailslot and can read messages from it. See also *process*.

management information base (MIB)   A set of objects used by *SNMP* to manage devices. MIB objects represent various types of information about a device.

mandatory user profile   This represents a user environment profile that cannot be changed by the user. If the profile is unavailable, the user will be unable to log on to the Windows NT enterprise.

map   To translate one value into another.

MAPI   See *Messaging Application Programming Interface*.

mapped I/O (or **mapped file I/O**)   This is the file I/O that is performed by reading and writing to virtual memory that is backed by a file.

MDI   See *multiple document interface*.

media access control (MAC)   The lower of the two sublayers of the data–link layer in the IEEE 802 network model.

Media Control Interface (MCI)   High-level control software that provides a device-independent interface to multimedia devices and media files. MCI includes a command-message interface and a command-string interface.

memory   A temporary storage area for information and applications.

memory object   A number of bytes allocated from the heap.

message   A structure or set of parameters used for communicating information or a request. Every event that happens in the system causes a message to be sent. Messages can be passed between the operating system and an application, different applications, threads within an application, and windows within an application.

message loop   A program loop that retrieves messages from a thread's message queue and dispatches them.

Messaging Application Program Interface (MAPI)   A set of calls used to add mail-enabled features to other Windows-based applications. It is one of the WOSA (Windows Open Systems Architecture) technologies.

metafile   A collection of structures that stores a picture in a device-independent format. (There are two metafile formats   the enhanced format and the Windows format.)

MIB   See *management information base*.

Microsoft Disk Operating System (MS-DOS)   The dominant operating system for personal computers from the introduction of the IBM personal computer until the introduction of Windows 95 and Windows NT 4.0.

MIDI   See *Musical Instrument Digital Interface*.

minidriver   The part of the device driver that is written by the hardware manufacturer, and provides device-specific functionality.

MS-DOS See *Microsoft Disk Operating System.*

MS-DOS-based application An application designed to run under MS-DOS. Windows NT 4.0 supports most MS-DOS-based applications except those that communicate directly to hardware devices.

multiple document interface (MDI) A specification that defines the standard user interface for Windows-based applications. An MDI application enables the user to work with more than one document at the same time. Microsoft Word is an example of an MDI application. Each of the documents is displayed in a separate window inside the application's main window.

multitasking The process by which an operating system creates the illusion that many tasks are executing simultaneously on a single processor. See also *cooperative multitasking* and *preemptive multitasking.*

multithreading The ability of a process to have multiple, simultaneous paths of execution (*threads*).

Musical Instrument Digital Interface (MIDI) A standard protocol for communication between musical instruments and computers.

N

name registration The way a computer registers its unique name with a name server on the network, such as a *WINS* server.

name resolution The process used on the network to determine the address of a computer by using its name.

named pipe A one-way or two-way pipe used for communications between a server process and one or more client processes. A server process specifies a name when it creates one or more instances of a named pipe. Each instance of the pipe can be connected to a client. Microsoft SQL Server clients use named pipes to communicate with the SQL Server.

NBF transport protocol   NetBEUI frame protocol. A descendant of the NetBEUI protocol, which is a Transport layer protocol, not the programming interface NetBIOS.

NCB   See *network control block*.

NDIS   See *network device interface specification*.

NetBEUI transport   NetBIOS (Network Basic Input/Output System) Extended User Interface. A transport protocol designed for use on small subnets. It is not routable, but it is fast.

NetBIOS interface   A programming interface that allows I/O requests to be sent to and received from a remote computer. It hides networking hardware from applications.

NetBIOS Over TCP/IP   The networking module that provides the functionality to support NetBIOS name registration and resolution across a TCP/IP network.

network   A group of computers and other devices that can interact by means of a shared communications link.

network adapter driver   Software that implements the lower layers of a network, providing a standard interface to the network card.

network basic input/output system (NetBIOS)   A software interface for network communication. See *NetBIOS interface*.

network control block (NCB)   A memory structure used to communicate with the NetBIOS interface.

Network DDE DSDM service   The Network DDE DSDM (DDE share database manager) service manages shared DDE conversations. It is used by the *Network DDE service*.

Network DDE service   The Network DDE (dynamic data exchange) service provides a network transport and security for DDE conversations. Network DDE is supported in Windows NT 4.0 for backwards compatibility, as most of its functions are superseded by OLE.

network device driver   Software that coordinates communication between the network adapter card and the computer's hardware and other software, controlling the physical function of the network adapter cards.

network device interface specification (NDIS)   In Windows networking, the interface for network adapter drivers. All transport drivers call the NDIS interface to access network adapter cards.

network directory   See *shared directory*.

Network File System (NFS)   A service for distributed computing systems that provides a distributed file system, eliminating the need for keeping multiple copies of files on separate computers. Usually used in connection with UNIX computers.

network ID   The portion of the IP address that identifies a group of computers and devices located on the same logical network. Separated from the Host ID using the *subnet mask*.

Network Information Service (NIS)   A service for distributed computing systems that provides a distributed database system for common configuration files.

network interface card (NIC)   An adapter card that connects a computer to a network.

network operating system (NOS)   The operating system used on network servers, such as Windows NT Server or Novell NetWare.

network provider   The Windows NT 4.0 component that allows Windows NT 4.0 to communicate with the network. Windows NT 4.0 includes providers for Microsoft networks and for Novell NetWare networks. Other network vendors may supply providers for their networks.

network transport   This can be either a particular layer of the OSI Reference Model between the network layer and the session layer, or the protocol used between this layer on two different computers on a network.

network-interface printers Printers with built-in network cards, such as Hewlett-Packard laser printers equipped with Jet Direct cards. The advantage of network-interface printers is that they can be located anywhere on the network.

New Technology file system (NTFS) The native file system used by Windows NT 4.0 which supplies file and directory security, sector sparing, compression, and other performance characteristics.

NIC See *network interface card.*

NIS See *Network Information Service.*

NOS See *network operating system.*

NTFS See *Windows NT file system.*

O

object A particular instance of a class. Most of the internal data structures in Windows NT 4.0 are objects.

object linking and embedding (OLE) The specification that details the implementation of Windows objects, and the interprocess communication that supports them.

OCR See *Optical Character Recognition.*

OEM See *original equipment manufacturer.*

OLE See *object linking and embedding.*

Open Systems Interconnect (OSI) The networking architecture reference model created by the ISO.

operating system (OS) The software that provides an interface between a user or application and the computer hardware. Operating system services usually include memory and resource management, I/O services, and file handling. Examples include Windows NT 4.0, Windows NT, and UNIX.

Optical Character Recognition (OCR)   A technology that is used to generate editable text from a graphic image.

original equipment manufacturer (OEM)   Software that is sold by Microsoft to OEMs only includes the operating system versions that are preloaded on computers before they are sold.

OS   See *operating system*.

OSI   See *Open Systems Interconnect*.

P-Q

PAB   See *personal address book*.

packet   A transmission unit of fixed maximum size that consists of binary information representing both data, addressing information, and error-correction information, created by the data-link layer.

page   A unit of memory used by the system in managing memory. The size of a page is computer-dependent (the Intel 486 computer, and therefore, Windows NT 4.0, uses 4K pages).

page map   An internal data structure used by the system to keep track of the mapping between the pages in a process's virtual address space, and the corresponding pages in physical memory.

paged pool   The portion of system memory that can be paged to disk.

paging file   A storage file (PAGEFILE.SYS) the system uses to hold pages of memory swapped out of RAM. Also known as a *swap file*.

parity   Refers to an error-checking procedure in which the number of 1's must always be the same (either even or odd) for each group of bits transmitted without error. Also used in the main RAM system of a computer to verify the validity of data contained in RAM.

partition   A partition is a portion of a physical disk that functions as though it were a physically separate unit. See also *system partition*.

partition table   The partition table contains entries showing the start and end points of each of the primary partitions on the disk. The partition table can hold four entries.

password   A security measure used to restrict access to computer systems. A password is a unique string of characters that must be provided before a logon or an access is authorized.

path   The location of a file or directory. The path describes the location in relation to either the root directory, or the current directory; for example, C:\WINNT\System32. Also, a graphic object that represents one or more shapes.

PCI   See *Peripheral Component Interconnect*.

PCMCIA   See *Personal Computer Memory Card International Association*.

performance monitoring   The process of determining the system resources an application uses, such as processor time and memory. Done with the Windows NT 4.0 Performance Monitor.

Peripheral Component Interconnect (PCI)   The local bus being promoted as the successor to VL. This type of device is used in most Intel Pentium computers and in the Apple PowerPC Macintosh.

persistent connection   A network connection that is restored automatically when the user logs on. In Windows NT 4.0, persistent connections are created by selecting the Reconnect at Logon check box.

personal address book (PAB)   One of the information services provided with the Microsoft Exchange client included with Windows NT 4.0. It is used to store the names and e-mail addresses of people you correspond with.

Personal Computer Memory Card International Association (PCMCIA)   The industry association of manufacturers of credit card-sized adapter cards (PC cards).

PIF   See *program information file*.

pixel   Short for picture element, a dot that represents the smallest graphic unit of measurement on a screen. The actual size of a pixel is screen-dependent, and varies according to the size of the screen and the resolution being used. (Also known as pel.)

platform   The hardware and software required for an application to run.

Plug and Play   A computer industry specification, intended to ease the process of configuring hardware.

Plug and Play BIOS   A BIOS with responsibility for configuring Plug and Play cards and system board devices during system power-up; provides runtime configuration services for system board devices after startup.

p-node   A NetBIOS implementation that uses point-to-point communications with a name server to resolve names as IP addresses

Point to Point Protocol (PPP)   The industry standard that is implemented in dial-up networking. PPP is a line protocol used to connect to remote networking services, including Internet Service Providers. Prior to the introduction of PPP, another line protocol, SLIP, was used.

pointer   The arrow-shaped cursor on the screen that follows the movement of a mouse (or other pointing device) and indicates which area of the screen will be affected when you press the mouse button. The pointer may change shape during certain tasks.

port   The socket to which you connect the cable for a peripheral device. See also *I/O address*.

port ID   The method TCP and UDP use to specify which application running on the system is sending or receiving the data.

Postoffice   The message store used by Microsoft Mail to hold the mail messages. It exists only as a structure of directories on disk, and does not contain any active components.

PostScript   A page-description language, developed by Adobe Systems, Inc., that offers flexible font capability and high-quality graphics. PostScript uses English-like commands to control page layout and to load and scale fonts.

PPP   See *Point to Point Protocol*.

preemptive multitasking   A multitasking technique that breaks time up into timeslices, during which the operating system allows a particular program thread to run. The operating system can interrupt any running thread at any time. Preemptive multitasking usually results in the best use of CPU time, and overall better perceived throughput. See also *cooperative multitasking*.

primary partition   A primary partition is a portion of a physical disk that can be marked for use by an operating system. There can be up to four primary partitions (or up to three, if there is an extended partition) per physical disk. A primary partition cannot be subpartitioned.

print device   Refers to the actual hardware device that produces printed output.

print monitor   Keeps track of printers and print devices. Responsible for transferring information from the print driver to the printing device, including any necessary flow control.

print provider   A software component that allows the client to print to a network printer. Windows NT 4.0 includes print providers for Microsoft networks and Novell networks.

printer driver   The component that translates GDI objects into printer commands.

printer fonts   Fonts that are built into your printer.

priority class   A process priority category (high, normal, or idle) used to determine the scheduling priorities of a process's threads. Each priority class has five levels. See also *thread*.

private memory   Memory owned by a process, and not accessible by other processes.

privileged instruction Processor-privileged instructions have access to system memory and the hardware. Privileged instructions can only be executed by Ring 0 components.

process The virtual address space, code, data, and other operating system resources such as files, pipes, and synchronization objects that make up an executing application. In addition to resources, a process contains at least one thread that executes the process's code.

profile A set of data describing a particular configuration of a computer. This information can describe a user's preferences (user profile) or the hardware configuration. Profiles are usually stored in the Registry, for example, the key HKEY_USERS contains the profiles for the various users of the computer.

program file A file that starts an application or program. A program file has an .EXE, .PIF, .COM, or .BAT file name extension.

program information file (PIF) Windows NT 4.0 stores information about how to configure the virtual machine for running MS-DOS applications in PIF files.

Programmable Read-Only Memory (PROM) A type of integrated circuit usually used to store a computer's BIOS. PROM chips, once programmed, can only be read from, not written to.

PROM See *Programmable Read-Only Memory*.

properties In Windows NT 4.0, the dialog boxes that are used to configure a particular object.

protocol A set of rules and conventions by which two computers pass messages across a network. Protocols are used between instances of a particular layer on each computer. Windows NT 4.0 includes NetBEUI, TCP/IP, and IPX/SPX–compatible protocols. See also *communications protocol*.

provider The component that allows Windows NT 4.0 to communicate with the network. Windows NT 4.0 includes providers for Microsoft and Novell networks.

R

RAM   See *random access memory*.

random-access memory (RAM)   The RAM memory in a computer is the computer's main memory, where programs and data are stored while the program is running. Information stored in RAM is lost when the computer is turned off.

read-only   A device, document, or file is read-only if you are not permitted to make changes to it.

read-write   A device, document, or file is read-write if you can make changes to it.

reboot   To restart a computer. To reboot a Windows NT 4.0 computer, click the Start Button, choose Shutdown, and then choose Restart Your Computer.

redirector   The networking component that intercepts file I/O requests and translates them into network requests. Redirectors (also called network clients) are implemented as installable file system drivers in Windows NT 4.0

REG_BINARY   A data type for Registry value entries that designates binary data.

REG_DWORD   A data type for Registry value entries that designates data represented by a number that is 4 bytes long.

REG_SZ   A data type for Registry value entries that designates a data string that usually represents human readable text.

Registry   Windows NT 4.0's and Windows NT's binary system configuration database.

Registry Editor (REGEDT32.EXE)   A utility supplied with Windows NT 4.0 that allows the user to view and edit Registry keys and values.

Registry key   A Registry entry that can contain other Registry entries.

remote access service (RAS)   A Windows NT Executive service that provides remote networking access to the Windows NT Enterprise for telecommuters, remote users system administrators, and home users. See also *dial-up networking*.

remote administration   The process of administrating one computer from another computer across a network.

remote initiation program load (RIPL)   A technique that allows a workstation to boot by using an image file on a network server instead of a disk.

remote procedure call (RPC)   An industry-standard method of interprocess communication across a network. Used by many administration tools.

Requests for Comments (RFCs)   The official documents of the Internet Engineering Task Force that specify the details for protocols included in the TCP/IP family.

requirements   The conceptual design and functional description of a software product, and any associated materials. Requirements describe the features, user interface, documentation, and other functions the product will provide.

resource   Windows resources include icons, cursors, menus, dialog boxes, bitmaps, fonts, keyboard-accelerator tables, message-table entries, string-table entries, version data, and user-defined data. The resources used by an application are either part of the system, or private resources stored in the application's program file. Also, a part of a computer system that can be assigned to a running process, such as a disk drive or memory segment.

RFC   See *Requests for Comments.*

RIP   See *routing information protocol.*

RIPL   See *remote initiation program load.*

ROM   See *read-only.*

router   A computer with two or more network adapters, each attached to a different subnet. The router forwards packets on a subnet to the subnet that they are addressed to.

routing   The process of forwarding packets until they reach their destination.

routing information protocol (RIP)   A protocol that supports dynamic routing. Used between routers.

RPC   See *remote procedure call.*

RPC server   The program or computer that processes remote procedure calls from a client.

S

SAM Database   The Registry database that contains the user and group account information, as well as user account policies. It is managed by the User Manager or User Manager for Domains utility.

screen buffer   a memory buffer that holds a representation of an MS-DOS VM's logical screen.

screen saver   Pictures or patterns that appear on your screen when your computer has not been used for a certain amount of time. Originally intended to protect the monitor from damage, modern screen savers are used mostly for their entertainment value.

scroll   To move through text or graphics (up, down, left, or right) in order to see parts of the file that cannot fit on the screen.

scroll arrow   An arrow on either end of a scroll bar that you use to scroll through the contents of the window or list box.

scroll bar   A bar that appears at the right and bottom edge of a window or list box whose contents are not completely visible. The scroll bar consists of two scroll arrows and a scroll box, which you use to scroll through the contents.

scroll box   In a scroll bar, a small box that shows where the information currently visible is, relative to the contents of the entire window.

SCSI   See *Small Computer System Interface*.

Security ID (SID)   The unique, randomly generated, alphanumeric identifier assigned by Windows NT when a new user, group, trust, or other security object is created.

sequence number   Sequence numbers are used by a receiving node to properly order packets.

Serial Line Internet Protocol (SLIP)   The predecessor to PPP, SLIP is a line protocol supporting TCP/IP over a modem connection. SLIP support is provided for Windows NT 4.0. See also *Point to Point Protocol*.

server   A computer or application that provides shared resources to clients across a network. Resources include files and directories, printers, fax modems, and network database services. See also *client*.

server message block (SMB)   A block of data that contains a work request from a workstation to a server, or that contains the response from the server to the workstation. SMBs are used for all network communications in a Microsoft network.

server service   An Executive Service that makes resources available to the workgroup or domain for file, print, and other RPC services.

service   A process that performs a specific system function and often provides an application programming interface (API) for other processes to call. Windows NT 4.0 services Computer Browser, Server, and Workstation.

session   A layer of the OSI reference model that performs name recognition and the functions needed to allow two applications to communicate over the network. Also, a communication channel established by the session layer.

share   In Microsoft networking, the process of making resources, such as directories and printers, available for network users.

share name   The name that a shared resource is accessed by on the network.

shared directory   A directory that has been shared so that network users can connect to it.

shared memory   Memory that two or more processes can read from and write to.

shared network directory   See *shared directory*.

shared resource   Any device, data, or program that is used by more than one other device or program. Windows NT 4.0 can share directories and printers.

sharepoint   A shared network resource, or the name that one is known by.

shell   The part of an operating system that the user interacts with. The Windows NT 4.0 shell is Windows Explorer.

shortcut key   a combination of keys that results in the execution of a program, or selection of an option, without going through a menu.

shut down   The process of properly terminating all running programs, flushing caches, and preparing the system to be powered off.

signaled   One of the possible states of a mutex.

SIMM   See *Single In-Line Memory Module*.

Simple Mail Transfer Protocol (SMTP)   The application layer protocol that supports messaging functions over the Internet.

Simple Network Management Protocol (SNMP)   A standard protocol for the management of network components. Windows NT 4.0 includes an SNMP agent.

Single In-Line Memory Module (SIMM)   One of the types of RAM chips.

SLIP   See *Serial Line Internet Protocol*.

Small Computer System Interface (SCSI)   Pronounced "scuzzy," a standard for connecting multiple devices to a computer system. SCSI devices are connected in a daisy chain, which can have up to seven devices (plus a controller) on it.

SMB   See *server message block.*

SMTP   See *Simple Mail Transfer Protocol.*

SNMP   See *Simple Network Management Protocol.*

socket   A channel used for incoming and outgoing data defined by the Windows Sockets API. Usually used with TCP/IP.

socket services   The protected-mode VxD that manages PCMCIA sockets adapter hardware. It provides a protected-mode PCMCIA Socket Services 2.x interface for use by *Card Services.* A socket services driver is required for each socket adapter.

source directory   The directory where files in a copy or move operation start out in.

spooler   A scheduler for the printing process. It coordinates activity among other components of the print model and schedules all print jobs arriving at the print server.

static VxD   A VxD that is loaded at system startup.

string   A sequence of characters representing human-readable text.

subdirectory   A directory within a directory.

subkey   A Registry key contained within another Registry key. All Registry keys are subkeys except for the six top-level keys.

subnet   On the Internet, any lower network that is part of the logical network identified by the network ID.

subnet mask   A 32-bit value that is used to distinguish the network ID portion of the IP address from the host ID.

swap file   A special file on your hard disk that is used to hold memory pages that are swapped out of RAM. Also called a *paging file.*

syntax   The order in which you must type a command and the elements that follow the command.

system directory   The directory that contains the Windows DLLs and drivers. Usually c:windows\system.

system disk   A disk that contains the files necessary to start an operating system.

system partition   The volume that contains the hardware-specific files needed to load Windows NT 4.0.

T

TAPI   See *Telephony Application Program Interface*.

TCP/IP transport   Transmission Control Protocol/Internet Protocol. The primary wide area network (WAN) transport protocol used on the worldwide Internet, which is a worldwide internetwork of universities, research laboratories, government and military installations, organizations, and corporations. TCP/IP includes standards for how computers communicate and conventions for connecting networks and routing traffic, as well as specifications for utilities.

TCP   See *Transmission Control Protocol*.

TDI   See *transport driver interface*.

Telephony Application Program Interface (TAPI)   An API that enables applications to control modems and telephony equipment in a device-independent manner. TAPI routes application function calls to the appropriate "Service Provider" DLL for a modem.

telnet   The application layer protocol that provides virtual terminal service on TCP/IP networks.

terminate- and stay-resident (TSR)   A technique used by MS-DOS applications that allows more than one program to be loaded at a time.

text file   A file containing only ASCII letters, numbers, and symbols, without any formatting information except for carriage return/linefeeds.

thread   The basic entity to which the operating system allocates CPU time. A thread can execute any part of the application's code, including a part currently being executed by another thread (re-entrancy). Threads cannot own resources; instead, they use the resources of the process they belong to.

thread local storage   A storage method in which an index can be used by multiple threads of the same process to store and retrieve a different value for each thread. See also *thread*.

thunking   The transformation between 16-bit and 32-bit formats, which is carried out by a separate layer in the *VDM*.

timeout   If a device is not performing a task, the amount of time the computer should wait before detecting it as an error.

toolbar   A frame containing a series of shortcut buttons providing quick access to commands, usually located below the menu bar, although many applications provide "dockable" toolbars which may be moved to different locations on the screen.

Transmission Control Protocol (TCP)   A connection-based protocol, responsible for breaking data into packets, which the IP protocol sends over the network. This protocol provides a reliable, sequenced communication stream for internetwork communication.

Transmission Control Protocol/Internet Protocol (TCP/IP)   The primary wide area network used on the worldwide Internet, which is a worldwide internetwork of universities, research laboratories, military installations, organizations, and corporations. TCP/IP includes standards for how computers communicate and conventions for connecting networks and routing traffic, as well as specifications for utilities.

transport driver interface (TDI)   The interface between the session layer and the network layer, used by network redirectors and servers to send network-bound requests to network transport drivers.

App
A

transport protocol   Defines how data should be presented to the next receiving layer in the networking model and packages the data accordingly. It passes data to the network adapter card driver through the *NDIS* interface, and to the redirector through the transport driver interface.

TrueType fonts   Fonts that are scalable and sometimes generated as bitmaps or soft fonts, depending on the capabilities of your printer. TrueType fonts can be sized to any height, and they print exactly as they appear on the screen. They are stored as a collection of line and curve commands, together with a collection of hints that are used to adjust the shapes when the font is scaled.

trust relationship   A security relationship between two domains in which the resource domain "trusts" the user of a trusted account domain to use its resources. Users and groups from a trusted domain can be given access permissions to resources in a trusting domain.

TSR   See *terminate- and stay-resident.*

U

UDP   See *user datagram protocol.*

UNC   See *universal naming convention.*

Unimodem   The universal modem driver used by *TAPI* to communicate with modems. It uses modem description files to control its interaction with VCOMM.

uninterruptible power supply (UPS)   A battery-operated power supply connected to a computer to keep the system running during a power failure.

universal naming convention (UNC)   Naming convention, including a server name and share name, used to give a unique name to files on a network. The format is as follows:

    \\servername\sharename\path\filename

UPS   See *uninterruptible power supply.*

UPS service   A software component that monitors an uninterruptible power supply, and shuts the computer down gracefully when line power has failed and the UPS battery is running down.

usability   A determination of how well users can accomplish tasks using a software product. Usability considers the characteristics of a product such as software, manuals, tutorials, help, and so on.

user account   Refers to all the information that identifies a user to Windows NT 4.0, including user name and password, group membership, and rights and permissions.

user datagram protocol (UDP)   The transport protocol offering a connectionless-mode transport service in the Internet suite of protocols. See also *Transport Control Protocol.*

user name   A unique name identifying a user account in Windows NT 4.0. User names must be unique, and cannot be the same as another user name, workgroup, or domain name.

V

value entry   A parameter under a key or subkey in the Registry. A value entry has three components: name, type, and value. The value component can be a string, binary data, or a DWORD.

VDM   See *virtual DOS machine.*

VFAT   See *virtual file allocation table.*

virtual DOS machine (VDM)   A virtual machine provides a complete MS-DOS environment and a character-based window in which to run an MS-DOS-based application. Every MS-DOS application runs in its own *VDM.*

virtual file allocation table (VFAT)   See *file allocation table.*

App
A

virtual machine (VM)   An environment created by the operating system in memory. By using virtual machines, the application developer can write programs that behave as though they own the entire computer. For example, this leaves the job of sorting out which application is receiving keyboard input at the moment to Windows NT 4.0.

virtual memory   The technique by which Windows NT 4.0 uses hard disk space to increase the amount of memory available for running programs.

visual editing   The ability to edit an embedded object in place, without opening it into its own window. Implemented by OLE.

VL   VESA local bus standard for a bus that allows high-speed connections to peripherals, which preceded the PCI specification. Due to limitations in the specification, usually only used to connect video adapters into the system.

VM   See *virtual machine*.

volume   A partition that has been formatted for use by the file system.

VxD   Virtual device driver. The x represents the type of device—for example, a virtual device driver for a display is a VDD and a virtual device driver for a printer is a VPD.

W

wild card   A character that is used to represent one or more characters, such as in a file specification. The question mark (?) wild card can be used to represent any single character, and the asterisk (*) wild card can be used to represent any character or group of characters that might match that position in other file names.

Win32 API   The 32-bit application programming interface used to write 32-bit Windows-based applications. It provides access to the operating system and other functions.

window handle   A 32-bit value that uniquely identifies a window to Windows NT 4.0.

window name   A text string that identifies a window for the user.

Windows Internet Name Service (WINS)   A name resolution service that resolve Windows networking computer names to IP addresses in a routed environment. A WINS server handles name registrations, queries, and releases.

Windows NT   The portable, secure, 32-bit preemptive-multitasking member of the Microsoft Windows operating system family. Windows NT server provides centralized management and security, advanced fault tolerance, and additional connectivity. Windows NT Workstation provides operating system and networking functionality for computers without centralized management.

Windows NT file system (NTFS)   The native file system used by Windows NT. Windows NT 4.0 can detect, but not use, NTFS partitions.

WINS   See *Windows Internet Name Service.*

wizard   A Windows NT 4.0 tool that asks you questions and performs a system action according to your answers. For example, you can use the Add Printer Wizard to add new printer drivers or connect to an existing network printer.

workgroup   A collection of computers that are grouped for viewing purposes or resource sharing, but which do not share security information. Each workgroup is identified by a unique name. See also *domain.*

workstation service   This is the Windows NT computer's redirector. It redirects requests for network resources to the appropriate protocol and network card for access to the server computer.

WYSIWYG   Stands for What You See Is What You Get.

X-Z

X.25   A connection-oriented network facility.

x86-based computer   A computer using a microprocessor equivalent to an Intel 80386 or higher chip. Only x86-based computers can run Windows NT 4.0.

X.121   The addressing format used by X.25 base networks.

X.400   An international messaging standard used in electronic mail systems.

XModem/CRC   A communications protocol for transmitting binary files that uses a cyclic redundancy check (CRC) to detect any transmission errors. Both computers must be set to transmit and receive eight data bits per character.

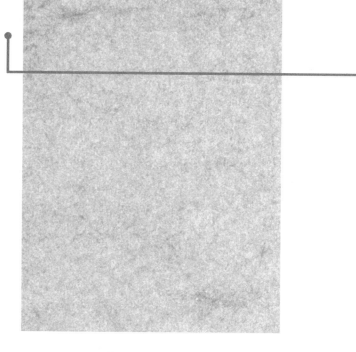

Certification Checklist

In addition to a resource like this book, this list of tasks tells you what you need to know to get on with the certification process.

Getting Started

Once you have decided to start the certification process, you should use the following list as a guideline for getting you started:

1. Get the Microsoft Roadmap to Education and Certification. (See "The Certification Roadmap" sidebar at the end of this appendix.)

2. Use the Roadmap Planning Wizard to determine *your* certification path.

3. Take the Windows NT Server 4.0 Enterprise Assessment Exams located on the CD that accompanies this book to determine *your*

competency level. For Microsoft products other than Windows NT 4.0, you can use the Assessment Exams located on the Roadmap to get a feel for the type of questions that appear on the exam. (See the "Assessment Exams" section in Appendix C.)

Getting Prepared

Getting started is one thing, but getting prepared to take the certification exam is a rather difficult process. The following guidelines will help you prepare for the exam:

1. Use the training materials listed in the Planning Wizard:
   - Microsoft Online Institute (MOLI). (See the section "Microsoft Online Training Institute, (MOLI)" in Appendix C.)
   - Self-Paced Training. (See the section "Self-Paced Training," in Appendix C.)
   - Authorized Technical Education Center. (ATEC). (See the section "Training Resources," in Appendix C.)
   - Additional study materials listed in the Roadmap.

2. Review the section "How Should I Prepare for the Exam?" in Appendix C.

3. Review the Exam Prep Guide on the Roadmap.

4. Gain experience with Windows NT 4.0.

Getting Certified

Call Sylvan Prometric at 1-800-755-EXAM to schedule your exam at a location near you. (See the section "How Do I Register for the Exam?" in Appendix C, and Appendix D, "Testing Tips.")

Getting Benefits

Microsoft will send your certification kit approximately 2–4 weeks after you pass the exam. This kit qualifies you to become a Microsoft Certified Professional. (See the section "Benefits Up Close and Personal," in the Introduction to this book.)

The Certification Roadmap

The Microsoft Roadmap to Education and Certification is an easy-to-use Windows-based application that includes all the information you need to plan a successful training and certification strategy. The Roadmap:

- Provides comprehensive information on the requirements for Microsoft Certified Professional certifications, with detailed exam topic outlines and preparation guidelines.
- Includes detailed outlines and prerequisites for Microsoft courses that are related to specific certification exams, helping you determine which courses teach the skills you need to meet your certification goals.
- Includes information on related Microsoft products and services.
- Helps you create a personal training and certification plan and print a to-do list of required certification activities.

You can request the Roadmap from Microsoft. In the U.S. and Canada, call 1-800-636-7544. Outside the U.S. and Canada, contact your local Microsoft office.

Or you can download it at the following online addresses:

- The Internet: **www.microsoft.com/train_cert/**
- The Microsoft Network (MSN): Go To MOLI, Advising Building, E&C Roadmap.
- Microsoft TechNet: Search for Roadmap and install from the built-in setup link.

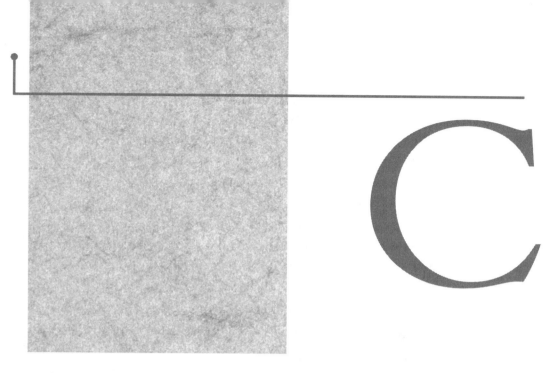

How Do I Get There from Here?

Becoming certified requires a certain level of commitment. The information in this appendix will answer some of the questions you may have about the certification process.

What Will I Be Tested On?

You should be able to apply your knowledge and experience with Windows NT 4.0 to perform the following tasks:

- ◆ Plan for, install, and troubleshoot Windows NT Server 4.0 in the enterprise.

- ◆ Install software or hardware and run applications.

- ◆ Answer "how-to" questions from users.

◆ Tune and optimize your Windows NT Server 4.0.

◆ Customize the Windows NT Server 4.0 system and user environments, especially as it pertains to the enterprise.

◆ Install, manage, and configure the network components of Windows NT Server 4.0.

◆ Create and manage domain user accounts.

◆ Create, manage, and secure network resources.

◆ Troubleshoot systems and solve network hardware or software problems.

◆ Recommend software products, versions, or upgrades.

◆ Collect requests for additional software features and functions.

To successfully complete the Windows NT Server 4.0 Enterprise Exam, you should be able to apply, according to Microsoft, "a comprehensive set of skills to the tasks necessary to administer, implement, and troubleshoot Microsoft Windows NT Server 4.0 in an enterprise computing environment."

Analysis Is Good, but Synthesis Is Harder

Microsoft Certified Professional Exams test for specific cognitive skills needed for the job functions being tested. Educational theorists postulate a hierarchy of cognitive levels, ranging from most basic (knowledge) up to the most difficult (evaluation), and a set of skills associated with each level:

◆ *Knowledge* is the lowest cognitive level at which you can identify, define, locate, recall, state, match, arrange, label, outline, and recognize items, situations, and concepts. Questions that ask for definitions or recitation of lists of characteristics test at this level.

◆ *Comprehension*, the level built immediately upon knowledge, requires that you translate, distinguish between, give examples, discuss, draw conclusions, estimate, explain, indicate, and paraphrase, rather than simply play back answers learned by rote.

◆ *Application* is the level at which hands-on activities come into play. Questions at this level ask you to apply, calculate, solve, plot, choose, demonstrate, design a procedure, change, interpret, or operate.

◆ *Analysis*, one of the top three levels, requires a thorough grounding in the skills required at the lower levels. You operate at this level when you analyze, state conclusions, detect logic errors, compare and contrast, break down, make an inference from, map one situation or problem to another, diagnose, diagram, or discriminate.

◆ *Synthesis* (which is harder than analysis) requires some creativity and the ability to rebuild and reintegrate what may have been disassembled during analysis. This level requires you to construct a table or graph, design, formulate, integrate, generalize, predict, arrange, propose, tell in your own words, or show the relationship between concepts.

◆ *Evaluation*, the highest cognitive level, is based on all the skills accumulated at the lower levels. At this level, you assess, apply standards, decide, indicate fallacies, weigh, show the relationship between, summarize, decide, look at situations and tell what is likely to occur, or make a judgment.

App
C

Exam Objectives

The following list of objectives defines the specific skills Microsoft wants the exam to measure. As you review the list, you can see the level at which the Windows NT Server 4.0 Enterprise Exam tests your knowledge and ability to implement, maintain, and troubleshoot the operating system. When an objective or item on the exam includes a verb or verb phrase associated with a given cognitive level (see the preceding section, "Analysis Is Good, but Synthesis Is Harder"), it is asking you to perform at that cognitive level.

For example, the exam objective "Installing Windows NT Server 4.0 to perform various server roles" asks you to perform at the Analysis level because it asks you to make a determination between three server roles—primary domain controller, backup domain controller, and member server. It's a good idea to be prepared to be tested at the Analysis level or higher for each objective.

You should review the following objectives and be able to apply the listed skills to the tasks described earlier in the section "What Will I Be Tested on?"

Planning

You will be tested for the following planning skills:

◆ Planning the implementation of a directory services architecture, considering appropriate domain models, single logon access, and resource access across domains.

◆ Configure disk drives for various requirements such as fault tolerance.

◆ Install and configure protocols as appropriate for the domain including TCP/IP, DHCP, WINS, NWLINK, DLC, and AppleTalk.

Installation and Configuration

You will be tested for your understanding of the installation process, as well as the various methods and tools available to configure the Windows NT system and user environment. Specific topics include:

◆ Choosing and installing the appropriate server role for Windows NT Server 4.0—for example, primary or secondary domain controller, and member server.

◆ Configuring and binding protocols.

◆ Configuring core services such as Directory Replicator and Computer Browser.

◆ Configuring hard disks to provide redundancy, fault tolerance, and improved performance.

- Creating, adding, and configuring printers, including setting up printer pools and setting printer priorities.
- Configuring Windows NT Server 4.0 for client support such as Windows NT Workstation, Windows 95, and Macintosh.

Managing Resources

You will be tested on your ability to manage disk, file, and print resources, and to create and manage user and group accounts. Specific topics include:

- Managing user and group accounts including user rights, account policies, and auditing changes to the account database.
- Creating and managing policies and profiles for local and roaming users, as well as system policies.
- Remotely administering servers from Windows 95 and NT Workstation clients.
- Managing disk resources through sharing, permissions, file and folder security, and auditing.

App
C

Connectivity

You will be tested for your understanding of Windows NT 4.0 Networking and interoperability issues, including:

- Configuring interoperability among Windows NT Server and Novell NetWare servers through Gateway Services and the Migration Tool.
- Installing and configuring multiprotocol routing for the Internet, the BOOTP/DHCP Relay Agent, and IPX.
- Installing and configuring Internet Information Server and other Internet services including Web services, DNS, and intranets.
- Installing and configuring Remote Access Service including implementing communications access, protocols, and security.

Monitoring and Optimization

You will be tested on your ability to track and optimize system performance using a variety of tools. Specific topics include:

◆ Implementing and using Performance Monitor to measure system performance through the use of baseline measurement object tracking (processor, memory, disk, and network).

◆ Implementing and using Network Monitor to monitor network traffic through data collection, analysis, and filtering.

◆ Identifying performance bottlenecks.

◆ Optimizing server performance to achieve specific results, such as controlling network traffic and server load balancing.

Troubleshooting

You will be tested on your understanding of basic Windows NT 4.0 concepts, processes, and functions, and your ability to choose the correct course of action to resolve problem situations. Specific topics include choosing the appropriate course of action to take to resolve:

◆ Installation failures

◆ Boot failures

◆ Configuration errors such as backing up and restoring the NT Registry, and editing the Registry

◆ Printing problems

◆ RAS problems

◆ Connectivity problems

◆ Resource access and permission problems

◆ Fault-tolerance failures such as backup, mirroring, and striping with parity

◆ Blue-screen problems, configuring a memory dump, and using Event Viewer (Event Log service)

What Kinds of Questions Can I Expect?

The Windows NT Server 4.0 Enterprise Certification Exam includes two types of multiple choice items: single-answer and multiple-answer.

Single-Answer Multiple-Choice Item

A single-answer multiple-choice item presents a problem and a list of possible answers. You must select the best answer to the given question from a list. Each answer is preceded by an `OptionButton` control.

For example: You will be supporting a group of 10 account executives all running Windows NT Workstation on their computers. Occasionally, each account executive will need to share files with some or all of the other account executives. Two of the account executives have printers that all of them will use. You do not expect the group to grow by any more than five more persons. Which computing model will best meet their needs?

    a) The Workgroup Model

    b) The Single Domain Enterprise Model

    c) The Master Domain Enterprise Model

    d) The Complete Trust Enterprise Model

Your response to a single-answer multiple-choice item is scored as either correct (1 or more points) or incorrect (0 points).

The answer to the above question is A, The Workgroup Model.

Multiple-Answer Multiple-Choice Item

A multiple-answer multiple-choice item presents a problem and a list of possible answers. You must select the best answer to the given question from a list. The question is often (but not always) followed by a phrase indicating the number of correct answers, such as "Pick two." Each answer is preceded by a `CheckBox` control.

For example: Which of the following is part of the Kernel mode of the Windows NT architecture? (Select three)

a) WIN32 Subsystem

b) HAL

c) Executive Services

d) Device Driver support

Your response to a multiple-answer multiple-choice item is also scored as either correct (1 or more points) or incorrect (0 points). Your response scores all points only if all the correct answers are selected.

The answer to the above question is B, HAL; C, Executive Services; and D, Device Driver support.

How Should I Prepare for the Exam?

The best way to prepare for the Windows NT Server 4.0 Enterprise Certified Exam is to study, learn, and master Windows NT Server 4.0. If you'd like a little more guidance, Microsoft recommends these specific steps:

1. Identify the objectives you'll be tested on. (See the section "Exam Objectives" earlier in this appendix.)
2. Assess your current mastery of those objectives.
3. Practice tasks and study the areas you haven't mastered.

The following are some tools and techniques, in addition to this book, that may offer a little more help.

Assessment Exams

Microsoft provides self-paced practice, or assessment exams, that you can take at your own computer. *Assessment exams* let you answer questions that are very much like the items in the actual certification exams. Your assessment exam score doesn't necessarily predict what your score will be on the actual exam, but its immediate feedback lets you determine the areas requiring extra study. The assessment exams also offer an additional advantage: They use the same computer-based testing tool as the certification exams, so you don't have to learn how to use the tool on exam day.

An assessment exam exists for almost every certification exam. You can find a complete list of available assessment exams in the Certification Roadmap available from Microsoft.

Microsoft Resources

A number of useful resources available from Microsoft are:

- *Windows NT Server 4.0.* A key component of your exam preparation is your actual use of the product. Gain as much real-world experience with Windows NT 4.0 as possible. As you work with the product, study the online and printed documentation, focusing on areas relating to the exam objectives.

- *Microsoft TechNet.* An information service for support professionals and system administrators. If you're a TechNet member, you receive a monthly CD full of technical information.

Note To join TechNet, refer to the TechNet section in the Microsoft Education and Certification Roadmap (see "The Certification Roadmap" sidebar in Appendix B). ∎

- *Microsoft Developer Network.* A technical resource for Microsoft developers. If you're a member of the Developer Network, you can receive information on a regular basis through the Microsoft Developer Network CD, *Microsoft Developer Network News,* or the Developer Network forum on CompuServe.

Note To join the Microsoft Developer Network, refer to the Microsoft Developer Network section in the Certification Roadmap. ∎

- *Implementing and Supporting Microsoft Windows NT Server 4.0 in the Enterprise Exam Preparation Guide.* A Microsoft publication that provides important specifics about the Windows NT Server 4.0

App C

Enterprise test. The *Exam Preparation Guide* is updated regularly to reflect changes and is the source for the most up-to-date information about Exam 70-68. It can be obtained through Microsoft's World Wide Web site—**www.microsoft.com**.

> **Note** The exam preparation guide can change at any time without prior notice, solely at Microsoft's discretion. Before you register for an exam, make sure that you have the current exam preparation guide by contacting one of the following sources:
>
> - *Microsoft Sales Fax Service.* Call 800-727-3351 in the United States and Canada. Outside the U.S. and Canada, contact your local Microsoft office.
> - *CompuServe.* **GO MSEDCERT**, Library Number 5.
> - *Internet.* Anonymous FTP to **ftp.microsoft.com**, /Services/ MSEdCert/Certification/ExamPreps.
> - *Sylvan Prometric.* Call 800-755-EXAM in the U.S. and Canada. Outside the U.S. and Canada, contact your local Sylvan office. ▪

Microsoft Online Training Institute (MOLI)

The *Microsoft Online Training Institute (MOLI)* on The Microsoft Network (MSN) is an interactive learning and information resource where Learning Advisors (instructors) pair their expert knowledge, guidance, and motivation with electronic self-study materials.

You may access MOLI at its main Classroom Building site on the Internet at **http://moli.microsoft.com**.

You enroll in a class, pay a small tuition fee (to cover the cost of materials and the Learning Advisor's time and expertise), and then receive a shortcut to the classroom. As a student, you can participate in class by interacting with a Learning Advisor and fellow students online via Exchange (e-mail), bulletin boards, forums, or other online communication services available through MSN. You control your own time by studying when and where you choose, working at your own speed, and attending the virtual "class" as often or as little as you want.

Only students enrolled in a class can participate in its online chat sessions and view the contents of the classroom, such as courseware and other materials provided by the Learning Advisor. In addition to MOLI campus resources, you have access to several other resources:

◆ The Assignments BBS gives you access to courseware assignments, test questions that measure subject-matter comprehension, chapter review guides, lab assignments, and information about certification exam topics. You can take advantage of these resources anytime.

◆ One or more chat sessions per week allow you to supplement class courseware, interact with other classmates to solve real-life situations, and get expert advice.

◆ The Notes BBS lets students download and play files, tips, tools, and resources available through Microsoft.

Self-Paced Training

If you prefer to learn on your own, you can obtain Microsoft Official Curriculum training (as well as non-Microsoft Official Curriculum courses) in self-paced formats. Self-paced training kits are available through courses offered on the Microsoft Online Training Institute with materials available in book, computer-based training (CBT), and mixed-media (book and video) formats.

Microsoft Approved Study Guides, such as this book, are self-paced training materials developed by Independent Courseware Vendors (ICVs) to help you prepare for MCP exams. The Study Guides include both single self-paced training courses and series of training courses that map to one or more MCP exams.

Self-training kits and study guides are often available through Microsoft authorized training centers, or you can purchase them where books from Microsoft Press are sold.

Other Online Resources

Both MSN and CompuServe (**GO MECFORUM**) provide access to technical forums for open discussions and questions about Microsoft products. Microsoft's Web site (**http:\\www.microsoft.com**) also allows you to access information about certification and education programs.

Training Resources

Microsoft product groups have designed training courses to support the certification process. The Microsoft Official Curriculum is developed by Microsoft course designers, product developers, and support engineers to help you prepare for MCP exams.

Authorized Technical Education Centers (ATECs), such as Productivity Point International, are approved by Microsoft to provide training on Microsoft products and related technologies. By enrolling in a course taught by a Microsoft Solution Provider ATEC, you receive high-end technical training on the design, development, implementation, and support of enterprise-wide solutions using Microsoft operating systems, tools, and technologies.

You also may take MOC courses via face-to-face training offered by *Microsoft Authorized Academic Training Program (AATP)* institutions. AATP schools use authorized materials and curriculum designed for the MCP program and deliver Microsoft authorized materials, including the Microsoft Official Curriculum, over an academic term.

Supporting Microsoft Windows NT Server 4.0-Enterprise Technologies, course number 689, available from Microsoft authorized training institutions, may help you prepare for the exam. Course 689 is five days long.

For a referral to an AATP or Productivity Point ATEC in your area, call 800-SOLPROV.

Suggested Reading and Internet Sites

When you're looking for additional study aids, check out the books and online sites listed in Appendix F, "Suggested Reading."

How Do I Register for the Exam?

Registering for the Windows NT Server 4.0 Enterprise certification exam is simple:

1. Contact Sylvan Prometric at (800) 755-EXAM, with the examination number (70-68), your social security number, and credit card ready.

2. Complete the registration procedure by phone. (Your SSN becomes the ID attached to your private file; the credit card takes care of the $100 test fee.) Request contact information for the testing center closest to you.

3. After you receive the registration and payment confirmation letter from Sylvan Prometric, call the testing center to schedule your exam. When you call to schedule, you'll be provided with instructions regarding the appointment, cancellation procedures, ID requirements, and information about the testing center location.

You can verify the number of questions and time allotted for your exam at the time of registration. You can schedule exams up to six weeks in advance, or as late as one working day ahead, but you must take the exam within one year of your payment. To cancel or reschedule your exam, contact Sylvan Prometric at least two working days before your scheduled exam date.

 Note At some locations, same-day registration (at least two hours before test time) is available, subject to space availability. ■

App
C

Testing Tips

You've mastered the required tasks to take the exam. After reviewing and re-reviewing the exam objectives, you're confident that you have the skills specified in the exam objectives. You're ready to perform at the highest cognitive level. And it's time to head for the testing center. This appendix covers some tips and tricks to remember.

Before the Test

Make sure you take care of the following items:

◆ Wear comfortable clothing. You want to focus on the exam, not on a tight shirt collar or pinching pair of shoes.

◆ Allow plenty of travel time. Get to the testing center 10 or 15 minutes early; nothing's worse than rushing in at the last minute. Give yourself time to relax.

◆ If you've never been to the testing center before, make a trial run a few days before to make sure that you know the route to the center.

◆ Carry with you at least two forms of identification, including one photo ID (such as a driver's license or company security ID). You will have to show them before you can take the exam.

Remember that the exams are closed-book. The use of laptop computers, notes, or other printed materials is not permitted during the exam session.

At the test center, you'll be asked to sign in. The test administrator will give you a Testing Center Regulations form that explains the rules that govern the examination. You will be asked to sign the form to indicate that you understand and will comply with its stipulations.

When the administrator shows you to your test computer, make sure that:

◆ The testing tool starts up and displays the correct exam. If a tutorial for using the instrument is available, you should be allowed time to take it.

Note   If you have any special needs, such as reconfiguring the mouse buttons for a left-handed user, you should inquire about them when you register for the exam with Sylvan Prometric. Special configurations are not possible at all sites, so you should not assume that you will be permitted to make any modifications to the equipment setup and configuration. Site administrators are *not* permitted to make modifications without prior instructions from Sylvan. ■

◆ You have a supply of scratch paper for use during the exam. (The administrator collects all scratch paper and notes made during the exam before your leave the center.) Some centers are now providing you with a wipe-off board and magic marker to use instead of paper. You are not permitted to make any kind of notes to take with you, due to exam security.

◆ You find out if your exam includes additional materials or exhibits. If any exhibits are required for your exam, the test administrator will provide you with them before you begin the exam and collect them from you at the end of the exam.

◆ The administrator tells you what to do when you complete the exam.

◆ You get answers to any and all of your questions or concerns before the exam begins.

As a Microsoft Certification examination candidate, you are entitled to the best support and environment possible for your exam. If you experience any problems on the day of the exam, inform the Sylvan Prometric test administrator immediately.

During the Test

The testing software lets you move forward and backward through the items, so you can implement a strategic approach to the test:

1. Go through all the items, answering the easy questions first. Then go back and spend time on the harder ones. Microsoft guarantees that there are no trick questions. The correct answer is always among the list of choices. Also, test questions can be marked and returned to later. If you encounter a question that you are not sure about, mark it and go back to it later. Chances are that you may gain some insight into how to answer the marked question from another subsequent question.

2. Eliminate the obviously incorrect answer first to clear away the clutter and simplify your choices.

3. Answer all the questions. You aren't penalized for guessing, so it can't hurt.

4. Don't rush. Haste makes waste (or substitute the cliché of your choice).

After the Test

When you have completed an exam:

- The testing tool gives you immediate, online notification of your pass or fail status, except for beta exams. Because of the beta process, your results for a beta exam are mailed to you approximately six to eight weeks after the exam.

- The administrator gives you a printed Examination Score Report indicating your pass or fail status and your exam results by section.

- Test scores are automatically forwarded to Microsoft within five working days after you take the test. If you pass the exam, you receive confirmation from Microsoft within two to four weeks.

If you don't pass a certification exam:

- Review your individual section scores, noting areas where your score must be improved. The section titles in your exam report generally correspond to specific groups of exam objectives.

- Review the exam information in this book; then get the latest Exam Preparation Guide and focus on the topic areas that need strengthening.

- Intensify your effort to get your real-world, hands-on experience and practice with Windows NT 4.0.

- Try taking one or more of the approved training courses.

- Review the suggested readings listed at the end of this appendix or in the Exam Preparation Guide.

- Take (or re-take) the Windows NT 4.0 Assessment Exam.

- Call Sylvan Prometric to register, pay, and schedule the exam again.

Contacting Microsoft

Microsoft encourages feedback from exam candidates, especially suggestions for improving any of the exams or preparation materials.

To provide program feedback, to find out more about Microsoft Education and Certification materials and programs, to register with Sylvan Prometric, or to get other useful information, check the following resources.

 Note Outside the United States or Canada, contact your local Microsoft office or Sylvan Prometric testing center. ■

Microsoft Certified Professional Program

(800) 636-7544

e-mail to **mcp@msprograms.com**

For information about the Microsoft Certified Professional program and exams, and to order the Microsoft Roadmap to Education and Certification.

Sylvan Prometric Testing Centers

(800) 755-EXAM

To register to take a Microsoft Certified Professional Exam at any of more than 700 Sylvan Prometric testing centers around the world.

Microsoft Sales Fax Service

(800) 727-3351

For Microsoft Certified Professional Exam Preparation Guides and Microsoft Official Curriculum course descriptions and schedules.

Education Program and Course Information

(800) SOLPROV

For information about Microsoft Official Curriculum courses, Microsoft education products, and the Microsoft Solution Provider Authorized Technical Education Center (ATEC) program, where you can attend a Microsoft Official Curriculum course, and to obtain the Microsoft Roadmap to Education and Certification.

Microsoft Certification Development Team

Fax: (206) 936-1311

To volunteer for participation in one or more exam development phases or to report a problem with an exam. Address written correspondence to:

> Certification Development Team
> Microsoft Education and Certification
> One Microsoft Way
> Redmond, WA 98052

Microsoft TechNet Technical Information Network

(800) 344-2121

For support professionals and system administrators to obtain information about or order the Microsoft TechNet CD series subscription. (Outside the U.S. and Canada, call your local Microsoft subsidiary for information.)

Microsoft Developer Network (MSDN)

(800) 759-5474

The official source for software development kits, device driver kits, operating systems, and information about developing applications for Microsoft Windows and Windows NT.

Microsoft Technical Support Options

(800) 936-3500

For information about the technical support options available for
Microsoft products, including technical support telephone numbers and
Premier Support options. (Outside the U.S. and Canada, call your local
Microsoft subsidiary for information.)

Microsoft Online Institute (MOLI)

(800) 449-9333

e-mail to **MOLI_Quest@MSN.COM**

Internet site: **http://moli.microsoft.com**

For information about Microsoft's new online training program.

Suggested Reading

Titles from Que

Que Corporation offers a wide variety of technical books for all levels of users. The following are some recommended titles, in alphabetical order, that can provide you with additional information on many of the exam topics and objectives.

Note The final version of Windows NT 4.0 Workstation and Server was released in late August, 1996. Books with a publisher's date earlier than this were probably written based on the beta versions of the Windows NT 4.0 software. This note should by no means discourage you from considering these books for purchase, nor is it meant to reflect negatively on the authorship or content, especially where Windows NT concepts are concerned. However, the final versions of software sometimes introduce subtle changes in look and feel which may not exactly match a description given in the book. ▪

Tip

To order any books from Que Corporation or other imprints of Macmillan Computer Publishing (SAMS, New Riders Publishing, Ziff-Davis Press, and others), call 800-428-5331, visit Macmillan's Information SuperLibrary on the World Wide Web (**http://www.mcp.com**), or check your local bookseller.

Windows NT 4.0 Installation and Configuration Handbook

Author: Jim Boyce

ISBN: 0–7897–0818–3

Special Edition Using Windows NT Server 4.0

Author: Roger Jennings

ISBN: 0–7897–0251–7

Other Titles

Advanced Windows, by Jeffrey Richter (Microsoft Press; ISBN 1–55615–677–4)

Inside Windows NT Server 4.0, by Drew Heywood (New Riders Publishing; ISBN: 1–56205–649–2)

Managing Windows NT Server, by Howard F. Hilliker (New Riders Publishing; ISBN: 1–56205–576–3)

Microsoft Windows NT Workstation Resource Kit (Version 4.0) (Microsoft Press; ISBN: 1–57231–343–9)

Microsoft Windows NT Server 4.0 Resource Kit (Microsoft Press; ISBN: 1–57231–344–7)

Professional Windows NT Server Resource Kit, by New Riders Publishing (New Riders Publishing; ISBN: 1–56205–703–0)

Windows NT Server Professional Reference, by Karanjit S. Siyan, Ph.D. (New Riders Publishing; ISBN: 1-56205-659-X)

Windows NT Registry Troubleshooting, by Rob Tidrow (New Riders Publishing; ISBN: 1-56205-660-3)

Windows NT Server 4 Security, Troubleshooting, and Optimization, by New Riders Publishing (New Riders Publishing; ISBN: 1-56205-601-8)

Windows NT 4 Server Unleashed, by Jason Garms, et al (SAMS Publishing; ISBN: 0-672-30933-5)

Windows NT 4.0 Overview

This appendix provides an overview of the features and functionality of Microsoft Windows NT Workstation and Server 4.0. Topics discussed in this appendix include:

◆ Providing a list of features and functionality common to the Windows NT product line past and present, and exploring certain specific characteristics in more detail.

◆ Understanding when an installation of Windows NT Workstation or Server is appropriate given the needs of the clients involved, the level of administration desired, and the level of security required.

◆ Introducing the basic architecture of the Windows NT operating system and explaining the features and functions that are new to version 4.0.

◆ Comparing Microsoft's Workgroup model with its Enterprise model of network communication.

Microsoft Windows NT Features Overview

Microsoft Windows NT is a 32-bit operating system designed to provide fast and efficient performance for power computer users such as software developers, CAD programmers, and design engineers. Because it provides better performance for existing 16-bit applications (both MS-DOS and Windows), as well as 32-bit applications developed specifically for the operating system, Windows NT is increasingly found on the desks of business users. These performance enhancements include:

◆ Multiple platform support

◆ Preemptive multitasking

◆ Expanded processing support

◆ Expanded memory support

◆ Expanded file system support

◆ Enhanced security

◆ Network and communications support

Multiple Platform Support

Microsoft Windows NT is engineered to run on several hardware platforms. The *Hardware Abstraction Layer*, or *HAL*, component of the Windows NT architecture isolates platform-specific information for the operating system—for example, how to interact with a RISC-based processor as opposed to an Intel x86 processor. This makes Windows NT a highly portable system through the recompilation of only a few pieces of code such as the HAL. Windows NT supports Intel x86 and Pentium-based computers and RISC-based computers such as MIPS R4000, DEC Alpha AXP, and PowerPC.

Preemptive Multitasking

All processes in Windows NT are given at least one thread of operation. A *thread* represents a piece of code relating to a process. For example, loading a file may require several threads to carry out the process—locating the file on disk, allocating RAM for the file, and moving it into that allocated memory space. Many processes and applications written for Windows and Windows NT have multiple threads associated with them. Windows NT can treat each thread of a process independently of the others, providing a greater degree of control over the overall performance of the system.

Each thread also is given a processing priority based on its function. For example, an operating system process such as memory allocation receives a higher priority for its threads than a file save process. Each thread is given a specific amount of time with the processor. This is sometimes called *time-slicing*. Higher priority threads are processed ahead of lower priority threads. All the threads of one priority are processed first, before those of the next priority, and so on. This process is called *preemptive multitasking*.

In addition, certain threads, primarily those that are system-related, are processed in the protected mode of the processor (known as *ring 0*) and thus are protected from other processes and crashes. Other threads, those relating to application functions such as file printing, run in the unprotected mode of the processor. This means that while they may be given their own memory space, other "poorly written" applications (and their threads) might try to "butt in" resulting in what is generally referred to as a *General Protection* or *GP fault*.

Microsoft and Windows NT have taken several precautions to ensure that this does not happen in Windows NT. Supporting both multitasking and multithreading gives applications excellent processing support and protection against system hangs and crashes.

App

G

Expanded Processing Support

Microsoft Windows NT provides *symmetric multiprocessing* with support for OEM implementations of up to 32 processors. Every process that runs under Windows NT has at least one thread of operation or programming code associated with it. A process might be user-generated such as the writing of a file to disk or printing a document; or system-generated such as validating a user logon or providing read access to a file.

Symmetric multiprocessing enables the Windows NT operating system to load balance process threads across all available processors in the computer, as opposed to *asymmetric multiprocessing* in which the operating system takes control of one processor and directs application threads to other available processors.

Expanded Memory Support

Windows NT supports computers with up to 4G of RAM and theoretic file or partition sizes of up to 16 exabytes (though this number will vary depending on the type of hardware you have). An *exabyte* is one billion gigabytes. You might consider that to be a theoretical number, and to a certain extent it is. However, it was not that long ago that MIS departments debated the wisdom of purchasing 10M disk drives for their users' computers because they felt that the drives would never be filled.

Expanded File System Support

Windows NT provides support for the MS-DOS FAT (File Allocation Table) file system as well as its own NTFS (New Technology File System). Previous versions of Windows NT also supported OS/2's HPFS (High Performance File System). Version 4.0 no longer provides support for HPFS.

NTFS provides a high level of security in the form of file and directory level permissions similar to those found in other network operating systems such as trustee rights used in Novell's NetWare. NTFS also provides transaction tracking to help recover data in the event of system failure and *sector sparing*, which identifies potentially bad disk storage space and moves data to good storage. NTFS also provides data compression implemented as a file or directory property.

Enhanced Security

Security begins with Windows NT's WINLOGON and Net Logon processes which authenticate a user's access to a computer, workgroup, or enterprise by validating the user name and password and assigning each its own security identifier. In addition to this mandatory logon, Windows NT offers share-level resource control, security auditing functions, and file and directory level permissions (in NTFS partitions).

Network and Communications Support

Windows NT is designed to provide several internetworking options. The NetBEUI, NWLINK (IPX/SPX), TCP/IP, AppleTalk, and DLC protocols are all supported and included. Windows NT also is supported on Novell NetWare networks, Microsoft LAN Manager, IBM LAN Server and SNA networks, Banyan VINES, and DEC PATHWORKS.

Through *Remote Access Service (RAS)*, Windows NT offers a secure dial-up option for clients and servers. RAS clients can remotely access any shared network resource to which they have been given access through RAS' gateway functions, such as shared folders and printers.

In a Windows NT network valid workstation, clients include Microsoft Windows NT workstations and servers, Windows 3.x, MS-DOS, Windows for Workgroups, Windows 95, OS/2, Novell NetWare (client/server), and Macintosh.

Choosing Windows NT Workstation or Server

The difference in choosing when to use Windows NT Workstation or Windows NT Server is not necessarily the difference between desktop

App
G

and enterprise computing. Both Windows NT Workstation and Windows NT Server provide the capability to make resources available on the network and thus act as a "server." For that matter, a Windows NT Server could be made part of a workgroup of Windows NT Workstations to act as the resource server for that workgroup. Choosing Windows NT Workstation or Windows NT Server really comes down to the features specific to each product and the type of network model that will be implemented. The following sections discuss the differences between Windows NT Workstation and Windows NT Server.

Microsoft Windows NT Workstation

Microsoft Windows NT Workstation is designed for the so-called power user, such as developers or CAD designers, but is increasingly becoming the desktop operating system of choice for end-user business computing because of its robust feature set as described in the last section. In addition to those features and functions which are common to both Windows NT Workstation and Windows NT Server, Windows NT Workstation offers the following specific characteristics:

- ◆ Unlimited outbound peer-to-peer connections
- ◆ Ten inbound client connections for resource access
- ◆ Can be a RAS client or server, but supports only one remote dial-in session
- ◆ Retail installation supports two processors for symmetric multiprocessing
- ◆ Acts as an import server for Directory Replication Services

Microsoft Windows NT Server

Windows NT Server is designed to provide file, print, and application service support within a given network model. While it also can be used as a desktop system, it is engineered to provide optimum performance when providing network services—for example, by optimizing memory differently for application servers than for domain controllers. In addition to the features and functions described previously, Windows NT Server offers the following:

◆ Allows as many inbound connections to resources as there are valid client licenses (virtually unlimited).

◆ Support for as many as 256 remote dial-in RAS sessions.

◆ Retail installation supports as many as four processors for symmetric multiprocessing.

◆ Provides a full set of services for application and network support such as:

- Services for Macintosh allowing client support for Macintosh computers

- Gateway Service for NetWare allowing Windows NT clients to access Novell NetWare file and print resources

- Directory Replication Service for copying of directory structures and files from a source Windows NT server computer to a target Windows NT server or workstation computer

◆ Provides full integration into the Microsoft BackOffice suite including System Management Server, SNA Server, and SQL Server.

New Features and Functions in Windows NT 4.0

This newest version of Windows NT continues Microsoft's commitment to reliable, performance-driven, network-ready operating systems by incorporating the power, features, and functions of the Windows NT operating system with the object-oriented Windows 95 user interface. Enhanced features and functions common to both Windows NT 4.0 Workstation and Server include:

◆ Windows 95 user interface

◆ Windows Explorer

◆ Hardware profiles

App
G

- ◆ Enhanced dial-up networking support
- ◆ NDS-aware client services for Novell NetWare 4.x
- ◆ Integrated Microsoft Exchange Client
- ◆ Internet Explorer 2.0
- ◆ Web services

Windows 95 User Interface

All the basic features of Microsoft's Windows 95 interface have been integrated into Windows NT 4.0. This includes updated or enhanced system utilities like the Performance Monitor (called the System Monitor in Windows 95), as well as additional utilities such as the Windows Explorer, Network Neighborhood, Briefcase, Desktop shortcuts, Microsoft Network support, and the Recycle Bin.

Windows Explorer

This feature of the interface replaces the File Manager utility. It provides excellent browsing capabilities for management of drives, directories, files, and network connections. Explorer presents the user's data access information as a hierarchy of drives, desktop, network connections, folders, and files. The browsing capabilities of Explorer offer not only browsing of file and directory names, but also of data strings within files. Throughout this book and its labs, you will use Windows Explorer to access files and folders, set permissions, create and manage shared folders, and more.

 Note Though Windows Explorer replaces the File Manager utility by default, File Manager is still available and can be launched by the user.

File Manager can be run by following these simple steps:

1. Choose Start from the taskbar.
2. Choose Run from the Start menu.
3. Enter the File Manager file name, **winfile.exe**.
4. Choose OK.

Microsoft recommends using File Manager only until you become comfortable with Windows Explorer. File Manager is still available for transition purposes only. ■

Hardware Profiles

Perhaps one of the most useful enhancements to Windows NT 4.0 is the support for multiple hardware profiles. First introduced in Windows 95, this feature enables you to create hardware profiles to fit various computing needs. The most common example for using hardware profiles would be with portable computers. You can create separate profiles to support the portable when it is in use by itself, and for when it is positioned in a docking station.

> **Note**   *Plug and Play* is a much appreciated feature of Windows 95. Note that while the Plug and Play service has been included with Windows NT 4.0, "hot" plug and play—that is to say, the ability for the operating system to recognize a configuration change on-the-fly and implement it—will not be fully supported until the next major release of Windows NT. Windows NT 4.0 does, however, recognize some hardware changes when it restarts. For example, additional memory or a new hard disk will be automatically detected by Windows NT the next time you boot up. ■

Enhanced Dial-Up Networking Support

The RAS Client service now is installed as *Dial-Up Networking*. In addition, Windows NT 4.0 provides the Dial-Up Networking Monitor for monitoring user connections and devices as well as Remote Access Admin for monitoring remote user access to a RAS Server.

Windows NT 4.0 also offers Telephony API version 2.0 (TAPI) and universal modem driver (Unimodem) support which provides communications technology for Fax applications, the Microsoft Exchange client, the Microsoft Network (MSN), and Internet Explorer.

App
G

NDS Aware Client Service for Novell NetWare 4.x

Microsoft provides an enhanced version of its Client Services for NetWare (CSNW) with Windows NT 4.0 which supplies compatibility with Novell NetWare servers (versions 3.x and higher) running NetWare Directory Services (NDS). This allows users to view NetWare shared resources organized in an hierarchical tree format.

Integrated Microsoft Windows Messaging

Microsoft *Windows Messaging* is Microsoft's newest electronic mail product. Windows Messaging is included with Windows NT 4.0 and enables users to send and receive mail, embed objects in mail messages, and integrate mail functionality into Microsoft applications.

Internet Explorer 2.0

Microsoft's Internet Explorer 2.0 is included with Windows NT 4.0 to enable users access to the Internet. However, Microsoft now has Internet Explorer 3.0 available through its various Internet sites (**www.microsoft.com**, for example). Watch for Microsoft to continue to enhance this product and make upgrades widely (and cheaply) available.

Note   Internet Explorer requires that the TCP/IP protocol be installed, and a connection made to the Internet or an organization's intranet for file and htm searching and connection. ■

Web Publishing

Microsoft includes Web publishing services in Windows NT 4.0 which allow you to develop, publish, and manage Web pages, FTP, and Gopher services for your company's intranet, or for smaller peer-to-peer networks. With Windows NT 4.0 Workstation, Microsoft provides *Peer Web Services (PWS)* for smaller workgroup-based Web publishing. With Windows NT 4.0 Server, Microsoft provides *Internet Information Services (IIS)* designed for heavy intranet and Internet usage.

Integrated Network Monitor Agent

Windows NT Server 4.0 includes a version of the Network Monitor utility which is included with Microsoft's System Management Server BackOffice product. *Network Monitor* provides a full range of network analysis tools for tracking and interpreting network traffic, frames, and so on.

Last but Certainly Not Least

Of all the features contained in Windows NT 4.0, there is one from which you will obtain the most productivity. It also is an example of enhancements made to Windows NT's Open GL and direct draw video support. This is of course, PINBALL! Yes, there is a new game added to Windows NT 4.0 and it is quite an addition. As mentioned, it does take full advantage of changes to Windows NT's architecture and enhancements for video support. Try it out!

Note Pinball is installed in the Games folder which can be found by choosing Start, Programs, Accessories, Games. If you have not installed your games, you can use the Add/Remove Programs applet in the Control Panel to add them. In the applet, choose the Windows Setup tab, highlight Accessories, choose Details, and select Games. Choose OK. Be sure to have your source files or CD handy because Windows NT will prompt you for them. ■

In addition to these features which Windows NT Workstation and Server 4.0 share, Windows NT Server 4.0 offers the following specific list of features and functions:

- ◆ DNS Name Server and enhanced support
- ◆ Integrated support for multiprotocol routing
- ◆ Enhanced support for BOOTP and DHCP routing
- ◆ Remote reboot support for Windows 95 clients
- ◆ New remote server administration tools for Windows 95 clients
- ◆ Installation wizards for most utility program installations

App
G

Basic Architecture of Windows NT 4.0

An integral part of any understanding of Windows NT is a discussion of the internal architecture of the Windows NT operating system. There are several resources available for an in-depth coverage of this topic. However, this basic overview will provide the building blocks and concepts needed to comprehend Windows NT security, service support, and other topics covered in this book.

The Windows NT 4.0 architecture consists of two primary processing areas: user or application mode, and kernel or privileged processor mode. The user mode, as it implies, provides operating system support primarily for user applications and the environment.

The kernel mode provides operating system support services for just about everything else including kernel processing, memory management, hardware access, and so on. These kernel mode services are referred to as the *Executive Services*.

User (Application) Mode

The user mode of the operating system provides application processing support. Applications in Windows NT run in one of three subsystems provided by the operating system: WIN32, OS/2, and POSIX. The primary subsystem, and that which is loaded at boot time, is WIN32. Win32 supports both 32-bit Windows and Win95 applications, as well as 16-bit DOS and Windows applications.

> **Note**   OS/2 was designed and implemented by IBM to support 32-bit applications in an object-oriented environment. POSIX stands for *Portable Operating System Interface for UNIX* and was originally an IEEE effort to standardize portability of applications across UNIX-based environments. ▪

The OS/2 subsystem provides support for 1.x character-based OS/2 applications. POSIX provides support for POSIX-based applications. Any application program calls from these two subsystems that read/

write to the display are forwarded to the WIN32 subsystem. Any other calls to drivers or other Executive Services are communicated directly to the kernel mode.

In Windows NT version 3.51, the USER and GDI (Graphics Device Interface) portions of the operating system were included in the WIN32 subsystem, thus in user mode. The USER is the Window Manager and responds to user input on-screen. The GDI processes graphics primitives such as pixels, lines, fills, and so on. The GDI also performs graphics rendering for print files.

If an application needed either the user or GDI for processing, it would have to create an *IPC (InterProcess Communication)* to it. This would involve a context switch from user mode to kernel mode (ring 0 to ring 3 of the processor) as well as 64K buffering. Then, another context switch would take place back to user mode. This, obviously, involves some time and decreases overall performance.

Windows NT version 4.0 moves the USER and GDI into the kernel mode. This move significantly improves application performance by eliminating the 64K buffer and leaving only a kernel transition. The benefit can be seen particularly in those applications that involve direct draw to the screen such as Pinball, as well as in multimedia applications such as QuickTime.

Kernel (Privileged Processor) Mode

Kernel mode provides support for all major operating system functions. It controls access to memory and the execution of privileged instructions. All kernel mode processes run in the protected mode of the processor, ring 0. As such, the applications running in user mode are effectively buffered from direct access to hardware. Thus, 16-bit applications which are designed to access hardware directly will not run successfully under Windows NT. These would have to be rewritten to "talk" to the Windows NT kernel mode services.

The kernel mode consists of three parts: Executive Services, HAL, and Windows NT kernel.

App

G

Executive Services

This is the largest part of kernel mode. The Executive Services provide support for processes, threads, memory management, I/O, IPC, and security. It is here that most Windows NT services and process managers execute. It also is here where device driver support is provided, including Windows NT's network architecture support drivers, protocols, and so on. It is written mostly in portable C code which helps make Windows NT portable across platforms. It is this C code that needs to be recompiled in order to accommodate different platforms such as Dec Alpha, PowerPC, and MIPS.

Windows NT Kernel

The Windows NT kernel provides support for thread management and context switching, synchronization among services and processes in Executive Services, multiprocessor load balancing, and exception and interrupt handling.

HAL (Hardware Abstraction Layer)

The HAL provides hardware platform support. It isolates specific platform details from the Executive Services and the Windows NT kernel. It is largely due to the HAL, that those 16-bit applications that like to talk directly to hardware are unable to run. It can be said, therefore, that users' applications are effectively isolated from base hardware interaction under Windows NT. HAL does it for you.

Windows NT Virtual Memory Management

One of the Executive Services managers is the *Virtual Memory Manager*. The memory architecture of Windows NT is a 32-bit, demand-based flat model. This model allows the Virtual Memory Manager to access up to 4G of RAM—generally far more than the amount of physical RAM installed in most computers.

If you recall Windows' swap file model, you're aware of two types of swap files: permanent and temporary. Both swap files managed available RAM in 4K pieces using an internal Windows algorithm called the *LRU (Least Recently Used)*. Essentially, the LRU said that the piece of code in memory that was least recently accessed by a process was liable to be swapped to disk when more RAM was needed for a current process. On computers with the minimal required RAM for Windows, there could be a considerable amount of swapping that takes place.

The main difference between permanent and temporary swap files is that a permanent swap file has a preallocated amount of space reserved on the disk. Temporary swap files begin at 2M and then "grow" as needed to a predetermined amount. Thus, while a permanent swap file actually provided better swap performance because the space was always there and available, it also reduced the amount of available disk storage. Similarly, while temporary swap files did not reduce the amount of disk storage available up front, more resource was expended in finding additional storage space when the swap file needed to "grow."

Windows NT combines the "best" of these swap files. The Windows NT pagefile (PAGEFILE.SYS) is created when Windows NT is installed and generally defaults to an initial, preallocated size (permanent swap files) of 12 plus physical RAM and a maximum size of three times physical RAM (depending on the amount of disk space available). So, on a computer with 16M of physical RAM, the default initial pagefile size would be 28M (12+16M) and the maximum size would be about 48M (3*16M). Windows NT will boot with the initial size pagefile available. The pagefile subsequently grows as applications are loaded and demands for physical RAM increase.

It is important to realize that while Windows NT allows addressing of up to 4G of physical RAM, the Virtual Memory Manager can allocate up to 2G of *virtual* storage for *each* application. Another 2G is allocated for all system (kernel mode) processing. The Virtual Memory Manager addresses application memory.

1. When an application is loaded, the Virtual Memory Manager assigns it virtual memory addresses in physical RAM.
2. The data is then moved in pages out of physical RAM and into the pagefile.

App
G

3. As the data is needed by the application, it calls for the virtual memory addresses.

4. The Virtual Memory Manager moves those pages on demand into available locations in physical RAM.

This process of assigning virtual addresses to the application effectively hides the organization of physical RAM from the application. The various pages of the application may wind up in non-contiguous space in physical RAM (that is, in sectors which may be distributed at different locations on the disk rather than next to each other). But as the Virtual Memory Manager is providing it with its addresses, it really doesn't care—because it doesn't know. This allows Windows NT to make the most efficient use of available physical RAM, and provides an overall performance increase for application processing.

Windows NT Cache Manager

The final aspect of the Windows NT Architecture that we will discuss is the Windows NT Cache Manager. As one might expect by now, the tried-and-true Windows and DOS SMARTDrive disk cache manager is no more. It has been replaced by an operating system-driven Cache Manager that runs as part of the Executive Services, and thus in kernel mode. Its actual physical size depends on the amount of physical RAM installed. Windows NT's cache competes for RAM with other applications and processes, and thus is automatically sized by the Cache Manager working in synch with the Memory Manager.

The Cache Manager provides an intelligent read-ahead/write-back operation. It predicts the next read location based on the history and locations of the last three reads. It also performs *lazy writes*—that is, using the processor when it is not being accessed by any other process—to update the file on disk while maintaining data in memory for quick access.

Internet Resources for Windows NT

Microsoft's Windows operating system series (Windows 95, Windows NT 4.0 Workstation, Windows NT Server 4.0) has become quite popular. The amount of new information and programs that become available each day is staggering. If you don't want to wait for the next super book or next month's magazine, you can go online to get new information. You can get a lot of information through commercial online services such as CompuServe, America Online, or The Microsoft Network (MSN). You'll find more variety, and potentially more useful information, on the Internet, however.

That's where this appendix comes in. It points you to some of the best resources on the Internet for Windows NT information and programs, and earlier versions, as well as version 4.0. Keep in mind that there are hundreds of Internet sites for each Windows NT site that you find in this appendix. I didn't include most of them because they contain links to the other sites. The result is a Web of Windows NT pages, all linked together, that contains nothing but links.

This chapter teaches you about:

◆ *FTP Servers.* It's usually easier to find shareware programs on the World Wide Web, but this sample of FTP sites collects so many programs in a few areas that they're worth checking out.

◆ *Mailing lists.* Sometimes it's easier to let the information you want come to you, instead of going out onto the Internet to look for it. Mailing lists deliver information directly to your mailbox.

◆ *World Wide Web.* There's little doubt that the Web is the hottest resource on the Internet. You find a variety of Web pages dedicated to Windows NT, including personal and corporate Web pages.

On the Web

You can find shortcuts to the Internet address described here at Que's Web site at:

http://www.quecorp.com

FTP Servers

The FTP servers in this section contain large collections of Windows NT shareware programs. They are all well organized, so you can quickly find the program you're looking for. Note that most of these sites are indexed by **Shareware.com**.

TIP

If you don't have an FTP client, you can use your Web browser to access FTP servers. Type **ftp://** followed by the FTP address in your Web browser's address bar.

Microsoft

FTP address: **ftp://ftp.microsoft.com**

This is the place to look for updated drivers, new files for Windows NT, and sometimes free programs. My favorite part of this FTP site is the

Knowledge Base articles that answer common questions about most of Microsoft's programs. If you're having trouble finding your way around, look for a file called DIR.MAP.TXT, which tells you what the different folders have in them. Here's what you find under each of the folders on this site:

- **/BUSSYS.** Files for business systems, including networking, mail, SQL Server, and Windows NT. Here you can find some knowledge base links specific to Windows NT. The Knowledge Base entries related to Windows NT reflect all versions of Windows NT.

- **/DESKAPPS.** Files for all of Microsoft's desktop applications, including Access, Excel, PowerPoint, Project, and Word. You can also find information for the Home series, including games and Works.

- **/DEVELPR.** The place to look if you're a developer. There are folders for Visual C++, Visual Basic, various utilities, the Microsoft Developer Network, and more. If you subscribe to the *Microsoft Systems Journal*, check here to find the source code for articles.

- **/KBHELP.** Microsoft's Knowledge Base folder. A *knowledge base*, in this context, is a help file that contains common questions and answers about Microsoft products. This folder contains one self-extracting, compressed file for each Microsoft product. There is not a lot of information here as yet about Windows NT 4.0. However, this is still a good area to keep scanning for the newest data.

- **/SOFTLIB.** The folder to check out if you're looking for up-dated drivers, patches, or bug fixes. This folder contains more than 1,500 files, though, so you need to check out INDEX.TXT to locate what you want.

- **/PEROPSYS.** For personal operating systems. If you're looking for back issues of *WINNEWS*, look in the **WIN_NEWS** folder. There are other folders relating to all versions of Windows, MS-DOS, and Microsoft hardware.

◆ **/SERVICES.** Contains information about TechNet, Microsoft educational services, sales information, and so on.

 Note   Many of the folders on the Microsoft FTP site have two files that you should read: README.TXT and INDEX.TXT.

README.TXT describes the type of files you find in the current folder and any subfolders. It also may describe recent additions and files that have been removed.

INDEX.TXT describes each file in the folder. It's a good idea to search for the file you want in INDEX.TXT before trying to pick it out of the listing. Note that Microsoft's site is constantly changing, so you'll want to check back here often. ■

Walnut Creek

FTP address: **ftp://ftp.cdrom.com**

I consider myself lucky to get on this FTP site; it's incredibly popular. Walnut Creek sells CD-ROMs that are packed with freeware and shareware programs. Files from these CD-ROMs are available from the Walnut Creek FTP site, too. Here are some folders that you can find for Windows NT:

    alpha
    incoming
    intel

 Tip
This site is usually very crowded. If you get onto this site, don't let yourself get disconnected by taking a coffee break; it could be a while before you get on again.

Mailing Lists

Windows NT-related mailing lists keep your mailbox full of messages. There's a lot of noise generated by these lists, but you can find a lot of gems, too. This section describes two of the most popular ones: DevWire and WinNews.

Microsoft DevWire

This is for Windows programmers. You'll find news and product information, such as seminar schedules and visual tool release schedules. To subscribe, send an e-mail to **DevWire@microsoft.nwnet.com** and type **subscribe DevWire** in the body of your message.

Microsoft WinNews

This weekly newsletter keeps you up-to-date on the latest happenings at Microsoft. You also find product tips and press releases. To subscribe, send an e-mail to **enews99@microsoft.nwnet.com** and type **subscribe winnews** in the body of your message.

World Wide Web

The explosive growth of Windows Web pages is evident if you search for the keyword **Windows NT** using Yahoo!, WebCrawler, Excite, or Lycos. You can find thousands of Web pages dedicated to Windows NT, some from the corporate community such as Microsoft or Symantec. Many more exist from individuals who want to make their mark on the world by sharing what they know about Windows NT.

The Web pages in this section are only a start. Many contain links to other Windows NT sites. Before you know it, your Windows NT favorite places list will grow by leaps and bounds.

Microsoft Corporation

URL address: **http://www.microsoft.com**

Microsoft's Web site contains an amazing amount of information about its products, services, plans, job opportunities, and more. You can find the two most useful Windows NT Web pages by clicking the Products link or the Support link.

Here's what you find on each:

◆ *Products link.* This Web page contains links for most Microsoft products, including Windows NT. You find links to Microsoft pages for Windows 95, Office, BackOffice, Windows NT Workstation, and more. The bulletin board on this page also contains the latest information about Microsoft products.

◆ *Support link.* The Support Desktop Web page provides access to the Microsoft Knowledge Base, which you can use to search for articles based on keywords that you specify. It also contains links to the Microsoft Software Library and Frequently Asked Questions (FAQ) Web pages.

This site is best viewed with Microsoft's Internet Explorer. You can get your own copy of Internet Explorer at **http://www.microsoft.com/ windows/ie/ie.htm**.

TIP
And it's free, too.

Other Windows NT-Related Web Sites

Chancellor and Chancellor Windows NT Resource Site

URL address: **http://www.chancellor.com/ntmain.html**

Info Nederland Windows NT Information Site

URL address: **http://nt.info.nl/english/default.htm**

Windows NT Magazine

URL address: **http://www.winntmag.com**

Windows NT Administration FAQ

URL address: **http://ftech.com/classes/admin/admin.htm**

Using the CD-ROM

The tests on this CD-ROM consist of performance-based questions. This means that rather than asking you what function an item would fulfill (knowledge-based question), you will be presented with a situation and asked for an answer that shows your capability of solving the problem.

Using the Self-Test Software

The program consists of three main test structures:

◆ *Self-Assessment Test.* This would typically be the test you take first. This test is meant to give you a sense of where your strengths and weaknesses are regarding Windows NT Server 4.0 in the enterprise. You will get immediate feedback on your answer. It will either be correct and you will be able to go to the next question, or it will be incorrect and the system will recommend what part of the study guide to research and you will be prompted to try again.

◆ *Chapter-End Test.* After reading a chapter from the study guide, you will have the option to take a mini-test consisting of questions relevant only to the given chapter. You will get immediate feedback on your answer, as well as an indication of what subsection to find the answer should your response be incorrect.

◆ *Mastery Test.* This is the big one. This test is different from the two others in the sense that feedback is not given on a question-by-question basis. It simulates the exam situation, so you will give answers to all questions and then get your overall score. In addition to the score, for all wrong answers you will get pointers as to where in the study guide you need to study further. You will also be able to print a report card featuring your test results.

All test questions are of the multiple-choice type offering four possible answers. The answers are all labeled A, B, C, and D. There will always be either one or two alternatives representing the right answer; thus, a right answer might be "A and D" or any other combination.

Equipment Requirements

To run the self-test software, you must have *at least* the following equipment:

◆ IBM-compatible PC I386

◆ Microsoft DOS 5.0

◆ Microsoft Windows 3.x

◆ 4M of RAM

◆ 256-color display adapter

◆ Double-speed CD-ROM drive

To take full advantage of the software and run it at a more acceptable speed, however, the following equipment is recommended:

◆ IBM–Compatible I486 DX

◆ Microsoft Windows 3.1 or better

◆ 8M of RAM

◆ 256-color display adapter or better

◆ Quad speed CD-ROM drive

Running the Self-Test Software

The self-test software runs directly from the CD-ROM, and does not require you to install any files to your hard drive. After you have followed these simple start-up steps, you will find the software very intuitive and self-explanatory.

If you are using Windows 3.x, Windows NT 3.x, or Windows for Workgroups:

1. Insert the disk in your CD drive.

2. Select Run from the File menu of your Windows Program Manager, click Browse, and select the letter of your CD drive (typically D).

3. Double-click the file name dtique95.exe and the self-test program will be activated.

If you are using Windows 95 or Windows NT 4.0:

1. Insert the disk in your CD drive.

2. Click the Start button on the Windows taskbar, select Run, and click Browse. Select My Computer and double-click dtique95.exe.

As soon as dtique95 executes, you will be in the program, then follow instructions or click your selections.

Sample Tests

The tests in this appendix are performance-based questions designed to test your problem-solving capabilities. The questions are divided into three main test structures:

◆ *Self-Assessment Test*. This would typically be the test you take first. This test is meant to give you a sense of where your strengths and weaknesses are on Windows NT 4.0 Workstation.

◆ *Chapter-End Test*. After reading a chapter from the study guide you will have the option to take a mini-test consisting of questions relevant only to the given chapter. These questions are listed in order of the chapters in this book.

◆ *Mastery Test*. This test simulates the exam situation, so you will give answers to all questions and then get your overall score.

All test questions are of multiple choice type offering four possible answers. The answers are all labeled A, B, C, and D. There will always be either one or two alternatives representing the right answer; thus, a right answer might be "A & D" or any other combination.

Note These questions are also included on the CD-ROM that accompanies this book. See Appendix I, "Using the CD-ROM," for information on how to access these questions and run the software included with the CD. ∎

Self-Assessment Test

Note The answers to these questions can be found in order at the end of this section. The resource line following the correct answer is the chapter and section in the book where information regarding that question is located. ■

Question #1

Resource: Chapter 17, "RIP for IPX Routing"

RIP for IPX can support _____ hops.

   A. 4

   B. 8

   C. 16

   D. 32

App

J

Question #2

Resource: Chapter 22, "Events and Event Log Viewer"

By default, events are ordered in all event logs?

   A. By oldest first

   B. By event importance

   C. By newest last

   D. By newest first

Question #3

Resource: Chapter 7, "Remotely Managing through the Command Line"

Carl's Windows NT computer in Rolling Meadows is acting strangely while connected to the network. You would like to view the network settings in Carl's computer. You plan to use a command-line utility to view the network settings on Carl's computer and record them in a text file. Which utilities will you use to accomplish this?

A. WINMSDP.EXE and the RCMD files

B. WINMSDP.EXE and the Registry Editor

C. RCMD and the Registry Editor

D. Windows Diagnostics Utility and the Registry Editor

Question #4

Resource: Chapter 8, Entire Chapter

If a group of workstations on a network are never to contain any shared resources, how can you optimize these workstations so they will never send host announcements to the master browser?

A. Disable the workstation service

B. Disable the server service

C. Disable the browser service

D. Disable the alerter service

Question #5

Resource: Chapter 13, "Examining the Windows NT Security Model"

A user's effective access to a resource is determined by:

A. Comparing the rights of the user with the permissions assigned through the ACL of the resource.

B. Comparing the permissions in the access token of the user with the permissions assigned through the ACL of the resource.

C. Comparing the user and group SID entries in the user's access token with the permissions assigned through the ACL of the resource.

D. Comparing the user and group SID entries in the user's access token with the user rights listed in the ACL of the resource.

Question #6

Resource: Chapter 15, "Installation of Windows 95 Server Tools"

To install server tools on a Windows 95 platform:

   A. Run Setup.bat from the CD-ROM, Clients\Srvtools\Win95 folder.

   B. Run Setup.bat from the CD-ROM, Clients\Srvtools\Windows folder.

   C. Run Setup.exe from the CD-ROM, Clients\Srvtools\Windows folder.

   D. Access Control Panel on the Windows 95 client computer and select the Add/Remove Programs ICON.

Question #7

Resource: Chapter 17, "Networks, Network Segments, and the Purpose of Routers"

Routers work up to the _____ layer in the OSI Network Model.

   A. Physical

   B. Data Link

   C. Network

   D. Transport

Question #8

Resource: Chapter 5, "AppleTalk"

The AppleTalk protocol is used in Windows NT to provide:

   A. Access to Macintosh computers.

   B. Access to IBM mainframes for terminal emulation.

   C. Access to Novell resources.

   D. Access to HP JetDirect Printers on the network.

App
J

Question #9

Resource: Chapter 5, "DHCP"

DHCP is a Windows NT service used to:

A. Dynamically map NetBIOS names and IP addresses.

B. Dynamically allocate IP address to DHCP clients.

C. Dynamically configure PDC to BDC synchronization.

D. Dynamically provide automatic logon validation.

Question #10

Resource: Chapter 13, "Assigning File and Folder Permissions"

The manager of the Accounting department wants to make next year's budget templates available for the staff accountants to review beginning next month. Staff accountants are already members of a global group called Accountants in CORPDOMAIN. The templates will be stored on the department resource server called ACCT1 in a folder called BUDGET97 on an NTFS partition. The folder has been shared with the default permission, which you do not want to change. How would you further secure the folder's contents so that it is available only to the Accounting department staff?

A. Use User Manager for Domains to create a local group on the resource server called Accountants. Make the global accountants group a member of the local accountants group. Assign the Accountants group permission to use the folder through User Manager for Domains.

B. Use User Manager for Domains to create a local group on the resource server called Accountants. Make the global accountants group a member of the local accountants group. Assign the appropriate User Rights to the Accountants group to access the BUDGET97 share.

C. Use User Manager for Domains to create a local group on the resource server called Accountants. Make the global accountants group a member of the local accountants group. Use the Security tab on the properties sheet for the folder to assign permissions to the Accountants group.

D. Use User Manager for Domains to create a local group on the resource server called Accountants. Make the global accountants group a member of the local accountants group. Use the Sharing tab on the properties sheet for the folder to assign permissions to the Accountants group.

Question #11

Resource: Chapter 9, "Disk Striping"

A Windows NT file and print server has been configured with striping with parity across 4 disk drives. Users have complained of poor response time. Checking the event view you discover there are disk errors. What steps should you take?

A. Reformat the logical drive.

B. Replace the failed drive.

C. Disk administrator select regenerate and restart the server.

D. Restore data from backup.

Question #12

Resource: Chapter 7, "HKEY_LOCAL_MACHINE"

Which of the following statements best describes HKEY_LOCAL_MACHINE?

A. HKEY_LOCAL_MACHINE contains all the system configuration data needed to boot and run the Windows NT operating system successfully including services, device drivers, and hardware profiles.

B. HKEY_LOCAL_MACHINE displays only the current system configuration settings, including those used to boot Windows NT for the current session.

C. HKEY_LOCAL_MACHINE contains all the configuration settings particular to the currently logged on user.

D. HKEY_LOCAL_MACHINE contains default file association and DDE setting data for the system.

App

J

Question #13

Resource: Chapter 9, "Disk Controllers"

Which disk controller has the highest throughput?

    A. IDE standard

    B. SCSI-2 Bus mastering

    C. Fast SCSI-2

    D. PCI with SCSI

Question #14

Resource: Chapter 9, "Disk Striping, Disk Controllers"

You have SCSI and IDE controllers, and 3 disks for each controller to install on the BDC you are building. What configurations can you use?

    A. Logical drive

    B. Striping with no parity

    C. Striping with parity

    D. Mirroring

Question #15

Resource: Chapter 9, "Hardware Controller RAID"

What hardware RAID configurations can be implemented?

    A. 0

    B. 1

    C. 5

    D. 10

Question #16

Resource: Chapter 5, "Planning the Size of Directory Services Database"

What type of account, by default, has inherent built-in system rights associations?

   A. Computer account

   B. User account

   C. Local group account

   D. Global group account

Question #17

Resource: Chapter 22, "Write Debugging Information To:"

By default, CrashDump will be placed in the _____ folder.

   A. %systemRoot%\System32

   B. %systemRoot%\System32\Debug

   C. %SystemRoot%\System32\MemoryDump

   D. %systemRoot%\

App

J

Question #18

Resource: Chapter 10, "Windows NT 4.0 Print Process"

You have created four printers. Each of them will be used by a specific group of users. Name all the steps which are required to successfully make the printer available to the appropriate users.

   A. Share each printer.

   B. Set the share permissions for each printer so that only the appropriate group has access.

   C. Set the printer permissions for each printer so that only the appropriate group has access.

   D. Create a printer pool so that each group can access all the print devices.

Question #19

Resource: Chapter 7, "Examining the Windows NT Boot Process"

Which of the following boot files is essential to the boot phase of the boot process?

A. NTLDR

B. NTDETECT.COM

C. NTOSKRNL.EXE

D. BOOT.INI

Question #20

Resource: Chapter 7, "HKEY_LOCAL_MACHINE"

Which of the following keys in HKEY_LOCAL_MACHINE have corresponding directory files in the Windows NT system directory?

A. System

B. Software

C. Hardware

D. Security

Question #21

Resource: Chapter 7, "Troubleshooting the Boot Process"

Jonas accidentally deleted the BOOT.INI file from his C: drive. Windows NT has been installed in the WINNT subdirectory on C:. What effect will the missing BOOT.INI have?

A. There will be no noticeable effect on the boot process. Windows NT will boot as always.

B. The BOOT.INI file provides the ARC path information that Windows NT needs to find the Windows NT system files. If it is missing, Windows NT will display a message that it cannot find the NTOSKRNL file and fail to boot.

C. If the BOOT.INI file is missing, Windows NT will not display the Boot menu during boot up. Windows NT will look for the Windows NT system files on the boot partition in the default directory name (WINNT).

D. The BOOT.INI file is not needed on RISC-based systems.

Question #22

Resource: Chapter 19, "What Are These Types of Connections?"

RAS Accepts what kind of Inbound connections? (Pick all that apply)

A. ISDN

B. Modem

C. X.25

D. PPP

Question #23

Resource: Chapter 16, "File and Print Services for NetWare"

What do you need to do for your existing Novell NetWare clients to access a new Windows NT Server without changing the client software? (Pick one)

A. Install File and Print Services for NetWare on the Windows NT Server.

B. Install File and Print Services for NetWare on the Novell NetWare Server.

C. Install Gateway (and Client) Services for NetWare on the Windows NT Server.

D. Install Gateway (and Client) Services for NetWare on the Novell NetWare Server.

App

J

Question #24

Resource: Chapter 10, "Windows NT 4.0 Print Process"

There are three downward compatible print devices connected to the print server in MIS. MIS Managers and Project Leaders should always be able to print to the first available printer. Help Desk staff and Developers should be able to print only to their specified print device. What will best accomplish this task?

A. Create a printer for each device and assign the appropriate groups access only to their printer. Give the Manager's printer a priority of 1, Help Desk's printer a priority of 50, and Developer's printer a priority of 99.

B. Create a printer for each device and assign the appropriate groups access only to their printer. Give the Manager's printer a priority of 99, Help Desk's printer a priority of 50, and Developer's printer a priority of 1.

C. Create a printer for each device and assign the appropriate groups access only to their printer. Make the Manager's printer a printer pool by associating it with each print device.

D. Create a printer for each device and assign the appropriate groups access only to their printer. Make each printer a printer pool by associating it with each print device.

Question #25

Resource: Chapter 3, "The NetLogon Service and Pass-Through Authentication"

The Finance domain trusts the Marketing domain. What NetLogon function allows a user from the Marketing domain to log on and validate from a computer that participates in the Finance domain?

A. Directory Replication

B. Pass-Through Authentication

C. Trust Validation

D. Access Control Lists

Question #26

Resource: Chapter 10, "Windows NT 4.0 Print Process"

Which of the following sets of Windows NT network clients do not require print drivers to be manually installed on the local computer?

A. All Microsoft Network clients

B. Windows NT and Windows 95

C. Windows NT, Windows 95, Windows for Workgroups 3.11

D. Windows NT, Windows 95, LAN Manager v2.x for DOS

Question #27

Resource: Chapter 9, "Disk Striping"

What is the minimum number of drives needed for striping with no parity?

A. 32

B. 3

C. 2

D. 1

Question #28

Resource: Chapter 13, "Determining Access when Using Share and NTFS Permissions"

Team Leaders need to be able to modify files contained in the share TOOLS. While you were on vacation, your trusted sidekick modified the permissions for the share and the folder. The two exhibits show what the permissions look like now. Team Leaders complain that they are unable to modify their files. What should you do?

A. Fire your trusted sidekick.

B. Change the TOOLS NTFS permission for Team Leaders to Change, and the share permission to Read.

C. Change the TOOLS NTFS permission for the Team Leaders to Change.

D. Remove Team Leaders from the ACL for the TOOLS share.

App

J

Question #29

Resource: Chapter 21, "Traffic Generated when Using Trusted Accounts; Optimizing Trust Traffic"

The ABCCorp domain is configured as a Master Domain model. 5000 user accounts are managed in the ABC-MIS domain in Chicago. Resource domains trust ABC-MIS. At the ABC-WEST resource domain, the print administrator is managing access to her printers by adding the appropriate user accounts from ABC-MIS to the ACL for each of five printers. Access will be managed for 300 users. ABC-WEST is connected to ABC-MIS via a slow WAN link. Every time she accesses the ABC-MIS account domain to display the list of users, the list takes several seconds to generate. The process is taking longer than she thinks it should. What can you suggest to improve performance and minimize network traffic? Choose the best answer.

A. Upgrade the WAN link to a higher speed.

B. Create local groups on the print servers in ABC-WEST and add the users to the local groups. Use the local groups to assign printer permissions.

C. Create global groups in ABC-MIS for the users that need printer access in ABC-WEST. Add the global groups to local groups on the print servers in ABC-WEST, and assign printer permissions to the local groups.

D. There is nothing you can do to improve performance. The same amount of trust traffic is generated whether you use user accounts or group accounts across the trust.

Question #30

Resource: Chapter 7, "BOOT.INI"

The BOOT.INI file on my computer looks like this:

[Boot Loader]

   timeout=15

   default=multi(0)disk(2)rdisk(1)partition(3)\winnt40

[Operating Systems]

multi(0)disk(**2**)rdisk(1)partition(3)\winnt40=Windows NT 4.0
Workstation

multi(0)disk(**2**)rdisk(1)partition(3)\winnt40=Windows NT 4.0
Workstation [VGA Mode] /basevideo c:\=MS-DOS

What can I infer from this file?

A. The timeout value before Windows NT loads is 15 seconds.
Windows NT system files can be found on the third partition of
the second physical disk attached to the first controller card.

B. The timeout value before Windows NT loads is 15 seconds, and
DOS is the default operating system.

C. The timeout value before Windows NT loads is 15 seconds.
Windows NT system files can be found on the third partition of
the first physical disk attached to the first controller card.

D. The controller card is a SCSI adapter.

Question #31

Resource: Chapter 13, "Managing Shares and Permissions Remotely"

Which tool(s) can you use to remotely manage shares across the domain?

A. User Manager for Domains

B. Server Manager

C. Windows Explorer

D. Network Neighborhood

Question #32

Resource: Chapter 4, Entire Chapter

Kite Flyers Corporation has two global locations, London and New
York. MIS manages the users in both locations in two account domains.
There are five departments: Accounting, Marketing, MIS, HR, and Corporate. Each has its own set of network resources that its staff accesses,
and some resources that everyone in the company uses.

Primary Goals: Give all employees a single logon account that they can use to access their resources. Let MIS be able to manage the account domains from any location. Let each department manage their own resources. Let certain delegated users act as print operators for printers in each department.

Secondary Goals: Centralize resources by department. Let all delegated users be able to manage any domain's printers. Allow as much flexibility as possible for printer management.

Solution: Implement a Multiple Master Domain model. Have all resource domains trust the account domain, and let the account domains trust each other. Create a global group called KFPRINT in each account domain and add the delegated users to it. Add KFPRINT from both account domains to the local Print Operators groups on the print servers in each domain.

A. The solution satisfies none of the goals.

B. The solution satisfies all the primary goals and all the secondary goals.

C. The solution satisfies both primary goals, but only one secondary goal.

D. The solution satisfies two primary goals and two secondary goals.

Question #33

Resource: Chapter 10, "Windows NT 4.0 Print Process"

Nicole calls to say that her print jobs seem to have stopped running. You check the printer that she sent the jobs to and see that the jobs are stuck in queue. What steps should you take to clear the stuck jobs? Select all that apply.

A. Select the stuck jobs and choose Document, Cancel.

B. Select Printer, Purge Printer.

C. Use the Control Panel applet Services to stop and restart the Spooler service.

D. Select each stuck job and change its priority.

Question #34

Resource: Chapter 12, "Group Management in Domains"

On a Windows NT Server in DomainA, you have stored a sales database and a marketing database, and have also shared a color printer. Five of the users in the domain are sales persons, five are marketers, and the rest are programmers. The users should be able to access their respective databases, but only the team leaders for sales, marketing, and programmers should be able to access the color printer. Which group strategy is the best?

- A. Create local groups for sales, marketing, and team leaders and assign the appropriate user accounts to the appropriate groups. Then, assign permissions for each resource to the appropriate group.

- B. Create global groups for sales, marketing, and team leaders and assign the appropriate user accounts to the appropriate groups. Then, assign permissions for each resource to the appropriate global group.

- C. Create global groups for sales, marketing, and team leaders and assign the appropriate user accounts to the appropriate groups. Following Microsoft's suggested strategy, create local groups for each and assign the global group to the local group. Then assign permissions for each resource to the appropriate local group.

- D. Simply assign the appropriate users access to the resources that they need access to.

Question #35

Resource: Chapter 5, "Physical Disk Monitoring Considerations"

Disk performance counters in Performance Monitor are turned off by default. From the choices below, indicate the correct syntax required to activate the counters.

- A. Diskperf On
- B. Diskperf Off
- C. Diskperf –n
- D. Diskperf –y

App
J

Question #36

Resource: Chapter 19, "What is PPTP?"

The Point-to-Point Tunneling Protocol does what? (Pick one)

A. Establishes a connection via the modem for the RAS server and RAS client to communicate.

B. Establishes a connection via X.25 for the RAS server and RAS client to communicate.

C. Enhances authentication with a longer key.

D. Encrypts all data between the client and server.

Question #37

Resource: Chapter 2, "Taking the Enterprise Challenge"

Which of the following scenarios defines the correct application for a domain? (Choose two)

A. A domain might be centered around the organizational hierarchy of a company with accounts and resources centered in the departments that will manage them.

B. A domain might represent the regional nature of an organization by establishing a domain for each region and then connecting them by trust relationships.

C. A domain might represent a small group of workstations each of which is managed by the owner of the workstation, and each of which maintains its own list of accounts and resources.

D. A domain might be best characterized as a peer-to-peer configuration of Windows NT Server computers.

Question #38

Resource: Chapter 8, Entire Chapter

A WINS database is used to:

A. Dynamically map IP addresses to network adapter card names

B. Dynamically map IP addresses to subnet masks

C. Dynamically map IP addresses to computer names

D. Dynamically map IP addresses to a user name

Question #39

Resource: Chapter 3, "Setting Up a Trust Relationship"

Which of the following are requirements for setting up a successful trust relationship? Choose all that apply.

A. A domain controller in each domain must be up and accessible.

B. There can be no current sessions between the PDCs of each domain.

C. You must have an administrator-level account.

D. You must have access to a computer running User Manager for Domains.

Question #40

Resource: Chapter 5, "Location of the Enterprise Administrator"

By pausing the Netlogon service on the PDC, the PDC will continue to:

A. Perform logon validations.

B. Perform directory services database synchronization with the BDCs.

C. Perform pass-through authentication.

D. Perform logon validation but not pass-through authentication.

Question #41

Resource: Chapter 20, "Monitoring Network-Related Objects"

After monitoring your heavily accessed file and print server, you determine that both the Server>Pool Paged Failures and Server>Pool Nonpaged Failures counters are unusually and consistently higher than normal. The Server service memory property is configured for Balanced memory usage. What should you do to reduce the number of Pool Paged and Pool Nonpaged failures?

App

J

A. Add more memory. Balanced is an appropriate setting for a file and print server.

B. Change the Server service memory configuration to Minimize Memory Used.

C. Change the Server service memory configuration to Maximize Throughput for File Sharing.

D. Change the Server service memory configuration to Load Balance Throughput for Virtual Memory.

Question #42

Resource: Chapter 6, "Selecting the Appropriate Server Role"

How many BDCs are recommended for 5,000 users?

A. 0

B. 2

C. 3

D. 5

Question #43

Resource: Chapter 13, "Sharing Resources and Determining Network Access"

The TOOLS folder has been shared to the Developers group with Change permission. DOOM is a subdirectory under TOOLS. Team Leaders should have access only to DOOM with Read permissions. What can you do to accomplish this?

A. Add Team Leaders to the TOOLS share with Read permission.

B. Create a new share called DOOM and give Team Leaders Read permission to it.

C. Add Team Leaders to the TOOLS share with Change permission.

D. Add Team Leaders to the TOOLS share with No Access and to the DOOM subdirectory with Read.

Question #44

Resource: Chapter 21, "Understanding Network Monitor"

Which of the following features is provided by the full version of Network Monitor that comes with Microsoft's System Management Server? Choose all that apply.

A. Direct monitoring of remote computer traffic.

B. Determining which protocol consumed the most bandwidth.

C. Identifying which physical disk has the most I/O activity for a network session.

D. Capturing local network traffic to and from the computer running the utility.

Question #45

Resource: Chapter 17, "RIP for IPX Routing"

RIP for IP and DHCP Relay can support _____ hops.

A. 4

B. 8

C. 16

D. 32

Question #46

Resource: Chapter 7, "Managing Remote Access to the Registry"

As the manager of the MIS department, you would like to delegate responsibility for remote management of the Windows NT registries on all the domain controllers to three key staff members. These three are members of the Domain Admins global group for the domain, as are all your staff members. How would you restrict remote access to the appropriate three persons?

A. Give the Remote Command Service utilities only to those three persons.

B. Modify the ACL for the HKEY_LOCAL_MACHINE\System\ CurrentControlSet\Control\SecurePipeServers\Winreg subkey on each domain controller so that only those three persons have access.

C. Modify the RemoteAccess parameter values for HKEY_LOCAL_ MACHINE\System\CurrentControlSet\Control\RemoteControl subkey on each domain controller so that only those three persons are listed.

D. Do nothing. Only these three can remotely manage the Registry by default.

Question #47

Resource: Chapter 11, Entire Chapter

Your assistant called and wants to know why he cannot use his server tools from his Windows 95 client with a 386DX/66. Your answer is

A. He does not have the correct protocol.

B. Insufficient hardware.

C. He is not an Backup operator.

D. The server is off-line

Question #48

Resource: Chapter 13, "Assigning File and Folder Permissions"

You have modified NTFS permissions for the file DOOM.DOC so that Team Leaders have Full Control. For all other files and folders, Team Leaders should have Read access. Using the exhibit, how can you best accomplish this?

A. Select Replace Permissions on Subdirectories and deselect Replace Permissions on Existing Files.

B. Select Replace Permissions on Subdirectories.

C. Deselect Replace Permissions on Existing Files.

D. Set permissions on each file and folder individually.

Question #49

Resource: Chapter 21, "What Does a Frame Look Like?"

Which of the following are components of an Ethernet 802.3 frame? Choose all that apply.

A. Source and Destination address

B. Length of the frame

C. Data contained in the frame such as IP and TCP information.

D. Type of frame

Question #50

Resource: Chapter 4, "Understanding the Master Domain Model"

Kite Flyers Corporation has opened offices in London and Tokyo. Each office maintains its own resources, though all users are managed in the corporate headquarters. Which domain model is best suited to this organization?

A. Single domain model

B. Master domain model

C. Multiple Master domain model

D. Complete Trust domain model

Question #51

Resource: Chapter 8, Entire Chapter

An IP address consists of what two parts in the following order from left to right?

A. A network address and a workstation address

B. A workstation address and a network address

C. A subnet mask address and a default gateway address

D. A default gateway address and a subnet mask address

App
J

Question #52

Resource: Chapter 13, "Effective File and Folder Permissions"

The manager of the Accounting department wants to make next year's budget templates available for the staff accountants to review beginning next month. Staff accountants are already members of a global group called Accountants in CORPDOMAIN. The templates will be stored on the department resource server called ACCT1 in a folder called BUDGET97 on an NTFS partition. The folder has been shared with the default permission. The global accountants group has been added to a local group called Accountants on ACCT1. You would like everyone to be able to see the files, but only the accounting staff should be able to make changes. What do you need to do?

X
No correct
answer)

A. Change the share permission to only Accountants with Change permission.

B. Assign the Accountants group the NTFS permission Change to the BUDGET97 folder.

C. Change the share permission to Everyone with No Access and assign the Accountants group the NTFS permission Change for the BUDGET97 folder.

D. Change the share permission to Everyone with Read and assign the Accountants group the NTFS permission Change for the BUDGET97 folder.

Question #53

Resource: Chapter 10, "Additional LPD Device Information"

A print job can be directed directly to a UNIX host print device, and its status checked using which two command-line utilities?

A. LPD and LPR

B. LPD and LPQ

C. LPR and IPCONFIG

D. LPR and LPQ

Question #54

Resource: Chapter 6, "Maximizing the Resources by Server Role"

The Security Accounts Manager (SAM) database is approximately 15M. What is the recommended memory size?

    A. 24M

    B. 32M

    C. 48M

    D. 64M

Question #55

Resource: Chapter 13, "Sharing Resources and Determining Network Access"; "Examining the Windows NT Security Model"

The manager of the Accounting department wants to make next year's budget templates available for the staff accountants to review beginning next month. Staff accountants are all members of the global group Accountants in the domain CORPDOMAIN. The templates will be stored on the department resource server called ACCT1 in a folder called BUDGET97. A local group called Budget has been created to manage access to the budget templates. None of the partitions on ACCT1 are formatted with NTFS. How would you make the folder available only to the Accounting department staff? Choose all that apply.

    A. Share the BUDGET97 directory.

    B. Add the Accountants group to the ACL for the share.

    C. Remove the Everyone group from the ACL for the share.

    D. Give the Accountants group read and write permissions at the folder level.

Question #56

Resource: Chapter 21, "File Session Frames"

Which of the following steps need to take place before a file session can be established between two computers using the TCP/IP protocol? Choose all that apply.

A. The user must register its name with the WINS server.

B. Name resolution must take place.

C. Address resolution must take place.

D. A TCP Session must be established.

Question #57

Resource: Chapter 17, "TCP/IP Routing"

Indicate the utility used from the command prompt to manually maintain a static IP routing table.

A. Route

B. IPXRoute

C. IPConfig

D. PING

Question #58

Resource: Chapter 11, "CHAPTER 11"

TCP/IP and DHCP are supported for what clients?

A. Lan Manager 2.2c for MS-DOS

B. Lan Manager 2.2c for OS2

C. Microsoft network client for MS-DOS

D. Microsoft Windows 95

Question #59

Resource: Chapter 14, "User Profiles ; Default User Profiles"

As you create new users you would like them to assume the same default environment settings such as common application groups, startup programs, and company logo as wallpaper. Which steps will achieve this?

A. Modify the appropriate changes in the Default User and All Users profile folders in WINNT\Profiles. When a new user is created, that user's profile will begin with the settings from these two.

B. Create a System Policy file that contains the appropriate settings for the Default User and save it in the WINNT\SYSTEM32\REPL\IMPORT\SCRIPTS subdirectory on the validating computer.

C. Create a template user account and modify the settings for that account. Create new accounts by copying the template.

D. Create a system policy file for each set of users modifying the settings as appropriate for each user.

Question #60

Resource: Chapter 12, "Remote Account Management Tips"

You need to be able to remotely manage the account database on two trusted domains. Which steps must take place for this to happen successfully?

A. Do nothing. You can remotely manage accounts through a trust by default.

B. Use User Manager for domains and choose User, Select Domain from the menu to choose the remote domain you want to administer.

C. Make your account a member of the Account Operators group in the trusted domains.

D. Give your user account Full Control access to the SAM hive file in WINNT\SYSTEM32\CONFIG.

Question #61

Resource: Chapter 21, "Account Database Synchronization"

Under what circumstances might a full database synchronization take place between a PDC and a BDC? Choose the best two.

A. Every synchronization event replicates the entire account databases.

B. Full synchronization occurs when the BDC is first installed.

C. Full synchronization may occur when the change log on the PDC becomes full and begins to overwrite existing information before the PDC can contact the BDC for updates.

D. Only changes are copied whenever synchronization occurs.

Question #62

Resource: Chapter 21, "Optimizing Logon Validation"

ABCCorp network consists of 5,000 users located in three office locations: New York, Chicago, and San Francisco. The current plan is to locate one PDC and one BDC in the corporate headquarters in Chicago. How could you optimize this configuration to make logging on more efficient for the users and minimize network traffic? Choose the best two answers.

A. Create two more BDCs to accommodate the 5,000 users. Microsoft recommends one BDC for every 2,000 users.

B. Create a trust relationship among all the offices.

C. Locate one BDC in each location so that logon validation takes place locally.

D. Do nothing. This configuration is optimized.

Question #63

Resource: Chapter 7, "What is the Last Known Good Control Set"; Table 7.7, "Service Subkey Parameters"

Under what circumstances will the Last Known Good control set load automatically?

A. If the system itself detects a critical error during the boot process, it will automatically load Last Known Good.

B. If the system detects an ErrorControl value of 0 or 1, it will automatically load Last Known Good.

C. If the system detects a failed control set, it will automatically load Last Known Good on the next boot.

D. Last Known Good is always selected from the screen during the boot process.

Question #64

Resource: Chapter 3, "Group Management in the Domain"

The Finance domain trusts the Marketing domain. You would like to give Sheila, Frank, and Pat the responsibility of backing up all the domain controllers and servers in the Finance Domain. Which is the best course of action?

A. Add Sheila, Frank, and Pat to the Backup Operators group in the Marketing domain, and then add that Backup Operators group to the local Backup Operators groups on each domain controller and server in the Finance domain.

B. Create a global group in the Marketing domain called Global Backup and add Sheila, Frank, and Pat to it. Add Global Backup to the local Backup Operators groups on each domain controller and server in the Finance domain.

C. Create a global group in the Marketing domain called Global Backup and add Sheila, Frank, and Pat to it. Add Global Backup to the local Backup Operators group on the primary domain controller and the local Backup Operators groups on each server in the Finance domain.

D. Create new accounts for Sheila, Frank, and Pat on each domain controller and server in the Finance domain and add them to the local Backup Operators groups on each domain controller and server in the Finance domain.

Question #65

Resource: Chapter 12, "Troubleshooting Accounts, Policies, and Profiles"

A user is having problems logging on to the network and is seeing a variety of messages. Which of the following things would you check to troubleshoot?

A. The user is entering the correct username and password.

B. The username is case-sensitive.

C. The domain controller is up and accessible.

D. The user's account requires a mandatory profile that is accessible.

Question #66

Resource: Chapter 10, "DLC Printing"

From the choices below, list the steps required to install a network interface printer using the DLC protocol.

A. Install the DLC protocol on the print server and shut down and restart.

B. Start the Print Wizard, select Add Printer, then select Add Port.

C. Select the Hewlett-Packard Network Port and click the New Port button.

D. Select a MAC address from the available addresses and supply a printer name in the Add Hewlett-Packard Network Peripheral Port dialog box.

Question #67

Resource: Chapter 7, "Emergency Repair Disk"

The master boot record of Sal's Windows NT computer became corrupted and he can no longer boot to Windows NT. How can you restore the master boot record on Sal's computer?

A. Create a Windows NT boot disk with the NTLDR file on it. Boot from this disk and copy the NTLDR file from it to the system partition of Sal's computer.

B. Create an Emergency Repair Disk. Boot from this disk and choose Inspect Boot Sector from the menu to repair the master boot record.

C. Create an Emergency Repair Disk. Boot from a Windows NT startup disk and choose Repair, using the Emergency Repair Disk when prompted. Choose Inspect Boot Sector to repair the MBR.

D. Create a Windows NT boot disk with the NTLDR file and the fixdisk.exe program on it. Boot from this disk and run fixdisk /c: where c: is the system partition.

Question #68

Resource: Chapter 3, "Local versus Global Accounts"

The Finance domain trusts the Marketing domain. Sheila has just joined the Marketing group as a short-term contractor. Sheila needs access to a Finance database to complete her project. What type of account would you create for Sheila?

A. Create a global account for Sheila in the Marketing domain.

B. Create a local account for Sheila in the Marketing domain.

C. Create a global account for Sheila in the Marketing Domain and a global account for Sheila in the Finance domain.

D. Create a local account for Sheila in the Marketing domain and a global account for Sheila in the Finance domain.

Question #69

Resource: Chapter 13, "Local versus Domain Access Token"; "Sharing Resources and Determining Network Access"

The manager of the Accounting department wants to make next year's budget templates available for the staff accountants to review beginning next month. Staff accountants are all members of the Accountants global group in CORPDOMAIN. The templates will be stored on the department resource server called ACCT1 in a folder called BUDGET97. None of the partitions on ACCT1 are formatted with NTFS. How would you make the folder available only to the Accounting department staff?

A. Use User Manager for Domains to create a local group on the resource server called Accountants. Make the global Accountants group a member of the local Accountants group. Assign permission to use the folder to the Accountants group through User Manager for Domains.

B. Use User Manager for Domains to create a local group on the resource server called Accountants. Make the global Accountants group a member of the local Accountants group. Assign the appropriate User Rights to the Accountants group to access the BUDGET97 share.

C. Use User Manager for Domains to create a local group on the resource server called Accountants. Make the global Accountants group a member of the local Accountants group. Use the Security tab on the properties sheet for the folder to assign permissions to the Accountants group.

D. Use User Manager for Domains to create a local group on the resource server called Accountants. Make the global Accountants group a member of the local Accountants group. Use the Sharing tab on the properties sheet for the folder to assign permissions to the Accountants group.

Question #70

Resource: Chapter 2, "Domain Model"

Which of the following characteristics best apply to a domain network model? (Choose two)

A. Resource access is provided by permitting access to users and groups that are members of the domain.

B. User and group accounts are maintained on each workstation that is a member of the domain.

C. A domain network model provides a relatively low level of resource security.

D. Resource and account management is centralized.

Question #71

Resource: Chapter 20, "Monitoring Memory"

Desiree, a Visual Basic developer, has noticed that her system's performance has decreased since she began work on a large VB application.

You have used Performance Monitor to determine that the pagefile usage has increased. You also notice that the pagefile, Windows NT system files, and the VB application are all stored on the same partition. In addition, the working set for the VB application shows that it consistently requires 16M for itself. What solutions can you recommend? Name all that apply.

A. Add more RAM in the computer.

B. Move the pagefile to a disk partition other than the system or application partition.

C. Increase the maximum size for the pagefile.

D. Create multiple page files.

Question #72

Resource: Chapter 10, "Introducing and Examining the Print Process"; "Troubleshooting Printing"

There are three hundred Windows NT and Windows 95 client computers that print to five printers on a print server. You have received upgraded print drivers for two of the print devices connected to this print server. What must you do to ensure that all clients can continue to access all the print devices?

A. Install the upgraded print drivers on all the client computers that need to use those print devices.

B. Install the upgraded print drivers on all the client computers.

C. Install the upgraded print drivers only on the Windows NT client computers.

D. Do nothing. The print server can download the new drivers to the clients the next time they make a print request.

Question #73

Resource: Chapter 12, "Understanding User and Group Accounts"; "Creating a New User"

Your boss has advised you that BrownC has left the company and asks that you delete his account. Later, your boss hires BrownC back as a consultant and tells you to put his account back on the network. BrownC calls you the next day and informs you gruffly that he can no longer access any of the network resources that he used to. How do you troubleshoot?

A. Use the Registry to set BrownC's SID back to what it was before you deleted his account. He will then be able to access all the old resources.

B. Deleting BrownC's account also deleted his SID. Because security in Windows NT is linked to the user's SID, you will need to reestablish all the network resource access that BrownC used to have.

C. Use the Emergency Repair Disk or your last network backup to copy BrownC's old account back to the Registry.

D. Leave the company and get hired back as a consultant yourself.

Question #74

Resource: Chapter 8, Entire Chapter

Protocols are installed by accessing the network icon in the Control Panel and:

A. Selecting the Protocol tab and selecting the Add button.

B. Selecting the Protocol tab and selecting the protocol.

C. Selecting the Protocol tab and choosing all protocols.

D. Selecting the Protocol tab, nothing else has to be selected.

Question #75

Resource: Chapter 11, Entire Chapter

What clients support Remoteboot?

A. Lan Manager 2.2c for MS-DOS

B. Lan Manager 2.2c for OS2

C. Microsoft network client for MS-DOS

D. Microsoft Windows 95

Question #76

Resource: Chapter 11, Entire Chapter

To create a Macintosh Accessible Volume on the server, you must have which of the following.

A. Pentium 166Mhz processor

B. FAT partition

C. NTFS partition

D. Windows NT Workstation

Question #77

Resource: Chapter 3, "Understanding the Nature of a Trust Relationship"

The Finance domain users need to access a laser printer in the Marketing domain. The Marketing domain users need to access a scanner in the Finance domain. How many trust relationships need to be created to facilitate the sharing of these two network resources?

A. Create one two-way trust relationship between Finance and Marketing.

B. Create two one-way trust relationships, one from Finance to Marketing and the other from Marketing to Finance.

C. Create two one-way trust relationships from Finance to Marketing. One can handle the shared laser printer, and the other the scanner.

D. Create one trust relationship between Finance and Marketing. A trust relationship is always bi-directional.

Question #78

Resource: Chapter 8, Entire Chapter

If Windows NT is configured for Auto frame type detection and multiple IPX frame types are detected on the network, Windows NT will:

A. Automatically default to 802.3

B. Automatically default to 802.2

C. Automatically configure itself to all IPX frame types detected

D. Automatically default to the first IPX frame type detected

Question #79

Resource: Chapter 20, "System Performance with Performance Monitor"

Which objects would be most beneficial to include in a log file when creating a baseline measurement of your system's performance? Choose all that apply.

A. Memory

B. TCP/IP

C. Processor

D. Physical and Logical Disk

Question #80

Resource: Chapter 10, "Windows NT 4.0 Print Process"

Elaine was the print administrator for the LotsOf Print Corporation, but has left the country to pursue a career as an opera singer. You need to assign a new print administrator. What will you need to do concerning ownership of the LotsOf Print Corporation printers that Elaine created and managed?

A. Do nothing. Printers are not owned by a user; they are owned by the system.

B. Make the new print administrator a Print Operator. The new print administrator can then take ownership of the printers in LotsOf Print Corporation.

C. Give ownership of the printers to the new print administrator.

D. Give the new administrator Full Control permission over the printers. Full Control automatically assigns ownership to that user.

Question #81

Resource: Chapter 10, "Windows NT 4.0 Print Process"

There is one high-speed network print device connected to the print server in MIS. MIS Managers and Project Leaders should always be able to print to this printer regardless of who has submitted print jobs. Help Desk staff should be able to print ahead of Developers. What will best accomplish this task?

A. Create three printers, each associated with the device, and assign the appropriate groups access only to their printer. Give the Manager's printer a priority of 1, Help Desk's printer a priority of 50, and Developer's printer a priority of 99.

B. Create three printers, each associated with the device, and assign the appropriate groups access only to their printer. Give the Manager's printer a priority of 99, Help Desk's printer a priority of 50, and Developer's printer a priority of 1.

C. Create three printers, each associated with the device, and assign the appropriate groups access only to their printer. Make the Manager's printer a printer pool by associating it with each print device.

D. Create three printers associated with the device and assign the appropriate groups access only to their printer. Make each printer a printer pool by associating it with each print device.

Question #82

Resource: Chapter 12, "Default Group Accounts"

Everyone should be able to read the files in a certain directory. How-ever, the user who created the file should be able to modify it. What do you need to do?

A. Do nothing. By default, only the creator of a file has access to it. Windows NT restricts resource access by default.

B. Give the group Everyone read access and the Creator Owner group change access. By default, Windows NT allows everyone complete access to resources.

C. Give the group Everyone read access and the Creator Owner group change access. By default, Windows NT restricts resource access.

D. Give the group Everyone read access and the Users group change access. Windows NT will automatically determine who the owner of the file is and restrict the other users.

Question #83

Resource: Chapter 8, Entire Chapter

By default, all BDCs on the same subnet in a domain will become:

A. A domain master browser

B. A potential browser

C. A backup browser

D. A non-browser

Question #84

Resource: Chapter 15, "Remote Server Management"

The reason that server tools are not installed on Windows NT Server installations is:

A. The server tools applications and utilities are already installed but must be run from a domain controller.

B. The server tools applications and utilities are not available for member servers.

C. The server tools applications and utilities cannot be run from the server platform.

D. The server tools applications and utilities are already installed and available for use.

Question #85

Resource: Chapter 4, "Understanding the Role of the Domain for Directory Services"

Which of the following characteristics can be applied to a domain? Choose all that apply.

A. A domain is a logical grouping of computers.

B. A domain depends entirely on the physical layout of the network.

C. A domain provides the foundation for implementing Directory Services.

D. A domain does not depend on the physical location of computers and users.

Question #86

Resource: Chapter 10, "Windows NT 4.0 Print Process"

Michelle has been selected to assist you as a print administrator in the Dry Gulch office, since you, yourself, are unable to travel there frequently, though you'd really like to. What is the minimum level of access you need to give Michelle so that she can perform basic print management tasks such as creating and sharing printers and managing print jobs?

A. Make Michelle a member of the Print Operators local group on her print server.

B. Make Michelle a member of the Server Operator local group on her print server.

    C. Make Michelle a member of the Administrators local group on her print server.

    D. Give Michelle Full Control permission for each printer on her print server.

Question #87

Resource: Chapter 12, "User Rights"

You want to give a particular domain user the ability to back up files on a server, but not be able to restore files. How can you accomplish this?

    A. Make the domain user a member of the Backup Operators group on the server.

    B. Make the domain user a member of the Server Operators group on the server.

    C. Create a new local group called BACKUP ONLY on the server and make the domain user a member of it. Assign this new group to the Backup Files and Directories User Right.

    D. Give the user read-only access to all the files.

Question #88

Resource: Chapter 17, "AppleTalk Routing"

Network types can have network numbers or network ranges associated with them. Which type of network can have only one network number associated with it?

    A. LocalTalk

    B. EtherTalk

    C. TokenTalk

    D. FDDI

Question #89

Resource: Chapter 12, "Account Policy"; "Audit Policy"

You suspect that someone is trying to log on to the network unauthorized. What is the best step you can take to increase security and determine who might be doing this?

A. Enable Account Lockout in the Account Policy requiring the Administrator to unlock the account.

B. Enable Account Lockout in the Account Policy requiring the Administrator to unlock the account. Enable auditing of unsuccessful logons and logoffs and monitor these events in the Event Viewer.

C. Advise users to change their passwords more frequently and not to use obvious passwords.

D. Increase the minimum password length in Account Policy.

Question #90

Resource: Chapter 8, Entire Chapter

If the AppleTalk protocol is installed on a Windows NT Workstation, other Windows NT users on the network can use the workstation:

A. To create Macintosh Accessible Volumes on Macintosh computers

B. To access Macintosh Accessible Volumes on Macintosh computers

C. To access Macintosh Accessible Volumes on the workstation and share files with Macintosh users

D. As a print server

Question #91

Resource: Chapter 21, "File Session Frames"

Which type of frames are involved in connecting to a shared resource once the session has been established?

A. SMB session frames

B. WINS resolution frames

C. NBT broadcast frames

D. TCP request frames

Question #92

Resource: Chapter 21, "WINS Frames"

When a computer registers with a WINS server, how many name registration frames are generated?

A. One name is registered for each computer.

B. A name is registered for the computer and for every service or application that supports the NetBIOS API. One frame registers all these names.

C. A name is registered for the computer and for every service or application that supports the NetBIOS API. One frame is generated for each name that needs to be registered.

D. NetBIOS names are not registered with the WINS server.

Question #93

Resource: Chapter 18, Entire Chapter

You have upgraded your Windows NT 3.5 FTP server to Windows NT 4.0. The plan for this machine is to make it an IIS. You are having trouble setting up the service and it will not complete. Why not?

A. WINS is not running.

B. DHCP is not running.

C. Gopher needs to be installed first.

D. FTP is still installed.

Question #94

Resource: Chapter 10, "Windows NT 4.0 Print Process"

The print device associated with a particular printer has failed. Several print jobs are waiting in queue in that printer. How can you service these print jobs?

    A. Connect to another remote printer. Open the printer manager window for the printer and drag the waiting print jobs to the remote printer manager window.

    B. Use the Ports tab properties for the printer to add a port for another remote printer. Deselect the current print port associated with the printer and select the remote port. Resume the printer.

    C. Do nothing. You must replace the failed print device before printing can resume.

    D. Use the Control Panel applet Services to stop the spooler service, configure it to connect to another remote printer, and restart it.

App
J

Question #95

Resource: Chapter 17, "RIP for IPX Routing"

Indicate the utility used from the command prompt to manually maintain an IPX routing table.

    A. Route

    B. IPXRoute

    C. IPConfig

    D. PING

Question #96

Resource: Chapter 12, "Creating a New User"

Under which of the following situations would you disable the user account rather than deleting it?

A. JaneD has left the company on maternity leave and plans to return in three months.

B. JohnB has taken an emergency medical leave of absence for possibly six or more months, but hopes to return full time.

C. JaniceD has left the company to take a job at Microsoft.

D. FrankP has taken a temporary team leader position in another department and will return when the project is completed.

Question #97

Resource: Chapter 10, "Troubleshooting Printing"

You are using a RISC-based computer as your print server. All your clients are either MS-DOS, Windows for Workgroups, Windows 95, or Windows NT running on Intel-based computers. What must you do to ensure that all your clients can print to the print devices managed by the RISC-based print server?

A. Install both RISC-based and Intel print drivers on the RISC-based print server. Install the appropriate print drivers only on the MS-DOS and Windows for Workgroups computers.

B. Install both RISC-based and Intel print drivers on the RISC-based print server. The client computers will receive the appropriate platform driver from the print server when they make a print request.

C. Install RISC-based print drivers on the RISC-based print server and Intel print drivers on the client computers. Windows NT will do the platform translation.

D. Install the Intel print drivers on the RISC-based print server and RISC-based print drivers on the client computers.

Question #98

Resource: Chapter 2, "Synchronization of Account and Security Information"

My domain consists of a PDC and three BDCs. My PDC is currently offline. Which functions can still take place on my network? Choose all that apply.

A. I can administer accounts through User Manager for Domains.

B. I can log on to the network.

C. I can use Server Manager to administer the other BDCs.

D. I can synchronize the domain controllers.

Question #99

Resource: Chapter 22, "Events and Event Log Viewer"

Audit events are placed in the _____ log in Event Viewer.

A. System

B. Security

C. Application

D. Audit

Question #100

Resource: Chapter 22, "Crash Dump Analysis Utilities"

The utility to verify the validity of a CrashDump is

A. Dumpflop.exe

B. Dumpexam.exe

C. Dumpchk.exe

D. Dump.exe

Question #101

Resource: Chapter 22, "Write Debugging Information To:"

For CrashDumps to be obtained, a pagefile must exist on the

A. System partition

B. Boot partition

C. NTFS partition

D. Data partition

Question #102

Resource: Chapter 21, "Understanding Network Monitor"

Which of the following features is provided by the version of Network Monitor that comes with Microsoft Windows NT Server 4.0?

A. Direct monitoring of remote computer traffic.

B. Determining which protocol consumed the most bandwidth.

C. Identifying which physical disk has the most I/O activity for a network session.

D. Capturing local network traffic to and from the computer running the utility.

Question #103

Resource: Chapter 20, "Monitoring the Processor"; "Monitoring Memory"; "Monitoring Disk Activity"

On your Windows NT 4.0 development workstation, you have concluded that performance as a whole has decreased. You are not sure which process is driving this, but you have noticed that your disk drive has had a lot more activity lately. What objects should you monitor through Performance Monitor to help you troubleshoot this situation?

A. Check the Processor>%Processor Time counter, determine the percent of disk I/O used for paging through the Memory>Pages/ Sec counter and the Logical Disk>Avg. Disk sec/Transfer counter, and the Process>Working Set for every process running.

B. Check the Processor>%Processor Time counter, determine the percent of disk I/O used for paging through the Memory>Pages/ Sec counter and the Logical Disk>Avg. Disk sec/Transfer counter. Track the Process>%Processor Time counter for every process running to determine which processes are pushing the processor excessively. Monitor the Process>Working Set counter for these processes in particular.

C. Check the Processor>%Processor Time counter, determine the percent of disk I/O used for paging through the Logical Disk>Disk Queue Length counter, and the Process>Working Set for every process running.

D. Check the Processor>%User Time counter, determine the percent of disk I/O used for paging through the Logical Disk>%Disk Time counter, and the Memory>Commit Limit counter for the pagefile.

Question #104

Resource: Chapter 19, "Troubleshooting RAS"

What programs can be used to troubleshoot RAS: (Pick all that apply)

A. Network Monitor

B. Dial-Up Networking Monitor

C. Remote Access Admin

D. Performance Monitor

Question #105

Resource: Chapter 21, "Optimizing Directory Replication Traffic"

Which of the following actions can serve to optimize network traffic associated with Directory Replication? Choose all that apply.

A. Lock directories that are not replicated frequently, or that you do not want to have replicated.

B. Maintain a shallow export directory tree structure.

C. Modify the interval value on the export server so that it does not check for changes in the export tree as frequently.

D. Remove the password from the Directory Replication service account.

Question #106

Resource: Chapter 20, "Monitoring the Processor"

Which Processor object counter would be useful to determine how much processor time is being utilized by application requests?

A. %Processor Time

B. %User Time

C. %Application Time

D. %Privileged Time

Question #107

Resource: Chapter 9, "Recovering from Hard Disk Failure"

Your Windows NT file server is configured with mirroring on one of the data drive partitions. Users have complained about the disk full errors and poor response time. You have 500M available on each drive. What steps do you take to remedy this situation?

A. Back up data, extend the mirrored partition, and restore data.

B. Back up data, break the mirror, create a larger mirror set, and restore data.

C. Implement disk duplexing.

D. Implement RAID5 on the free space, assign permissions to the users.

Question #108

Resource: Chapter 7, "HKEY_LOCAL_MACHINE\System\CurrentControlSet"

Which of the following HKEY_LOCAL_MACHINE\System\CurrentControlSet subkey would you use to determine which services and drivers contain dependencies on other services and service groups?

A. Control

B. Enum

C. Dependencies

D. Services

Question #109

Resource: Chapter 8, Entire Chapter

The Advanced button on the Microsoft TCP/IP Properties sheet allows for the addition of:

A. 5 additional WINS server IP addresses

B. 10 additional default gateways

C. 5 additional DHCP server IP addresses

D. 5 additional default gateways

Question #110

Resource: Chapter 22, "Start the Kernel Debugger"

Kernel Debugger commands can be entered after a _____ key sequence is entered.

A. Ctrl,G

B. Ctrl,C

C. Ctrl,K

D. Ctrl,Q

Question #111

Resource: Chapter 5, "Database Synchronization"

Users for the Discover America company are located in office A and office B connected by a slow WAN link. The PDC is located in office A and the BDC is located in office B. Because of the high level of security required, users are required to change their password every seven days. There is also a very large amount of network traffic due to resource

App J

access between the two offices. The administrator is getting complaints of intermittent slow resource access. Select the best solution from the choices below.

A. Install a BDC in office A.

B. Install a BDC in office A and a second BDC in office B.

C. Install a second BDC in office B.

D. Locate the BDC in office A.

Question #112

Resource: Chapter 13, "Managing Shares and Permissions Remotely"

Which tool(s) can you use to remotely manage file and folder permissions across the domain?

A. User Manager for Domains

B. Server Manager

C. Windows Explorer

D. Network Neighborhood

Question #113

Resource: Chapter 19, "RAS Installation"

RAS Supports what protocols? (Pick all that apply)

A. TCP/IP

B. IPX/SPX

C. NetBEUI

D. DLC

Question #114

Resource: Chapter 20, "Monitoring Disk Activity"

While tracking the performance of disk activity on a system, you notice that the measured value is always 0 although the disk appears to be heavily used. What is your evaluation of this situation?

A. The disk is a high performance unit and can handle the heavy disk I/O.

B. The wrong disk objects and counters have been selected for Performance Monitor.

C. The disk counters had not been enabled by typing DISKPERF -Y at a command prompt.

D. The disk has crashed.

Question #115

Resource: Chapter 20, "Monitoring Memory"

Frederick has recently loaded two more C++ applications to modify on his Windows NT 4.0 Workstation. He has noticed that when he boots and loads all his applications, Windows NT takes longer to respond to application requests. You use Performance Monitor and notice that pagefile usage has increased and that the Commit Limit for the pagefile drops rapidly when the applications are loaded. What is the best solution you can offer Frederick based on this data?

App J

A. Purchase more RAM for Frederick's computer.

B. Move the pagefile to another disk partition.

C. Increase the initial size of the pagefile so that it doesn't have to grow right away as the applications load.

D. Move the C++ applications to another disk partition.

Question #116

Resource: Chapter 3, "Understanding the Nature of a Trust Relationship"

The Finance domain trusts the Marketing domain. What implication can you draw from this relationship?

A. The Finance domain is the trusted domain and the Marketing domain is the trusting domain. Users from the Marketing domain can access resources in the Finance domain, but only log on at their own domain computers.

B. The Finance domain is the trusting domain and the Marketing domain is the trusted domain. Users from the Marketing domain can access resources in the Finance domain, but only log on at their own domain computers.

C. The Finance domain is the trusted domain and the Marketing domain is the trusting domain. Users from the Finance domain can access resources in the Marketing domain, and log on at computers in the Marketing domain.

D. The Finance domain is the trusting domain and the Marketing domain is the trusted domain. Users from the Finance domain can only access their own resources and log on at computers in their domain. Users from the Marketing domain can access resources in the Finance domain, and log on at computers in either the Finance domain or their own domain.

Question #117

Resource: Chapter 21, "Interpreting Frames in a Capture File"; "Analyzing Traffic between Domain Controllers"

Which of the following network services generate traffic between a client and a server computer? Choose all that apply.

A. NetBIOS name registration with a WINS server

B. Logon validation

C. Account database synchronization

D. DHCP IP address requests

Question #118

Resource: Chapter 10, "Windows NT 4.0 Print Process"

Which of the following steps apply to the Windows NT 4.0 print process on Windows NT computers? Select all that apply.

A. The GDI component of the client computer generates an enhanced metafile print job.

B. The bulk of the print process completes in the spooler on the client computer before forwarding the print job to the print server.

C. The print monitor controls access to the print devices and device ports and monitors status of the print job.

D. The local printer spooler makes a remote connection to the print server spooler and copies the print job there.

Question #119

Resource: Chapter 14, "Creating the Server-Based Profile"

There are five summer interns joining the company this year for a three month period. You want to give them access to the network, but you want to restrict their environment settings to specific programs, colors, and so on. They should not be able to change the settings. What steps are involved?

A. Change the NTUSER.DAT file in the shared directory to NTUSER.MAN.

B. Through the User Profiles tab in the System applet, copy the profile of the account that has the appropriate environment settings to a shared directory on a central server.

C. Create a user account and make the appropriate changes to that account's environment settings.

D. Specify the location and file name of the profile in each summer intern's account properties.

Question #120

Resource: Chapter 18, Entire Chapter

You are responsible for a small company local area network and have implemented an intranet. Your manager is concerned that the confidential data might get out to the competition. What can you do to help?

A. Tell the manager it's okay, the data is old anyway.

App

J

B. Tell the manager you do not have Internet access.

C. Use PWS instead.

D. Use Microsoft Windows NT IE in place of the Windows 95 version.

Question #121

Resource: Chapter 8, Entire Chapter

Which of the following parameters can be configured manually with the NWLink protocol?

A. IP address

B. Frame type

C. Subnet mask

D. DHCP scope

Question #122

Resource: Chapter 15, "Remote Server Management"

Server tools are designed to be installed on which of the following clients?

A. Windows 95

B. Windows for Workgroups 3.11

C. Windows NT 4.0 and 3.5/3.51 Workstations

D. Windows NT 4.0 Server

Question #123

Resource: Chapter 10, "TCP/IP Printing"

From the choices below, indicate the step that is NOT required when installing and configuring a printing device using the TCP/IP protocol.

A. Enter the IP address of the remote controller servicing the print device in the Add LPR Compatible Printer dialog box.

B. Enter the name of the remote controller servicing the print device in the Add LPR Compatible Printer dialog box.

C. Enter the IP address of the print device in the Add LPR Compatible Printer dialog box.

D. Enter the IP address of the print server in the Add LPR Compatible Printer dialog box.

Question #124

Resource: Chapter 15, "Creating a Server Tools Share Using Network Client Administrator"

The default share name for the server tools share is:

A. SrvTools

B. ClientTools

C. SetupAdm

D. ServerTools

Question #125

Resource: Chapter 8, Entire Chapter

The Registry location for the NetBEUI protocol parameters is HKEY_LOCAL_MACHINE\System\CurrentControlSet\Services\...:

A. NetBEUI\Parameters

B. NetBIOS\Parameters

C. NBF\Parameters

D. NetBEUI\NBF\Parameters

Question #126

Resource: Chapter 8, Entire Chapter

When the directory replicator service is configured, a user account must be created. Why is a user account required?

A. The administrator must log on to the computer with the user account and manually start and stop the replicator service.

B. The replicator service will log on to the computer as the user and use the account to perform directory replication.

C. The replicator service will not log on to the computer as the user, but will use the account in case the replicator service fails.

D. The administrator uses this account to perform administrative duties once the replicator service is configured.

Question #127

Resource: Chapter 4, "Understanding the Single Domain Model"

Kite Flyers Corporation consists of 300 employees located in a single office complex. Which domain model would best suit this organization?

A. Single domain model

B. Master domain model

C. Multiple Master domain model

D. Complete Trust domain model

Question #128

Resource: Chapter 17, "AppleTalk Routing"

What service must be installed on a Windows NT 4.0 Server to allow it to function as an AppleTalk router?

A. RPC

B. GSNW

C. FDDI

D. SFM

Question #129

Resource: Chapter 21, "File Session Frames"

When a TCP session is established, three frames are generated known as the TCP three-way handshake. Which of the following frames are part of the three-way handshake? Choose all that apply.

    A. TCP Request from the client to the server.

    B. TCP Name resolution request from the client to the WINS server.

    C. TCP Request Acknowledgment from the server to the client.

    D. TCP Session establishment from the client to the server.

Question #130

Resource: Chapter 5, "Database Synchronization"

What Windows NT service provides pass-through authentication?

    A. Netlogon

    B. Browser

    C. Alerter

    D. Network DDE

Question #131

Resource: Chapter 6, "Backup Domain Controller"

The PDC must go offline to add more memory. What do you do?

    A. Install a new PDC to take over the role.

    B. Add the new memory and bring the PDC back online.

    C. Promote a server to PDC.

    D. Promote the BDC to PDC.

App
J

Question #132

Resource: Chapter 4, Entire Chapter

Kite Flyers Corporation is a relatively small company with about 1,000 employees. They are located in the same office complex. There are five departments: Accounting, Marketing, MIS, HR, and Corporate. Each has its own set of network resources that its staff accesses, and some resources that everyone in the company uses.

Primary Goals: Give all employees a single logon account that they can use to access their resources. Let each department manage their own resources.

Secondary Goal: Centralize resources by department.

Solution: Implement a single domain model and make all resource servers members of the domain.

   A. The solution satisfies none of the goals.

   B. The solution satisfies both primary goals and the secondary goal.

   C. The solution satisfies both primary goals, but not the secondary goal.

   D. The solution satisfies one primary goal and the secondary goal.

Question #133

Resource: Chapter 21, "WINS Frames"

What types of traffic are associated with the WINS service?

   A. WINS Registration

   B. WINS Time Out

   C. WINS Query Request

   D. WINS Address Request

Question #134

Resource: Chapter 3, "Setting Up a Trust Relationship"

The Finance domain users need to access a printer resource in the Marketing domain. You are going to set up a trust relationship to facilitate the sharing of this resource. Which two steps need to take place?

A. The Finance domain must identify the Marketing domain as its trusted domain.

B. The Marketing domain must permit the Finance domain to trust it—the Marketing domain must make Finance its trusting domain.

C. The Finance domain must permit the Marketing domain to trust it—the Finanace domain must make Marketing its trusting domain.

D. The Marketing domain must identify the Finance domain as its trusted domain.

Question #135

Resource: Chapter 16, "Gateway (and Client) Services for NetWare"

Gateway (and Client) Services for NetWare is: (Pick one)

A. sold as a part of Services for Netware

B. included with Windows NT Workstation

C. included with Windows NT Workstation and Server

D. included with Windows NT Server

Question #136

Resource: Chapter 15, "Required Resources for Windows 95"

To install server tools on a Windows 95 client computer, the following resources and services are required.

A. Client for Novell Networks installed.

B. 3M of free disk space.

C. 8M of memory.

D. Client for Microsoft Networks installed.

Question #137

Resource: Chapter 13, "Understanding the Concept of Ownership"

The person that created DOOM.DOC on server ACCT1 is no longer with the company. Cathy, a member of Team Leaders, will be assuming responsibility for the DOOM project, and needs to become the owner of DOOM.DOC. How can this be accomplished? Choose all that apply.

A. Give Cathy the Take Ownership of Files and Folders User Right on the server ACCT1.

B. Give Cathy the Take Ownership permission on the file DOOM.DOC.

C. Tell Cathy to just take ownership of the file.

D. Give the Team Leaders group the Take Ownership permission for DOOM.DOC.

Question #138

Resource: Chapter 12, "Account Policy"

To provide a greater level of security, you have decided to create an account policy that requires a minimum password length of eight characters, requires that users change their passwords at least once a month, and does not allow users to use the same password twice in two months. Which Account Policy settings are appropriate?

A. Max Password Age: 60; Min Password Age: 30; Min Password Length: 8; Password Uniqueness: 2

B. Max Password Age: 30; Min Password Age: 30; Min Password Length: 8; Password Uniqueness: 6

C. Max Password Age: 30; Min Password Age: 10; Min Password Length: 8; Password Uniqueness: 6

D. Max Password Age: 60; Min Password Age: 30; Min Password
Length: 8; Password Uniqueness: 1

Question #139

Resource: Chapter 22, "Connect the Host and Target Computers"

What kind of connection can be established between the Host computer and the Target computer for the Host computer to monitor the Boot process on the Target computer?

A. Null Modem connection using a COM port

B. Normal Network connection using a Network Adapter Card

C. Modem connection using a COM port

D. Modem connection using a LPT port

Question #140

Resource: Chapter 4, "Understanding the Complete Trust Domain Model"

Kite Flyers Corporation was formed from three different regional companies located in San Francisco, Chicago, and Atlanta. Each company already had its own Windows NT network configured as a Single Domain model. It is necessary that all the users in the new company be able to log on to the network, no matter which office they work from, and still be able to access their resources. Which domain model provides the best solution for this scenario?

A. Multiple Master domain model. Create two one-way trusts between San Francisco and Chicago, and between Chicago and Atlanta.

B. Master domain model. Have San Francisco and Atlanta create one-way trusts to Chicago.

C. Complete Trust model. Have all domains trust each other for a total of three trusts.

D. Complete Trust model. Have all domains trust each other for a total of six trusts.

Question #141

Resource: Chapter 15, "Installation of Windows 3.1 and Windows for Workgroups 3.11 Server Tools"

Indicate the two files that contain settings that must be appended to the Config.sys and Autoexec.bat respectively when installing server tools on a Windows for Workgroup platform.

A. New-conf.sys and New-vars.bat.

B. New-config.sys and New-vars.bat.

C. New-vars.bat and New-config.sys.

D. New-auto.bat and New-vars.sys.

Question #142

Resource: Chapter 12, "Default User Accounts"

Which of the following statements is true about the default user accounts created in Windows NT Server 4.0?

A. The Administrator account is enabled and can be renamed; the Guest account is enabled and cannot be renamed.

B. The Administrator account is enabled and cannot be renamed; the Guest account is disabled and cannot be renamed.

C. The Administrator account is enabled and can be renamed; the Guest account is disabled and can be renamed.

D. The Administrator account is disabled and cannot be renamed; the Guest account is enabled and can be renamed.

Question #143

Resource: Chapter 13, "Sharing Resources and Determining Network Access"

The administrator of the TOOLS shared folder wants to limit access to the folder only to the Developers group. To accomplish this, she gives the Everyone group NO ACCESS, and the Developers group Change access. The Developers complain that they cannot access any file in TOOLS. What else must the administrator do?

A. Share the files in the TOOLS folder.

B. Remove the Everyone group.

C. Give the Developers group Full Control.

D. Format the partition as NTFS and assign NTFS permissions in addition to the share permissions.

Question #144

Resource: Chapter 21, "Suggestions for Optimizing Browser Traffic"

The KITEMASTERS corporate network consists of 6000 users located across five regional locations, each on its own subnet. About half the users have Windows NT Workstation 4.0 computers, and the rest have Windows 95 computers. These computers are frequently restarted throughout the day. There is one PDC and BDC located in the MIS department, and a BDC in each regional location. Each location also has one or more Windows NT Server 4.0 computers for resource management.

Using Network Monitor, you have noticed that there is an unusually high percentage of Browser traffic generated throughout the day. How can you optimize traffic associated with the Browser while letting users continue to browse for resources? Choose the best two answers.

A. You cannot configure Browser parameters.

B. Configure the Windows 95 and Windows NT Workstation 4.0 computers to never become browsers.

C. Disable the Server service on user computers which will not be sharing resources in the network.

D. Disable the Computer Browser service on all user computers.

App
J

Question #145

Resource: Chapter 22, "STOP Messages During Installation"

The major cause of STOP errors during the installation process is?

A. Incompatible software.

B. Incompatible hardware.

C. Incompatible Windows NT setup program.

D. It is impossible to get STOP errors during installation.

Question #146

Resource: Chapter 21, "Account Database Synchronization"

Built-in local groups and their members are contained in which accounts database?

A. SAM Accounts Database

B. Local Security Accounts Database

C. SAM Built-In Database

D. Account synchronization database

Question #147

Resource: Chapter 2, "Centralized Account Administration"

Which statements best describe the roles of the primary and backup domain controllers for a domain?

A. The primary and backup domain controllers authenticate users equally.

B. The primary domain controller authenticates users, while the backup domain controller maintains the domain's account database.

C. The primary domain controller's primary responsibility is to maintain the master account database; the backup domain controller's primary responsibility is to authenticate users' requests to log on to the network.

D. The accounts database can be managed from either the primary or the backup domain controller.

Question #148

Resource: Chapter 5, "Planning Protocol Selection of a Network Enterprise"

Pam is a manager in a training development corporation of 200 users using Windows NT Workstations connected over a LAN using the NetBEUI protocol. The corporation has just purchased a new office building. Pam decides to relocate 30 of the 200 users and computers to the new building and connects the two buildings together through a router. Now employees in the new building cannot see resources in the original facility, and the users in the original facility cannot connect to resources in the new building. Select the two best solutions to the problem.

A. Install NWLink on all workstations.
B. Install AppleTalk on all workstations.
C. Configure NetBEUI to use the router.
D. Install TCP/IP on all workstations.

Question #149

Resource: Chapter 8, Entire Chapter

A DHCP reservation is assigned to a:

A. Computer
B. Network Adapter Card
C. Domain
D. Workgroup

Question #150

Resource: Chapter 8, Entire Chapter

When configuring GSNW on Windows NT Server, a group called _____ must be set up on the Novell Server.

A. NTUserGateway

B. NovellGateway

C. NetBIOSGateway

D. NTGateway

Question #151

Resource: Chapter 3, "Group Management in the Domain"

The Finance domain trusts the Marketing domain. You would like the administrators of the Marketing domain to be able to administer the servers in the Finance domain. What should you do to facilitate this?

A. Make the Domain Admins group from the Marketing domain a member of the local Administrators group on each server on the Finance domain.

B. Make the Administrators group from the Marketing domain a member of the local Administrators group on each server in the Finance domain.

C. Make the Domain Admins group from each server in the Finance domain a member of the local Administrators group in the Marketing domain.

D. Do nothing. When a trust is established, the Administrators group from the trusted domain is automatically added to the local administrator groups on the servers in the trusting domain.

Question #152

Resource: Chapter 2, "Single Network Logon"

Windows NT 4.0's Directory Services answers the enterprise challenge of providing one logon account and password by:

A. Having each member of the domain maintain a copy of the account database.

B. Allowing a user the ability to log on to any computer that is a member of the domain or the enterprise, and be able to access the same network resources.

C. Allowing a user the ability to log on only to any computer in their domain and access resources in that domain.

D. Making the user's logon account domain-independent.

Question #153

Resource: Chapter 13, "Troubleshooting Security"

Fred is a member of the Developers group. The Developers group has been given the NTFS permission Full Control to the TOOLS folder. Fred is changing jobs and has been given NO ACCESS to the file DOOM.DOC, which is contained in the TOOLS folder. Later, Fred logs on and deletes the file DOOM.DOC. Luckily, you can restore the file from your tape backup. How can you prevent Fred from deleting the file again, but still maintain the original level of access for him and the Developers group?

A. Fire Fred.

B. Give the Developers group Special Access with all options selected for the TOOLS folder. Then give Fred NO ACCESS to the file.

C. Give the Developers group Change access at the folder level.

D. Give Fred NO ACCESS at the folder level.

Question #154

Resource: Chapter 3, "Troubleshooting Trust Relationships"

You created a trust between Finance and Marketing so that users in the Marketing domain can access resources managed in the Finance domain. However, Marketing users are unable to access resources. What would you check?

A. Has the trust been completed by both domains?

B. Was the trust broken?

C. Has appropriate access been granted to the users?

D. Is the trust set up in the correct direction?

Question #155

Resource: Chapter 2, "Taking the Enterprise Challenge"

When planning a large wide area network for an enterprise, Microsoft advocates implementing a structure that supports the following characteristics: (Choose all that apply)

A. Single network logon regardless of location or domain affiliation.

B. Easy user access to network resources regardless of the location of the user or the resource in the enterprise.

C. Decentralized account and resource administration.

D. Synchronization of account and security information across the enterprise.

Question #156

Resource: Chapter 14, "Server-Based User Profiles"; "Mandatory Profiles"

You would like your users to receive default environment settings when they log on, but not allow them to change their own settings and save them as part of their own personal profiles. What type of server profile will accomplish this?

A. Server-based mandatory profile

B. Server-based user profile

C. Local user profile

D. Local system policy

Question #157

Resource: Chapter 11, Entire Chapter

What clients and services disks can you create with network administrator tool?

A. Microsoft Windows 95

B. Microsoft Windows NT Workstation

C. Microsoft Windows for Workgroups

D. LAN Manager 2.2c clients

Question #158

Resource: Chapter 10, "Windows NT 4.0 Print Process"

What is the purpose of the print monitor SFMMON.DLL?

A. SFMMON.DLL monitors Macintosh print jobs routed using AppleTalk protocol to network print devices.

B. SFMMON.DLL is the System File Manager print monitor which tracks print jobs sent directly to or printed directly from a file.

C. SFMMON.DLL is the software print job compression DLL which compresses the print job before it is sent from the local print spooler to the print server.

D. SFMMON.DLL is not a valid print monitor.

Question #159

Resource: Chapter 7, "Service Dependencies"

Which two utilities would you use to determine whether a service failed to start and why?

A. Server Manager to view service startup values, and Windows Diagnostics to view service dependencies.

B. Event Viewer to view stopped services, and Windows Diagnostics to view service dependencies.

    C. Control Panel\System to view service startup values, and Windows Diagnostics to view service dependencies.

    D. Event Viewer to view stopped services, and Server Manager to view service startup values.

Question #160

Resource: Chapter 18, Entire Chapter

You are responsible for a small company that has three locations in Chicago. You want to be sure the new software updates are available to all the appropriate installers throughout the company. Which publishing service(s) would you use?

    A. WWW

    B. FTP

    C. GOPHER

    D. NETSCAPE

Question #161

Resource: Chapter 5, "Network Monitoring Considerations"

What two applications can be used to store and view data collected with the Performance Monitor?

    A. Microsoft Notepad

    B. Microsoft SQL

    C. Microsoft Excel

    D. Microsoft Calculator

Question #162

Resource: Chapter 13, "Local Versus Domain Access Tokens"

Permissions for the BUDGET shared folder on ACCT1 are as shown in the following exhibit. ACCT1 is a member server of the FINANCE domain. Finance is a trusting domain of CORPDOMAIN. There is a global group called FinanceMgrs that must have Read access to the folder and its files. How would you make this happen?

A. Click the Add button and add the FinanceMgrs global group from FINANCE to the ACL with Read permission.

B. Click the Add button, choose CORPDOMAIN from the From Domain list, and add the FinanceMgrs global group from CORPDOMAIN to the ACL with Read permission.

C. Click the Add button and add the FinanceMgrs global group from CORPDOMAIN to the Accountants local group on ACCT1.

D. You cannot add users from another domain to this ACL.

Question #163

Resource: Chapter 21, "Account Database Synchronization"

User, group, and computer accounts are contained in which account database?

A. SAM Accounts Database

B. Local Security Accounts Database

C. SAM Built-In Database

D. Account Synchronization Database

Question #164

Resource: Chapter 10, "Troubleshooting Printing"

Which of the following steps is appropriate to take when trouble-shooting a failed print job?

A. Verify that the appropriate print port has been defined and configured by printing a test page.

B. Delete and recreate the printer.

C. Determine whether the print device is online and connected.

D. Resubmit the print job to a file and then copy the file to a printer port to see if it is successful.

App

J

Question #165

Resource: Chapter 20, "Monitoring Network-Related Objects"

You are analyzing network activity between your network clients and a server. You plan to use Network Monitor to monitor network traffic generated by and received by the server, and Performance Monitor to track system performance relating to network traffic. What types of objects would facilitate your analysis? Choose all that apply.

A. Redirector

B. Server

C. Protocol

D. Frame

Question #166

Resource: Chapter 2, "Synchronization of Account and Security Information"

My domain consists of a PDC and three BDCs. One of my BDCs has gone down. Which functions can still take place on my network? Choose all that apply.

A. I can administer accounts through User Manager for Domains.

B. I can log on to the network.

C. I can use Server Manager to administer the PDC and the other BDCs.

D. I can synchronize the domain controllers.

Question #167

Resource: Chapter 20, "Monitoring Disk Activity"; "Monitoring System Performance with Performance Monitor"

Which of the following counters will provide you with the total number of bytes transferred during disk I/O for all the disks in your computer?

A. Logical Disk>Disk Bytes/sec, Total instance

B. Logical Disk>Disk Bytes/sec, for each partition instance

C. Physical Disk>Disk Bytes/sec, Total instance

D. Physical Disk>Disk Bytes/sec, for each disk instance

Question #168

Resource: Chapter 12, "Renaming, Copying, and Deleting Accounts"; "Home Directory"

You are creating multiple user accounts for salespersons, marketers, and programmers. Each set of accounts belongs to the same relative groups (sales users in SALES, marketing users in MARKETING, and programmer users in PROGRAMMERS), uses the same logon scripts (SALES.BAT, MARKET.BAT, PROGRAM.BAT), and saves data in a home directory relative to each group (sales users under USERS\SALES, marketing users under USERS\MARKETERS, programmer users under USERS\PROGRAMMERS). What is the most efficient way to create these users?

App
J

A. Create a separate account for each user. As you create the user, use the %USERNAME% environment variable when specifying the home directory to let Windows NT create it for you.

B. Create a template for each type of user. Make the appropriate choices and entries for groups, logon script, and home directory. Use the %USERNAME% environment variable when specifying the home directory to let Windows NT create them for you. Then, create each user by copying the appropriate template.

C. Create all the users without specifying group membership. After they are all created, select each group of users by Ctrl+clicking them and create the appropriate group.

D. You must create each user individually.

Question #169

Resource: Chapter 7, "Hardware"

Which HKEY_LOCAL_MACHINE\Hardware subkey displays data collected by NTDETECT.COM, NTOSKRNL.EXE, or a hardware recognizer during the bootup process?

A. DeviceMap

B. Description

C. ResourceMap

D. OwnerMap

Question #170

Resource: Chapter 5, "Planning Effective WAN Performance"

Donna, a system administrator in office A, has been getting calls from users in office B complaining that logon validation is extremely slow every morning. The PDC and three BDCs are located in office A, which is connected to office B with a 56K link. What is the best way to correct the problem?

A. Do nothing except tell the users to get to work 15 minutes earlier and log on before the crowd.

B. Relocate two BDCs from office A to office B.

C. Upgrade the 56K line to 256K line.

D. Install and configure two more BDCs in office A.

Question #171

Resource: Chapter 22, "BugCheck Information"

The first four lines of the _____ section are critical to finding the cause of the STOP error.

A. BugCheck Information

B. Driver Information

C. Kernel Build Number and Stack Dump

D. Debug Port Information

Question #172

Resource: Chapter 16, "Gateway (and Client) Services for NetWare"

You have clients which only have the Microsoft client installed, but need access to a Novell NetWare server. How can you allow these clients to have access to the NetWare server? (Pick all that apply)

A. Install Gateway (and Client) Services for NetWare on the Novell Server.

B. Install Gateway (and Client) Services for NetWare on the Windows NT Server.

C. Install the Novell NetWare requestor on the client.

D. Install File and Print Services for NetWare on the Windows NT Server.

Question #173

Resource: Chapter 8, Entire Chapter

RIP for NWLink will allow a Windows NT computer to act as a:

A. IP Router

B. AppleTalk Router

C. IPX Router

D. DLC Router

Question #174

Resource: Chapter 15, "Windows NT 4.0 Workstation Server Tools"

What server tool is NOT installed on a Windows NT 3.5/3.51 Workstation platform?

A. Services for Macintosh

B. System Policy Editor

C. Remote Access Administrator

D. User Profile Editor

Question #175

Resource: Chapter 10, "Windows NT 4.0 Print Process"

The printer for a network print device has been configured to print documents at all times. Pam plans to send a large complex graphics document that she would like to have tomorrow morning. This job will take at least one hour to complete. What can you do to minimize the effect that printing this document will have on other documents in the queue?

A. Select Pam's document and pause it. Resume printing after hours when print jobs are at a minimum.

B. Modify the printer schedule so that it only prints documents after hours.

C. Modify the document schedule for Pam's document so that it only prints between 1:00 A.M. and 3:00 A.M.

D. Do nothing. The printer automatically holds long jobs until short jobs finish spooling and printing.

Question #176

Resource: Chapter 20, "Creating a Performance Monitor Log"; "Summarizing Performance Monitoring and Optimization"

You plan to use Performance Monitor to help predict and troubleshoot server activity under various conditions. Which of the following would be the best way to begin?

A. Create and monitor a real-time chart during peak activity and note the percent of processor usage during these periods.

B. Create a series of baseline logs of specific objects (processor, memory, disk, and network), each representing a different condition. Use these to predict activity under those conditions and to troubleshoot abnormal system activity.

C. Create a baseline log measuring system activity during periods of average activity. Compare this against real-time charts created during peak activity on the system.

D. Network Monitor would be a better tool to predict system activity.

Question #177

Resource: Chapter 13, "Effective Permissions"

Ned is a member of the Developers group at Springfield Technologies. He has been promoted to team leader for his group. He needs to edit the DOOM.DOC file in the Tools folder, but does not have Write access. What must you do to give Ned access to DOOM.DOC?

A. Do nothing. The next time Ned logs on, his permissions will change.

B. Change the Developers group permission to Change.

C. Add Ned to the Team Leaders group.

D. Change the Team Leaders group permission to Full Control.

Question #178

Resource: Chapter 19, "RAS Installation"

Who can install RAS on an Windows NT Server? (Pick all that apply)

A. Administrator

B. Any member of the Administrators group

C. Any member of the PowerUsers group

D. Any member of the RAS group

Answer Key for Self-Assessment Test

Question	Correct Answer
1	B
2	D
3	A
4	B
5	C
6	D
7	C
8	A
9	B
10	C
11	B,C
12	A
13	D
14	A,B,C,D
15	A,B,C,D
16	C
17	D
18	A,C
19	A
20	A,B,D
21	C
22	A,B,C,D
23	A
24	C
25	B

Question	Correct Answer
26	B
27	C
28	C
29	C
30	~~C~~ A
31	B,C
32	B
33	A,B,C
34	C
35	D
36	D
37	A,B
38	C
39	B,C,D
40	B
41	C
42	~~D~~ C
43	B
44	A,B,D
45	~~C~~ B
46	B
47	B
48	A
49	A,B,C,D
50	B
51	A
52	~~A,B~~ no correct answer

continues

continued

Question	Correct Answer
53	D
54	C
55	A,B,C
56	B,C,D
57	A
58	A,C,D
59	A,B
60	B,C
61	B,C
62	A,C
63	A
64	C
65	A,C,D
66	A,B,C,D
67	C
68	A
69	D
70	A,D
71	A,B,D
72	D
73	B
74	A
75	A
76	C
77	B
78	B
79	A,C,D

Question	Correct Answer
80	B
81	B
82	B
83	C
84	D
85	A,C,D
86	A
87	C
88	A
89	B
90	D
91	A
92	C
93	D
94	B
95	B
96	A,B,D
97	A
98	A,C
99	B
100	C
101	B
102	D
103	B
104	B,C
105	A,B,C
106	B

continues

continued

Question	Correct Answer
107	B
108	D
109	D
110	B
111	D
112	C
113	A,B,C
114	C
115	C
116	D
117	A,B,D
118	A,C,D
119	A,B,C,D
120	B
121	B
122	A,B,C
123	D
124	C
125	C
126	B
127	A
128	D
129	A,C,D
130	A
131	B
132	C
133	A,D

Question	Correct Answer
134	C,D
135	D
136	B,C,D
137	A,B,D
138	C
139	A,C
140	D
141	A
142	A,C
143	B
144	B,C
145	B
146	C
147	C
148	A,D
149	B
150	D
151	A
152	B
153	B
154	A,B,C,D
155	A,B,D
156	A
157	A,C,D
158	A
159	B
160	A,B

continues

App
J

continued

Question	Correct Answer
161	B,C
162	B
163	A
164	A,C,D
165	A,B,C
166	A,B,C,D
167	C
168	B
169	B
170	B
171	A
172	B,C
173	C
174	B
175	C
176	B
177	C
178	A,B

Chapter Tests

Note The answers to these questions can be found in order at the end of this section. The resource line following each question number is the section in the book where information regarding that question is located. ■

Chapter 2

Question #02-01

Resource: "Workgroup Model"

Which of the following characteristics best apply to a workgroup network model? Choose two.

A. A workgroup network model provides a high level of security for resource access.

B. The workgroup model is best applied to smaller (fewer than 20) workstation groups.

C. A workgroup model is identified by its domain controller.

D. Each Windows NT computer participating in a workgroup must maintain a list of users that will be accessing the resources on that computer.

Question #02-02

Resource: "Domain Model"

Which of the following characteristics best apply to a domain network model? Choose two.

A. Resource access is provided by permitting access to users and groups that are members of the domain.

B. User and group accounts are maintained on each workstation that is a member of the domain.

C. A domain network model provides a relatively low level of resource security.

D. Resource and account management is centralized.

Question #02-03

Resource: "Taking the Enterprise Challenge"

When planning a large wide area network for an enterprise, Microsoft advocates implementing a structure that supports the following characteristics: (Choose all that apply)

A. Single network logon regardless of location or domain affiliation.

B. Easy user access to network resources regardless of the location of the user or the resource in the enterprise.

C. Decentralized account and resource administration.

D. Synchronization of account and security information across the enterprise.

Question #02-04

Resource: "Taking the Enterprise Challenge"

Which of the following scenarios define the correct application for a domain? Choose two.

A. A domain might be centered around the organizational hierarchy of a company with accounts and resources centered in the departments that will manage them.

B. A domain might represent the regional nature of an organization by establishing a domain for each region and then connecting them by trust relationships.

C. A domain might represent a small group of workstations each of which is managed by the owner of the workstation, and each of which maintains its own list of accounts and resources.

D. A domain might be best characterized as a peer-to-peer configuration of Windows NT Server computers.

Question #02-05

Resource: "Taking the Enterprise Challenge"

The identity of the domain is established by the implementation of a:

A. Windows NT 4.0 Server

B. Any Windows NT 4.0 Workstation or Server that maintains an account database

C. A domain controller

D. A peer-to-peer network model

Question #02-06

Resource: "Single Network Logon"

Windows NT 4.0's Directory Services answers the enterprise challenge of providing one logon account and password by:

A. Having each member of the domain maintain a copy of the account database.

B. Allowing a user the ability to log on to any computer that is a member of the domain or the enterprise, and be able to access the same network resources.

C. Allowing a user the ability to log on only to any computer in their domain and access resources in that domain.

D. Making the user's logon account domain–independent.

Question #02-07

Resource: "Centralized Account Administration"

Which statements best describe the roles of the primary and backup domain controllers for a domain?

A. The primary and backup domain controllers authenticate users equally.

B. The primary domain controller authenticates users, while the backup domain controller maintains the domain's account database.

App

J

C. The primary domain controller's primary responsibility is to maintain the master account database; the backup domain controller's primary responsibility is to authenticate users' requests to log on to the network.

D. The accounts database can be managed from either the primary or the backup domain controller.

Question #02-08

Resource: "Network Resource Access"

In the ABC enterprise, it has been determined that the MIS department will manage all user and group accounts, while each department in the organization should be able to administer its own resources using the same enterprise account database without having to worry about user management. Which response best answers this need?

A. All resources and accounts must participate in the same domain. Establish one domain controller, create all the user and group accounts, and then let each resource administrator assign permissions to their resources.

B. The MIS department will be given their own domain called the account domain from which they can create and manage all user and group accounts. Each department could be given its own domain for the purpose of managing its own resources. The resource administrators can use the accounts from the account domain with no other modifications.

C. The MIS department will be given their own domain called the account domain from which they can create and manage all user and groups accounts. Each department could be given its own domain for the purpose of managing its own resources. By creating trust relationships between the resource domains and the account domain, each resource manager will be able to secure their resources using the enterprise account database.

D. Directory Services does not support this type of management structure.

Question #02-09

Resource: "Synchronization of Account and Security Information"

My domain consists of a PDC and three BDCs. One of my BDCs has gone down. Which functions can still take place on my network? Choose all that apply.

    A. I can administer accounts through User Manager for Domains.

    B. I can log on to the network.

    C. I can use Server Manager to administer the PDC and the other BDCs.

    D. I can synchronize the domain controllers.

Question #02-10

Resource: "Synchronization of Account and Security Information"

My domain consists of a PDC and three BDCs. My PDC is currently offline. Which functions can still take place on my network? Choose all that apply.

    A. I can administer accounts through User Manager for Domains.

    B. I can log on to the network.

    C. I can use Server Manager to administer the other BDCs.

    D. I can synchronize the domain controllers.

Chapter 3

Question #03-01

Resource: "Understanding the Nature of a Trust Relationship"

Which of the following Directory Services goals are met by trust relationships? Select all that apply.

    A. Provide users a single logon account that can be used anywhere within the enterprise to log on to the network.

B. Centralize management of accounts and resources.

C. Maintain separate user accounts for resource access on each resource server in the enterprise.

D. Facilitate access to network resources regardless of their domain location.

Question #03-02

Resource: "Understanding the Nature of a Trust Relationship"

The Finance domain users need to access a laser printer in the Marketing domain. The Marketing domain users need to access a scanner in the Finance domain. How many trust relationships need to be created to facilitate the sharing of these two network resources?

A. Create one two-way trust relationship between Finance and Marketing.

B. Create two one-way trust relationships, one from Finance to Marketing and the other from Marketing to Finance.

C. Create two one-way trust relationships from Finance to Marketing. One can handle the shared laser printer, and the other the scanner.

D. Create one trust relationship between Finance and Marketing. A trust relationship is always bi-directional.

Question #03-03

Resource: "Understanding the Nature of a Trust Relationship"

The Finance domain trusts the Marketing domain. What implication can you draw from this relationship?

A. The Finance domain is the trusted domain and the Marketing domain is the trusting domain. Users from the Marketing domain can access resources in the Finance domain, but only log on at their own domain computers.

B. The Finance domain is the trusting domain and the Marketing domain is the trusted domain. Users from the Marketing domain can access resources in the Finance domain, but only log on at their own domain computers.

C. The Finance domain is the trusted domain and the Marketing domain is the trusting domain. Users from the Finance domain can access resources in the Marketing domain, and log on at computers in the Marketing domain.

D. The Finance domain is the trusting domain and the Marketing domain is the trusted domain. Users from the Finance domain can only access their own resources and log on at computers in their domain. Users from the Marketing domain can access resources in the Finance domain, and log on at computers in either the Finance domain or their own domain.

App

J

Question #03-04

Resource: "Understanding the Nature of a Trust Relationship"

The Finance domain trusts the Marketing domain. The Marketing domain trusts the Accounting domain. Users in the Accounting domain need to access a database resource in the Finance domain. What needs to happen to facilitate the sharing of that resource?

A. Nothing. Because Finance already trusts Marketing and Marketing already trusts Accounting, Finance can share the database resource directly to Accounting users through the trusts.

B. Create a one-way trust from the Accounting domain to the Finance domain.

C. Create a one-way trust from the Finance domain to the Accounting domain.

D. Create a reverse trust from Accounting to Marketing, and from Marketing to Finance.

Question #03-05

Resource: "Setting Up a Trust Relationship"

Which of the following are requirements for setting up a successful trust relationship? Choose all that apply.

A. A domain controller in each domain must be up and accessible.

B. There can be no current sessions between the PDCs of each domain.

C. You must have an administrator-level account.

D. You must have access to a computer running User Manager for Domains.

Question #03-06

Resource: "Setting Up a Trust Relationship"

The Finance domain users need to access a printer resource in the Marketing domain. You are going to set up a trust relationship to facilitate the sharing of this resource. Which two steps need to take place?

A. The Finance domain must identify the Marketing domain as its trusted domain.

B. The Marketing domain must permit the Finance domain to trust it—the Marketing domain must make Finance its trusting domain.

C. The Finance domain must permit the Marketing domain to trust it—the Finance domain must make Marketing its trusting domain.

D. The Marketing domain must identify the Finance domain as its trusted domain.

Question #03-07

Resource: "The NetLogon Service and Pass-Through Authentication"

Which Windows NT Server service allows a user to log on at computers in domains in which they have no account through the trust relationship to a computer or domain in which they do have an account?

A. NetLogon Service

B. Directory Replication Service

C. Account Synchronization Service

D. Self Service

Question #03-08

Resource: "The NetLogon Service and Pass-Through Authentication"

The Finance domain trusts the Marketing domain. What NetLogon function allows a user from the Marketing domain to log on and validate from a computer that participates in the Finance domain?

A. Directory Replication

B. Pass-Through Authentication

C. Trust Validation

D. Access Control Lists

Question #03-09

Resource: "Local versus Global Accounts"

The Finance domain trusts the Marketing domain. Sheila has just joined the Marketing group as a short-term contractor. Sheila needs access to a Finance database to complete her project. What type of account would you create for Sheila?

A. Create a global account for Sheila in the Marketing domain.

B. Create a local account for Sheila in the Marketing domain.

C. Create a global account for Sheila in the Marketing Domain and a global account for Sheila in the Finance domain.

D. Create a local account for Sheila in the Marketing domain and a global account for Sheila in the Finance domain.

Question #03-10

Resource: "Group Management in the Domain"

Which statement best represents Microsoft's recommended group strategy for managing resources effectively?

A. Create a local group in the domain database and add the users from the domain to that local group. Create a local group on the resource computer and make the domain local group a member of the resource local group.

B. Create a global group in the domain database and add the users from the domain to that global group. Create a global group on the resource computer and make the domain global group a member of the resource global group.

C. Create a global group in the domain database and add the users from the domain to that global group. Create a local group on the resource computer and make the domain global group a member of the resource local group.

D. Create a local group on the resource computer and add the domain users directly to the local group.

Question #03-11

Resource: "Group Management in the Domain"

The Finance domain trusts the Marketing domain. You would like the administrators of the Marketing domain to be able to administer the servers in the Finance domain. What should you do to facilitate this?

A. Make the Domain Admins group from the Marketing domain a member of the local Administrators group on each server on the Finance domain.

B. Make the Administrators group from the Marketing domain a member of the local Administrators group on each server in the Finance domain.

C. Make the Domain Admins group from each server in the Finance domain a member of the local Administrators group in the Marketing domain.

D. Do nothing. When a trust is established, the Administrators group from the trusted domain is automatically added to the local administrator groups on the servers in the trusting domain.

Question #03-12

Resource: "Group Management in the Domain"

The Finance domain trusts the Marketing domain. You would like to give Sheila, Frank, and Pat the responsibility of backing up all the domain controllers and servers in the Finance Domain. Which is the best course of action?

A. Add Sheila, Frank, and Pat to the Backup Operators group in the Marketing domain, and then add that Backup Operators group to the local Backup Operators groups on each domain controller and server in the Finance domain.

B. Create a global group in the Marketing domain called Global Backup and add Sheila, Frank, and Pat to it. Add Global Backup to the local Backup Operators groups on each domain controller and server in the Finance domain.

C. Create a global group in the Marketing domain called Global Backup and add Sheila, Frank, and Pat to it. Add Global Backup to the local Backup Operators group on the primary domain controller and the local Backup Operators groups on each server in the Finance domain.

D. Create new accounts for Sheila, Frank, and Pat on each domain controller and server in the Finance domain and add them to the local Backup Operators groups on each domain controller and server in the Finance domain.

App J

Question #03-13

Resource: "Resource Management Across Trusts"; "Group Management in the Domain"

The Finance domain trusts the Marketing domain. The Finance domain shares a color laser printer that the CAD users in Marketing need to use from time to time. There is a global group in Marketing called CAD USERS. There is a local group on the print server in Finance called COLOR USERS that has Print permission to the color laser printer. How would you grant the Marketing CAD users permission to the color laser printer? Select the best answer (Microsoft's recommended solution).

A. In the Permissions dialog box for the color laser printer, choose Add and select the Marketing domain from the list of valid domains. Then select CAD USERS from the list of global groups in the Marketing database.

B. Add the CAD USERS global group from Marketing to the COLOR USERS local group on the print server.

C. Create a global group in Finance called MARKETING CAD USERS. Add the CAD USERS global group from Marketing to the MARKETING CAD USERS global group in Finance. Then add the MARKETING CAD USERS global group to the COLOR USERS local group on the print server.

D. You can't do this because the trust is in the wrong direction.

Question #03-14

Resource: "Troubleshooting Trust Relationships"

You created a trust between Finance and Marketing so that users in the Marketing domain can access resources managed in the Finance domain. However, Marketing users are unable to access resources. What would you check?

A. Has the trust been completed by both domains?

B. Was the trust broken?

C. Has appropriate access been granted to the users?

D. Is the trust set up in the correct direction?

Chapter 4

Question #04-01

Resource: "Understanding the Role of the Domain for Directory Services"

Which of the following characteristics can be applied to a domain? Choose all that apply.

A. A domain is a logical grouping of computers.

B. A domain depends entirely on the physical layout of the network.

C. A domain provides the foundation for implementing Directory Services.

D. A domain does not depend on the physical location of computers and users.

Question #04-02

Resource: "User and Group Accounts"

One factor that will definitely affect the type of domain model that you implement is:

A. The number of user and group accounts.

B. The physical location and grouping of users.

C. The type of wide area network connections you have in place.

D. The location of network servers.

Question #04-03

Resource: "Understanding the Single Domain Model"

Kite Flyers Corporation consists of 300 employees located in a single office complex. Which domain model would best suit this organization?

A. Single domain model

B. Master domain model

C. Multiple Master domain model

D. Complete Trust domain model

Question #04-04

Resource: "Understanding the Master Domain Model"

Kite Flyers Corporation has opened offices in London and Tokyo. Each office maintains its own resources, though all users are managed in the corporate headquarters. Which domain model is best suited to this organization?

A. Single domain model

B. Master domain model

C. Multiple Master domain model

D. Complete Trust domain model

Question #04-05

Resource: "Understanding the Multiple Master Domain Model"

Kite Flyers Corporation has experienced tremendous growth and now has between 10,000 and 15,000 employees located across its three global locations Chicago, London, and Tokyo. Resources are managed in each location as well as the users located in those offices. Which model best suits this organization?

A. Single domain model

B. Master domain model

C. Multiple Master domain model

D. Complete Trust domain model

Question #04-06

Resource: "Understanding the Master Domain Model"

Kite Flyers Corporation has its corporate headquarters in New York and branch offices in Chicago and San Francisco. Resource domains have been set up in each location and all accounts are managed by MIS in New York. The main goals of directory services are met. Which domain model does this represent and how many trusts need to be established?

A. Master domain model. The account domain in New York must trust each resource domain in each location, therefore three one-way trusts need to be established.

B. Complete Trust model. All domains must trust each other. Because there are 4 domains, 4*(4–1) or 12 trusts must be established.

C. Master domain model. Each resource domain must trust the account domain in New York, therefore three one-way trusts need to be established.

D. Master domain model. The account and resource domains must trust each other. Therefore, two one-way trusts must be established between each resource domain and the account domain, or 6 total.

Question #04-07

Resource: "Understanding the Complete Trust Domain Model"

Kite Flyers Corporation was formed from three different regional companies located in San Francisco, Chicago, and Atlanta. Each company already had its own Windows NT network configured as a Single Domain model. It is necessary that all the users in the new company be able to log on to the network, no matter which office they work from, and still be able to access their resources. Which domain model provides the best solution for this scenario?

A. Multiple Master domain model. Create two one-way trusts between San Francisco and Chicago, and between Chicago and Atlanta.

B. Master domain model. Have San Francisco and Atlanta create one-way trusts to Chicago.

C. Complete Trust model. Have all domains trust each other for a total of three trusts.

D. Complete Trust model. Have all domains trust each other for a total of six trusts.

Question #04-08

Resource: "Understanding Global Groups in the Domain Models; Master Domain Model"

Which of the following statements best represents Microsoft's groups strategy for the Master Domain model?

A. Create global groups in the resource domains to manage local resources. Create local groups in the account domains to manage users. Add the resource domains' global groups to the account domain's local groups.

B. Create local groups on the resource servers in the resource domains to manage access to resources. Group users into appropriate global groups in the account domain. Add the global groups from the account domain to the local groups in the resource domains.

C. Create local groups on the resource servers in the resource domains to manage access to resources. Create global groups in the resource domains and add to them global users from the account domain. Make the global groups from the resource domain members of the local groups on the resource servers.

D. Create local groups on the resource servers in the resource domains to manage access to resources. Add global users from the account domain to the local resource groups.

Question #04-09

Resource: "Multiple Master Domain Model"

Kite Flyers Corporation has configured a Multiple Master domain model with accounts managed by MIS in the KFCORPA and KFCORPB domains. Resource domains are located in Seattle, Houston, and Boston. Certain users—whose accounts might be in either KFCORPA or KFCORPB—have been selected to provide backup functions for all the domains. Which of the following represents the most flexible solution for this scenario?

A. Create a global backup group called KFBACKUP in KFCORPA and in KFCORPB. Add the user accounts that reside in KFCORPA to its KFBACKUP global group, and add the users that reside in KFCORPB to its KFBACKUP global group. Add both KFCORPA\KFBACKUP and KFCORPB\KFBACKUP to the local Backup Operators groups in each resource domain.

B. Create a global backup group called KFBACKUP in KFCORPA. Add the users from KFCORPA and KFCORPB to KFBACKUP. Add KFBACKUP from KFCORPA to the local Backup Operators groups in each resource domain.

C. Create a global backup group called KFBACKUP in KFCORPA and in KFCORPB. Add the user accounts that reside in KFCORPA to its KFBACKUP global group, and add the users that reside in KFCORPB to its KFBACKUP global group. Add both KFCORPA\KFBACKUP and KFCORPB\KFBACKUP to the local Backup Operators groups in each resource domain and to the local Backup Operators groups for KFCORPA and KFCORPB.

D. Create a global backup group called KFBACKUP in KFCORPA. Add the users from KFCORPA and KFCORPB to KFBACKUP. Add KFBACKUP from KFCORPA to the local Backup Operators groups in each resource domain and to the local Backup Operators groups in KFCORPA and KFCORPB.

App
J

Question #04-10

Resource: Entire Chapter, especially, "Understanding the Single Domain Model"

Kite Flyers Corporation is a relatively small company with about 1,000 employees. They are located in the same office complex. There are five departments: Accounting, Marketing, MIS, HR, and Corporate. Each has its own set of network resources that its staff accesses, and some resources that everyone in the company uses.

Primary Goals: Give all employees a single logon account that they can use to access their resources. Let each department manage its own resources.

Secondary Goal: Centralize resources by department.

Solution: Implement a single domain model and make all resource servers members of the domain.

   A. The solution satisfies none of the goals.

   B. The solution satisfies both primary goals and the secondary goal.

   C. The solution satisfies both primary goals, but not the secondary goal.

   D. The solution satisfies one primary goal and the secondary goal.

Question #04-11

Resource: Entire Chapter, especially, "Understanding the Master Domain Model"

Kite Flyers Corporation is a relatively small company with about 1,000 employees. They are located in the same office complex. There are five departments: Accounting, Marketing, MIS, HR, and Corporate. Each has its own set of network resources that its staff accesses, and some resources that everyone in the company uses.

Primary Goals: Give all employees a single logon account that they can use to access their resources. Let each department manage its own resources.

Secondary Goal: Centralize resources by department.

Solution: Implement a master domain model and have all resource domains trust the account domain.

  A. The solution satisfies none of the goals.
  B. The solution satisfies both primary goals and the secondary goal.
  C. The solution satisfies both primary goals, but not the secondary goal.
  D. The solution satisfies one primary goal and the secondary goal.

Question #04-12

Resource: Entire Chapter, especially, "Understanding the Role of the Domain for Directory Services"

Kite Flyers Corporation is a relatively small company with about 1,000 employees. They are located in the same office complex. There are five departments: Accounting, Marketing, MIS, HR, and Corporate. Each has its own set of network resources that its staff accesses, and some resources that everyone in the company uses.

Primary Goals: Give all employees a single logon account that they can use to access their resources. Let each department manage its own resources.

Secondary Goal: Centralize resources by department.

Solution: Give each department its own domain and let each manage its own users and resources.

  A. The solution satisfies none of the goals.
  B. The solution satisfies both primary goals and the secondary goal.
  C. The solution satisfies both primary goals, but not the secondary goal.
  D. The solution satisfies the secondary goal.

Question #04-13

Resource: Entire Chapter, especially, "Understanding the Multiple Master Model"; "Managing Global Groups in the Domain Models"

Kite Flyers Corporation has two global locations, London and New York. MIS manages the users in both locations in two account domains. There are five departments: Accounting, Marketing, MIS, HR, and Corporate. Each has its own set of network resources that its staff accesses, and some resources that everyone in the company uses.

Primary Goals: Give all employees a single logon account that they can use to access their resources. Let MIS be able to manage the account domains from any location. Let each department manage its own resources. Let certain delegated users act as print operators for printers in each department.

Secondary Goals: Centralize resources by department. Let all delegated users be able to manage any domain's printers. Allow as much flexibility as possible for printer management.

Solution: Implement a Multiple Master Domain model. Have all resource domains trust the account domain, and let the account domains trust each other. Create a global group called KFPRINT in each account domain and add the delegated users to it. Add KFPRINT from both account domains to the local Print Operators groups on the print servers in each domain.

A. The solution satisfies none of the goals.

B. The solution satisfies all the primary goals and all the secondary goals.

C. The solution satisfies both primary goals, but only one secondary goal.

D. The solution satisfies two primary goals and two secondary goals.

Question #04-14

Resource: Entire Chapter, especially, "Understanding the Single Domain Model"; "Managing Global Groups in the Domain Models"

Kite Flyers Corporation has two global locations, London and New York. MIS manages the users in both locations in two account domains. There are five departments: Accounting, Marketing, MIS, HR, and Corporate. Each has its own set of network resources that its staff accesses, and some resources that everyone in the company uses.

Primary Goals: Give all employees a single logon account that they can use to access their resources. Let MIS be able to manage the account domains from any location. Let each department manage its own resources. Let certain delegated users act as print operators for printers in each department.

Secondary Goals: Centralize resources by department. Let all delegated users be able to manage any domain's printers. Allow as much flexibility as possible for printer management.

Solution: Implement a Single Domain model. Have all resource servers become members of the domain. Create a global group called KFPRINT. Add KFPRINT to the local Print Operators groups on the print servers in each domain.

A. The solution satisfies none of the goals.

B. The solution satisfies all the primary goals and all the secondary goals.

C. The solution satisfies all primary goals but only one secondary goal.

D. The solution satisfies two primary goals and two secondary goals.

Question #04-15

Resource: Entire Chapter, especially, "Understanding the Multiple Master Model"; "Managing Global Groups in the Domain Models"

Kite Flyers Corporation has two global locations, London and New York. MIS manages the users in both locations in two account domains. There are five departments: Accounting, Marketing, MIS, HR, and Corporate. Each has its own set of network resources that its staff accesses, and some resources that everyone in the company uses.

Primary Goals: Give all employees a single logon account that they can use to access their resources. Let MIS be able to manage the account domains from any location. Let each department manage its own resources. Let certain delegated users act as print operators for printers in each department.

Secondary Goals: Centralize resources by department. Let all delegated users be able to manage any domain's printers. Allow as much flexibility as possible for printer management.

Solution: Implement a Multiple Master Domain model. Have all resource domains trust the account domain, and let the account domains trust each other. In each account domain, create a global group for print operators for each department's resource domain called, for example, ACCT-PRINT, MARK-PRINT, MIS-PRINT, HR-PRINT and CORP-PRINT. Add the appropriate global group to the local Print Operators groups on the print servers in their respective domains.

A. The solution satisfies none of the goals.

B. The solution satisfies all the primary goals and all the secondary goals.

C. The solution satisfies all primary goals but only one secondary goal.

D. The solution satisfies two primary goals and two secondary goals.

Chapter 5

Question #05-01

Resource: "Physical Disk Monitoring Considerations"

Disk performance counters in performance monitor are turned off by default. From the following choices, indicate the correct syntax required to activate the counters.

A. Diskperf On

B. Diskperf Off

C. Diskperf -n

D. Diskperf -y

Question #05-02

Resource: "Network Monitoring Considerations"

TCP/IP objects do not appear as choices to monitor in Performance Monitor unless the _____ service is installed.

A. DHCP

B. WINS

C. SNMP

D. DNS

Question #05-03

Resource: "Network Monitoring Considerations"

What two applications can be used to store and view data collected with Performance Monitor?

A. Microsoft Notepad

B. Microsoft SQL

C. Microsoft Excel

D. Microsoft Calculator

Question #05-04

Resource: "Planning Effective WAN Performance"

Donna, a system administrator in office A, has been getting calls from users in office B complaining that logon validation is extremely slow every morning. The PDC and three BDCs are located in office A, which is connected to office B with a 56K link. What is the best way to correct the problem?

A. Do nothing except tell the users to get to work 15 minutes earlier and log on before the crowd.

B. Relocate two BDCs from office A to office B.

C. Upgrade the 56K line to 256K line.

D. Install and configure two more BDCs in office A.

Question #05-05

Resource: "Pass–Through Authentication"

When does pass-through authentication occur?

A. When logging on from a member server to a domain.

B. When logging on to a workstation.

C. When logging on from a workstation to a domain.

D. When logging on from a workstation to a trusted domain.

Question #05-06

Resource: "Database Synchronization"

What Windows NT service provides pass-through authentication?

A. Netlogon

B. Browser

C. Alerter

D. Network DDE

Question #05-07

Resource: "Database Synchronization"

Users for the Discover America company are located in office A and office B connected together by a slow WAN link. The PDC is located in office A and the BDC is located in office B. Because of the high level of security required, users are required to change their password every seven days. There is also a very large amount of network traffic due to resource access between the two offices. The administrator is getting complaints of intermittent slow resource access. Select the best solution from the following choices.

A. Install a BDC in office A.

B. Install a BDC in office A and a second BDC in office B.

C. Install a second BDC in office B.

D. Locate the BDC in office A.

Question #05-08

Resource: "Database Synchronization"

What would happen if the Netlogon ReplicationGovernor parameter were set to a value of 0?

A. PDC to BCD synchronization would never occur.

B. PDC to BCD synchronization would occur every 100 seconds.

C. Is the default ReplicationGovernor parameter value.

D. PDC to BCD synchronization would occur every 100 minutes.

Question #05-09

Resource: "Planning Protocol Selection of a Network Enterprise"

Pam is a manager in a training development corporation of 200 users using Windows NT Workstations connected over a LAN using the NetBEUI protocol. The corporation has just purchased a new office building. Pam decides to relocate 30 of the 200 users and computers to the new building and connects the two buildings together through a router. Now employees in the new building cannot see resources in the original facility, and the users in the original facility cannot connect to resources in the new building. Select the two best solutions to the problem.

A. Install NWLink on all workstations.

B. Install AppleTalk on all workstations.

C. Configure NetBEUI to use the router.

D. Install TCP/IP on all workstations.

Question #05-10

Resource: "DHCP"

DHCP is a Windows NT service used to:

A. Dynamically map NetBIOS names and IP addresses.

B. Dynamically allocate IP address to DHCP clients.

C. Dynamically configure PDC to BDC synchronization.

D. Dynamically provide automatic logon validation.

Question #05-11

Resource: "DLC"

The DLC protocol is used with Windows NT to provide:

A. Access to Macintosh computers.

B. Access to IBM mainframes for terminal emulation.

C. Access to Novell resources.

D. Access to HP JetDirect Printers on the network.

Question #05-12

Resource: "AppleTalk"

The AppleTalk protocol is used in with Windows NT to provide:

A. Access to Macintosh computers.

B. Access to IBM mainframes for terminal emulation.

C. Access to Novell resources.

D. Access to HP JetDirect Printers on the network.

Question #05-13

Resource: "Planning the Size of Directory Services Database"

What type of account, by default, has inherent built-in system rights associations?

A. Computer account

B. User account

C. Local group account

D. Global group account

Question #05-14

Resource: "Global Group Accounts"

Global groups can contain which of the following?

A. User accounts from a trusted domain.

B. Local group accounts from the local domain.

C. User accounts from the local domain.

Question #05-15

Resource: "Location of the Enterprise Administrator"

By pausing the Netlogon service on the PDC, the PDC will continue to:

A. Perform logon validations.

B. Perform directory services database synchronization with the BDCs.

C. Perform pass-through authentication.

D. Perform logon validation but not pass-through authentication.

Chapter 6

Question #06-01

Resource: "Selecting the Appropriate Server Role"

How many BDCs are recommended for 5,000 users?

A. 0

B. 2

C. 3

D. 5

Question #06-02

Resource: "Maximizing the Resources by Server Role"

I want to improve network printing for my users. What would be the best course of action?

A. Make the local SQL server a print server, too.

B. Add print services and more RAM to the existing file server.

C. Add a print server to my PDC.

D. Relocate a remote print server near the users.

Question #06-03

Resource: "Maximizing the Resources by Server Role"

The Security Accounts Manager (SAM) database is approximately 15M. What is the recommended memory size?

A. 24M

B. 32M

C. 48M

D. 64M

Question #06-04

Resource: "Backup Domain Controller"

The PDC must go offline to add more memory. What do you do?

A. Install a new PDC to take over the role.

B. Add the new memory and bring the PDC back online.

C. Promote a server to PDC.

D. Promote the BDC to PDC.

Question #06-05

Resource: "Maximizing the Resources by Server Role"

I have a large SQL server database on an application server. All employees have access to the data. What two resources can best improve performance?

A. More memory and a newer network interface card.

B. More memory and faster disk drive.

C. More memory and a second processor.

D. More network interface cards and more disk drives.

Chapter 7

Question #07-01

Resource: "HKEY_LOCAL_MACHINE"

Which of the following keys in HKEY_LOCAL_MACHINE have corresponding directory files in the Windows NT system directory?

A. System

B. Software

C. Hardware

D. Security

Question #07-02

Resource: "Examining the Windows NT Boot Process"

Which of the following boot files is essential to the boot phase of the boot process?

A. NTLDR

B. NTDETECT.COM

C. NTOSKRNL.EXE

D. BOOT.INI

Question #07-03

Resource: "Sidebar, Boot Process for RISC-based Computers"

While looking at the files on my RISC-based computer, I notice that NTLDR, NTDETECT.COM, and BOOT.INI are missing. What impact will this have on the boot process on this computer?

A. The boot process relies on these files to govern the boot and load phases. Missing or corrupt files will result in error messages and failed boots.

B. It will have no impact on the boot process because RISC-based computers do not rely on these files.

C. The BOOT.INI is not an essential file. Windows NT will look for the default Windows NT system directory.

D. NTLDR is always needed to direct the boot process. NTDETECT.COM and BOOT.INI are not necessary on RISC-based computers.

Question #07-04

Resource: "BOOT.INI"

The BOOT.INI file on my computer looks like this:

[Boot Loader]

   timeout=15

   default=multi(0)disk(2)rdisk(1)partition(3)\winnt40

[Operating Systems]

   multi(0)disk(2)rdisk(1)partition(3)\winnt40=Windows NT 4.0 Workstation

   multi(0)disk(2)rdisk(1)partition(3)\winnt40=Windows NT 4.0 Workstation [VGA Mode] /basevideo c:\=MS-DOS

What can I infer from this file?

A. The timeout value before Windows NT loads is 15 seconds. Windows NT system files can be found on the third partition of the second physical disk attached to the first controller card.

B. The timeout value before Windows NT loads is 15 seconds, and DOS is the default operating system.

C. The timeout value before Windows NT loads is 15 seconds. Windows NT system files can be found on the third partition of the first physical disk attached to the first controller card.

D. The controller card is a SCSI adapter.

Question #07-05

Resource: "Troubleshooting the Boot Process"

Jonas accidentally deleted the BOOT.INI file from his C: drive. Windows NT has been installed in the WINNT subdirectory on C:. What effect will the missing BOOT.INI have?

A. There will be no noticeable effect on the boot process. Windows NT will boot as always.

B. The BOOT.INI file provides the ARC path information that Windows NT needs to find the Windows NT system files. If it is missing, Windows NT will display a message that it cannot find the NTOSKRNL file and fail to boot.

C. If the BOOT.INI file is missing, Windows NT will not display the Boot menu during bootup. Windows NT will look for the Windows NT system files on the boot partition in the default directory name (WINNT).

D. The BOOT.INI file is not needed on RISC–based systems.

Question #07-06

Resource: "Troubleshooting the Boot Process"

I have booted Windows NT and received the message:

Windows NT could not start because the following file is missing or corrupt: \winnt root\system32\ntoskrnl.exe

How can I recover this file?

A. Boot with the Emergency Repair Disk and choose Verify Windows NT System Files.

B. Boot with the Windows NT Startup disk, choose Repair, and then Verify Windows NT System Files from the Emergency Repair Disk.

C. Find a working Windows NT computer and use the EXPAND command to expand the compressed version of this file from the installation source directory. Then copy the file to the system directory on the problem computer.

D. Boot with a Windows NT Boot Disk and copy the file from this disk.

Question #07-07

Resource: "HKEY_LOCAL_MACHINE"

Which of the following statements best describes HKEY_LOCAL_MACHINE?

A. HKEY_LOCAL_MACHINE contains all the system configuration data needed to boot and run the Windows NT operating system successfully including services, device drivers, and hardware profiles.

B. HKEY_LOCAL_MACHINE displays only the current system configuration settings, including those used to boot Windows NT for the current session.

C. HKEY_LOCAL_MACHINE contains all the configuration settings particular to the currently logged on user.

D. HKEY_LOCAL_MACHINE contains default file association and DDE setting data for the system.

Question #07-08

Resource: "Hardware"

Which HKEY_LOCAL_MACHINE\Hardware subkey displays data collected by NTDETECT.COM, NTOSKRNL.EXE, or a hardware recognizer during the bootup process?

A. DeviceMap

B. Description

C. ResourceMap

D. OwnerMap

Question #07-09

Resource: "System Policy Editor"

You have decided to modify the logon process for all of your Windows NT users so that a legal notice displays before they log on, warning against unauthorized access. What would be the best way to accomplish this?

A. Use the Windows NT Registry Editor to modify the Legal Notice Caption and Legal Notice Text parameters for WINLOGON on each Windows NT computer.

B. Use the System applet in the Control Panel to set the values for Legal Notices on each of the Windows NT computers.

C. Use the System Policy Editor to create a default policy for every Windows NT computer that contains the appropriate legal notice settings and store it in the NETLOGON share of every domain controller.

D. Use the Legal Notice utility from the Resource Kit to set these values remotely for each Windows NT computer.

Question #07-10

Resource: "Managing Remote Access to the Registry"

As the manager of the MIS department, you would like to delegate responsibility for remote management of the Windows NT registries on all the domain controllers to three key staff members. These three are members of the Domain Admins global group for the domain, as are all your staff members. How would you restrict remote access to the appropriate three persons?

A. Give the Remote Command Service utilities only to those three persons.

B. Modify the ACL for the HKEY_LOCAL_MACHINE\System\CurrentControlSet\Control\SecurePipeServers\Winreg subkey on each domain controller so that only those three persons have access.

C. Modify the RemoteAccess parameter values for HKEY_LOCAL_MACHINE\System\CurrentControlSet\Control\RemoteControl subkey on each domain controller so that only those three persons are listed.

D. Do nothing. Only these three can remotely manage the Registry by default.

Question #07-11

Resource: "Remotely Managing Through the Command Line"

Carl's Windows NT computer in Rolling Meadows is acting strangely while connected to the network. You would like to view the network settings in Carl's computer. You plan to use a command-line utility to view the network settings on Carl's computer and record them in a text file. Which utilities will you use to accomplish this?

A. WINMSDP.EXE and the RCMD files

B. WINMSDP.EXE and the Registry Editor

C. RCMD and the Registry Editor

D. Windows Diagnostics Utility and the Registry Editor

Question #07-12

Resource: "HKEY_LOCAL_MACHINE\System\Select"

How can you determine which ControlSet entry refers to the Last Known Good control set?

A. The ControlSet entry with the highest number increment is always the Last Known Good control set.

B. Look at the control set number referenced by the LastKnownGood parameter entry for the HKEY_LOCAL_MACHINE\SYSTEM\Select subkey.

C. Restart the computer and load the Last Known Good control set, noting which control set number Windows NT displays on the screen.

D. Use Windows Diagnostics to find which control set maps to Last Known Good.

Question #07-13

Resource: "What Is the Last Known Good Control Set?"; Table 7.7, "Service Subkey Parameters"

Under what circumstances will the Last Known Good control set load automatically?

A. If the system itself detects a critical error during the boot process, it will automatically load Last Known Good.

B. If the system detects an ErrorControl value of 0 or 1, it will automatically load Last Known Good.

C. If the system detects a failed control set, it will automatically load Last Known Good on the next boot.

D. Last Known Good is always selected from the screen during the boot process.

Question #07-14

Resource:

"HKEY_LOCAL_MACHINE\System\CurrentControlSet"

Which of the following HKEY_LOCAL_MACHINE\System\CurrentControlSet subkey would you use to determine which services and drivers contain dependencies on other services and service groups?

A. Control

B. Enum

C. Dependencies

D. Services

Question #07-15

Resource:

"HKEY_LOCAL_MACHINE\System\CurrentControlSet\Services"

The following parameter values display in the Registry Editor when you select the HKEY_LOCAL_MACHINE\System\CurrentControlSet\Services\Replicator subkey.

DependOnGroup: REG_MULTI_SZ:

DependOnService: REG_MULTI_SZ: LanmanWorkstation LanmanServer

DisplayName: REG_SZ: Directory Replicator

ErrorControl: REG_DWORD: 0x1

ImagePath: REG_EXPAND_SZ: %SystemRoot%\System32\lmrepl.exe

ObjectName: REG_SZ: LocalSystem

Start: REG_DWORD: 0x3

Type: REG_DWORD: 0x10

Which of the following statements can be inferred from these settings? Choose all that apply.

A. The Directory Replicator service has no group dependencies.

B. The Directory Replicator service depends on the LanmanWorkstation and LanmanServer services being loaded successfully.

C. If the Directory Replicator service does not load, the boot process will still continue.

D. If the Directory Replicator service does not load, the Last Known Good control set is loaded automatically.

Question #07-16

Resource: "Emergency Repair Disk"

The master boot record of Sal's Windows NT computer became corrupted and he can no longer boot to Windows NT. How can you restore the master boot record on Sal's computer?

A. Create a Windows NT boot disk with the NTLDR file on it. Boot from this disk and copy the NTLDR file from it to the system partition of Sal's computer.

B. Create an Emergency Repair Disk. Boot from this disk and choose Inspect Boot Sector from the menu to repair the master boot record.

C. Create an Emergency Repair Disk. Boot from a Windows NT startup disk and choose Repair, using the Emergency Repair Disk when prompted. Choose Inspect Boot Sector to repair the MBR.

D. Create a Windows NT boot disk with the NTLDR file and the fixdisk.exe program on it. Boot from this disk and run fixdisk /c: where c: is the system partition.

App
J

Question #07-17

Resource: "Service Dependencies"

Which two utilities would you use to determine whether a service failed to start and why?

A. Server Manager to view service startup values, and Windows Diagnostics to view service dependencies.

B. Event Viewer to view stopped services, and Windows Diagnostics to view service dependencies.

C. Control Panel\System to view service startup values, and Windows Diagnostics to view service dependencies.

D. Event Viewer to view stopped services, and Server Manager to view service startup values.

Chapter 8

Question #08-01

Resource: Entire Chapter

Which of the following protocols is not considered routable?

A. TCP/IP

B. NetBEUI

C. NWLink

D. AppleTalk

Question #08-02

Resource: Entire Chapter

Protocols are installed by accessing the network icon in the Control Panel and:

A. Selecting the Protocol tab and selecting the Add button.

B. Selecting the Protocol tab and selecting the protocol.

C. Selecting the Protocol tab and choosing all protocols.

D. Selecting the Protocol tab, nothing else has to be selected.

Question #08-03

Resource: Entire Chapter

The Registry location for the NetBEUI protocol parameters is
HKEY_LOCAL_MACHINE\System\CurrentControlSet\Services\…:

A. NetBEUI\Parameters

B. NetBIOS\Parameters

C. NBF\Parameters

D. NetBEUI\NBF\Parameters

Question #08-04

Resource: Entire Chapter

The NWLink protocol by itself can be used to communicate with:

A. Novell Servers

B. Windows NT Workstations

C. Macintosh Workstations

D. Novell Clients for client/server applications

Question #08-05

Resource: Entire Chapter

Which of the following parameters can be configured manually with
the NWLink protocol?

A. IP address

B. Frame type

C. Subnet mask

D. DHCP scope

Question #08-06

Resource: Entire Chapter

If Windows NT is configured for Auto frame type detection and multiple IPX frame types are detected on the network, Windows NT will:

A. Automatically default to 802.3

B. Automatically default to 802.2

C. Automatically configure itself to all IPX frame types detected

D. Automatically default to the first IPX frame type detected

Question #08-07

Resource: Entire Chapter

The CSNW redirector will allow a Windows NT Workstation to communicate with:

A. Novell Servers

B. Windows NT Workstations

C. Macintosh Workstations

D. Novell Clients for client/server applications

Question #08-08

Resource: Entire Chapter

When configuring GSNW on Windows NT Server, a group called _____ must be set up on the Novell Server.

A. NTUserGateway

B. NovellGateway

C. NetBIOSGateway

D. NTGateway

Question #08-09

Resource: Entire Chapter

RIP for NWLink will allow a Windows NT computer to act as a:

A. IP Router

B. AppleTalk Router

C. IPX Router

D. DLC Router

Question #08-10

Resource: Entire Chapter

An IP address of 191.191.191.191 will have a default subnet mask of:

A. 255.255.255.0

B. 255.255.0.0

C. 255.0.0.0

D. 0.0.0.0

Question #08-11

Resource: Entire Chapter

An IP address consists of what two parts in the following order from left to right?

A. A network address and a workstation address

B. A workstation address and a network address

C. A subnet mask address and a default gateway address

D. A default gateway address and a subnet mask address

App
J

Question #08-12

Resource: Entire Chapter

The Advanced button on the Microsoft TCP/IP Properties sheet allows for the addition of:

A. 5 additional WINS server IP addresses

B. 10 additional default gateways

C. 5 additional DHCP server IP addresses

D. 5 additional default gateways

Question #08-13

Resource: Entire Chapter

A DHCP server eliminates the need to manually configure:

A. A DHCP scope

B. A WINS database

C. An IP address and subnet mask for DHCP clients

D. An IP address and subnet mask for non-DHCP clients

Question #08-14

Resource: Entire Chapter

A DHCP reservation is assigned to a:

A. Computer

B. Network Adapter Card

C. Domain

D. Workgroup

Question #08-15

Resource: Entire Chapter

A WINS database is used to:

A. Dynamically map IP addresses to network adapter card names

B. Dynamically map IP addresses to subnet masks

C. Dynamically map IP addresses to computer names

D. Dynamically map IP addresses to a user name

Question #08-16

Resource: Entire Chapter

The DLC protocol is used on Windows NT 4.0 computers to:

A. Communicate with HP JetDirect printing devices

B. Communicate with AppleTalk Postscript printing devices

C. Communicate with Novell file servers and client computers

D. Communicate with IBM mainframes and front end processors

Question #08-17

Resource: Entire Chapter

If the AppleTalk protocol is installed on a Windows NT Workstation, other Windows NT users on the network can use the workstation:

A. To create Macintosh Accessible Volumes on Macintosh computers

B. To access Macintosh Accessible Volumes on Macintosh computers

C. To access Macintosh Accessible Volumes on the workstation and share files with Macintosh users

D. As a print server

Question #08-18

Resource: Entire Chapter

By default, all BDCs on the same subnet in a domain will become:

A. A domain master browser

B. A potential browser

C. A backup browser

D. A non–browser

Question #08-19

Resource: Entire Chapter

Within a single workgroup, there will be a master browser elected for:

A. Each protocol

B. Every 32 computers

C. Every 12 users

D. Only one protocol

Question #08-20

Resource: Entire Chapter

If a group of workstations on a network are never to contain any shared resources, how can you optimize these workstations so they will never send host announcements to the master browser?

A. Disable the workstation service

B. Disable the server service

C. Disable the browser service

D. Disable the alerter service

Question #08-21

Resource: Entire Chapter

When the directory replicator service is configured, a user account must be created. Why is a user account required?

A. The administrator must log on to the computer with the user account and manually start and stop the replicator service.

B. The replicator service will log on to the computer as the user and use the account to perform directory replication.

C. The replicator service will not log on to the computer as the user, but will use the account in case the replicator service fails.

D. The administrator uses this account to perform administrative duties once the replicator service is configured.

Chapter 9

Question #09-01

Resource: "Windows NT Controller Software RAID"

What Windows NT software RAID configurations are supported?

A. 1

B. 2

C. 5

D. 10

Question #09-02

Resource: "Hardware Controller RAID"

What hardware RAID configurations can be implemented?

A. 0

B. 1

C. 5

D. 10

Question #09-03

Resource: "Recovering from Hard Disk Failure"

A Windows NT Server has been configured with striping across 6 disk drives and one of the drives have failed to spin up. How can you recover your data?

App

J

A. Add the new drive and select Regenerate.

B. Add the new drive and do nothing. Windows NT does it automatically.

C. Create a new stripe set and restore data from the backup.

D. Delete the stripe set and add it back.

Question #09-04

Resource: "Disk Striping"

A Windows NT file and print server have been configured with striping with parity across 4 disk drives. Users have complained of poor response time. Checking the event view, you discover there are disk errors. What steps should you take?

A. Reformat the logical drive.

B. Replace the failed drive.

C. Disk administrator select regenerate and restart the server.

D. Restore data from backup.

Question #09-05

Resource: "Disk Striping"

What is the minimum number of drives needed for striping with no parity?

A. 32

B. 3

C. 2

D. 1

Question #09-06

Resource: "What Is Fault Tolerance?"

Your assistant called and wants to know why he cannot set up his mirrored disk on his workstation. Your answer is:

    A. He does not have the correct password.

    B. Only RAID5 is available for workstations.

    C. Striping with no parity is not available for workstations.

    D. RAID1 is not available to workstations.

Question #09-07

Resource: "Disk Striping"; "Disk Controllers"

You have SCSI and IDE controllers, and 3 disks for each controller to install on the BDC you are building. What configurations can you use?

    A. Logical drive.

    B. Striping with no parity.

    C. Striping with parity.

    D. Mirroring.

Question #09-08

Resource: "Disk Controllers"

You have a file and print server configured for striping with no parity using one ISA controller and four disk drives. You want to increase the read and write performance. What is the best option to use?

    A. Add a second ISA controller to your configuration.

    B. Add a fifth drive to your configuration.

    C. Format the stripe set as an NTFS partition.

    D. Replace the one ISA controller with two BUS master ISA controllers.

Question #09-09

Resource: "Recovering from Hard Disk Failure"

Your Windows NT file server is configured with mirroring on one of the data drive partitions. Users have complained about the disk full errors and poor response time. You have 500M available on each drive. What steps do you take to remedy this situation?

App

J

A. Backup data, extend the mirrored partition, and restore data.

B. Backup data, break the mirror, create a larger mirror set, and restore data.

C. Implement disk duplexing.

D. Implement RAID5 on the free space, assign permissions to the users.

Question #09-10

Resource: "Disk Controllers"

Which disk controller has the highest throughput?

A. IDE standard

B. SCSI-2 Bus mastering

C. Fast SCSI-2

D. PCI with SCSI

Chapter 10

Question #10-01

Resource: "Windows NT 4.0 Print Process"

Which of the following sets of Windows NT network clients do not require print drivers to be manually installed on the local computer?

A. All Microsoft Network clients

B. Windows NT and Windows 95

C. Windows NT, Windows 95, Windows for Workgroups 3.11

D. Windows NT, Windows 95, LAN Manager v2.x for DOS

Question #10-02

Resource: "Windows NT 4.0 Print Process"

Which of the following steps applies to the Windows NT 4.0 print process on Windows NT computers? Select all that apply.

A. The GDI component of the client computer generates an enhanced metafile print job.

B. The bulk of the print process completes in the spooler on the client computer before forwarding the print job to the print server.

C. The print monitor controls access to the print devices and device ports and monitors status of the print job.

D. The local printer spooler makes a remote connection to the print server spooler and copies the print job there.

Question #10-03

Resource: "Windows NT 4.0 Print Process"

Nicole calls to say that her print jobs seem to have stopped running. You check the printer that she sent the jobs to and see that the jobs are stuck in queue. What steps should you take to clear the stuck jobs? Select all that apply.

A. Select the stuck jobs and choose Document, Cancel.

B. Select Printer, Purge Printer.

C. Use the Control Panel applet Services to stop and restart the Spooler service.

D. Select each stuck job and change its priority.

Question #10-04

Resource: "Windows NT 4.0 Print Process"

Several users have called you within the past half-hour to complain that their print jobs are not printing. In fact, they get system messages that tell them that the spooler is not responding. You have verified that the spooler directory partition does not have adequate free space to hold all the print jobs sent to it. What steps should you take to resolve this situation?

Appendix J   Sample Tests

A. Use the Control Panel applet Services to more frequently stop and restart the Spooler service to keep the print jobs from becoming fragmented.

B. Change the location of the spool directory to a partition with enough disk space by modifying the HKEY_LOCAL_MACHINE\System\CurrentControlSet\Control\Print\Printers DefaultSpoolDirectory parameter.

C. Change the location of the spool directory to a partition with enough disk space by modifying the HKEY_Current_User\Control\Print\Printers\Spool SpoolDirectory parameter.

D. If the partition is formatted with NTFS, compress the spool directory.

Question #10-05

Resource: "Windows NT 4.0 Print Process"

If the final print output is corrupted, what print process component should you check?

A. Spooler service on the client computer.

B. Spooler service on the print server.

C. Print processor on the print server.

D. Print monitor on the client computer.

Question #10-06

Resource: "Windows NT 4.0 Print Process"

Which print monitor is loaded with TCP/IP and tracks print jobs targeted for TCP/IP print hosts?

A. IPMON.DLL

B. LPDMON.DLL

C. LPRMON.DLL

D. LOCALMON.DLL

Question #10-07

Resource: "Windows NT 4.0 Print Process"

What is the purpose of the print monitor SFMMON.DLL?

A. SFMMON.DLL monitors Macintosh print jobs routed using AppleTalk protocol to network print devices.

B. SFMMON.DLL is the System File Manager print monitor which tracks print jobs sent directly to or printed directly from a file.

C. SFMMON.DLL is the software print job compression DLL which compresses the print job before it is sent from the local print spooler to the print server.

D. SFMMON.DLL is not a valid print monitor.

Question #10-08

Resource: "Additional LPD Device Information"

A print job can be directed directly to a UNIX host print device, and its status checked using which two command-line utilities?

A. LPD and LPR

B. LPD and LPQ

C. LPR and IPCONFIG

D. LPR and LPQ

Question #10-09

Resource: "Windows NT 4.0 Print Process"

Michelle has been selected to assist you as a print administrator in the Dry Gulch office, since you, yourself, are unable to travel there frequently, though you'd really like to. What is the minimum level of access you need to give Michelle so that she can perform basic print management tasks such as creating and sharing printers and managing print jobs?

App
J

A. Make Michelle a member of the Print Operators local group on her print server.

B. Make Michelle a member of the Server Operator local group on her print server.

C. Make Michelle a member of the Administrators local group on her print server.

D. Give Michelle Full Control permission for each printer on her print server.

Question #10-10

Resource: "Windows NT 4.0 Print Process"

You have created four printers. Each of them will be used by a specific group of users. Name all the steps which are required to successfully make the printer available to the appropriate users.

A. Share each printer.

B. Set the share permissions for each printer so that only the appropriate group has access.

C. Set the printer permissions for each printer so that only the appropriate group has access.

D. Create a printer pool so that each group can access all the print devices.

Question #10-11

Resource: "Windows NT 4.0 Print Process"

Elaine was the print administrator for the LotsOf Print Corporation, but has left the country to pursue a career as an opera singer. You need to assign a new print administrator. What will you need to do concerning ownership of the LotsOf Print Corporation printers that Elaine created and managed?

A. Do nothing. Printers are not owned by a user; they are owned by the system.

B. Make the new print administrator a Print Operator. The new print administrator can then take ownership of the printers in LotsOf Print Corporation.

C. Give ownership of the printers to the new print administrator.

D. Give the new administrator Full Control permission over the printers. Full Control automatically assigns ownership to that user.

Question #10-12

Resource: "Windows NT 4.0 Print Process"

The print device associated with a particular printer has failed. Several print jobs are waiting in queue in that printer. How can you service these print jobs?

A. Connect to another remote printer. Open the printer manager window for the printer and drag the waiting print jobs to the remote printer manager window.

B. Use the Ports tab properties for the printer to add a port for another remote printer. Deselect the current print port associated with the printer and select the remote port. Resume the printer.

C. Do nothing. You must replace the failed print device before printing can resume.

D. Use the Control Panel applet Services to stop the spooler service, configure it to connect to another remote printer, and restart it.

Question #10-13

Resource: "Windows NT 4.0 Print Process"

There are three downward-compatible print devices connected to the print server in MIS. MIS Managers and Project Leaders should always be able to print to the first available printer. Help Desk staff and Developers should be able to print only to their specified print device. What will best accomplish this task?

App
J

A. Create a printer for each device and assign the appropriate groups access only to their printer. Give the Manager's printer a priority of 1, Help Desk's printer a priority of 50, and Developer's printer a priority of 99.

B. Create a printer for each device and assign the appropriate groups access only to their printer. Give the Manager's printer a priority of 99, Help Desk's printer a priority of 50, and Developer's printer a priority of 1.

C. Create a printer for each device and assign the appropriate groups access only to their printer. Make the Manager's printer a printer pool by associating it with each print device.

D. Create a printer for each device and assign the appropriate groups access only to their printer. Make each printer a printer pool by associating it with each print device.

Question #10-14

Resource: "Windows NT 4.0 Print Process"

There is one high-speed network print device connected to the print server in MIS. MIS Managers and Project Leaders should always be able to print to this printer regardless of who has submitted print jobs. Help Desk staff should be able to print ahead of Developers. What will best accomplish this task?

A. Create three printers, each associated with the device, and assign the appropriate groups access only to their printer. Give the Manager's printer a priority of 1, Help Desk's printer a priority of 50, and Developer's printer a priority of 99.

B. Create three printers, each associated with the device, and assign the appropriate groups access only to their printer. Give the Manager's printer a priority of 99, Help Desk's printer a priority of 50, and Developer's printer a priority of 1.

C. Create three printers, each associated with the device, and assign the appropriate groups access only to their printer. Make the

Manager's printer a printer pool by associating it with each print device.

D. Create three printers associated with the device and assign the appropriate groups access only to their printer. Make each printer a printer pool by associating it with each print device.

Question #10-15

Resource: "Windows NT 4.0 Print Process"

The printer for a network print device has been configured to print documents at all times. Pam plans to send a large complex graphics document that she would like to have tomorrow morning. This job will take at least one hour to complete. What can you do to minimize the effect that printing this document will have on other documents in the queue?

A. Select Pam's document and pause it. Resume printing after hours when print jobs are at a minimum.

B. Modify the printer schedule so that it only prints documents after hours.

C. Modify the document schedule for Pam's document so that it only prints between 1:00 A.M. and 3:00 A.M.

D. Do nothing. The printer automatically holds long jobs until short jobs finish spooling and printing.

Question #10-16

Resource: "Troubleshooting Printing"

Which of the following steps is appropriate to take when troubleshooting a failed print job?

A. Verify that the appropriate print port has been defined and configured by printing a test page.

B. Delete and re-create the printer.

C. Determine whether the print device is online and connected.

D. Resubmit the print job to a file and then copy the file to a printer port to see if it is successful.

Question #10-17

Resource: "Troubleshooting Printing"

You are using a RISC-based computer as your print server. All your clients are either MS-DOS, Windows for Workgroups, Windows 95, or Windows NT running on Intel-based computers. What must you do to ensure that all your clients can print to the print devices managed by the RISC-based print server?

A. Install both RISC-based and Intel print drivers on the RISC-based print server. Install the appropriate print drivers only on the MS-DOS and Windows for Workgroups computers.

B. Install both RISC-based and Intel print drivers on the RISC-based print server. The client computers will receive the appropriate platform driver from the print server when they make a print request.

C. Install RISC-based print drivers on the RISC-based print server and Intel print drivers on the client computers. Windows NT will do the platform translation.

D. Install the Intel print drivers on the RISC-based print server and RISC-based print drivers on the client computers.

Question #10-18

Resource: "Introducing and Examining the Print Process"; "Troubleshooting Printing"

There are 300 Windows NT and Windows 95 client computers that print to five printers on a print server. You have received upgraded print drivers for two of the print devices connected to this print server. What must you do to ensure that all clients can continue to access all the print devices?

A. Install the upgraded print drivers on all the client computers that need to use those print devices.

B. Install the upgraded print drivers on all the client computers.

C. Install the upgraded print drivers only on the Windows NT client computers.

D. Do nothing. The print server can download the new drivers to the clients the next time they make a print request.

Question #10-19

Resource: "DLC Printing"

From the following choices, list the steps required to install a network interface printer using the DLC protocol.

A. Install the DLC protocol on the print server and shut down and restart.

B. Start the Print Wizard, select Add Printer, then select Add Port.

C. Select the Hewlett-Packard Network Port and click the New Port button.

D. Select a MAC address from the available addresses and supply a printer name in the Add Hewlett-Packard Network Peripheral Port dialog box.

Question #10-20

Resource: "TCP/IP Printing"

From the following choices, indicate the step that is NOT required when installing and configuring a printing device using the TCP/IP protocol.

A. Enter the IP address of the remote controller servicing the print device in the Add LPR Compatible Printer dialog box.

B. Enter the name of the remote controller servicing the print device in the Add LPR Compatible Printer dialog box.

C. Enter the IP address of the print device in the Add LPR Compatible Printer dialog box.

D. Enter the IP address of the print server in the Add LPR Compatible Printer dialog box.

Chapter 11

Question #11-01

Resource: Entire Chapter

What clients and services disks can you create with network administrator tool?

A. Microsoft Windows 95

B. Microsoft Windows NT Workstation

C. Microsoft Windows for Workgroups

D. Lan Manager 2.2c clients

Question #11-02

Resource: Entire Chapter

TCP/IP and DHCP are supported for what clients?

A. Lan Manager 2.2c for MS-DOS

B. Lan Manager 2.2c for OS2

C. Microsoft network client for MS-DOS

D. Microsoft Windows 95

Question #11-03

Resource: Entire Chapter

What clients support Remoteboot?

A. Lan Manager 2.2c for MS-DOS

B. Lan Manager 2.2c for OS2

C. Microsoft network client for MS-DOS

D. Microsoft Windows 95

Question #11-04

Resource: Entire Chapter

Windows 95 and TCP/IP support which of the following services?

A. DHCP

B. WINS

C. DNS

D. Protected mode drivers

Question #11-05

Resource: Entire Chapter

You just created a startup disk with the ne2000 interface card selected and NetBEUI. You installed the disk and cannot connect to the server. What may be the problem?

A. Old NIC driver.

B. DHCP server is offline.

C. Server only uses NetBEUI.

D. Server only uses TCP/IP.

Question #11-06

Resource: Entire Chapter

Your assistant called and wants to know why he cannot use his Server tool User Manager for Domains from his Windows 95 client. Your answer is:

A. He does not have the correct protocol.

B. He needs Windows NT Workstation.

App

J

C. He is not an administrator.

D. The server is offline.

Question #11-07

Resource: Entire Chapter

Your assistant called and wants to know why he cannot use his server tools from his Windows 95 client with a 386DX/66. Your answer is:

A. He does not have the correct protocol.

B. Insufficient hardware.

C. He is not a Backup operator.

D. The server is offline.

Question #11-08

Resource: Entire Chapter

To create a Macintosh Accessible Volume on the server, you must have which of the following?

A. Pentium 166Mhz processor

B. FAT partition

C. NTFS partition

D. Windows NT Workstation

Chapter 12

Question #12-01

Resource: "Default User Accounts"

Which of the following statements is true about the default user accounts created in Windows NT Server 4.0?

A. The Administrator account is enabled and can be renamed; the Guest account is enabled and cannot be renamed.

B. The Administrator account is enabled and cannot be renamed; the Guest account is disabled and cannot be renamed.

C. The Administrator account is enabled and can be renamed; the Guest account is disabled and can be renamed.

D. The Administrator account is disabled and cannot be renamed; the Guest account is enabled and can be renamed.

Question #12-02

Resource: "Default Group Accounts"

Everyone should be able to read the files in a certain directory. However, the user who created the file should be able to modify it. What do you need to do?

A. Do nothing. By default, only the creator of a file has access to it. Windows NT restricts resource access by default.

B. Give the group Everyone read access and the Creator Owner group change access. By default, Windows NT allows everyone complete access to resources.

C. Give the group Everyone read access and the Creator Owner group change access. By default, Windows NT restricts resource access.

D. Give the group Everyone read access and the Users group change access. Windows NT will automatically determine who the owner of the file is and restrict the other users.

Question #12-03

Resource: "Group Management in Domains"

On a Windows NT Server in DomainA, you have stored a sales database and a marketing database, and have also shared a color printer. Five of the users in the domain are salespersons, five are marketers, and the rest are programmers. The users should be able to access their respective databases, but only the team leaders for sales, marketing, and programmers should be able to access the color printer. Which group strategy is the best?

A. Create local groups for sales, marketing, and team leaders and assign the appropriate user accounts to the appropriate groups. Then, assign permissions for each resource to the appropriate group.

B. Create global groups for sales, marketing, and team leaders and assign the appropriate user accounts to the appropriate groups. Then, assign permissions for each resource to the appropriate global group.

C. Create global groups for sales, marketing, and team leaders and assign the appropriate user accounts to the appropriate groups. Following Microsoft's suggested strategy, create local groups for each and assign the global group to the local group. Then assign permissions for each resource to the appropriate local group.

D. Simply assign the appropriate users access to the resources that they need access to.

Question #12-04

Resource: "Creating a New Local or Global Group"

What are the differences between a local group and a global group? Choose all that apply.

A. Local groups can be created on workstations, servers, and domain controllers, while global groups can only be created and maintained on a domain controller.

B. Local groups can contain local users, domain users, and global groups, while global groups can contain only users from their domain.

C. Local groups can contain local users, domain users, global groups, and other local groups, while global groups can contain only users from their domain.

D. Local groups can be used for managing resources only on the local computer, while global groups can be used to manage resources on any computer that participates in the domain.

Question #12-05

Resource: "Naming Conventions"; "Considerations Regarding Passwords"; "Creating a New User"

Which of the following sets of usernames and passwords are acceptable for Windows NT ?

Username – Password

A. First Ass't Comptroller – FirstComp

B. FirstAsstCompt – 1stComp

C. FirstAss★tCompt – COMP1

D. AssComp1 – 123COMPTROLLER1

Question #12-06

Resource: "Understanding User Manager for Domains"; "Creating a New User"

Your workstations are members of a domain called Titan. You need to create user accounts so that two shifts of temporary employees can log on to the same computer, but only during their shift.

A. Use User Manager for domains on each local Windows NT Workstation to create the temporary accounts and assign each the appropriate logon hours.

B. Use User Manager on each local Windows NT Workstation to create the temporary accounts and assign each the appropriate logon hours.

C. Use User Manager for domains on the domain controller for Titan to create domain accounts for the temporary employees and assign each the appropriate logon hours.

D. Use User Manager on the domain controller for Titan to create local group accounts for the temporary employees and assign each the appropriate logon hours.

App
J

Question #12-07

Resource: "Understanding User and Group Accounts"; "Creating a New User"

Your boss has advised you that BrownC has left the company and asks that you delete his account. Later, your boss hires BrownC back as a consultant and tells you to put his account back on the network. BrownC calls you the next day and informs you gruffly that he can no longer access any of the network resources that he used to. How do you troubleshoot?

A. Use the Registry to set BrownC's SID back to what it was before you deleted his account. He will then be able to access all the old resources.

B. Deleting BrownC's account also deleted his SID. Because security in Windows NT is linked to the user's SID, you will need to reestablish all the network resource access that BrownC used to have.

C. Use the Emergency Repair Disk or your last network backup to copy BrownC's old account back to the Registry.

D. Leave the company and get hired back as a consultant yourself.

Question #12-08

Resource: "Creating a New User"

Under which of the following situations would you disable the user account rather than deleting it?

A. JaneD has left the company on maternity leave and plans to return in three months.

B. JohnB has taken an emergency medical leave of absence for possibly six or more months, but hopes to return full time.

C. JaniceD has left the company to take a job at Microsoft.

D. FrankP has taken a temporary team leader position in another department and will return when the project is completed.

Question #12-09

Resource: "Renaming, Copying, and Deleting Accounts"; "Home Directory"

You are creating multiple user accounts for salespersons, marketers, and programmers. Each set of accounts belongs to the same relative groups (sales users in SALES, marketing users in MARKETING, and programmer users in PROGRAMMERS), uses the same logon scripts (SALES.BAT, MARKET.BAT, PROGRAM.BAT), and saves data in a home directory relative to each group (sales users under USERS\SALES, marketing users under USERS\MARKETERS, programmer users under USERS\PROGRAMMERS). What is the most efficient way to create these users?

A. Create a separate account for each user. As you create the user, use the %USERNAME% environment variable when specifying the home directory to let Windows NT create it for you.

B. Create a template for each type of user. Make the appropriate choices and entries for groups, logon script, and home directory. Use the %USERNAME% environment variable when specifying the home directory to let Windows NT create them for you. Then, create each user by copying the appropriate template.

C. Create all the users without specifying group membership. After they are all created, select each group of users by Ctrl+clicking them and create the appropriate group.

D. You must create each user individually.

Question #12-10

Resource: "Account Policy"

To provide a greater level of security, you have decided to create an account policy that requires a minimum password length of eight characters, requires that users change their passwords at least once a month, and does not allow users to use the same password twice in two months. Which Account Policy settings are appropriate?

A. Max Password Age: 60; Min Password Age: 30; Min Password Length: 8; Password Uniqueness: 2

B. Max Password Age: 30; Min Password Age: 30; Min Password Length: 8; Password Uniqueness: 6

C. Max Password Age: 30; Min Password Age: 10; Min Password Length: 8; Password Uniqueness: 6

D. Max Password Age: 60; Min Password Age: 30; Min Password Length: 8; Password Uniqueness: 1

Question #12-11

Resource: "Account Policy"; "Audit Policy"

You suspect that someone is trying to log on to the network unauthorized. What is the best step you can take to increase security and determine who might be doing this?

A. Enable Account Lockout in the Account Policy requiring the Administrator to unlock the account.

B. Enable Account Lockout in the Account Policy requiring the Administrator to unlock the account. Enable auditing of unsuccessful logons and logoffs and monitor these events in the Event Viewer.

C. Advise users to change their passwords more frequently and not to use obvious passwords.

D. Increase the minimum password length in Account Policy.

Question #12-12

Resource: "User Rights"

You want to give a particular domain user the ability to back up files on a server, but not be able to restore files. How can you accomplish this?

A. Make the domain user a member of the Backup Operators group on the server.

B. Make the domain user a member of the Server Operators group on the server.

C. Create a new local group called BACKUP ONLY on the server and make the domain user a member of it. Assign this new group to the Backup Files and Directories User Right.

D. Give the user read-only access to all the files.

Question #12-13

Resource: "Troubleshooting Accounts, Policies, and Profiles"

A user is having problems logging on to the network and is seeing a variety of messages. Which of the following things would you check to troubleshoot?

A. The user is entering the correct username and password.

B. The username is case-sensitive.

C. The domain controller is up and accessible.

D. The user's account requires a mandatory profile that is accessible.

Question #12-14

Resource: "Remote Account Management Tips"

You need to be able to remotely manage the account database on two trusted domains. Which steps must take place for this to happen successfully?

A. Do nothing. You can remotely manage accounts through a trust by default.

B. Use User Manager for domains and choose User, Select Domain from the menu to choose the remote domain you want to administer.

C. Make your account a member of the Account Operators group in the trusted domains.

D. Give your user account Full Control access to the SAM hive file in WINNT\SYSTEM32\CONFIG.

Chapter 13

Question #13-01

Resource: "Local versus Domain Access Token"; "Sharing Resources and Determining Network Access"

The manager of the Accounting department wants to make next year's budget templates available for the staff accountants to review beginning next month. Staff accountants are all members of the Accountants global group in CORPDOMAIN. The templates will be stored on the department resource server called ACCT1 in a folder called BUDGET97. None of the partitions on ACCT1 are formatted with NTFS. How would you make the folder available only to the Accounting department staff?

A. Use User Manager for Domains to create a local group on the resource server called Accountants. Make the global Accountants group a member of the local Accountants group. Assign permission to use the folder to the Accountants group through User Manager for Domains.

B. Use User Manager for Domains to create a local group on the resource server called Accountants. Make the global Accountants group a member of the local Accountants group. Assign the appropriate User Rights to the Accountants group to access the BUDGET97 share.

C. Use User Manager for Domains to create a local group on the resource server called Accountants. Make the global Accountants group a member of the local Accountants group. Use the Security tab on the properties sheet for the folder to assign permissions to the Accountants group.

D. Use User Manager for Domains to create a local group on the resource server called Accountants. Make the global Accountants group a member of the local Accountants group. Use the Sharing tab on the properties sheet for the folder to assign permissions to the Accountants group.

Question #13-02

Resource: "Sharing Resources and Determining Network Access"; "Examining the Windows NT Security Model"

The manager of the Accounting department wants to make next year's budget templates available for the staff accountants to review beginning next month. Staff accountants are all members of the global group Accountants in the domain CORPDOMAIN. The templates will be stored on the department resource server called ACCT1 in a folder called BUDGET97. A local group called Budget has been created to manage access to the budget templates. None of the partitions on ACCT1 are formatted with NTFS. How would you make the folder available only to the Accounting department staff? Choose all that apply.

A. Share the BUDGET97 directory.

B. Add the Accountants group to the ACL for the share.

C. Remove the Everyone group from the ACL for the share.

D. Give the Accountants group read and write permissions at the folder level.

Question #13-03

Resource: "Examining the Windows NT Security Model"

A user's effective access to a resource is determined by:

A. Comparing the rights of the user with the permissions assigned through the ACL of the resource.

B. Comparing the permissions in the access token of the user with the permissions assigned through the ACL of the resource.

C. Comparing the user and group SID entries in the user's access token with the permissions assigned through the ACL of the resource.

D. Comparing the user and group SID entries in the user's access token with the user rights listed in the ACL of the resource.

Question #13-04

Resource: "Local versus Domain Access Tokens"

The Sales department recently acquired a laser quality printer with an envelope feed that has been installed on their print server called SalesPrint. The sales staff is already a member of the local group SALES on SalesPrint. The print operator shared the printer with the default permission. The sales staff can access the printer, but so can everyone else in the domain. What else must you do to ensure that only sales staff can access the printer?

A. Assign the Sales group print access to the printer.

B. Assign the Sales group print access to the printer, and remove the Everyone group.

C. Do nothing else.

D. Assign the Sales group print access to the printer, and give the Everyone group Read access.

Question #13-05

Resource: "Examining Access Control Lists"

The permission list defining access to a resource resides:

A. With the resource and is called the Access Control List.

B. With the user and is called the User Rights Policy.

C. With the user and is called the Access Control List.

D. With the resource and is called the User Rights Policy.

Question #13-06

Resource: "How ACLs Determine Access"

Arlo, a member of the Developers group, is currently editing the file DOOM.DOC in the share TOOLS. The administrator of the share changes permission to the Developers group from Change to Read. Arlo continues to make changes to the document. What else must the administrator do to restrict Arlo's access?

A. Take Arlo out of the Developers group.

B. Give Arlo No Access explicitly.

C. Disconnect Arlo from the resource.

D. Nothing. Arlo must disconnect from the share and then reconnect before the new permission will take effect.

Question #13-07

Resource: "Sharing Resources and Determining Network Access"

The administrator of the TOOLS shared folder wants to limit access to the folder only to the Developers group. To accomplish this, she gives the Everyone group NO ACCESS, and the Developers group Change access. The Developers complain that they cannot access any file in TOOLS. What else must the administrator do?

A. Share the files in the TOOLS folder.

B. Remove the Everyone group.

C. Give the Developers group Full Control.

D. Format the partition as NTFS and assign NTFS permissions in addition to the share permissions.

Question #13-08

Resource: "Effective Permissions"

Ned is a member of the Developers group at Springfield Technologies. He has been promoted to team leader for his group. He needs to edit the DOOM.DOC file in the Tools folder, but does not have Write access. What must you do to give Ned access to DOOM.DOC?

A. Do nothing. The next time Ned logs on, his permissions will change.

B. Change the Developers group permission to Change.

C. Add Ned to the Team Leaders group.

D. Change the Team Leaders group permission to Full Control.

Question #13-09

Resource: "Sharing Resources and Determining Network Access"

The TOOLS folder has been shared to the Developers group with Change permission. DOOM is a subdirectory under TOOLS. Team Leaders should have access only to DOOM with Read permissions. What can you do to accomplish this?

A. Add Team Leaders to the TOOLS share with Read permission.

B. Create a new share called DOOM and give Team Leaders Read permission to it.

C. Add Team Leaders to the TOOLS share with Change permission.

D. Add Team Leaders to the TOOLS share with No Access and to the DOOM subdirectory with Read.

Question #13-10

Resource: "Assigning File and Folder Permissions"

The manager of the Accounting department wants to make next year's budget templates available for the staff accountants to review beginning next month. Staff accountants are already members of a global group called Accountants in CORPDOMAIN. The templates will be stored on the department resource server called ACCT1 in a folder called BUDGET97 on an NTFS partition. The folder has been shared with the default permission, which you do not want to change. How would you further secure the folder's contents so that it is available only to the Accounting department staff?

A. Use User Manager for Domains to create a local group on the resource server called Accountants. Make the global accountants group a member of the local accountants group. Assign the Accountants group permission to use the folder through User Manager for Domains.

B. Use User Manager for Domains to create a local group on the resource server called Accountants. Make the global accountants group a member of the local accountants group. Assign the

appropriate User Rights to the Accountants group to access the
BUDGET97 share.

C. Use User Manager for Domains to create a local group on the
resource server called Accountants. Make the global accountants
group a member of the local accountants group. Use the Security
tab on the properties sheet for the folder to assign permissions to
the Accountants group.

D. Use User Manager for Domains to create a local group on the
resource server called Accountants. Make the global accountants
group a member of the local accountants group. Use the Sharing
tab on the properties sheet for the folder to assign permissions to
the Accountants group.

Question #13-11 *No correct answer!*

Resource: "Effective File and Folder Permissions"

The manager of the Accounting department wants to make next year's
budget templates available for the staff accountants to review beginning
next month. Staff accountants are already members of a global group
called Accountants in CORPDOMAIN. The templates will be stored
on the department resource server called ACCT1 in a folder called
BUDGET97 on an NTFS partition. The folder has been shared with
the default permission. The global accountants group has been added to
a local group called Accountants on ACCT1. You would like everyone
to be able to see the files, but only the accounting staff should be able
to make changes. What do you need to do?

A. Change the share permission to only Accountants with Change
permission.

B. Assign the Accountants group the NTFS permission Change to
the BUDGET97 folder.

C. Change the share permission to Everyone with No Access and
assign the Accountants group the NTFS permission Change for
the BUDGET97 folder.

D. Change the share permission to Everyone with Read and assign
the Accountants group the NTFS permission Change for the
BUDGET97 folder.

Question #13-12

Resource: "Determining Access When Using Share and NTFS Permissions"

Team Leaders need to be able to modify files contained in the share TOOLS. While you were on vacation, your trusted sidekick modified the permissions for the share and the folder. The two exhibits show what the permissions look like now. Team Leaders complain that they are unable to modify their files. What should you do?

A. Fire your trusted sidekick.

B. Change the TOOLS NTFS permission for Team Leaders to Change, and the share permission to Read.

C. Change the TOOLS NTFS permission for the Team Leaders to Change.

D. Remove Team Leaders from the ACL for the TOOLS share.

Question #13-13

Resource: "Assigning File and Folder Permissions"

You have modified NTFS permissions for the file DOOM.DOC so that Team Leaders have Full Control. For all other files and folders, Team Leaders should have Read access. Using the exhibit, how can you best accomplish this?

A. Select Replace Permissions on Subdirectories and deselect Replace Permissions on Existing Files.

B. Select Replace Permissions on Subdirectories.

C. Deselect Replace Permissions on Existing Files.

D. Set permissions on each file and folder individually.

Question #13-14

Resource: "Understanding the Concept of Ownership"

The person that created DOOM.DOC on server ACCT1 is no longer with the company. Cathy, a member of Team Leaders, will be assuming responsibility for the DOOM project, and needs to become the owner of DOOM.DOC. How can this be accomplished? Choose all that apply.

A. Give Cathy the Take Ownership of Files and Folders User Right on the server ACCT1.

B. Give Cathy the Take Ownership permission on the file DOOM.DOC.

C. Tell Cathy to just take ownership of the file.

D. Give the Team Leaders group the Take Ownership permission for DOOM.DOC.

Question #13-15

App
J

Resource: "Troubleshooting Security"

Fred is a member of the Developers group. The Developers group has been given the NTFS permission Full Control to the TOOLS folder. Fred is changing jobs and has been given NO ACCESS to the file DOOM.DOC, which is contained in the TOOLS folder. Later, Fred logs on and deletes the file DOOM.DOC. Luckily, you can restore the file from your tape backup. How can you prevent Fred from deleting the file again, but still maintain the original level of access for him and the Developers group?

A. Fire Fred.

B. Give the Developers group Special Access with all options selected for the TOOLS folder. Then give Fred NO ACCESS to the file.

C. Give the Developers group Change access at the folder level.

D. Give Fred NO ACCESS at the folder level.

Question #13-16

Resource: "Local versus Domain Access Tokens"

Permissions for the BUDGET shared folder on ACCT1 are as shown in the following exhibit. ACCT1 is a member server of the FINANCE domain. Finance is a trusting domain of CORPDOMAIN. There is a global group called FinanceMgrs that must have Read access to the folder and its files. How would you make this happen?

A. Click the Add button and add the FinanceMgrs global group from FINANCE to the ACL with Read permission.

B. Click the Add button, choose CORPDOMAIN from the From Domain list, and add the FinanceMgrs global group from CORPDOMAIN to the ACL with Read permission.

C. Click the Add button and add the FinanceMgrs global group from CORPDOMAIN to the Accountants local group on ACCT1.

D. You cannot add users from another domain to this ACL.

Question #13-17

Resource: "Managing Shares and Permissions Remotely"

Which tool(s) can you use to remotely manage shares across the domain?

A. User Manager for Domains

B. Server Manager

C. Windows Explorer

D. Network Neighborhood

Question #13-18

Resource: "Managing Shares and Permissions Remotely"

Which tool(s) can you use to remotely manage file and folder permissions across the domain?

A. User Manager for Domains

B. Server Manager

C. Windows Explorer

D. Network Neighborhood

Chapter 14

Question #14-01

Resource: "User Profiles"; "Default User Profiles"

As you create new users, you would like them to assume the same default environment settings such as common application groups, startup programs, and company logo as wallpaper. Which steps will achieve this?

A. Modify the appropriate changes in the Default User and All Users profile folders in WINNT\Profiles. When a new user is created, that user's profile will begin with the settings from these two.

B. Create a System Policy file that contains the appropriate settings for the Default User and save it in the WINNT\SYSTEM32\REPL\IMPORT\SCRIPTS subdirectory on the validating computer.

C. Create a template user account and modify the settings for that account. Create new accounts by copying the template.

D. Create a system policy file for each set of users modifying the settings as appropriate for each user.

Question #14-02

Resource: "Creating the Server-Based Profile"

There are five summer interns joining the company this year for a three-month period. You want to give them access to the network, but you want to restrict their environment settings to specific programs, colors, and so on. They should not be able to change the settings. What steps are involved?

A. Change the NTUSER.DAT file in the shared directory to NTUSER.MAN.

B. Through the User Profiles tab in the System applet, copy the profile of the account that has the appropriate environment settings to a shared directory on a central server.

C. Create a user account and make the appropriate changes to that account's environment settings.

D. Specify the location and file name of the profile in each summer intern's account properties.

Question #14-03

Resource: "Server–Based User Profiles"; "Mandatory Profiles"

You would like your users to receive default environment settings when they log on, but not allow them to change their own settings and save them as part of their own personal profiles. What type of server profile will accomplish this?

A. Server-based mandatory profile

B. Server-based user profile

C. Local user profile

D. Local system policy

Question #14-04

Resource: "Working with the System Policy Editor"

You would like to modify the Registry settings of a remote Windows NT 4.0 computer so that users will receive a legal notice warning when they log on. Which of the following provides the best way of accomplishing this?

A. Use Server Manager and connect to the remote computer.

B. Use the System Policy Editor. Connect to the remote computer and open the local Registry.

C. Use User Profile Editor to make a UNC connection to the remote computer and access its Registry.

D. Microsoft does not support remote management of the Registry.

Question #14-05

Resource: "Default and Specific User and Computer Settings"

You plan to create a policy file that will be used by all the users in your domain. You want certain default settings for the users and their Windows NT computers to be downloaded automatically when they log on. You also will assign specific settings to specific users and groups. Which of the following steps need to take place to accomplish this goal?

A. Modify the Default Computer policy options as desired.

B. Create a system policy file called NTCONFIG.POL and save it in the NETLOGON share of each domain controller.

C. Set individual policy options for the specific users and groups.

D. Create separate system policy files for each user and group and save these in the users' home directories.

Chapter 15

Question #15-01

Resource: "Remote Server Management"

Server tools are designed to be installed on which of the following clients?

A. Windows 95

B. Windows for Workgroups 3.11

C. Windows NT 4.0 and 3.5/3.51 Workstations

D. Windows NT 4.0 Server

Question #15-02

Resource: "Remote Server Management"

The reason that server tools are not installed on Windows NT Server installations is:

App
J

A. The server tools applications and utilities are already installed but must be run from a domain controller.

B. The server tools applications and utilities are not available for member servers.

C. The server tools applications and utilities cannot be run from the server platform.

D. The server tools applications and utilities are already installed and available for use.

Question #15-03

Resource: "Required Resources for Windows 95"

To install server tools on a Windows 95 client computer, the following resources and services are required.

A. Client for Novell Networks installed.

B. 3M of free disk space.

C. 8M of memory.

D. Client for Microsoft Networks installed.

Question #15-04

Resource: "Installation from the CD-ROM"

To install server tools on a Windows NT Workstation, Intel platform:

A. Run Setup.bat from the server CD-ROM, Clients folder.

B. Run Setup.bat from the server CD-ROM, Clients\Srvtools folder.

C. Run Setup.bat from the server CD-ROM, Clients\Srvtools\Winnt folder.

D. Run Setup.bat from the server CD-ROM, Clients\Srvtools\Winnt\I386 folder.

Question #15-05

Resource: "Installation from the CD-ROM"

Once server tools are installed on a Windows NT Workstation, they can be run from:

A. The <winntroot>\System32 folder.

B. The Start Menu, Programs, Server Tools group.

C. The Start Menu, Programs, Administrative Tools group.

D. Any manually made program group provided the executables are placed in that group.

Question #15-06

Resource: "Creating a Server Tools Share Using Network Client Administrator"

What server administrative tool is used to copy the server tools from the CD-ROM and automatically create a shared folder?

A. Network Server Tools Administrator

B. Network Client Administrator

C. Network Server Tools Manager

D. Network Server Manager

Question #15-07

Resource: "Creating a Server Tools Share Using Network Client Administrator"

The default share name for the server tools share is:

A. SrvTools

B. ClientTools

C. SetupAdm

D. ServerTools

Question #15-08

Resource: "Installation of Windows 95 Server Tools"

To install server tools on a Windows 95 platform:

A. Run Setup.bat from the CD-ROM, Clients\Srvtools\Win95 folder.

B. Run Setup.bat from the CD-ROM, Clients\Srvtools\Windows folder.

C. Run Setup.exe from the CD-ROM, Clients\Srvtools\Windows folder.

D. Access Control Panel on the Windows 95 client computer and select the Add/Remove Programs ICON.

Question #15-09

Resource: "Windows NT 4.0 Workstation Server Tools"

What server tool is NOT installed on a Windows NT 3.5/3.51 Workstation platform?

A. Services for Macintosh

B. System Policy Editor

C. Remote Access Administrator

D. User Profile Editor

Question #15-10

Resource: "Installation of Windows 3.1 and Windows for Workgroups 3.11 Server Tools"

Indicate the two files that contain settings that must be appended to the Config.sys and Autoexec.bat, respectively, when installing server tools on a Windows for Workgroup platform.

A. New-conf.sys and New-vars.bat.

B. New-config.sys and New-vars.bat.

C. New–vars.bat and New–config.sys.

D. New–auto.bat and New–vars.sys.

Chapter 16

Question #16-01

Resource: "Gateway (and Client) Services for NetWare"

Gateway (and Client) Services for NetWare is: (Pick one)

A. Sold as a part of Services for Netware

B. Included with Windows NT Workstation

C. Included with Windows NT Workstation and Server

D. Included with Windows NT Server

Question #16-02

Resource: "File and Print Services for NetWare"

You need for your existing Novell NetWare clients to access a new Windows NT Server without changing the client software. Do you: (Pick one)

A. Install File and Print Services for NetWare on the Windows NT Server.

B. Install File and Print Services for NetWare on the Novell NetWare Server.

C. Install Gateway (and Client) Services for NetWare on the Windows NT Server.

D. Install Gateway (and Client) Services for NetWare on the Novell NetWare Server.

Question #16-03

Resource: "Gateway (and Client) Services for NetWare"

You have clients which only have the Microsoft client installed, but need access to a Novell NetWare server. How can you allow these clients to have access to the NetWare server? (Pick all that apply)

A. Install Gateway (and Client) Services for NetWare on the Novell Server.

B. Install Gateway (and Client) Services for NetWare on the Windows NT Server.

C. Install the Novell NetWare requestor on the client.

D. Install File and Print Services for NetWare on the Windows NT Server.

Question #16-04

Resource: "Migration Tool for NetWare"

When migrating NetWare servers to Windows NT, what are the options passwords? (Pick all that apply)

A. Set them to blank.

B. Set them to the user name.

C. Set them to a password set in a map file.

D. Set them to a random password from a dictionary.

Question #16-05

Resource: "Gateway (and Client) Services for NetWare"

Gateway (and Client) Services for NetWare require what to function: (Pick one)

A. A user with membership in an NTGATEWAY group on the Windows NT Server

B. A user with membership in an NTGATEWAY group on the Novell NetWare Server

C. Supervisor access to the Novell NetWare Server

D. A Translation file which translates Windows NT user names to Novell NetWare user names

Chapter 17

Question #17-01

Resource: "Multiprotocol Routing"

Indicate, from the following choices, which routing options are available with a Windows NT 4.0 Server installation.

A. IP Routing

B. IPX Routing

C. DHCP Relay

D. AppleTalk Routing

Question #17-02

Resource: "Networks, Network Segments, and the Purpose of Routers"

Why is NetBEUI protocol routing not supported in Windows NT 4.0 installations?

A. Because NetBEUI maintains its own route tables and requires no additional services to handle routing.

B. Because NetBEUI cannot be installed on Windows NT 4.0 Server.

C. Because NetBEUI uses either RIP for IP or RIP for IPX, which-ever is installed.

D. Because NetBEUI is not a routable protocol.

Question #17-03

Resource: "Networks, Network Segments, and the Purpose of Routers"

Routers work up to the _____ layer in the OSI Network Model.

   A. Physical

   B. Data Link

   C. Network

   D. Transport

Question #17-04

Resource: "Networks, Network Segments, and the Purpose of Routers"

From the following choices, indicate which are considered functions of a router.

   A. They can pass information packets from one protocol to another such as TCP/IP to IPX.

   B. They cannot pass information packets from one protocol to another such as TCP/IP to IPX.

   C. They can pass information packets from one network segment to another, even though each segment may use a different media type such as Ethernet or Token Ring.

   D. They can pass information packets from one network segment to another, but only if each segment is the same media type such as Ethernet or Token Ring.

Question #17-05

Resource: "RIP for IPX Routing"

RIP for IP and DHCP Relay can support _____ hops.

   A. 4

   B. 8

C. 16

D. 32

Question #17-06

Resource: "RIP for IPX Routing"

RIP for IPX can support _____ hops.

A. 4

B. 8

C. 16

D. 32

Question #17-07

Resource: "TCP/IP Routing"

Indicate the utility used from the command prompt to manually maintain a static IP routing table.

A. Route

B. IPXRoute

C. IPConfig

D. PING

Question #17-08

Resource: "RIP for IPX Routing"

Indicate the utility used from the command prompt to manually maintain an IPX routing table.

A. Route

B. IPXRoute

C. IPConfig

D. PING

Question #17-09

Resource: "AppleTalk Routing"

What service must be installed on a Windows NT 4.0 Server to allow it to function as an AppleTalk router?

A. RPC

B. GSNW

C. FDDI

D. SFM

Question #17-10

Resource: "AppleTalk Routing"

Network types can have network numbers or network ranges associated with them. Which type of network can have only one network number associated with it?

A. LocalTalk

B. EtherTalk

C. TokenTalk

D. FDDI

Chapter 18

Question #18-01

Resource: Entire Chapter

You are responsible for a small company that has three locations in Chicago. You want to be sure the new software updates are available to all the appropriate installers throughout the company. Which publishing service(s) would you use?

A. WWW

B. FTP

C. GOPHER

D. NETSCAPE

Question #18-02

Resource: Entire Chapter

You are responsible for a small company local area network and have implemented the intranet. Your manager is concerned that the confidential data might get out to the competition. What can you do to help?

A. Tell the manager it's okay; the data is old, anyway.

B. Tell the manager you do not have Internet access.

C. Use PWS instead.

D. Use Microsoft Windows NT IE in place of the Windows 95 version.

Question #18-03

Resource: Entire Chapter

What clients are supported for the Internet Explorer?

A. Microsoft Windows

B. Lan Manager 2.2c for OS2

C. UNIX

D. Microsoft Windows 95

Question #18-04

Resource: Entire Chapter

You have upgraded your Windows NT 3.5 FTP server to Windows NT 4.0. The plan for this machine is to make it an IIS. You are having trouble setting up the service and it will not complete. Why not?

A. WINS is not running.

B. DHCP is not running.

C. Gopher needs to be installed first.

D. FTP is still installed.

Chapter 19

Question #19-01

Resource: "What Are These Types of Connections?"

RAS accepts what kind of inbound connections? (Pick all that apply)

A. ISDN

B. Modem

C. X.25

D. PPP

Question #19-02

Resource: "What Are These Types of Connections?"

Which technology allows RAS to utilize two ISDN channels? (Pick one)

A. PPTP

B. PPP

C. Multi-link PPP

D. SLIP

Question #19-03

Resource: "What Is PPTP"

The Point-to-Point Tunneling Protocol does what? (Pick one)

A. Establishes a connection via the modem for the RAS server and RAS client to communicate.

B. Establishes a connection via X.25 for the RAS server and RAS client to communicate.

C. Enhances authentication with a longer key.

D. Encrypts all data between the client and server.

Question #19-04

Resource: "User Security Options"

Callback security can be set up how? (Pick all that apply)

A. Not to call back.

B. To call back to a predefined number.

C. To call back to a user-assigned number.

D. To call back and require a voiceprint match.

Question #19-05

Resource: "RAS Installation"

Who can install RAS on an Windows NT Server: (Pick all that apply)

A. Administrator

B. Any member of the administrators group

C. Any member of the PowerUsers group

D. Any member of the RAS group

Question #19-06

Resource: "RAS Installation"

RAS Supports what protocols? (Pick all that apply)

A. TCP/IP

B. IPX/SPX

C. NetBEUI

D. DLC

Question #19-07

Resource: "Troubleshooting RAS"

What programs can be used to troubleshoot RAS: (Pick all that apply)

A. Network Monitor

B. Dial-Up Networking Monitor

C. Remote Access Admin

D. Performance Monitor

Chapter 20

Question #20-01

Resource: "Monitoring Memory"

Frederick has recently loaded two more C++ applications to modify on his Windows NT 4.0 Workstation. He has noticed that when he boots and loads all his applications, Windows NT takes longer to respond to application requests. You use Performance Monitor and notice that pagefile usage has increased and that the Commit Limit for the pagefile drops rapidly when the applications are loaded. What is the best solution you can offer Frederick based on this data?

A. Purchase more RAM for Frederick's computer.

B. Move the pagefile to another disk partition.

C. Increase the initial size of the pagefile so that it doesn't have to grow right away as the applications load.

D. Move the C++ applications to another disk partition.

Question #20-02

Resource: "Monitoring Memory"

Desiree, a Visual Basic developer, has noticed that her system's performance has decreased since she began work on a large VB application. You have used Performance Monitor to determine that the pagefile usage has increased. You also notice that the pagefile, Windows NT system files and the VB application are all stored on the same partition. In addition, the working set for the VB application shows that it consistently requires 16M for itself. What solutions can you recommend? Name all that apply.

A. Add more RAM in the computer.

B. Move the pagefile to a disk partition other than the system or application partition.

C. Increase the maximum size for the pagefile.

D. Create multiple pagefiles.

Question #20-03

Resource: "Monitoring the Processor"

Which Processor object counter would be useful to determine how much processor time is being utilized by application requests?

A. %Processor Time

B. %User Time

C. %Application Time

D. %Privileged Time

Question #20-04

Resource: "Monitoring Processes"

Which Process object counter would be useful in determining the amount of memory required by an application?

A. %Application Memory

B. Commit Limit

C. Working Set

D. Avg. Disk sec\Transfer

Question #20-05

Resource: "Monitoring Memory"

Which Memory object counter would help to identify when to right-size the pagefile?

A. %Pagefile

B. Commit Limit

C. Working Set

D. %Disk Time

Question #20-06

Resource: "Monitoring the Processor"; "Monitoring Memory"; "Monitoring Disk Activity"

On your Windows NT 4.0 development workstation, you have concluded that performance as a whole has decreased. You are not sure which process is driving this, but you have noticed that your disk drive has had a lot more activity lately. What objects should you monitor through Performance Monitor to help you troubleshoot this situation?

A. Check the Processor>%Processor Time counter, determine the percent of disk I/O used for paging through the Memory>Pages/Sec counter and the Logical Disk>Avg. Disk sec/Transfer counter, and the Process>Working Set for every process running.

B. Check the Processor>%Processor Time counter, determine the percent of disk I/O used for paging through the Memory>Pages/Sec counter and the Logical Disk>Avg. Disk sec/Transfer counter. Track the Process>%Processor Time counter for every process running to determine which processes are pushing the processor excessively. Monitor the Process>Working Set counter for these processes in particular.

C. Check the Processor>%Processor Time counter, determine the percent of disk I/O used for paging through the Logical Disk>Disk Queue Length counter, and the Process>Working Set for every process running.

D. Check the Processor>%User Time counter, determine the percent of disk I/O used for paging through the Logical Disk>%Disk Time counter, and the Memory>Commit Limit counter for the pagefile.

Question #20-07

Resource: "Monitoring Disk Activity"

Which counter will provide you with the total percent of time spent servicing disk requests for a given partition on a disk?

A. Logical Disk>%Disk Time

B. Logical Disk>Disk Queue Length

C. Physical Disk>%Disk Time

D. Physical Disk>Disk Queue Length

Question #20-08

Resource: "Monitoring Disk Activity"; "Monitoring System Performance with Performance Monitor"

Which of the following counters will provide you with the total number of bytes transferred during disk I/O for all the disks in your computer?

A. Logical Disk>Disk Bytes/sec, Total instance

B. Logical Disk>Disk Bytes/sec, for each partition instance

C. Physical Disk>Disk Bytes/sec, Total instance

D. Physical Disk>Disk Bytes/sec, for each disk instance

Question #20-09

Resource: "System Performance with Performance Monitor"

Which objects would be most beneficial to include in a log file when creating a baseline measurement of your system's performance? Choose all that apply.

A. Memory

B. TCP/IP

C. Processor

D. Physical and Logical Disk

Question #20-10

Resource: "Creating a Performance Monitor Log"; "Summarizing Performance Monitoring and Optimization"

You plan to use Performance Monitor to help predict and troubleshoot server activity under various conditions. Which of the following would be the best way to begin?

A. Create and monitor a real-time chart during peak activity and note the percent of processor usage during these periods.

B. Create a series of baseline logs of specific objects (processor, memory, disk and network), each representing a different condition. Use these to predict activity under those conditions and to troubleshoot abnormal system activity.

C. Create a baseline log measuring system activity during periods of average activity. Compare this against real-time charts created during peak activity on the system.

D. Network Monitor would be a better tool to predict system activity.

Question #20-11

Resource: "Monitoring Disk Activity"

While tracking the performance of disk activity on a system, you notice that the measured value is always 0 although the disk appears to be heavily used. What is your evaluation of this situation?

A. The disk is a high performance unit and can handle the heavy disk I/O.

B. The wrong disk objects and counters have been selected for Performance Monitor.

C. The disk counters had not been enabled by typing DISKPERF -Y at a command prompt.

D. The disk has crashed.

Question #20-12

Resource: "Monitoring Network-Related Objects"

You are analyzing network activity between your network clients and a server. You plan to use Network Monitor to monitor network traffic generated by and received by the server, and Performance Monitor to track system performance relating to network traffic. What types of objects would facilitate your analysis? Choose all that apply.

A. Redirector

B. Server

C. Protocol

D. Frame

Question #20-13

Resource: "Monitoring Network-Related Objects"

After monitoring your heavily accessed file and print server, you determine that both the Server>Pool Paged Failures and Server>Pool Nonpaged Failures counters are unusually and consistently higher than normal. The Server service memory property is configured for Balanced memory usage. What should you do to reduce the number of Pool Paged and Pool Nonpaged failures?

A. Add more memory. Balanced is an appropriate setting for a file and print server.

B. Change the Server service memory configuration to Minimize Memory Used.

C. Change the Server service memory configuration to Maximize Throughput for File Sharing.

D. Change the Server service memory configuration to Load Balance Throughput for Virtual Memory.

Chapter 21

Question #21-01

Resource: "Understanding Network Monitor"

Which of the following features is provided by the full version of Network Monitor that comes with Microsoft's System Management Server? Choose all that apply.

A. Direct monitoring of remote computer traffic.

B. Determining which protocol consumed the most bandwidth.

C. Identifying which physical disk has the most I/O activity for a network session.

D. Capturing local network traffic to and from the computer running the utility.

Question #21-02

Resource: "Understanding Network Monitor"

Which of the following features is provided by the version of Network Monitor that comes with Microsoft Windows NT Server 4.0?

A. Direct monitoring of remote computer traffic.

B. Determining which protocol consumed the most bandwidth.

C. Identifying which physical disk has the most I/O activity for a network session.

D. Capturing local network traffic to and from the computer running the utility.

Question #21-03

Resource: "Exploring Network Frames"

A broadcast frame:

A. Is always directed to a specific computer by its IP, IPX, or MAC address.

B. Is sent to all hosts on the network via the unique destination address FFFFFFFF.

C. Is sent to a subset of computers on the network depending on how the computer has registered itself on the network.

D. Is a multicast frame that is directed to a specific computer on the network.

Question #21-04

Resource: "What Does a Frame Look Like?"

Which of the following are components of an Ethernet 802.3 frame? Choose all that apply.

A. Source and Destination address

B. Length of the frame

C. Data contained in the frame such as IP and TCP information

D. Type of frame

Question #21-05

Resource: "Implementing Network Monitor"

In your network, you would like to remotely monitor traffic on all your Windows NT 4.0 Server and Workstation computers, as well as your Windows 95 computers. Which of the following steps needs to take place?

A. Install the Network Monitor agent on all the computers and the Windows NT Server 4.0 version of Network Monitor on the computer that will remotely monitor the computers.

B. Install the Network Monitor agent on all the computers and the SMS full version of Network Monitor on the computer that will remotely monitor the computers.

C. Install only the Windows NT Server 4.0 version of Network Monitor on the computer that will remotely monitor the computers.

D. Install only the SMS full version of Network Monitor on the computer that will remotely monitor the computers.

Question #21-06

Resource: "Interpreting Frames in a Capture File"; "Analyzing Traffic Between Domain Controllers"

Which of the following network services generate traffic between a client and a server computer? Choose all that apply.

A. NetBIOS name registration with a WINS server

B. Logon validation

C. Account database synchronization

D. DHCP IP address requests

Question #21-07

Resource: "DHCP Frames"

What types of network traffic are associated with the DHCP service?

A. DHCP Address Request

B. DHCP Lease Renewal

C. DHCP Time Out

D. DHCP Replication

Question #21-08

Resource: "WINS Frames"

What types of traffic are associated with the WINS service?

A. WINS Registration

B. WINS Time Out

C. WINS Query Request

D. WINS Address Request

Question #21-09

Resource: "WINS Frames"

When a computer registers with a WINS server, how many name registration frames are generated?

    A. One name is registered for each computer.

    B. A name is registered for the computer and for every service or application that supports the NetBIOS API. One frame registers all these names.

    C. A name is registered for the computer and for every service or application that supports the NetBIOS API. One frame is generated for each name that needs to be registered.

    D. NetBIOS names are not registered with the WINS server.

App
J

Question #21-10

Resource: "File Session Frames"

Which of the following steps need to take place before a file session can be established between two computers using the TCP/IP protocol? Choose all that apply.

    A. The user must register its name with the WINS server.

    B. Name resolution must take place.

    C. Address resolution must take place.

    D. A TCP Session must be established.

Question #21-11

Resource: "File Session Frames"

When a TCP session is established, three frames are generated known as the TCP three-way handshake. Which of the following frames are part of the three-way handshake? Choose all that apply.

    A. TCP Request from the client to the server.

    B. TCP Name resolution request from the client to the WINS server.

C. TCP Request Acknowledgment from the server to the client.

D. TCP Session establishment from the client to the server.

Question #21-12

Resource: "File Session Frames"

Which type of frames are involved in connecting to a shared resource once the session has been established?

A. SMB session frames

B. WINS resolution frames

C. NBT broadcast frames

D. TCP request frames

Question #21-13

Resource: "Optimizing Logon Validation"

ABCCorp network consists of 5,000 users located in three office locations: New York, Chicago, and San Francisco. The current plan is to locate one PDC and one BDC in the corporate headquarters in Chicago. How could you optimize this configuration to make logging on more efficient for the users and minimize network traffic? Choose the best two answers.

A. Create two more BDCs to accommodate the 5,000 users. Microsoft recommends one BDC for every 2,000 users.

B. Create a trust relationship among all the offices.

C. Locate one BDC in each location so that logon validation takes place locally.

D. Do nothing. This configuration is optimized.

Question #21-14

Resource: "Suggestions for Optimizing Browser Traffic"

The KITEMASTERS corporate network consists of 6,000 users located across five regional locations, each on its own subnet. About half the users have Windows NT Workstation 4.0 computers, and the rest have Windows 95 computers. These computers are frequently restarted throughout the day. There is one PDC and BDC located in the MIS department, and a BDC in each regional location. Each location also has one or more Windows NT Server 4.0 computers for resource management.

Using Network Monitor, you have noticed that there is an unusually high percentage of Browser traffic generated throughout the day. How can you optimize traffic associated with the Browser while letting users continue to browse for resources? Choose the best two answers.

App
J

A. You cannot configure Browser parameters.

B. Configure the Windows 95 and Windows NT Workstation 4.0 computers to never become browsers.

C. Disable the Server service on user computers which will not be sharing resources in the network.

D. Disable the Computer Browser service on all user computers.

Question #21-15

Resource: "Account Database Synchronization"

Under what circumstances might a full database synchronization take place between a PDC and a BDC? Choose the best two.

A. Every synchronization event replicates the entire account databases.

B. Full synchronization occurs when the BDC is first installed.

C. Full synchronization may occur when the change log on the PDC becomes full and begins to overwrite existing information before the PDC can contact the BDC for updates.

D. Only changes are copied whenever synchronization occurs.

Question #21-16

Resource: "Account Database Synchronization"

Built-in local groups and their members are contained in which accounts database?

- A. SAM Accounts Database
- B. Local Security Accounts Database
- C. SAM Built-In Database
- D. Account Synchronization Database

Question #21-17

Resource: "Account Database Synchronization"

User, group, and computer accounts are contained in which accounts database?

- A. SAM Accounts Database
- B. Local Security Accounts Database
- C. SAM Built-In Database
- D. Account Synchronization Database

Question #21-18

Resource: "Traffic Generated when Using Trusted Accounts"; "Optimizing Trust Traffic"

The ABCCorp domain is configured as a Master Domain model. 5,000 user accounts are managed in the ABC-MIS domain in Chicago. Resource domains trust ABC-MIS. At the ABC-WEST resource domain, the print administrator is managing access to her printers by adding the appropriate user accounts from ABC-MIS to the ACL for each of five printers. Access will be managed for 300 users. ABC-WEST is connected to ABC-MIS via a slow WAN link. Every time she accesses the ABC-MIS account domain to display the list of users, the list takes several seconds to generate. The process is taking longer than she thinks it should. What can you suggest to improve performance and minimize network traffic? Choose the best answer.

A. Upgrade the WAN link to a higher speed.

B. Create local groups on the print servers in ABC-WEST and add the users to the local groups. Use the local groups to assign printer permissions.

C. Create global groups in ABC-MIS for the users that need printer access in ABC-WEST. Add the global groups to local groups on the print servers in ABC-WEST, and assign printer permissions to the local groups.

D. There is nothing you can do to improve performance. The same amount of trust traffic is generated whether you use user accounts or group accounts across the trust.

Question #21-19

App J

Resource: "Optimizing Directory Replication Traffic"

Which of the following actions can serve to optimize network traffic associated with Directory Replication? Choose all that apply.

A. Lock directories that are not replicated frequently, or that you do not want to have replicated.

B. Maintain a shallow export directory tree structure.

C. Modify the interval value on the export server so that it does not check for changes in the export tree as frequently.

D. Remove the password from the Directory Replication service account.

Chapter 22

Question #22-01

Resource: "STOP Messages During Installation"

The major cause of STOP errors during the installation process is?

A. Incompatible software.

B. Incompatible hardware.

C. Incompatible Windows NT setup program.

D. It is impossible to get STOP errors during installation.

Question #22-02

Resource: "STOP Error Screen Layout and Section Meanings"

The third major area of a STOP screen displays?

A. Debug Port Status Indicator Information

B. BugCheck Information

C. Driver Information

D. Kernel Build Number and Stack Dump Information

Question #22-03

Resource: "BugCheck Information"

The first four lines of the _____ section are critical to finding the cause of the STOP error.

A. BugCheck Information

B. Driver Information

C. Kernel Build Number and Stack Dump

D. Debug Port Information

Question #22-04

Resource: "Write Debugging Information To:"

By default, CrashDump will be placed in the _____ folder.

A. %systemRoot%\System32

B. %systemRoot%\System32\Debug

C. %SystemRoot%\System32\MemoryDump

D. %systemRoot%\

Question #22-05

Resource: "Write Debugging Information To:"

For CrashDumps to be obtained, a pagefile must exist on the

A. System partition

B. Boot partition

C. NTFS partition

D. Data partition

Question #22-06

Resource: "Write Debugging Information To:"

For CrashDumps to be obtained, the pagefile must be at least _____ megabytes larger than the physical size of memory.

A. 1

B. 2

C. 4

D. 8

Question #22-07

Resource: "Crash Dump Analysis Utilities"

The utility to verify the validity of a CrashDump is

A. Dumpflop.exe

B. Dumpexam.exe

C. Dumpchk.exe

D. Dump.exe

Question #22-08

Resource: "Dumpexam.exe"

Reference to the most recently installed Service pack Symbols files must be listed _____ in the Dumpexam utility command line.

App J

A. Last

B. First after the normal Symbols files reference

C. Second

D. First

Question #22-09

Resource: "Connect the Host and Target Computers"

What kind of connection can be established between the Host computer and the Target computer for the Host computer to monitor the Boot process on the Target computer?

A. Null Modem connection using a COM port

B. Normal Network connection using a Network Adapter Card

C. Modem connection using a COM port

D. Modem connection using an LPT port

Question #22-10

Resource: "Start the Kernel Debugger"

Kernel Debugger commands can be entered after a _____ key sequence is entered.

A. Ctrl,G

B. Ctrl,C

C. Ctrl,K

D. Ctrl,Q

Question #22-11

Resource: "Events and Event Log Viewer"

Audit events are placed in the _____ log in Event Viewer.

A. System

B. Security

C. Application

D. Audit

Question #22-12

Resource: "Events and Event Log Viewer"

By default, events are ordered in all event logs?

A. By oldest first

B. By event importance

C. By newest last

D. By newest first

Answer Key for Chapter Tests

Chapter 2

Question	Answer
02–01	B,D
02–02	A,D
02–03	A,B,D
02–04	A,B
02–05	C
02–06	B
02–07	C
02–08	C
02–09	A,B,C,D
02–10	*β*A,C

Chapter 3

Question	Answer
03–01	A,B,D
03–02	B
03–03	D
03–04	C
03–05	B,C,D
03–06	C,D
03–07	A
03–08	B
03–09	A
03–10	C
03–11	A
03–12	C
03–13	B
03–14	A,B,C,D

Chapter 4

Question	Answer
04–01	A,C,D
04–02	A
04–03	A
04–04	B
04–05	C
04–06	C
04–07	D
04–08	B

Question	Answer
04–09	C
04–10	C
04–11	B
04–12	D
04–13	B
04–14	D
04–15	C

Chapter 5

Question	Answer
05–01	D
05–02	C
05–03	B,C
05–04	B
05–05	A, C, D
05–06	A
05–07	D
05–08	A
05–09	A,D
05–10	B
05–11	B,D
05–12	A
05–13	C
05–14	C
05–15	B

App
J

Chapter 6

Question	Answer
06–01	~~D~~ C
06–02	D
06–03	C
06–04	B
06–05	C

Chapter 7

Question	Answer
07–01	A,B,D
07–02	A
07–03	B
07–04	~~C~~ A
07–05	C
07–06	B,C,D
07–07	A
07–08	B
07–09	C
07–10	B
07–11	A
07–12	B
07–13	A
07–14	D
07–15	A,B,C
07–16	C
07–17	B

Chapter 8

Question	Answer
08–01	B
08–02	A
08–03	C
08–04	B,D
08–05	B
08–06	B
08–07	A
08–08	D
08–09	C
08–10	B
08–11	A
08–12	D
08–13	C
08–14	B
08–15	C
08–16	A,D
08–17	D
08–18	C
08–19	A
08–20	B
08–21	B

Chapter 9

Question	Answer
09–01	A,C
09–02	A,B,C,D

continues

Question	Answer
09–03	C
09–04	B,C
09–05	C
09–06	D
09–07	A,B,C,D
09–08	D
09–09	B
09–10	D

Chapter 10

Question	Answer
10–01	B
10–02	A,C,D
10–03	A,B,C
10–04	B
10–05	C
10–06	C
10–07	A
10–08	D
10–09	A
10–10	A,C
10–11	B
10–12	B
10–13	C
10–14	B
10–15	C
10–16	A,C,D
10–17	A

Question	Answer
10–18	D
10–19	A,B,C,D
10–20	D

Chapter 11

Question	Answer
11–01	A,C,D
11–02	A,C,D
11–03	A
11–04	A,B,C,D
11–05	D
11–06	C
11–07	B
11–08	C

Chapter 12

Question	Answer
12–01	A
12–02	B
12–03	C
12–04	A,B,D
12–05	B
12–06	C
12–07	B
12–08	A,B,D
12–09	B
12–10	C
12–11	B

continues

App
J

Question	Answer
12–12	C
12–13	A,C,D
12–14	B,C

Chapter 13

Question	Answer
13–01	D
13–02	A,B,C
13–03	C
13–04	B
13–05	A
13–06	D
13–07	B
13–08	C
13–09	B
13–10	C
13–11	A,B ~~no correct answer~~
13–12	C
13–13	A
13–14	A,B,D
13–15	B
13–16	B
13–17	B,C
13–18	C

Chapter 14

Question	Answer
14–01	A,B
14–02	A,B,C,D

Question	Answer
14-03	A
14-04	B
14-05	A,B,C

Chapter 15

Question	Answer
15-01	A,B,C
15-02	D
15-03	B,C,D
15-04	C
15-05	A,D
15-06	B
15-07	C
15-08	D
15-09	B
15-10	A

Chapter 16

Question	Answer
16-01	D
16-02	A
16-03	B,C
16-04	A,B,C
16-05	B

Chapter 17

Question	Answer
17–01	A,B,C,D
17–02	D
17–03	C
17–04	B,C
17–05	~~C~~ B
17–06	B
17–07	A
17–08	B
17–09	D
17–10	A

Chapter 18

Question	Answer
18–01	A,B
18–02	B
18–03	A,D
18–04	D

Chapter 19

Question	Answer
19–01	A,B,C,D
19–02	C
19–03	D
19–04	A,B,C
19–05	A,B
19–06	A,B,C
19–07	B,C

Chapter 20

Question	Answer
20-01	C
20-02	A,B,D
20-03	B
20-04	C
20-05	B
20-06	B
20-07	A
20-08	C
20-09	A,C,D
20-10	B
20-11	C
20-12	A,B,C
20-13	C

Chapter 21

Question	Answer
21-01	A,B,D
21-02	D
21-03	B
21-04	A,B,C,D
21-05	B
21-06	A,B,D
21-07	A,B
21-08	A,D
21-09	C
21-10	B,C,D

continues

App
J

Question	Answer
21–11	A,C,D
21–12	A
21–13	A,C
21–14	B,C
21–15	B,C
21–16	C
21–17	A
21–18	C
21–19	A,B,C

Chapter 22

Question	Answer
22–01	B
22–02	C
22–03	A
22–04	D
22–05	B
22–06	A
22–07	C
22–08	D
22–09	A,C
22–10	B
22–11	B
22–12	D

Mastery Test

 Note The answers to these questions can be found in order at the end of this section. ∎

Question #1

Global groups can contain which of the following?

A. User accounts from a trusted domain.

B. Local group accounts from the local domain.

C. User accounts from the local domain.

D. Local group accounts from the local domain.

Question #2

By default, events are ordered in all event logs?

A. By oldest first

B. By event importance

C. By newest last

D. By newest first

Question #3

To install server tools on a Windows NT Workstation, Intel platform:

A. Run Setup.bat from the server CD-ROM, Clients folder.

B. Run Setup.bat from the server CD-ROM, Clients\Srvtools folder.

C. Run Setup.bat from the server CD-ROM, Clients\Srvtools\Winnt folder.

D. Run Setup.bat from the server CD-ROM, Clients\Srvtools\Winnt\I386 folder.

App

J

Question #4

If a group of workstations on a network are never to contain any shared resources, how can you optimize these workstations so they will never send host announcements to the master browser?

A. Disable the workstation service

B. Disable the server service

C. Disable the browser service

D. Disable the alerter service

Question #5

Which of the following Directory Services goals are met by trust relationships? Select all that apply.

A. Provide users a single logon account that can be used anywhere within the enterprise to log on to the network.

B. Centralize management of accounts and resources.

C. Maintain separate user accounts for resource access on each resource server in the enterprise.

D. Facilitate access to network resources regardless of their domain location.

Question #6

To install server tools on a Windows 95 platform:

A. Run Setup.bat from the CD-ROM, Clients\Srvtools\Win95 folder.

B. Run Setup.bat from the CD-ROM, Clients\Srvtools\Windows folder.

C. Run Setup.exe from the CD-ROM, Clients\Srvtools\Windows folder.

D. Access Control Panel on the Windows 95 client computer and select the Add/Remove Programs ICON.

Question #7

Routers work up to the _____ layer in the OSI Network Model.

A. Physical

B. Data Link

C. Network

D. Transport

Question #8

The AppleTalk protocol is used in with Windows NT to provide:

A. Access to Macintosh computers.

B. Access to IBM mainframes for terminal emulation.

C. Access to Novell resources.

D. Access to HP JetDirect Printers on the network.

App

J

Question #9

TCP/IP objects do not appear as choices to monitor in Performance Monitor unless the _____ service is installed.

A. DHCP

B. WINS

C. SNMP

D. DNS

Question #10

The manager of the Accounting department wants to make next year's budget templates available for the staff accountants to review beginning next month. Staff accountants are already members of a global group called Accountants in CORPDOMAIN. The templates will be stored on the department resource server called ACCT1 in a folder called BUDGET97 on an NTFS partition. The folder has been shared with the default permission, which you do not want to change. How would you further secure the folder's contents so that it is available only to the Accounting department staff?

A. Use User Manager for Domains to create a local group on the resource server called Accountants. Make the global accountants group a member of the local accountants group. Assign the Accountants group permission to use the folder through User Manager for Domains.

B. Use User Manager for Domains to create a local group on the resource server called Accountants. Make the global accountants group a member of the local accountants group. Assign the appropriate User Rights to the Accountants group to access the BUDGET97 share.

C. Use User Manager for Domains to create a local group on the resource server called Accountants. Make the global accountants group a member of the local accountants group. Use the Security tab on the properties sheet for the folder to assign permissions to the Accountants group.

D. Use User Manager for Domains to create a local group on the resource server called Accountants. Make the global accountants group a member of the local accountants group. Use the Sharing tab on the properties sheet for the folder to assign permissions to the Accountants group.

Question #11

Within a single workgroup, there will be a master browser elected for:

A. Each protocol

B. Every 32 computers

C. Every 12 users

D. Only one protocol

Question #12

A Windows NT file and print server has been configured with striping with parity across 4 disk drives. Users have complained of poor response time. Checking the event view you discover there are disk errors. What steps should you take?

A. Reformat the logical drive.

B. Replace the failed drive.

C. Disk administrator select regenerate and restart the server.

D. Restore data from backup.

Question #13

Kite Flyers Corporation has experienced tremendous growth and now has between 10,000 and 15,000 employees located across its three global locations Chicago, London, and Tokyo. Resources are managed in each location as well as the users located in those offices. Which model best suits this organization?

A. Single domain model.

B. Master domain model.

C. Multiple Master domain model.

D. Complete Trust domain model.

Question #14

Which of the following statements best describes HKEY_LOCAL_MACHINE?

A. HKEY_LOCAL_MACHINE contains all the system configuration data needed to boot and run the Windows NT operating system successfully including services, device drivers, and hardware profiles.

B. HKEY_LOCAL_MACHINE displays only the current system configuration settings, including those used to boot Windows NT for the current session.

App

J

C. HKEY_LOCAL_MACHINE contains all the configuration settings particular to the currently logged on user.

D. HKEY_LOCAL_MACHINE contains default file association and DDE setting data for the system.

Question #15

Which disk controller has the highest throughput?

A. IDE standard

B. SCSI-2 Bus mastering

C. Fast SCSI-2

D. PCI with SCSI

Question #16

The CSNW redirector will allow a Windows NT Workstation to communicate with:

A. Novell Servers

B. Windows NT Workstations

C. Macintosh Workstations

D. Novell Clients for client/server applications

Question #17

Once server tools are installed on a Windows NT Workstation, they can be run from:

A. The <winntroot>\System32 folder.

B. The Start Menu, Programs, Server Tools group.

C. The Start Menu, Programs, Administrative Tools group.

D. Any manually made program group provided the executables are placed in that group.

Question #18

What are the differences between a local group and a global group?
Choose all that apply.

A. Local groups can be created on workstations, servers, and domain controllers, while global groups can only be created and maintained on a domain controller.

B. Local groups can contain local users, domain users, and global groups, while global groups can contain only users from their domain.

C. Local groups can contain local users, domain users, global groups, and other local groups, while global groups can contain only users from their domain.

D. Local groups can be used for managing resources only on the local computer, while global groups can be used to manage resources on any computer that participates in the domain.

App
J

Question #19

Gateway (and Client) Services for NetWare require what to function:
(Pick one)

A. A user with membership in an NTGATEWAY group on the Windows NT Server

B. A user with membership in an NTGATEWAY group on the Novell NetWare Server

C. Supervisor access to the Novell NetWare Server

D. A Translation file which translates Windows NT user names to Novell NetWare user names

Question #20

What hardware RAID configurations can be implemented?

A. 0

B. 1

C. 5

D. 10

Question #21

In your network, you would like to remotely monitor traffic on all your Windows NT 4.0 Server and Workstation computers, as well as your Windows 95 computers. Which of the following steps needs to take place?

A. Install the Network Monitor agent on all the computers and the Windows NT Server 4.0 version of Network Monitor on the computer that will remotely monitor the computers.

B. Install the Network Monitor agent on all the computers and the SMS full version of Network Monitor on the computer that will remotely monitor the computers.

C. Install only the Windows NT Server 4.0 version of Network Monitor on the computer that will remotely monitor the computers.

D. Install only the SMS full version of Network Monitor on the computer that will remotely monitor the computers.

Question #22

You have created four printers. Each of them will be used by a specific group of users. Name all the steps which are required to successfully make the printer available to the appropriate users.

A. Share each printer.

B. Set the share permissions for each printer so that only the appropriate group has access.

C. Set the printer permissions for each printer so that only the appropriate group has access.

D. Create a printer pool so that each group can access all the print devices.

Question #23

You have decided to modify the logon process for all of your Windows NT users so that a legal notice displays before they log on, warning against unauthorized access. What would be the best way to accomplish this?

A. Use the Windows NT Registry Editor to modify the Legal Notice Caption and Legal Notice Text parameters for WINLOGON on each Windows NT computer.

B. Use the System applet in the Control Panel to set the values for Legal Notices on each of the Windows NT computers.

C. Use the System Policy Editor to create a default policy for every Windows NT computer that contains the appropriate legal notice settings and store it in the NETLOGON share of every domain controller.

D. Use the Legal Notice utility from the Resource Kit to set these values remotely for each Windows NT computer.

Question #24

I have booted Windows NT and received the message:

Windows NT could not start because the following file is missing or corrupt: \winnt root\system32\ntoskrnl.exe

How can I recover this file?

A. Boot with the Emergency Repair Disk and choose Verify Windows NT System Files.

B. Boot with the Windows NT Startup disk, choose Repair, and then Verify Windows NT System Files from the Emergency Repair Disk.

C. Find a working Windows NT computer and use the EXPAND command to expand the compressed version of this file from the installation source directory. Then copy the file to the system directory on the problem computer.

D. Boot with a Windows NT Boot Disk and copy the file from this disk.

Question #25

Which of the following keys in HKEY_LOCAL_MACHINE have corresponding directory files in the Windows NT system directory?

A. System

B. Software

C. Hardware

D. Security

Question #26

I have a large SQL server database on an application server. All employees have access to the data. What two resources can best improve performance?

A. More memory and a newer network interface card.

B. More memory and faster disk drive.

C. More memory and a second processor.

D. More network interface cards and more disk drives.

Question #27

There are three downward-compatible print devices connected to the print server in MIS. MIS Managers and Project Leaders should always be able to print to the first available printer. Help Desk staff and Developers should be able to print only to their specified print device. What will best accomplish this task?

A. Create a printer for each device and assign the appropriate groups access only to their printer. Give the Manager's printer a priority of 1, Help Desk's printer a priority of 50, and Developer's printer a priority of 99.

B. Create a printer for each device and assign the appropriate groups access only to their printer. Give the Manager's printer a priority of 99, Help Desk's printer a priority of 50, and Developer's printer a priority of 1.

C. Create a printer for each device and assign the appropriate groups access only to their printer. Make the Manager's printer a printer pool by associating it with each print device.

D. Create a printer for each device and assign the appropriate groups access only to their printer. Make each printer a printer pool by associating it with each print device.

Question #28

Which of the following sets of usernames and passwords are acceptable for Windows NT ?

Username – Password

A. First Ass't Comptroller – FirstComp

B. FirstAsstCompt – 1stComp

C. FirstAss*tCompt – COMP1

D. AssComp1 – 123COMPTROLLER1

Question #29

The Finance domain trusts the Marketing domain. What NetLogon function allows a user from the Marketing domain to log on and validate from a computer that participates in the Finance domain?

A. Directory Replication

B. Pass–Through Authentication

C. Trust Validation

D. Access Control Lists

Question #30

Team Leaders need to be able to modify files contained in the share TOOLS. While you were on vacation, your trusted sidekick modified the permissions for the share and the folder. The two exhibits show what the permissions look like now. Team Leaders complain that they are unable to modify their files. What should you do?

App
J

A. Fire your trusted sidekick.

B. Change the TOOLS NTFS permission for Team Leaders to Change, and the share permission to Read.

C. Change the TOOLS NTFS permission for the Team Leaders to Change.

D. Remove Team Leaders from the ACL for the TOOLS share.

Question #31

The ABCCorp domain is configured as a Master Domain model. 5000 user accounts are managed in the ABC-MIS domain in Chicago. Resource domains trust ABC-MIS. At the ABC-WEST resource domain, the print administrator is managing access to her printers by adding the appropriate user accounts from ABC-MIS to the ACL for each of five printers. Access will be managed for 300 users. ABC-WEST is connected to ABC-MIS via a slow WAN link. Every time she accesses the ABC-MIS account domain to display the list of users, the list takes several seconds to generate. The process is taking longer than she thinks it should. What can you suggest to improve performance and minimize network traffic? Choose the best answer.

A. Upgrade the WAN link to a higher speed.

B. Create local groups on the print servers in ABC-WEST and add the users to the local groups. Use the local groups to assign printer permissions.

C. Create global groups in ABC-MIS for the users that need printer access in ABC-WEST. Add the global groups to local groups on the print servers in ABC-WEST, and assign printer permissions to the local groups.

D. There is nothing you can do to improve performance. The same amount of trust traffic is generated whether you use user accounts or group accounts across the trust.

Question #32

The BOOT.INI file on my computer looks like this:

[Boot Loader]

timeout=15

default=multi(0)disk(2)rdisk(1)partition(3)\winnt40

[Operating Systems]

multi(0)disk(2)rdisk(1)partition(3)\winnt40=Windows NT 4.0 Workstation

multi(0)disk(2)rdisk(1)partition(3)\winnt40=Windows NT 4.0 Workstation [VGA Mode] /basevideo c:\=MS-DOS

What can I infer from this file?

A. The timeout value before Windows NT loads is 15 seconds. Windows NT system files can be found on the third partition of the second physical disk attached to the first controller card.

B. The timeout value before Windows NT loads is 15 seconds, and DOS is the default operating system.

C. The timeout value before Windows NT loads is 15 seconds. Windows NT system files can be found on the third partition of the first physical disk attached to the first controller card.

D. The controller card is a SCSI adapter.

Question #33

Which tool(s) can you use to remotely manage shares across the domain?

A. User Manager for Domains

B. Server Manager

C. Windows Explorer

D. Network Neighborhood

Question #34

A DHCP server eliminates the need to manually configure:

A. A DHCP scope

B. A WINS database

C. An IP address and subnet mask for DHCP clients

D. An IP address and subnet mask for non-DHCP clients

Question #35

What would happen if the Netlogon ReplicationGovernor parameter were set to a value of 0?

A. PDC to BCD synchronization would never occur.

B. PDC to BCD synchronization would occur every 100 seconds.

C. Is the default ReplicationGovernor parameter value.

D. PDC to BCD synchronization would occur every 100 minutes.

Question #36

One factor that will definitely affect the type of domain model that you implement is:

A. The number of user and group accounts.

B. The physical location and grouping of users.

C. The type of wide area network connections you have in place.

D. The location of network servers.

Question #37

Which of the following are requirements for setting up a successful trust relationship? Choose all that apply.

A. A domain controller in each domain must be up and accessible.

B. There can be no current sessions between the PDCs of each domain.

C. You must have an administrator-level account.

D. You must have access to a computer running User Manager for Domains.

Question #38

By pausing the Netlogon service on the PDC, the PDC will continue to:

A. Perform logon validations.

B. Perform directory services database synchronization with the BDCs.

C. Perform pass-through authentication.

D. Perform logon validation but not pass-through authentication.

Question #39

After monitoring your heavily accessed file and print server, you determine that both the Server>Pool Paged Failures and Server>Pool Nonpaged Failures counters are unusually and consistently higher than normal. The Server service memory property is configured for Balanced memory usage. What should you do to reduce the number of Pool Paged and Pool Nonpaged failures?

A. Add more memory. Balanced is an appropriate setting for a file and print server.

B. Change the Server service memory configuration to Minimize Memory Used.

C. Change the Server service memory configuration to Maximize Throughput for File Sharing.

D. Change the Server service memory configuration to Load Balance Throughput for Virtual Memory.

Question #40

The TOOLS folder has been shared to the Developers group with Change permission. DOOM is a subdirectory under TOOLS. Team Leaders should have access only to DOOM with Read permissions. What can you do to accomplish this?

A. Add Team Leaders to the TOOLS share with Read permission.

B. Create a new share called DOOM and give Team Leaders Read permission to it.

C. Add Team Leaders to the TOOLS share with Change permission.

D. Add Team Leaders to the TOOLS share with No Access and to the DOOM subdirectory with Read.

Question #41

Which of the following features is provided by the full version of Network Monitor that comes with Microsoft's System Management Server? Choose all that apply.

A. Direct monitoring of remote computer traffic.

B. Determining which protocol consumed the most bandwidth.

C. Identifying which physical disk has the most I/O activity for a network session.

D. Capturing local network traffic to and from the computer running the utility.

Question #42

As the manager of the MIS department, you would like to delegate responsibility for remote management of the Windows NT registries on all the domain controllers to three key staff members. These three are members of the Domain Admins global group for the domain, as are all your staff members. How would you restrict remote access to the appropriate three persons?

A. Give the Remote Command Service utilities only to those three persons.

B. Modify the ACL for the HKEY_LOCAL_MACHINE\System\ CurrentControlSet\Control\SecurePipeServers\Winreg subkey on each domain controller so that only those three persons have access.

C. Modify the RemoteAccess parameter values for HKEY_LOCAL_MACHINE\System\CurrentControlSet\ Control\RemoteControl subkey on each domain controller so that only those three persons are listed.

D. Do nothing. Only these three can remotely manage the Registry by default.

Question #43

Your assistant called and wants to know why he cannot use his server tools from his Windows 95 client with a 386DX/66. Your answer is:

A. He does not have the correct protocol.

B. Insufficient hardware.

C. He is not Backup operator.

D. The server is off-line.

Question #44

When does pass-through authentication occur?

A. When logging on from a member server to a domain.

B. When logging on to a workstation.

C. When logging on from a workstation to a domain.

D. When logging on from a workstation to a trusted domain.

Question #45

You have modified NTFS permissions for the file DOOM.DOC so that Team Leaders have Full Control. For all other files and folders, Team Leaders should have Read access. Using the exhibit, how can you best accomplish this?

App

J

A. Select Replace Permissions on Subdirectories and deselect Replace Permissions on Existing Files.

B. Select Replace Permissions on Subdirectories.

C. Deselect Replace Permissions on Existing Files.

D. Set permissions on each file and folder individually.

Question #46

An IP address consists of what two parts in the following order from left to right?

A. A network address and a workstation address

B. A workstation address and a network address

C. A subnet mask address and a default gateway address

D. A default gateway address and a subnet mask address

Question #47

The manager of the Accounting department wants to make next year's budget templates available for the staff accountants to review beginning next month. Staff accountants are already members of a global group called Accountants in CORPDOMAIN. The templates will be stored on the department resource server called ACCT1 in a folder called BUDGET97 on an NTFS partition. The folder has been shared with the default permission. The global accountants group has been added to a local group called Accountants on ACCT1. You would like everyone to be able to see the files, but only the accounting staff should be able to make changes. What do you need to do?

A. Change the share permission to only Accountants with Change permission.

B. Assign the Accountants group the NTFS permission Change to the BUDGET97 folder.

C. Change the share permission to Everyone with No Access and assign the Accountants group the NTFS permission Change for the BUDGET97 folder.

D. Change the share permission to Everyone with Read and assign the Accountants group the NTFS permission Change for the BUDGET97 folder.

Question #48

A print job can be directed directly to a UNIX host print device, and its status checked using which two command-line utilities?

A. LPD and LPR

B. LPD and LPQ

C. LPR and IPCONFIG

D. LPR and LPQ

Question #49

The Security Accounts Manager (SAM) database is approximately 15M. What is the recommended memory size?

A. 24M

B. 32M

C. 48M

D. 64M

Question #50

You just created a startup disk with the ne2000 interface card selected and NetBEUI. You installed the disk and cannot connect to the server. What may be the problem?

A. Old NIC driver.

B. DHCP server is off-line.

C. Server only uses NetBEUI.

D. Server only uses TCP/IP.

Question #51

A Windows NT Server has been configured with striping across 6 disk drives and one of the drives has failed to spin up. How can you recover your data?

A. Add the new drive and select Regenerate.

B. Add the new drive and do nothing. Windows NT does it automatically.

C. Create a new stripe set and restore data from the backup.

D. Delete the stripe set and add it back.

Question #52

A broadcast frame:

A. Is always directed to a specific computer by its IP, IPX, or MAC address.

B. Is sent to all hosts on the network via the unique destination address FFFFFFFF.

C. Is sent to a subset of computers on the network depending on how the computer has registered itself on the network.

D. Is a multicast frame that is directed to a specific computer on the network.

Question #53

Which of the following steps need to take place before a file session can be established between two computers using the TCP/IP protocol? Choose all that apply.

A. The user must register its name with the WINS server.

B. Name resolution must take place.

C. Address resolution must take place.

D. A TCP Session must be established.

Question #54

Arlo, a member of the Developers group, is currently editing the file DOOM.DOC in the share TOOLS. The administrator of the share changes permission to the Developers group from Change to Read. Arlo continues to make changes to the document. What else must the administrator do to restrict Arlo's access?

A. Take Arlo out of the Developers group.

B. Give Arlo No Access explicitly.

C. Disconnect Arlo from the resource.

D. Nothing. Arlo must disconnect from the share and then reconnect before the new permission will take effect.

Question #55

You need to be able to remotely manage the account database on two trusted domains. Which steps must take place for this to happen successfully?

A. Do nothing. You can remotely manage accounts through a trust by default.

B. Use User Manager for domains and choose User, Select Domain from the menu to choose the remote domain you want to administer.

C. Make your account a member of the Account Operators group in the trusted domains.

D. Give your user account Full Control access to the SAM hive file in WINNT\SYSTEM32\CONFIG.

Question #56

Under what circumstances might a full database synchronization take place between a PDC and a BDC? Choose the best two.

A. Every synchronization event replicates the entire account databases.

B. Full synchronization occurs when the BDC is first installed.

App
J

C. Full synchronization may occur when the change log on the PDC becomes full and begins to overwrite existing information before the PDC can contact the BDC for updates.

D. Only changes are copied whenever synchronization occurs.

Question #57

ABCCorp network consists of 5,000 users located in three office locations: New York, Chicago, and San Francisco. The current plan is to locate one PDC and one BDC in the corporate headquarters in Chicago. How could you optimize this configuration to make logging on more efficient for the users and minimize network traffic? Choose the best two answers.

A. Create two more BDCs to accommodate the 5,000 users. Microsoft recommends one BDC for every 2,000 users.

B. Create a trust relationship among all the offices.

C. Locate one BDC in each location so that logon validation takes place locally.

D. Do nothing. This configuration is optimized.

Question #58

Under what circumstances will the Last Known Good control set load automatically?

A. If the system itself detects a critical error during the boot process, it will automatically load Last Known Good.

B. If the system detects an ErrorControl value of 0 or 1, it will automatically load Last Known Good.

C. If the system detects a failed control set, it will automatically load Last Known Good on the next boot.

D. Last Known Good is always selected from the screen during the boot process.

Question #59

What types of network traffic are associated with the DHCP service?

   A. DHCP Address Request

   B. DHCP Lease Renewal

   C. DHCP Time Out

   D. DHCP Replication

Question #60

A user is having problems logging on to the network and is seeing a variety of messages. Which of the following things would you check to troubleshoot?

   A. The user is entering the correct username and password.

   B. The username is case-sensitive.

   C. The domain controller is up and accessible.

   D. The user's account requires a mandatory profile that is accessible.

Question #61

From the choices below, list the steps required to install a network interface printer using the DLC protocol.

   A. Install the DLC protocol on the print server and shutdown and restart.

   B. Start the Print Wizard, select Add Printer, then select Add Port.

   C. Select the Hewlett-Packard Network Port and click the New Port button.

   D. Select a MAC address from the available addresses and supply a printer name in the Add Hewlett-Packard Network Peripheral Port dialog box.

App
J

Question #62

Which print monitor is loaded with TCP/IP and tracks print jobs targeted for TCP/IP print hosts?

   A. IPMON.DLL

   B. LPDMON.DLL

   C. LPRMON.DLL

   D. LOCALMON.DLL

Question #63

The master boot record of Sal's Windows NT computer became corrupted and he can no longer boot to Windows NT. How can you restore the master boot record on Sal's computer?

   A. Create a Windows NT boot disk with the NTLDR file on it. Boot from this disk and copy the NTLDR file from it to the system partition of Sal's computer.

   B. Create an Emergency Repair Disk. Boot from this disk and choose Inspect Boot Sector from the menu to repair the master boot record.

   C. Create an Emergency Repair Disk. Boot from a Windows NT startup disk and choose Repair, using the Emergency Repair Disk when prompted. Choose Inspect Boot Sector to repair the MBR.

   D. Create a Windows NT boot disk with the NTLDR file and the fixdisk.exe program on it. Boot from this disk and run fixdisk /c: where c: is the system partition.

Question #64

Which Windows NT Server service allows a user to log on at computers in domains in which they have no account through the trust relationship to a computer or domain in which they do have an account?

   A. NetLogon Service

   B. Directory Replication Service

C. Account Synchronization Service

D. Self Service

Question #65

For CrashDumps to be obtained, the pagefile must be at least _____ megabytes larger than the physical size of memory.

A. 1

B. 2

C. 4

D. 8

Question #66

There are three hundred Windows NT and Windows 95 client computers that print to five printers on a print server. You have received upgraded print drivers for two of the print devices connected to this print server. What must you do to ensure that all clients can continue to access all the print devices?

A. Install the upgraded print drivers on all the client computers that need to use those print devices.

B. Install the upgraded print drivers on all the client computers.

C. Install the upgraded print drivers only on the Windows NT client computers.

D. Do nothing. The print server can download the new drivers to the clients the next time they make a print request.

Question #67

Your boss has advised you that BrownC has left the company and asks that you delete his account. Later, your boss hires BrownC back as a consultant and tells you to put his account back on the network. BrownC calls you the next day and informs you gruffly that he can no longer access any of the network resources that he used to. How do you troubleshoot?

A. Use the Registry to set BrownC's SID back to what it was before you deleted his account. He will then be able to access all the old resources.

B. Deleting BrownC's account also deleted his SID. Because security in Windows NT is linked to the user's SID, you will need to reestablish all the network resource access that BrownC used to have.

C. Use the Emergency Repair Disk or your last network backup to copy BrownC's old account back to the Registry.

D. Leave the company and get hired back as a consultant yourself.

Question #68

Protocols are installed by accessing the network icon in the Control Panel and:

A. Selecting the Protocol tab and selecting the Add button.

B. Selecting the Protocol tab and selecting the protocol.

C. Selecting the Protocol tab and choosing all protocols.

D. Selecting the Protocol tab, nothing else has to be selected.

Question #69

To create a Macintosh Accessible Volume on the server, you must have which of the following?

A. Pentium 166Mhz processor

B. FAT partition

C. NTFS partition

D. Windows NT Workstation

Question #70

The Finance domain users need to access a laser printer in the Marketing domain. The Marketing domain users need to access a scanner in the Finance domain. How many trust relationships need to be created to facilitate the sharing of these two network resources?

A. Create one two-way trust relationship between Finance and Marketing.

B. Create two one-way trust relationships, one from Finance to Marketing and the other from Marketing to Finance.

C. Create two one-way trust relationships from Finance to Marketing. One can handle the shared laser printer, and the other the scanner.

D. Create one trust relationship between Finance and Marketing. A trust relationship is always bidirectional.

Question #71

Which objects would be most beneficial to include in a log file when creating a baseline measurement of your system's performance? Choose all that apply.

A. Memory

B. TCP/IP

C. Processor

D. Physical and Logical Disk

Question #72

Elaine was the print administrator for the LotsOf Print Corporation, but has left the country to pursue a career as an opera singer. You need to assign a new print administrator. What will you need to do concerning ownership of the LotsOf Print Corporation printers that Elaine created and managed?

A. Do nothing. Printers are not owned by a user; they are owned by the system.

B. Make the new print administrator a Print Operator. The new print administrator can then take ownership of the printers in LotsOf Print Corporation.

C. Give ownership of the printers to the new print administrator.

D. Give the new administrator Full Control permission over the printers. Full Control automatically assigns ownership to that user.

Question #73

Which Process object counter would be useful in determining the amount of memory required by an application?

A. %Application Memory

B. Commit Limit

C. Working Set

D. Avg. Disk sec\Transfer

Question #74

Your assistant called and wants to know why he cannot use his Server tool User Manager for Domains from his Windows 95 client. Your answer is:

A. He does not have the correct protocol.

B. He needs Windows NT Workstation.

C. He is not an administrator.

D. The server is off-line.

Question #75

There is one high-speed network print device connected to the print server in MIS. MIS Managers and Project Leaders should always be able to print to this printer regardless of who has submitted print jobs. Help Desk staff should be able to print ahead of Developers. What will best accomplish this task?

A. Create three printers, each associated with the device, and assign the appropriate groups access only to their printer. Give the Manager's printer a priority of 1, Help Desk's printer a priority of 50, and Developer's printer a priority of 99.

B. Create three printers, each associated with the device, and assign the appropriate groups access only to their printer. Give the Manager's printer a priority of 99, Help Desk's printer a priority of 50, and Developer's printer a priority of 1.

C. Create three printers, each associated with the device, and assign the appropriate groups access only to their printer. Make the Manager's printer a printer pool by associating it with each print device.

D. Create three printers associated with the device and assign the appropriate groups access only to their printer. Make each printer a printer pool by associating it with each print device.

Question #76

What server administrative tool is used to copy the server tools from the CD-ROM and automatically create a shared folder?

A. Network Server Tools Administrator

B. Network Client Administrator

C. Network Server Tools Manager

D. Network Server Manager

Question #77

You plan to create a policy file that will be used by all the users in your domain. You want certain default settings for the users and their Windows NT computers to be downloaded automatically when they log on. You also will assign specific settings to specific users and groups. Which of the following steps need to take place to accomplish this goal?

A. Modify the Default Computer policy options as desired.

B. Create a system policy file called NTCONFIG.POL and save it in the NETLOGON share of each domain controller.

C. Set individual policy options for the specific users and groups.

D. Create separate system policy files for each user and group and save these in the users' home directories.

Question #78

Michelle has been selected to assist you as a print administrator in the Dry Gulch office, since you, yourself, are unable to travel there frequently, though you'd really like to. What is the minimum level of access you need to give Michelle so that she can perform basic print management tasks such as creating and sharing printers and managing print jobs?

A. Make Michelle a member of the Print Operators local group on her print server.

B. Make Michelle a member of the Server Operator local group on her print server.

C. Make Michelle a member of the Administrators local group on her print server.

D. Give Michelle Full Control permission for each printer on her print server.

Question #79

You want to give a particular domain user the ability to back up files on a server, but not be able to restore files. How can you accomplish this?

A. Make the domain user a member of the Backup Operators group on the server.

B. Make the domain user a member of the Server Operators group on the server.

C. Create a new local group called BACKUP ONLY on the server and make the domain user a member of it. Assign this new group to the Backup Files and Directories User Right.

D. Give the user read-only access to all the files.

Question #80

Your workstations are members of a domain called Titan. You need to create user accounts so that two shifts of temporary employees can log on to the same computer, but only during their shift.

A. Use User Manager for domains on each local Windows NT Workstation to create the temporary accounts and assign each the appropriate logon hours.

B. Use User Manager on each local Windows NT Workstation to create the temporary accounts and assign each the appropriate logon hours.

C. Use User Manager for domains on the domain controller for Titan to create domain accounts for the temporary employees and assign each the appropriate logon hours.

D. Use User Manager on the domain controller for Titan to create local group accounts for the temporary employees and assign each the appropriate logon hours.

Question #81

Network types can have network numbers or network ranges associated with them. Which type of network can have only one network number associated with it?

A. LocalTalk

B. EtherTalk

C. TokenTalk

D. FDDI

Question #82

The permission list defining access to a resource resides:

A. With the resource and is called the Access Control List.

B. With the user and is called the User Rights Policy.

C. With the user and is called the Access Control List.

D. With the resource and is called the User Rights Policy.

Question #83

You suspect that someone is trying to log on to the network unauthorized. What is the best step you can take to increase security and determine who might be doing this?

A. Enable Account Lockout in the Account Policy requiring the Administrator to unlock the account.

B. Enable Account Lockout in the Account Policy requiring the Administrator to unlock the account. Enable auditing of unsuccessful logons and logoffs and monitor these events in the Event Viewer.

C. Advise users to change their passwords more frequently and not to use obvious passwords.

D. Increase the minimum password length in Account Policy.

Question #84

If the AppleTalk protocol is installed on a Windows NT Workstation, other Windows NT users on the network can use the workstation:

A. To create Macintosh Accessible Volumes on Macintosh computers

B. To access Macintosh Accessible Volumes on Macintosh computers

C. To access Macintosh Accessible Volumes on the workstation and share files with Macintosh users

D. As a print server

Question #85

Which type of frames are involved in connecting to a shared resource once the session has been established?

A. SMB session frames.

B. WINS resolution frames.

C. NBT broadcast frames.

D. TCP request frames.

Question #86

When a computer registers with a WINS server, how many name registration frames are generated?

A. One name is registered for each computer.

B. A name is registered for the computer and for every service or application that supports the NetBIOS API. One frame registers all these names.

C. A name is registered for the computer and for every service or application that supports the NetBIOS API. One frame is generated for each name that needs to be registered.

D. NetBIOS names are not registered with the WINS server.

Question #87

You have upgraded your Windows NT 3.5 FTP server to Windows NT 4.0. The plan for this machine is to make it an IIS. You are having trouble setting up the service and it will not complete. Why not?

A. WINS is not running.

B. DHCP is not running.

C. Gopher needs to be installed first.

D. FTP is still installed.

Question #88

The print device associated with a particular printer has failed. Several print jobs are waiting in queue in that printer. How can you service these print jobs?

A. Connect to another remote printer. Open the printer manager window for the printer and drag the waiting print jobs to the remote printer manager window.

B. Use the Ports tab properties for the printer to add a port for another remote printer. Deselect the current print port associated with the printer and select the remote port. Resume the printer.

C. Do nothing. You must replace the failed print device before printing can resume.

D. Use the Control Panel applet Services to stop the spooler service, configure it to connect to another remote printer, and restart it.

Question #89

Indicate the utility used from the command prompt to manually maintain an IPX routing table.

A. Route

B. IPXRoute

C. IPConfig

D. PING

Question #90

Under which of the following situations would you disable the user account rather than deleting it?

A. JaneD has left the company on maternity leave and plans to return in three months.

B. JohnB has taken an emergency medical leave of absence for possibly six or more months, but hopes to return full time.

C. JaniceD has left the company to take a job at Microsoft.

D. FrankP has taken a temporary team leader position in another department and will return when the project is completed.

Question #91

You are using a RISC-based computer as your print server. All your clients are either MS-DOS, Windows for Workgroups, Windows 95, or Windows NT running on Intel-based computers. What must you do to ensure that all your clients can print to the print devices managed by the RISC-based print server?

A. Install both RISC-based and Intel print drivers on the RISC-based print server. Install the appropriate print drivers only on the MS-DOS and Windows for Workgroups computers.

B. Install both RISC-based and Intel print drivers on the RISC-based print server. The client computers will receive the appropriate platform driver from the print server when they make a print request.

C. Install RISC-based print drivers on the RISC-based print server and Intel print drivers on the client computers. Windows NT will do the platform translation.

D. Install the Intel print drivers on the RISC-based print server and RISC-based print drivers on the client computers.

Question #92

Kite Flyers Corporation has two global locations, London and New York. MIS manages the users in both locations in two account domains. There are five departments: Accounting, Marketing, MIS, HR, and Corporate. Each has its own set of network resources that its staff accesses, and some resources that everyone in the company uses.

Primary Goals: Give all employees a single logon account that they can use to access their resources. Let MIS be able to manage the account domains from any location. Let each department manage its own resources. Let certain delegated users act as print operators for printers in each department.

Secondary Goals: Centralize resources by department. Let all delegated users be able to manage any domain's printers. Allow as much flexibility as possible for printer management.

Solution: Implement a Single Domain model. Have all resource servers become members of the domain. Create a global group called KFPRINT. Add KFPRINT to the local Print Operators group on the print servers in each domain.

A. The solution satisfies none of the goals.

B. The solution satisfies all the primary goals and all the secondary goals.

C. The solution satisfies all primary goals but only one secondary goal.

D. The solution satisfies two primary goals and two secondary goals.

Question #93

Audit events are placed in the _____ log in Event Viewer.

A. System

B. Security

C. Application

D. Audit

Question #94

Which technology allows RAS to utilize two ISDN channels? (Pick one)

A. PPTP

B. PPP

C. Multi-link PPP

D. SLIP

Question #95

If the final print output is corrupted, what print process component should you check?

A. Spooler service on the client computer.

B. Spooler service on the print server.

C. Print processor on the print server.

D. Print monitor on the client computer.

Question #96

Call back security can be setup how? (Pick all that apply)

A. Not to call back.

B. To call back to a predefined number.

C. To call back to a user assigned number.

D. To call back and require a voice print match.

Question #97

For CrashDumps to be obtained, a pagefile must exist on the

A. System partition

B. Boot partition

C. NTFS partition

D. Data partition

Question #98

On your Windows NT 4.0 development workstation, you have concluded that performance as a whole has decreased. You are not sure which process is driving this, but you have noticed that your disk drive has had a lot more activity lately. What objects should you monitor through Performance Monitor to help you troubleshoot this situation?

A. Check the Processor>%Processor Time counter, determine the percent of disk I/O used for paging through the Memory>Pages/ Sec counter and the Logical Disk>Avg. Disk sec/Transfer counter, and the Process>Working Set for every process running.

B. Check the Processor>%Processor Time counter, determine the percent of disk I/O used for paging through the Memory>Pages/ Sec counter and the Logical Disk>Avg. Disk sec/Transfer counter. Track the Process>%Processor Time counter for every process running to determine which processes are pushing the processor excessively. Monitor the Process>Working Set counter for these processes in particular.

C. Check the Processor>%Processor Time counter, determine the percent of disk I/O used for paging through the Logical Disk>Disk Queue Length counter, and the Process>Working Set for every process running.

D. Check the Processor>%User Time counter, determine the percent of disk I/O used for paging through the Logical Disk>%Disk Time counter, and the Memory>Commit Limit counter for the pagefile.

Question #99

What programs can be used to troubleshoot RAS? (Pick all that apply)

A. Network Monitor

B. Dial-Up Networking Monitor

C. Remote Access Admin

D. Performance Monitor

Question #100

Which of the following actions can serve to optimize network traffic associated with Directory Replication? Choose all that apply.

A. Lock directories that are not replicated frequently, or that you do not want to have replicated.

B. Maintain a shallow export directory tree structure.

C. Modify the interval value on the export server so that it does not check for changes in the export tree as frequently.

D. Remove the password from the Directory Replication service account.

Question #101

What clients are supported for the Internet Explorer?

A. Microsoft Windows

B. Lan Manager 2.2c for OS2

C. UNIX

D. Microsoft Windows 95

Question #102

Kernel Debugger commands can be entered after a
_____ key sequence is entered.

A. Ctrl,G

B. Ctrl,C

C. Ctrl,K

D. Ctrl,Q

Question #103

App

J

Which of the following characteristics best apply to a workgroup network model? Choose two.

A. A workgroup network model provides a high level of security for
resource access.

B. The workgroup model is best applied to smaller (fewer than 20)
workstation groups.

C. A workgroup model is identified by its domain controller.

D. Each Windows NT computer participating in a workgroup must
maintain a list of users that will be accessing the resources on that
computer.

Question #104

Which tool(s) can you use to remotely manage file and folder permissions across the domain?

A. User Manager for Domains

B. Server Manager

C. Windows Explorer

D. Network Neighborhood

Question #105

RAS Supports what protocols? (Pick all that apply)

A. TCP/IP

B. IPX/SPX

C. NetBEUI

D. DLC

Question #106

While tracking the performance of disk activity on a system, you notice that the measured value is always 0 although the disk appears to be heavily used. What is your evaluation of this situation?

A. The disk is a high performance unit and can handle the heavy disk I/O.

B. The wrong disk objects and counters have been selected for Performance Monitor.

C. The disk counters have not been enabled by typing DISKPERF - Y at a command prompt.

D. The disk has crashed.

Question #107

In the ABC enterprise, it has been determined that the MIS department will manage all user and group accounts, while each department in the organization should be able to administer its own resources using the same enterprise account database without having to worry about user management. Which response best answers this need?

A. All resources and accounts must participate in the same domain. Establish one domain controller, create all the user and group accounts, and then let each resource administrator assign permissions to their resources.

B. The MIS department will be given its own domain called the account domain from which they can create and manage all user and group accounts. Each department could be given its own domain for the purpose of managing its own resources. The resource administrators can use the accounts from the account domain with no other modifications.

C. The MIS department will be given its own domain called the account domain from which they can create and manage all user and group accounts. Each department could be given its own domain for the purpose of managing its own resources. By creating trust relationships between the resource domains and the account domain, each resource manager will be able to secure their resources using the enterprise account database.

D. Directory Services does not support this type of management structure.

Question #108

Which of the following statements best represents Microsoft's groups strategy for the Master Domain model?

A. Create global groups in the resource domains to manage local resources. Create local groups in the account domain to manage users. Add the resource domains' global groups to the account domain's local groups.

B. Create local groups on the resource servers in the resource domains to manage access to resources. Group users into appropriate global groups in the account domain. Add the global groups from the account domain to the local groups in the resource domains.

C. Create local groups on the resource servers in the resource domains to manage access to resources. Create global groups in the resource domains and add to them global users from the account domain. Make the global groups from the resource domain members of the local groups on the resource servers.

D. Create local groups on the resource servers in the resource domains to manage access to resources. Add global users from the account domain to the local resource groups.

Question #109

Why is NetBEUI protocol routing not supported in Windows NT 4.0 installations?

A. Because NetBEUI maintains its own route tables and requires no additional services to handle routing.

B. Because NetBEUI cannot be installed on Windows NT 4.0 Server.

C. Because NetBEUI uses either RIP for IP or RIP for IPX, which-ever is installed.

D. Because NetBEUI is not a routable protocol.

Question #110

Which of the following parameters can be configured manually with the NWLink protocol?

A. IP address

B. Frame type

C. Subnet mask

D. DHCP scope

Question #111

From the choices below, indicate the step that is NOT required when installing and configuring a printing device using the TCP/IP protocol.

A. Enter the IP address of the remote controller servicing the print device in the Add LPR Compatible Printer dialog box.

B. Enter the name of the remote controller servicing the print device in the Add LPR Compatible Printer dialog box.

C. Enter the IP address of the print device in the Add LPR Compatible Printer dialog box.

D. Enter the IP address of the print server in the Add LPR Compatible Printer dialog box.

Question #112

Reference to the most recently installed Service pack Symbols files must be listed _____ in the Dumpexam utility command line.

  A. Last

  B. First after the normal Symbols files reference

  C. Second

  D. First

Question #113

I want to improve network printing for my users. What would be the best course of action?

  A. Make the local SQL server a print server, too.

  B. Add print services and more RAM to the existing file server.

  C. Add a print server to my PDC.

  D. Relocate a remote print server near the users.

Question #114

The default share name for the server tools share is:

  A. SrvTools

  B. ClientTools

  C. SetupAdm

  D. ServerTools

Question #115

You would like to modify the Registry settings of a remote Windows NT 4.0 computer so that users will receive a legal notice warning when they log on. Which of the following provides the best way of accomplishing this?

App

J

A. Use Server Manager and connect to the remote computer.

B. Use the System Policy Editor. Connect to the remote computer and open the local Registry.

C. Use User Profile Editor to make a UNC connection to the remote computer and access its Registry.

D. Microsoft does not support remote management of the Registry.

Question #116

Kite Flyers Corporation consists of 300 employees located in a single office complex. Which domain model would best suit this organization?

A. Single domain model

B. Master domain model

C. Multiple Master domain model

D. Complete Trust domain model

Question #117

What service must be installed on a Windows NT 4.0 Server to allow it to function as an AppleTalk router?

A. RPC

B. GSNW

C. FDDI

D. SFM

Question #118

When a TCP session is established, three frames are generated known as the TCP three-way handshake. Which of the following frames are part of the three-way handshake? Choose all that apply.

A. TCP Request from the client to the server.

B. TCP Name resolution request from the client to the WINS server.

C. TCP Request Acknowledgment from the server to the client.

D. TCP Session establishment from the client to the server.

Question #119

What Windows NT service provides pass-through authentication?

- A. Netlogon
- B. Browser
- C. Alerter
- D. Network DDE

Question #120

The third major area of a STOP screen displays?

- A. Debug Port Status Indicator Information
- B. BugCheck Information
- C. Driver Information
- D. Kernel Build Number and Stack Dump Information

App
J

Question #121

Which statement best represents Microsoft's recommended group strategy for managing resources effectively?

- A. Create a local group in the domain database and add the users from the domain to that local group. Create a local group on the resource computer and make the domain local group a member of the resource local group.
- B. Create a global group in the domain database and add the users from the domain to that global group. Create a global group on the resource computer and make the domain global group a member of the resource global group.
- C. Create a global group in the domain database and add the users from the domain to that global group. Create a local group on the resource computer and make the domain global group a member of the resource local group.
- D. Create a local group on the resource computer and add the domain users directly to the local group.

Question #122

The identity of the domain is established by the implementation of:

A. A Windows NT 4.0 Server.

B. Any Windows NT 4.0 Workstation or Server that maintains an account database.

C. A domain controller.

D. A peer-to-peer network model.

Question #123

The Finance domain trusts the Marketing domain. The Finance domain shares a color laser printer that the CAD users in Marketing need to use from time to time. There is a global group in Marketing called CAD USERS. There is a local group on the print server in Finance called COLOR USERS that has Print permission to the color laser printer. How would you grant the Marketing CAD users permission to the color laser printer? Select the best answer (Microsoft's recommended solution).

A. In the Permissions dialog box for the color laser printer, choose Add and select the Marketing domain from the list of valid domains. Then select CAD USERS from the list of global groups in the Marketing database.

B. Add the CAD USERS global group from Marketing to the COLOR USERS local group on the print server.

C. Create a global group in Finance called MARKETING CAD USERS. Add the CAD USERS global group from Marketing to the MARKETING CAD USERS global group in Finance. Then add the MARKETING CAD USERS global group to the COLOR USERS local group on the print server.

D. You can't do this because the trust is in the wrong direction.

Question #124

What types of traffic are associated with the WINS service?

A. WINS Registration

B. WINS Time Out

C. WINS Query Request

D. WINS Address Request

Question #125

The following parameter values display in the Registry Editor when you select the HKEY_LOCAL_MACHINE\System\CurrentControlSet\Services\Replicator subkey:

DependOnGroup: REG_MULTI_SZ:

DependOnService: REG_MULTI_SZ: LanmanWorkstation LanmanServer

DisplayName: REG_SZ: Directory Replicator

ErrorControl: REG_DWORD: 0x1

ImagePath: REG_EXPAND_SZ: %SystemRoot%\System32\lmrepl.exe

ObjectName: REG_SZ: LocalSystem

Start: REG_DWORD: 0x3

Type: REG_DWORD: 0x10

Which of the following statements can be inferred from these settings? Choose all that apply.

A. The Directory Replicator service has no group dependencies.

B. The Directory Replicator service depends on the LanmanWorkstation and LanmanServer services being loaded successfully.

C. If the Directory Replicator service does not load, the boot process will still continue.

D. If the Directory Replicator service does not load, the Last Known Good control set is loaded automatically.

Question #126

While looking at the files on my RISC-based computer, I notice that NTLDR, NTDETECT.COM, and BOOT.INI are missing. What impact will this have on the boot process on this computer?

A. The boot process relies on these files to govern the boot and load phases. Missing or corrupt files will result in error messages and failed boots.

B. It will have no impact on the boot process because RISC-based computers do not rely on these files.

C. The BOOT.INI is not an essential file. Windows NT will look for the default Windows NT system directory.

D. NTLDR is always needed to direct the boot process. NTDETECT.COM and BOOT.INI are not necessary on RISC-based computers.

Question #127

Your assistant called and wants to know why he cannot set up his mirrored disk on his workstation. Your answer is:

A. He does not have the correct password.

B. Only RAID5 is available for workstations.

C. Striping with no parity is not available for workstations.

D. RAID1 is not available to workstations.

Question #128

The person that created DOOM.DOC on server ACCT1 is no longer with the company. Cathy, a member of Team Leaders, will be assuming responsibility for the DOOM project, and needs to become the owner of DOOM.DOC. How can this be accomplished? Choose all that apply.

A. Give Cathy the Take Ownership of Files and Folders User Right on the server ACCT1.

B. Give Cathy the Take Ownership permission on the file DOOM.DOC.

C. Tell Cathy to just take ownership of the file.

D. Give the Team Leaders group the Take Ownership permission for DOOM.DOC.

Question #129

To provide a greater level of security, you have decided to create an account policy that requires a minimum password length of eight characters, requires that users change their passwords at least once a month, and does not allow users to use the same password twice in two months. Which Account Policy settings are appropriate?

A. Max Password Age: 60; Min Password Age: 30; Min Password Length: 8; Password Uniqueness: 2

B. Max Password Age: 30; Min Password Age: 30; Min Password Length: 8; Password Uniqueness: 6

C. Max Password Age: 30; Min Password Age: 10; Min Password Length: 8; Password Uniqueness: 6

D. Max Password Age: 60; Min Password Age: 30; Min Password Length: 8; Password Uniqueness: 1

Question #130

What kind of connection can be established between the Host computer and the Target computer for the Host computer to monitor the Boot process on the Target computer?

A. Null Modem connection using a COM port

B. Normal Network connection using a Network Adapter Card

C. Modem connection using a COM port

D. Modem connection using a LPT port

Question #131

The Finance domain trusts the Marketing domain. The Marketing domain trusts the Accounting domain. Users in the Accounting domain need to access a database resource in the Finance domain. What needs to happen to facilitate the sharing of that resource?

A. Nothing. Because Finance already trusts Marketing and Marketing already trusts Accounting, Finance can share the database resource directly to Accounting users through the trusts.

B. Create a one-way trust from the Accounting domain to the Finance domain.

C. Create a one-way trust from the Finance domain to the Accounting domain.

D. Create a reverse trust from Accounting to Marketing, and from Marketing to Finance.

Question #132

How can you determine which ControlSet entry refers to the Last Known Good control set?

A. The ControlSet entry with the highest number increment is always the Last Known Good control set.

B. Look at the control set number referenced by the LastKnownGood parameter entry for the HKEY_LOCAL_MACHINE\SYSTEM\Select subkey.

C. Restart the computer and load the Last Known Good control set, noting which control set number Windows NT displays on the screen.

D. Use Windows Diagnostics to find which control set maps to Last Known Good.

Question #133

Indicate the two files that contain settings that must be appended to the Config.sys and Autoexec.bat respectively when installing server tools on a Windows for Workgroups platform.

A. New-conf.sys and New-vars.bat

B. New-config.sys and New-vars.bat

C. New-vars.bat and New-config.sys

D. New-auto.bat and New-vars.sys

Question #134

The administrator of the TOOLS shared folder wants to limit access to the folder only to the Developers group. To accomplish this, she gives the Everyone group NO ACCESS, and the Developers group Change access. The Developers complain that they cannot access any file in TOOLS. What else must the administrator do?

A. Share the files in the TOOLS folder.

B. Remove the Everyone group.

C. Give the Developers group Full Control.

D. Format the partition as NTFS and assign NTFS permissions in addition to the share permissions.

Question #135

The KITEMASTERS corporate network consists of 6000 users located across five regional locations, each on its own subnet. About half the users have Windows NT Workstation 4.0 computers, and the rest have Windows 95 computers. These computers are frequently restarted throughout the day. There is one PDC and BDC located in the MIS department, and a BDC in each regional location. Each location also has one or more Windows NT Server 4.0 computers for resource management.

App
J

Using Network Monitor, you have noticed that there is an unusually high percentage of Browser traffic generated throughout the day. How can you optimize traffic associated with the Browser while letting users continue to browse for resources? Choose the best two answers.

A. You cannot configure Browser parameters.

B. Configure the Windows 95 and Windows NT Workstation 4.0 computers to never become browsers.

C. Disable the Server service on user computers which will not be sharing resources in the network.

D. Disable the Computer Browser service on all user computers.

Question #136

Built-in local groups and their members are contained in which accounts database?

A. SAM Accounts Database

B. Local Security Accounts Database

C. SAM Built-In Database

D. Account Synchronization Database

Question #137

Which of the following protocols is not considered routable?

A. TCP/IP

B. NetBEUI

C. NWLink

D. AppleTalk

Question #138

Pam is a manager in a training development corporation of 200 users using Windows NT Workstations connected over a LAN using the NetBEUI protocol. The corporation has just purchased a new office building. Pam decides to relocate 30 of the 200 users and computers to the new building and connect the two buildings together through a router. Now employees in the new building cannot see resources in the original facility, and the users in the original facility cannot connect to resources in the new building. Select the two best solutions to the problem.

A. Install NWLink on all workstations.

B. Install AppleTalk on all workstations.

C. Configure NetBEUI to use the router.

D. Install TCP/IP on all workstations.

Question #139

A DHCP reservation is assigned to a:

A. Computer

B. Network Adapter Card

C. Domain

D. Workgroup

Question #140

When configuring GSNW on Windows NT Server, a group called _____ must be set up on the Novell Server.

A. NTUserGateway

B. NovellGateway

C. NetBIOSGateway

D. NTGateway

Question #141

The Finance domain trusts the Marketing domain. You would like the administrators of the Marketing domain to be able to administer the servers in the Finance domain. What should you do to facilitate this?

A. Make the Domain Admins group from the Marketing domain a member of the local Administrators group on each server on the Finance domain.

B. Make the Administrators group from the Marketing domain a member of the local Administrators group on each server in the Finance domain.

C. Make the Domain Admins group from each server in the Finance domain a member of the local Administrators group in the Marketing domain.

D. Do nothing. When a trust is established, the Administrators group from the trusted domain is automatically added to the local administrator groups on the servers in the trusting domain.

Question #142

Which counter will provide you with the total percent of time spent servicing disk requests for a given partition on a disk?

A. Logical Disk>%Disk Time

B. Logical Disk>Disk Queue Length

C. Physical Disk>%Disk Time

D. Physical Disk>Disk Queue Length

Question #143

The DLC protocol is used on Windows NT 4.0 computers to:

A. Communicate with HP JetDirect printing devices

B. Communicate with AppleTalk Postscript printing devices

C. Communicate with Novell file servers and client computers

D. Communicate with IBM mainframes and front end processors

Question #144

Windows NT 4.0's Directory Services answers the enterprise challenge of providing one logon account and password by:

A. Having each member of the domain maintain a copy of the account database.

B. Allowing a user the ability to log on to any computer that is a member of the domain or the enterprise, and be able to access the same network resources.

C. Allowing a user the ability to log on only to any computer in their domain and access resources in that domain.

D. Making the user's logon account domain-independent.

Question #145

The Sales department recently acquired a laser quality printer with an envelope feed that has been installed on their print server called SalesPrint. The sales staff is already a member of the local group SALES on SalesPrint. The print operator shared the printer with the default permission. The sales staff can access the printer, but so can everyone else in the domain. What else must you do to ensure that only sales staff can access the printer?

A. Assign the Sales group print access to the printer.

B. Assign the Sales group print access to the printer, and remove the Everyone group.

C. Do nothing else.

D. Assign the Sales group print access to the printer, and give the Everyone group Read access.

Question #146

Fred is a member of the Developers group. The Developers group has been given the NTFS permission Full Control to the TOOLS folder. Fred is changing jobs and has been given NO ACCESS to the file DOOM.DOC, which is contained in the TOOLS folder. Later, Fred logs on and deletes the file DOOM.DOC. Luckily, you can restore the file from your tape backup. How can you prevent Fred from deleting the file again, but still maintain the original level of access for him and the Developers group?

A. Fire Fred.

B. Give the Developers group Special Access with all options selected for the TOOLS folder. Then give Fred NO ACCESS to the file.

C. Give the Developers group Change access at the folder level.

D. Give Fred NO ACCESS at the folder level.

Question #147

An IP address of 191.191.191.191 will have a default subnet mask of:

A. 255.255.255.0

B. 255.255.0.0

C. 255.0.0.0

D. 0.0.0.0

Question #148

You created a trust between Finance and Marketing so that users in the Marketing domain can access resources managed in the Finance domain. However, Marketing users are unable to access resources. What would you check?

A. Has the trust been completed by both domains?

B. Was the trust broken?

C. Has appropriate access been granted to the users?

D. Is the trust set up in the correct direction?

Question #149

When planning a large wide area network for an enterprise, Microsoft advocates implementing a structure that supports the following characteristics: (Choose all that apply)

A. Single network logon regardless of location or domain affiliation.

B. Easy user access to network resources regardless of the location of the user or the resource in the enterprise.

C. Decentralized account and resource administration.

D. Synchronization of account and security information across the enterprise.

Question #150

What is the purpose of the print monitor SFMMON.DLL?

A. SFMMON.DLL monitors Macintosh print jobs routed using AppleTalk protocol to network print devices.

B. SFMMON.DLL is the System File Manager print monitor which tracks print jobs sent directly to or printed directly from a file.

C. SFMMON.DLL is the software print job compression DLL which compresses the print job before it is sent from the local print spooler to the print server.

D. SFMMON.DLL is not a valid print monitor.

Question #151

You are responsible for a small company that has three locations in Chicago. You want to be sure the new software updates are available to all the appropriate installers throughout the company. Which publishing service(s) would you use?

A. WWW

B. FTP

C. GOPHER

D. NETSCAPE

Question #152

Windows 95 and TCP/IP support which of the following services?

A. DHCP

B. WINS

C. DNS

D. Protected mode drivers

Question #153

Kite Flyers Corporation is a relatively small company with about 1,000 employees. They are located in the same office complex. There are five departments: Accounting, Marketing, MIS, HR, and Corporate. Each has its own set of network resources that its staff accesses, and some resources that everyone in the company uses.

Primary Goals: Give all employees a single logon account that they can use to access their resources. Let each department manage their own resources.

Secondary Goal: Centralize resources by department.

Solution: Implement a master domain model and have all resource domains trust the account domain.

   A. The solution satisfies none of the goals.

   B. The solution satisfies both primary goals and the secondary goal.

   C. The solution satisfies both primary goals, but not the secondary goal.

   D. The solution satisfies one primary goal and the secondary goal.

Question #154

What two applications can be used to store and view data collected with performance monitor?

   A. Microsoft Notepad

   B. Microsoft SQL

   C. Microsoft Excel

   D. Microsoft Calculator

Question #155

Permissions for the BUDGET shared folder on ACCT1 are as shown in the following exhibit. ACCT1 is a member server of the FINANCE domain. Finance is a trusting domain of CORPDOMAIN. There is a global group called FinanceMgrs that must have Read access to the folder and its files. How would you make this happen?

A. Click the Add button and add the FinanceMgrs global group from FINANCE to the ACL with Read permission.

B. Click the Add button, choose CORPDOMAIN from the From Domain list, and add the FinanceMgrs global group from CORPDOMAIN to the ACL with Read permission.

C. Click the Add button and add the FinanceMgrs global group from CORPDOMAIN to the Accountants local group on ACCT1.

D. You cannot add users from another domain to this ACL.

Question #156

User, group, and computer accounts are contained in which account database?

A. SAM Accounts Database

B. Local Security Accounts Database

C. SAM Built-In Database

D. Account Synchronization Database

Question #157

Which Memory object counter would help to identify when to right-size the pagefile?

A. %Pagefile

B. Commit Limit

C. Working Set

D. %Disk Time

Question #158

Several users have called you within the past half-hour to complain that their print jobs are not printing. In fact, they get system messages that tell them that the spooler is not responding. You have verified that the spooler directory partition does not have adequate free space to hold all the print jobs sent to it. What steps should you take to resolve this situation?

A. Use the Control Panel applet Services to more frequently stop and restart the Spooler service to keep the print jobs from becoming fragmented.

B. Change the location of the spool directory to a partition with enough disk space by modifying the HKEY_LOCAL_MACHINE\System\CurrentControlSet\Control\Print\Printers DefaultSpoolDirectory parameter.

C. Change the location of the spool directory to a partition with enough disk space by modifying the HKEY_Current_User\Control\Print\Printers\Spool SpoolDirectory parameter.

D. If the partition is formatted with NTFS, compress the spool directory.

Question #159

Which of the following steps is appropriate to take when troubleshooting a failed print job?

A. Verify that the appropriate print port has been defined and configured by printing a test page.

B. Delete and re-create the printer.

C. Determine whether the print device is online and connected.

D. Resubmit the print job to a file and then copy the file to a printer port to see if it is successful.

Question #160

You are analyzing network activity between your network clients and a server. You plan to use Network Monitor to monitor network traffic generated by and received by the server, and Performance Monitor to track system performance relating to network traffic. What types of objects would facilitate your analysis? Choose all that apply.

A. Redirector

B. Server

C. Protocol

D. Frame

Question #161

My domain consists of a PDC and three BDCs. One of my BDCs has gone down. Which functions can still take place on my network? Choose all that apply.

A. I can administer accounts through User Manager for Domains.

B. I can log on to the network.

C. I can use Server Manager to administer the PDC and the other BDCs.

D. I can synchronize the domain controllers.

Question #162

Which of the following counters will provide you with the total number of bytes transferred during disk I/O for all the disks in your computer?

A. Logical Disk>Disk Bytes/sec, Total instance

B. Logical Disk>Disk Bytes/sec, for each partition instance

C. Physical Disk>Disk Bytes/sec, Total instance

D. Physical Disk>Disk Bytes/sec, for each disk instance

Question #163

From the choices below, indicate which are considered functions of a router.

A. They can pass information packets from one protocol to another such as TCP/IP to IPX.

B. They cannot pass information packets from one protocol to another such as TCP/IP to IPX.

App

J

C. They can pass information packets from one network segment to another, even though each segment may use a different media type such as Ethernet or Token Ring.

D. They can pass information packets from one network segment to another, but only if each segment is the same media type such as Ethernet or Token Ring.

Question #164

You are creating multiple user accounts for salespersons, marketers, and programmers. Each set of accounts belongs to the same relative groups (sales users in SALES, marketing users in MARKETING, and programmer users in PROGRAMMERS), uses the same logon scripts (SALES.BAT, MARKET.BAT, PROGRAM.BAT), and saves data in a home directory relative to each group (sales users under USERS\SALES, marketing users under USERS\MARKETERS, programmer users under USERS\PROGRAMMERS). What is the most efficient way to create these users?

A. Create a separate account for each user. As you create the user, use the %USERNAME% environment variable when specifying the home directory to let Windows NT create it for you.

B. Create a template for each type of user. Make the appropriate choices and entries for groups, logon script, and home directory. Use the %USERNAME% environment variable when specifying the home directory to let Windows NT create them for you. Then, create each user by copying the appropriate template.

C. Create all the users without specifying group membership. After they are all created, select each group of users by Ctrl+clicking them and create the appropriate group.

D. You must create each user individually.

Question #165

The first four lines of the _____ section are critical to finding the cause of the STOP error.

    A. BugCheck Information

    B. Driver Information

    C. Kernel Build Number and Stack Dump

    D. Debug Port Information

Question #166

When migrating NetWare servers to Windows NT, what are the options passwords? (Pick all that apply)

    A. Set them to blank.

    B. Set them to the user name.

    C. Set them to a password set in a map file.

    D. Set them to a random password from a dictionary.

Question #167

What server tool is NOT installed on a Windows NT 3.5/3.51 Workstation platform?

    A. Services for Macintosh

    B. System Policy Editor

    C. Remote Access Administrator

    D. User Profile Editor

Question #168

The printer for a network print device has been configured to print documents at all times. Pam plans to send a large complex graphics document that she would like to have tomorrow morning. This job will take at least one hour to complete. What can you do to minimize the effect that printing this document will have on other documents in the queue?

    A. Select Pam's document and pause it. Resume printing after hours when print jobs are at a minimum.

    B. Modify the printer schedule so that it only prints documents after hours.

App

J

C. Modify the document schedule for Pam's document so that it only prints between 1:00 AM and 3:00 AM.

D. Do nothing. The printer automatically holds long jobs until short jobs finish spooling and printing.

Question #169

You have a file and print server configured for striping with no parity using one ISA controller and four disk drives. You want to increase the read and write performance. What is the best option to use?

A. Add a second ISA controller to your configuration.

B. Add a fifth drive to your configuration.

C. Format the stripe set as an NTFS partition.

D. Replace the one ISA controller with two BUS master ISA controllers.

Question #170

What Windows NT software RAID configurations are supported?

A. 1

B. 2

C. 5

D. 10

Question #171

Indicate, from the choices below, which routing options are available with a Windows NT 4.0 Server installation.

A. IP Routing

B. IPX Routing

C. DHCP Relay

D. AppleTalk Routing

Question #172

You plan to use Performance Monitor to help predict and troubleshoot server activity under various conditions. Which of the following would be the best way to begin?

A. Create and monitor a real-time chart during peak activity and note the percent of processor usage during these periods.

B. Create a series of baseline logs of specific objects (processor, memory, disk, and network), each representing a different condition. Use these to predict activity under those conditions and to troubleshoot abnormal system activity.

C. Create a baseline log measuring system activity during periods of average activity. Compare this against real-time charts created during peak activity on the system.

D. Network Monitor would be a better tool to predict system activity.

Question #173

The DLC protocol is used with Windows NT to provide:

A. Access to Macintosh computers.

B. Access to IBM mainframes for terminal emulation.

C. Access to Novell resources.

D. Access to HP JetDirect Printers on the network.

Question #174

Ned is a member of the Developers group at Springfield Technologies. He has been promoted to team leader for his group. He needs to edit the DOOM.DOC file in the Tools folder, but does not have Write access. What must you do to give Ned access to DOOM.DOC?

A. Do nothing. The next time Ned logs on, his permissions will change.

B. Change the Developers group permission to Change.

App

J

C. Add Ned to the Team Leaders group.

D. Change the Team Leaders group permission to Full Control.

Question #175

The NWLink protocol by itself can be used to communicate with:

A. Novell Servers

B. Windows NT Workstations

C. Macintosh Workstations

D. Novell Clients for client/server applications

Question #176

Who can install RAS on a Windows NT Server? (Pick all that apply)

A. Administrator

B. Any member of the administrators group

C. Any member of the PowerUsers group

D. Any member of the RAS group

Answer Key for Mastery Test

Question	Answer	Resource
1	C	**Resource:** Chapter 5 "Global Group Accounts"
2	D	**Resource:** Chapter 22 "Events and Event Log Viewer"
3	C	**Resource:** Chapter 15 "Installation from the CD-ROM"
4	B	**Resource:** Chapter 8 Entire Chapter
5	A,B,D	**Resource:** Chapter 3 "Understanding the Nature of a Trust Relationship"

Question	Answer	Resource
6	D	**Resource:** Chapter 15 "Installation of Windows 95 Server Tools"
7	C	**Resource:** Chapter 17 "Networks, Network Segments, and the Purpose of Routers"
8	A	**Resource:** Chapter 5 "AppleTalk"
9	C	**Resource:** Chapter 5 "Network Monitoring Considerations"
10	C	**Resource:** Chapter 13 "Assigning File and Folder Permissions"
11	A	**Resource:** Chapter 8 Entire Chapter
12	B,C	**Resource:** Chapter 9 "Disk Striping"
13	C	**Resource:** Chapter 4 "Understanding the Multiple Master Domain Model"
14	A	**Resource:** Chapter 7 "HKEY_LOCAL_MACHINE"
15	D	**Resource:** Chapter 9 "Disk controllers"
16	A	**Resource:** Chapter 8 Entire Chapter
17	A,D	**Resource:** Chapter 15 "Installation from the CD-ROM"

App

J

continues

continued

Question	Answer	Resource
18	A,B,D	**Resource:** Chapter 12 "Creating a New Local or Global Group"
19	B	**Resource:** Chapter 16 "Gateway (and Client) Services for NetWare"
20	A,B,C,D	**Resource:** Chapter 9 "Hardware Controller RAID"
21	B	**Resource:** Chapter 21 "Implementing Network Monitor"
22	A,C	**Resource:** Chapter 10 "Windows NT 4.0 Print Process"
23	C	**Resource:** Chapter 7 "System Policy Editor"
24	B,C,D	**Resource:** Chapter 7 "Troubleshooting the Boot Process"
25	A,B,D	**Resource:** Chapter 7 "HKEY_LOCAL_MACHINE"
26	C	**Resource:** Chapter 6 "Maximizing the Resources by Server Role"
27	C	**Resource:** Chapter 10 "Windows NT 4.0 Print Process"
28	B	**Resource:** Chapter 12 "Naming Conventions"; "Considerations Regarding Passwords"; "Creating a New User"
29	B	**Resource:** Chapter 3 "The NetLogon Service and Pass-through Authentication"

Question	Answer	Resource
30	C	**Resource:** Chapter 13 "Determining Access when Using Share and NTFS Permissions"
31	C	**Resource:** Chapter 21 "Traffic Generated when Using Trusted Accounts"; "Optimizing Trust Traffic"
32	C A.	**Resource:** Chapter 7 "BOOT.INI"
33	B,C	**Resource:** Chapter 13 "Managing Shares and Permissions Remotely"
34	C	**Resource:** Chapter 8 Entire Chapter
35	A	**Resource:** Chapter 5 "Database Synchronization"
36	A	**Resource:** Chapter 4 "User and Group Accounts"
37	B,C,D	**Resource:** Chapter 3 "Setting Up a Trust Relationship"
38	B	**Resource:** Chapter 5 "Location of the Enterprise Administrator"
39	C	**Resource:** Chapter 20 "Monitoring Network-Related Objects"
40	B	**Resource:** Chapter 13 "Sharing Resources and Determining Network Access"

App
J

continues

continued

Question	Answer	Resource
41	A,B,D	**Resource:** Chapter 21 "Understanding Network Monitor"
42	B	**Resource:** Chapter 7 "Managing Remote Access to the Registry"
43	B	**Resource:** Chapter 11 Entire Chapter
44	A,C,D	**Resource:** Chapter 5 "Pass-Through Authentication"
45	A	**Resource:** Chapter 13 "Assigning File and Folder Permissions"
46	A	**Resource:** Chapter 8 Entire Chapter
47	A,B	**Resource:** Chapter 13 "Effective File and Folder Permissions"
48	D	**Resource:** Chapter 10 "Additional LPD Device Information"
49	C	**Resource:** Chapter 6 "Maximizing the Resources by Server Role"
50	D	**Resource:** Chapter 11 Entire Chapter
51	C	**Resource:** Chapter 9 "Recovering from hard disk failure"
52	B	**Resource:** Chapter 21 "Exploring Network Frames"

Question	Answer	Resource
53	B,C,D	**Resource:** Chapter 21 "File Session Frames"
54	D	**Resource:** Chapter 13 "How ACLs Determine Access"
55	B,C	**Resource:** Chapter 12 "Remote Account Management Tips"
56	B,C	**Resource:** Chapter 21 "Account Database Synchronization"
57	A,C	**Resource:** Chapter 21 "Optimizing Logon Validation"
58	A	**Resource:** Chapter 7 "What is the Last Known Good Control Set"; Table 7.7, "Service Subkey Parameters"
59	A,B	**Resource:** Chapter 21 "DHCP Frames"
60	A,C,D	**Resource:** Chapter 12 "Troubleshooting Accounts, Policies, and Profiles"
61	A,B,C,D	**Resource:** Chapter 10 "DLC Printing"
62	C	**Resource:** Chapter 10 "Windows NT 4.0 Print Process"
63	C	**Resource:** Chapter 7 "Emergency Repair Disk"
64	A	**Resource:** Chapter 3 "The NetLogon Service and Pass-through Authentication"

App
J

continues

continued

Question	Answer	Resource
65	A	**Resource:** Chapter 22 "Write Debugging Information To:"
66	D	**Resource:** Chapter 10 "Introducing and Examining the Print Process"; "Troubleshooting Printing"
67	B	**Resource:** Chapter 12 "Understanding User and Group Accounts"; "Creating a New User"
68	A	**Resource:** Chapter 8 Entire Chapter
69	C	**Resource:** Chapter 11 Entire Chapter
70	B	**Resource:** Chapter 3 "Understanding the Nature of a Trust Relationship"
71	A,C,D	**Resource:** Chapter 20 "System Performance with Performance Monitor"
72	B	**Resource:** Chapter 10 "Windows NT 4.0 Print Process"
73	C	**Resource:** Chapter 20 "Monitoring Processes"
74	C	**Resource:** Chapter 11 Entire Chapter
75	B	**Resource:** Chapter 10 "Windows NT 4.0 Print Process"
76	B	**Resource:** Chapter 15 "Creating a Server Tools Share Using Network Client Administrator"

Question	Answer	Resource
77	A,B,C	**Resource:** Chapter 14 "Default and Specific User and Computer Settings"
78	A	**Resource:** Chapter 10 "Windows NT 4.0 Print Process"
79	C	**Resource:** Chapter 12 "User Rights"
80	C	**Resource:** Chapter 12 "Understanding User Manager for Domains"; "Creating a New User"
81	A	**Resource:** Chapter 17 "AppleTalk Routing"
82	A	**Resource:** Chapter 13 "Examining Access Control Lists"
83	B	**Resource:** Chapter 12 "Account Policy"; "Audit Policy"
84	D	**Resource:** Chapter 8 Entire Chapter
85	A	**Resource:** Chapter 21 "File Session Frames"
86	C	**Resource:** Chapter 21 "WINS Frames"
87	D	**Resource:** Chapter 18 Entire Chapter
88	B	**Resource:** Chapter 10 "Windows NT 4.0 Print Process"
89	B	**Resource:** Chapter 17 "RIP for IPX Routing"
90	A,B,D	**Resource:** Chapter 12 "Creating a New User"

continues

App **J**

continued

Question	Answer	Resource
91	A	**Resource:** Chapter 10 "Troubleshooting Printing"
92	D	**Resource:** Chapter 4 Entire Chapter, especially "Understanding the Single Domain Model"; "Managing Global Groups in the Domain Models"
93	B	**Resource:** Chapter 22 "Events and Event Log Viewer"
94	C	**Resource:** Chapter 19 "What Are These Types of Connections?"
95	C	**Resource:** Chapter 10 "Windows NT 4.0 Print Process"
96	A,B,C	**Resource:** Chapter 19 "User Security Options"
97	B	**Resource:** Chapter 22 "Write Debugging Information To:"
98	B	**Resource:** Chapter 20 "Monitoring the Processor"; "Monitoring Memory"; "Monitoring Disk Activity"
99	B,C	**Resource:** Chapter 19 "Troubleshooting RAS"
100	A,B,C	**Resource:** Chapter 21 "Optimizing Directory Replication Traffic"
101	A,D	**Resource:** Chapter 18 Entire Chapter

Question	Answer	Resource
102	B	**Resource:** Chapter 22 "Start the Kernel Debugger"
103	B,D	**Resource:** Chapter 2 "Workgroup Model"
104	C	**Resource:** Chapter 13 "Managing Shares and Permissions Remotely"
105	A,B,C	**Resource:** Chapter 19 "RAS Installation"
106	C	**Resource:** Chapter 20 "Monitoring Disk Activity"
107	C	**Resource:** Chapter 2 "Network Resource Access"
108	B	**Resource:** Chapter 4 "Understanding Global Groups in the Domain Models"; "Master Domain Model"
109	D	**Resource:** Chapter 17 "Networks, Network Segments, and the Purpose of Routers"
110	B	**Resource:** Chapter 8 Entire Chapter
111	D	**Resource:** Chapter 10 "TCP/IP Printing"
112	D	**Resource:** Chapter 22 "Dumpexam.exe"
113	D	**Resource:** Chapter 6 "Maximizing the Resources by Server Role"

App
J

continues

continued

Question	Answer	Resource
114	C	**Resource:** Chapter 15 "Creating a Server Tools Share Using Network Client Administrator"
115	B	**Resource:** Chapter 14 "Working with the System Policy Editor"
116	A	**Resource:** Chapter 4 "Understanding the Single Domain Model"
117	D	**Resource:** Chapter 17 "AppleTalk Routing"
118	A,C,D	**Resource:** Chapter 21 "File Session Frames"
119	A	**Resource:** Chapter 5 "Database Synchronization"
120	C	**Resource:** Chapter 22 "STOP Error Screen Layout and Section Meanings"
121	C	**Resource:** Chapter 3 "Group Management in the Domain"
122	C	**Resource:** Chapter 2 "Taking the Enterprise Challenge"
123	B	**Resource:** Chapter 3 "Resource Management Across Trusts"; "Group Management in the Domain"
124	A,D	**Resource:** Chapter 21 "WINS Frames"

Question	Answer	Resource
125	A,B,C	**Resource:** Chapter 7 "HKEY_LOCAL_MACHINE\ System\CurrentControlSet\Services"
126	B	**Resource:** Chapter 7 "Sidebar, Boot Process for RISC-based Computers"
127	D	**Resource:** Chapter 9 "What Is Fault Tolerance"
128	A,B,D	**Resource:** Chapter 13 "Understanding the Concept of Ownership"
129	C	**Resource:** Chapter 12 "Account Policy"
130	A,C	**Resource:** Chapter 22 "Connect the Host and Target Computers"
131	C	**Resource:** Chapter 3 "Understanding the Nature of a Trust Relationship"
132	B	**Resource:** Chapter 7 "HKEY_LOCAL_MACHINE\ System\Select"
133	A	**Resource:** Chapter 15 "Installation of Windows 3.1 and Windows for Workgroups 3.11 Server Tools"
134	B	**Resource:** Chapter 13 "Sharing Resources and Determining Network Access"

continues

App
J

continued

Question	Answer	Resource
135	B,C	**Resource:** Chapter 21 "Suggestions for Optimizing Browser Traffic"
136	C	**Resource:** Chapter 21 "Account Database Synchronization"
137	B	**Resource:** Chapter 8 Entire Chapter
138	A,D	**Resource:** Chapter 5 "Planning Protocol Selection of a Network Enterprise"
139	B	**Resource:** Chapter 8 Entire Chapter
140	D	**Resource:** Chapter 8 Entire Chapter
141	A	**Resource:** Chapter 3 "Group Management in the Domain"
142	A	**Resource:** Chapter 20 "Monitoring Disk Activity"
143	A,D	**Resource:** Chapter 8 Entire Chapter
144	B	**Resource:** Chapter 2 "Single Network Logon"
145	B	**Resource:** Chapter 13 "Local versus Domain Access Tokens"
146	B	**Resource:** Chapter 13 "Troubleshooting Security"
147	B	**Resource:** Chapter 8 Entire Chapter

Question	Answer	Resource
148	A,B,C,D	**Resource:** Chapter 3 "Troubleshooting Trust Relationships"
149	A,B,D	**Resource:** Chapter 2 "Taking the Enterprise Challenge"
150	A	**Resource:** Chapter 10 "Windows NT 4.0 Print Process"
151	A,B	**Resource:** Chapter 18 Entire Chapter
152	A,B,C,D	**Resource:** Chapter 11 Entire Chapter
153	B	**Resource:** Chapter 4 Entire Chapter, especially "Understanding the Master Domain Model"
154	B,C	**Resource:** Chapter 5 "Network Monitoring Considerations"
155	B	**Resource:** Chapter 13 "Local versus Domain Access Tokens"
156	A	**Resource:** Chapter 21 "Account Database Synchronization"
157	B	**Resource:** Chapter 20 "Monitoring Memory"
158	B	**Resource:** Chapter 10 "Windows NT 4.0 Print Process"
159	A,C,D	**Resource:** Chapter 10 "Troubleshooting Printing"

continues

continued

Question	Answer	Resource
160	A,B,C	**Resource:** Chapter 20 "Monitoring Network-Related Objects"
161	A,B,C,D	**Resource:** Chapter 2 "Synchronization of Account and Security Information"
162	C	**Resource:** Chapter 20 "Monitoring Disk Activity"; "Monitoring System Performance with Performance Monitor"
163	B,C	**Resource:** Chapter 17 "Networks, Network Segments, and the Purpose of Routers"
164	B	**Resource:** Chapter 12 "Renaming, Copying, and Deleting Accounts"; "Home Directory"
165	A	**Resource:** Chapter 22 "BugCheck Information"
166	A,B,C	**Resource:** Chapter 16 "Migration Tool for NetWare"
167	B	**Resource:** Chapter 15 "Windows NT 4.0 Workstation Server Tools"
168	C	**Resource:** Chapter 10 "Windows NT 4.0 Print Process"
169	D	**Resource:** Chapter 9 "Disk Controllers"
170	A,C	**Resource:** Chapter 9 "Windows NT Controller Software RAID"

Question	Answer	Resource
171	A,B,C,D	**Resource:** Chapter 17 "Multiprotocol Routing"
172	B	**Resource:** Chapter 20 "Creating a Performance Monitor Log"; "Summarizing Performance Monitoring and Optimization"
173	B,D	**Resource:** Chapter 5 "DLC"
174	C	**Resource:** Chapter 13 "Effective Permissions"
175	B,D	**Resource:** Chapter 8 Entire Chapter
176	A,B	**Resource:** Chapter 19 "RAS Installation"

App
J

Lab Exercises

Chapter 7 Lab Exercises— Troubleshooting with the NT Registry

For this exercise it is assumed that you have two Windows NT computers at your disposal. Although they might be Windows NT Workstations, it is assumed that you have them configured, as suggested in Lab1, as primary domain controllers called DOMAINA and DOMAINB. It is further assumed that you have installed the Windows NT Server 4.0 Resource Kit utilities on both computers.

PART 1

1. Log on to both computers as Administrator. The password should be the same on both computers.

2. Use the Windows NT Registry Editor to view the start value for the Workstation service in HKEY_LOCAL_ MACHINE\System\CurrentControlSet\Services\ LanmanWorkstation: Start = 0×2. Recall from the chapter that a start value of 2 means that the service starts automatically during the system initialization of the boot process.

3. On DOMAINA, use the Control Panel Services applet to select the Workstation service and Stop the service. Do not actually stop the service, but do note the other services that depend on it. Write them down. At the least, you will note the Computer Browser, NETLOGON, Messenger, and Alerter services. Change the Workstation service startup setting from Automatic to Disabled. Restart the computer.

4. After the computer restarts, log back in as Administrator. Note the dependency error message that you receive.

5. Open Event Viewer, and look for the most recent EventLog entry. Right above that entry, look for the first Service Control Manager stop entry. Beginning with this entry, read each subsequent stop entry, noting the services and dependencies that failed to start. Which service caused these errors (could it be a Workstation service such as a Lanman Workstation service)? Attempt to map a drive from DOMAINA to a share on DOMAINB. Can you do it? (No, because the workstation service processes such requests for remote resources and it is disabled.) Attempt to map a drive from DOMAINB to a share on DOMAINA. Can you do so? (Yes, because the Server service not the workstation service on DOMAINA responds to remote requests for resource access.)

6. Open the Windows NT Registry Editor on DOMAINA and find the HKEY_LOCAL_MACHINE\System\Current ControlSet\Services\LanmanWorkstation subkey. Note how its start value has changed from 0×2 to 0×4. Go back to the section "Understanding HKEY_LOCAL_MACHINE\ System\CurrentControlSet\Services" to review what 0×4 means (service-disabled). Double-click the Start entry to display the string editor and replace the string value with 2. Restart the computer.

7. After the computer restarts, log on as Administrator. Check the Event Viewer for any additional stop value entries. Were there any? (Not if you made the appropriate change to the Registry as indicated in step 6.)

8. From DOMAINA, try again to map a drive to a share on DOMAINB. Are you successful this time? (Yes.) The work-station service is now loaded and running.

PART 2

For this exercise, you will introduce a problem on computer DOMAINA and remotely resolve it through DOMAINB.

1. Log on to both computers as Administrator as in PART 1.

2. On DOMAINA, Use Windows Explorer to copy the RCMDSVC.EXE and OEMNSVRC.INF files from the Windows NT Resource Kit directory (usually c:\NTRESKIT) to the WINNT\SYSTEM32 folder. Share c:\ntreskit as NTRESKIT.

3. Open the Network Properties dialog box and switch to the Services tab. Choose the Add button and then choose Re-mote Command Server from the list. Choose OK, close the Network Properties dialog box, and do not restart the com-puter.

4. Use the Control Panel Services applet to configure the startup setting for Remote Command Server to be automatic.

5. Now use the Registry Editor on DOMAINA to find the HKEY_ LOCAL_MACHINE\System\CurrentControlSet\ Services\ Mouclass subkey. Double-click its Start parameter entry to display the string editor and change the value to 4.

6. Restart the computer and log on as Administrator. Note that you no longer have mouse support.

7. Now switch to computer DOMAINB. Open a command prompt window and enter the command **RCMD \\DOMAINA**. This establishes a remote management session between DOMAINB and DOMAINA running the Remote Command Server service. The command line now represents a command line on DOMAINA.

8. At the prompt, switch to the NTRESKIT directory and type **WINMSDP** to display the report options that you may choose from. In this case, because the mouse failed to start, you will use the /R switch to generate a list of driver settings from the Registry on DOMAINA. Enter **WINMSDP /R**. When it completes, it will generate a text file called MSDRPT.TXT stored in the current folder.

9. Open another command prompt window. You can now view the text file using the command-line editor EDIT.COM. Enter **EDIT \\DOMAINA\NTRESKIT\ MSDRPT.TXT** to view the file. Knowing that a Start value of 4 means that the service or device driver is disabled, scroll through the file until you find the MOUSE CLASS DRIVER entry. Note its start type is 4. You must change it back to 1 in order to enable mouse support for DOMAINA. Here are two options for modifying the Registry.

OPTION A

1. Start the Registry Editor on DOMAINB. Choose **R**egistry, **S**elect Computer. Enter **DOMAINA**, or select it from the browse list. The Registry Editor will now display the HKEY_LOCAL_ MACHINE subtree from DOMAINA.

2. Find the HKEY_LOCAL_MACHINE\System\Current Control Set\Services\MouClass subkey. Double-click the Start parameter entry and change it back to 1.

3. At your RCMD command prompt, enter the command **SHUTDOWN**. This is another Resource Kit utility stored in the NTRESKIT folder.

4. Back on DOMAINA, log in as Administrator and verify that mouse support is reestablished.

OPTION B

1. Open another command prompt window. Create a text file called MOUSEFIX.INI using the following command:

```
Edit \\domaina\ntreskit\mousefix.ini
```

Make the following entries:

```
\Registry\Machine
 System
  CurrentControlSet
   Services
   MouClass
    Start = REG_DWORD 1
```

2. Now switch to the RCMD prompt and enter the following command: **regini d:\ntreskit\mousfix.ini**.

3. Execute the Shutdown command to restart DOMAINA: **Shutdown \\DOMAINA**.

4. Log in as Administrator on DOMAINA and verify that mouse support has been restored.

Chapter 8 Lab Exercises

Exercise 1

In this exercise, you install the TCP/IP protocol and manually configure an IP Address and Subnet Mask. It is assumed that only the NetBEUI protocol is presently installed and the source files are located on the C drive of your computer in a folder ntsrv.

1. Log on to your domain controller as the administrator and open up the Network application by selecting Start, Settings, Control Panel, Network Icon.

2. Select the Protocols tab in the Network properties dialog box and choose the Add button.

3. From the list of available protocols in the Select Network Protocol dialog box, select the TCP/IP Protocol and choose OK.

4. A TCP/IP Setup dialog box appears asking you if you wish to use a DHCP server? Answer NO to continue.

5. When the Windows NT Setup dialog box appears, type the location of the source file in the space provided (**C:\ntsrv**) and choose Continue. Files will be copied and the TCP/IP protocol and related services will be installed. Notice that the TCP/IP protocol appears in the network protocols window on the Network properties sheet.

6. Choose Close on the Network properties sheet. (Bindings will be reviewed and configured.)

7. A Microsoft TCP/IP Properties sheet appears to manually configure an IP address, subnet mask, and default gateway. Enter an IP Address of **131.107.2.x** where x is a unique assigned number. Change the default Subnet Mask from 255.255.0.0 to **255.255.255.0**. Leave the Default Gateway entry blank.

Note You may require a different IP address and subnet mask because of your local network characteristics. Make sure you supply a unique IP address, or error messages indicating a duplicate IP address on the network will result.

8. When the Networks Settings Change dialog box appears asking you to shut down and restart your computer, select YES.

Exercise 2

In this exercise you install the DHCP Service to become a DHCP server and to configure a scope of address. You also designate a group of address to be excluded from the scope and add an address reservation. It is assumed that the NetBEUI and TCP/IP protocols are presently installed and the source files are located on your computer in a folder ntsrv on your C drive.

1. Log on to your domain controller as the administrator and open up the Network application by selecting Start, Settings, Control Panel, Network Icon.

2. Select the Services tab in the Network properties dialog box and choose the Add button.

3. From the list of available services in the Select Network Services dialog box, select Microsoft DHCP Server and choose OK.

4. When the Windows NT Setup dialog box appears, type the location of the source file in the space provided (**C:\ntsrv**) and choose Continue. Files will be copied, and the DHCP server service will be installed. An information box appears stating that if any adapters are using DHCP to obtain an IP address, they are now required to use a static IP address.

5. Press OK. Notice that the DHCP server appears in the network services window on the Network properties sheet.

App
K

6. Choose Close on the Network properties sheet. (Bindings will be reviewed and configured.)

7. When the Networks Settings Change dialog box appears asking you to shut down and restart your computer, select YES.

8. When your computer restarts, log on to your domain controller as the administrator and open up the DHCP Manager application by selecting Start, Programs, Administrative Tools, DHCP Manager. The DHCP Manager Application dialog box appears.

9. From the Scope drop-down menu, select Create. A Create Scope (Local) configuration sheet appears.

10. In the IP Address Pool Start Address entry box, enter **131.107.2.150** and in the IP Address Pool Stop Address entry box, enter **131.107.2.199**. In the IP Address Pool Subnet Mask entry box, enter **255.255.255.0**.

11. In the Exclusion Range Start Address entry box, enter **131.107.2.170** and in the Exclusion Range Start Address entry box, enter **131.107.2.180** and select Add. The range of address will appear in the Exclusion Addresses window.

12. In the Lease Duration portion of the screen, ensure the Limited To radio button is selected and change the lease duration from the default value of 3 days to 1 day and enter OK.

13. A DHCP Manager question box appears telling you the scope was created successfully but is not activated yet. It then asks if you would like to activate the scope now. Click YES.

14. The new scope will appear under the Local Machine entry on the DHCP Manager dialog box with the light bulb on (this means the scope is active). If the new scope does not appear automatically, double-click the Local Machine entry.

15. On the DHCP Manager dialog box, select the newly created scope. From the Scope drop-down menu, select Add Reservations. The Add Reserved Clients information screen appears.

16. Review the required information for this screen. Notice the network number automatically appears in the IP Address portion of the screen. Why did this happen?

    _____

    _____

    (Because of the starting address and subnet mask values entered when the scope was created.)

17. Enter a value of your IP address used in Exercise 1, Step 7 in the IP Address entry box.

For the next step, a unique identifier is required to associate a specific network card with this reservation. To obtain a network card and a unique MAC address, perform the following steps:

   1. Start up a Command Prompt

   2. Type **ipconfig /all**

   3. Record the Physical Address (this is the unique identifier)

18. Enter your 12-digit MAC address in the Unique Identifier entry box.

19. Enter your computer name in the Client Name entry box, choose Add, and then Close.

20. From the DHCP Manager dialog box, select the Scope drop-down menu and select Active Leases. Make sure the reservation you added is present. Remove the reservation by selecting Delete and Close DHCP Manager.

App
K

Exercise 3

In this exercise you install the WINS Service on your computer to become a WINS server. It is assumed that the NetBEUI and TCP/IP protocols are presently installed and the source files are located on the C drive of your computer in a folder ntsrv.

1. Log on to your domain controller as the administrator and open up the Network application by selecting Start, Settings, Control Panel, Network Icon.

2. Select the Services tab in the Network properties dialog box and choose the Add button.

3. From the list of available services in the Select Network Services dialog box, select Windows Internet Name Service and choose OK.

4. When the Windows NT Setup dialog box appears, type the location of the source file in the space provided (**C:\ntsrv**) and choose Continue. Files will be copied and the WINS server service will be installed.

5. Choose Close on the Network properties sheet. (Bindings will be reviewed and configured.)

6. When the Networks Settings Change dialog box appears asking you to shut down and restart your computer, select YES.

7. When your computer restarts, log on to your domain controller as the administrator and open up the WINS Manager application by selecting Start, Programs, Administrative Tools, WINS Manager. The DHCP Manager application dialog box appears.

8. Your IP address should appear in the WINS Manager under the WINS Server window. Double-click your IP address. The statistics screen on the right side of the dialog box should refresh.

9. From the Mappings drop-down menu, select Show Database. View the Show Database [Local] Mappings window. How many entries are in the database pertaining to your computer?_____. List the entries in the database for your computer in the spaces provided below.

    _____

    _____

    _____

    _____

    (Answers will vary; however, at least two entries should be registered in the database pertaining to the local computer. There may be a browser entry, a domain entry, a computer entry, and a user entry.)

10. Choose Close and then exit from WINS Manager.

Exercise 4

In this exercise you install the DNS Service and manually configure an alias computer name. You then PING the alias to ensure proper configuration. It is assumed that the NetBEUI and TCP/IP protocols are presently installed and the source files are located on the C drive of your computer in a folder ntsrv.

1. Log on to your domain controller as the administrator and open up the Network application by selecting Start, Settings, Control Panel, Network Icon.

2. Select the Services tab in the Network properties dialog box and choose the Add button.

3. From the list of available services in the Select Network Services dialog box, select Microsoft DNS Server and choose OK.

4. When the Windows NT Setup dialog box appears, type the location of the source file in the space provided (**C:\ntsrv**)

and choose Continue. Files will be copied and the DNS server service will be installed.

5. Choose Close on the Network properties sheet. (Bindings will be reviewed and configured.)

6. When the Networks Settings Change dialog box appears asking you to shut down and restart your computer, select YES.

7. When your computer starts, log on to your domain controller as the administrator and open up the Network application by selecting Start, Settings, Control Panel, Network Icon.

8. Select the Protocols tab in the Network properties dialog box, choose the TCP/IP protocol, and choose Properties.

9. In the Microsoft TCP/IP Properties sheet, select DNS.

10. In the Domain box, type **<your first name>.com**. Your computer name appears in the Host Name box. Do not alter your computer name.

11. Select the Add button below the DNS Service Search Order window and enter your IP address in the TCP/IP DNS Server dialog box and click Add.

12. Select OK to close the Microsoft TCP/IP Properties window and OK to close the Network application.

13. Open the DNS Manager application by selecting Start, Programs, Administrative Tools, DNS Manager. The DNS Manager application dialog box appears.

14. Select the DNS drop-down menu and select New Server. The Add DNS Server dialog box appears. Enter your computer name or your IP address in the space provided, and click OK. Your DNS server should appear under the Server List, and Cache should appear under your DNS Server name or IP address.

15. Select the DNS drop-down menu and select New Zone. The Creating new zone for <computer name> dialog box appears. Select the Primary radio button and select Next.

16. In the Creating new zone for <computer name> dialog box, type the same name entered in step 10 (**your first name.com**) and press the TAB key. Verify that <your first name>.com.dns appears in the zone file box. Select Next, then Finish. Verify that your new zone name appears under your server name on the left pane of the dialog box and that an NS record and an SOA record appear under Zone Info on the right pane in the dialog box.

17. Right-click your zone name in the left pane and select New Record. In the Record Type Window select the A Record. Enter your Host Name and your Host IP Address and clear the Create Associated PTR Record. Click OK.

18. Right-click your zone name in the left pane and select New Record. In the Record Type Window select the CNAME Record. Enter an alias name of your choice in the Alias Name box and click OK.

19. In the For Host DNS box, type your computer name and your DNS domain name separated by a period (Example: <computer name>.<your first name>.com.) and click OK.

20. Close the Domain Name Service Manager application.

21. Start a command prompt window.

22. Type **PING** <alias name>.

Chapter 10 Lab Exercises

It is assumed that you have installed the computers as outlined in Lab 1 and that DOMAINB trusts DOMAINA. This lab requires that a printer be attached to one of your computers, and it is

App
K

assumed that it is connected to DOMAINA. Installing Windows 95 print drivers is also an option, if you have the Windows 95 CD-ROM handy.

Exercise 1

Even if you have installed your printer already, complete this exercise on DOMAINA. Pay close attention to the screens, messages, and options available to you. Refer back to the chapter text to highlight and clarify screens.

1. Start the Add Printer Wizard. (My Computer, Printers, Add Printer; or Start, Settings, Printers. Add Printer.)

2. You will install the printer on your local computer. Choose My Computer.

3. Select the port that your print device is attached to.

4. Select the manufacturer and model of the print device connected to your computer.

5. Set this to be your print default.

6. Call it Managers Printer and share the printer as NTPRINT. If you have the Windows 95 source CD-ROM available, select Windows 95 from the list of additional print drivers to support.

7. Print a test page to verify that your configuration works.

8. If necessary, enter the appropriate path to the Windows NT source files to complete installation.

Exercise 2 (Optional)

If you have a network TCP/IP printer available that you can use and are allowed to manage, be sure to add the TCP/IP protocol to your computer and repeat Exercise 1. For step 3, choose Add Port and select Local Port. Enter the IP address of the network printer.

Exercise 3

1. On DOMAINB, start the Add Printer Wizard.

2. This time choose Network Printer Server to connect to the printer you just created on Computer1.

3. From the Connect to Printer browse screen, expand through the Microsoft Windows Network entries to find the printer you created on Computer1 called NTPRINT and select it.

   OR

   Type in the UNC path to the printer as follows: **\\Computer1\NTPRINT**.

4. Make this the default printer on DOMAINB.

5. Complete the installation. A network printer icon will be displayed in the Printers folder.

6. Use Notepad to create and save a short text document called PRINT.TXT. (Suggested content: If you can read this, printing was successful.)

7. Print PRINT.TXT to the network printer you just connected to. Was printing successful? Yes.

8. On DOMAINA, open the NTPRINT Print Manager window and pause the shared printer.

9. Resubmit PRINT.TXT on Computer2.

10. In the NTPRINT window, select the PRINT.TXT print job and explore the document properties. Schedule the job to print at the next half-hour.

11. Resume the printer and wait until the next half-hour to see your print job print.

Exercise 4

For additional practice installing and configuring printers, complete this exercise after reading Chapter 12, "Domain Users and Groups."

1. On DOMAINA, open the NTPRINT properties sheet and select the Scheduling tab.

2. Set the priority to the highest setting (99).

3. On the Security tab, choose Permissions.

4. Remove Everyone and add Managers with Print permission.

5. Close NTPRINT properties.

6. Create another printer for the same print device on the same port. Call it Staff Printer and share it as STAFFPRT.

7. After it is created, open its properties and select the Scheduling tab.

8. Set the priority to the lowest setting (1).

9. On the Security tab, choose Permissions.

10. Remove Everyone and add MIS with Print permission.

11. Close STAFFPRT properties.

12. Create a user called Bert and a user called Fred. Make Bert a member of the Print Operators group on DOMAINA.

13. Log on to DOMAINA as Bert.

14. Open both NTPRINT and STAFFPRT windows. Pause NTPRINT and STAFFPRT.

15. Create a text document called TESTP1.TXT with the text `This is a test print - 1` and print to NTPRINT. You should see it queued in the NTPRINT window.

16. Log on to DOMAINB from DOMAINA as Fred.

17. Connect to STAFFPRT and make it the default.

18. Create a text document called STAFFP1.TXT with the text This is a staff test print - 1 and print to STAFFPRT. You should see it queued in the STAFFPRT window on DOMAINA.

19. Create two more documents on DOMAINA (TESTP2.TXT and TESTP3.TXT with similar text) and on DOMAINB (STAFFP2.TXT and Staffp3.TXT with similar text) and print them to their respective printers. You will see them queued.

20. Resume STAFFPRT then NTPRINT. In what order did the print jobs print? Chances are that because STAFFPRT was resumed first, its low priority STAFFp1.TXT job was sent to the print device ahead of TESTP1.TXT. Nevertheless, before any other staff jobs print, the Managers' jobs will print first because their print queue associated with the same printer has a higher priority than staff print jobs.

If your computer had a previous printer setup, restore it as your default now, if you like.

Chapter 12 Lab Exercises—Working with User Manager for Domains

This exercise assumes that you have installed and configured your computers as outlined in Lab 1. Complete this exercise on both DOMAINA and DOMAINB. This exercise along with the Chapter 3 "Trust Relationships" labs will give a complete picture of account management in a Directory Services environment.

1. Log on to both PDCs as Administrator.

2. Create a trust relationship so that DOMAINB trusts DOMAINA (DOMAINA is trusted). Refer back to Chapter 3, "Trust Relationships" if you are unsure of how to do this. While you are in User Manager for Domains, select Policies,

Audit from the menu and enable Success and Failure audits for Logon and Logoff, File and Object Access, and User and Group Management. Also, set the account policy so that lockout is enabled after three bad logon attempts with a lockout duration of Forever (until Admin unlocks).

3. Using Windows Explorer, create and share a directory called USERS on DOMAINA.

4. Using Notepad, create the following logon script called JEDI.BAT and save it in the WINNT\SYSTEM32\REPL\IMPORT\SCRIPTS subdirectory on DOMAINA.

```
@echo Welcome to the Jedi Warriors network!
@echo off
Pause
```

5. Open User Manager for Domains. Choose User, Select Domain from the menu. Select DOMAINA from the list of domains, or enter it in the Domain text box. The account database for DOMAINA will be displayed.

6. Use User Manager for Domains to create the following user accounts on DOMAINA. Require all users to change their password when they log on (check User Must Change Password at Next Logon). In the Profiles button for each, enter the JEDI.BAT logon script you created in step 1, and enter the following home directory: **\\DOMAINA\Users\%USERNAME%**.

New Users

Username	Full Name	Description	Password
NancyA	Nancy Acton	Acquisitions Editor	password
MaryM	Mary Miller	Executive Editor	password
JohnC	John Cook	Cool Dude	password
EmmettR	Emmett Rollins	Trainer Extraordinaire	password
DonD	Don Davidson	Acquisitions Editor	password

7. Log off and log back on to DOMAINA as Administrator on DOMAINB. Start User Manager for Domains. Note that you are now viewing the account database for DOMAINB. This is because of the trust you created, and because you added DOMAINA\Domain Admins to DOMAINB\ Administrators. Create the following group accounts:

New Groups

Group Name	Description	Members
ZanyGroup	They're Wild	NancyA MaryM JohnC
StraightArrows	Don't Step out of Line	NancyA
KindGroup	Cool People	EmmettR

8. Create the following template accounts. Require the user to change password at next logon. Choose the Groups button, remove the Users group for each, and add in the corresponding group you created in step 3 (StraightArrows for StraightTemp, ZanyGroup for ZanyTemp, KindGroup for KindTemp). Choose the Profile button for each and enter in the login script you created (jedi.bat) and the following home directory: **\\DOMAINA\USERS\ %USERNAME%**.

New Users

Username	Full Name	Description	Password
StraightTemp	Straight Arrows Template	Straight	stemplate
ZanyTemp	Zany Template	Zany	ztemplate
KindTemp	Bad Guys Template	Kind	ktemplate

App
K

9. Create the following accounts by copying the appropriate template you created in step 4. Notice which elements of the template account are copied (description, password options, group, and profile information) and which you need to fill in (username, full name, and password).

   StraightArrows
   PatK, Pat Kooper, password
   BrianS, Brian Short, password
   ZanyGroup
   LorraineS, Lorraine Schubert, password
   KindGroup
   DonE, password

10. Use Windows Explorer to confirm that the home directories for each account were created. Log on from DOMAINB as NancyA and confirm that the login script runs, and that Nancy can access her home directory on DOMAINA. Can Nancy view the Event Viewer Security log? (No, she is not an administrator.)

11. Log off and log back on as NancyA three times with the wrong password. Note the message that NT displays each time. Log on a fourth time with the correct password. Note that the message now indicates that the account is locked out. Log off and log back on as Administrator.

12. Unlock NancyA through User Manager for Domains. Open the Event Viewer Security log. Look for the entries with the lock icon. Find the three bad logon attempts (category: Account Management), as well as the entry that recorded the account lockout. Which Security Log entry records the event when the administrator unlocks the account? (Look for category: Account Management, event number 642 toward the top of the list; detail: User account changed.) Toward the bottom of the list, find the entries that correspond to the

creation of the user and global group accounts. Note that each user was added to the global group Domain Users automatically, and that this event was recorded. Familiarize yourself with the entries that correspond to the creation of each user and group.

Chapter 13 Lab Exercises

This set of labs is most effective if you use both computers, and if you have one NTFS partition created on each computer. It is assumed that you have installed the computers as outlined in Lab1.

If you do not currently have an NTFS partition, but have an existing FAT partition that you can convert to NTFS (other than the boot partition), use the following steps to convert it to NTFS:

1. Open a DOS prompt window.

2. At the prompt type **CONVERT D: /FS:NTFS**, where D: represents the letter of the partition that you are converting.

3. Press Enter. If there are any files in use by NT on that partition such as the pagefile, you will see a message to the effect that you must reboot for the conversion to take effect. Do so; otherwise, NT will convert the partition when you press Enter.

If you do not have a partition that you can convert, but do have at least 50M of free disk space available, you can use Disk Administrator to create an NTFS partition. Follow these steps:

1. Start Disk Administrator. If this is the first time you are starting this utility, click OK to the start up message.

2. Click the free disk space available in the graphic screen provided.

3. From Partition on the menu, choose Create.

App
K

4. Specify the total size of the partition and choose OK. It should be at least 50M, but can be no smaller than 10M.

5. Choose Partition, Commit Changes Now.

6. From Tools, choose Format and NTFS.

7. When format is complete, exit Disk Administrator.

PART 1

Log on to both domain controllers as Administrator. Remove any trust relationships between DOMAINA and DOMAINB.

1. Using Windows Explorer, create the following folders and files on both computers in the NTFS partition. Place a couple lines of text in each file (you don't need to get fancy now).

\TOOLS	DOOM.TXT	(Create new text file)
	BUDGET97.DOC	(Create new WordPad file)
\TOOLS\DATA	MEMO.DOC	
	WELCOME.TXT	

2. Share TOOLS as TOOLS.

3. Use User Manager for Domains to create local groups called Managers, MIS, and Sales on DOMAINB.

4. Remove Everyone from the ACL for the share. Add the Managers group with Change and the Sales group with Read.

5. Create new users called SimpsonC and SmithS and global groups called GSALES and GMANAGERS on DOMAINA. Add SimpsonC to GSALES and SmithS to GMANAGERS.

6. Log on as SimpsonC on DOMAINA.

7. Using Network Neighborhood, access the TOOLS share on DOMAINB. Can you access it? NT will tell you that you

have used an incorrect password or username to access the share. Recall that in an untrusted environment, you must either create a valid account for every user that needs access to shared resources in the domain or be able to connect as a valid user. Cancel from the dialog box.

8. Establish a trust relationship from DOMAINB to DOMAINA (DOMAINB trusts DOMAINA). Add the DOMAIN ADMINS global group from DOMAINA to the Administrators local group on DOMAINB.

9. Add the GSALES global group from DOMAINA to the Sales local group on DOMAINB, and add the GMANAGERS global group from DOMAINA to the Managers local group on DomainB.

10. On DOMAINA, access the TOOLS share again. Your access should now be successful because you have established a trust and added the GSALES global group to the Sales local group. Disconnect from the share.

App
K

PART 2

1. On DOMAINA, log on as SmithS.

2. Connect to the TOOLS share on DOMAINB.

3. Open the file DOOM.TXT, make a change to the file, and close it.

4. Log off, and log on as SimpsonC.

5. Connect to the TOOLS share on DOMAINB.

6. Open the file DOOM.TXT and make a change to the file. Can you save the file? Note that NT will not let you save changes made to the file because SimpsonC is a member of the Sales group, which has been given Read access to the file. Do not close the file.

7. On DOMAINB, use User Manager for Domains to make SimpsonC a member of the GMANAGERS global group on DOMAINA.

8. On DOMAINA, try to access the file and save changes again. Can you do it? Note that you still will not be able to save your changes because SimpsonC's access token for the domain still reflects the old group membership. Close the file, disconnect from the share, reconnect, and attempt to modify the file again. Could you do it? (No. SimpsonC's access token still contains the original group membership information.)

9. Log off and log back on as SimpsonC again. Try to access the file again to modify it and save changes. Could you do it this time? (Yes, because by logging in again, SimpsonC's access token was updated to reflect the change in group membership.)

PART 3

1. On DOMAINB share the folder DATA as DATA$. Give only Managers Change permission to the share.

2. Log on as SmithS on DOMAINA.

3. Using Network Neighborhood, look for the DATA share in the list of shares for DOMAINB. You should not see it because the $ makes it a hidden share.

4. Right-click Network Neighborhood and choose Map Network Drive. In the path box type **\\DOMAINB\DATA$** and choose OK. You should have been able to access the share.

5. Modify the file called MEMO.DOC in DATA and save your changes.

6. Disconnect from the share and log off.

PART 4

Log on to DOMAINB as Administrator and make the following changes:

◆ Modify the NTFS permissions for the TOOLS folder. Remove Everyone and add Managers with Read and Administrators with Full Control.

◆ Modify the NTFS permissions for the DATA folder. Remove Everyone and add Sales with Change and MIS with Add. (You may need to take control on the folder as Administrator before you can make this change.)

1. On DOMAINB, log on to DOMAINA as SmithS.

2. Use Windows Explorer to expand the NTFS partition. Open the file BUDGET97.DOC in TOOLS and modify it.

3. Can you save your changes? Note that the NTFS permission for Managers is Read. Because SmithS is a member of Managers and he is accessing the resource locally (on the same computer as the resource resides), he gets Read access to the file and therefore cannot save changes.

4. On DOMAINA, use User Manager for Domains to create a new user in DOMAINA called Bert and a global group called GMIS. Add Bert to GMIS and GMANAGERS. Add GMIS to the local MIS group on DOMAINB.

5. On DOMAINB, log off and log back on as Bert from DOMAINA.

6. Use Windows Explorer to access the DATA folder. Because MIS has only Add permission, you cannot access the DATA folder.

7. Use Notepad to create a document called BERT.TXT. Try to save it in the DATA folder. (Access denied.) Try to save it in

App
K

the TOOLS folder. (You only have Read access, so you can't write a file to this folder.) Save it in the root directory of the NTFS partition.

8. Open a DOS prompt window. At the prompt copy the file BERT.TXT from the root of the NTFS partition to the TOOLS\DATA directory. Note that you *can* do this because you have Add permission to the DATA folder.

9. Log off.

PART 5

1. Log on as SimpsonC on DOMAINA.

2. Access the TOOLS share on DOMAINB through Windows Explorer.

3. Open the file DOOM.TXT and modify it.

4. Save your changes. Can you do it? (Not this time. The share permission is Change for Managers, and the NTFS permission is Read for Managers. When accessing a resource through a share, the more restrictive of the permissions will become the effective permissions. Thus, your effective permission is Read and you cannot save changes.)

5. Log on as Administrator on DOMAINB.

6. Change the NTFS permission for Managers on TOOLS to Full Control.

7. On DOMAINA, reconnect to the share and try to modify and save the file again. This time you can because the effective permission is Change (the more restrictive of the share permission—Change—and the NTFS permission—Full Control.)

8. As SmithS, create a new file called SmithS.TXT in the TOOLS directory on DOMAINB.

9. Log off.

10. As Administrator on DOMAINB, change the NTFS permission for managers on TOOLS to Change.

PART 6

1. Log on as Bert from DOMAINA on the DOMAINB domain controller.

2. Locate the TOOLS folder on DOMAINB.

3. Locate the file Smiths.TXT and display its Security sheet (right–click, Properties, Security).

4. Choose Ownership to see that SmithS is the owner.

5. Can you take ownership of the file? (No, because you only have Change permission.)

6. Log off and log back on as Administrator.

7. Add Bert from DOMAINA to the ACL for the file SmithS.TXT on DOIMAINB with the NTFS Special Access Take Ownership permission.

8. Log on DOMAINB as Bert again, and try to take ownership of the file. This time you can, because you have the permission to do so. Verify that Bert is now the owner of SmithS.TXT.

App
K

PART 7

1. Log on as Administrator on DOMAINA.

2. Use Windows Explorer to map drive K to the D$ share on DOMAINB (where D is the letter of the NTFS partition on DOMAINB).

3. Select K in Windows Explorer and create a new folder there called REMOTE.

4. Right-click the new folder and select the Security tab in the folder's properties. Add the Administrators group with Full Control and the Managers group with Change. Remove the Everyone group.

5. Close Windows Explorer and open Server Manager.

6. Choose Computer, Select Domain from the menu. Enter DOMAINB in the Domain text box or select it from the list.

7. Choose DOMAINB domain controller from the computer list. Then choose Computer, Shared Directories from the menu.

8. Choose New Share. Create a share called REMOTE with the path **D:\REMOTE** (where D represents the NTFS partition on DOMAINB). Leave the permissions at the default. Choose OK and close Server Manager.

9. Log off and log back in on DOMAINA as SmithS. Verify that you can access the REMOTE share on DOMAINB and create and save a file there.

Chapter 14 Lab Exercises—Working with Profiles and Policies

It is assumed that you have completed Chapter 12 Lab "Working with User Manager for Domains."

PART 1

Complete this exercise from DOMAINA.

1. Log on as NancyA. Modify your environment settings by changing the screen colors, adding a wallpaper, and creating a shortcut to Solitaire on the desktop.

2. Log off and log on again as Administrator.

3. Use Windows Explorer to find the WINNT\PROFILES directory. Notice the new subdirectory structure for NancyA with the file NTUSER.DAT in the NancyA subdirectory. Expand that subdirectory to find the Desktop subdirectory and notice the shortcut to Solitaire located there.

4. Find the WINNT\PROFILES\Default User subdirectory. Expand it to display the Desktop subdirectory. Create a shortcut here for Solitaire (right-click and drag the Solitaire icon from WINNT\SYSTEM32). Also, rename the NTUSER.DAT file in Default User to NTUSER.OLD and copy the NTUSER.DAT file from NancyA.

5. Create a new user called PAT with no password and no password options selected.

6. Log on as PAT. Notice that the Solitaire shortcut and the environment settings became part of PAT's profile. This will be true not only for each new user you create, but also for any previous user who has not yet logged on for the first time and thus created his or her own profile.

7. Log back on as Administrator. Use Windows Explorer to delete the NTUSER.DAT file from WINNT\PROFILES\Default User and rename NTUSER.OLD back to NTUSER.DAT.

PART 2

1. Use Windows Explorer to create a new directory called Profiles in the root directory of DOMAINB. Right-click it. Select Sharing, choose Shared As, and select OK.

2. On DOMAINA, delete the account PAT. Create a new user account called MEG with no password and no password options selected. Choose Profile and in User Profile Path enter the following: **\\DOMAINB\profiles\ntuser.dat**.

App
K

3. Start the System applet from the Control Panel and switch to the User Profiles tab. You will note an entry for Account Deleted. This was PAT that you deleted in step 2. Select this entry and choose Delete and Yes.

4. In the list, select the entry for NancyA and choose Copy To.

5. In the Copy Profile To text box enter **\\DOMAINB\ profiles**, or choose Browse to find the shared folder in Network Neighborhood. Select Permitted to Use; select Change and choose MEG from the list (be sure to select Show Users). Choose OK and exit from System.

6. Log on as MEG. Notice that MEG received her profile from DOMAINB and that her environment settings match NancyA.

7. On DOMAINA, log off and log back in again as Administrator. Open the properties for MEG in User Manager and change the profile file reference from NTUSER.DAT to NTUSER.MAN.

8. Log in as MEG. Notice that you are unable to log in because you have referenced a mandatory profile that does not exist.

9. Log back in as Administrator. Delete the account MEG.

PART 3

1. On DOMAINB, start the System Policy Editor.

2. Choose File, Connect and connect to DOMAINA. Now choose File, Open Registry to open the Registry on DOMAINA.

3. Modify the Local User options as follows: Under Shell, Restrictions, choose Remove Run Command from Start Menu.

4. Modify the Local Computer options as follows: Under Windows NT System, Logon choose Logon Banner (note

the two settings that you can modify in the lower half of the dialog box when you select this option), and Do Not Display Last Logged On User Name.

5. Save the changes and close System Policy Editor.

6. Log on as MaryM on DOMAINA. Confirm that the system policy options you selected in steps 3 and 4 have been implemented.

PART 4

1. On DOMAINB, start the System Policy Editor.

2. Choose File, New Policy.

3. Modify the Default User options as follows: Under Desktop choose Color Scheme and select Tan from the Scheme Name list box.

4. Modify the Default Computer options as follows: Under Windows NT System, Logon choose Logon Banner modifying the text to read `Unauthorized users will be shot!`, and choose Do Not Display Last Logged On User Name.

5. Choose Edit, Add User and create a policy for EmmettR. Modify the policy as follows: Under Control Panel, Display select Restrict Display and check all five settings. Under Shell, Restrictions select Remove Run command from Start Menu and Hide Network Neighborhood.

6. Choose Edit, Add Group and create a group policy for ZanyGroup. Under Desktop, choose Color Scheme and select Rose. Create a group policy for KindGroup. Under Restrictions choose Remove Find Command from Start Menu.

7. Save the policy file as NTCONFIG.POL in the NETLOGON share of DOMAINA.

App
K

8. From DOMAINB, log on to DOMAINA as NancyA. Note the legal notice dialog box that displays. This is a result of the Default Computer policy setting you made. Because NancyA is also a member of ZanyGroup, the color scheme should also have changed. Log off and log back on as EmmettR. Confirm the policy settings you implemented for this account. EmmettR is a member of the KindGroup group. Do you expect to see the Find command removed from the Start menu as indicated by the KindGroup group policy? (No, as the group policy is ignored if a user has a specific user policy.) On DOMAINA (or remotely from DOMAINB) log off and log back on as Administrator. Create a new user called DonD and add it to the KindGroup group. From DOMAINB, log on to DOMAINA as DonD. Check to see whether the Find command has been removed from the Start menu as set in the KindGroup group policy.

Chapter 15 Lab Exercises

The first exercise of this lab assumes that at least one Windows NT server installation is available to use Network Client Administrator to create a shared folder to be used to install server tools on client computers on the network.

If a Windows NT 4.0 Workstation is available, exercise 2 has you install server tools on that platform. If a Windows 95 platform is available, exercise 3 has you install server tools on that platform.

Exercise 1

Complete this exercise from your domain controller.

1. Log on to your PDC and start the Network Client Administrator utility. (Start, Programs, Administrative Tools, Network Client Administrator.)

2. When the Network Client Administrator selection box appears, select the Copy Client-based Network Administration Tools and choose Continue.

3. When the Share Client-based Network Administration Tools appears, enter the path where the server tools source files are located (example: F:\Clients). Accept the default Destination Path and Share Name and press OK.

4. When the files are copied to the selected folder, a Network Client Administrator information box appears. Read the message and choose OK.

5. Another Network Client Administrator information box appears stating the Network Administration Tools are now available, choose OK.

6. On the Network Client Administrator selection box, select Exit.

Exercise 2

Complete this exercise from a Windows NT Workstation computer if available on the network.

1. Log on to a Windows NT 4.0 Workstation on the network with the administrator account.

2. Map to the network share created in exercise 1.

3. Double-click the Winnt folder.

4. Double-click Setup.bat.

5. A MS-DOS prompt will start and the server tools files will be copied to your computer. Record the server tools .exe files that were copied in the spaces below.

————————— , ————————— , —————————

Dhcpadmin.exe   Poledit.exe   Rasadmin.exe

_____ , _____ , _____

Rplmgr.exe   Srvmgr.exe   Usrmgr.exe

_____ .

Winsmgr.exe

6. Press any key to continue.

7. Right-click the Start button and choose Open.

8. When the Start Menu appears, choose the File drop-down menu, select New, Folder, and type Server Tools.

9. Open Explorer and locate the <winntroot>\System32 folder.

10. Locate the server tools .exe files one at a time, as recorded in step 5, and with the primary mouse button, drag each file to the Server Tools folder created in step 9.

    (Hint: Position the Explorer window and the Start Menu window so each can be viewed.)

11. Click the Start button, hover over the Server Tools selection, and choose Shortcut to Usrmgr.exe.

12. From the User drop-down menu, choose Select Domain and from the Select Domain window, select Domain A.

13. View the user and group accounts from that domain.

14. Close User Manager.

Exercise 3

Complete this exercise from a Windows 95 computer, if available on the network.

1. Start Windows 95, open the Control Panel, and select the Add/Remove Programs ICON.

2. Select the Windows Setup tab from the Add/Remove Programs Properties sheet and click the Have Disk button.

3. When the Install from Disk dialog box appears, enter the
   path to the server tools source files created in exercise 1
   (Example: <computername>\SetupAdm\Win95).

4. When the Have Disk property sheet appears, select the check
   box next to the Windows NT Server Tools item and click
   Install.

5. After the server tools are installed, click Start, Programs,
   Windows NT Server Tools, and select User Manager for
   Domains.

6. From the User drop-down menu, choose Select Domain and
   from the Select Domain window, select Domain A.

7. View the user and group accounts from that domain.

8. Close User Manager.

Chapter 20 Lab Exercises— Performance Monitor Lab

PART 1

1. At a command prompt on one of your computers type:
   DISKPERF –Y.

2. If your computer has more than 16M RAM installed, modify
   the boot.ini file so that you only boot with 16M of RAM.
   To the line under [Operating Systems] that contains the
   location of the Windows NT 4.0 workstation system files,
   add the switch: /MAXMEM:16. (Remember that Boot.ini is
   a read-only file.)

3. Shutdown and restart Windows NT to enable the Performance Monitor disk objects and their counters.

4. Start the Windows Explorer utility and Pinball.

5. Start the Performance Monitor from the Administrative Tools group and add the following objects and counters to a new chart:

Object	Counter	Instance
Processor	%Processor Time	0
Process	%Processor Time	Perfmon, Explorer, Pinball
Process	Working Set	Perfmon, Explorer, Pinball
Memory	Commit Limit	default
Memory	Pages/Sec	default
Logical Disk	Avg. Disk sec/ Transfer	pagefile drive
Logical Disk	%Disk Time	pagefile drive

6. Track the values of each of the counters you added to the chart especially noting the working set values for Performance Monitor, Windows Explorer, and Pinball (about 2.2M, 175K, and 184K, respectively). Note also the Commit Limit for the pagefile (will vary). (Hint: Press Ctrl+H to highlight each line graph.)

7. Switch to Explorer and create a new folder called PERFMON on the same drive as the pagefile. Switch to Pinball and start the demo game.

8. Track the activity of the chart again and note the average values for each of the counters in the chart. Note any significant changes. In particular, you should have noticed a spike for %Processor Time for the processor and each of the three

processes driven proportionately as each one performed its activity (creating the folder, running the demo game, and updating the chart with the new statistics). Notice the flurry in disk counter activity initially, and then how it settles once the actions are performed. Notice, too, the increased amount of memory required by Pinball and Performance Monitor to correspond with their activities. Multiply Pages/Sec and Avg. Disk sec/Transfer to obtain the percent of Disk I/O related to pagefile activity. It will be well below Microsoft's suggested 10 percent threshold.

9. Switch to Windows Explorer. Copy only the files from the WINNT directory into the PERFMON folder. While the copy is taking place, switch to the Performance Monitor and note the Pages/Sec and Avg. Disk sec/Transfer. These have all peaked at or near the top of the scale. Multiply the average value for each together to obtain a percentage. This should be just over 10 percent and indicates that for this activity, the percent of disk I/O related to pagefile activity was greater than Microsoft's recommended 10 percent. If this was consistently above 10 percent, you might consider adding more RAM.

10. Open the BOOT.INI file and remove the /MAXMEM:16 switch. Restart Windows NT.

11. If you have more than 16M RAM installed, repeat steps 4-9 and note the differences. (All disk values and %processor times should be less, though they will vary depending on the amount of additional RAM you have.)

12. Close Windows Explorer and Pinball.

PART 2

1. With Performance Monitor still running, select View, LOG. Choose Add to Log and add each of the following objects to

the log: Logical Disk, Memory, Process, and Processor. Then choose Done.

2. Select Options, LOG. Enter PERF1.LOG for the log name and save it in the PERFMON folder. Set the interval to 1 second and choose Start Log.

3. Start Pinball and run the demo. Start Windows Explorer and create a new folder called PERFMON2 on the same partition as PERFMON. Copy everything from PERFMON into PERFMON2.

4. Switch to Performance Monitor. Wait another minute, and then select Options, LOG, Stop Log. Save the log file.

5. Select File, New Chart to clear and reset the chart view for new values.

6. Select Options, Data From. Under Log File, find and select the PERF1.LOG file you just created. Choose OK.

7. Select Edit, Add to Chart. Note the entries listed represent those you collected during the log process. Add the following objects and counters to the chart as you did before. This time, the chart will represent static data collected from the log.

Object	Counter	Instance
Processor	%Processor Time	0
Process	%Processor Time	Perfmon, Explorer, Pinball
Process	Working Set	Perfmon, Explorer, Pinball
Memory	Commit Limit	default
Memory	Pages/Sec	default
Logical Disk	Avg. Disk sec/ Transfer	pagefile drive
Logical Disk	%Disk Time	pagefile drive

8. Note the average values for each during the log period.

9. Choose Edit, Time Window to change the time range to show only the period of peak activity. Note how the average values change.

10. Close Performance Monitor.

PART 3

This lab uses both computers and monitor remote server performance. On the server that is monitored remotely, modify the boot.ini file and restart the computer so that it runs with only 16M of RAM. (Refer to PART 1 of this lab for instructions on how to do this.) Also, enable disk counters on both computers by typing **DISKPERF –y** at a command prompt and restarting the computers. The computer running Performance Monitor is referred to as the local computer and the other as the remote computer. It is not necessary that the computers participate in a trust relationship. However, the Administrator accounts and passwords must match in order to perform remote administration.

1. Start Performance Monitor on the local computer. Select View, LOG. Choose Add to Log and add each of the following objects to the log. Then choose Done.

   From the local computer:
   Logical Disk, Memory, Processor, Redirector
   From the remote computer:
   Logical Disk, Memory, Processor, Server

2. Select Options, LOG. Enter **REMOTE.LOG** for the log name and save it in the PERFMON folder. Set the interval to 1 second and choose Start Log.

3. Start Windows Explorer on the remote computer and create a new folder called REMOTE on the same partition as the pagefile. Perform this step remotely from the local computer.

4. Copy everything from the PERFMON directory on the local computer into the REMOTE directory on the remote computer.

5. Start User Manager for Domains on the local computer and change to the other domain (choose User, Select Domain). Create three new users and three new global groups, adding the three users to each new global group.

6. Switch to Performance Monitor. Wait another minute, and then select Options, LOG, Stop Log. Save the log file.

7. Select File, New Chart to clear and reset the chart view for new values.

8. Select Options, Data From. Under Log File, find and select the REMOTE.LOG file you just created. Choose OK.

9. Select Edit, Add to Chart. Note the entries listed represent those you collected during the log process. Add the following objects and counters to the chart as you did before. This time, the chart will represent static data collected from the log.

From the local computer:

Object	Counter	Instance
Processor	%Processor Time	0
Memory	Commit Limit	default
Memory	Pages/Sec	default
Logical Disk	Avg. Disk sec/Transfer	pagefile drive
Logical Disk	%Disk Time	pagefile drive
Redirector	Bytes Total/sec	default
Redirector	Current Commands	default
Redirector	Reads Denied/sec	default
Redirector	Writes Denied/sec	default

Object	Counter	Instance
Processor	%Processor Time	0
Memory	Commit Limit	default
Memory	Pages/Sec	default
Logical Disk	Avg. Disk sec/Transfer	pagefile drive
Logical Disk	%Disk Time	pagefile drive
Server	Bytes Total/sec	default
Server	Pool Nonpaged Failures	default
Server	Pool Paged Failures	default

10. Note the average values for each during the log period.

11. Use Edit, Time Window to change the time range to show only the periods of peak activity. Note how the average values change. Determine at what point the remote server was accessed to create the new folder, copy the data, and create the new accounts. At any point did either the Redirector or Server counters indicate high values (greater than 2)? Results will vary based on your computer configuration. However, what could you conclude if they were high values? You could conclude that the server may be a bottleneck, especially if the Server>Pool Nonpaged Failures or Pool Paged Failures counters were high. If either of these were high (greater than 2), modify the boot.ini file on the remote computer so that it can be restarted to recognize all the memory (presuming that it has more than 16M of RAM). Then repeat this exercise creating a log file called REMOTE2, and create a different folder and accounts. Note whether the Server counters are lower when more RAM is available.

12. Close Performance Monitor.

App
K

Chapter 21 Lab Exercises—Working with Network Monitor

It is assumed that you have two Windows NT computers at your disposal and that you have them configured as suggested in Lab1 as primary domain controllers called DOMAINA and DOMAINB. Also, the DOMAINB PDC can be restarted as a backup domain controller to DOMAINA.

The best way to become familiar with Network Monitor is to use it. This lab helps you to create some Network Monitor capture files. You then take these files and work back through this chapter to identify the frames discussed throughout. This may seem tedious, but it gives you some experience using the tool and identifying frames relating to specific events.

Before completing this exercise, be sure to isolate your computers from the rest of your network. The first part of this exercise works best if you have Windows NT Workstation or Windows 95 installed on one of the computers—say DOMAINB.

PART 1

1. If you have not already installed TCP/IP as your primary protocol, do so on DOMAINA. Configure DOMAINA to be a DHCP server. You can use 131.107.2.250 as the IP address of the DHCP server. For the scope address range, you can use 131.107.2.251 to 131.107.2.255. Add the DHCP server IP address as the router address to the scope if you desire. Also, install the WINS service on DOMAINA.

2. If you have Windows 95 or Windows NT Workstation 4.0 installed on the other computer, start it up and configure the computer to join DOMAINA. If not, start up the second computer as DOMAINB with no trust relationships. The

second computer is referred to as the client for the rest of this exercise.

3. Configure the client to obtain its IP address from the DHCP server. Also, tell the client to use DOMAINA as the WINS server. After the client has restarted, open a command prompt window and issue the command **IPCONFIG /RELEASE**. Close the command prompt window.

4. Share a directory on DOMAINA and create a text file in it.

PART 2

Do this if the client is a Windows 95 or NT Workstation computer:

1. At DOMAINA, start up Network Monitor.

2. Shut down and restart the client.

3. When the client shuts down, but before it restarts, start the capture cycle in Network Monitor. As you perform each of the following steps, watch the Network Monitor screen as it captures frames.

4. Start up the client. Log in to DOMAINA.

5. Using Network Neighborhood, browse for the shared directory you created in PART 1 and open the file. Make a modification to the file, save it, and close it.

6. Using Windows Explorer, connect a network drive to the shared directory on DOMAINA. Copy the text file from the shared directory to a directory on your computer. Disconnect the network drive and close Windows Explorer.

7. Log off and shut down the client.

8. On DOMAINA, stop the capture and view the data. Save the capture file as CLIENT1.CAP. Go back through the

chapter and find the frames in the CLIENT1.CAP file that reference the DHCP IP address process, the WINS resolution process, logging on, establishing the file session and accessing the file in the shared directory, disconnecting the network drive, and logging off. Notice, too, the browser broadcasts. Note the number of frames involved and the size of each. Look at the details of each also to determine which frames are broadcast to the subnet, and which are directed to a specific computer.

PART 3

Do this if the other computer is a PDC (DOMAINB):

1. At DOMAINA, start up Network Monitor.

2. Shut down and restart the client.

3. When the client shuts down, but before it restarts, start the capture cycle in Network Monitor. As you perform each of the following steps, watch the Network Monitor screen as it captures frames.

4. Start up the client. Log in to DOMAINB as administrator.

5. Using Network Neighborhood, browse for the shared directory you created in PART 1 and open the file. Make a modification to the file, save it, and close it.

6. Establish a trust relationship between DOMAINA and DOMAINB so that DOMAINA is trusted and DOMAINB is trusting. Create a shared directory on DOMAINB, giving full control access to the administrator account on DOMAINA. Also, give the DOMAIN USERS group on DOMAINA Read access to the shared directory on DOMAINB. Log off and log on as Administrator in DOMAINA from the DOMAINB computer.

7. Using Windows Explorer on DOMAINA, connect a network drive to the shared directory on DOMAINB. Copy the text file from the shared directory on DOMAINA to the shared directory on DOMAINB. Disconnect the network drive and close Windows Explorer.

8. On DOMAINA, stop the capture and view the data. Save the capture file as CLIENT2.CAP. Go back through the chapter and find the frames in the CLIENT2.CAP file that reference the DHCP IP address process, the WINS resolution process, establishing the file session and accessing the file in the shared directory, establishing the trust, adding a user to the share's ACL across the trust, using pass-through authentication to access the resource across the trust, logging in across the trust, disconnecting the network drive and logging off. Notice, too, the browser broadcasts. Note the number of frames involved and the size of each. Look at the details of each also to determine which frames are broadcast to the subnet, and which are directed to a specific computer.

App
K

PART 4

Do this with the client configured as a BDC for DOMAINA:

1. On DOMAINA, start Network Monitor.

2. Restart the other computer as a BDC for DOMAINA.

3. Before you restart the other computer, start a new capture in Network Monitor.

4. Add two new user accounts to DOMAINA. Create two new global groups and add both users and the administrator account to each group.

5. Using Server Manager, force replication to take place between the two domain controllers (select the PDC, choose Computer, then Synchronize Entire Domain).

6. Create a simple login script and place it in the WINNT\
   SYSTEM32\Repl\Export\Scripts subdirectory on
   DOMAINA.

7. Configure Directory Replication so that DOMAINA
   exports to DOMAINB.

8. Confirm that the login script file was replicated from the
   WINNT\SYSTEM32\Repl\Export\Scripts subdirectory
   on DOMAINA to the WINNT\SYSTEM32\Repl\Import\
   Scripts subdirectory on DOMAINB.

9. On DOMAINA, stop the capture and view the data. Save
   the capture file as CLIENT3.CAP. Go back through the
   chapter and find the frames in the CLIENT3.CAP file that
   reference the account synchronization process and the directory replication process. Note the number of frames related
   to each of the processes involved with each step you performed in the exercise, as well as the detail information for
   each frame.

Index

configuration
parameters, 427–429
Frame Type parameter,
192–203
Gateway Service for
Netware (GSNW),
195–197
multiple frame types,
configuring, 194–195
RIP for NWLink IPX/
SPX Compatible
Transport Service,
configuring, 198–199
selecting, 102–103

**NWLinkIPX values
(Registry), 201–202**

O

**Object Linking and
Embedding (OLE), 655**

**ObjectName parameter
(Services parameter),
173**

objects, 502–513, 655
Cache, 494
instances, 492
Logical Disk, 494,
508–510
%Disk Time counter,
509
Avg. Disk Bytes/
Transfer counter,
509
Avg. Disk sec/
Transfer counter,
509

Current Disk Queue
Length counter,
509
Disk Bytes/sec
counter, 509
Memory, 494, 505
Commit Limit
counter, 506
Committed Bytes
counter, 506
Pages/Sec counter,
507
monitoring,
Performance Monitor,
492–495
network-related,
511–516
Objects, 494
Paging File, 494
Physical Disk, 508–510
%Disk Time counter,
509
Avg. Disk Bytes/
Transfer counter,
509
Avg. Disk sec/
Transfer counter,
509
Current Disk Queue
Length counter,
509
Disk Bytes/sec
counter, 509
Process, 494, 504–505
Working Set, 505
Processor, 494
Interrupts/Sec
counter, 503
Privileged Time
counter, 502

Processor Time
counter, 502
User Time counter,
502
Processor object,
502–504
Redirector, 494
Network Errors/sec
counter, 512
Reads Denied/sec
counter, 512
Writes Denied/sec
counter, 512
Server, Pool Paged
Failures, 512
Server Work Queues,
Queue Length
counter, 504
System, 494
Thread, 494

**Objects (Performance
Monitor core object),
494**

**OCR (Optical Character
Recognition), 655**

**OEM (Original
Equipment
Manufacturer), 655**

**OLE (Object Linking
and Embedding), 655**

one way trusts, 46–47
creating, 51
managing users, 52–62

**Open Registry
command (File menu),
402**

**Open Systems
Interconnect,** *see* **OSI**

Complete and Return this Card
for a *FREE* Computer Book Catalog

Thank you for purchasing this book! You have purchased a superior computer book written expressly for your needs. To continue to provide the kind of up-to-date, pertinent coverage you've come to expect from us, we need to hear from you. Please take a minute to complete and return this self-addressed, postage-paid form. In return, we'll send you a free catalog of all our computer books on topics ranging from word processing to programming and the internet.

Mr. ☐   Mrs. ☐   Ms. ☐   Dr. ☐

Name (first) ☐☐☐☐☐☐☐☐☐☐☐   (M.I.) ☐   (last) ☐☐☐☐☐☐☐☐☐☐☐☐☐☐☐☐☐☐☐

Address ☐☐☐☐☐☐☐☐☐☐☐☐☐☐☐☐☐☐☐☐☐☐☐☐☐☐☐☐☐☐☐

☐☐☐☐☐☐☐☐☐☐☐☐☐☐☐☐☐☐☐☐☐☐☐☐☐☐☐☐☐☐☐

City ☐☐☐☐☐☐☐☐☐☐☐☐☐☐☐☐☐   State ☐☐   Zip ☐☐☐☐☐   ☐☐☐☐

Phone ☐☐☐   ☐☐☐   ☐☐☐☐   Fax ☐☐☐   ☐☐☐   ☐☐☐☐

Company Name ☐☐☐☐☐☐☐☐☐☐☐☐☐☐☐☐☐☐☐☐☐☐☐☐☐☐☐☐

E-mail address ☐☐☐☐☐☐☐☐☐☐☐☐☐☐☐☐☐☐☐☐☐☐☐☐☐☐☐☐☐

1. Please check at least (3) influencing factors for purchasing this book.

Front or back cover information on book .... ☐
Special approach to the content .... ☐
Completeness of content .... ☐
Author's reputation .... ☐
Publisher's reputation .... ☐
Book cover design or layout .... ☐
Index or table of contents of book .... ☐
Price of book .... ☐
Special effects, graphics, illustrations .... ☐
Other (Please specify): _____ ☐

2. How did you first learn about this book?

Saw in Macmillan Computer Publishing catalog .... ☐
Recommended by store personnel .... ☐
Saw the book on bookshelf at store .... ☐
Recommended by a friend .... ☐
Received advertisement in the mail .... ☐
Saw an advertisement in: _____ ☐
Read book review in: _____ ☐
Other (Please specify): _____ ☐

3. How many computer books have you purchased in the last six months?

This book only .... ☐   3 to 5 books .... ☐
2 books .... ☐   More than 5 .... ☐

4. Where did you purchase this book?

Bookstore .... ☐
Computer Store .... ☐
Consumer Electronics Store .... ☐
Department Store .... ☐
Office Club .... ☐
Warehouse Club .... ☐
Mail Order .... ☐
Direct from Publisher .... ☐
Internet site .... ☐
Other (Please specify): _____ ☐

5. How long have you been using a computer?

☐ Less than 6 months   ☐ 6 months to a year
☐ 1 to 3 years   ☐ More than 3 years

6. What is your level of experience with personal computers and with the subject of this book?

	With PCs	With subject of book
New	☐	☐
Casual	☐	☐
Accomplished	☐	☐
Expert	☐	☐

Source Code ISBN: 0-7897-1191-5

7. Which of the following best describes your job title?

- Administrative Assistant ☐
- Coordinator ☐
- Manager/Supervisor ☐
- Director ☐
- Vice President ☐
- President/CEO/COO ☐
- Lawyer/Doctor/Medical Professional ☐
- Teacher/Educator/Trainer ☐
- Engineer/Technician ☐
- Consultant ☐
- Not employed/Student/Retired ☐
- Other (Please specify): _____ ☐

8. Which of the following best describes the area of the company your job title falls under?

- Accounting ☐
- Engineering ☐
- Manufacturing ☐
- Operations ☐
- Marketing ☐
- Sales ☐
- Other (Please specify): _____ ☐

9. What is your age?

- Under 20 ☐
- 21-29 ☐
- 30-39 ☐
- 40-49 ☐
- 50-59 ☐
- 60-over ☐

10. Are you:

- Male ☐
- Female ☐

11. Which computer publications do you read regularly? (Please list)

_____
_____
_____
_____
_____
_____
_____
_____
_____
_____

Comments: _____
_____
_____

Fold here and scotch-tape to mail.

Check out Que® Books
on the World Wide Web
http://www.quecorp.com

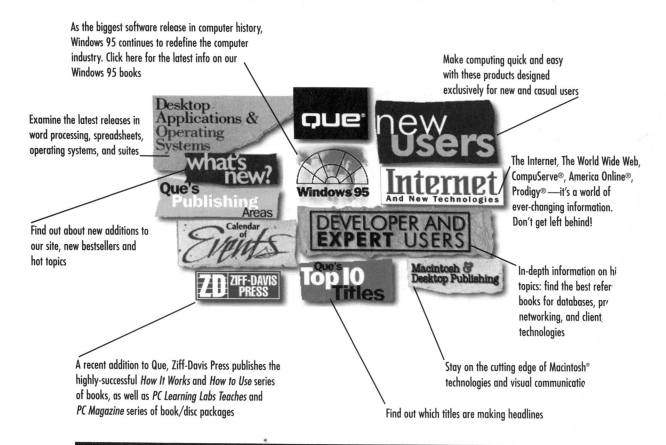

As the biggest software release in computer history, Windows 95 continues to redefine the computer industry. Click here for the latest info on our Windows 95 books

Make computing quick and easy with these products designed exclusively for new and casual users

Examine the latest releases in word processing, spreadsheets, operating systems, and suites

The Internet, The World Wide Web, CompuServe®, America Online®, Prodigy®—it's a world of ever-changing information. Don't get left behind!

Find out about new additions to our site, new bestsellers and hot topics

In-depth information on hi topics: find the best refer' books for databases, pr' networking, and client, technologies

A recent addition to Que, Ziff-Davis Press publishes the highly-successful *How It Works* and *How to Use* series of books, as well as *PC Learning Labs Teaches* and *PC Magazine* series of book/disc packages

Stay on the cutting edge of Macintosh® technologies and visual communicatic

Find out which titles are making headlines

With 6 separate publishing groups, Que develops products for many specific market segmer areas of computer technology. Explore our Web Site and you'll find information on best-' titles, newly published titles, upcoming products, authors, and much more.

- Stay informed on the latest industry trends and products available
- Visit our online bookstore for the latest information and editions
- Download software from Que's library of the best shareware and fre

Before using this disc, please read Appendix I, "Using the CD-ROM," for information on how to install the disc and what programs are included on the disc. If you have problems with this disc, please contact Macmillan Technical Support at (317) 581-3833. We can be reached by e-mail at **support@mcp.com** or on CompuServe at **GO QUEBOOKS**.

License Agreement

By opening this package you are agreeing to be bound by the following:

This software is copyrighted and all rights are reserved by the publisher and its licensers. You are licensed to use this software on a single computer. You may copy the software for backup or archival purposes only. Making copies of the software for any other purpose is a violation of United States copyright laws. THIS SOFTWARE IS SOLD AS IS, WITHOUT WARRANTY OF ANY KIND, EITHER EXPRESSED OR IMPLIED, INCLUDING BUT NOT LIMITED TO THE IMPLIED WARRANTIES OF MERCHANTABILITY AND FITNESS FOR A PARTICULAR PURPOSE. Neither the publisher nor its licensers, dealers, or distributors assumes any liability for any alleged or ~tual damages arising from the use of this software. (Some states do not ~v exclusion of implied warranties, so the exclusion may not apply ~.)

~e contents of the disc and the compilation of the software are ~d and protected by United States copyright laws. The indi- ~ms on this disc are copyrighted by the authors or owners ~. Each program has its own use permissions and limita- ~program, you must follow the individual requirements ~iled for each. Do not use a program if you do not ~nsing agreement.